Politics and Governance in the UK

Second edition

Politics and Governance in the UK

Michael Moran

palgrave
macmillan

First edition 2005
Second edition 2011

Published by
PALGRAVE MACMILLAN

Palgrave Macmillan in the UK is an imprint of Macmillan Publishers Limited,
registered in England, company number 785998, of Houndmills, Basingstoke,
Hampshire RG21 6XS.

Palgrave Macmillan in the US is a division of St Martin's Press LLC,
175 Fifth Avenue, New York, NY 10010.

Palgrave Macmillan is the global academic imprint of the above companies
and has companies and representatives throughout the world.

Palgrave® and Macmillan® are registered trademarks in the United States,
the United Kingdom, Europe and other countries.

ISBN 978–0–230–28998–7   hardback
ISBN 978–0–230–28999–4   paperback

This book is printed on paper suitable for recycling and made from fully
managed and sustained forest sources. Logging, pulping and manufacturing
processes are expected to conform to the environmental regulations of the
country of origin.

A catalogue record for this book is available from the British Library.

A catalog record for this book is available from the Library of Congress.

10 9 8 7 6 5 4 3 2 1
20 19 18 17 16 15 14 13 12 11

Printed and bound in China

Summary of contents

Contents

List of illustrative material

IMAGES

BRIEFINGS

PEOPLE IN POLITICS

TIMELINES

DOCUMENTING POLITICS

POLITICAL ISSUES

DEBATING POLITICS

EUROPEANIZING

Preface to the second edition

I must begin by restating my great debt to the readers of the drafts of the first edition of this book: their guidance has continued to shape this second edition. I have burdened for a second time my friend Neill Nugent, who gave his usual invaluable comments on my draft of Chapter 5 for this edition. Jon Tonge's comments on a draft of Chapter 11 saved me from many errors of fact and interpretation. Four anonymous referees for Palgrave Macmillan gave invaluable comments on a draft of the manuscript. As usual I am deeply indebted to Steven Kennedy: without his constant encouragement I would never have completed the work of producing this edition. I must also now thank another Palgrave Macmillan stalwart, Stephen Wenham, who has seen this edition from conception to birth, and who has been a tower of strength throughout. Special thanks are due to Keith Povey and Nick Fox who did a brilliant job copy editing a messy manuscript, and to Helen Caunce for all her work on the companion web site to the book. Shaun Steele has once again contributed fresh cartoons in his inimitable witty style, and allowed the reproduction of several from the first edition. For corrections of particular points of detail in the first edition I am also indebted to Cameron Dron, Salla Maarit Juga and Robert Nagaji. For any remaining errors I alone am responsible.

Michael Moran
University of Manchester

Acknowledgements

The author and publishers would like to thank the following who have kindly given permission for the use of copyright material: PA photos for Images 1.1, 13.1, 14.3, 17.2, 18.2, 22.1, 23.2; Palgrave Macmillan for Figure 6.1 and Image 5.1; the British Retail Consortium for Documenting Politics 9.1; *Political Studies* for Table 13.3; The Labour Party for Image 15.1 (the 'Labour Rose' logo is a registered emblem of the Labour Party); Oxford University Press for Figure 17.1 and 19.3; Patrick Dunleavy for Figure 19.2.

Crown copyright material in Image 3.1; Documenting Politics 4.1, 5.2, 6.1, 7.1, 7.2, 7.3, 7.4, 7.5, 9.1, 9.3, 9.4, 10.1, 12.1, 19.1, 19.3, 21.1, 22.1 and 22.2; Figures 4.2, 6.2, 12.1 and 20.1; Briefing 7.2, 9.4 and 22.6; and Table 12.2 and 18.1 is reproduced by permission of the controller of Her Majesty's Stationery Office under click licence P2009000114. Documenting Politics 1.2 and 6.1 are reproduced under Crown copyright waiver. Documenting Politics 5.1 and 5.3 are European Union copyright.

Particular thanks to Clive Lacey at the Foreign and Commonwealth Office for his help in obtaining Image 3.1.

List of abbreviations

BBC	British Broadcasting Corporation
BSE	bovine spongiform encephalopathy
CCTV	closed-circuit television
CFSP	common foreign and security policy
CND	Campaign for Nuclear Disarmament
DEFRA	Department of the Environment, Food and Rural Affairs
DTI	Department of Trade and Industry
DUP	Democratic Unionist Party
ECJ	European Court of Justice
ECSC	European Coal and Steel Community
EEC	European Economic Community
EMU	European Monetary Union
EP	European Parliament
EU	European Union
FCO	Foreign and Commonwealth Office
FSA	Financial Services Authority
GDP	gross domestic product
GP	general practitioner
HFEA	Human Fertilization and Embryology Authority
HSE	Health and Safety Executive
IRA	Irish Republican Army
IT	information technology
JHA	justice and home affairs
LGA	Local Government Association
MEPs	Members of the European Parliament
MPs	Members of Parliament
NATO	North Atlantic Treaty Organisation
NFU	National Farmers' Union
NHS	National Health Service
PAYE	Pay as you earn
PC	personal computer
PFI	Private Finance Initiative
RSPB	Royal Society for the Protection of Birds
RSPCA	Royal Society for the Prevention of Cruelty to Animals
SDLP	Social Democratic and Labour Party
SDP	Social Democratic Party
SEA	Single European Act
SNP	Scottish Nationalist Party
SOCPO	Society of Personnel Officers in Local Government
SOPO	Society of Procurement Officers in Local Government
UK	United Kingdom
UN	United Nations
US	United States
UUP	Ulster Unionist Party
VAT	value added tax
WHO	World Health Organization
WTO	World Trade Organization

Introduction

WHAT THIS BOOK IS ABOUT

This book is an introduction to the study of British politics for the beginning student. I assume little or no prior knowledge of British society, or British history or, obviously, of political life in the UK. I have tried to make the language of the text as accessible as possible, and to provide as comprehensive a survey as possible.

The book is therefore aimed at a wide audience. It is primarily intended for readers studying the subject at undergraduate level, though I have tried to write in the plainest English, with the intention of making it accessible also for students at AS and A2 level. I have two main aims: to give the reader as comprehensive a picture as is possible, within the available space, of political life in Britain; and to open up for the reader some of the important questions and debates in the study of British politics. Of course any student of politics soon realizes that these two aims cannot be divorced. No picture of British politics is drawn innocently from life; it is the result of a whole set of assumptions brought, consciously and unconsciously, to the act of composing that picture. Description cannot be separated from theory. Indeed one of my intentions throughout is to make explicit the assumptions about the character of British politics which underpin my descriptions.

Put more formally, the aims of the book are:

- to provide a comprehensive introduction to the context, ideas, institutions, practices and policies that are most important in British political life;
- to provide an introduction to the main analytical issues and theoretical debates in the study of British politics.

The learning objectives of the book need to be more fully stated. By the end of the book student readers should have grasped the following:

- They should know fundamental institutional information about the workings of British politics.

- They should be able to think of British politics as a system of *multilevel governance*, stretching from the level of the European Union to the most local of political systems, and should appreciate what this means for the strategies and tactics employed by the most important actors in British political life. Below I explain what 'governance' here means.
- They should understand that British politics amounts to much more than the political institutions located in London, but now encompasses distinct systems of government in the different nations of the UK.
- They should realize that British politics is now also European politics: that Britain is – regardless of whether people like it or not – a part of the political system of the European Union.

THE INTELLECTUAL STRUCTURE OF THE BOOK

The structure of a book is never the result of simple choices. Even mundane features – like the order of chapters – often arise from important presuppositions and conceal key implications. Since a main aim of the book is to communicate how the study of British politics is affected by the theoretical 'lenses' used, it is only right that some of the assumptions governing this book's structure should themselves be laid bare.

Five important preoccupations lie at the heart of the book, and have shaped its organization:

Taking territorial decentralization seriously. The events of recent years require that we undergo a change of mindset in approaching the British political system. For much of the twentieth century Britain had a highly centralized system of government. This centralization partly reflected the domination – both in numbers and wealth – of one nation, England, and the dominance in turn of one city, London. The capital's predominance was particularly remarkable, whether we measured it by concentration of economic resources, concentration of the great institutions of culture like the mass media, or concentration of important political institutions. That history of centralization naturally coloured the way the British political system was pictured: the institutions that were put at the centre were mostly the institutions of the capital. In the study of British politics most roads led to London. There were good justifications for shaping the study of politics in this way. The reality of power and decision indeed meant that it was mostly what happened in London that mattered. It still matters a great deal, and that explains why what, for shorthand, in this book is called 'The Westminster System' occupies several long chapters. But in recent years things have changed. It is not enough to take this historically centralized state of affairs for granted. It must be recognized as the product of a particular set of hierarchies; and those hierarchies must be exposed and examined. That exposure and examination is made easier because in political life itself those very hierarchies have been seriously challenged: in Ireland for decades; in Scotland and Wales more recently; and more recently still in the revival and reinvention of many English provincial cities and in the stirrings of a movement for regional government. The devolution reforms put in place by the Labour Government after 1997 attempted to respond to these challenges. The predominant power still lies with London institutions, but these reforms have accelerated the establishment of distinctive national political systems in the British Isles. Moreover, since the publication of the first edition, these reforms have been more securely established, even in the difficult arena of Northern Ireland.

Taking Europe seriously. The devolution reforms referred to above are often thought of as weakening the centre 'from below'. But there is also a big challenge to the London focused picture coming from a very different direction – the European Union. Of course even the very beginner to British politics knows that membership of the European Union – which stretches back to the original accession to the European Economic Community, the Common Market, in 1973 – is of outstanding importance. But understanding the significance of membership demands more than acknowledging this fact. It too demands a change in mindset. It is not enough to think of the Union as an important influence from 'outside' or 'above'. It is necessary to think of Britain as a European political system: that is, as a system of politics so woven into the government of the European Union that the two cannot easily be disentangled. That explains two big features of the book: the space given to European institutions and issues; and, something that is not obvious from simple inspection of the contents, the extent to which the European dimension is built into the substance of the discussion in individual chapters. In this edition I have also recognized Europeanization by more systematically high-

lighting it in the boxed features: most chapters now contain a briefing box which examines Europeanization.

Taking institutions seriously. A generation ago in political science institutions were assigned only subordinate importance. It was widely believed that social, economic and cultural forces mattered above all in shaping politics, and that institutional life mostly reflected these wider and deeper forces. But since the mid-1980s political science has rediscovered institutions and formal organization (March and Olsen 1984 is the key text.) The rediscovery is particularly important for British politics. 'Europeanization' has opened Britain to systems where formal organization and written rules – for example in written constitutions – are very important. There are numerous examples in this text showing how the influence of Europe has made the practice of government in Britain more elaborately codified. There are also numerous examples showing that there is much more formal organization than in the past which regulates the relations between the state and its citizens – which are particularly important themes in, for instance, Chapters 5 and 21–3. Moreover, there are numerous examples showing that interest representation is increasingly populated by formal organizations. Finally, we will see that some of the greatest reforms of recent years – such as the devolution reforms discussed in Chapter 10 – have precisely been about changing the institutional shape of government.

Taking democracy seriously. By this phrase I mean the following. All official accounts of the British system of government take pride in picturing it as democratic. Even critics of this official view usually only dissent because, while wanting democracy, they deny that it has been realized. Only a few authoritarians publicly argue that we should not have democratic government. This almost universal consensus about the desirability of democracy provides a powerful set of tools with which to evaluate British government. 'Democracy' is a hotly contested idea, but plainly it implies beliefs about the distribution of power, about participation in politics and about controls over government. An important purpose of the chapters that follow is to tackle the difficult matter of the reality or otherwise of British democracy. I try to show that we should take democratic claims seriously, and to show how we can evaluate the worth of these claims.

Taking theory seriously. The study of British politics was for a long time theoretically innocent – a kind of high level current affairs. And indeed we need to be attuned to the everyday political world. But we also need to realize that there are no innocent descriptions of that world – all our accounts are suffused with theoretical assumptions. One thing I have tried to do in these pages is to make the assumptions more explicit – more visible and therefore more open to challenge by the student reader. That explains, for example, why so much of the opening and closing chapters are devoted to examinations of the theoretical frameworks which we can use to make sense of British politics.

SOME PARTICULAR CHANGES FROM THE FIRST EDITION

In organizing the chapters I have made several important changes beyond the obvious ones: that is, those needed to take account of the passage of time. Readers of the first edition felt, rightly, that there were too many 'contextual' chapters, on history, society and economy, delaying the task of grappling with the core features of British politics. I have greatly compressed this contextual material. The first edition contained a chapter (20) on understanding policy, which sought to relate the study to contemporary political issues. But that chapter succeeded all too well in being contemporary: it became obvious that the issues dealt with were quickly outmoded, leaving the student reader, I suspect, puzzled as to their relevance. The proper place, I concluded, for contemporary comment was in the updates on the book website. That chapter therefore disappears in this edition.

A word should also be said about something more mundane: how the chapters open and close. Under 'Aims' I start each chapter in the same way: with a short, bald summary of what is coming. Under 'Review' I end each chapter, not with a summary, but with my 'take' on what have been the main themes of the chapter. The reader might not agree with the themes I have highlighted; indeed, for the student reader a useful exercise, and a prompt to active reading, is to compare my view of the important themes with his or her own view.

I have also changed the format of the 'Further Reading'. Any teacher knows that organizing further reading presents a dilemma: you want to offer as wide a range as possible; but offer too wide a range and the student is discouraged and confused about where to start. My solution in this edition is brutal: I offer for each chapter a single 'absolutely essential' item, and then follow this with a brief bibliographical essay. In the website accompanying the book I then offer, as with the first edition, a much longer list. I am sure many readers will disagree with my idea of the 'essential', but it has the merit of giving the student reader a very clear starting point.

THE TITLE OF THE BOOK

Why 'governance' in the title? The choice acknowledges the increasing use of the word in recent years to describe what is going on in the governing process in Britain. 'Governance' brings a new stress on the importance of coordination and bargaining, in place of issuing commands. It also reflects something not apparent from the title alone: that the governing process is increasingly 'multilevel' and 'multi-agency': in other words, the business of governing involves drawing together a wide range of different institutions at many levels of a governing system. The development of devolution and the growing importance of Europe have both been important in reinforcing this multilevel system. The succeeding chapters show time and again that the complexity of modern society means that numerous agencies typically have to be involved in the governing process. Governing can never be a solitary vice, or virtue; it necessarily involves coordination between many different bodies.

I try in the pages that follow to use 'governance' as a summary description of the whole process and to reserve 'government' for the institutions of, for instance, the Westminster or the devolved governing systems. The significance of this usage should not be exaggerated: 'governance' here is a shift of nuance rather than a wholesale shift of meaning. By contrast, in some other accounts it is indeed a shift in meaning: some radical versions of the 'governance' approach picture the state as a transformed 'network' state. I examine the pros and cons of this radical view in the concluding chapter.

A NOTE ON PRESENTATION

This book will be in the main used as part of a course and, obviously, how it is used will be determined by the needs of the individual course. But a note is needed about two features, to explain why I have developed them: the 'visuals' – boxes, photos, charts, tables, graphs – and the website that accompanies the book.

The visuals build on the innovations of a generation of textbooks that appeared in the 1990s. These departed from the traditional presentation of the book as a block of text. The innovations were a real breakthrough, exploiting technological developments in setting and printing, allowing a better conveyance of material to readers. They also exploited something that everyone experiences in their daily lives: an idea or a fact is best understood and remembered if it is presented in more than one form. The choice of visuals nevertheless needs to be highly self-conscious if it is not simply to become a gimmick or just a way of breaking up blocks of text. I intend the book to be, within the limits of an introductory text, comprehensive and self-contained. Although most students will, naturally, wish to read widely beyond these chapters, my intention is that the beginning reader should not have to go beyond the book to understand its contents. The visuals, therefore, are intended to ensure that all the central concepts used, the historical and social features invoked and the technical terms employed are explained without breaking up the flow of the text. The contents of the boxes, charts and other visual material represent my judgement of what the beginning reader needs by way of extra explanation and illustration. No doubt I have not made all the right choices and I appeal to readers to tell me where I have made mistakes so that later editions can be improved.

For the most part the meaning of the various features is self-evident, but it is worth highlighting seven:

- *Briefing boxes* are the commonest form of boxed material. This is where I try economically to summarize facts and ideas that, if inserted into the body of the text, would break up the flow, but which are nevertheless particularly important for the student.
- *Documenting politics* boxes try to give the student the raw flavour of political life: I use extracts from Parliamentary debates, official documents and private (leaked) memos to show what language the political class uses to talk to itself, to talk *to* the rest of us and to talk *about* the rest of us.
- *People in politics* boxes recognize that politics is a people business and that personalities matter. I usually group three figures together, normally to give some perspective, historical or otherwise, to their significance. The cartoons by Shaun Steele put faces to text. Cartoons are used in homage to the great British tradition of political caricature.
- *Images* are used because political life is lived as vividly through images as through ideas. Most of these images are photographs, in the main taken by me. When people are asked to conjure up British politics they are likely to turn to images – of people like the Prime Minister or of buildings like the Houses of Parliament. I grew up in traditional rural Ireland in the 1950s and my sense of the authority of the Irish state is still conveyed by memories of the old coins that pictured icons of rural Ireland: the hen on the penny, the salmon on the two shilling (ten pence) coin. The images in this book are intended to illustrate how politics is represented to us. Those selected are usually deliberately mundane and everyday, precisely because they surround us and – like the icons of the state on coins – seep more or less unacknowledged into everyday consciousness.
- *Political issues* boxes recognize that politics is about much more than institutions, structures or people: it is about issues that form the stuff of everyday political argument. For virtually every chapter I have taken an issue linked to a main theme of the chapter, to convey some of the life of real politics in action. These boxes are intended to be self-contained narratives and do not therefore come with an extra annotation.
- *Debating politics* boxes come at the end of each chapter. The study of British politics is a contested subject, and debating these contested issues, as much as learning institutional detail, is central to its study. The debates are numerous and endless; each single debate box can do no more than select one area of contestation. Like the *Political issues* boxes these are self-contained and have no external annotation.
- *Europeanizing* boxes are a new feature. They are designed to highlight a major feature of the book: that the UK system is now constantly being reshaped by the impact of membership of the EU. 'Europeanization' is the common summary way of describing this phenomenon; it shows that there is no longer a simple division to be made between 'domestic' UK politics and the politics of the EU.

Beyond the special cases of the last two categories of boxes, all the other visual features are annotated, and these annotations are an integral part of the features, since they try to explain both the placing of the feature and the point of the particular material chosen.

The website linked to the book also tries to exploit technology to communicate more effectively. Virtually all students now have access to the Web, and the site for the book has two purposes. First, on it is placed material (self-assessment tests to measure comprehension of the text), which it would simply be too bulky to put into hard copy. Second, the site is used to solve one of the main problems of textbooks: trying to cover social and political life in an up-to-date way. The traditional text is, just because of the mechanics of book production, inevitably several months out of date even when it first appears. The website contains regular updates of all important developments that affect the text. Over five years of updates are available in the first-edition archive at http://www. palgrave.com/politics/moran/students/Update.htm.

Though I have provided a website linked to the text, I have not provided guides to websites in my 'Further Reading' at the end of chapters. The omission is deliberate. As a glance at the sources for the boxed material will show, I have used the Web widely in writing the book. In the age of Google it is all too easy to search the Web. But this is an extremely inefficient way for the beginner to study a subject, and it runs the risk of detaching the beginner from what is essential: embedding knowledge in developed scholarly understanding. The Web is an important tool in the study of Britain. It is vital for the student, for example in electronically accessing academic journals or in gathering original material for projects or dissertations. But it is a distraction for the beginner.

CHAPTER 1

Why politics matters and why British politics matters

CONTENTS

AIMS

This chapter:

- ☐ Explains why we study politics

- ☐ Explains why we study the politics of a special sort of institution, the state

- ☐ Explains why we study British politics

- ☐ Sketches some of the main themes that we encounter when we study British politics

- ☐ Anticipates some of the ways we can 'frame' British politics theoretically

WHY STUDY POLITICS?

Why study politics? Indeed, why be concerned with political life at all? For most citizens – including citizens of the UK – the answers to these questions are pretty obvious: there are no good reasons either to study politics or to take an active part in political life. Politics is a popular subject in most universities and in further education, but beyond these places the study of politics really is a minority interest – more accessible, say, than the study of theoretical physics, but not able to attract more interest among the wider population. The reader of this book is engaged in a minority activity. And the reader of this book who is engaged actively in politics is engaged in a more unusual activity still. There are perhaps no more than 100,000 really committed political activists in this country – by which I mean people for whom, beyond work and the immediate demands of family life, politics is a seriously time consuming activity. By contrast, surveys tell us that an apparently marginal activity like dressmaking and knitting is actually engaged in by 3 per cent of all *men* over the age of sixteen – about 700,000 in all. About double that number of people regularly play skittles or ten-pin bowling. So one way to put politics into perspective is to realize that it is a lot less popular than either knitting or skittles.

But if politics is a minority interest, even in a democracy, it is nevertheless a matter of the utmost importance – in a quite literal sense, a matter of life and death. We soon start to see this if we consider some of the commonest definitions of politics and political life, such as those illustrated in Documenting Politics 1.1. There are important differences in emphasis in the different definitions collected in that box, but we can nevertheless find in there a common theme. *Politics is a social activity involving the attempt to choose between competing views and interests in institutions.* It immediately becomes obvious that politics can happen in any of a variety of institutions: there is politics in families, in colleges and in business firms. It also immediately becomes obvious why politics is so important: the failure to make these choices by peaceful means, and to carry them out effectively and peacefully, has catastrophic results. Consider, for instance, the life of people unfortunate enough to live in poverty stricken countries of Africa, like the Democratic Republic of Congo. What single thing would transform their life: a great medical advance, a great advance in biotechnology which would make farming more productive? Neither of these things: their lives would be transformed for the better by peace and the creation of a stable system of government, because since the then Belgian Congo achieved independence over 50 years ago it has been racked by civil

DOCUMENTING POLITICS 1.1

Defining politics

- 'Politics are now nothing more than a means of rising in the world' (Samuel Johnson, English writer, 1709–84).
- 'Politics is perhaps the only profession for which no preparation is thought necessary' (Robert Louis Stevenson, Scottish writer, 1850–94).
- 'Whoever could make two ears of corn or two blades of grass to grow upon a spot of ground where only one grew before, would deserve better of mankind, and do more essential service to his country than the whole race of politicians put together' (Jonathan Swift, Irish writer, 1667–1745).

Definitions from students and practitioners are, predictably, more restrained:

- 'A human being is naturally a political animal' (Aristotle, Greek philosopher, 384–322 BC, *Ethics*).
- 'Politics is the art of the possible' (Bismarck, Prince Otto von, German statesman, 1815–98).
- 'Politics: who gets what, when, how' (Harold Lasswell, American political scientist, title of introduction to political science, 1950).
- 'A political system (is) any persistent pattern of human relationships that involves, to a significant extent, control, influence, power, or authority' (Robert Dahl, American political scientist, 1984:10).

- There is a popular cynicism about politics and politicians illustrated by our first three quotations. But our second four, though very different in their emphasis, all fasten on one key feature: that some form of political action is a necessary condition of all social life.

wars. Understanding politics, if we want to make the world a better place for our fellow human beings, is more urgent even than understanding medicine, biology or physics.

Because Britons – the most likely readers of this book – usually live in peace and security they naturally take the contribution of politics to our well-being for granted. But not all Britons, for when these conditions disappear we see immediately how important they are. That is the lesson of the last 40 years in the history of Northern Ireland. What single development transformed the lives of the people of Northern Ireland? The answer is obvious: the political settlement that finally brought a measure of peace to the province following the Belfast Agreement of 1998. (See Chapter 11 for more.) Indeed, when the first long standing ceasefire in the province began in 1994 the transformation took place: not only did the threat of violence diminish, but everything from the biggest things – like the state of the economy – to the smallest – like the ability of people in Belfast to enjoy the life of their city on a Saturday night – was transformed.

Of course these are very dramatic examples of the way politics matters in all our lives. But it is not just a matter of the way politics determines the biggest issues, like the very conditions of peaceful existence. Politics shapes every detail of our lives, from the most dramatic to the most mundane. And it does this for a particular historical reason: the importance of the institution called 'the state' in a country like the UK.

WHY STUDY THE STATE?

We began above by defining politics in very general terms – essentially as a social activity, which could be carried out in a whole variety of institutional settings. That is why we can and do speak of the internal politics of a college or a tennis club. But in Europe from the seventeenth century – most observers, if pressed for a single date, would choose the Treaty of Westphalia in 1648 – a very particular institution began to take on responsibility for managing the political process in societies. That institution we normally call 'the state'. Many social sciences study politics as a general social process, but the study of the politics connected with the state is usually done within the field of political studies or political science. That is just a matter of the convenient division of labour in academic work. Courses conventionally called 'politics' or 'government' are mostly concerned with this state-focused system of politics, and books like this one share the same preoccupation. The state is not the whole of politics; but since the seventeenth century it has been a very important part of politics.

Why is this, and why is so much of modern political studies preoccupied with the state? What emerged out of the Treaty of Westphalia was a particular political form, the essence of which is contained in the most famous definition of the state, one offered by a founding father of the social sciences, the German sociologist Max Weber: 'the state is a human community that (successfully) claims *the monopoly of the legitimate use of physical force* within a given territory' (See Briefing 1.1).

There are three elements of this definition to notice. First, the state is a territorial entity, as indeed a glance at a weather map of the UK in your morning paper will show. Second, the state claims to monopolize the means of coercion in this territory. This does not mean that physical coercion by other means does not take place; but it does mean that the state claims that coercion can only legitimately take place with its consent. The word 'legitimacy' gets at the third feature of the state: the claim to monopoly is tied to a claim to being the *legitimate* supreme power in a given territory.

What does 'legitimacy' mean? It involves the state making a special kind of claim to the loyalties of the population. The idea is once again well conveyed by Max Weber, who linked the idea of legitimacy to the idea of *authority*. If I have power over you that means that I have the capacity, whether you like it or not, to get you to do something you would not otherwise do. But if I exercise authority I command you, not simply through fear or money, but because you recognize my moral right to demand your obedience: I have a legitimate right to get you to obey. This idea of *legitimate* authority conveys a key claim of the modern state.

The notion of legitimate authority opens up another key feature of the state: why and how states are in practice obeyed. States have great powers of coercion: they can take away our property, our liberty and even our lives, by war or execution. But if we only obeyed the state through fear of coercion its power would be quite limited. We would disobey whenever we thought the state might not discover our disobedience, and that in turn would entail the state investing huge resources in spying and controlling its population. Some famous modern dictatorships of the twentieth century have indeed done exactly that, and as a result they have turned out to be quite inefficient. The states most effective in commanding obedience have ruled by legitimate authority rather than fear.

Legitimate authority can rest on various grounds. Weber again made a famous distinction between three sorts of authority. *Traditional authority* rests on custom, often based on right of succession, for instance the kind of authority claimed by a hereditary monarchy. Leaders with some extraordinary personal quality that commands obedience claim *charismatic authority.* *Rational–legal authority* is claimed on the grounds that the person or institution wielding it does so because of certain agreed rules and procedures.

BRIEFING 1.1

Max Weber's definition of state and of authority

Weber on the state: 'the relation between the state and violence is an especially intimate one ... the state is a human community that (successfully) claims the *monopoly of the legitimate use of physical force* within a given territory'.

Weber on the three grounds that can confer the legitimacy for domination:

- Traditional: 'the authority of the eternal yesterday ... traditional domination exercised by the patriarch and the patrimonial prince of yore'.
- Charismatic: 'the authority of extraordinary and personal gift of grace (charisma)' exercised by 'the great demagogue, or the political party leader'.
- Rational–legal authority: 'by virtue of the belief in the validity of legal statute and functional competence based on rationally created *rules*'.

■ Max Weber (1864–1920) was a key figure in the development of modern social science. But like all great social observers his apparently universal statements grew out of particular historical experiences. His most often quoted statements on the state and authority, summarized above, come from a lecture entitled 'Politics as a Vocation' delivered in Munich, the capital of Bavaria in 1918. The Great War (1914–18) had led to the collapse of three empires: Germany, Austro-Hungary and Tsarist Russia. Weber had been a supporter of the Monarchy in Germany; now he lived through upheaval, civil war, dictatorship and the threat of Communist Revolution. His view of the state as an institution that secured authority in a territory was inseparable from this experience of collapse and turmoil.

Source: Weber, 1918/1948.

One reason Weber's classification is so important is that it throws light on the changing nature of legitimate authority in the state. Traditional authority was typically in the past claimed by monarchs. We can see faint traces in the case of the present British monarchy: the Queen is monarch through right of succession, even though the line of succession was often falsified. The original charismatic leader was the Pope, who claims to wield authority as the anointed successor of Christ. 'Charisma' is a word of Greek origins, and its original literal meaning conveys the idea of being an anointed one, marked with divine qualities. As a sign of this, at the coronation of a Pope the new Pontiff is anointed with an oil called chrism; and an even fainter sign can be seen in the fact that the coronation of a monarch in Britain also involves being anointed with oil of chrism. (Readers of this book who have been confirmed will know of a fainter echo yet: at the Christian ceremony of confirmation anointing with chrism takes place as a sign of joining the elect of the church.) The genius of Weber's notion of charisma lay not in the way it interpreted the past, but how it anticipated a

terrible future. Elaborated at the start of the twentieth century, it anticipated the kind of authority claimed by the most notorious dictatorships of the twentieth century: both Hitler in Nazi Germany (1933–45) and Stalin in Soviet Russia (died 1953) were pictured as having superhuman, god-like qualities of leadership.

The other great form of authority in our age is rational–legal authority, which is now closely associated with the modern democratic state such as exists in Britain. From the core notion of rational legality – that the exercise of authority is rule bound – come several key ideas in modern politics, especially democratic politics. As our example of the British Monarchy shows, there are faint traces of both traditional and charismatic authority in modern British government. But the most important source of authority claimed by the state in Britain is rational legality: it is to be obeyed because what it does is governed by explicit rules covering both the substance of what it can do and the ways it can do it. (To help make the point, Documenting Politics 1.2 provides an everyday example of the exercise of rational–legal authority in Britain.) This idea that state authority is rule bound is also, as we will now see, central to an equally important claim made by the state in Britain: that it is democratic.

WHY STUDY DEMOCRACY?

Until the twentieth century democracy was usually spoken of in hostile terms. That hostile tradition began at the very dawn of political theory. The Greek political philosopher Aristotle classified democracy as a form of tyranny, because it was a form of class rule: rule in the interests of the poor, propertyless masses in a society. That is why, until the twentieth century, it was viewed with hostility or suspicion, at least by anyone with property. But it is now most commonly thought of in procedural terms: democratic governments are democratic because they have been chosen by particular rules, usually involving winning some sort of majority in elections where all or most adults have the right to take part. In Britain, although formally we still speak of Her Majesty's Government, implying that authority is traditional, in reality the government's authority rests on the fact that it won a General Election and has a majority in the House of Commons. 'Democracy', in this meaning, has shrunk to something quite narrow: it refers to a procedure (periodic elections involving most of the adult population), which selects the Government.

Commanding a majority in the House of Commons is also critical to another aspect of rational–legal authority. A majority gives the capacity, in most cases, to pass laws, and a government's ability to command obedience only stretches to those areas where it is backed by properly enacted laws. Not only do we not feel obliged to obey government if it makes demands beyond the law; we are entitled to, and often do, challenge it in the courts. In short, in Britain, the rational–legal authority of government is not only bound up with the fact that it has won a majority under defined rules of political competition, but that its claims to obedience rest on properly passed laws. This notion of the rule of law is thus central to claims to authority. That is why in our illustration (Documenting Politics 1.2) rational–legal authority is illustrated by a tax demand received by me. If I do not pay the tax the authorities will seek a court judgement against me, seizing my property to the value of the demand (plus an additional fine). But I can successfully appeal against the demand if I can show that the authorities have not acted in accordance with the law – for instance, if they have not applied the legally stated tax rate in calculating my bill. (This is the theory; later in the book, especially in Chapters 21 and 22, we will examine how far this opti-

IMAGE 1.1 ■ The tank and the piper

Photo: Maurice McDonald/PA/EMPICS

■ Max Weber (Briefing 1.1) defined the state by its monopoly of coercion. But we also know that physical force is not enough: states need symbols that arouse loyalty. The photo, taken during the military campaign in Iraq, encapsulates the two elements: the tank has for more than a century been a hugely effective instrument of military action; the regimental piper has an even longer lineage, symbolizing the attachment of soldiers to their regiment, the Crown and the state.

mistic view of British government as constrained by law fits the reality.)

In some political systems, but not yet in Britain, this notion of government under law is given a special force by a written constitution. A constitution lays down the most important rules of political procedure: for instance, how elections are to be organized, the powers of different branches of government, and the rights of citizens against government. As we will see, one of the peculiarities of Britain is that, while it undoubtedly has a constitution, it does not have it in the form of a single written document.

The theory of modern democracy thus claims that it is a form of rule involving the selection of government by some majority and the exercise of restraint on government by compelling it to act only in accordance with the law. This theory in turn entails another key idea: accountability. Periodic elections are of course one important way in which governments are obliged to be held accountable – literally, to give an account of their stewardship over the preceding period. One of the marks of democratic government is the existence of a wide range of formal and informal practices and institutions designed to ensure that government is held accountable for its actions. We shall see that the different meanings of

DOCUMENTING POLITICS 1.2

The tax demand as rational–legal authority

■ The tax demand (received by the author) illustrates the most important kind of authority identified by Weber, now at the heart of the modern state: rational–legal authority. The power of the Inland Revenue (or HM Revenue and Customs as it is now called) to issue the demand derives solely from the law. The substance of the demand – the size of the bill – is the product of calculations according to explicit rules, referred to in the demand. And the ability to enforce the demand depends on the calculation having been made according to the rules: hence the invitation to the recipient to examine and if appropriate disagree with the calculation.

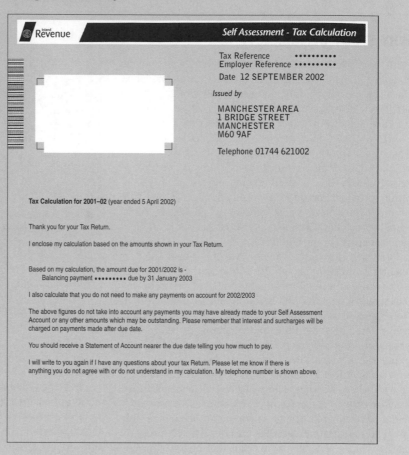

Inland **Revenue**

Self Assessment - Tax Calculation

Tax Reference •••••••••
Employer Reference •••••••••

Date 12 SEPTEMBER 2002

Issued by

MANCHESTER AREA
1 BRIDGE STREET
MANCHESTER
M60 9AF

Telephone 01744 621002

Tax Calculation for 2001–02 (year ended 5 April 2002)

Thank you for your Tax Return.

I enclose my calculation based on the amounts shown in your Tax Return.

Based on my calculation, the amount due for 2001/2002 is -
        Balancing payment •••••••• due by 31 January 2003

I also calculate that you do not need to make any payments on account for 2002/2003

The above figures do not take into account any payments you may have already made to your Self Assessment Account or any other amounts which may be outstanding. Please remember that interest and surcharges will be charged on payments made after due date.

You should receive a Statement of Account nearer the due date telling you how much to pay.

I will write to you again if I have any questions about your tax Return. Please let me know if there is anything you do not agree with or do not understand in my calculation. My telephone number is shown above.

accountability, and the tests of accountability, are central to debates about whether we do indeed have effective democracy in Britain.

Weber's famous definition of the state opened up for us the important notion of authority. But two other linked elements in his definition open up another key political concept: his notion that the state claims a monopoly of authority, and claims it in a bounded territory. These are encapsulated in the idea of sovereignty – a notion that was central to the emergence of the state as a key political unit after the Treaty of Westphalia in 1648. In legal theory, sovereignty – the idea that a state commanded supreme authority in its own territory – was at the core of statehood. As we will see, it has turned out to be one of the most difficult and contested ideas in modern British politics.

States in the seventeenth century could make these Weber-like claims, but in practice they often had very little impact on the daily lives of the populations over whom they ruled. The state in the twenty-first century is a very different matter – as the example of Britain below will show.

WHY STUDY BRITISH POLITICS?

Why should anyone be interested in the study of British politics? There are two linked answers: they partly have to do with the importance of Britain, and they partly have to do with the lives of those who live in Britain. Imagine first posing the question to someone who did not live in Britain. The British political system would

TABLE 1.1   **Britain as a rich and privileged country: the British and the poorest on earth**

	Britain	*Poorest countries on earth**
Life expectancy (years)	79	59
Infant mortality rates (per live 1,000 births)	5	78
Gross national income, per head (US$)	45,390	524
Internet users (per 100 people)	79.4	3.7

* The figures are for the poorest countries identified by the World Bank for its 'low income' set – a collective portrait of the poorest countries on earth.

■ The table summarizes the single most important feature of social and economic life in Britain: it is one of a small number of fabulously rich countries by the standards of most of the world's population (and by the standards of most Britons of earlier generations). The figures compare Britain with the poorest countries as identified in its country profiles by the World Bank. Some of the figures directly measure the huge disparities in income, such as that for gross national income per head. Some measure fundamental differences in life chances, such as those for mortality, adult and infant. Some measure access to modern technology which most Britons now take for granted.

Source: Calculated from World Bank Development Indicators 2009: www.worldbank.org.

nevertheless be highly relevant. Britain is an exceptionally important member of the international state system, because it is one of a small number of rich and powerful states that belong to what is sometimes called the 'first world'. It is also a member, in the European Union, of an organization which, as we shall see, is one of the most important economic and political players in world politics.

Britain also has a special historical significance in the development of the wider global system. The Industrial Revolution, which Britain pioneered in the eighteenth century, created the first industrial society, clearing a path in economics and politics which many other leading nations have followed. In short, you do not have to be particularly interested in Britain for its own sake to find the study of British politics important; you just have to be interested in our modern world and how we got here.

For those who live in Britain the importance of politics is greater still. A century ago most people who lived in Britain could go through their daily lives without being significantly touched by the state: if you had wandered round a British town a century ago the only big public employer you would have seen evidence of, for example, would have been the Post Office (then, as now, it was publicly owned). But during the twentieth century the British state, like the states of other democracies, emerged as a major influence on the lives of all citizens. The typical reader of this book is probably a student at a university or at a college for 16–19 year olds, and most of his or her contemporaries will profess themselves entirely uninterested in government and politics. Yet

their lives are profoundly shaped by what goes on in the political arena and by what government does. Just consider some of the ways. They will almost certainly have been born in a hospital run by the National Health Service, a state funded and state controlled body. Bar a small minority they will have been educated in state schools – schools entirely funded by government and, over the last couple of decades, subjected to close control by central government as to what they teach and how they teach. And now, if in further or higher education, the story will be repeated. Although students in higher education in England pay an annual fee, that fee nowhere near covers the cost, most of which comes from taxation raised by central government. And as in schools, what is taught, and how it is taught, is increasingly prescribed by agencies of central government.

This sketch is just a miniature of the way government now looms large in the life of all of us. Figure 1.1 presents a summary measure of the long-term growth in the scale of government spending over this last century. (More recent changes are examined later, especially in Chapter 20.)

British politics is an important subject of study because of its size and historical importance, so we try to make sense of it for academic reasons. But there are also reasons why as citizens we should study it. Those reasons are summarized below.

Understanding. Anyone who follows the daily arguments that go on in British politics – in the House of Commons or in the media – will know that they are highly charged. They resemble more the argument of a

FIGURE 1.1 ■ The growth in the scale of government over a century (% gross domestic product accounted for by general government spending)

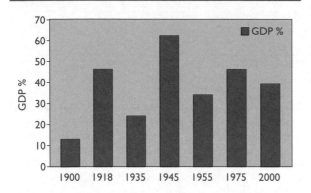

■ The chart highlights the changing scale of spending by government at various points over the course of the twentieth century. It measures 'general government spending' – a broad measure – as a proportion of gross domestic product, the commonest measure of the size of the wider economy. It thus measures both the growing absolute scale of government and also its changing relative importance in the wider economy. It is a summary of why studying British government is so important: government is easily the biggest institution in British society. The great financial crisis that began in 2007 had a dramatic effect on the scale of government commitments; this is discussed in Chapter 20.

Source: Calculated from Clark and Dilnot 2002:3.

courtroom, where competing prosecutors and defenders do battle, than the atmosphere of a scientific laboratory or a seminar room. But politics also needs to be understood in a manner just as dispassionately as we try to understand the workings of the natural world. In the broadest sense of the term the study of politics thus needs to be 'scientific'. This does not mean that the key elements we study in politics – who are after all human beings – are like the key elements that a chemist or an astronomer studies. Nor does it mean that we expect to be able to develop the sort of highly formal, mathematically expressed theories common in the physical sciences. (Nevertheless in some areas, like the most sophisticated study of elections, mathematical formality is quite well advanced.) 'Science' is a word with a root in Latin and by origin it denotes only knowledge and its systematic study. To speak of the need to study British politics scientifically is thus only to speak of the need to study it as systematically and dispassionately as possible; to develop accounts of how the various parts of the system operate; and to debate the accuracy of those

accounts, not by reference to our subjective views, but by reference to agreed bodies of evidence.

Effective citizenship. Britain is run, we will discover, by an activist minority numbered in tens, rather than hundreds, of thousands. Some readers of this book will eventually form a part of that minority. There are many ways of getting knowledge about how the system of government operates in order to have an effective say in government, and practical participation in politics is one. But that sort of knowledge only comes with long experience. Not everyone wants to wait 20 years to pick up the hard truths about the realities of political power; systematic study is a way of short-circuiting that extended learning through experience.

Making government effective. Governments make decisions and put those decisions into effect. Nothing guarantees that they are wise decisions or, if they are, that wise decisions actually take effect. One of the main lessons of the study of British government in recent years, we will see in these pages, is that good government is more than a matter of good intentions or good people. It also depends on how government is run. Getting things wrong can be catastrophic. Northern Ireland, for instance, was very badly run between the 1920s and the 1960s, and part of what was bad about how it was run can be found in the way government in the province was organized. Between the end of the 1960s and the 1990s several thousand people paid with their lives for that bad history. Lesser, but still great fiascos, occur every day. Government manages the economy, sometimes for better, sometimes for worse. Look around your neighbourhood. Is the way it is laid out – the amount of green space, the safety of the roads, the quality of the buildings – satisfactory? If not, at least some of the blame can be laid at the door of government in its role as the planner of our local environment. Understanding how government is organized, and how it fails or succeeds in particular policies, does not guarantee that we can produce more effective government; but without this knowledge we have no chance at all of improving the quality of our governing institutions.

THREE BIG QUESTIONS ABOUT BRITISH POLITICS

We have been answering questions about the reasons for studying politics, and studying British politics in particular. It is time to turn to more particular questions: those that focus on British politics itself. These questions anticipate the most important themes that recur throughout the pages of the rest of this book, and we

BRIEFING 1.2

Why we cannot take success in government for granted

■ Northern Ireland was ruled from the 1920s to the 1960s by sectarian devolved government which systematically discriminated against Catholics and Irish nationalists (whom it mostly treated as the same). Governments of both parties in Westminster turned a blind eye. At the end of the 1960s civil strife resulted. Since then governments of both parties have struggled with the consequences, the most disastrous of which have been the loss of over 3,000 lives.

■ The Poll Tax was introduced in the 1980s by Mrs Thatcher's government, and almost as quickly abandoned. It was intended to be a new way of levying taxes by local government. It led to large scale civil disobedience, did huge damage to local government finance and wasted about £1.5 billion in public money.

■ In 2007–08 the British banking system came close to complete collapse because regulators, especially in the Bank of England and the Financial Services Authority, incompetently regulated the business practices of banks, who made huge, grossly imprudent loan commitments. The complete collapse was avoided; but we all continue to bear the price in both paying for huge financial support for the banks and in the way the failed banking system has damaged the rest of the economy leading, for instance, to rapid rises in unemployment.

■ Government successfully carries out many complex tasks. But the very scale of the modern state in Britain means that when things go wrong, they often go wrong in a spectacular fashion. Success has to be worked for, and as the three cases show, when it is not achieved the result is a fiasco, often, as in the case of Northern Ireland, on the scale of a grand tragedy.

will return to them in the final chapter. Three are sketched below because they recur so commonly in later pages.

Who has power in Britain and under what conditions do they exercise that power?

This is the most fundamental of all questions about British government, and for very obvious reasons. The struggle for power lies at the heart of all political life, and it bears in particular on the most important moral claim made about British government: that it is democratic. As Briefing 1.3 illustrates, there are many meanings that can be attributed to democracy, and many ways of conceiving 'power'. But at the very minimum the theory that Britain is democratic demands two things: that power be widely distributed and that those who exercise power should do so in an open way according to clear rules and be held accountable for its exercise. In terms of the theories outlined in Briefing 1.3 power in Britain should at least match the requirements of the 'pluralist' model of power distribution.

An equally important claim about British government concerns not the direct question of the distribution of power, but the conditions under which it is exercised:

that the system of government is constitutional. What this amounts to is the claim that government is constrained by law and that the liberties of citizens are protected by the independent power of law. It is easy to see that we could all live under such a system of limited, constrained government even if the system were not democratic in the sense of allowing us a positive say in the making of policy. We will see that the claim that the British system is constitutional in this sense is intensely debated. The preference for imposing constitutional limitations on government goes alongside a powerful apparatus – through, for instance, Official Secrets legislation – ensuring secrecy in the operation of a large part of the state machine. In institutions like the security services the state has bodies that can seriously infringe the liberties of citizens. In at least one part of the kingdom – Northern Ireland – many of the established mechanisms for ensuring liberty, such as jury trial for some categories of offence, were suspended for a generation on the grounds that this suspension was needed to combat the bigger threat to liberty posed by terrorism. Some claim that in the 'war against terror' the British government colluded in the torture of citizens (see Political Issues 1.1). Britain is also quite special in not

BRIEFING 1.3

Theories of democratic government

	Class rule	Direct democracy	Elitist democracy	Pluralist democracy
How are decisions made?	By direct participation of the poor and propertyless.	By direct participation of all people, either in assemblies or through devices like referenda.	By political and administrative elites; the former elected through competition by parties for the popular vote.	By political and administrative elites, and by numerous competing organized interests and opinion groups.
In whose interests?	Those without property.	Decisions reflect the general will of the community, as expressed by choices made after collective deliberation.	Decisions reflect the balance of power between competing elites, modified by the need to compete for the popular vote every four or five years.	Decisions reflect the balance of power between different groups at different times, no one interest dominates and no interest has a monopoly of the different means of exercising power over decision.
Influence in Britain.	Almost nil.	Historically nil; some growth in the use of referenda, public opinion polling and a few experiments with mass electronic voting allowing direct popular say in particular decisions.	Was the dominant form of democratic rule in Britain throughout the twentieth century following the creation of near universal adult voting rights after 1918.	Is the commonest 'official' approved account of how Britain has been, and continues to be, governed.

■ 'Democracy' comes in many forms. Before the twentieth century most people thought of democracy as 'class rule', and were fearful of it. 'Direct democracy' was long associated with small communities since it was believed that only when numbers were small was real direct participation in decisions possible. 'Elitist democracy' was the dominant academic theory of how democracy functioned for most of the second half of the twentieth century. Its intellectual father is the great Austrian social scientist Joseph Schumpeter (1883–1950): his masterpiece, *Capitalism, Socialism and Democracy* (1943), offered a vision of democracy as the competitive struggle for the popular vote by elites. 'Pluralist democracy' is a close cousin of elitism, but it stresses the importance of popular participation through the web of organized (and unorganized) interests and opinions in society, and sees group organization and participation and voting in elections as complementary.

POLITICAL ISSUES 1.1

Liberal freedoms under pressure: torture and the war on terror

We saw in Briefing 1.1 that a defining feature of the state is its ability to impose coercion. But coercion is supposed to be limited by the rules of liberal democracy. Torture, whatever precise definition it is given, is acknowledged to be 'out of bounds' under the rules of liberal democracy. But what happens in a world where terror threats are global and cooperation occurs between states, some of whom are liberal democracies and some of whom are not? 'Rendition' illustrates the problem. It refers to the practice of a liberal democracy, the US, 'rendering' suspects to jurisdictions where there are not liberal safeguards against torture, and then using the evidence gained. The US admits that it has used rendition; the UK has now admitted that it assisted the US in the process of despatching suspects for rendition; there are allegations by suspects that they were tortured with the complicity of the UK authorities.

The case illuminates three key issues about state power:

- It shows the critical connection between national citizenship and the exercise of power: the state makes a clear distinction here between the rights of British nationals and foreigners.
- It illuminates in a particularly clear way the heart of coercive state power.
- It illuminates one of the central dilemmas of a liberal democracy, such as Britain claims to be: how far the safe-guards conventional in a liberal democracy, like those against imprisonment without trial, can defensibly be violated.

having a written constitution that incorporates a bill of rights for citizens – one of the main legal mechanisms used in other democratic countries to try to ensure that citizen liberties are protected. But we will also see that Britain has undergone a constitutional revolution in recent years, and we will want to discover how far this has strengthened the forces making the exercise of power open and accountable.

Is British central government 'hollowed-out' government?

Arguments about power and accountability assume that there is some worthwhile power to be struggled over. Yet in recent years doubts have grown over the degree to which power actually is any longer exercised at the traditional centre of British government, in London. The argument is that the centre is being 'hollowed out', that power is forcibly being distributed across many levels of society – and that, as a result, government in Britain is necessarily 'multilevel' government: policy is made and executed at many different levels and is the result of bargaining and manoeuvring by a wide range of forces at these different levels. The biggest problem for the 'centre' is trying to coordinate this multilevel system in

order to produce some consistency and effectiveness in what government does.

Three big forces lie behind these claims. First, the spectacular policy failures illustrated in Briefing 1.2 show that modern government is a highly complex business. (There is further discussion of policy fiascos in Chapters 19 and 23.) British government was traditionally very centralized in London, but this centralization makes government highly vulnerable to policy disasters. Only by recognizing that the power to shape successful policy is nowadays distributed widely through many social networks can governments have any hope of governing effectively. The age of successful policy made by command from the centre in London is at an end, though governments in London do not necessarily recognize this fact.

Second, British government is being 'hollowed-out' from the top, as a result of our membership of the European Union. A large number of important decisions, especially about the critical matter of economic policy, can no longer be made independently in London; at best they have to be negotiated through the institutions of the European Union, mostly in Brussels. This second force obviously connects to one of the major themes of this book: the thoroughgoing interpenetration between the institutions of government in Britain and the institutions of government in the European Union. These changes now date back a long time: they can be traced to Britain's original entry into what was then the European Economic Community in 1973, something we look at in more detail in Chapters 2 and 5.

But the third force is more recent: it is produced by the large scale constitutional changes introduced by the new Labour Government after 1998, especially the establishment of devolved executives for Wales and Scotland. This last change, according to the hollowing-out theory, amounts to hollowing out 'from below'. This form of hollowing-out may be the most important of all: it forms a big theme of Chapters 10 and 11, which examine the experience of devolved government in the UK.

Can the British state manage the economy in an age of globalization?

The election of a new Conservative Government under Margaret Thatcher in 1979 was a momentous event in British politics – perhaps the single most momentous peacetime event in British politics during the twentieth century. Mrs Thatcher remained Prime Minister for over 11 years, the longest tenure of any Prime Minister of modern times. The 1980s were the decade of 'Thatcherism': unusually, a whole political programme was identified with a leading politician. Thatcherism produced revolutionary changes in Britain. It transformed economic life: it greatly reduced the power of trade unions; it sold off many large publicly owned industries, like gas and telecommunications, and disposed of over a million council house dwellings to sitting tenants; it forced numerous industries to abandon restrictions on competition. It also transformed government: as we will see, for instance in Chapter 7, it fundamentally reorganized the structure of the civil service. Thatcherism also led to a wider transformation of political life. The Labour Party spent the 1980s trying to work out how to cope with Mrs Thatcher, suffering three successive election defeats at her hands (in 1979, 1983 and 1987). It ended up by accepting most of the elements of the Thatcher revolution.

But there was a more fundamental strategic importance in the victory of Thatcherism which went beyond everyday struggles between the parties. Thatcherism involved embracing the full forces of globalization – something that is described more fully in the next chapter. New Labour after 1997 fully accepted the idea that the only successful economy was an economy that competed in a lightly regulated fashion in world markets – especially in world financial markets. And for much of the 1990s and the early years of the new millennium it

seemed that this prescription worked: at any rate successive British Prime Ministers and Chancellors of the Exchequers lectured foreigners and Britons alike about the need to embrace freely competitive global markets. The great world financial crisis of 2007–09 brought that era to an end. It has been succeeded by a world recession which has been particularly severe in the UK. As the British government struggled to avoid the complete collapse of the banking system in 2008, measures were taken – like the nationalization of banks – which would have been unthinkable even a few months before. The state has once again emerged as a major force controlling economic life. The big questions are now whether, and on what terms, the British state can effectively control economic life. These are themes we return to in the concluding chapter.

FRAMING BRITISH POLITICS THEORETICALLY

The issues sketched here are many and complicated, and in our concluding chapter we will see that they intersect with a variety of competing accounts of how British politics has been changing over the last generation. One reason they are complicated is that the way we think about British politics, and the way we investigate it, is a product of a series of usually barely articulated assumptions that we make about the social world. These are sometimes summarized as arising from positions of ontology and epistemology. Ontology refers to a fundamental position which we all hold, but about which we hardly ever think: is there a world 'out there' which exists independently of us, or is 'reality' fundamentally a construct of our subjective understanding of the world? Epistemology is related to this, but bears much more directly on the kind of evidence we can rely on as being able to gather information about the social world, of which of course the political world is a part. One position is that we can indeed gather evidence about social/political worlds in much the same way as we can gather evidence about the natural world. An alternative position is that, since we are, as human beings, embedded in social and political worlds, the kind of knowledge we can have is different from the kind of knowledge that can be gathered about a physical world which is not marked by human consciousness. When we study politics, not only are we studying it as political beings, but the political 'world' consists of other human beings like ourselves.

These abstractions may seem a long way from the everyday conduct of British politics, but they soon lead to very clear conclusions – and to very different conclusions. For instance, if ontologically we accept that there

DEBATING POLITICS 1.1

The study of politics: practically useful or practically useless?

THE STUDY OF POLITICS IS OF PRACTICAL IMPORTANCE	THE STUDY OF POLITICS IS PRACTICALLY USELESS
▶ Most of the big sources of human misery are political in origin: wars, revolution, poverty. Curing or alleviating these would immeasurably benefit humanity.	▶ After more than 2,000 years of studying politics we are still no nearer remedying the political causes of human misery.
▶ Governments frequently perpetrate policy disasters and it is important to understand the causes of those disasters.	▶ Understanding disasters after they have occurred is like locking the stable door when the horse has bolted.
▶ British democracy demands informed citizens – and being informed about how government operates is a vital kind of information.	▶ Most citizens get by, and get active in politics, without opening a single academic text or attending a single politics lecture.
▶ The study of politics in a university or college provides a valuable training for a political career.	▶ None of the greatest British Prime Ministers studied politics at university: Mrs Thatcher studied chemistry; neither David Lloyd George nor Winston Churchill studied at a university.

is indeed a 'real' world out there that exists independently of our perceptions, and if we accept that it is possible to understand that political world in much the same way as a scientist understands nature, then we are very quickly led to the conclusion that we can study British politics 'scientifically': that we can offer statements about British political 'reality' that can stand independently of our own individual preferences, just as the statements of the chemist or physicist about the physical world can stand independently of the scientific researcher's individual preferences. But if we ontologically doubt an objectively existing reality, and if we doubt that we can separate our nature as social beings from the way we experience the social world, we are led in a very different direction: to the one made influential by Bevir and Rhodes, in which the point of studying British politics is to explicate competing interpretations of the world of British politics held by the actors in the political system. Hence that alternative direction is usually labelled 'interpretivism' (Bevir and Rhodes 2003, 2006, 2010.) In one direction, therefore, we are led, ultimately, to the attempt to construct scientific laws of political behaviour in Britain; in the contrary direction we are led to the exploration of the subjective perceptions of those engaged in politics, and indeed to the intersection between those perceptions and our own.

It may seem alarming to the beginning student to be confronted with these radically different choices, and it would indeed be alarming if the beginner were required to make some initial decision between them. Fortunately, the implications are much less drastic; indeed, the worst thing to do would be to decide to 'plump' for or against the notion of, say, a science of British politics. What we can draw from these discussions is the importance of being conscious from the beginning about what we are doing. It is important, in reading any study of British politics, to ask oneself: what are the ontological and epistemological assumptions that underpin this study? More simply: what is assumed in the study about the nature of political reality and how knowledge of it can be gathered?

The reader might reasonably respond: suppose it is not clear what the assumptions are in any particular study? Indeed, they often will not be clear, or may indicate confusion and contradiction in ontology and epistemology. But this is precisely why we need to learn to interrogate accounts of British politics. Indeed, just about the most striking feature of the study of British politics until recently was the lack of any consciousness about issues of ontology and epistemology. It was a decidedly untheoretical part of the discipline of political studies and had grown out of a highly practical interest in the workings of British government – indeed many of its leading authors had had direct experience of government. That practical orientation had its strengths: it kept the author's feet on the ground, so to speak, by emphasizing the importance of engaging directly with the world of government. But it also meant that the perceptions and preoccupations of the powerful and well placed were often taken at face value. For instance, since the powerful and well placed in Britain are mostly to be found in London, the overwhelming preoccupation of the academic study of British politics has been with the world of central government in London: with what, in this book, is described as the Westminster system. Students of the subject tended to equate British politics with this system – to work, quite unconsciously, with a 'Westminster model' of politics to the exclusion of much else. That covered not only the substance of the subjects studied, but also the problems identified: the 'problems' of British politics tended to be the problems that preoccupied those who dominated at the metropolitan centre.

We need to be conscious about the ontological and epistemological assumptions that underpin our own study of British politics; and we need to be particularly conscious about how far our understandings are taken unthinkingly from the world view of the powerful. That applies in the same measure to this book as to everything else. While in the following pages I have tried to escape the dominance of the Westminster model, I can offer no guarantee of success. Thus for the beginning student embarking on this book a very useful exercise is to read the following pages with an attitude of interrogating scepticism about its treatment of the British political world.

Review OF CHAPTER 1

Five themes have dominated this chapter:

◖▶ The importance of politics as an activity for securing for any community the basics of a peaceful and prosperous life.

◖▶ The importance of the state as an arena where the most vital political issues are contested.

◖▶ The importance of the British system of government, both for anyone interested in government across the rich industrial nations and for anyone who actually lives in Britain.

◖▶ The importance of studying British government in the light of hotly contested questions about the nature of power and democracy, the nature of decision making in Britain, and the impact of the era of Thatcherism in Britain.

◖▶ The importance of reading accounts of British politics in a spirit of interrogation and scepticism.

FURTHER READING

ESSENTIAL
If you read only one book for this chapter it should be Dryzek and Dunleavy (2009) which comprehensively surveys theories of the democratic state and of the nature of politics.

RECOMMENDED
The classic introduction to the nature of politics is Crick (2000). A standard American work which is particularly strong on the study of power and authority is Dahl (1984). Professor Crick chaired a committee on the teaching of citizenship: its report (Crick 1998) is a very good introduction to the study of the subject in a British setting. Harrison (1996) provides a clear, compressed, thematic introduction to British politics covering more than a century. The whole of section 1 of Flinders et al. (2009) surveys the history of the study of British models. A very good introduction to the historically controversial meaning of democracy is Macpherson (1971). Bevir and Rhodes (2010) is advanced but very rewarding. Furlong and Marsh (2010) is the best entry to the often highly abstract debates about ontology and epistemology.

Britain: a capitalist democracy

CONTENTS

AIMS

This chapter :

- [ ] Explains the significance of combining capitalism with democracy, as is done in the UK

- [ ] Describes the history of capitalist democracy in Britain

- [ ] Describes the main tensions between capitalism and democracy in governing Britain

- [ ] Describes how capitalist democracy in Britain compares with some other important 'models' of democratic capitalism

- [ ] Describes how recent changes in British society have altered the character of capitalist democracy in Britain

CAPITALISM AND DEMOCRACY

We saw in the Introduction, and in Chapter 1, that most accounts of politics in Britain picture it as some sort of democracy – even if fully democratic politics is only an aspiration, providing a standard against which we can evaluate the reality of governing Britain. But politics cannot be isolated from the wider society, and one feature of that wider society – the way the economy functions – is critical to understanding the way Britain is governed. The economy of Britain is capitalist.

'Capitalism' is a word often used polemically – either as a term of approval or disapproval. But here it is used descriptively. A capitalist economy has two distinguishing features. First, it allocates resources primarily through market forces: that is, through price mechanisms which signal demand, and generate supply, of goods and services. Second, the most important economic institutions – firms – are privately owned. Thus the twin institutions of market allocation and private property define a capitalist economy.

Even this summary description immediately alerts us to an important implication: capitalist economies come in many shapes and sizes. There is no society where all goods and services are allocated by market mechanisms: societies conventionally labelled 'capitalist' differ in the degree to which they rely on the market or, alternatively, use the state for allocation. Likewise, there is no society where all productive resources are privately owned. Every capitalist economy is a mixed economy of public and private ownership; the key difference lies in the composition of the mix.

Combining a political system organized on democratic lines with an economy organized on capitalist lines has great consequences for British politics. The diversity that a capitalist economy produces helps underpin the workings of democratic politics. In our examination of the representation of interests in later chapters, for instance, we will see that the variety of interests created by the market economy – variety of firms, industries, sectors – is an important spur to the organization of the competing interests that are an essential part of healthy democratic life. Not all capitalist economies, it is true, are also democracies. If we look around the world we can find many examples – in Latin America, in some of the states of the old Soviet Union – where free markets are combined with undemocratic systems. But on the other hand it is hard to find a democratic political system that does not have a capitalist economy. Being capitalist does not guarantee democracy, but it helps a lot.

Nevertheless, uniting democratic politics and capitalist economics creates powerful tensions, and we shall see that they are particularly acute in Britain. The origin

IMAGE 2.1 ■ The symbolic representation of wealth and capitalism: the Royal Exchange in the City of London

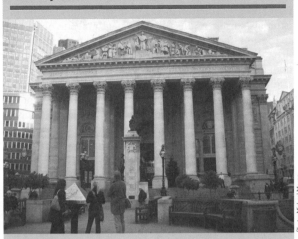

Photo: Michael Moran

■ A Royal Exchange building has stood on this site in the centre of the City of London since an original building was opened by Queen Elizabeth I in 1571. The present building was erected in 1844. On the pediment are inscribed the words: 'The earth is the Lord's and the fullness thereof' – a Victorian unifying of God and Mammon. It was the original physical place where London's trading took place. With the rise of electronic trading its function has now changed: it is a shopping centre trading the brands associated with the most luxurious end of capitalism, such as Hermès and Tiffany, where the bankers of London can go to spend some of their bonuses (see Political Issues 2.1).

of these tensions lies in the way democracy and capitalism rest on different principles of social organization. At the heart of modern democratic politics in Britain, for instance, is a presumption of equality in citizenship. How far that presumption is realized in practice is, we shall see, a recurrent source of argument, but the presumption is well established. It lies behind basic principles of political organization, such as underpin the electoral system: the principle of 'one person, one vote', in which everybody – regardless of property, capacity or education – is entitled to cast a vote that counts equally in elections. It lies behind the workings of the judicial system, in the presumption that all are equal in the eyes of the law. (How far these principles and presumptions actually guide behaviour are examined in subsequent chapters.)

By contrast, the principles of a capitalist economy presume inequality in the distribution of productive resources and in the outcomes of market forces. The stock of wealth is distributed unequally, as are the continuing rewards of economic activity, in profits and incomes. This inequality is not accidental: it is a designed feature of the market system. Both friends and foes of capitalist economics recognize that inequality is one of its inherent characteristics. Defenders of this feature of a capitalist order argue that inequality of outcomes – in the form of profits, for instance, for the most successful firms – are necessary to encourage enterprise and risk taking. This is not just a theoretical matter. The most enduring feature of the capitalist economy in Britain is the way it indeed in practice has allocated economic resources in a strikingly unequal way; and as we shall see this inequality has grown in recent decades.

The tension between the presumptions of equality that underpin democratic citizenship, and the realities of inequality in the capitalist economy, lies at the heart of British politics. The divisions and inequalities created by the market economy permeate the political system and constantly inhibit the ability to realize the egalitarian principles of democratic citizenship. How the state should respond to inequalities is a key and enduring problem of democratic politics. Simply: how far should the power of the state be used to reshape the workings of the capitalist economy, notably to moderate the inequalities which it produces? How far, indeed, is it possible for the state effectively to engage in the task of moderation? The tension between democratic principles and capitalist economics is not the only source of tension in Britain, but it is an overwhelmingly important one. That tension, as we shall in the next section, has deep historical roots.

THE HISTORY OF CAPITALIST DEMOCRACY IN BRITAIN

Britain was a capitalist society before it was a democracy, and this particular historical sequence has had important consequences for modern British politics. The critical historical event in the British economy occurred in the middle decades of the eighteenth century when, to use an image popular with economic historians, the economy 'took off' in the Industrial Revolution. By the middle of the nineteenth century the fact of Britain's pioneering voyage into industrialism had exerted a huge impact on British politics and society – an impact that continues to be felt. That impact could be summed up in three ways: physical; social; international.

Physical

The Industrial Revolution changed the physical face of Britain. Before it, the country was primarily a rural society with an agricultural economy, and most of the population lived in small towns and villages. By the middle of the nineteenth century manufacturing industry, and extractive industries like mining, were the dominant employers. Britain had become an urban society: that is, the majority of the population now lived in large towns and in cities that had grown rapidly in a short time. Manchester's population, for instance, grew from 89,000 to 303,000 between 1811 and 1851.

Social

These changes in the physical face of Britain were accompanied by huge changes in social structure and social relations, and these in turn had immense political consequences. Much of the political history of the nineteenth century – especially the history of the party system and the electoral system – was about trying to work out these consequences. Two sets should be highlighted.

First, the physical and geographical consequences were at the base of long running political issues and tensions. The political system before the Industrial Revolution was organized for a rural society, and moreover a rural society dominated by a hereditary aristocracy that had its wealth primarily in land. A critical problem for most of the nineteenth century concerned what to do in response to the growth, not just of new industries, but also of the vast cities – like Manchester and Birmingham – that had spread so rapidly due to industrial change. A large amount of institutional reform in the nineteenth century – for instance in local government and in the electoral system – was an attempt to address the problem of how to create systems of government for these new urban centres and how to incorporate them into existing national institutions, like the House of Commons.

Second, there were momentous changes in the class system and in its relations with politics. The Industrial Revolution created great new classes. A class of industrial capitalists founded the enterprises – in cotton, steel, shipbuilding, rail – that were characteristic of the Industrial Revolution. These industries employed a numerically much larger class of workers, mostly manual workers.

These class consequences of the creation of the first national system of industrial capitalism dominated the domestic history of Britain in the nineteenth century – and, indeed, continue to shape much of the pattern of politics. Constitutional change in the first half of that century was mainly concerned with trying to accommodate the claims of the new industrial capitalists and the new cities like Manchester and Birmingham that they dominated. For example, the first great piece of electoral reform in the century, the 1832 Reform Act, mostly extended Parliamentary representation to the new owners of property created by economic change and to the cities of the Industrial Revolution. In the 1867

People in Politics 2.1

Three who made the modern British state

Elizabeth I (reigned 1558–1603)

The Tudor Monarchs ruled from 1485–1603 and Elizabeth was the last and the greatest. She consolidated the Protestantism that had started with the Reformation begun by her father Henry, finally wiping out the Catholic Church as a rival power to the state. Under her the Church of England was settled as the official keeper of the state religion. She also consolidated central executive power. The defeat of an invading Spanish Armada in 1588 was soon mythologized as a great feat of national defence. National mythologies were also developed by the great burst of creative theatre that coincided with her reign, notably in the historical dramas of Shakespeare. And long after her death the concept of a glorious 'Elizabethan Age' had become central to notions of British, and especially English, national identity.

Oliver Cromwell (1599–1658)

Born of minor gentry in Huntingdon in 1599, he emerged as the leading general of the Parliamentary forces in the English Civil War (1642–49). He played a key part not only in the military defeat of the Crown but in the political debates that arose out of the conflict. Following the defeat of the Royalists and the execution of King Charles I in 1649 he emerged as the most powerful figure in the state. He imposed a brutal military settlement on Ireland, and in the execution of the King decisively banished the royalist claim to rule by absolute monarchy. Though he contemptuously dismissed Parliament, and though the monarchy was restored following Cromwell's death, his impact was decisive: after it, the Monarchy was always limited and a long process of decline in its powers began.

David Lloyd George (1863–1945)

He was the most creative political figure of the early decades of the twentieth century. From 1905 to 1922 he served continuously in the Cabinet, from 1908–15 as Chancellor. His period as Chancellor was marked by radical social policy innovations – such as the introduction of old age pensions – that helped found the modern welfare state. This radicalism also provoked fierce opposition and resulted in a decisive curtailment of the power of the House of Lords. As Prime Minister in 1916–22 he presided over the great wartime expansion of state controls. In 1918 he split from, and broke, the Liberal Party, thus allowing Labour to supplant it as the Conservatives' main opponents for the whole of the twentieth century.

Cartoons: Shaun Steele

■ Many historical figures have shaped the British state, but these three were decisive. In all three cases there is a distinctive combination: a mix of great military demands coupled with a powerfully commanding personality.

Reform Act there was some limited extension of the vote to the most prosperous of *male* manual workers, but even the progressive extensions of the suffrage later in the century maintained two key principles: that the right to vote should be restricted to those who owned some specified amount of property and that it should be restricted to men. (The two were connected since property laws made it difficult for women, especially married women, to own property independently.) It was not until the Representation of the People Act of 1918 that something like a modern democratic system of suffrage emerged: entitlement to a vote was then in the case of men disconnected from property, being extended to all adult males (aged 21 and over). But property was still used to restrain the political power of women: those aged 30 and over were given the vote, but only if they were ratepayers or married to ratepayers. The qualifying conditions and age for women to vote were made equal to that of men only in 1928, while the qualifying age for everyone was reduced to 18 in 1969.

This summary of electoral reform emphasizes a key feature of the history of British capitalist democracy: the country developed industrial capitalism long before it developed democratic politics. The general election that was held in the immediate aftermath of the end of the First World War, at the close of 1918, can credibly be said to mark the beginning of formal democracy: 'formal' meaning that for the first time the bare conditions for the existence of democracy – competitive elections on something close to universal adult suffrage – were established. The years immediately succeeding the end of the War were also marked by other developments that we now recognize as central to the modern political system. In the 1918 General Election the party system that dominated Britain for the rest of the twentieth century crystallized. Conservatives and Labour emerged as the two dominant parties and the Liberals, who had been the Conservatives' main opponents for over half a century, were pushed to the margins of politics. The emergence of this two-party system also coincided with the rise of class based political conflict in Britain, since (in very broad terms) the Conservatives established themselves as the party of property owners and the Labour Party presented itself as the party of the newly enfranchised working class.

Something like the organization of the system of government that characterized Britain for most of the twentieth century also matured at around this time. In 1910, the end of a long struggle for power between the House of Lords (which was dominated by traditional aristocratic interests) and the House of Commons was settled in favour of the latter, through a law that greatly reduced the ability of the Lords to obstruct legislation passed in the Commons. By 1918 a series of reforms in the civil service, which had originated in proposals dating from as long back as the mid-1850s, finally produced a unified civil service, one which recruited by competitive selection rather than connections. In 1921 the establishment of the Irish Free State redefined for the remainder of the century the boundaries of the UK, creating an independent Irish state in 26 of the 32 counties of Ireland. In the 1920s itself the foundation of the BBC, and the development of radio as a means of mass communication, heralded other important long-term developments: the creation of a national system of mass communication controlled from the capital and the rise of a system of political communication (including mass campaigning by the parties) which relied heavily on that mass communication, rather than the sort of face to face contacts which had been the norm in the nineteenth century. From the 1920s most important events, and most political propaganda, were communicated via mass media – first by radio and, from the early 1950s, by television.

In summary, *domestically* the development of democratic capitalism involved grafting democratic institutions onto a system of industrial capitalism which had established itself in a non-democratic society in the nineteenth century.

International

The Industrial Revolution shaped British capitalist democracy domestically, but it was also critical for the country's wider role in the international economic and political system, and for elite conceptions of that role. The Industrial Revolution was not just a domestic event; it was part of the shaping of a global market economy, and Britain's pioneering position made it for much of the nineteenth century the dominant actor in that economy – indeed, made it the dominant world power, economically, militarily and diplomatically. Economically the country was well ahead of the pack until the last quarter of the century, when national competitors like Germany and the US began to catch up. Militarily, Britain was the dominant sea power throughout most of the century. Moreover, the country used its military muscle to help enforce an international trading system that opened up global markets to British goods and services. But the most visible sign of its military predominance was imperial reach. When Britain lost the American colonies in the 1780s it seemed destined to return to its historic position: a small trading nation on the margins of international politics. But in the century that followed it created a vast territorial empire on the Indian subcontinent and in Africa. It complemented this empire with more informal domination in other parts of the globe, such as

Timeline 2.1

The rise of universal suffrage in Britain

	Measure	Main provisions
1832	Reform Act	Abolishes 'rotten boroughs', constituencies with no or few electors owned by rich patrons; creates new constituencies in the growing urban/industrial districts; extends voting rights to middle-class property owners.
1867	Representation of the People Act	Relaxes property qualifications so as to enfranchise many skilled male manual workers; creates more new constituencies in urban/industrial districts.
1884	Representation of the People Act	Adds 2.5 million new voters by enfranchising virtually all male householders and many tenants.
1918	Representation of the People Act	Votes for all men over 21 and women over the age of 30 who were ratepayers or married to ratepayers.
1928	Representation of the People Act	Reduces the qualifying age for voting for women to 21.
1948	Representation of the People Act	Abolishes plural voting for business and professional classes: the practice of giving an extra vote to owners of businesses and graduates of some prestigious universities.
1969	Representation of the People Act	Reduces the qualifying age for voting from 21 to 18.

■ The spread of the franchise was not simply a matter of the mere quantitative extension in the numbers of voters: it consisted in the principle of gradually severing the connection between property ownership and the vote. The connection was vital to most nineteenth-century thinkers about these matters, since they feared that a democracy of the 'propertyless' would confiscate property. The old principles of advantaging property lingered remarkably late: notice that only in 1948 was a separate 'business vote' (based on location of business property) abolished. The struggle to extend the franchise overlapped with, but was in key respects distinct from, the struggle to enfranchise women.

parts of the Middle East and Latin America. Diplomatically, as the dominant economic and military power, Britain was the conductor of the international system – the 'hegemon', in the specialized language of international relations theory. It used its hegemonic position to promote one of the great features of this period: the creation of an economy that was increasingly organized on a global scale. London was the world's dominant financial centre; the pound sterling was the dominant global currency; and the 'Gold Standard' – which involved a commitment to exchange holdings of sterling for gold on demand – helped create an open, international, trading system with Britain at its centre.

British dominance – economic, military and diplomatic – was comparatively brief. It probably reached its height right in the middle of the century: the Great Exhibition in London in 1851, which celebrated British manufacturing achievements, was a symbol of that moment. By the closing decades of the century other national competitors were starting to supplant Britain in world markets, and the First World War destroyed the open global system of trading which it had regulated. The country remained an important capitalist economy, but other national ways of organizing capitalism now became prominent. The national peculiarities of British capitalist democracy became increasingly evident.

BRITISH CAPITALIST DEMOCRACY IN COMPARATIVE PERSPECTIVE

Not all democracies are alike, and not all capitalist economic systems are alike. Britain is part of a bigger family of democratic capitalist nations. The things that make it distinctive are critical to understanding its politics. Four distinctive features can be identified here.

Historical trajectory

The fact that the UK was the first industrial society helped shape the broad features of both its system of government and the system of political conflict. We have already seen that one critical consequence concerned the timing of the development of industrial capitalism and democracy: the revolution that produced the first industrial society was accomplished before the rise of anything resembling democratic politics. The system of competitive democracy that emerged in Britain from 1918 also had features which made party competition distinctive, certainly when compared with other large European states, like Germany, France and Italy. The depth and completeness of industrialization considerably 'simplified' the social and cultural system. The democratic politics that emerged after 1918 were dominated by a vocabulary of class politics, with arguments about more cultural forms of division, like religion and territory, marginalized.

Both the Labour Party and the Conservative Party had retained some distinct cultural and geographical roots. The Labour Party inherited many loyalties of Protestant dissenting sects like Methodism, and of Irish Catholic immigrants; and it also inherited, from the Liberal Party that it displaced, much electoral support in the Celtic nations of Britain. By contrast, the Conservatives were a party of religious Anglicanism, and of England, especially of the English suburbs in the south-east. Nevertheless, after 1918 the two parties faced each other as class alliances, and the language of religious differences largely disappeared from the politics of the British mainland. There was nothing like the religious 'confessional' parties that existed across Europe, or the parties based on agriculture which persisted in, for instance, much of Scandinavia.

Economic structure

Beyond the fact of deep industrialization there were other important structural legacies of the country's economic history. By far the most important of these was a cleavage in the British economy that remains critical even today: between financial institutions, especially those organized in the City of London, and manufacturing interests. In many of the great national capitalist

FIGURE 2.1 ■ How Britain dominated the world economy at the height of the Industrial Revolution (percentage share of world exports in 1870)

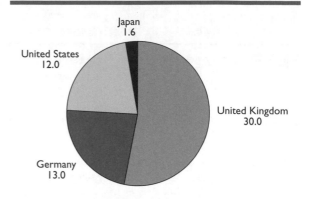

Source: Calculated from Alford (1996:7).

■ These figures date from 1870 – just about the high point of British industrial and imperial power. They show how far ahead Britain was of its main competitors at the height of the Industrial Revolution and how far this lead rested on its domination of global markets. They also alert us to how much ground was made up by some of those competitors: look at the share enjoyed by Japan, which by the second half of the twentieth century had far outstripped that of Britain.

systems that rose to challenge British dominance in the late nineteenth century – like Germany and Japan – there was no big divide between industry and finance; financial institutions were important in providing the resources for industrial investment, and partly as a result were closely involved in the ownership and control of industrial enterprise. Large investment banks (Germany) or corporate networks that governed constellations of firms (Japan) symbolized this close integration. In the UK, on the other hand, the relationship between industry and finance was largely mediated via the stock market. Owners of enterprises expressed their views, not by direct involvement in firm governance, but by buying and selling shares. This distinctiveness is partly due to the City of London's role in shaping the global connections of the British economy and the British state. As we saw earlier, for a large part of the nineteenth century Britain was the regulator of the global economy, especially of the global financial system. The institutions of the City were global players: Lloyds organized the global maritime insurance market; great merchant banks like Rothschild financed projects abroad like building the Suez Canal or constructing the railway system of Latin America; the Bank of England managed the international financial system through the Gold Standard.

Beside all this the workings of the domestic economy were fairly marginal. That in turn has bequeathed an economic structure with a very distinctive territorial character. London had once been a significant centre of industry, and part of the provinces – like the industrial belt along the Clyde in Scotland, and parts of Lancashire and Yorkshire – were once the great centres of wealth in the UK. But for over a hundred years now the territorial structure of the British economy has had two distinctive features: (i) London, and the economy of the south-east which is linked to the capital, has been by virtually any measure the most prosperous centre; (ii) that prosperity has rested largely on the financial sector in the City and the associated service industries upon which it draws (the point is further symbolized in Image 2.1).

Work and welfare

In some official accounts Britain is spoken of as the pioneer, not only of the Industrial Revolution but also of the Welfare State. But the truth is more complicated. In a famous study published over two decades ago the Scandinavian social scientist Gosta Esping-Andersen identified 'three worlds of welfare' (Esping-Andersen 1990.) One world, closely identified with Scandinavia, used welfare services provided by the state to manage and change the consequences of markets, especially the inequalities produced by labour markets. A second, identified with Germany and with many mid-European states that were influenced by Germany, organized welfare around the existing structures of capitalist labour markets. In practice, what this meant was that benefits were closely tied to position in the labour market, and thus were unequally distributed according to the structure of the market. Thus in this second 'world' the welfare state reflected the inequalities of the economic system, rather than, as in the Scandinavian model, seeking to modify them. But it is Esping-Andersen's third world that most interests us, for it is where he placed the UK. This third world provided a 'residual' welfare state. What this meant was that welfare services were largely conceived as a fairly minimal 'safety net' for those who, for instance, were thrown out of the labour market by unemployment. The UK thus resembled some other Anglo-Saxon welfare systems, most importantly the US: it made little attempt to use the welfare state to modify the consequences of markets; it provided a narrow range of services and benefits; and it spent comparatively low amounts on welfare. Esping-Andersen's typology, and especially his characterization of Britain, has aroused considerable debate. The National Health Service, for

example, which was established in 1948, seems anything but 'residual': it guaranteed – and broadly still guarantees – to everyone in the community free and equal access to health care. It is also the case that welfare spending – including spending on the NHS – has risen to levels comparable with those of our big European neighbours. But the NHS nevertheless well illustrates Esping-Andersen's characterization of the British system as 'residual'. It operated tight systems of centralized financial control which limited what the population could in practice get by way of health care. The access to free and equal care in reality amounted to access rationed by doctors, especially by general practitioners, who treated most of the population and who could determine whether patients should be referred further for care, for instance in hospitals. The NHS therefore, despite its apparent generosity, strikingly illustrates a distinctive feature of the relations between the state, the economy and welfare in the UK.

Business regulation

Capitalist democracy is formally a system which joins, as we have seen, two modes of social organization animated by different principles: by those of equal citizenship, on the one hand, and by those of market competition and the unequal allocation of productive resources, on the other. This inevitably creates tensions, especially between business, which is the main actor in the economic system, and the system of democratic politics. How this tension is managed is a key to the way any capitalist democracy operates and certainly has been a key to its operation in the British case. Indeed we can already see the peculiar British sources of tension here. Business already existed as a powerful system in Britain before the development of even formal democratic politics in 1918: the two dominant political parties before 1914 were both business friendly parties. Even more important, business largely controlled its own affairs. In the immensely powerful and prestigious financial sector that operated from the City of London 'self-regulation' ruled. That is, it was virtually universally accepted that markets should run their own affairs, with the minimum of interference from either the law or the state. But even where there was a history of public control – for instance in respect of health and safety at work, or in control of the consequences for public health of industrial pollution – it was established that any controls exercised by public bodies should be wielded in a consensual and cooperative way: that is, controls should be limited by the willingness of regulated enterprises to accept them, and there should be a minimum of legal enforcement or adversarial pursuit of those enterprises that broke the law.

For almost a century – since 'formal democracy' began in 1918 –relations between markets and the state in Britain have been shaped by the attempt to preserve as much as possible of this history of business independence. The attempt has not always been successful. The central state in Britain was transformed after 1914: it became used to intervening in the regulation of social and economic life, and it took into public ownership many important industries. The key problem for business was how to ensure that this newly assertive democracy with a history of intervention did not destroy the ability of business to control its own affairs. Some parts of business were more successful in this than others. The most successful was the City of London, which organized itself under the Bank of England – then a privately owned institution – to run City markets after 1918 through a series of 'self-regulatory' bodies that the markets themselves controlled. The Bank of England was nationalized in 1946, but this made virtually no difference to the independent system of self-regulation (for more on the Bank, see Image 7.1). And while, as we shall see shortly, great changes came over the regulation of markets in the 1980s and 1990s, this culture of self-regulation remained powerful. As we shall also see shortly, at the heart of the great economic crisis that hit capitalist democracy after 2007 was a crisis in this historically established system of business regulation.

BRITAIN AS AN ANGLO-SAXON CAPITALIST DEMOCRACY

It will be plain from the last section that the shape of capitalist democracy in Britain is in part a product of the distinctive economic and political history of the UK. But this does not mean that Britain is unique. Indeed, one of the most productive ideas in the study of capitalist democracy in recent years has been the notion that while, naturally, individual national capitalist democracies all have their own special characteristics, there are distinct models of capitalism, and these models group nations into distinctive families. Britain has commonly been pictured as a member of the family of Anglo-Saxon (or even more commonly Anglo-American) nations. It is not difficult to see why, if we look back at features summarized in the earlier sections of this chapter. Some of the notable features the country shares with the US are highly deregulated markets, especially financial and labour markets, and a system of corporate ownership in which stock exchanges play a central part. Esping-Andersen's account also grouped it in the same 'world of welfare' as the US. Before the great economic crisis that

FIGURE 2.2 ■ Unequal Britain: how it compares with other leading economies

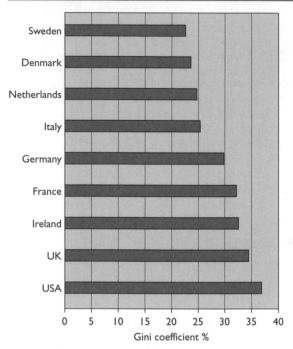

Source: Atkinson (2000:367).

■ This reproduces an attempt to compare income inequality in Britain and other leading economies by the leading British student of wealth and income distribution. The technical measure used is the 'Gini coefficient' and the simplest intuitive interpretation is that the higher the coefficient – and thus here the higher the bar chart – the more unequal is income distribution. Britain belongs to a class of high inequality countries. The most recent authoritative report on inequality in Britain (National Equality Panel 2010:30) confirms the continuation of the differences identified by Atkinson.

began in 2007 political leaders in Britain were fond of picturing Britain as an example of a deregulated Anglo-Saxon model which more tightly controlled European systems like France and Germany would be well advised to follow.

But in fact the evidence on the extent to which the UK is an Anglo-American rather than a European system is mixed. In some respects developments in last three decades have made the UK more closely resemble the kind of capitalist democracy that is practised in the US; in some respects, capitalism in Britain has become 'Europeanized' – more regulated and more bound by the notion that the market should serve social functions and be controlled with this purpose in mind. The evidence for the 'Americanization' of capitalist democracy in Britain is fourfold.

The US consciously adopted as a model

Since at least the election of Mrs Thatcher as Prime Minister in 1979, successive British governments have been impressed by the American economic model and have tried to introduce key elements of it into the UK. Of the five Prime Ministers who have held office since 1979 – Thatcher, Major, Blair, Brown and Cameron – not one was an enthusiast for European style regulated markets, and at least two – Thatcher and Brown – have been conscious admirers of American society.

American models of deregulation copied

But it is not just a matter of the personal preferences of political leaders. It is also the case that two of the great stories of economic policy in recent years have been American inspired: they concern the deregulation of financial and labour markets.

The deregulation of financial markets began in earnest in Britain in the 1980s. In 1986 the 'big bang' on the London Stock Exchange overnight abolished a long-established series of controls over who could do business and over price competition. This followed a similar 'big bang' in American financial markets in the 1970s and was designed to establish the City of London as at least the equal of New York as a world financial centre. In this it succeeded: over the next 20 years London emerged as the leading financial centre in Europe, its trading practices closely tied to American patterns.

In deregulating labour markets the UK started from a different position from the US, where there was a long history of fragmented and weak unionism. But the Thatcher governments of the 1980s made great strides in labour market deregulation. They privatized many publicly owned industries where labour organization had been strong; they confronted some of the most powerful and militant unions either directly or through sympathetic employers – notably in coal mining and printing – and destroyed their power; they introduced legal restrictions over the capacity of unions to take industrial action, and made those restrictions effective; and, by exposing firms to the full force of competition in global markets, they contributed to a change in the balance of power in the workplace, which made managers more influential and organized labour less so. The Labour Government that succeeded the Conservatives after their long tenure of office in 1997 not only did not reverse these changes, it embraced them. Moreover, under the leadership of Tony Blair (1994–2007) the Labour leadership consciously tried to distance itself from what had been historically the Party's most important ally – the trade union movement.

American models of business ownership copied

The impact of the deregulation of financial markets was not confined to those markets alone. Deregulation here involved the triumph of models of business that put share ownership aggressively traded on stock exchanges at its centre. State ownership shrank substantially as a whole series of publicly owned industries – in energy, water, telecommunications and numerous others – were 'privatized': that is, ownership was sold to private interests, typically via stock market flotation. Historically established models of 'mutual' ownership – such as building societies owned and controlled by members – were 'demutualized': that is, turned into private enterprises with shares again traded on the stock exchange. Above all, the period saw the triumph of a model of ownership directly copied from the US that put the maximization of 'shareholder value' at the centre of the life of the enterprise. On this theory the only 'stakeholders' that mattered in guiding the affairs of an enterprise were the shareholders, to the exclusion of groups like employees and consumers – whose interests were deemed to be adequately protected by the workings of competitive markets.

American levels of inequality approached

In the generation spanning the Second World War and the 1970s there was a sustained debate in Britain about how far state intervention had succeeded in modifying the inequalities produced by market capitalism. The evidence was mixed and it was hard to come to an unambiguous conclusion. But we can say with certainty that this generation was certainly not one where inequality greatly increased. At the least, it could be said that the state made little impact; at the most, it could be claimed that some redistribution of wealth and income in the direction of more equality had been achieved. For the last 30 years, however, there can be no argument: inequality significantly increased, and this increased inequality could be traced at least in part to the features summarized above. Intergenerational social mobility – the process by which, especially through the education system, people enter classes higher than that of their parents – had been an important feature of British society in the generation following on from the Second World War; the extent of that mobility slowed greatly in the succeeding generation. But even more striking changes took place in wealth and income inequality. 'Wealth' can be taken as referring to the 'stock' of wealth that we own at any one time; 'income' to the stream of

EUROPEANIZING 2.1

Europeanizing capitalist democracy in Britain

That the United Kingdom was a distinctive, 'Anglo-Saxon' model of capitalist democracy was an article of faith for successive governments in the 1990s. But in many ways the UK model has converged on a European norm. Levels of spending on welfare now approximate those of other leading EU member states. And key areas of the government of the economy and society now live under European jurisdiction. Two outstanding examples are Health and Safety at Work, where the regulatory regime is substantially shaped by Brussels, and the regulation of the environment, where for over two decades Directives from the EU have been critical to shaping not only the content of the regulations, but also the shape of the institutions within Britain that enforce them.

wealth that we receive, most obviously from our work. On both measures those at the very top of the hierarchy considerably increased the gap between themselves and the rest, and in this respect Britain closely followed an American pattern.

In summary, a generation after the landmark electoral victory that brought Mrs Thatcher to office in 1979, and irrevocably changed the shape of British politics, we can also say that the shape of the wider society has changed. Britain looks much more like an American style model of capitalist democracy now than it did in 1979. Deregulated financial and labour markets, a 'shareholder value' conception of the purpose of the business enterprise, sharp increases in the wealth of the richest: all fit that picture.

But the story is not just a tale of Americanization, and it is not a story of a single line of development over the years following the Conservative victory in 1979. We have to differentiate, in particular, between the years of Conservative rule and those of Labour since 1997. The political scientist Andrew Gamble has argued that Britain is not simply Americanized, but is poised 'between Europe and America' – the title of his important study (Gamble 2003.) In other words, it is subject to competing pressures. The one political event of the 1970s that can claim to exceed the 1979 general election result in momentousness was the entry of the UK into the (then) European Economic Community (EEC; Common Market) in 1973. From that event follows one of the main themes of this text: the increasing Europeanization of British society and the British political system. Four forces, in summary, have drawn the UK closer to a European model of capitalism.

Europeanization of policy making

One of the things we shall see time and again in later chapters is that policy-making institutions at all levels in Britain have turned increasingly to face the European Union (EU). They participate in European institutions, notably in the policy-making machinery that surrounds the European Commission in Brussels and, increasingly, the European Parliament (EP). Thus for all the admiration of American ways that undoubtedly exists in the minds of important political leaders, the daily reality of the policy-making system is that it is turned more to Brussels than to Washington or New York.

Europeanization of economic life

The financial markets of the City of London are indeed closely integrated with American financial markets, but the most striking feature of trading patterns in the UK in the last generation is the growing importance of traffic and trading with our fellow members of the EU, especially with the larger members like Germany and France. Indeed Britain's importance as a location for American investment owes a lot to the fact that it is a member of the EU: firms come to Britain to invest in Europe, not just in Britain alone.

Europeanization of business regulation

The story of business regulation has not just been one about the wholesale deregulation of financial and labour markets under American inspiration, although that is an important thread. One reason the trade union movement in Britain has shifted in recent decades from hostility to support for membership of the EU is that the Union has emerged as an important source of pressure for closer regulation of economic life. European regulation, often with the aim of creating common regulatory conditions across the European Single Market, includes areas like the packaging of goods and the regulation of health and safety at work and the environment. All impose new rules, usually legal in character, on the conduct of the business enterprise. In some instances British

POLITICAL ISSUES 2.1

Bankers, bonuses and inequality

We have noticed (p. 29) that the very richest in business became fabulously richer in Britain in the great era of deregulated markets, and the most fabulously well rewarded were concentrated in banking. The end of that era in the great economic crisis that began in 2007 dramatically illustrated one of the key issues in capitalist democracy in Britain: how much inequality is acceptable? The state was obliged virtually to take over large parts of the banking sector. Fierce arguments surrounded the rewards top bankers had received and the terms under which they had left the posts of the banks which they had led to ruin. The fiercest arguments surrounded Sir Fred Goodwin, chief executive officer of the Royal Bank of Scotland, who retired at 50 on a pension of over £700,000 per annum, having led the bank to ruin. The government led a campaign – ultimately successful – to 'claw back' some of Sir Fred's pension. But behind the particular issue here lay the big questions that have recurred in this chapter:

- How much economic inequality is desirable in a market economy, where it is common to argue that the most enterprising should be highly rewarded?
- How far should the state intervene, either by persuasion or the law, to regulate top salaries and other rewards?
- How far should the existence of an international market in top executives mean that rates in Britain have to be bid up to attract the best in the world – in short, how far are top executives subject to the same kinds of market forces as star footballers?

Governments have, in the name of a deregulated economy, secured 'derogations' (exemptions) from these regulations, but only in a minority of very high profile instances. Even in these instances some of the most important derogations have been ended. The Conservative Governments before 1997 had declined to sign the Charter of Fundamental Social Rights, an important statement of welfare commitments inserted in the Maastricht Treaty, the most significant Treaty signed by members of the EU in the 1990s. Mr Blair's new Labour Government did sign up to the Charter, though this still left space for many particular derogations.

The 'European' impact of Labour

Labour displaced the Conservatives as the governing party in Westminster in 1997, and under two Prime Ministers (Blair 1997–2007; Brown 2007–10) enjoyed a tenure of office almost as long as that of the Conservatives after 1979. Labour endorsed many of the policies pursued by its Conservative predecessors that caused the surge in inequality after 1979, notably the deregulation of financial and labour markets. But it also used state power to try to redistribute income and wealth from rich to poor – a classic function of demo-cratic politics under capitalist democracy. The most thorough study of the impact of these efforts concludes that it did have a significant effect in a number of ways: in using the taxation system to help the very poorest; in using the education system, especially state financed preschool education, to improve the chances and the performance of the poorest (Hills et al. 2009). It invested heavily in public services, especially after 2001, for instance bringing the historically low levels of health care spending up to the levels of other large European member states. As we have seen, it adopted the Social Chapter from the Maastricht Treaty which its Conservative predecessors had rejected. In summary, away from the very top and the very bottom of the social ladder it succeeded in narrowing inequalities. It was at these extremes, however, that it had least impact. In particular, the gap between the very richest and the rest continued to widen under Labour, principally because of the effect of deregulated markets.

Labour's record was therefore mixed, but it did not amount to anything as straightforward as reinforcing the inequalities of Anglo-American capitalism. New Labour was enthusiastic about many things American; but during its tenure of office it also made British capitalist

DEBATING POLITICS 2.1

Capitalism: friend or enemy of British democracy?

CAPITALISM PROMOTES DEMOCRATIC POLITICS IN BRITAIN	CAPITALISM UNDERMINES DEMOCRATIC POLITICS IN BRITAIN
▶ Capitalism promotes free markets and this freedom underpins political freedom. ▶ Private property counters the power of the central state. ▶ Capitalism promotes competition between interests and this is also the heart of democratic politics. ▶ Though capitalist systems are often undemocratic, democracy has been unable to survive outside capitalist economies.	▶ British capitalism in recent decades has created inequalities incompatible with democratic citizenship. ▶ Economic resources are the key to political influence; in capitalism they are in the hands of a wealthy minority. ▶ All democratically elected governments have to work within the constraints set by private property. ▶ The poorest under unequal capitalism are also the least likely to be well organized politically.

democracy markedly more 'European'. Moreover, events over which Labour had little control near the end of its tenure dramatically changed the environment within which capitalist democracy functioned in Britain.

The impact of economic crisis

The history of capitalist democracy in Britain can be read as a set of powerful tensions between American and European influences, particularly in the regulation of business life. But from 2007 momentous changes took place; all damaged the notion that an Anglo-American style deregulated model of capitalism was the pattern of the future with which European systems would have to adapt. The American system itself entered a profound economic crisis; moreover, that crisis is agreed by most observers to have its origins in the deregulated financial markets that the US pioneered. The crisis not only discredited whole parts of the business elite in the US; it forced the system away from deregulation, often in the direction of hitherto virtually unimaginable policies, such as taking into public ownership major financial institutions. What is more, the crisis rapidly engulfed the UK and had similar institutional and intellectual consequences: it forced the state to nationalize much of the banking system and to put almost inconceivably large sums of public money behind the rest; it destroyed the case for the deregulation of financial markets which had been a hallmark of British economic policy since the 1980s; and it destroyed the intellectual

case for the supposed superiority of the British model of competitive capitalism.

It also had an important consequence for British capitalist democracy: it changed the balance between democracy and capitalism, to the advantage of the former. The model of deregulated capitalism that became influential from the close of the 1970s had important implications for democratic politics: in effect, it narrowed the domains of politics and expanded the domains of markets. At the most visible level this took the form of shifting important economic sectors from the public to the private domain, through privatization. More subtly, it involved the notion that market actors were the best judges of how to organize economic life, and it involved also the notion that the democratic state should stand back from controls. But in the great crisis after 2007 the state was drawn back into areas that it had evacuated for a generation. Not only did it acquire ownership of key parts of the British economy, it was also drawn into a whole set of issues – for instance to do with what constituted appropriate rewards for business – that for many decades had been thought to be the business of the markets, and which, as we saw above, the markets settled by further vastly enriching the already wealthy. In short, it reinvigorated the question that always lies at the root of capitalist democracy: what balance is to be struck between the inequalities of the business system and the egalitarian principles of democratic politics?

Review OF CHAPTER 2

Four themes have dominated this chapter:

◖▶ The engrained tensions between capitalist markets and democratic politics.

◖▶ The unique historical trajectory of capitalist democracy in Britain.

◖▶ The tension that exists in Britain between an 'American' and a more 'European' model of capitalism.

◖▶ The radical impact on British capitalist democracy of a crisis which is still unfolding: the great economic crisis that began in 2007.

FURTHER READING

ESSENTIAL

If you read only one book for this chapter it should be Gamble (2003), a sustained reflection on the nature and history of the British state.

RECOMMENDED

Coates (2000b) sets Britain internationally as a model of capitalism. Halsey and Webb (2000) is still valuable because it surveys British economy and society across the twentieth century. Colley (1996) is a famous study in the making of Britishness. Harrison (1996) is an extended survey of the historical development of domestic politics, while Gamble (1981/1994) is standard on British 'decline' in the world. Gamble (2009) is the most interesting of a spate of books on the significance of the great financial crisis that began in 2007. Hills et al. (2009) is a balanced and very well documented 'audit' of the impact of New Labour on inequality.

CHAPTER **3**

Britain in a globalizing world

AIMS

The chapter starts from a self-evident assumption: Britain may be a set of islands, but it can only be understood within the setting of the wider world. This chapter:

- [ ] Describes two overlapping sets of foreign relations that are critical to British government: Britain in the global economy and Britain in the international political system created by a world of separate sovereign states

- [ ] Describes how Britain traditionally managed these relations

- [ ] Shows how this traditional model is changing

- [ ] Describes the main influences causing change

BRITAIN AND THE GLOBAL ECONOMY

Look at a simple map of the world – even the traditional schoolroom globe. It makes clear the underlying point of this chapter: that Britain is a collection of islands, but one located in a wider world. Nowhere is this more evident than in considering the British economy. All economies develop what economists call a 'division of labour': a system where people specialize in different trades and services. That division of labour can be seen in something as comparatively simple as the local economy of a town or district. Just consult the Yellow Pages of your local telephone directory to see how refined and elaborate a division of labour can exist even in quite small communities: it will show the development of specialized trades of which you were not even aware.

What is true of the modest and limited economy of a local community is even truer of the global economy. Since the sixteenth century there has been developing a global economy where different parts of the world occupy different positions in the division of labour. Countries or regions specialize in different economic sectors, depending on climate, natural resources or the skills of the population. Understanding Britain's place in this global economy depends on understanding the different places it has occupied in this evolving system. We already know something of this from Chapter 2. We saw there that Britain pioneered the world's first Industrial Revolution. In terms of the global division of labour, in the nineteenth century the country specialized with great success in two fields: in the production of manufactured goods for export; and, through the world importance of the City of London, in channelling financial resources into economic development right across the globe. In the twentieth century, as we also saw in Chapter 2, it lost its specialized roles, notably in manufacturing exports. But despite all these changes it still stands out in four key respects in the global economy: it is rich; market capitalist; a world financial centre; and a major trader.

Britain is rich

For over a century public debate about the economy in Britain has been dominated by an assumption that in this country we have serious economic problems. But looked at against a wider global setting a rather different picture emerges: Britons live in incredibly fortunate economic circumstances. They belong to a small group of outstandingly rich economies. The most obvious contrast is with a group of economies, mostly clustered in Africa below the Sahara, which are extremely poor. The total wealth of each of these nations is, measured in standard ways, often less than the turnover of a single business corpora-

FIGURE 3.1 ■ **Britain and the premier world league of the wealthy**

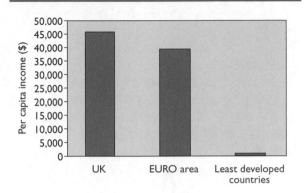

Source: Calculated from World Bank Development Indicators 2009 (www.world-bank.org).

■ These figures, derived from World Bank sources for 2009, measure a standard indicator of wealth. 'Per capita' income is a form of average: we simply divide total wealth by total population. The World Bank divides countries into wealth categories: Britain belongs to the very richest, the high income group. The middle bar is for the countries of the Eurozone, to which the UK does not belong; the tiny third bar is for the poorest countries in the World Bank collection. Suppose the wealth of someone were indicated by their height: as the figure suggests the British, alongside their fortunate neighbours in the Eurozone, would be giants; those unfortunate enough to live in the poorest countries would be tiny.

tion in a rich nation. Most of the populations of these countries live in the direst poverty. They are part of what the economist Paul Collier calls 'the bottom billion' – the poorest people on earth (Collier 2008.) They do not get to eat enough of even the simplest food to ensure their good health; they do not have the basic public facilities, like reliable sources of clean water, to protect them against infectious disease; they are always at risk of sudden death in famine; and even when they do not die of famine they die young by British standards, worn out by lack of decent food and exposure to a myriad of diseases. Most of the people of these countries live lives of hardship virtually inconceivable, let alone experienced, by any imaginable reader of this book. Viewing Britain in the world requires us to maintain a variety of perspectives: in part viewing where Britain stands within the club of the rich; but in part viewing it as one of a small club of the rich distinguished from the mass of humanity across the globe.

But Britain is not only rich. It is part of a select group of very rich nations, mostly clustered around Western

BRIEFING 3.1

Britain and the global financial crisis

The global financial crisis originated in 2007 in parts of the American home loan industry, but quickly spread internationally. The UK was particularly deeply affected. In September 2007 a major bank, Northern Rock, collapsed and had to be taken over by the state. In 2008 the whole banking system came close to collapse, part of a threatened global systemic collapse. Disaster was only avoided by a hugely expensive rescue of some big banks, like the Royal Bank of Scotland, and an even more expensive scheme to, in effect, underwrite the assets of the wider banking system. The 2008 collapse of the whole system was only avoided by what the Bank of England described as the greatest banking support operation since before the First World War.

■ In the last chapter we stressed the way the UK economy was integrated in the global economy; the great financial crisis from 2007 was a graphic illustration of this. An accessible, authoritative account is in Turner (2009).

Europe and North America. It is a group that commands a disproportionate share of the globe's resources. This is a premier league of wealth, and Britain has been in this league for at least a couple of centuries. What is more, this premier league is getting richer all the time. (This is indisputable. There is a complex debate about whether the poor at the same time are getting more impoverished or are sharing modestly in wealth growth.) Beyond the two national groups identified here – the long term very rich and the very poor – there are nations which have changed their status over a century or so. For example, Japan 'joined' the premier league of wealth over the course of the twentieth century. By contrast, Argentina was one of the richest countries on earth at the start of the twentieth century; it now has difficulty in feeding, let alone employing, parts of its population. Within the group of the very wealthy there have also been changes in the rankings in the league of wealth over time.

Most of the debates about the failings of the British economy are about the fact that, while becoming ever more fabulously wealthy, Britain in the course of the twentieth century slipped down the rankings of the super-wealthy. That is a serious matter, because this process of decline has inflicted great suffering, mostly through unemployment caused by the decline and disappearance of particular industries. But the single most important fact about Britain in the world economy remains: it is a securely rich society.

Britain is market capitalist

We have already encountered a definition of what it means to be market capitalist: it involves an economy where most wealth takes the form of privately owned property and where resources are allocated chiefly by

the workings of supply and demand in markets. Britain has been a market capitalist economy since at least the beginning of the Industrial Revolution in the middle of the eighteenth century. If we look across the globe now we find that most nations aspire to market capitalism, but in the fairly recent past taking market capitalism seriously made Britain fairly unusual. Even up to the late 1980s a large part of the globe – stretching more or less continuously from the borders of West Germany to China – was governed by Marxist dictatorships which claimed to run their economies according to socialist, anti-capitalist principles: that is, property was mostly owned by the state and resources were allocated by government, not by market demand. If we had gone further back in the twentieth century, to the 1930s, we would have found large parts of the globe governed by another rival to market capitalism: some of the most important countries of Western Europe, like Germany, as well as Japan and some parts of Latin America, were governed by regimes which allowed private property but which tried to suppress the market as a mechanism for allocating resources. The commonest label for this alternative to market capitalism was Fascism.

The domination of the market capitalist model now gives Britain a special significance in the world economy. It makes the country one of the pioneers of the system of economic organization that seems to be the pattern for the foreseeable future across the globe; and as we saw in Chapter 2 it allows us to compare the kind of capitalism practised in Britain with that practised elsewhere.

Britain is a world financial centre

We have seen that Britain was the dominant financial power in the world during the nineteenth century. It no longer occupies that dominant position, but it remains one of the world's leading centres where financial trading takes place. That is still true even after the great financial crisis that began in 2007. The most important reason for this is the City of London, which is one of the three dominant financial capitals on earth. (The other two are New York and Tokyo.) We have seen some of the domestic consequences of this importance – notably the way the economy of London singled itself out from the rest of the British economy. The country's financial importance amounts to a further development in the specialized global division of labour: the British lead in manufacturing has disappeared, but it specializes heavily in the provision of financial services for large parts of the globe. This specialization has produced, in London and the south-east, an economy of high prosperity and employment; it is therefore a key feature of the domestic British economy and society. But it also gives the country a special international importance. Financial services encompass activities like trading in currencies, debt raising for governments and firms, and dealings in the shares of firms. These are activities that in recent decades have been organized on a unified, global scale. London's dominance means that it is part of a global system of round the clock, round the year trading. If manufacturing can be thought of as the muscle of an economy, financial services are its nerves; and Britain, through London, is part of the nerve centre of the global economy.

Britain is a trading economy

All national economies live partly by trading with the world around them. But some trade more than others, because some are more self-sufficient than others. For example the US, which is of course a continent wide economy, is able to produce most of its goods and services within its own borders. But Britain has comparatively few natural resources, and its climate means that the range of food that it can grow is limited. Self-sufficiency is impossible, at least at present high standards of living: a glance at the product origins of the goods in any supermarket greengrocery or wine section will show the daily reality of this fact. The global division of labour is therefore especially important to Britain, because it is only by importing a huge variety of goods that it can maintain the standard of life of a rich country. And, conversely, it is only by exporting either goods or services, like those carried out in the City of London, that it can pay for the products that make a high standard of living possible. If we think back for a moment to Chapter 2 we can see that this state of affairs is a continuation of a feature that was central to Britain from the very start of its Industrial Revolution: its economy is bound in with

FIGURE 3.2 ■ Britain as a trading nation: exports and imports as percentage of GDP

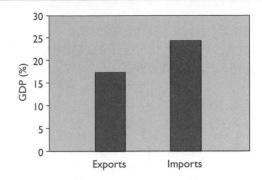

Source: Calculated from World Bank Global Indicators 2010 (http://data.worldbank.org/indicator).

■ The figures (for the year 2008) measure against a standard indicator (gross domestic product) the magnitude of exports and imports in the economy. They show that Britain's is a strikingly open economy. But they also reveal an important structural feature of that economy: we are a net importer. A private household that consistently spent more money than it brought in would soon go bankrupt. How does the British economy avoid this? In part because we have other sources of overseas income, notably the income from investments abroad on which the profits can be 'repatriated'.

the fate of the world economy to an unusual degree. This in turn affects many important domestic policy problems. Whether the British economy prospers or not depends critically on relations with, and the condition of, the rest of the world. It depends, for instance, on the following:

● whether other countries allow British goods and services freely to circulate in their home markets;
● how competitive British goods and services are, whether measured by price or quality;
● how buoyant generally is the wider world economy.

In short, issues of global economic policy are uniquely important to Britain.

Britain is a trading economy but not all parts of the world are equally important to it as traders. Britain actually shares an important characteristic with the rest of the club of rich capitalist countries: they trade increasingly, but increasingly they trade with each other, not with the poorer parts of the world. Thus trading patterns 'lock in' Britain even more tightly to the most economically privileged and powerful part of the globe. This fact in turn has consequences for the patterns examined in the next section.

BRITAIN IN THE INTERNATIONAL POLITICAL SYSTEM: THE TRADITIONAL MODEL OF MANAGEMENT

Britain is part of a world of nations. If we look at a map of the globe we will find that every square kilometre is either claimed by some sovereign state or – as in the case of parts of Antarctica – is under some system of shared dominion. It is usual to date the beginning of this world 'state system' from the Peace of Westphalia, whose conclusion in 1648 brought to an end the Thirty Years War in Europe. This international system of states that claim sovereign control over their own territory is thus long established. Moreover, dismantling empires like those of Britain in the last 50 years has multiplied the number of states. In 1945, when the UN was founded, it consisted of 51 member states; now there are 191.

British government has to manage the country's relations with this world of states. But this management has not always been done in the same way, and it is helpful to distinguish a 'traditional' model that was built up out of the Westphalian system with more recent patterns. (This traditional model was not unique to Britain. On the contrary, Britain practised it precisely because it was the norm for other powers.) Traditionally, managing Britain's interests in the world of states was done by three means.

Specialized domestic institutions

The most important and enduring of these actually still exists. It is the Foreign Office whose political head (the Foreign Secretary) is always a leading member of any British government. The Foreign Office's comprehensive management of Britain's foreign relations covers a huge range, including the organization of public, highly ceremonial occasions, such as the visit of a foreign head of state to Britain; and, the most secret, the management of a large network of spies by which Britain (like many other nations) tries to spy on the rest of the world. In the past other domestic institutions have also been important: for instance, at the height of Empire, a separate Colonial Office was an important domestic institution in managing relations with imperial possessions.

Specialized institutions abroad

Of these, the most important are embassies. Britain still maintains separate embassies for virtually all nations, and always for all important ones. Before global communication and travel became comparatively easy, embassies often enjoyed a high level of autonomy in how they managed relations with 'their' state. The Diplomatic Service, which was the career of the most important embassy staff, was a distinct Service within British government. The heads of embassies – ambassadors – were often major figures in their own right. Embassy buildings were often imposing, acting as major statements of national power and prestige (see Image 3.1).

Alliances

One of the main functions of both 'domestic' institutions like the Foreign Office and of embassies was to maintain, or create, alliances with other nation states in the 'world of nations'. These alliances could range from informal friendly relations to elaborately specified treaties detailing the obligations of Britain and the other signatories, in the event of such occurrences as an attack by a third party, such as another state. These alliances could often shift in a historically drastic manner. Britain's relations with Germany and with the US in the twentieth century provide the most striking illustration. In the first half of the century Britain fought two world wars against Germany and created a powerful alliance with the US. Yet at the start of that century foreign policy makers in Britain were still debating the uncertain question of whether it would be better for Britain to go to war with Germany or with the US. The choice, and the way it was made in favour of a long term alliance with the US, shows that, in the traditional model of foreign relations, calculations of the national interest were the most important influence on the alliances made by Britain. As we shall see, in the conduct of foreign affairs the UK, like other sovereign governments, continues to be very hard headed.

The traditional model of managing Britain's place in the world can be summarized in three ways:

- foreign policy was a specialized area dominated by a few institutions, notably the foreign office and the diplomatic service;
- there was heavy reliance on management of foreign relations country by country, through relatively autonomous embassies;
- alliances and treaties were struck between Britain and other sovereign nations in an ad hoc fashion depending on which foreign alliance was held to serve Britain's short-term interests.

There are still important elements of this traditional 'model' in place: for example, the Foreign Office and individual embassies still retain great influence, and still stand as important physical symbols of national prestige (see Image 3.1). But it has gradually been modified over the last 50 years, a process which is continuing.

IMAGE 3.1 ■ Icons of government: the physical face of the British state abroad

■ When Britain was a world superpower the British embassy in any foreign capital was a building of great importance. Embassies, and their ambassadors, played a large independent part in conducting foreign policy. The independence has now declined, and the importance of Britain as a power has declined. But embassies can still be used to try to make an important statement about national 'image'. Contrast the two examples here: the traditional 'grandeur' of the British embassy in Prague, a mansion dating from the seventeenth century, with the equally striking, but self-consciously modern, image presented by the new embassy specially built in Brasilia, the capital of Brazil, opened in 1961 – a modern building to match a purpose built modern capital.

MODIFYING THE TRADITIONAL MODEL OF MANAGEMENT

The traditional model of managing Britain's place in the international political system has been modified in three important ways.

Foreign policy has ceased to be a uniquely specialized policy field

The divide between 'domestic' and 'foreign' policy is no longer automatically recognized. This is partly because most important areas of domestic policy are now seen as having a 'foreign policy' aspect. Areas as traditionally domestic as crime management, control of immigration, customs control, health care and education: all are seen as impossible to manage without coordination with powers abroad. Conversely, traditional areas of foreign policy are now seen as impinging in important ways on the management of government at home. The management of the world economy, which is periodically discussed at 'summits' of the leading industrial nations, or bargained over in the WTO, has obvious effects on the domestic management of the British economy. At a more particular level, Britain's large arms exporting industry depends heavily on the kind of alliances and deals made in foreign negotiations – and the prosperity of that industry in turn affects the jobs of tens of thousands at home. Foreign secretaries can no longer treat foreign affairs as their unique domain. Decision making has to be shared, and not only with the most important figures in the Government, like the Prime Minister and the Chancellor of the Exchequer. Virtually every Cabinet Minister, and every government department, will have a continuing interest in foreign affairs.

Specialized institutions have lost much of their autonomy

The most important effect here is observable in the case of embassies and ambassadors, which were a product of a historical epoch when international communication was slow. In the early nineteenth century it could take weeks to communicate between London and embassies abroad; now it can be done instantaneously via email and secure telephone. As these examples show, part of the reason for the change is technological: embassies can now be incorporated into communications almost as easily as if they were located in London. But the decline of autonomy is also due to changes in policy priorities. As Britain declined in the twentieth century from the status of a major world power, the point of foreign relations changed. Britain was no longer a main manager of the international political system. The job of embassies became increasingly mundane, notably trying to improve British commercial relations and to promote British exports.

DOCUMENTING POLITICS 3.1

How the foreign and the domestic are entwined: the case of steel tariffs

'In a joint effort between the FCO, DTI and other Departments, trade teams in London and our Posts in Washington, Brussels and Geneva pulled together to win major concessions for UK industry at the outset of the steel trade dispute with the US.

In March 2002 the Bush Administration announced a programme of tariffs on steel imports to the US ... Whitehall and our Embassy in Washington worked with UK companies to mitigate the effects of steel tariffs for UK producers and workers. The Embassy reported, early on, the likelihood of tariffs, and was able to advise the FCO and DTI of key players for lobbying efforts and the best timing for deployment. The companies provided ample substantive justification for their request, and were pleased with the advice and high-level lobbying support from us. Trade policy teams in London, Washington, Brussels and Geneva worked together to provide a full picture of action in capitals and the implications for UK interests.

This team effort paid off. At the end of the first round of the exclusion process, some 70% of UK steel exports were free of the tariffs. A good example of joined-up government.'

■ The boastful and partisan tone of this extract derives from its origin, in the annual report of the Foreign and Commonwealth Office, essentially a piece of propaganda both for the FO and for the government in power. But it illustrates very well the hard headed nature of modern diplomacy, notably the extent to which it involves the active defence of private corporate interests by the state. It also shows how far modern foreign policy is now conducted in a world of multilevel institutions. Among those central to this story are: our embassies abroad; the Foreign Office itself; the Department of Trade and Industry (DTI) as it was then known, the department that speaks for industrial interests at home; the European Commission, the key institution in the European Union, whose importance for the British economy is spelled out in Chapter 5; the WTO which tries to adjudicate on trade disputes of this kind; and the US Government, the promoter of the biggest and richest economy in the world.

Source: Foreign and Commonwealth Office 2003.

The nature of alliances and treaties has changed

When Britain was a great power it made alliances with states as and when it seemed to suit its individual interests. But as its power and prestige declined, it increasingly relied on participation in alliances and institutions as one of a number of states, albeit often an important one. Three examples illustrate the point. For over 60 years the most important military alliance of which Britain has been a member is NATO. This is an organization, dominated by the US, with its own command hierarchy and command headquarters. A second example is the UN, which was founded in 1945 to try to promote collective international security. As a legacy of its former great power status Britain is one of a small number of states with a permanent place on the UN Security Council, the most important decision making body of that organization. A third example anticipates a major theme of this whole book, and is discussed in more detail in Chapter 5: much of Britain's foreign relations are now conducted through the institutions of the EU. Two important examples are negotiations on trade relations in the WTO, where the Union negotiates on behalf of its member states; and bargaining over treaties to control climate change, where Britain again negotiates as part of the EU because the Union plays such a large part in environmental regulation.

In the 'new model' of managing Britain's international political relations, therefore, we can see three important developments:

- at home, foreign policy is much more closely integrated into the wider domestic system of policy making;
- this integration has greatly reduced the autonomy of traditional foreign policy-making institutions;
- Britain's foreign relations are increasingly managed collectively in institutions with other states.

WHY THE TRADITIONAL MODEL HAS CHANGED

Some of the reasons for the changes summarized here have already been referred to: for instance, the rise of rapid means of global communication and easier travel now make it much simpler to manage foreign relations from London rather than relying on far flung embassies. But at the root of the changes lie long-term developments in the nature of the international economic and political system, and of Britain's place in that system.

People in Politics 3.1

Three who made modern British foreign policy

Ernest Bevin (1881–1951)

Bevin was the greatest trade union leader in Britain in the years between the two world wars and only entered government as a result of the great crisis of war, in 1940. He became Foreign Secretary in the Labour Government elected in 1945 and throughout the next six years was one of its dominant personalities. He set the direction of British Foreign Policy for the next 60 years: scepticism about European unification, and a commitment to an alliance with the US. He was one of the architects of NATO, a military alliance dominated by the Americans, which opposed the Soviet Union when it was one of the two world superpowers.

Edward Heath (1916–2005)

Only Prime Minister for just over three and a half years (1970–74) but he changed the direction of British Foreign Policy in one vital respect: he led the Government which negotiated the terms of British entry into the then EEC in 1973. A decade earlier he had also unsuccessfully tried to negotiate entry into the original Common Market. He thus critically modified, though did not extinguish, the 'Eurosceptic' tone of British Foreign Policy set by Ernest Bevin. He spent the years following his deposition as leader of the Conservative Party (1975) advocating closer integration between Britain and the EU, in an increasingly 'Euro-sceptic' Conservative Party.

Margaret Thatcher (1925–)

By common consent the most forceful peacetime Prime Minister in modern British history, in some respects reinforced the pro-European direction of Mr Heath: under her Britain became increasingly integrated into the wider European economy. But in the later years of her Premiership she became hostile to European integration, and out of office became the focus of a powerful Euro-sceptic movement in the Conservative Party. She also throughout the 1980s reinforced the strength of the Anglo-American alliance, thus continuing work begun by Ernest Bevin a generation before. The fact that for two decades Britain has been America's closest military ally testifies to her influence.

Cartoons: Shaun Steele

■ These three great figures are important because they left different, indelible prints on British foreign policy. But they are also important because their policies encapsulate the tensions about where Britain should locate itself in the international power system. Bevin was a convinced 'Atlanticist', who strengthened the alliance with the US; Heath decisively pushed the country in a European direction; and in Mrs Thatcher's foreign policy career she was alternately Europeanist and Atlanticist.

EUROPEANIZING 3.1

Europeanizing British foreign policy

There are numerous instances in this book of British politicians, British governing institutions and British interest groups seeking to shape policy through the institutions of the EU. But the Europeanization of British foreign policy in some key instances goes beyond that: the Union has supplanted the individual member state as the bargaining unit in international negotiations. It concludes agreements as a sovereign actor, binding its own member states in the process. Two important examples are:

- The international high politics of climate change negotiation. The Union, not individual members, negotiates from an agreed common position in the landmark international meetings, such as the Kyoto and Montreal climate summits. The UK position is therefore set by common Union position.
- The international high politics of trade negotiation. In the complex trade negotiations that now surround the workings of the WTO, which regulates much of the conditions of international competition, the Union again acts as the common voice of all member states.

This does not mean that an individual state like Britain has no voice. But it does decisively Europeanize these areas of foreign policy because voice depends critically on ability to influence what the Union adopts as the common negotiating position.

■ Europeanization is a major theme of this text; and the shaping power of Europeanization is perhaps nowhere greater than in the sphere of foreign policy, as this feature shows.

Increasing global interdependence

The growth of an increasingly interdependent economic and political global system is one of the most important reasons why foreign policy is no longer viewed as a distinct domain separate from domestic policy. The 'global dimension' exists in economic production, in crime control, in regulation of broadcasting and telecommunications, and in a host of other fields: this helps to explain why virtually every department of government now feels it must have a say over some aspect of foreign policy. For example, the rise of immigration as a major issue for government inside Britain, and the changing sources of immigration, are due to wider changes in the nature of the international political system. The rise of immigration as a problem for governments at home is also due to the difficulty of policing national borders in a world of increasing global movement of goods and people. The fact that the British Government has to manage the economy in a world of global economic organization is now a commonplace in discussions of economic policy. But as examples like crime control and immigration show there is now a global dimension to

virtually everything that government attempts to do domestically.

American domination

From the beginning of the twentieth century it became obvious, even in Britain, that the country was no longer the supreme world power and was being challenged by the two rising powers of the US and Germany. In the two great wars of the twentieth century (1914–18 and 1939–45) America eventually intervened on the side of Britain. After the Second World War the US replaced Britain as a world superpower. Since then, all British governments have followed essentially the same foreign policy strategy: to position Britain as a close ally, and junior partner, of the US. The calculation has been that since we are living in an American dominated world Britain's best interests are served by an alliance with the dominant power. This helps to explain, for instance, why Britain's most important military alliance for over 60 years has been through the American dominated NATO.

One important legacy of great power status, and of the conviction that Britain is an especially important partner of the US, is British military power. Britain rapidly acquired nuclear weapons – then thought to be the badge of the superpower – after the Second World War. It remains one of a small number of countries that possess nuclear weapons, though it is virtually completely reliant on American rockets to deliver these – and the weapons are virtually useless without the means of delivery. The country also retains a most unusual conventional military capability, brought about by high levels of spending. We have been emphasizing how the 'traditional' model of foreign relations have changed over time. But here we see two striking continuities: the importance of war and the importance of the arms economy to Britain.

Britain still uses force as an important means of managing its foreign relations. Since the early 1980s alone it has participated in five important military campaigns: to recover the Falkland Islands colony from Argentina after that country invaded in 1982; to expel the Iraqi invaders from Kuwait in 1991, as an important part of a multinational force led by the US; to intervene in the civil war in the Balkans in 1999 as the leading member of a NATO force; to help the Americans conquer Afghanistan in 2001–02, following the terrorist attacks on the US on 11 September 2001, and then to prosecute a continuing war against the Taliban in that country; and to invade Iraq as the main ally of the US in 2003.

We saw in Chapter 2 that British manufacturing suffered a long historical decline. One exception to this is arms manufacturing and export where Britain remains a world leader. There is a connection between the importance of war and the importance of arms production. At the start of the twentieth century British firms were important in helping to build the Japanese Navy, thus laying the foundations of a military power that Britain then had to fight in the Second World War. At the end of the twentieth century British firms were important in equipping the Iraqi dictator Saddam Hussein, who then had to be fought in the invasion of 2003.

The rise and fall of the Soviet Union

One reason Britain – and other West European states – so quickly became junior allies of the American superpower after 1945 was fear of a new superpower that had arisen in Eastern Europe, the Soviet Union. The Marxist doctrines and dictatorial system of the Soviet Union were a threat to both capitalism and democracy. For over 40 years there was a 'cold war' across the globe. The war was 'cold' because it involved little open military conflict, in Europe at least. Both superpowers had nuclear weapons and were held back by the fear of mutual nuclear annihilation. The Soviet Union controlled a set of Marxist dictatorships across Eastern Europe. It was

believed that only American nuclear protection defended Western Europe against Soviet ambitions. This naturally helped to support alliances like NATO and to encourage Britain to cultivate its place as a junior ally of the US.

The Soviet Empire in Eastern Europe collapsed dramatically at the end of the 1980s. This was followed in 1991 by the collapse of the Soviet Union itself. But these collapses, though they changed much, did not change Britain's role as a junior ally of the US. In the 1990s, as we saw above, it fought a number of wars alongside the US. The collapse of the Soviet Union, though it removed a threat to democracy and capitalism in Western Europe, also meant that in the 1990s America was now the single and unchallenged superpower. This made even stronger the logic of Britain's long-term strategy, which was to seek influence in foreign relations as an ally of this superpower. The collapse of Soviet power in Eastern Europe and over large parts of Asia has made these areas unstable, and has drawn in the US and its ally in a policing role.

The rise of the EU as a regional power

The most important factors cited so far as influences changing the traditional model of foreign relations – such as the rise of America to superpower position and the collapse of the Soviet Union – have all pointed Britain in a particular direction: to strengthening its role as a junior partner of the US in an American dominated world. But the rising importance of the EU potentially pulls Britain in very different directions. In Chapter 5 we will see that the Government of Britain and of the EU are now so intertwined that it is hard in many instances to make any clear separation between the two. Not surprisingly, this is having important consequences for managing Britain's place in the international political system. It is the best example of one of the big changes identified earlier: the tendency for Britain now to be an international actor, not as a separate sovereign state, but as one member of a group. As we have noticed, in some important fields such as international trade negotiations in the WTO, Britain effectively has no separate presence at all. Since the EU is a single trading unit all important trade negotiations have to be carried on by the Union collectively. This does not mean that Britain has no influence – but it does mean that influence has to start by shaping the collective position adopted by the Union as a whole. Britain can no longer take independent decisions on these key aspects of foreign economic policy. The Union is an economic superpower. Its economic interests are often sharply opposed to those of the US. Here, then, is one important area where Britain is often constrained from acting as a junior ally of the US.

POLITICAL ISSUES 3.1

The Iraq War of 2003–09

When British troops finally withdrew from an active combat role in Iraq in 2009, an important phase finished in one of the most divisive foreign policy issues in modern British politics. The war involved the invasion of Iraq in 2003, the toppling of the regime headed by Saddam Hussein, and the attempt to create a new political regime in the country. The invasion was led by the US, with the UK as its main ally. The war had many claimed justifications, the most important of which was that the Saddam regime possessed 'weapons of mass destruction' which could be used against Iraq's neighbours and even further afield. A successful military campaign which toppled Saddam rapidly in 2003 was followed by a succession of catastrophes: large scale loss of Iraqi lives as the occupying forces tried to maintain order; the emergence of rival groupings struggling for power, often violently, in Iraq; revelation in 2004 of large scale abuse and torture of Iraqi prisoners by American forces; allegations of abuse and torture against British forces, some of which, though not all, turned out to be fabricated; growing hostility in both the British and the American electorates to the military operation; and increasing pressure on the British government publicly to separate itself from support for American policies. The war raised many issues, most of which are still unresolved at the time of writing. For the conduct of British foreign policy the most important issues were:

- How closely should the UK ally itself in foreign policy with the US over an issue where there were deep divisions between member states of the EU?
- 'Weapons of mass destruction' were not discovered. How far should foreign policy decisions be made on the basis of secret intelligence, in this case about the existence of weapons of mass destruction, which could not be tested in the public arena?
- How far should a government go in making foreign policy commitments which are intensely opposed by a large section – by some measures the majority – of its domestic electorate?
- How can wars claimed to be aimed at threats of terrorism be reconciled with the preservation of civil liberties at home?

TENSIONS AND CHOICES IN BRITAIN'S INTERNATIONAL RELATIONS

Discussion of the forces that have contributed to the changing model of managing Britain's international relations returns us to a key theme examined at the end of Chapter 2. The collapse of the Soviet Union has made more severe the tension between Britain's position as an EU member and its historically established close alliance with the US. The collapse of Soviet power strengthened the tendency for Britain to position herself as a junior partner in an American dominated world order. But the removal of much of the threat of Soviet power had a rather different effect across the rest of the EU. Freed from the threat of Soviet domination, the Union has felt able to act increasingly independently of the US. The passing away of the Soviet Empire has led, as we shall

see in Chapter 5, to the entry of a large number of new members who were formerly under the control of the Soviet Union. In some key cases a divide has opened up between the UK and other leading members of the EU in their attitude to the exercise of American power. After a series of terrorist attacks in America on 11 September 2001 the US began to pursue a much more active policy of military intervention, for instance in Afghanistan and Iraq. It tried to do this mainly with the support of the UN. In these efforts Britain has stood out from other leading members of the Union in its willingness to support the US, both in diplomatic negotiations to secure UN support and on the battlefield.

Thus Britain finds herself pulled between American and European influences, often trying to conciliate between the two. It is at a historical crossroads marked by divergent signposts, one pointing to a European

DEBATING POLITICS 3.1

American junior partner or European regional power?

THE CASE FOR AN AMERICAN PARTNERSHIP

- The US will be the dominant superpower for the foreseeable future, and the collapse of the Soviet Union has left it as the unchallenged sole world superpower: it makes sense to stay in close alliance with it.
- Britain is the most important European centre of American investment in Europe.
- The US was Britain's key ally in the two great world wars of the twentieth century.
- Britain and the US share important cultural features, such as a common language.
- The British and American economies share important structural features: notably, they are lightly regulated by comparison with the economies of the leading members of the EU.

THE CASE FOR EUROPEAN REGIONAL POWER

- The EU is emerging as an important world economic power and it makes sense to maximize UK influence within its institutions.
- The EU is the most important trading partner for the UK and can be expected to become more so.
- Britain's democratic institutions and cultures are shared with most important member states of the EU.
- The EU will largely regulate the British economy unless we take the radical step of withdrawal – so it makes sense to maximize influence over how that regulation works.
- Full membership of an enlarged EU offers Britain a part in a largely self-sufficient European-wide economy with protection from both American power and global economic disturbances.

future, the other to a future as a junior partner of the US. One effect of the tensions created by the need to choose between the two routes has been to make the domestic management of foreign policy an especially important preoccupation at the top of British government. When we come to examine the core executive in Chapter 6 we will see that foreign policy management is one of its key concerns. This active management is needed because British government internally is not united. Some institutions, and some important personalities, will incline towards the American 'signpost' at the crossroads; some will incline towards the European. The core executive is constantly trying to sort out these tensions.

Review OF CHAPTER 3

Four main themes have been developed in this chapter:

- British government lives in a world of other nation states and has to manage British interests in that world.

- Britain's economy makes it particularly sensitive to global developments.

- The traditional division between the management of foreign policy and the management of the rest of government at home has been eroding for over half a century.

- The dominant strategy of British governments for at least 60 years has been to position the country as a junior ally of the US, but this is now seriously complicated by the influences of EU membership.

FURTHER READING

ESSENTIAL

If you read only one book it should be Hirst et al. (2009): the latest edition of the most stimulating, authoritative and partly sceptical study of the economic globalization which has done so much to transform the traditional model of foreign relations.

RECOMMENDED

A vast, stimulating and highly readable panorama of the history of the international system in which Britain plays a key part is Kennedy (1989). Judt (2007) has become an instant classic, surveying the history of Europe, notably important on the period not covered by Kennedy: the world since the collapse of the Soviet Empire in 1989. The most important scholarly study of the European movement is Milward (1992).

CHAPTER 4

Cultures, constitutions and British political culture

AIMS

This chapter:

- Explains why we need to explore the political culture and the constitution together

- Locates the sources of the constitution

- Describes the sources of, and the content of, constitutional change

- Describes the traditional pattern of the political culture and how it is changing

- Shows that there is a close connection between constitutional change and cultural change

POLITICAL CULTURES AND THE CONSTITUTION

Constitutions are at the heart of democratic politics. Formally, a constitution prescribes the rules of the game in a system of government: it describes both rules by which decisions in government can be made, and defines the broad boundaries of the content of those decisions – laying down the range of potential powers of government, in other words. Put in this bald way it may seem that constitutions are rather specialized and even stilted. But the living constitution of a country is itself a part of something bigger: the thing that we conventionally call the 'political culture'. This refers to the understandings that shape how the whole range of political life is conducted: how we all view politics and politicians; how we view the purpose of government; and how we view the way we should sort out our political differences. Thus understanding the constitution has to involve much more than understanding the formal legal rules that lay out how government should be conducted; it demands understanding how those rules connect to the wider political cultural understandings in the community.

A good example of the connection is the relationship between the constitution and the vital question of whether a political system is democratic. A constitution does not have to be democratic: we can find numerous examples historically where 'the rules of the game' are not democratic; but part of the essence of modern democratic government is that the state is subject to explicit constraints. It cannot act arbitrarily, but has to observe some rules of the game. That is one reason why a common alternative summary of the system of government in Britain is 'constitutional democracy'. Of course a continuing question in this book is: how accurate is that summary description?

The state has to be subject to constitutional restraints, but the form of these restraints varies enormously. One of the common kinds of variation concerns the extent to which a constitution is *codified*. The most highly developed kind of codification occurs when we can identify a single written document called a 'constitution'. If we were, for instance, examining political life in the US our natural starting point would be precisely this: a document originally written in 1787 and subsequently amended 26 times. The American constitution is a document, even with all its amendments, of only about 8,000 words – the length, in other words, of a typical student project.

By contrast, the British constitution is more elusive. It is sometimes said that Britain is distinguished by the fact that it has an unwritten constitution. This is not strictly correct, because as we shall see shortly many

key elements of the constitution are indeed written, some in the form of law. But it is true that the constitution is not systematically codified in a single document. We have an uncodified constitution which comes from a wide range of sources, and which takes many forms: it is what might be called an eclectic, 'pick and mix' constitution. The fact that the constitution is uncodified and eclectic has a number of implications. Three are especially important.

First, the uncodified and eclectic nature of the constitution means that its nature depends heavily on constitutional understandings. But it is the nature of understandings that different groups understand them differently. As the author of one of the first great studies of the constitution put it: 'we live under a system of tacit understandings. But the understandings themselves are not always understood' (Low 1904:12). The result is that both the boundaries of the constitution, and even the meaning of its core content, are widely contested. The British constitution should not therefore be conceived as a single definitive, settled set of rules. Conflict about the meaning of the constitution is one important way in which wider political conflict is expressed in Britain.

That emphasizes once again the connection between the constitution and the wider political culture. This introduces the second key point: the uncodified and eclectic nature of the constitution means that it cannot be conceived as a set of formal doctrines; it is an expression of, and is closely connected to, the wider *political culture* of the community. 'Political culture' is the term we apply to what might be thought of as the wider pattern of popular understandings about the rules of the game of government. Not many people think about the nature of the British constitution; but most of us have a view about the system of government in Britain. Do we trust the institutions of government to act fairly and truthfully? Do we believe that the UK should remain united under the single symbol of the Crown? Do we approve of the most important institutions and practices of British politics, such as universal suffrage? These attitudes form the core components of the political culture.

Third, the shifting and uncertain meaning of the British constitution makes it ideally suited to performing two very different functions. These were famously identified in the greatest of all books on the constitution as the *dignified* and the *efficient* (see Documenting Politics 4.1). In making this distinction the nineteenth-century political commentator Walter Bagehot argued that the 'dignified' elements of the constitution were important in creating loyalty and political attachment to the system of rule. His most important example was the monarchy, which performed no serious governing function but which inspired popular loyalty to the system of

DOCUMENTING POLITICS 4.1

Walter Bagehot on the monarchy as a 'dignified' institution

'The best reason why Monarchy is a strong government is that it is an intelligible government. The mass of mankind understand it, and they hardly anywhere in the world understand any other ... A *family* on the throne is an interesting idea also. It brings down the pride of sovereignty to the level of petty life. No feeling could seem more childish than the enthusiasm of the English at the marriage of the Prince of Wales. They treated as a great political event, what, looked at as a matter of pure business, was very small indeed. But no feeling could be more like common human nature as it is, and as it is likely to be. The women – one half of the human race at least – care fifty times more for a marriage than a ministry.'

■ The passages here can be found on pp. 82 and 85 of the 1963 edition of *The English Constitution*. Bagehot was a worldly journalist, a distinguished editor of *The Economist*. He thought of politics, even in this age before the rise of democracy, as the art of manipulating popular beliefs; hence the distinction between highly public, 'dignified' bodies like the monarchy, that commanded public loyalty, and the real, informal and often hidden practical mechanisms of government. Notice also the reflection – common for the time – of the view that women were especially likely to care for the dignified over the efficient. Yet, despite the lapse of time, the passages on the Prince of Wales's wedding (in the 1860s) have an uncanny application to the present Prince of Wales's first wedding (in 1981). His second wedding to his long-term mistress (in 2005) was a much more low key event, reflecting the decline of this kind of Royal 'magic'.

government. By contrast, Bagehot argued that the 'efficient' elements of a constitution concerned those parts where the rules of the governing game were actually specified and operated. The exact words used by Bagehot can mislead in our time. The Royal Family remains a 'dignified' part of the constitution, but a glance at any tabloid newspaper will show that its members often behave in a very undignified way. Often the 'efficient' parts of the constitution work in a blundering, inef-

fective way – something we will see in Chapter 19 when we examine fiascos in British government. But the heart of Bagehot's argument stands: that some elements of the constitution are there to induce loyalty to the system of rule, and some are there actually to guide the practice of government. The importance of the 'dignified' function of the constitution, however, makes the meaning of the constitution even more contested and uncertain, since different interests and groups will want to attach the magic of 'constitutional' to their own view of what the system of rule should be.

WHERE WILL WE FIND THE CONSTITUTION?

This simple question is the obvious first step in identifying the British constitution. Yet it is actually a more difficult question than appears at first sight, and for a highly revealing reason. Because the constitution is eclectic and uncodified its sources are many and varied; and for this reason we can stress different sources depending on what we want to make of the constitution. There are six important sources we can look to in identifying the constitution.

'Normal' statutes

It is hardly surprising to find that the law of the land is an important source of the constitution. It stretches historically as far back at least as the constitutional turmoil of the seventeenth century. For instance the law of habeas corpus passed in 1679 put explicit legislative restraints on the power of the state – which at that time largely meant the Crown – to detain subjects without trial: it codified on the statute book what had long before been a common law remedy. At the other end of the historical spectrum, two more recent pieces of legislation significantly qualify the protections of habeas corpus. The Prevention of Terrorism Act was originally passed in 1974 as a 'temporary' measure following horrific bomb attacks on the British mainland, at the height of a bombing campaign by Irish Republicans. It has been renewed each year since. It proscribes certain organizations on the criterion that they are implicated in terrorism and gives police the power to detain and exclude persons from Great Britain on the grounds that they are suspected of terrorism. In December 2001, following terrorist attacks on the World Trade Center in New York in September of that year, the Anti-Terrorism, Crime and Security Emergency Act was passed. It greatly strengthened the power of the state to restrict civil liberties. These examples emphasize the point made earlier: the constitution is not a single, consistent set of provisions but rather a set of domains where different

EUROPEANIZING 4.1

Europeanizing the constitution

Much of the pressure for the constitutional revolution of recent years has been 'domestic' – from pressure internal to the UK. But even a quick glance at Timeline 4.1 below will show the importance of the EU: arguably, the modern era of constitutional change begins with our accession to the original Common Market in 1973; the Single European Act of 1986 transformed the rules of economic decision making; the Treaties of Maastricht (1992) and Lisbon (2009) continued this transformation. Possibly the single most important constitutional innovation – the passage of the Human Rights Act 1998 – incorporated into UK law the provisions of a Europe-wide convention on human rights. Thus the constitution has not just been revolutionized in recent decades; it has been Europeanized.

views of the 'rules of the government game' are contested.

'Superstatutes'

Until recently it was commonly argued that there were no distinct constitutional statutes in Britain: any statute, from the most momentous for civil liberty to the most mundane, was passed through Parliament in the same way, and could be repealed in the same way. Parliament was the supreme arbiter of the constitution. In the words of A. V. Dicey, the most influential constitutional theorist of the nineteenth century, Parliament 'has, under the English constitution, the right to make or unmake any law whatsoever' (Bradley 2000:27). It is doubtful if this is any longer the case. There now exist a set of laws that restrict government in Britain in unique ways. The most obvious of these arise from our obligations as signatories of the various treaties that govern our membership of the EU. While these obligations are embodied in statute passed by Parliament it is hard to imagine that Parliament could repeal them – for instance to withdraw from the EU – except in the most dramatic circumstances. The same is true of the laws that led to the establishment of a Scottish Parliament and a Welsh Assembly in 1999. Likewise the principle of hereditary membership of the House of Lords was all but abolished by the Labour Government in the House of Lords Act of that year, and it is hard to imagine a return to the previous state of affairs; the statute has a special quality marking it out from 'normal' legislation. All of these statutes have the character of a constitutional Rubicon: once crossed there is no going back – they are irreversible changes in the constitutional order.

Law shaped by judges

Notice the word 'shaped' rather than 'made' here. It recognizes that Parliament has in the last analysis been the source of law; but it also recognizes an important role for judicial decisions. Judges have until recently been reluctant to review and strike down law passed by Parliament. But they have been able to exercise a huge influence on the way law is put into effect. In part the influence comes through an accumulation of decisions in the courts. We usually summarize this as the 'common law': a law that comes out of customary understandings and the accumulation of cases decided by judges over centuries. But judges have also felt able to practise 'judicial review'. Since Parliamentary statutes are typically general in character their application in any particular instance can be unclear and contested. And it is in the interpretation and clarification of meaning that judicial review is important: judges can pronounce on the mind of Parliament even when (especially when) Parliament's mind is not obvious.

Institutional rules

Many of the most important governing institutions in Britain have their own internal 'rule books' and these are so central to the way government life is conducted that they can be considered part of the Constitution. The best example is *Erskine May*, the bible covering matters of procedure in the House of Commons. It originated as a codification of the rules of Commons behaviour by a nineteenth-century clerk to the Commons, Sir Thomas Erskine May (1815–86), and each successive edition has governed the conduct of business in the Commons.

Conventions

The original title of Erskine May's handbook of parliamentary practice (see McKay 2004) was *A Treatise upon the Law, Privileges, Proceedings, and Usages of Parliament* (1844). The variety of sources of parliamentary authority, and especially the reference to

Timeline 4.1

The spread of 'superstatutes' in defining the constitution

	Statute	Main effect
1972	UK government signs Treaty of Accession to EEC	Confirms British membership of 'common market' from January 1973 and subjects British government to the law of the Community as interpreted by the ECJ.
1986	Single European Act (SEA)	Commits British governments to implementation of final measures to create free movement of goods, services and people across the EEC.
1993	Maastricht Act	Confirms UK as signatory of Maastricht Treaty: creates EU; extends range of decisions taken by majority decision of members of the Union.
1998	Scotland Act	Following referendum supporting devolved powers in 1997, creates an elected Scottish Parliament and Scottish Executive in 1999 with control of most domestic policy and some tax raising power.
1998	Government of Wales Act	Following referendum supporting some devolved power in 1997, creates an elected Welsh Assembly with a Cabinet and First Minister, but with no tax raising power and more limited control of policy than in Scotland.
1998	Human Rights Act	Incorporates into law the provisions of the European Convention on Human Rights.
1999	House of Lords Act	Removes from Lords all but 92 specially selected hereditary peers.
2009	Treaty of Lisbon	Expands powers of EU and narrows areas where (UK) government has a veto.

■ Three features should be noticed about this box. First, it illustrates a long-term development which we highlight again at the end of the chapter: the shift from a constitution dominated by informal conventions to one increasingly laid down in law. Second, it shows how important has been the membership of the (now) EU in this process. Third, it shows how far the election of New Labour brought constitutional innovation to the centre of policy making.

'usages', catches the importance of constitutional conventions and perfectly expresses the historically uncodified and eclectic character of the constitution in Britain. Conventions are understandings that guide behaviour; and like understandings in any walk of life they can vary in the degree to which they are openly expressed, and can vary in the degree to which they actually do shape behaviour. A convention of social life with which most readers will be familiar is the convention that teachers do not swear at students. But we know that what is viewed as swearing varies from place to place and time to time; and we know that in extreme exasperation teachers have been driven to swear. A parallel example in British government is provided by the convention (sometimes called doctrine) of collec-

tive ministerial responsibility. This is a convention that decrees that members of the British Cabinet (see Chapter 6) are publicly bound to defend a collective policy decision made by Cabinet. The convention undoubtedly does constrain the public utterances of Cabinet members; even if they disagree privately with what has been decided they will in many cases at least keep their disagreement publicly silent. But the way the convention works shows how elastic is the idea of a convention and how much fiction it contains. The convention originated when the Cabinet normally debated in full session all important policy matters and tried to arrive at a common view. But as we will discover in Chapter 6 this kind of collective debate hardly ever now happens. Most business is done in bodies like

Cabinet committees. Ministers can thus often find themselves publicly committed to policies without ever being present at the debate where the decision was made.

Cabinet ministers cope with the convention of collective responsibility in this changed world in various ways. They stretch the meaning of 'public' disagreement. While remaining silent 'on the record' they can 'off the record' brief journalists about their dissent; the fact of a minister's disagreement is reported but with no sources named. They can informally let their allies outside government know of their dissent. This is then often reported as 'friends' of the minister briefing journalists about internal Cabinet disagreements. There have been a few occasions when Cabinets were so divided that they have agreed openly to license disagreement on an issue (the political equivalent of the exasperated teacher actually swearing). The most famous came in 1975, when members of the then Labour Cabinet campaigned on different sides in the referendum on the country's continuing membership of the EEC. Coalition governments of the kind that took office in Westminster after the May 2010 general election increase the likelihood of this licensed open disagreement. But this open breach with the convention is less important than the continuous informal leaking of disagreements by Cabinet ministers as they battle with each other over policy and career ambitions.

The shifting and uncertain meaning of conventions is one of the most important mechanisms in the British constitution. It allows the rules of the game to be adapted to the demands of the most powerful, and it helps the process by which interests can struggle to appropriate the magic of 'constitutional dignity' to their own view of the rules of the governing game. But conventions have an added importance. For the most part they cover the daily conduct of business, as the example of the convention of collective ministerial responsibility shows. But they shade off into the larger understandings described below, and thus are the point where the constitution as conventionally understood shades off into the wider character of the political culture.

Cultural understandings

Most constitutional conventions of the sort described above can and do change, and are often abandoned. It is not hard to imagine the doctrine of collective Cabinet responsibility being openly abandoned – for instance, if the innovation of May 2010 persists and we have a series of governments composed of coalitions from different parties. But suppose a government proposed reinstating the link between property ownership and the right to vote that was broken by the long struggle for universal adult suffrage described in Chapter 2 (p. 25). It is not hard to imagine here that the attempt would provoke widespread popular resistance. The example shows that at the foundations of the constitution lie features engrained in the wider political culture: understandings that are thought to be the moral core of the system of government. Like conventions, these cultural understandings can themselves be elusive, will shift over time and will often not command universal support. The understanding that there should be universal suffrage unqualified by property is a good example of this. It is a comparatively recent understanding: only in 1948 were the last property qualifications finally abolished. It is also uncertain as to its exact meaning: until 1969 an 'adult' was anyone over 21; after that, anyone over 18; and some reformers would like to reduce the age to 16. And there are undoubtedly some traditionalists – though numerically few – who actually would like to see property or educational qualifications reinstated as a precondition of an entitlement to vote.

THE DOMAINS OF THE CONSTITUTION: THE CORE AND THE CONTESTED

I have stressed the diverse sources of the constitution and the shifting and contested nature of many key constitutional understandings. Does this mean that the constitution has no settled identifiable existence? Is it simply a fiction that can be dreamt up by whichever group is most powerful?

The answer is that the meaning of the British constitution is not a fiction, but its meaning is uncertain. The reason takes us back to Bagehot's insight about the functions of a constitution: that it is invoked as a symbol to command loyalty and obedience and is also a practical means of specifying the rules of the game of government. The symbolic importance of the constitution means that it will be given different meanings by different powerful groups in different circumstances. But these groups cannot simply invent the constitution to suit themselves. The constitution is best thought of as a series of domains or territories. The boundaries of all these domains are often contested, but some are more contested than others. We can express this by a simple distinction between the *core domains* of the constitution and the *contested domains* of the constitution: between its heartland and its more disputed outer regions. And we will see that one of the fascinating features of the constitution is that the core and contested domains shift over time.

BRIEFING 4.1

Two groups that contest the domains of the constitution: Unlock Democracy and Liberty

Unlock Democracy is an independent pressure group for constitutional reform. It is the direct descendant of 'Charter 88', which as the name implies dated from a 'charter' drafted in 1988 which argued for major constitutional reform in a number of areas. These included devolution, electoral reform and the framing of a written constitution including a bill of rights. Although some of these changes have been partly achieved, Unlock Democracy has now widened its campaigning to encompass issues like lobbying transparency, electoral fraud and parliamentary accountability. Its existence shows how there is now no end to constitutional campaigning: the constitution is a perennially contested series of domains. Unlock Democracy also uses the modern 'soft technologies' of lobbying and campaigning which we discuss in later chapters (see http://www.unlockdemocracy.org.uk/). Liberty traces its history back to 1934, when the National Council for Civil Liberties was formed. It shares many of the same values as Unlock Democracy, but is much more focused on campaigning on particular issues: it takes human rights cases through the UK courts and the European Court of Human Rights; it conducts research into current government policies that affect the rights of groups like refugees; it provides practical advice and training to human rights lawyers, runs specialist advice lines and offers guidance to individual members of the public who have fallen foul of the authorities (see www.liberty-human-rights-org.uk). These activities are intended to push the boundaries of individual rights as far as possible and limit the powers of the state as far as possible.

■ As the meaning of the constitution has become more and more uncertain, radical constitutional groups like Liberty and Unlock Democracy have emerged to contest key constitutional domains.

THE CORE DOMAINS OF THE CONSTITUTION

Four important core domains of the British constitution are described here.

Rule of law

Governments can change the law; they can manipulate it since the meaning of law is often unclear; and they do even on some occasions covertly break it. But they cannot openly breach the law. One technical but important expression of this is the legal doctrine of ultra vires. A literal translation from the Latin is 'beyond powers'; and one important practical meaning is that government decisions can be overturned in the courts if they are held not to be based on a capacity conferred by a law. Government ministers and their civil service advisors therefore spend a great deal of time in trying to gauge the state of law and gauging how far it limits or empowers them. As we will see later in this text (see notably Chapters 21 and 22) the rising importance of judicial review, and of the Human Rights Act, means

that they have to spend increasing amounts of time in making these calculations. The central value attached to the rule of law also explains why the Westminster Parliament remains central to the governing process. To introduce a policy innovation of any significance at all will require a change in law. That is why, as we will discover in Chapter 9, any government's legislative timetable in any particular year is at the heart of its governing activity.

Three developments have strengthened the significance of the rule of law as a central feature of the constitution: the long term expansion in the role of government in social life has meant that ever wider areas of life are covered by the statute book; our membership of the EU means that governments now have to ask not only whether what they are doing agrees with UK law, but whether it is consistent with the law of the EU; and the value attached to the rule of law means that citizens and pressure groups now increasingly use the courts to try to establish that some policies are in breach of (or are required by) the law. (Many important changes in policy relating to employment protection, we will see later, have come about in this way.) We return to the rising importance of law in the constitution in describing the changing constitution later in this chapter.

Procedural democracy

This second 'core' domain of the constitution refers to what might be called the bare bones of democratic life: the requirement to hold elections within specified periods; to allow those registered on the electoral roll to vote; and to organize the process of electoral registration so as to make it possible for all adults to register. It is easy to see that the bare bones of procedural democracy are a powerful influence on the conduct of political life. They are so engrained that it occurs to virtually nobody to even imagine changing them. Since the passage of the Parliament Act in 1911 the life of a Parliament has been limited to five years – in effect obliging the governing party to submit to a general election at least every fifth year. Or imagine the reaction if a government proposed a new Representation of the People Act restricting the right to vote to university graduates.

Yet even the bare bones of procedural democracy can change shape. Under the great crisis of world war the general election that was due in 1940 was postponed until 1945. And while governments do not dare attack head-on the principle of universal adult suffrage, it is qualified at the boundaries in numerous ways. For instance, most inmates of prisons and mental hospitals are disqualified from voting. Rules governing registration to vote – a precondition of actually voting – are framed so as to exclude, or make difficult, registration by many voters: for example, until recently registration had to be at a fixed address, so large numbers of the very poorest – the homeless – were disqualified. That these restrictions are not fixed by some clear theory of the democratic franchise is shown by recent changes relaxing some of the restrictions summarized here: remand prisoners can now vote; those who voluntarily enter a mental hospital may do so; and the homeless can qualify if they can give an address where correspondence can be collected.

Accountability

Try this simple thought experiment. Imagine a Cabinet minister who declined to answer questions in Parliament, and who told journalists to mind their own business when they asked questions about his or her department. Such a figure is actually very hard to conceive in Britain, and were one to appear would not last long in government. That expectation reflects a central constitutional value: that governments are obliged to be accountable at least in the bare sense of giving an account in public of what they are doing and why they are doing it. That requirement can be set aside in some circumstances, for example on the grounds that an account would be contrary to national security. Ministers can often decline to give an account by claiming some such exceptional dispensation, but they do not have to make that claim. They can also evade questioning, and indeed an important part of the skill of being a minister is fending off the questions of journalists and political opponents while giving away as little as possible. But they cannot just tell inquirers to push off and mind their own business – much as they might sometimes privately feel like so doing. The presumption of accountability, though its meaning and application are varied and contested, is a central constitutional value. One of the most famous modern examples of this occurred in 1997, when in a gruelling television interview the then Home Secretary refused to answer fourteen times the same question from an interviewer. But the exchange was repeated so often, and threatened to show the Home Secretary in such an unfavourable light, that he felt obliged to offer an extended defence of his behaviour in another bruising interview a few days later (see Documenting Politics 4.2).

Liberal freedoms

Liberal freedoms in the core domain of the constitution refer to the freedoms like those of the press, of speech and assembly. We can see how central they are to constitutional understandings by again performing a simple thought experiment. Imagine turning on the radio news tomorrow morning to find that all but government controlled papers had been closed; that any criticism of the government was outlawed; that no public meetings could be held without the permission of the Home Secretary. We would be in no doubt that major (and damaging) changes in the constitution had taken place.

But this example also shows just how uncertain and contested even is the 'heartland' of the constitution. The sudden abolition of one or all of these liberal freedoms would be a major and damaging change to the constitution. Yet all these liberal freedoms are constantly breached in some particulars, and there is constant debate about just how widely they can be set. Freedom of the press is not absolute: for instance, it is restricted by libel laws that are stricter than in many other democracies. Likewise freedom of speech is not absolute: it is not allowed, for instance, where its exercise would threaten public order, and making racist attacks is

DOCUMENTING POLITICS 4.2

The modern adversarial interview: Michael Howard and John Humphrys

Extract from On The Record Interview, Michael Howard and John Humphrys, 1997.

HUMPHRYS: But what's intrigued some people is that when Jeremy Paxman asked you that very question on Tuesday night you declined to answer it. He asked you the question fourteen times and the interview has been replayed on various other forms since then and you wouldn't answer it now ...

HOWARD: I wanted to be scrupulously accurate in answering that question. I'd been thinking of lots of other things that day. I wanted to check the documents, I did not want there to be any question at all of my giving an answer that wasn't entirely true and accurate. The next day I checked the records, I gave the answer, I did not threaten to overrule Derek Lewis.

HUMPHRYS: But surely the only reason you could have had for wanting to check the documents, the minutes or whatever they were, was that you yourself weren't sure whether you had threatened to overrule him or not.

HOWARD: This was a meeting that took place two and a half years ago and before answering a question to which I knew importance would be attached, I wanted to make absolutely sure that I got the right, honest and accurate answer and that's what I did.

HUMPHRYS: But there must have been some doubt in your mind therefore.

HOWARD: No, I just wanted to check absolutely that there was no question of my giving an answer that wasn't entirely accurate ...

HUMPHRYS: So you had to check the minutes to make sure that you hadn't said something about which you were sure ...

■ In May 1997 Michael Howard, then Home Secretary, was confronted in a famous interview by the BBC *Newsnight* interviewer Jeremy Paxman. Mr Paxman was interested in discovering whether the Home Secretary had given orders to the director of the Prison Service in a critical episode in the recent history of the Service – orders which would have exceeded his powers. Mr Howard initially declined to answer – and Mr Paxman repeated the question fourteen times, each time failing to extract a direct answer. The widespread assumption that he was declining to answer because he had indeed exceeded his powers was what Mr Howard now tried to counter in a radio interview a few days later with an interviewer with an almost equal reputation for ferocity, John Humphrys. The extract and the wider episode shows how far the broadcasting interview has emerged as the main method now of grilling Government ministers.

Source: www.bbc.co.uk/otr/int/howard/18.5.97.

prohibited. Freedom of assembly is not absolute: meetings and marches that might provoke racial violence or otherwise pose a threat to public order are often banned. In Northern Ireland the 'right to march' is governed by an elaborate set of rules administered by a specially appointed Parades Commission (see www.paradescommission.org).

The domain of liberal freedoms is one of the key domains of the constitution, not because it is settled and stable, but for the very opposite reason. It is a key area where disputes about the meaning of the constitution are conducted. Rival invocations of the meaning of what liberal freedoms are guaranteed by the constitution are one important means by which conflicting understandings of the constitution are expressed. The process returns us once again to Bagehot's insight about the importance of the constitution as a source of political loyalty and obedience: invoking the constitutional status of liberal freedoms is an important way in which advocates of particular meanings of these freedoms try to capture the magic of the constitution for their particular understandings.

IMAGES 4.1 and 4.2 ■ The dignified constitution made flesh

■ Bagehot identified the Monarchy as the key 'dignified' part of the constitution. Queen Victoria – monarch when Bagehot wrote – was the personal incarnation of this dignified role. Statues of the Queen like those pictured here can be found in numerous towns and cities. The two here, however, show how differently 'dignity' is revealed. Image 4.1 shows the Queen's pristine statue outside Belfast City Hall. Note the Union Jack flying above. Here the statue represents Protestant Union dominion in Ireland: see Chapter 11 for this history. Image 4.2 shows a similar statue in the centre of Manchester: but here, ignored, occasionally vandalized and usually covered with pigeon droppings.

THE CONTESTED DOMAINS OF THE CONSTITUTION

The contested territories of the constitution are important and revealing. We know that part of the appeal of the constitution in Britain is that it has a 'magic' to which contesting groups can appeal to give legitimacy to their view of what the rules of the political game should be. The areas of contestation therefore also tell us something about the nature of conflict and competition over how Britain should be ruled. And we will also find, as we sketch these contested domains, that we are also looking at a map of constitutional change in Britain: many of the areas now contested were once part of the core of the constitution. Four important contested domains are discussed here.

Territorial unity

The creation of the 'United Kingdom' is the result of an important historical ambition: to unite the different territories of the islands under a single Crown and a single Parliament. But we know that in the twentieth century it was sundered by one great civil war followed by secession: the 'Irish War of Independence' that led to the establishment of an 'Irish Free State' in 1922 following a treaty of 1921 (see Chapter 11 for more). Dismantling the Empire also amounted to a break up of territorial unity. When George VI was ceremonially crowned King in May 1937, having succeeded his brother the preceding year, he was also Emperor of India; when his daughter was crowned Elizabeth II in 1953 the title had disappeared because India had disappeared from the Empire into an independent republic.

For nearly 40 years the dominion of Parliament and Crown in Northern Ireland has been contested by a republican movement prepared to use acts of terrorism to separate the province from the UK. For a generation there have also been nationalist parties in both Wales and Scotland that have by peaceful means advocated separation from the UK. As we shall see in Chapter 10 that has now resulted in a separate Parliament for Scotland with distinct powers, and an Assembly in Wales that over the period since the beginning of devolution has evolved into a Parliament in all but name. We saw in Chapter 1 that the most influential modern definition of a state – that given by Max Weber – pictured it as a system of rule over a physically identifiable territory. The geographical boundaries of rule are thus central to any account of a country's constitution. In the case of the UK these boundaries are subject to sustained dispute.

Parliamentary supremacy

The territorial unity of the UK and doctrines of parliamentary supremacy are connected, because the parliament in question is the Westminster Parliament. This Parliament remains central to any understanding of the constitution: as we saw above, the rule of law remains a core part of the constitution and the Westminster Parliament is still a main source of the law. But this supremacy is now contested in two main ways. First, there is the constraining importance of what we above called 'superstatutes': legal commitments that arise out of legislation originally passed in Parliament but that now constrain its ability to exercise supremacy. The legal obligations of EU membership, as we shall see in Chapter 5, are a prime example of this: it has been estimated that 80 per cent of the rules that govern trade in the single market of the Union now originate in EU institutions, rather than in national parliaments like Westminster. Since 1998 the establishment of separate assemblies in Wales and Scotland has further diminished Westminster supremacy especially in the case of Scotland. The boundaries of this supremacy are now an even more contested domain of the constitution than the territorial boundaries of the UK itself.

But the most serious challenges to parliamentary supremacy have not come from the conscious transfer of power to other institutions. They have come from the rise of rival forms of representation. The Westminster Parliament owes its authority to territorial representation: the 'bare bones' of democracy that we sketched out above involve elections in territorially defined constituencies. But territory is not the only possible basis on which interests and ideas can be represented. An important alternative is sometimes called 'functional' representation. Groups claim legitimacy because they speak for members who perform functions in the community – as teachers, doctors, firefighters or accountants. Governments have to deal all the time with these functional groups, and a number of constitutional crises have arisen because the demands of functional and territorial representation could not be reconciled. That was true of some of the bitterest industrial disputes of the twentieth century: for instance, a 'general strike' called by all trade unions in 1926 and a strike by coalminers in 1973–74, in defiance of the government, which led to widespread social chaos and, eventually, the fall of the Government itself. The balance between the supremacy of a territorially elected parliament and groups claiming authority through functional representation is one of the most unstable and contested domains of the constitution.

Crown legitimacy

When Bagehot published his famous work in 1867 he put the Crown at the centre of the constitution. It was the most important way the 'dignified' constitutional function was performed, and was therefore vital to supporting the system of rule. It was strengthened in the twentieth century by the invention of a 'Royal Family' with a carefully managed public image that presented that Family as simultaneously glamorously remote but very ordinary in its family preoccupations. The dignified role of the Royal Family probably reached its highest point in the Second World War. The King and Queen insisted on staying at their palace in London for the express purpose of being bombed by the Germans, thus sharing the dangers of other Londoners. But in the last generation this dignified effect has worn away. Royal ceremonial at great public occasions is still commonplace. But a key device identified by Bagehot – the cultivation of an aura of magic and mystery – has disappeared. The troubles and foibles of royalty – sexual and financial – are now a commonplace of media reporting. While polling evidence shows little sustained support for a republic it shows also that the public routinely 'grades' different members of the royal family according to their performance, usually awarding high marks to the Queen herself, and much lower marks to most of the rest. This grading of performance profoundly undermines the cultivation of a remote, magical mystique. It turns being royal into just another job – like university teaching or train driving – where effectiveness at doing the job can be graded.

The Crown as pictured by Bagehot is therefore being pushed to the margins of the constitution, and is becoming decreasingly important in performing 'dignified' roles. At times of great national distress it is now common for Prime Ministers – most of whom have a gift for public communication – to play a consoling, dignified role. How far this marginalization continues depends on many factors, not least the intelligence with which the Monarchy manages its public roles. It is possible to imagine a reinvention of the Monarch's role in which the Crown once again assumes an important place in the emotional life of the nation, for instance by the development of something like the 'people's monarchies' so successful in parts of Scandinavia. Alternatively, it may simply become part of the celebrity world of the international demi-monde, like the royal family of Monaco, providing the same sort of tabloid entertainment as movie stars, footballers and contestants in reality TV shows.

Citizens not subjects

Traditionally the British were subjects, not citizens. That is, they had important legal protections such as those detailed above in my sketch of the rule of law. But these were not rights that they could claim against the authority of the state; rather, they were protections that they could claim by virtue of being subjects of the Crown. Protection was granted by the state, rather than being enforceable against the state. But the language of citizenship is now increasingly used to speak of rights in Britain. This is partly reflected in the rise of campaigning groups who simply do not accept the constitutional language of the subject and assert that individuals should have rights against the state as citizens. They include groups campaigning to reform the constitution, like Unlock Democracy, and groups dedicated to the defence of what they conceive as civil liberties, like Liberty. The passage of the Human Rights Act 1998 incorporates into law the provisions of an international charter, the European Charter of Human Rights. It thus has some of the features of what I have called a 'super-statute': it entrenches the rights of citizens against the state, and its language of 'rights' departs from the traditional language of concessions granted to subjects by the Crown.

We should not overstate the extent to which the language of 'subjection' is now contested by the language of 'citizenship'. The British Government – in the name of the Crown – retains the power to curb these rights in emergency conditions. It has done this in respect of the detention of some groups of suspects without trial in the search for terrorists after the 11 September 2001 bombing of the World Trade Center in New York. But the

FIGURE 4.1 ■ The decline of deference in Britain: the young are more likely to support disregarding authority and law (percentage of two age groups saying that different kinds of behaviour are never justified)

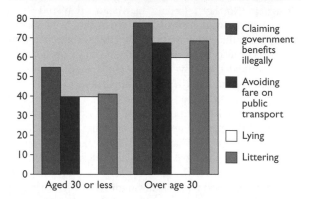

Source: Calculated from Hall (1999:448).

■ The political scientist Peter Hall combined responses to two large scale surveys to produce these figures, which relate to the 1980s and 1990s. They show a remarkably consistent pattern: older people are more disapproving of both law breaking and general antisocial behaviour than are young people. The inference is that this reflects a historical change – that the old are reflecting values from the past that are now, literally, dying out. We should, however, bear two cautions in mind: there is the possibility that the young are simply more frank than the old, and that the differences do not always reflect real differences in behaviour; and the possibility that the difference is simply age related, and that as people mature in years they adopt more socially responsible attitudes.

very acrimony this has created reveals the shift in assumptions that is taking place. The idea that we were 'subjects' of the Crown was once a settled part of the constitution; but this is now contested territory because of the rise of a vocabulary that pictures us as 'citizens' with rights that we can assert against state authority.

THE SOURCES OF CONSTITUTIONAL CHANGE AND CONFLICT

The British constitution is never a stable settlement. It performs Bagehot's 'dignified' function: whatever can convincingly be described as part of the constitution has conferred on it a special legitimacy. This is why it resembles a series of territories or domains over which conflicting groups compete. No domain is ever entirely settled, but some are more securely at the heart of the constitution than others. Obviously changes in what is at the heart of the constitution, and what is pushed to the margins or even excluded, depend on the operation of many forces. Three are identified here, because they help reinforce an important point: that there is a powerful connection between the constitution as narrowly understood and the wider political culture in Britain.

The decline of deference

The British constitution was traditionally a deferential constitution. Deference has many shades of meaning, but the core one is straightforward. It refers to a willingness to obey without undue questioning. That willingness can arise from a number of sources: from a belief, for instance, that others have an innate superiority in the art of government; or from a belief that some social groups are by birth or training uniquely suited to government. This latter deference was once an important part of the constitution. It explains, for example, why Bagehot set such store by the magic of monarchy. That was shorthand for a political culture in which the mass of the population accepted that social superiors in the aristocracy had a special entitlement to rule. Even when the aristocracy declined as an important source of political leadership in Britain – and that did not happen until the second half of the twentieth century – deference carried over into modern times in a special willingness to obey the authority figures of the state, like the police. It also showed itself in a special willingness to 'defer' to key ideas, such as the notion that one should scrupulously obey laws and the values that underlay those laws.

Changes in cultural patterns like deference are hard to document partly because cultural patterns are complex and partly because we often lack systematic evidence that will allow us to compare the past and the present. But there does seem to be compelling evidence that deference is declining (see Figure 4.1). Social deference has almost disappeared: aristocrats who seek elected office now usually find it expedient, indeed, to modify the evidence of their aristocratic origins, like their accents. Survey evidence shows a long-term decline in a special willingness to obey authority: for instance, a rising willingness, especially among the young, to claim that they would openly resist laws that they felt to be unjust. There is also some evidence from behaviour of a declining willingness to do something just because authority figures say so. In the 1980s a major reform of local government finance – the replacement of the rates on property by a tax levied on each individual – was destroyed by mass civil disobedience, especially in Scotland. The state has long prohibited consumption and

IMAGE 4.3 ■ A less deferential political culture in action

■ The photo is of a young demonstrator on one of the many mass demonstrations against the Iraq War in 2003. It showed how hitherto deferential and submissive people are now prepared to protest against the Westminster elite. Note the headband: in her own unique way the young demonstrator has broadened antiwar protest into a wider protest against the whole political–economic system.

sale of a wide range of narcotics, such as cannabis; but there is compelling evidence that this is disregarded by a large part of the population. Political demonstrations, from all ends of the political spectrum, now involve open use of civil disobedience: examples include opposition to construction projects like motorway or airport extensions; tax protests, such as those against fuel taxes which virtually brought the country to a halt briefly in the autumn of 2000; and generalized campaigns such as those against the perceived threats of globalization. There also seems to be a consistent pattern of lower trust in established elites: consider the view of the low trustworthiness of politicians in Figure 4.2.

The decline of deference is more, however, than a change in wider popular attitudes. There have been demonstrable long-term changes in the treatment of rulers in media reporting, and these too are signs of declining deference. This decline is one important reason for the damage inflicted in recent years on a once key 'dignified' part of the constitution: the Royal Family. The Royal Family now routinely provides material for the scandal sheets of newspapers. Historical evidence suggests that present royalty are no odder in behaviour than previous generations of royals: no more given to

FIGURE 4.2 ■ Don't trust me: I'm a politician (percentage expressing trust in different occupations to tell the truth)

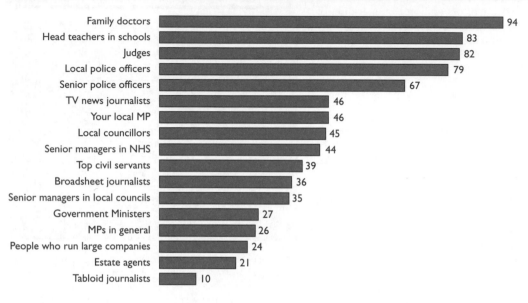

Family doctors	94
Head teachers in schools	83
Judges	82
Local police officers	79
Senior police officers	67
TV news journalists	46
Your local MP	46
Local councillors	45
Senior managers in NHS	44
Top civil servants	39
Broadsheet journalists	36
Senior managers in local councils	35
Government Ministers	27
MPs in general	26
People who run large companies	24
Estate agents	21
Tabloid journalists	10

Source: Committee on Standards in Public Life (2008:22).

■ The figure reports the proportion of a representative national sample who expressed trust in a variety of groups in the community to tell the truth. The survey was conducted for the Committee on Standards in Public Life in 2008. MPs, we can see, are among the least trusted group in the community. But notice that when citizens are asked about their own MP – putting a face to a more general category – the level of trust rises considerably. However, the survey pre-dated the great scandal of 2009 over MPs expenses.

marital infidelity, boorishness or drug use than the average royal in history. But in the past these were rarely reported. When King Edward VIII abdicated in 1936 to marry his mistress, the occasion was the first that the country at large knew that he actually had a mistress. In the case of the present heir to the throne there has been intimate reporting of the Prince of Wales, his late wife and her lovers, the Prince's own mistress, and the way she in turn became his wife.

Declining trust

The decline of deference helps to explain one of the most striking features of modern popular attitudes to politicians: the fact that politicians are among the least trusted of all groups in the community. There is a connection between declining deference and low trust because willingness to defer partly arises from a high level of trust: if I have strong faith in your integrity and competence I will be more willing to do what you command without questioning. The evidence of low trust comes from surveys where representative samples of the population have been asked about their willingness to

trust public authority figures like educators, the police and politicians. This survey evidence of course only reveals what people tell opinion pollsters, but other evidence supports it. Although there is widespread participation in a range of political demonstrations and protests, there is declining enthusiasm to participate in more conventional politics: membership of political parties is in long-term decline, and voter turnout is also in decline – themes to which we will turn in detail in Chapters 13, 14 and 17.

Of course taken by itself declining participation in official politics might easily be taken as a sign of satisfaction – arising from a feeling that government was run so well that one could let it run unhindered. But the evidence of surveys contradicts this complacent conclusion. In addition, the last two decades have been an era of sleaze and scandal at the top of British politics. In 2009 the House of Commons was convulsed by a long series of revelations of dubious, bizarre and possibly illegal manipulation of the Parliamentary expenses system by MPs. In 2010 former members of the Labour Cabinet were secretly filmed offering their services to

BRIEFING 4.2

From convention to codification: some recommendations of the Committee on Standards in Public Life

NUMBER AND TITLE OF REPORT	SUMMARY OF MAIN RECOMMENDATIONS
First Report: Standards in Public Life	All public bodies to draw up Codes of Conduct incorporating the Seven Principles of Public Life
Second Report: Local Public Spending Bodies	■ Set limits to terms of office of public appointments ■ Develop independent complaints processes ■ Establish codes for 'whistleblowers'
Third Report: Standards of Conduct in Local Public Bodies	■ Set new rules on declaration of interests by councillors ■ Replace existing National Code with codes tailored to individual councils ■ Create new framework for standards of discipline for councillors and officers
Fourth Report: Standards of Conduct of non-departmental public bodies, NHS Trusts and Local Public Spending Bodies	More open and transparent appointment rules in accordance with the principles of the Committee's First Report and specific recommendations of its Second Report (above)
Fifth Report: funding of political parties	■ Clear rules for full disclosure of all donations ■ Limit to total campaign spending in a general election ■ Regulation of any organization or individual spending more than £25,000 in a general election campaign
Sixth Report: Reinforcing Standards	The Report reviewed progress on implementing the recommendations of earlier reports, especially the First Report
Twelfth Report: MPs' Expenses and Allowances	■ Independent regulatory body should regulate MPs' expenses ■ Claims for mortgage relief and other housing expenses, and employment of family members, to be discontinued

■ This is only a sample of the full range of the Committee's work, and not all its recommendations have been implemented. But many have, and it is the one of the most important sources of pressure to shift constitutional understandings from the realm of informal understandings to formal codification.

Source: www.public-standards.gov.uk.

POLITICAL ISSUES 4.1

Irreversible constitutional reform: New Labour's big idea

The constitution is always changing, but until the late 1990s it tended to change piecemeal and often imperceptibly. After the return of Labour in 1997 the pace of change has accelerated, so much that constitutional reform looks like New Labour's 'big idea' – comparable to the big idea of the Conservatives in the 1980s of large scale privatization. Three radical innovations can be traced directly to New Labour: the virtual abolition of the hereditary element in the House of Lords, as part of an unfinished wider reconstruction of the composition of the Lords; the introduction of a new regime of human rights, notably in the Human Rights Act of 1998; and the creation of new devolved systems of government in Scotland, Wales and Northern Ireland (see Chapters 10 and 11). The years of the Blair governments, in particular, saw major changes in constitutional practice in fields as different as the regulation of political parties, the methods of making public appointments and the regulation of the declaration of interests by public servants. Most of these changes have involved more detailed written rules and have been connected to the activities of the Committee on Standards in Public Life (see Briefing 4.2). Like privatization these changes are now 'locked in': whatever opposing parties say by way of criticism, they cannot be reversed, just as Labour's opposition to the privatization in the 1980s was abandoned in the 1990s.

lobbyists for corporate interests. But these were only the latest in a series of grubby episodes. Two prominent public figures from the Conservative Party of the 1990s ended in jail for perjury: one was a former Cabinet minister and one a former Deputy Chairman of the Party (Jonathan Aitken and Jeffrey Archer). There were newspaper exposures of the willingness of backbench Members of Parliament to 'plant' parliamentary questions to ministers in return for personal payments. A campaign by the Prime Minister John Major in the early 1990s to assert the importance of traditional Victorian values was destroyed by the revelation of numerous sexual indiscretions by leading members of his government and Party. It later transpired that Mr Major had himself conducted a protracted illicit extra-marital affair with a fellow Conservative MP. In 1994 the same Prime Minister was obliged by the volume of scandal to establish a special Committee on Standards in Public Life. This is still in existence, and still investigating standards across a wide range of public life – and, as we shall see next, has made an important contribution to the rise of a more formally codified constitution.

The rise of codification

What would you do if your trust in someone – an authority figure like a priest or a lecturer – was badly damaged? If you were obliged to continue dealing with them a natural response would be to want to write down clearly what their obligations amounted to and to check closely that they were meeting those obligations. In

short, you would explicitly codify what had hitherto been only informally understood and probably never openly expressed. This describes an important change that is reshaping constitutional understandings in Britain. As we noted at the start of this chapter the British constitution was traditionally described as uncodified: more accurately, codification was piecemeal and fragmented, and many key parts of the constitution consisted of informal understandings. These 'conventions' are still important, but there is a growing tendency to codify understandings, mostly by the simple act of writing down what they mean. This may seem a trivial change, but it has momentous consequences. Once an understanding is written down it is much more difficult to keep it out of the public domain. And while words written down may often be ambiguous they are less ambiguous than unwritten understandings; they therefore provide an openly available standard against which behaviour can be judged. The rising importance of codification reflects wider social and cultural changes: a growing tendency to codify all kinds of hitherto informal social relations.

In the case of the constitution, the rise of codification has some obvious, particular origins. One of the most important is the influence of the Committee on Standards in Public Life originally established in 1994. The Committee has not only developed a set of general standards of conduct in public life but has produced detailed recommendations covering some of the most important institutions of government: for more open rules governing appointment to public bodies; for rules

DEBATING POLITICS 4.1

Political authority in Britain: democratic change or decay?

POLITICAL AUTHORITY IS SIMPLY BEING SUBJECTED TO MORE DEMOCRATIC SCRUTINY

▶ Unthinking deference to authority is in decline.
▶ The Committee on Standards in Public Life is obliging public bodies to obey clear rules and give clear accounts of their activities.
▶ Constitutional conventions are increasingly openly debated rather than being settled without public discussion.
▶ Constitutional 'lobby groups' like Liberty are increasingly contesting the meaning of the constitution.

POLITICAL AUTHORITY IN BRITAIN IS IN DECAY

▶ Trust in politicians is lower than among almost any other group in the community, and there are many cases of politicians acting in a scandalous way.
▶ Popular readiness to act unlawfully and dishonestly is growing.
▶ The power of the ceremonial role of the Monarchy is decaying.
▶ Media treatment of government figures is increasingly adversarial, treating the politician as a kind of permanent 'accused' in the dock.

regulating the relations between Members of Parliament and special interests; for rules governing the financing of political parties; and for rules governing standards of conduct in local government (see Briefing 4.2). Many of these recommendations are now embodied in written codes, and some are even embodied in laws. In later chapters – for example when we turn to political parties – we shall find widespread evidence of this growth in codification.

Law is the most developed form of codification. Laws are backed by the power of the state, and their breach attracts its coercive power. Governments that claim to be bound by the rule of law – as do governments in Britain – therefore have to frame laws carefully. Laws need to say as unambiguously as possible what obligations they impose, and on whom. Since they are backed by the state's coercive power – in the last analysis through the police and the courts – clear rules are needed: to show when coercion will be applied, how, and what safeguards citizens have against the improper use of that coercion. All these considerations make codification in law special: the rules are spelt out in an especially clear and elabo-

rate way. Hence embodying constitutional understandings in law moves the constitution further away again from its traditional uncodified, informal understandings. In recent years important laws have regulated key domains of the constitution, as the three following examples show:

● The Human Rights Act 1998, to which we have already referred, seeks to codify legally the relations between the state and the individual citizen.
● The Political Parties, Elections and Referendums Act of 2000 now legally codifies what was hitherto largely a matter of informal understanding: the roles of political parties and especially the conditions under which they can raise finance. It has also established an agency to regulate these activities in the form of the Electoral Commission.
● The legislation creating devolved government in Scotland and Wales, which we shall examine in Chapter 10, naturally codifies also the relations between the different levels of government in the newly created multilevel system.

Review OF CHAPTER 4

Four important themes have dominated this chapter:

◗ The very diverse sources of the constitution in Britain.

◗ The importance of the constitution's dual functions: the *dignified* and the *efficient*.

◗ The continually contested nature of the constitution.

◗ The gradual transformation of the constitution from a patchwork of informal understandings to something more explicitly and systematically codified.

FURTHER READING

ESSENTIAL

If you read only one book it should be the great classic of the constitution originally published in 1867 by Walter Bagehot, in the edition cited here as Bagehot (1867/1963) because this edition has an almost equally well celebrated long introduction by Richard Crossman, who was both an eminent politician and a writer on British politics.

RECOMMENDED

Political scientists used not to be much interested in the constitution, but since the first edition of this book two outstanding works have been published by eminent scholars of British politics: King (2007) and Bogdanor (2009). Chapter 4 of this book has been, in the widest sense, about the 'political culture' of the UK: about the understandings, popular and elite, which shape thinking and behaviour about the rules of the game. Two 'classics' are Almond and Verba (1963 and 1980.) The authoritative modern collection on constitutional theory and practice is Jowell and Oliver, now in its sixth edition (2007). Brazier (1999) is the best single-author study on the constitutional foundations of political practice. Hay (2007) has a lot to say about discontents with our political culture.

Europeanizing British politics

CONTENTS

AIMS

The aims of this chapter are to introduce the wider political system of the EU, a political system of which Britain is an important component part. This chapter:

- Summarizes the history of European integration, showing why it is so important in British politics

- Describes the main ways the EU now permeates British politics

- Shows, conversely, how deeply embedded is Britain in European political institutions

- Describes the EU as a legal creation and explains why that is so important

- Summarizes the way the 'Europeanization' of British politics has added key elements to the development of multilevel governance in Britain, and discusses the meaning of 'Europeanization'

BRITAIN AS A EUROPEAN POLITICAL SYSTEM

In a textbook on British politics, why do we begin our account of the institutional structure of the system with a chapter on institutions outside Britain – the political institutions of the EU? The answers not only justify the chapter – they tell us something very important about the system of government under which the British live. The reasons for treating Europe in such an important way are threefold:

Impact of the Union on British Government

A large amount of what government actually undertakes in Britain is done as a result of decisions taken by the institutions of the EU. We would utterly fail to grasp why and how government functions in Britain if we failed to grasp this fact.

Resources

A key issue in all government is: where do resources get allocated, and by whom? In British government, resource allocation is increasingly a European matter: the British contribute large amounts annually to the budget of the Union; and they receive annually large amounts in subsidies and grants. The size of the British contribution annually can vary widely because of fluctuations in the value of sterling against the euro. It can also vary depending on different measures used. As a result, competing estimates are used by partisans for and against the country's membership of the EU. But what is undeniable is that five of the big member states contribute the lions' share, and that Britain is always one of these big five. The level of contribution therefore has a twofold significance: it does indeed signal the scale of British commitment; but it is also symbolically invoked in the debates within Britain as a sign either of how burdensome is membership or as a sign of what a good bargain is the EU.

Impact on the wider political system

Because the EU is so important in decision making and in resource allocation, the British political system is increasingly organized along European lines: government runs itself so as to try to act effectively in Europe; pressure groups organize themselves to exert pressure in Brussels; and parties increasingly argue about how best to organize Britain as a member of the EU.

THE EU SINCE 1945

In 1945, most of Western Europe lay in ruins, and most of Eastern Europe – roughly east of the river Elbe – was now under the control of a new communist military superpower, the Soviet Union. Two great wars (1914–18 and 1939–45) had been fought largely because of rivalry between three west European nations: Germany, Britain and France. The outcome not only produced the untold suffering of the wars; such was the physical devastation and social dislocation that on several occasions after 1945 the people of Western Europe were on the verge of starvation.

These catastrophes eventually produced what we now call the EU. The origin of the movement for integration lay in the effort to solve the key problem in Europe that had led to the great wars: the inability of France and Germany to live in peace. The first important step was taken in 1951 with the signing of the Treaty of Paris, which founded the ECSC, an organization designed to integrate the coal and steel industries of six countries into a single unified market: Germany, France, Italy and the three Benelux countries (Belgium, the Netherlands and Luxembourg). These industries were targeted for a first stage of integration because they were then the foundations of military and industrial power: integrated coal and steel industries would make it exceptionally difficult for any single nation to build a separate military capacity such as led Germany to the aggressive military policies that produced war in 1939.

In 1955 at Messina in Italy a meeting of the six countries that had joined together in the ECSC attempted, successfully, to repeat for their wider economies what had been achieved in coal and steel. This agreement led to the signing in 1957 of the Treaty of Rome, the founding Treaty of a new EEC (colloquially called the Common Market), what we now know as the EU. The Treaty became effective at the start of 1958. The Messina meeting and the Treaty that it produced are momentous historical events in the history of Europe – easily the most momentous for Western Europe in the second half of the twentieth century. They were in part the product of a vision of a united Europe which was held by a number of public servants and politicians: the French civil servant Jean Monnet, the French politician Robert Schuman and the German politician Konrad Adenauer (see People in Politics 5.1).

But if there was a grand vision of what a united Europe would become, the first version of the Treaty of Rome seems, over 50 years later, quite modest in its ambitions – at least by the standards of what has now been achieved. The modesty of these practical ambitions is shown in three ways.

Modest formal powers

The formal powers of the institutions of the Community were very limited. The most important sign of this limita-

People in Politics 5.1

Three who shaped European integration

Konrad Adenauer (1876–1967)

German statesman. He was deprived of all political office by the Nazis in 1933. He helped found the Christian Democratic Party after German defeat in 1945 and was Chancellor (Prime Minister) of the Federal Republic of Germany, 1949–63, and simultaneously Foreign Minister, 1951–55. Adenauer's determination to stabilize a new German democracy by binding Germany into a new united Europe was the key element in German support for European unification.

Jean Monnet (1888–1979)

French public servant. He held numerous public offices before the Second World War and lived in exile when France was occupied by the Nazis, 1940–45. He made the blueprint for the ECSC (and was its President 1952–55), the forerunner of what became the EU. The 'Monnet method' – to use economic integration as a foundation for political integration – has been the key to the development of the EU.

Robert Schuman (1886–1963)

French statesman. His life and history graphically illustrate the tortured history of early twentieth-century Europe. He was educated mostly at German universities, but made his career in French public life. Briefly Prime Minister (1947–48) his greatest impact was as French Foreign Minister, 1948–52, when he gave his name to the plan that created the ECSC. He was President of the EP 1958–60.

Cartoons: Shaun Steele

■ Here are three key figures in the founding period of what became the EU. They shared the experience of economic depression and war in Europe in the first half of the twentieth century and conceived European integration as a way of ensuring that the experience was not repeated. Notice that none was British.

tion was a voting rule designed to ensure that the sovereign independence of no member country could be overruled: important decisions required unanimity among the national members.

Modest resources

The resources of the Common Market were few. Virtually the only sizable pot of money which it controlled was a fund designed to provide subsidies for agriculture, itself the product of the most important single economic bargain at its heart. The creation of a Common Market promised to open up the markets of other member nations to the industrial goods of the biggest, most efficient, industrial economy in Europe, that of Germany. In return Germany contributed a disproportionate amount to a common budget that was largely used to subsidize small farmers in the other countries, especially in France.

Modest economic aims

'Common Market' is in fact a misnomer, because it implies that the only ambition was to create a free trade area – an area where goods and services would be traded without the imposition of any national barriers. But from the beginning the aim was to create something more: a customs union, which means an area not only where there is internal free trade but also a common set of external tariffs imposed on all goods and services imported into the new union.

From the present vantage point of the EU these are modest aims, though in 1957 they were startlingly radical. They were, in particular, far too radical for British governments of the time, which declined to participate in either the ECSC or the original Common Market. How was this limited attempt to create a modest amount of European integration between six countries transformed into the present EU? Four important factors were at work.

Economic success

From the very beginning the various efforts at economic integration (both the ECSC and the Common Market) were accompanied by staggering economic success. The economies ruined by two world wars and the great depression of the 1930s were transformed by years of high economic growth in the 1950s and 1960s. For instance between 1950 and 1973 (the year when Britain joined the EEC) British economic growth was 3 per cent per annum; the corresponding German figure was exactly twice that; and the French figure was 5.1 per cent per annum. How far this economic transformation could be attributed to economic integration can be debated, but what mattered was what the association did

to belief in the whole European enterprise. It gave confidence to those with a vision of building a single Europe and created wide public support for their continuing efforts.

Enlargement

One of the most important results of this economic success was in Britain. The country had stood aside from the original Messina negotiations. Most of her initial reactions to the Common Market consisted in efforts to create alternatives – for example a European Free Trade Area – that, if successful, would have turned the integration movement into something much more limited than was envisioned by the Common Market's founders. The success of the economies of the Common Market, coupled with the continuing relative failure of the British economy, destroyed this effort to create an alternative. It led to a decade of attempts to join the Community. This culminated, finally, in British accession in 1973, which was accompanied by that of two other economies, Ireland and Denmark, which until then had been closely tied to Britain because it was an important market for their agricultural products. In the 1980s three Mediterranean countries joined after they had reconstructed their political systems along democratic lines following periods of dictatorship: Greece (1981) and Spain and Portugal (1986). A fourth wave in 1995 brought the total to 15: Austria, Finland and Sweden. The most dramatic enlargement occurred in May 2004 when ten new members joined – mostly states that had until the end of the 1980s been ruled by Communist dictatorships under the control of the Soviet Union. Bulgaria and Romania also joined as part of this wave, though their membership did not become active until 2007, at which point the Union consisted of 27 members (see Image 5.1).

Policy innovation

For much of the 1970s and 1980s the EU barely seemed to develop and the economies of the member states struggled with a succession of economic problems. The most important policy innovation breaking away from this stagnation was the programme to complete the Single Market that was formally launched by a treaty agreed by all member states (the SEA) in 1986. The SEA marked the moment when Europe decisively turned from the limited aims of the original Treaty of Rome – creating a customs union – to something much more active: building a single European economy where the movement of goods, services and labour would be as free as within the old national economies. Building this economy would not be possible without extensive political intervention by the institutions of

IMAGE 5.1 ■ The growth of the EU

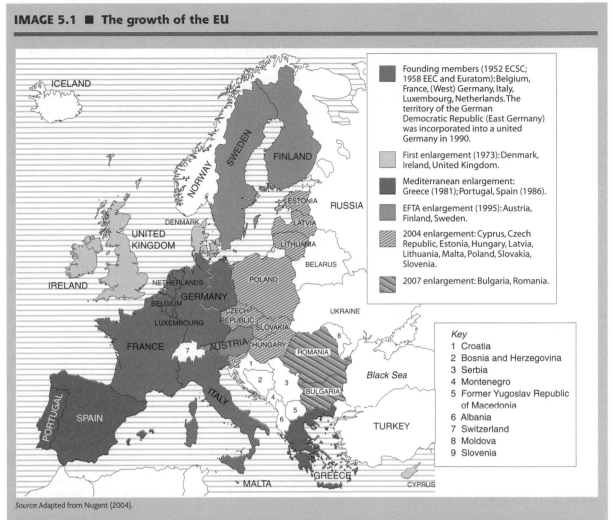

Founding members (1952 ECSC; 1958 EEC and Euratom): Belgium, France, (West) Germany, Italy, Luxembourg, Netherlands. The territory of the German Democratic Republic (East Germany) was incorporated into a united Germany in 1990.

First enlargement (1973): Denmark, Ireland, United Kingdom.

Mediterranean enlargement: Greece (1981); Portugal, Spain (1986).

EFTA enlargement (1995): Austria, Finland, Sweden.

2004 enlargement: Cyprus, Czech Republic, Estonia, Hungary, Latvia, Lithuania, Malta, Poland, Slovakia, Slovenia.

2007 enlargement: Bulgaria, Romania.

Key
1 Croatia
2 Bosnia and Herzegovina
3 Serbia
4 Montenegro
5 Former Yugoslav Republic of Macedonia
6 Albania
7 Switzerland
8 Moldova
9 Slovenia

Source: Adapted from Nugent (2004).

■ The map shows the growth of the EU over a period spanning more than 50 years: the very first integration involved the coal and steel industries of six West European states in 1952. This period of more than half a century has seen both geographical widening and institutional 'deepening' – the expansion of the original limited coverage of a couple of industries to the wholesale government of the economies of the member states. The biggest single enlargement measured by increase in members came in 2004 – the fifth enlargement identified here – and is a direct consequence of the collapse of the Soviet Empire in eastern Europe after 1989.

the EU to ensure that economic conditions across Europe would be regulated to give equality of competitive conditions across the whole Union: as it is often put, to create a 'level playing field' for all those competing in the markets of the Union. In other words, the commitment to completing the single market also meant a commitment to a great expansion in the powers of the institutions of Europe: it meant creating not just a single European economy but a unified system of economic government. The Treaty of Maastricht, signed in 1992 (though only ratified in

Britain the following year after bitter debate) was a further striking stage of policy innovation. It marked four key advances:

● It made provision for the creation of single European currency, an ambition realized, we shall see below, with the introduction of the euro in 1999. The euro is now the single currency for 16 of the 27 member states of the Union.

● It strengthened Europe's capacities in foreign, defence and social policy.

- As a symbol of the transformation from a narrowly economic to a more ambitiously political grouping it introduced the new name of the 'European Union'.
- It conferred on the people of the member states the common status of citizens of the new Union.

But change has not stopped there: as Briefing 5.3 (p. 82) shows the Treaty of Lisbon of 2009 takes further the construction of a system of government for the Union.

Crisis

As we have seen, the original moves to integration were the product of the ruinous historical crises of the first half of the twentieth century. The spread in the range and influence of the EU was greatly helped in the last two decades of that century by another crisis, the collapse of the Communist systems of eastern Europe and the dissolution of their controlling power, the Soviet Union, after 1989. This created a gap in the international power system that in the intervening years the EU began to fill by expanding its diplomatic and even its military capacities. It directly led to the accession of one new member, Finland, which had previously been limited in its foreign commitments by the domination of its immediate neighbour, the Soviet Union. It led to applications for membership from a large number of former Soviet bloc countries. In May 2004, as we noted above, ten new states joined, mostly from the former Soviet bloc. The enlargement added 75 million new European citizens, and necessitated, as we shall see below, important changes in institutions and policies.

EUROPE IN BRITAIN

The scope of EU power and influence in Britain

The influence of Britain's membership of the EU permeates numerous aspects of British government, and indeed of British life. The most important influences are fivefold: in the markets for goods and services; in the market for labour; in regional and environmental policy; in foreign economic policy; and in foreign diplomacy.

The *market for goods and services* is the first and most important area. Historically the Union above all has had an economic face. Membership involved both negative surrender of power by British government and positive acquisition of power by the institutions of the Union. The most obvious surrender is that, even on entry to the old EEC in 1973, British governments surrendered any right to impose import duties or other restrictions on the flow of goods from other members of the Union – just as

we acquired corresponding rights in other member states. These areas of 'negative integration', as they are sometimes called, have been joined now by 'positive' integration – the positive use of the power of the institutions of the EU to create equal competitive conditions right across the Union. This move to positive integration has grown stronger since the movement to complete a Single Market began in the 1980s. An important example of this is the power of the European Commission (the Union's most important institution, described below) directly to regulate competition between firms across the Union: the Commission has direct power to prosecute and fine firms which break EU competition regulations.

The *market for labour* provides examples of both the positive and negative power of the Union. Negatively, no government (or any other institution) can prohibit any citizen from any member state of the Union entering Britain to work – and conversely Britons have the same entitlement across the whole Union. (There are some transitional restrictions on free movement from the ten new members: for those who joined in 2004 lasting until 2011, and for the 2007 entrants, Bulgaria and Romania, until 2013.) Positively, a wide range of working conditions are now the subject of the Union's jurisdiction: they include health and safety at work, aspects of collective bargaining, and even working hours.

The examples of *regional and environmental policies* are striking instances of how the Union is now deeply woven into the fabric of domestic policy making. Europe is a major distributor of funds for the development of economically depressed regions (see Image 5.2). In environmental policy it is the single most important source of regulation – everything from the purity of the water that we drink to the purity of the air that we breathe is subject to EU originated regulations.

The *foreign economic policy* of Britain is now substantially conducted through the EU. For instance, because Europe is a single trading block with common rules governing trade and investment, agreements governing these with other trading nations have to be settled in common by the Union. This means that in international negotiations, such as those conducted within the framework of the WTO, the Union rather than individual separate members is the key negotiator.

Diplomacy and defence cannot be sealed off from economic policy, so in foreign affairs generally the Union's importance is growing. Any great international crisis that affects the interests of a member state like Britain is likely to draw in the Union in some role. From the 1990s (through the Treaties of Maastricht, 1992, and of Amsterdam, 1997) this participation has been increasingly regularized: Maastricht provided for a common foreign and security policy (though carefully drawn to

Timeline 5.1

Landmarks in European integration

1951   The Six sign the Treaty establishing the ECSC in Paris.

1955   The foreign ministers of the Six, meeting in Messina, decide to create a customs union covering their economies.

1957   The Treaty establishing the EEC is signed in Rome.

1973   First enlargement: Denmark, Ireland and the United Kingdom join the Community (Norway withdraws following a referendum).

1979   The first direct elections to the (then) 410-seat European Parliament are held.

1981   Second enlargement: Greece becomes a member.

1985   Jacques Delors is appointed President of the Commission. At the Luxembourg European Council the Ten agree to amend the Treaty of Rome and to revitalize the process of European integration by drawing up a Single European Act.

1986   Third enlargement: Portugal and Spain join. The SEA is signed in Luxembourg and The Hague.

1992   The Treaty on European Union is signed in Maastricht.

1995   Fourth enlargement: Austria, Finland and Sweden join the Union.

1997   'Consolidated' Treaty unifying all the preceding Treaties into a single document signed in Amsterdam.

2002   Euro coins and notes come into circulation, and the euro becomes the sole currency of the eurozone.

2004   Accession of ten new member states from middle and eastern Europe.

2007   Bulgaria and Romania join EU, bringing total number of members to 27.

2009   Lisbon Treaty in effect: see Briefing 5.3.

■ There are two important lessons here. The first is the most obvious, even from a casual glance: the movement to European integration is now deeply rooted, lasting more than half a century. The second is that the progress of integration comes in irregular spurts, often produced by great external changes: for example the developments since the early 1990s are inseparable from the collapse of the old Soviet ruled bloc of countries after 1989.

ensure any state could have a veto); while Amsterdam provided for the appointment of the Union's own High Representative for foreign and security policy. This has been further augmented by the Treaty of Lisbon of 2009 (see Briefing 5.3). The Union thus penetrates deeply into the policy world in Britain. What are the main instruments of this penetration?

The means of EU power and influence

The means of EU power and influence in Britain can be divided into the formal and the informal. The most important formal instruments are threefold: treaties, legislation and court rulings. In combination they specify areas where British decision makers are *obliged* to take action and other areas where they are *prohibited* from action.

Treaties (like those such as Rome and Maastricht discussed above) are the great legal compacts that bind the Union together. The legal obligations of the treaties explain, for instance, why British governments now do not have the right to impose tariffs on goods coming into Britain from elsewhere in the Union. Conversely, the treaties explain why any British goods can likewise be traded freely across the Union and why any British citizens can settle in any other member state. The chief institution 'policing' breaches of treaty law by either national governments or institutions like firms is the Commission: there have, for example, been several cases of British firms being fined for breaches of the Union's competition policy.

Directives are by far the most important instruments by which the Union 'legislates' on particular policies. For instance the whole Single Market Programme depended heavily on directives that were designed to ensure parity of competitive conditions in the different industries and sectors across the nations of the Union. The formal position is that directives are the result of joint decisions by the Council of Ministers and the European Parliament. The reality is that they emerge from a complicated process of negotiation in which interest groups and the Commission bargain hard over drafts, and this is often followed by more bargaining in the Council of Ministers, in the European Parliament and between the Parliament and the Council. The best way to think of directives is as a form of what is sometimes called 'framework legislation': a directive will apply across the whole Union, but will typically only prescribe certain goals to be achieved, not the exact means or timing. Directives are 'translated' into law at national level, and this process of translation often allows a large area of discretion to national states. This discretion even extends to the promptness with which directives are translated and enforced, there being large variations between different members.

Courts are a vital source of law precisely because of the discretion just referred to. No legislation ever covers all eventualities. Courts in substance make law by interpreting the meaning of legislation in particular circumstances. Later in the chapter we will examine in detail the workings in these respects of the most important EU legal institutions, notably the ECJ. To these formal sources, we can add three important informal means of influence.

The reputation of Commissioners. Members of the Commission, undoubtedly one of the most important institutions in the EU, have a high profile in many arguments about policy in Britain. It is increasingly common for Commissioners to give interviews to the British media and directly to take part in discussions within British Government. (This is described in more detail

DOCUMENTING POLITICS 5.1

Extract from the preamble to the Treaty of Rome 1957

HIS MAJESTY THE KING OF THE BELGIANS, THE PRESIDENT OF THE FEDERAL REPUBLIC OF GERMANY, THE PRESIDENT OF THE FRENCH REPUBLIC, THE PRESIDENT OF THE ITALIAN REPUBLIC, HER ROYAL HIGHNESS THE GRAND DUCHESS OF LUXEMBOURG, HER MAJESTY THE QUEEN OF THE NETHERLANDS,

DETERMINED to lay the foundations of an ever closer union among the peoples of Europe,

RESOLVED to ensure the economic and social progress of their countries by common action to eliminate the barriers which divide Europe,

ANXIOUS to strengthen the unity of their economies and to ensure their harmonious development by reducing the differences existing between the various regions and the backwardness of the less favoured regions,

DESIRING to contribute, by means of a common commercial policy, to the progressive abolition of restrictions on international trade,

HAVE DECIDED to create a EUROPEAN COMMUNITY.

■ There were actually two Rome Treaties. The lesser known created a joint authority for the management of nuclear power. This box reproduces the preamble – the aspirations – of the Treaty that created what is now the EU.

below.) The President of the Commission, the leading Commissioner, has, since the Presidency of Jacques Delors (1985–95), become a significant figure in arguments about Britain's place in the Union. The significance of this public reputation is reinforced by the fact that until 2004 there were always two British Commissioners, usually politicians with high name recognition within the UK, who did not hesitate to intervene in 'European' debates within the UK.

The allocation of Union resources. The Union has become a significant distributor of resources within

Britain, and these offer high profile opportunities both to influence policy priorities and to raise the profile of European institutions. A wide range of programmes funnels resources into public investment infrastructure and higher education. For instance, under the rules of regional development funding certain areas are designated as eligible for substantial funding especially for building projects; in higher education, the Union both funds extensive student exchange schemes and even a range of academic posts, all designed to encourage the study of Europe in Britain and to make Britons more European minded (Image 5.2 illustrates how assiduous is the Union in publicizing its contribution to public investment projects within Britain).

Propaganda and public relations. The Commission maintains its own office of representation in London and three other outposts in Cardiff, Edinburgh and Belfast. The office is unashamedly a means of propaganda and public relations. It pumps out a ceaseless stream of advocacy of the European 'idea', highly partial accounts of recent developments and constant attempts to demolish what it describes as the myths and mistakes of those in Britain who are sceptical of the EU or the European idea generally. It thus contributes to the symbolic presence of the Union in Britain. Just how common is that symbolic presence is illustrated again by Image 5.2. It is the very ordinariness of these images, the way they are encountered so often in everyday life, that so impressively testifies to the Union's success in propaganda and public relations: I guarantee that a ten-minute walk round any town or city centre will turn up one of these self-publicizing images.

The EU in the core executive

By far the most important presence of the EU in British politics is felt in the core executive, the area of government covering the most senior ministers and civil servants gathered at the apex of the big departments of state in London and in the machinery organized around the Cabinet Office and the Prime Minister in Downing Street. (The concept of the core executive and its organization is described more fully in Chapter 6.) The presence of the EU stretches right across the institutions of government, though naturally the magnitude of that presence varies by institution and has also changed over time. In summary the most 'Europe engaged' departments are: the Treasury; the Department for Business, Innovation and Skills; DEFRA; the Foreign and Commonwealth Office; and, increasingly since the 1990s, the Home Office. (Prime Ministers love to tinker with the machinery of the centre. These designations are correct at the time of writing, but you may well find that the labels change.) The Union's impact on the core

IMAGE 5.2 ■ **Europe in everyday life: the daily symbolic presence of the EU in Britain**

■ The image shows how pervasive is the EU presence in everyday life. It is a noticeboard on a public spending project of a kind that can be seen all over Britain: it advertises the fact that the project is part funded from the Union budget, and uses the occasion once again to publicize the EU symbols, notably its flag. The Union is very attentive to these symbols: grants for European funding include detailed instructions on the design of these boards, including on the relative size of EU symbols.

executive is displayed in four particularly important ways.

Organization of the core executive. Within British government most issues are handled by a 'lead' department – for example, on anything to do with immigration policy the Home Office would be the natural 'lead'. But very few issues of any importance arising from EU membership are confined in their implications to a single Department. Most, for instance, have some spending implications, so the Treasury is very commonly an interested party. Coordinating the cross-departmental management of issues is a particularly important function of the European Secretariat of the Cabinet Office. (The way Prime Ministers like to tinker with the machinery at the centre is illustrated here also: its latest name is the European and Global Issues Secretariat.)

Conflict and bargaining in the core executive. In the higher reaches of the core executive much of the bargaining and struggle that takes place over policy is about what stances to take up in bargaining within the EU itself. The most dramatic example of that is provided by the case of membership of the EMU, the project to

73

DOCUMENTING POLITICS 5.2

How membership of the European Union shapes every aspect of policy making in the core executive: the guidance given to policy makers

'There are very few areas of policy making that no longer have a European dimension of any kind. From areas of exclusive Community competence such as international trade to those where the Community involvement is more one of promotion of common interests and information sharing such as culture or sport, we need to be aware of how our decisions fit in to this context. The questions the policy maker must address early on include:

- What, if anything, is happening elsewhere in the EU – in other Member States or at the EU level?
- Experience of others in addressing similar problems can be very useful. Plus, if there is already an initiative at EU level, the UK should seek to be an influential part of it.
- If there is nothing happening at the EU level, should we seek concerted action at that level? Action at EU level may be more effective and can help to ensure that the UK competes on a level playing field.
- Maintenance of the Single Market is a key UK objective.
- Is the suggested policy compatible with European law? Any proposed policy must be in line with European law. As it has supremacy over national law (i.e. overrules contradictory national law), failure to ensure this could lead to legal challenge, the policy being overturned and damages.
- If the policy is within the context of an EU level initiative, then compatibility of that initiative should also be checked.
- Is the suggested policy compatible with the UK's European policy? The UK's aim is to be a positive and pro-active member of the EU. The UK is committed to transposing legislation promptly and implementing it fully.'

■ This is guidance from the Cabinet Office to all senior officials involved in making policy across the full range of government. It shows how far membership of the Union now demands that everyone concerned with formulating and implementing policy now has to 'think European' from the very start.

Source: Extracted from original at www.cabinet-office.gov.uk.

---

create a single currency already described above. Under two recent Prime Ministers (Major, 1990–97 and Blair, 1997–2007) the question of whether, or when, Britain should join the euro was the biggest single subject of debate about economic policy inside the core executive; it only receded under Prime Minister Brown (2007–10) because economic policy was overwhelmed by the crisis that began almost as soon as he entered 10 Downing Street.

The daily business of political leaders. The daily business of the most important political leaders is now as concerned with Europe as with domestic institutions; indeed in the daily round of business the two are woven together inextricably. A large part of the job of being Prime Minister, Chancellor, Foreign Secretary or Business Secretary is engaging in the diplomacy of negotiation with European colleagues, either opposite numbers in other member states or officials in Brussels.

Processing policy in the core executive. Just managing the daily business of government is now closely shaped by the fact of EU membership. We saw above that a major concern of the core executive – especially in the division of the Cabinet Office concerned with European issues – is coordinating European policy across government. But in individual departments specialized groups are charged with examining the European dimensions of policy. Documenting Politics 5.2 illustrates just how detailed and pervasive the guidance to 'think European' now is.

The EU in the wider political system

We already have a sense of how the EU permeates the political system, through such means as the media presence of prominent officials of the Union and the use of money both to influence policy and to raise the public profile of the Union. But the Union's presence in the wider political system is more pervasive than even this would suggest. Three signs of that presence are particularly noticeable.

In British political argument. For 50 years the question of what Britain's attitude to the movement for an integrated Europe should be has provided a major point of division and debate. It has periodically divided the two main governing parties, Conservative and Labour, and it has always divided those parties internally, just as it has internally divided most important interests in Britain – industry, finance and unions. Since the original decision in the early 1960s to apply for membership of what was then the Common Market, right through to the present divisions over our participation in a single European currency, the question of how to respond to the challenge of European integration has provided a major line of division in British politics. More generally, the Conservatives have now staked out a position as opponents to any increases in the power of the Union, and indeed claim that in government their policy is to 'repatriate' powers, such as those over many aspects of social and workplace policy.

In government beyond Whitehall. As we will see in later chapters on the devolved institutions established in Scotland and Wales by the Blair Government in 1999, Europe is potentially very important in the new devolved system. The administration of EU Structural Funds – which help finance large public works projects – are in the hands of the newly devolved institutions. For local government, too, the Union is also important: it is a potential source of funds for local development projects, and this has encouraged both active individual lobbying in Brussels and cooperation with other local governments in other member states of the Union.

In the resolution of political problems. The resources and (sometimes) the prestige of the EU on occasion play an important part in attempts to resolve difficult domestic problems. In the case of the Good Friday Agreement that attempted in 1998 to resolve the Northern Ireland problem, for instance, an important incentive to the parties to settle was the promise held out of significant sums of EU money to help rebuild the province's economy. (For the significance of the Good Friday Agreement see Chapter 11.) The photograph of a public spending project in Image 5.2 also shows how the Union reaches right down to local level.

In summary, we can say that the EU is not just an important external influence on British politics: since the country's original accession at the start of 1973 it has become incorporated into the workings of the political system itself. At the same time, the traffic has not been all one way: a large amount of what goes on in British government and politics is now designed to influence what happens in the rest of the EU.

BRITAIN IN EUROPE

Britain in the European Commission

Perhaps the single most important institution of the EU is the European Commission. This has three main functions. First, it is the main institutional initiator of policy proposals for the Union: for instance much of the preparatory work on the original proposals that led to the widening of the Single European Market from the middle of the 1980s came from within the Commission. Second, it is the most important means by which the terms of the treaties governing the Union are adhered to: for instance, it scrutinizes all subsidies paid by national governments to ensure that they do not infringe the Union's competition rules. Third, the Commission as a whole is the Union's 'civil service': it manages Union policies and negotiates – though it cannot finalize – international trade and cooperation agreements. For instance, the Commission leads negotiations on international trade rules with the WTO. Thus, while the formal range of decisions on which the Commission can act independently is limited, in practice it is a vital part of the Union's decision-making machinery.

These functions explain why, if we went to the Commission headquarters in Brussels, we would soon come across numerous instances of British political presence. But even these functions, impressive though they look, only hint at why national, including British, presence is so important in the life of the Commission. Perhaps the single most important feature of the EU is that it in effect operates an indirect system of government. In other words, having taken a decision it relies heavily on individual national institutions to implement that decision. In practice things are even more complex: the making of policy, and its implementation, cannot be separated into watertight compartments. The result is that, as far as British government is concerned, relations with the Commission consist of a virtually continuous dialogue and negotiation, both at many different levels and at all stages of the policy process. The responsibilities extend across the whole range of government; there is no government department that does not spend a large

BRIEFING 5.1

The structure and scale of the European Commission

POLICIES

- Agriculture and Rural Development
- Competition
- Economic and Financial Affairs
- Education and Culture
- Employment, Social Affairs and Equal Opportunities
- Energy and Transport
- Enterprise and Industry
- Environment
- Executive Agencies
- Maritime Affairs and Fisheries
- Health and Consumers
- Information Society and Media
- Internal Market and Services
- Joint Research Centre
- Justice, Freedom and Security
- Regional Policy
- Research
- Taxation and Customs Union

EXTERNAL RELATIONS

- Development
- Enlargement
- EuropeAid: Cooperation Office
- External Relations
- Humanitarian Aid
- Trade

GENERAL SERVICES

- Communication
- European Anti-Fraud Office
- Eurostat
- Publications Office
- Secretariat General

INTERNAL SERVICES

- Budget
- Bureau of European Policy Advisers
- Informatics
- European Commission Data Protection Officer
- Infrastructures and Logistics: Brussels
- Infrastructures and Logistics: Luxembourg
- Internal Audit Service
- Interpretation
- Legal Service
- Office for Administration and Payment of Individual Entitlements
- Personnel and Administration
- Translation

■ This conveys a picture of the Commission as a complex, comprehensive bureaucracy. The impression of complexity is accurate, but the impression of scale is not. Its total staff is – depending on how the counting is done – about 25,000, including all routine support staff; it has only 5,500 administrators. This imposes a particular style of doing business on the Commission: in formulating policy it relies heavily on specialized advisory committees, which are often dominated by experts and special interests; and in implementing policy it virtually relies totally on national level institutions.

amount of time consulting and negotiating with the Commission in Brussels.

The mode of appointing the Commission also increases the presence of national governments like that of Britain in Brussels. About 10 per cent of all Commission staff are UK nationals, and until the last enlargement two Commissioners came from the UK. (From 2004 this was reduced to one.) Although the appointment of Commissioners as a group – and of the President of the Commission – has to command the support of the European Parliament, in effect the British Government can presently nominate the British

Commissioner. Although there are powerful expectations that Commissioners will not act in their own national interests in managing their 'portfolio', nevertheless the effective power of nomination gives an important piece of patronage. There has been a tendency for this patronage to be shared between the two main Westminster political parties.

A more important lever of national influence still over the Commission comes in the nomination of the President of the Commission, its leading figure and one who can therefore, with sufficient skill and force of personality, deeply influence the direction of the EU. Thus the French President Jacques Delors (1985–95) is acknowledged to have played a big part in reviving the whole integration movement in the 1980s. Formally the President is nominated by the European Council; in practice the name is the result of horse-trading between member states. It is impossible for Britain, or any other member, to impose a particular President.

Until the Treaty of Nice it was possible formally to 'blackball' a candidate because unanimous support was required from member states. New voting rules introduced in Nice mean that selection of the President is now done through qualified majority voting; but the post is so sensitive that in practice strenuous efforts are made to ensure the emergence of a compromise candidate acceptable to all. Indeed even after Nice the UK in effect vetoed a candidate who was thought to be too enthusiastic about integration. This emphasizes the point that, whatever the formal rules, there is a great emphasis on consensus – especially consensus between the biggest members – in arriving at decisions.

The British Government is therefore an important player in all aspects of the life of the Commission, from the big initial choices about selecting Commissioners to the most detailed negotiations about the making of policies. It is an even more direct participant in the Council of Ministers.

Britain in the Council of Ministers

The 'Council', despite the singular, is actually a set of institutions: whenever the ministers from member states with responsibility for a particular domain assemble (for instance all finance ministers) they constitute a Council of Ministers. There are now ten specified Council domains, so a correspondingly appropriate set of separately constituted Councils. Naturally there are numerous meetings of the Council, covering the different policy domains, in the course of a year. In addition, the distinct title of 'European Council' is reserved for the meetings of heads of government, the 'summits' that take place at least four times yearly. Formally the Council makes decisions about policy based on proposals

from the Commission; in practice, the issues considered by meetings of the Council of Ministers come from a wide range of sources and, in respect of policy proposals, will be the result of a large amount of toing and froing with the Commission. Britain makes its voice heard in the Council by a variety of means.

The threat of veto. A range of policy areas – principally to do with common foreign and security policy and cooperation on justice and home affairs – are subject to a unanimity rule, though the range of these was considerably narrowed by the Lisbon Treaty. Since a policy cannot be agreed without the assent of all members, the British minister attending, like any other minister, can veto any policy not to the liking of the UK. In practice this veto is less useful than at first appears. The range of policies settled by qualified majority voting has tended to widen over time. But even when a veto is formally available, it must be used, or threatened, with subtlety. The Union is a community, and a member state that vetoed constantly would be viewed as an obstructive member of the community – something sustainable in the short, but not the long, term. Britain, like any other member state, has policies that it both wants to promote and kill. But where a unanimity rule applies, Britain must ensure that another member state does not kill the policies it favours. The natural way to do this is to horse trade: to agree not to veto a policy desired by another member state in return for a similar promise concerning policies that are in British interests. In practice, therefore, the 'veto' converts into an opportunity to influence policy by bargaining and compromise with other members of the Council of Ministers.

Bargaining in qualified majority voting. Some of the policy areas most important to the historical development of the Union (for example agriculture, transport, energy, environment) are largely decided by qualified majority voting, with countries assigned different weights. As we have noted, majority voting of this kind is becoming increasingly important and is a natural consequence of the expansion in the number of members. A unanimity rule when there only six founding members, or even the nine created by the accessions of 1973, could still allow policies to be made. But with 27 members, the threat that one single state could veto a decision obviously carries the danger of not being able to make policies at all. Majority voting is 'qualified' in an attempt to recognize the fact that member states vary greatly in size, power and wealth: members are allocated different voting weights, rather than being each given a single vote as would happen under 'simple' majority voting. It is also 'qualified' in a second sense. In simple majority voting 50 per cent plus one of votes carries the day. But the threshold for a majority in the Council has, after the 2004

BRIEFING 5.2

The UK and the tactics of qualified majority voting in the Council of Ministers

Total votes in the Council	345
Votes required for a qualified majority	255 (73.9%)
Number of votes allocated to the UK	29 (8.0%)

■ The simple arithmetic shows why the UK – like every other member of the Union – must build coalitions to influence decisions. Despite belonging to the group of members with the largest proportional allocation (alongside France, Germany and Italy), the UK needs lots of allies to be in a winning coalition. The procedure creates hurdles to success: proposals subject to Qualified Majority Voting require the support of over two-thirds of the individual national members of the Union. As we will see in Chapter 9 British governments are used to ruling by simple majorities in the Westminster Parliament; the EU demands a very different, more consensual, approach to decision making.

enlargement, been set in many cases at over 70 per cent. The present formula is summarized in Briefing 5.2. It is the result of hard bargaining, and is in turn intended to promote bargaining and compromise. The important consequence for the UK is that the country must form coalitions consisting of more than 50 per cent of the votes to carry the day. Indeed the practical working of the Union creates even more pressure to compromise. Up to now only about 20 per cent of decisions in any one year have been decided by a qualified majority vote. A commoner practice has been to try to bargain until a point is reached where there is unanimity, and for a very good reason: members that persistently lost majority votes would soon become disillusioned with the Union.

Summits in the European Council. The 'summits' of heads of government held four times or more a year as the 'European Council' give member states particularly important opportunities to bargain with each other, both formally in meetings and, perhaps even more important, informally. Indeed, under the Lisbon Treaty the European Council is now a formally designated EU institution. But the summits are only the tip of an iceberg. The British Prime Minister is engaged in a constant round of negotiations – sometimes face to face, sometimes by telephone or email – with other heads of government in the Union.

The Presidency. The Presidency (chair) of the European Council until recently rotated between all members for six monthly periods. Britain's periodic occupancy of the Presidency provided an opportunity, as it did for the other member states, both to play the lead in the Union's diplomacy with the rest of the world and to promote in a particularly visible way British policy priorities. A major feature of the Lisbon Treaty sees the European Council selecting a 'President' for a longer period of two and a half years: the details can be seen in Briefing 5.3.

This summary of the opportunities for influence offered by the Council of Ministers contains a particularly important lesson. British influence rests less on the exercise of particular powers – such as the power of veto – as on the ability of ministers and their advisors to build coalitions with other member states, and to bargain with member states that have different views and policy interests. This means that exercising influence in the Union is not something that just happens in the periodic meetings of the Council; it is a continuous process of negotiation that is meshed with the everyday business of government inside Britain. It also means that the growing importance of the Union in British Government has now added a new skill to the requirements of a successful minister within the UK: the ability successfully to bargain within EU institutions.

The British Government in Brussels

One important means by which Britain monitors the whole EU political system, and continually channels its views through that system, is via the Office of Permanent Representation in Brussels – Britain's 'embassy' to the EU, so to speak. The Office is rather like a 'mini-Whitehall' in Brussels, with desk officers overseeing all the major policy and departmental areas. Officials are formally seconded to the Foreign and Commonwealth Office during their Brussels tour of duty, but are usually

TABLE 5.1 National allocations of seats in the EP: examples

	Number of seats	*Percentage of seats*
Germany	99	12.6
UK	78	9.9
Poland	54	6.8
Netherlands	27	3.4
Ireland	13	1.6

■ Allocation of seats is *roughly* proportional to population: Germany has the largest allocation; the smallest goes to Malta with five seats. The UK has the second largest allocation, equal to Italy and France, behind Germany. But national allocations are only part of the picture. It is natural to expect members from the same nations to share some common positions and interests. But party groups crossing national frontiers, encompassing tendencies as various as conservatism, socialism and environmentalism, are well organized in the Parliament.

drawn from across the span of Whitehall departments. The role of the Office well illustrates how far the gap between governing in Brussels and governing in Whitehall is now quite unclear. The Office puts a large amount of effort in Brussels-style functioning as might an Embassy abroad: making as wide a range of contacts as possible in order to put the UK government's point of view. But a large proportion of time is also spent in Whitehall, serving on the interdepartmental committees that manage the processing of EU business in Whitehall, and more informally liaising with officials. Thus we see again how the processes in Brussels and in London are tightly stitched together.

Britain in the EP

The EP was first directly elected in 1979; now all its 751 members from the 27 member countries are subject to re-election every five years. (The UK is allocated 78 of these.) The shift to direct election, coupled with the periodic reconstruction of the Union's powers in successive treaties, have gradually augmented the functions of the Parliament, notably in three areas: legislation, budgetary decision making and supervision of the institutions of the Union. Legislation is formally the subject of co-decision with the Council of Ministers: that is, the Commission is the formal originator of proposals for legislation, which to succeed must be adopted by both the Council of Ministers and the Parliament. In practice the Commission and the Council are the two dominant actors. In the early decades of the history of the Union the Parliament was by far the least important of the major institutions, but its power has grown significantly, especially since the early 1990s. It is at least as important in the European system as, for instance, is a domestically elected assembly like the House of Commons in the Westminster system – and some

observers would claim that it is more so. In particular, measured by 'Westminster' standards the EP is probably a more effective amending body. One reason for this is that the resources of European Parliamentarians – 'back office' support like research assistants – are more impressive than those until very recently available to, for instance, members of the Westminster Parliament. Another reason is that, while there are party groupings of members of the EP, they are more fluid and less internally disciplined than in the domestic assemblies, giving individual European Parliamentarians more freedom to scrutinize and criticize.

The significance of the EP is generally undervalued within the UK. Its public visibility in Britain is reduced because it is now impossible simultaneously to occupy seats in the Westminster and the EPs. The most ambitious British politicians continue to prefer the former, guaranteeing it a higher domestic salience. (Nick Clegg, leader of the Liberal Democrats and from May 2010 Deputy Prime Minister, began his parliamentary life in the EP, but furthered his ambitions by switching to Westminster.) In addition, the basis of election to the Parliament – as we shall see when we consider electoral systems in Chapter 17 – has created very large constituencies and little incentive for members of the Parliament to connect directly with voters. This is reflected in the persistently low British 'turnout' in elections to the EP, compared to the Europe-wide 'norm' for the Parliament.

These undoubtedly important features of the EP should not, however, obscure its importance. Measured by the standards of influence we would apply to domestic elected assemblies it is a significant institution.

Britain in the EU lobbying system

Any system of government that takes important decisions – whether these involve distributing resources or exercising power and authority – affects interests in society and prompts those interests to organize so as to influence government. That is the simplest explanation for the existence of lobbying groups – groups that organize so as to influence the outcome of decisions. 'Lobbying' is an archaic image for an activity central to all modern government. The original 'lobby' was that of the House of Commons where special interests accosted Members of Parliament to try to influence laws. Now it is shorthand for the pervasive presence of numerous special interests in the governing process.

Groups end up in the governing process in different ways. Some 'spontaneously' emerge in society – out of businesses, churches, leisure groups and a myriad of other forms. Others are actually engineered into existence by governing institutions, which often find it immensely helpful to be able to work out, and even to implement, policy through such groups.

Both these effects can be seen in the case of the EU, and both shape the presence of British 'lobbies' in the EU. (In Chapter 8 we describe these patterns in more detail in 'setting' the Europeanization of interest representation into the wider system of interest group organization.)

Adaptation by pre-existing groups. When Britain became a member of the EEC in 1973 it already had a large and well organized lobbying system that was mostly focused on trying to shape the decisions of government in London. These groups included the familiar interests in society: those organized in professions, in trade unions, in numerous associations representing different sections of business, as well as a huge diversity of important groups representing every conceivable inclination and view. As the range and penetration of the EU grew, something unsurprising happened: this pre-existing world of groups increasingly organized itself to supplement its activities within Britain by lobbying within the EU. No significant British lobby group now lacks some representation in Brussels, principally aimed at influencing the Commission. The largest and best funded have their own permanent offices; others use the services of the increasingly large industry of professional lobbyists that operates in Brussels. Nor are they confined to Brussels: the EP is also a useful supplementary arena for lobbying, and as we will see below the European Court of Justice is an important focus of argument and pressure. A good example is provided by agriculture. One of the best-organized domestic interest groups is the National Famers Union, with over 200 full-time staff in its London headquarters. In cooperation with separate farming organizations from Scotland and Ulster it also maintains a Brussels office (the Brussels Office for Agriculture). But the NFU is also a leading member of the Committee of Agricultural Organisations in the EU (COPA), a Union-wide grouping of all the important national farming interest groups.

Groups created within Britain to exploit EU opportunities. The effect of the EU just described, although important, is the most conventional and obvious: membership of the Union obliged the pre-existing groups to adapt their lobbying tactics to reflect the creation of this new level of government. A second effect is more profound: many groups in Britain (and for that matter in other member states) have formed solely because of the country's membership of the EU. One of the most obvious examples is provided by the rise of the EU, in the last couple of decades, as a major player in regional development policy, through a succession of programmes designed to channel aid to poorer regions of the Union. But EU resources never come spontaneously; they have to be won competitively, usually by making an elaborate case and typically backed up with cofunding from other sources. Effective organization, both in putting together bids and in ensuring that those bids are presented to decision makers in the most favourable way, is one of the keys to success. Across Europe regional and local governments, intent on managing economic development, have organized so as more effectively to secure this funding. Organizing is encouraged by the very structure of the EU grant making process, because it is premised on the assumption that development projects will be partnerships, both between different public bodies and between public and private sector institutions. This process produces some often-novel attempts to organize a mix of public and private lobbying. Since 2000, for example, there has been a lobbying office in Brussels, run jointly by the North West Development Agency (an official public body) and other regional lobbying groups, designed to lobby for EU funds for the North West of England.

The world of lobbying in Europe is one of the prime examples of the key theme of this chapter: that the EU must not be considered simply as an important external influence on British politics. That image is inadequate because it misleadingly separates the Union from Britain; in practice, British and European lobbying are now entwined in a single system.

THE EU AS A LEGAL CREATION: COURTS, LAWS AND BRITISH POLITICS

It is necessary to deal in separate detail with the legal dimension to the EU, both because this is of profound and growing importance for Britain and because it adds a novel dimension to British politics. As we saw in Chapter

DOCUMENTING POLITICS 5.3

The language of European policy making: extract from a directive on the legal protection of designs

'Whereas it is unnecessary to undertake a full-scale approximation of the design laws of the Member States, and it will be sufficient if approximation is limited to those national provisions of law which most directly affect the functioning of the internal market; whereas provisions on sanctions, remedies and enforcement should be left to national law; whereas the objectives of this limited approximation cannot be achieved by the Member States acting alone ... '

■ Protection of copyright in designs is vital in any market and this directive is concerned with ensuring this in the Single Market. Notice how the directive, the single most important instrument of policy making in the Union, tries to balance two different considerations: common action ('limited approximation cannot be achieved by the Member States acting alone') and delegation to member states ('provisions on sanctions, remedies and enforcement should be left to national law'). Notice too that while the language is that of the legal draftsman, it is perfectly straightforward – contradicting the common British picture of 'EU language' as impenetrable.

Source: Nugent (2002:250).

4 Britain, famously, has not had a codified constitution. One result has been that – by contrast with countries in possession of a single, written, constitutional document – it has been hitherto impossible for citizens in Britain to appeal to courts against actions of government on the grounds that they violated some constitutionally entrenched rights (though of course actions of government could be overthrown on other grounds, such as that existing law did not sanction the exercise of authority.) The EU represents a very different conception of the exercise of state authority. It is the product of successive treaties, a series of conscious 'contracts' negotiated by members at various moments (such as the Treaty of Rome, and the Treaty of Accession that brought in Britain and others in 1973). These treaties attempt to lay out in an explicit form how the important institutions of the Union, like the Commission and the Council, will be constituted, and also attempt to lay out the principles governing the exercise of authority by these institutions. They thus amount to something close to a written constitution for the Union, attempting to specify, among other things, the extent of the Union's jurisdiction over its member states and over the citizens of those states. The latest, the Treaty of Lisbon, indeed originated as an explicit constitution that was rejected by voters in France and the Netherlands in 2005. Some critics of Lisbon indeed assert that it is in substance a constitution, labelled a 'treaty' merely for tactical purposes.

All written constitutions are subject to dispute in their interpretation, and the fundamental purpose of the European Court of Justice is to adjudicate in any cases of uncertainty about the scope of Union jurisdiction. In this sense it can be considered analogous to other constitutional courts, like the Supreme Court of the US. And like that Court the European Court of Justice has emerged as a very important centre for the government of the EU. Under the nomenclature introduced by the Lisbon Treaty, the 'Court of Justice of the EU' now actually refers to two institutions: the Court of Justice and the General Court. The former is of vital importance because, as the final 'referee' in any disputed view of the powers of the Union, it is the most public face of this judicial process. But the latter is more quantitatively important. As the title implies it is the first resort of most cases that go to the level of the Union's judicial institutions; the Court of Justice itself will only usually be invoked when the continuing dispute concerns a point of law rather than the substance of a case.

The Court: composition and significance

The Court of Justice consists of one judge from each member state, nominated by member governments for renewable terms of six years. A President of the Court is elected from among the judges. The issues dealt with by the Court, though they can have a momentous bearing on the other institutions of the Union and on the lives of citizens in all member states, usually involve complex arguments on points of law, and are therefore mostly conducted through written submissions and responses to those submissions, rather than through the sort of oral argument which is usual in British courts. The significance of the Court of Justice for Britain lies in three important effects of its judgements.

Effects on the wider integration process. Important decisions of the Court, even when not made with direct reference to Britain, have had a profound effect because they have shaped the whole nature of the

BRIEFING 5.3

The Treaty of Lisbon 2009

The Treaty of Lisbon came into force in December 2009. It introduces the most radical set of changes in the government of the EU since, at least, the Treaty of Maastricht of 1992. Among its most important provisions are: a President of the European Council to serve for two and a half years; a new 'High Representative' who will be in effect the Union's foreign minister; an expansion of the powers of European institutions like the Court and the Commission into areas like justice; an increase in the powers of the Parliament; removal of national vetoes from some key areas, such as climate change and energy security policy.

■ It took two referendums in Ireland and court cases in Germany and the Czech Republic before the Lisbon Treaty finally came into effect in December 2009.

process of European integration. Perhaps the greatest example is provided by the so-called Cassis de Dijon judgement of 1979. It shows graphically how abstruse and technical Court judgements can have great historical effects. Cassis de Dijon is a liqueur produced in France and the Court ruled that efforts to prevent its sale in other member states were unlawful. The principle behind the Court's decision was one of mutual recognition: that a product that met national standards in its own home state was entitled to circulate throughout the Union. The principle applies widely beyond the comparatively trivial original case, since it establishes an important principle on which much economic integration now proceeds. Applied generally, it means that a good need only conform to the standards in its own country of origin (concerning, in this instance, liquor production and marketing); member states must then mutually recognize each other's regulatory standards, thus allowing goods licensed in one country free circulation throughout the Union. Integration can thus happen without establishing centrally decided, single standards for the whole Union. The range of the Cassis de Dijon effect shows the subtlety of the connection between Court judgements and the integration process.

The principle of mutual recognition is not applied universally and mechanically. For instance, where mutual recognition raises issues of the safety of goods, or the competence of services, it can only apply when minimum standards have been negotiated to apply in all member states of the Union. This explains why, for instance, the entitlement of doctors qualified in one member country to practise across the Union depends on the negotiation of minimum training standards. But this very process of

negotiation – which often is largely determined by non-state bodies such as professional associations – is itself an important influence in stimulating the creation of Union-wide networks of groups and institutions.

Critical judgements directly affecting Britain. As the Cassis de Dijon judgement shows, the decisions of the Court do not have to directly concern the UK to have a profound effect within Britain. But the Court has also in a number of important cases handed down judgements that have obliged governments in Britain to change both policy and legislation, since under the Treaty of Union a government is obliged to observe its judgements. Among the most important of these are judgements which have obliged changes in equal opportunities legislation, for instance concerning equal treatment of men and women as far as pay and pensions are concerned.

Effects on the form of British political debates. Perhaps the most important influence of the Court involves what can be called anticipated reaction. Knowing that the Court has made judgements in the past, and can make judgements in the future, has influenced the whole nature of arguments about policy in Britain. The threat to take an issue to the European Court is in itself a resource that advocates of a policy now have at their disposal, since this forces a government to calculate whether it can win. If opponents of a group calculate that they might lose, this is in itself an incentive to compromise, since a loss at the European Court is a definitive defeat – not to mention the cost and embarrassment of a reversal to the British Government by a 'foreign' body. Thus, for the first time in history appeal to a 'Supreme Court' has itself become integral to the tactics used by the contending parties in

POLITICAL ISSUES 5.1

Britain and the euro

The 'eurozone' presently unites 16 members of the EU under a single currency, the euro. Since 2002 the euro has totally replaced the separate national currencies of those countries. The UK has so far declined to join the zone. In office before 1997 a deeply divided Conservative Government had adopted a 'wait and see' policy on the prospect of euro membership. In Opposition the Party moved virtually to a root and branch opposition to membership, though a large minority of leading figures from the 1990s, such as Michael Heseltine and Kenneth Clarke, remained in favour of joining. The incoming Labour Government agreed a set of 'tests' which would have to be met before joining; the tests were formally economic, but were so general that in practice their interpretation was a political judgement. They arose out of tensions between Prime Minister Blair and his then Chancellor, Gordon Brown: the Treasury had responsibility for deciding whether the tests are met, thus giving the Chancellor control over the government's decision. Labour had also committed to a referendum on the question of joining before a final decision was made The Labour Governments of 1997–2010, while containing many leading figures sympathetic to joining, feared a tabloid press which is virtually unanimously hostile to replacement of sterling by the euro. It also faced a public opinion which consistently polled against adoption of the new currency. The coalition government elected in May 2010 is not in favour of adoption, despite the historic support of the Liberal Democrats for adoption.

The case of the euro highlights a number of key issues:

- A powerful tension, both personal and one built into the nature of the institutions, between the Prime Minister and Chancellor, for control over big decisions of foreign economic policy.
- The enduring scepticism about not only the euro but the whole idea of the EU among the electorate at large.
- The great power of the tabloid press in the minds of politicians, shaping their fear of adopting positions to which the tabloids are hostile.

policy making. This also stretches to the drafting of legislation. The fact that a whole range of British law is now subject to review by what is in effect a constitutional court to determine its conformity with Treaty obligations has influenced the whole law writing process within Britain. Look back, for example, at Documenting Politics 5.2 to see how the guidance given to civil servants emphasizes how all decisions about policy now have to be made in the light of our obligations as EU members.

THE EUROPEANIZATION OF BRITISH POLITICS

The most important theme of this chapter is that British politics is, after several decades of membership of the EU, now thoroughly Europeanized. I have placed this

chapter at the head of our examination of specifically British institutions to emphasize this point; we have to look, in the succeeding chapters, at all the important institutions through European eyes. A summary account of what 'Europeanization' means is as follows. Europeanization is a process rather than a final product. In other words, it refers to sets of changes that are coming over Britain, changes that are still in progress. These changes can be considered under three headings.

Economic Europeanization

This is the most easily measurable change. Since the 1970s the British economy has become inextricably intertwined with the economies of the other member states of the Union. One simple measure of that is trade: nearly 60 per cent of UK exports now go to another member economy of the EU. A less tangible measure is

DEBATING POLITICS 5.1

The EU: weakening or strengthening British democracy?

WEAKENING BRITISH DEMOCRACY	STRENGTHENING BRITISH DEMOCRACY
▶ Membership transfers power from elected politicians in Westminster to an unelected Commission in Brussels which wields great practical influence.	▶ Membership of a Union where power ultimately rests on treaties gives powerful new legal safeguards to citizens against government.
▶ Brussels policy making is dominated by powerful special interests.	▶ The Council of Ministers is an institution where elected ministers from across Europe are obliged to bargain and compromise.
▶ The elected EP draws a low turnout in Britain and has huge constituencies that make it difficult for Euro MPs to connect to voters.	▶ The Commission's financial and personnel weaknesses oblige it to consult widely with affected interests before making policy proposals.
▶ The process of making policy in the Union is unclear and complex: lack of clarity results in deals done behind closed doors; complexity means that the normal citizen, as distinct from the policy professional, usually cannot make sense of what is going on.	▶ 'Indirect' government means that the Commission delegates most responsibility for policy implementation to the national level – thereby strengthening, rather than weakening, many British institutions.

that the rules (legal and otherwise) governing the conduct of economic life are becoming standardized across Europe: they include everything from big issues, for instance about the regulation of competition or recognition of trade unions, to the most detailed, like the packaging of products.

Europeanization of the process of government

This has been the main focus of this chapter, and it will re-emerge in the chapters that follow. It refers to two linked processes: the growing extent to which the business of government within Britain is carried out by reference to the EU; and the growing extent to which the activities of British Government involve participating in the business of governing the EU.

Europeanization of the political system

This refers to the wider interpenetration of the political system with the EU: the way political debate turns on the sort of tactics and strategies that should be adopted in our position as members of the Union; the way representing interests has acquired a European dimension; and the way the Union is itself present within Britain, allocating resources and intervening in the terms of political argument.

THE MEANING OF EUROPEANIZATION IN BRITAIN

'Europeanization' is one of the most closely studied and actively debated concepts in the study of the EU. The study of Europeanization generally has clarified the meaning of the term in a way that is highly illuminating for the UK experience. It is natural, at first sight, to think of Europeanization as a process by which the external influence of the EU reshapes the politics and policy of a member state of the Union. But this 'download' model – where measures and institutions are 'downloaded' from outside – now seems inadequate. Europeanization is a reciprocal process: that is, it involves a constant exchange between domestic politics and institutions and those of the Union. The workings of the Union's own institutions are deeply influenced by individual member states, and this is particularly true of a large member state like Britain. The policies of the Union in turn are shaped and reshaped at national level, notably by the business of implementation. And the fact of the Union's role is itself incorporated into the strategies and tactics of domestic actors: the way domestic actors in Britain try to anticipate the judgements of the Court of Justice, described above, is one instance of this.

Review OF CHAPTER 5

Three themes have dominated this chapter:

◖◗ A limited attempt to create an area of free trade between six economies in the 1950s has now been transformed into a hugely ambitious enterprise to create a common system of government across Europe.

◖◗ Britain was a late and reluctant participant in this transformation.

◖◗ Despite this late start the 'Europeanization' of British government and politics is now profound: the EU, far from being only an important external influence, is now woven into the everyday fabric of British government.

FURTHER READING

ESSENTIAL
If you read only one book it should be Nugent's (2010) overview of the government of the Union, now in its seventh edition.

RECOMMENDED
The most important historical study of the development of the Union is Milward (1992). George (1998), though now dating, is the standard history of the relations between Britain and the Union. Watts and Pilkington (2005) is also a helpful overview of the same subject. An exceptionally important chapter-length study of the Europeanization of the system of government is Bulmer and Burch (2000), while Bulmer et al. (2002) explore the impact of Europe on the devolved system. Bulmer and Burch (2009) do for the core executive what they had earlier done for the devolved system. The *Annual Review of the European Union* published by the Journal of Common Market studies is invaluable in keeping up to date on European developments.

CHAPTER 6

The core executive in the Westminster system

CONTENTS

AIMS

This chapter:

- Outlines the most important current general framework for understanding government at the centre: the 'core executive'

- Describes the institutions of the core executive

- Describes the main functions performed by these institutions and the way they are carried out

- Describes the tensions within the core executive

- Returns the discussion of the core executive to key debates about British government, notably about the location of power

UNDERSTANDING BRITISH GOVERNMENT: THE TRADITIONAL PYRAMID MODEL

Until recently when we spoke of 'the executive' in Britain we meant the executive in the Westminster system of government. But that is no longer the case. The devolved systems, as we shall discover in later chapters, are developing their own executive systems and these are not simply extensions of the Westminster model. The title of this chapter is therefore deliberately chosen: it is about executive politics in one part of UK government, albeit an exceptionally important part. Indeed, the next four chapters have this Westminster focus. It will help in making sense of both Westminster politics, and the politics of other levels of UK governance, to bear in mind throughout these chapters that we are surveying only one part of the governing system.

The traditional theory of British government pictures it as a kind of pyramid. At the top of the pyramid are the elected members of the executive – ministers drawn from Parliament, mostly elected to the House of Commons. And at the very tip of this pyramid are the ministers who head the most prestigious departments, and the Prime Minister as the political head of the government. This group of elected politicians takes the most important decisions. It receives advice from lower down the pyramid, especially from permanent civil servants, who also put the decisions of ministers into effect. This pyramid model has much to recommend it.

It highlights the importance of democratic control. It is important for our theories of British democracy, which say that the most important decisions in government should be taken by those selected by the people in competitive elections.

It highlights struggles for power. This is a feature which is undoubtedly central to the everyday workings of the top of central government: a constant struggle for power and status between different departments and the political heads of those different departments.

It highlights the debate about Prime Ministerial power. It has been the starting point for one of the most frequently argued theories of power at the centre in Britain: the theory that we are shifting to a system of Prime Ministerial Government, where the single figure of the Prime Minister is held increasingly to dominate British government.

But this pyramid has come to be seen as inadequate, for a number of reasons.

It involves an unrealistic division of labour in government. This division of labour in policy making between taking decisions, taking advice and putting decisions into effect is unrealistic. At the top of govern-

IMAGES 6.1 and 6.2 ■ The dignified and efficient faces of the core executive

Photos: Michael Moran

■ In Chapter 4 we encountered Walter Bagehot's distinction between the dignified and the efficient – between the ceremonial and the working faces of government. Here they are embodied in two images. The front face of 10 Downing Street shows the importance of image and presentation in government. It presents a public face of government as venerable (the house was originally a gentleman's residence of the eighteenth century) and as serene and elegant (the main door has ten coats of varnish to give it a beautiful sheen). A posse of press photographers wait outside to snap the comings and goings of the famous. Round the corner is a very different entrance, to the Cabinet Office. On the day I took the photograph it was even covered in tarpaulin for building work. Here the movers and shakers of the core executive quietly slip in and out of work. There are no photographers to record their comings and goings.

ment, where decisions are usually very complex and involve subtle judgement, no simple division exists between politics and administration.

It involves an unrealistic concept of a hierarchy of departments. The notion that departments are organized in a clear hierarchy is likewise unrealistic. The departmental structure of Westminster government is much more like a series of tribes – the Treasury tribe, the Home Office tribe – who have their own recognized territory, their own distinctive cultures and their own distinctive policies. The tribes are of course not equal: the Treasury tribe is more powerful and prestigious than the tribe at the Department for Culture, Media and Sport. But much of what goes on in government involves bargaining between the tribes over their territory and their policies.

It involves an unrealistic picture of Prime Ministerial power. In focusing on the Prime Minister the pyramid model both overstates and understates the importance of the individual who holds that office. It overstates the case because Prime Ministerial government is impossible – in the sense that the government machine at the centre is too complex and too much power is lodged with the departmental 'tribes' – for any single individual tightly to control government. And it understates the case because, in focusing on an individual, it risks missing what we will see to be a very important source of power: the growing machinery of decision making and policy coordination that surrounds the Prime Minister in Downing Street.

THE IDEA OF THE CORE EXECUTIVE

These points explain why the 'pyramid' notion of government, with a few powerful individuals at the top controlling the important decisions, has been increasingly replaced by the notion of a 'core executive'. Four key features mark out this notion.

It breaks down the policy/administration division

It identifies institutions and individuals that are at the heart of decision making in government. As a result, it downplays the traditional distinction between ministers and civil servants, and offers a more realistic picture of the way decisions are made at the heart of government.

It stresses interdependence and coordination

It focuses on a feature that is a fact of life in modern government: policy is not divided into separate 'boxes' labelled the economic, the educational or the social. At the centre of government, policy is interdependent, both

in the sense that decisions in one field often have big consequences for the rest of government, and in the sense that, at the centre, government is attempting to manage a stream of decisions which it has to coordinate and present as in some sense consistent. A good example of interdependence is provided by the mundane fact of money. The Treasury is permanently in the core executive because every time it agrees a substantial commitment of resources to one field – say education – it is denying that resource to another set of claimants. A second good example is the presentation of policy. In practice modern government is so complicated, and the decisions demanded of government so difficult, that governments often take wildly contradictory decisions. But they can never admit this, and a huge amount of energy goes into trying to convince the outside world – and indeed to convince government itself – that what it does in one area is quite consistent with what it is doing elsewhere.

It stresses roles more than structures

The concept of the core executive focuses on roles rather than on structures alone. We all play different roles, and some roles dominate our lives more than do others: my role as a university teacher is a big part of my life; my role as a supporter of the Irish national rugby team is more marginal. Some people and institutions are permanently part of the core executive. A good example is the Prime Minister, whose whole life is given over to managing the centre of government. But many people shift in and out. This is the case with most departmental ministers. A very senior minister like the Home Secretary, for example, will spend a large amount of working life operating in the core executive: formally, serving on committees in the Cabinet system, for example; less formally, negotiating the most important Home Office policies with other leading members of the core executive, like the Prime Minister. But the Home Secretary is chief of one of the departmental tribes and will spend a large amount of time on the business of that tribe. One of the biggest sources of tension inside the core executive as a whole, and in the lives of Ministers, is between the demands of their 'own' departments and the demands of business in the core executive.

It stresses decisions

The concept of the core executive alerts us to the fact that government is about doing things – about making decisions or trying to avoid making decisions. It is not about the relations between static 'blocks' like departments, or abstractions like ministers and civil servants. At the centre, life is a constant struggle to respond to one problem after another and to present and defend the

FIGURE 6.1 ■ The wiring of the core executive

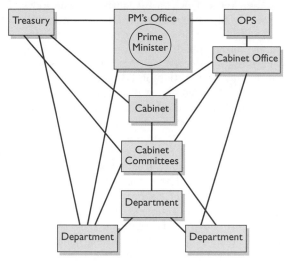

The core executive

Source: Smith (1999:6).

■ Smith's diagram of the core executive perfectly catches three of its key features. First, the office of Prime Minister is its heart. Second, it is not a simple hierarchy but an elaborate network of exchanges of communication and resources between a shifting population of institutions and individuals. Third, it pays little attention to one of the traditionally sacred divisions in British government: that between elected politicians (ministers) and appointed officials. Indeed, for the latter it also mixes together civil servants and 'political' appointments made by the Government of the day.

result to an outside world that is always intensely critical. There is no fixed agenda of business for the core executive; demands for decisions just flow in remorselessly. Nor are the boundaries of the core executive fixed. At the centre, government cannot pick and choose the subjects for decision. Often they will be self-evidently important: how to decide, say, our policy on the single European currency. Often they will be unexpected and detailed: a riot by drunken football fans abroad calls into question the government's law and order policy, and the machinery of the core executive suddenly has to be mobilized to respond. As a consequence, the boundaries of the core executive are constantly shifting. An issue that was once routine (managing football fans who travel abroad) suddenly rises right to the top of the concerns of the core executive. Individuals who normally work in obscurity within the Home Office tribe suddenly find themselves at meetings with the senior ministers and officials trying to explain how best to manage the problem.

In summary, we increasingly think of government in terms of the core executive because it focuses on government as an activity; and it encourages us to examine how the most important parts of government cope (or fail in coping) with the constant need to make, present and defend decisions.

THE MAIN COMPONENTS OF THE CORE EXECUTIVE

The boundaries of the core executive are flexible, but that does not mean that we cannot describe its most important components. Here we summarize three: the Prime Ministerial machine; the Cabinet machine; and the machinery of departmentalism.

The Prime Ministerial machine

At the heart of the core executive lies institutional machinery that is organized to serve the Prime Minister. We should beware of thinking of this in excessively personal terms – the complexity of government in Britain is too great for a single individual to control what is going on. But undoubtedly Prime Ministers have the potential to be immensely powerful within the core executive, and at least two recent Prime Ministers – Margaret Thatcher and Tony Blair – have at various periods of their time in office realized very fully that potential. The central place of the Prime Minister is reflected in the institutional machinery that has now grown up to support the office.

One of the features of the organization of the Prime Ministerial machine is that it is very sensitive to the moods of the particular Prime Minister. The details constantly change. This is partly because Prime Ministers always fret about whether they are being adequately served and partly because life at the centre has a frenetic, hothouse quality: little empires are constantly being built (and dismantled) as different people struggle for the ear of the Prime Minister and for their own personal advancement. The atmosphere is rather like that of the court of a monarch, where the skill consists in catching the ear and the eye of the powerful one. A small sign of this is that, between the various drafts of this chapter, the titles assigned to various components of the machine were changed, as were alterations in their formal organization. The practical consequence of this is that the best place to go for an up to date picture of organization is the latest official web page (www.number-10.gov.uk). Figure 6.2 provides an adapted version of the latest available 'organogram' provided by Number 10. In describing the components below I recognize the constantly shifting formal structure by identifying the 'functional components' of the machine: the functions that always have to be performed whatever particular structure the Prime Minister at the moment chooses.

The Private Office function. This is staffed by the civil service and is the single most important official form for managing the Prime Minister's business life: processing all advice and papers that come in both from elsewhere in government and from outside; managing the Prime Minister's day, and indeed the whole diary; managing all correspondence in and out of the office; and recording all Prime Ministerial meetings. There is a team of Private Secretaries who are generally civil servants marked out for a high flying career, headed by a Principal Private Secretary. The calibre of the last will be the highest the civil service can provide: most Principal Private Secretaries end up later in their career at or near the very top of the civil service. Supporting the Private Secretaries in turn is a cohort of more routine administrators and secretaries, who ensure that the office is staffed 24 hours a day.

The Policy analysis function. This consists of a mixture of civil servants and special advisers appointed by the Prime Minister from outside. The latter will often, though not invariably, be close political allies of the ruling party. If the Private Office function is designed to ensure that business is processed effectively, the policy analysis function is designed to provide specialist advice to the Prime Minister and to work with departmental ministers and civil servants to produce sound specialist advice and to chase policy implementation. The existence of this function is prompted by worries that bother all Prime Ministers: worries that they should not just be reacting to problems as they arise, but should be thinking ahead; worries that they lack the expert resources available to Cabinet Ministers who head big departments; worries that the policies they want to happen will not actually be implemented within departments. In practice, the actual roles played by the special advisers are heavily shaped by what Prime Ministers feel they need. They might spend time working on detailed policy problems; they might try to think about long-term strategy, something Prime Ministers are usually anxious to do but almost never get round to; or they might just as well suddenly be called on to draft a speech for the Prime Minister.

The press relations function. This is a permanent 24-hour-a-day operation. It manages the presentation of news from Number 10 and all the Prime Minister's relations with the media. It also tries to coordinate news management across government. The Official Spokesman (the gender insensitive language has not been changed) holds briefings virtually daily (indeed commonly twice daily) for the journalists who specialize in covering the core executive. Even the mechanics of managing all this are onerous: a Prime Minister, for example, often spends a large part of the working day giving press interviews. But this sort of news management is only part of the job. The core executive is at heart about policy coordination, and policy presentation is inseparable from coordination. So those who manage communications, and especially the Official Spokesman, are critical: they need to know the Prime Minister's mind and convey what is in it to the media. This is a 24-hour-a-day operation because in addition to presenting the Prime Minister's mind, the centre has to stand ready to respond at an instant to press enquiries about any urgent matter. And 'urgent' here can be almost anything, from a great international crisis to an embarrassment resulting from the private behaviour of a member of the Cabinet or even a member of the Prime Minister's family.

The party political function. Prime Ministers head the government of the whole nation, but they only get there in the first place because they head a political party. A critical measure of their success is how far they put into effect the policies of their party and how far they succeed in winning partisan general elections. The bottom line for any Prime Minister is success in winning partisan elections; otherwise he or she ceases to be Prime Minister and, almost certainly, ceases to be a prominent politician at all. This function is a recognition of these facts: it is designed to manage all those areas where the Prime Minister's role overlaps with party leadership duties. It is therefore staffed by the party of government.

It is straightforward to describe in broad terms these different functions performed by parts of the Number 10 machine. But it will be obvious to anyone who spends even a short time looking at the actual life of the Prime Minister that no easy division of labour exists between them. If we glance at Image 6.1, for instance, we will see that the public face of Downing Street is elegant and impressive. Notoriously, however, crammed into this house are cramped, often tiny, working offices. There is constant pressure on space. In Mr Blair's time, for instance, the Prime Minister's machine colonized the whole of the house next door, Number 12, which used to be occupied by the Chief Whip, and spread into part of Number 11, which is the house of the Chancellor of the Exchequer. Those inside are forced into close contact with each other all the time.

A few matters are very obviously party political and the job of the Political Office – for example, the Prime

FIGURE 6.2 ■ The core of the core executive: the components of the Cabinet Office and Prime Ministerial machine in 2010

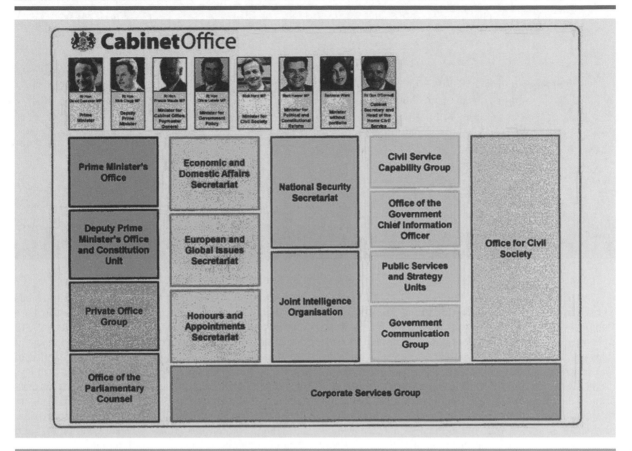

■ The 'organogram', supplied by the Cabinet Office in May 2010 is highly contingent. Prime Ministers fiddle endlessly with the structure (see also Political Issues 6.1). Indeed, this completely new organization chart was inserted after the delivery of the manuscript of this book.

Source: http://download.cabinetoffice.gov.uk/organogram/co-organogram.pdf.

Minister's relations with his own constituency party. But at root a Prime Minister's whole life is party political, since he functions in a political system dominated by adversarial competition between government and opposition. This sketch of the Prime Ministerial machine makes it look superficially impressive. But actually what is striking about this part of the core executive, relative to the responsibilities and public profile of the Prime Minster, is how little institutional support the office has, as Figure 6.2 illustrates. This is to some extent counterbalanced by the fact that the Cabinet Machinery is also to a large degree at the disposal of the Prime Minister.

The Cabinet machine

The Cabinet itself consists of the 20 or so leading ministers in Government and is chaired by the Prime Minister. In this bare sense it has hardly changed in over a century. But in that period, and especially in the last 50 years, both Cabinet roles and the machinery that surrounds them have been transformed. A century ago the Cabinet machinery meant only the Cabinet itself; there was not even a permanent arrangement for making a formal minute of what the Cabinet had discussed and decided. Now the machinery is elaborate, its most important components being as follows.

EUROPEANIZING 6.1

Europeanizing the core executive: the European and Global Issues Secretariat

This Secretariat, a division of the Cabinet Office, provides advice for the Prime Minister in all foreign 'summits', including EU summits. It also coordinates the European work of the core executive by providing the Secretariat for relevant Cabinet committees. It holds regular meetings with the UK's ambassador to the EU in Brussels. And, in its own words, 'it acts as the focal point within the Government for handling advice and guidance on ... EU matters'. It is an institutional expression of a major theme of this book: that EU membership is reshaping the system of government.

■ Bulmer and Burch (2009) have produced the authoritative study of the Europeanization of the core executive. This briefing shows how it works right at the heart – in the Cabinet Office.

Source: http://www.cabinetoffice.gov.uk/secretariats/european_secretariat.aspx.

The Cabinet itself. The Cabinet still usually meets weekly, normally chaired by the Prime Minister. The Cabinet will never lose significance as long as it is presently constituted. It contains all the big power figures – the most senior ministers – in a government, and so when big issues arise that divide the government it will always be important as an arena where those are argued out. But the Cabinet has increasingly taken on this character: a place where occasionally a really divisive issue is argued out, but otherwise a place which tends to do little more than hear reports of doings elsewhere, especially from the system of Cabinet Committees.

The system of Cabinet committees. A century ago the Cabinet had no permanent committees, and until the 1990s their existence was not even formally acknowledged. But we have known for a long time that the committee system of Cabinet is one of the most important means of processing business. At any one moment there will be in existence over 30 of these committees. Many will be permanent: for instance, there always has to be a committee charged with managing the Government's legislative timetable. Some will be set up in response to one of the many crises that are the stuff of life in the core executive: Prime Minister Brown established such a committee to deal with the economic crisis in 2008.

Why is the committee system so important? At the simplest level the answer is obvious: the volume of business in government is such that it would be impossible for Cabinet to cope were it to attempt to deal with all business in full session. But this resort to committees has reshaped the whole nature of power within the core executive, for three reasons. First, in almost all cases, to dominate an issue in government it is now necessary to dominate it in Cabinet committee, since the chance of appealing to full Cabinet or the Prime Minister, still less of winning that appeal, is slight. Second, Cabinet committees are now the main focus of activity for senior ministers within the core executive. They spend far more time attending committees than attending Cabinet, and Cabinet committee documents dominate their paperwork. Even when a committee is not actually meeting it provides a framework for business: much business consists of exchange of ministerial correspondence between members, often in the form of an exchange of letters with the chair checking agreement to a proposal. Finally, assignment to Cabinet committees is an important indicator of place in the political pecking order, with the prize as chair of the most important committees going to the most powerful ministers in government. This explains a superficially odd feature: some of the most important Cabinet committees are not much smaller than the full Cabinet. This is because, knowing that it is in committee that the key decisions will be taken, all the major figures demand the right of representation. This feature shows a powerful tension in the whole arrangement: the committee system exists with the avowed aim of doing business more efficiently; but the insistence of departments and ministers on being represented on committee means that the most important committees are often almost as unwieldy as the full Cabinet.

People in Politics 6.1

Grey eminences: three powerful figures behind the scenes in the history of the core executive

Hankey, Maurice (1877–1939)

Secretary, Committee on Imperial Defence 1912–38; Secretary War Cabinet 1916, Imperial War Cabinet 1915–18, Cabinet 1918–38. Hankey created the Cabinet Secretariat, mostly by exploiting the pressures of war. He then dominated it for over 20 years. His relatively unusual background by comparison with later Cabinet Secretaries (his early career was as a soldier) typified his status as an institutional pioneer. Not only was his career route unusual – his long tenure allowed him to dominate the system to a degree never later achieved.

Brook, Norman (1902–67)

Secretary to the Cabinet 1947–62; head of the Home Civil Service 1955–62. Brook entered the civil service in the Administrative class in 1925, after education at Wadham College Oxford. His career typified that of the civil service elite in the mid-twentieth century: progression from high early academic achievement, early appointment to the Administrative class as a recognition of future leadership of the Service, and domination of the administrative apparatus in the great years of war time crisis and post-war British decline.

Armstrong, Robert (1927–).

Secretary to the Cabinet, 1979–87, head of the Home Civil Service 1983–87. Armstrong entered the Administrative class in the Treasury in 1950, after an education at Christ Church Oxford, the most socially exclusive college in a socially exclusive university. He typified in education and style the administrative elite that governed Britain in its years of post-war decline, a style that put a premium on quick thinking, social skills and diplomatic subtlety. But he also served during his years at the very top the Prime Minister, Margaret Thatcher (1979–90), who most fundamentally challenged that style and sought to reverse decline.

Cartoons: Shaun Steele

■ Top civil servants are among the most important figures in the core executive. These three personalities from different eras were barely known to the general public at the time they exercised great power.

The Cabinet Office. This elaborate machinery of committees could not exist without a machinery of support – to prepare and circulate papers and to minute decisions and discussions. That is the fundamental job of the civil servants in the Cabinet Office. The Office originated in the decision – taken in the First World War – to appoint an official to record the minutes of Cabinet discussions and conclusions. Out of that has grown one of the most powerful parts of the machinery of government. The head of the Office, the Cabinet Secretary, is the most senior civil servant of all and will virtually work to the Prime Minister of the day as his most senior official adviser. The title of 'Cabinet Secretary' is potentially misleading since it suggests almost a passive, high-level, clerical role. In fact it is intensely political, and in recent decades the Cabinet Secretary has typically been one of the most powerful figures in government. Prime Ministers in turn often rely on the Cabinet Secretary to deal with delicate issues that they wish to keep at arms length. For instance, when Jonathan Aitken, a senior member of the Conservative Cabinet in the 1990s, was accused of impropriety it was the Cabinet Secretary, not the Prime Minister, who sought assurances from him as to the propriety of his conduct. (The assurances turned out to be lies.) Just as the Cabinet Secretary occupies a powerful and delicate political role, so the whole Cabinet Office is much more than an institution for preparing and circulating official papers, though this remains an important function. The Cabinet Office is also a key institution in attempting to perform what is in many ways the central function of the core executive: managing policy that will not fit neatly into existing departmental responsibilities. It tracks interdepartmental issues and advises when they need Cabinet committee consideration – in many ways the key task of the core executive. It sets agendas, writes committee position papers and, crucially, briefs the ministers who chair committees. One of its rarely publicized but vitally important functions is also to coordinate the machinery for both domestic and external security intelligence (for more details, see Chapter 21). And it is the critical bit of the machinery of government for trying to coordinate policy on the EU (see Documenting Politics 5.2 and Europeanizing 6.1). Thus it makes sense to distinguish between the Cabinet Secretariat, which is largely concerned with 'servicing' the Cabinet system, and the wider Cabinet Office which has important responsibilities for the management of the broader civil service system.

The machinery of departments

No matter how much Prime Ministers try to control and coordinate from the centre, British government is still at heart departmental. The departmental tribes command fierce loyalty from permanent civil servants, and even from their relatively short-lived ministerial heads. As we noted in passing earlier, some tribes are more powerful than others. Two need to be highlighted.

The Treasury is virtually a permanent part of the core executive. It is a comparatively small department, and that reflects its importance in formulating advice and making policy decisions, rather than assuming executive responsibility for putting policy into effect. Its political head, the Chancellor of the Exchequer, occupies a central part in the machinery of the core executive and almost invariably will have ready access to the Prime Minister. Its policy responsibilities encompass the whole of economic policy and it dominates decisions about the allocation of public spending. All governments believe, probably rightly, that their chances of re-election turn on the perceived success of economic policy. And all departments need money to carry out their responsibilities. Both these considerations reinforce the position of the Treasury at the centre.

The Foreign Office is central for two reasons. First, it is a critical institution in dealing with the EU, an increasingly vital part of British government, as we have already seen. Second, Prime Ministers define foreign affairs as a key part of their responsibility, so they naturally draw the Foreign Office into their domain.

DOING BUSINESS IN THE CORE EXECUTIVE

Most of what we have described so far is intended to give an overview of the institutional structure of the core executive in Britain. Now we need to turn to how this structure works. Government is important because it takes decisions, or decides to avoid making a decision, or tries to implement decisions where taken. This next section is all about how business is done in the core executive.

The very first condition for business to be processed by the core executive is that it must come to the attention of the executive machine. How does this happen? We can, broadly, observe three mechanisms.

Business comes in from departments

The core executive is part of the huge organizational machine that is British central government. Most business is processed in departments, and many issues start life quite far down a departmental hierarchy. The most important instrument of management is the file, even in this electronic era: usually a set of papers and written memos by civil servants about a particular issue. If we just did a count of decisions made within central government we would find that most are made by permanent

BRIEFING 6.1

The working days of Prime Ministers in different eras

William Gladstone's routine as Prime Minister 1880–85

'He rarely slept beyond 9 a.m., and until the official day began at 11 a.m. he read the newspapers and – if there was nothing especially urgent – literature. He would then have a meeting with the Chief Whip and deal with the day's letters and papers, which the Private Secretariat had sifted for him. In this period policy was often developed by correspondence. A lunch and then a walk would follow before he went to the House of Commons, where he remained, with breaks for tea and dinner, until the end of sitting. He would spend seven hours a day in the Commons chamber, sitting on the Treasury bench.'
(Kavanagh and Seldon 1999:37–8).

The working day of Prime Minister Brown, 2007–10

5.30 a.m.:	Rises
6 a.m.:	In office emailing and checking Internet for press stories
8 a.m.:	Breakfast
9 a.m.:	Meetings with senior advisors
10 a.m.–1 p.m.:	Cabinet, committee meetings; when Parliament is sitting Wednesday morning given up to preparing for PM's Question Time
1–2 p.m.:	Official lunch, or sandwich with family
2–5 p.m.:	Meetings in office, often with overseas visitors
5 p.m.:	Dinner with family
6 p.m.:	Brief appearance at public function (which he was known to hate)
6.30–9 p.m.:	In office to prepare for next day; respond to emails
9 p.m.:	If no late-night vote in Parliament relax in flat with family
11 p.m.:	Bedtime

■ These two descriptions show not only how the role of the Prime Minister has changed, but how much more stressful and busy life in the core executive has become. Gladstone, one of the greatest of nineteenth-century Prime Ministers, led a routine of what now looks like gentlemanly leisure. But even Mr Brown's diary does not fully convey the pressure of the workload: much of a PM's life is spent travelling, surviving on little sleep and then trying to catch up with the accumulated work on return.

Source: Henke 2008.

officials inside departments, not elected ministers or by others within the core executive. (This is not to mention something that will loom large in the next chapter: the importance of the executive agencies.) A complex mixture of things decides where the file lands for decision. A general principle is that matters should be decided at the lowest level possible, but what that level should be in any particular case can be affected by many things: a judgement about the substantive importance of the issue; precedents; whether it involves a clear shift in policy direction; even the simple urgency of being seen to do something. Most important of all, however, is perceived political sensitivity. Ministers will always want to know about an issue that is politically sensitive: that might damage or advance their careers or the fortunes of their Government. Quite often they will be alerted to it from outside the department – from being formally lobbied to hearing about the issue on the morning radio news. Most politicians are obsessed by the reporting of politics but pressure of work means that senior ministers have a highly unusual experience of reporting. Early morning broadcasting, like *Today*, can be particularly important because it is one of the few 'unfiltered' forms of news that senior Ministers receive as they prepare for work or are driven to the office. Part of the folklore of the Thatcher Premiership was that Mrs Thatcher could be reached, and impressed, by an appearance on *Today* as she cooked breakfast. Senior politicians hardly every watch television since they are usually out in the evening, and Ministers rely, again because of pressure of time, on digests and cuttings from the press prepared by their advisors and civil servants.

Political sensitivity is the overriding influence determining whether the issue will be brought to the attention of the minister. The end of the line within the department is when the file is put onto the minister's desk or into the 'red box' – the box that is usually replenished daily with the papers and files that require ministerial attention. Since most ministers spend their working day in a whirlwind of meetings, the contents of the red box will usually be dealt with in the small hours of the morning. At this point a minister may decide that an issue is so sensitive that it needs to go into the core executive, and going further can take many different forms: being formally processed by the machinery of the Cabinet, usually starting in cabinet committees; or being the subject of discussions of varying levels of formality with other senior figures.

But while this route into the core executive is very important because it will identify the issues that are most sensitive, it is quantitatively not the most important – after all, there is an obvious physical limit to the volume of papers that a minister can process through the red box. Many issues will go out of the department into the core executive early in their lives. Some are just preordained by the rules of government: legislative proposals prepared within a department, for instance, have to be dealt with by the Cabinet committee that settles the legislative timetable of the government of the day. A huge number of issues in government are cross departmental: a single department cannot settle them alone. These issues are naturally within the domain of the core executive.

Business comes from inside the core executive

If most decisions in British government start and end their lives within a single department, a minority of (usually particularly important ones) start and end their lives inside the core executive. Three kinds would, without question, be processed within the core executive. First, the Cabinet Office has managed over time to establish the convention that interdepartmental issues (its language) are naturally within its domain. An obvious example of this with which we are now familiar is the way the Office has established the right to process the range of European issues. Second, the core executive is the natural home for two areas of decision that are central to the lives of all governments: managing the legislative programme and managing the economy. The first is largely done through the network of Cabinet committees, including a committee charged with managing the whole legislative timetable itself. The second is centred on the Treasury. Third, at any one moment there will be a small number of issues that are so central to the survival of a government that they will never leave the core executive. Two very important examples of these from recent years involve economic policy and foreign policy: the former, the question of whether, and when, Britain should join the single European currency; the latter, the conduct of the war in Iraq which began with the invasion of that country in 2003.

Business comes from 'firefighting'

So far I have presented a picture of processing business that stresses routine and stability. And indeed it is the case that, because government is a machine, these are important features. Routines are established; precedents create conventions about who takes what decision, when and where; papers are produced for meetings. Precedent and conventional understandings about how business is processed are important not because individuals are necessarily conservative but because observing routines is the only way a large complicated machine can process a huge volume of business. But there is another roller coaster aspect to the business in the core executive, and it is one that is missed completely by this stress on routine. A large part of the job of the core executive is firefighting – managing crises that appear suddenly, often apparently out of nowhere. Sometimes these are huge matters of life and death. Every British Prime Minister in the last 25 years has been involved in a large scale war, and each of these was created by a short notice crisis: the Falklands, 1982; the Gulf War, 1990; the war against the Serbs in Kosovo in 1999; the wars in Afghanistan in 2002 and Iraq in 2003. Some issues of life and death just appear without notice: every British Prime Minister in the last 35 years has had to react in some way to violent deaths in Northern Ireland. The physical and emotional stress of these crises is immense. But equally a crisis can land in the core executive from

DOCUMENTING POLITICS 6.1

Edited extracts from the report of daily press briefings by the Prime Minister's spokesman, Monday 1 June 2009

Britain's Got Talent

Asked why the Prime Minister had spoken to the judges from *Britain's Got Talent* regarding the contestant Susan Boyle, the PMS (Prime Minister's Spokesman) said that the Prime Minister personally knew some of the judges and that this was a programme that he had always taken an interest in because it showed that there was a huge amount of untapped potential in the country.

Constitutional Reform

Asked why there had been a delay in the Prime Minister's idea of constitutional reform, the PMS said that there hadn't been a delay; the Prime Minister identified this as an important issue early on in his premiership and we were taking significant action in order to ensure that the executive was better held to account by Parliament.

■ This edited extract of a lobby briefing by the Prime Minister's Spokesman, taken from the 10 Downing Street website, shows the jumble of the trivial and the momentous which government has to manage for presentation: *Britain's Got Talent* was a TV variety talent show; constitutional reform was supposed to have been Prime Minister Brown's big idea.

Source: http://www.number10.gov.uk/Page19448.

something apparently quite minor. They can be totally trivial but intensely embarrassing: the children of two leading figures in the Labour Government after 1997 were apprehended by the police, causing a flurry of activity to manage the embarrassment. In 2002 the then Prime Minister's wife was involved in a series of revelations about the purchase of a flat for her son, involving an alleged confidence trickster who claimed to be her intermediary. At a moment when the country faced problems ranging from a strike of all firefighters to a possible war

in Iraq the resources of the core executive were substantially devoted to 'firefighting' the embarrassing revelation. Sometimes Ministers themselves cause short-term crises because their sexual or financial lives get into the newspapers. The Home Office is a particularly important source of comparatively minor issues that suddenly require the attention of the core executive, chiefly through its responsibilities for policing: issues as various as dangerous dogs, British football hooligans, binge drinking and escapes from jails have in recent years arisen in this way. To get a sense of how the large scale and tragic is often mixed up with the trivial on the agenda of the core executive, glance at Documenting Politics 6.1.

MANAGING THE COORDINATION OF POLICY IN THE CORE EXECUTIVE

One of the most difficult things in modern government is trying to ensure that policy fits together in some consistent way. Modern governments are huge and complex organizations, making large numbers of important decisions daily. Without constant effort, there is no reason to suppose that these decisions will be coordinated in a consistent way. On the contrary, every day of the week provides examples of one government department pursuing a policy that directly contradicts that of another. Sometimes the contradiction is inside the same department: in recent years British government has been unable to make up its mind, as a single mind, as to whether it wants people to use their cars more or less. A central task of the core executive is to try to ensure some coordination and consistency, even where it is absent. The attempt is made by three means: institutions; the formal rules for coordinating policy; and informal processes.

Institutions

The most important institution of coordination is the office of Prime Minister, the components of which we described earlier. We speak of the 'office' rather than the 'person' because this role attaches to the Prime Minister regardless of who is the individual occupant of the office. In any 'job description' of the office of Prime Minister, coordinating government policy and ensuring its consistency would be right at the top of the list. Nor is any Prime Minister likely to neglect this part of the job, for on doing it well can depend the life of the government – and therefore the Prime Minister's own job.

Prime Ministers have a number of means of shaping institutions to achieve coordination. They not only chair the Cabinet, but also chair some   of its important committees. They have extensive powers of appointment, including appointment to, and dismissal from, Cabinet, and while these cannot be used in an unrestrained way they do allow a Prime Minister to set the tone of the government – including influencing the likelihood that ministers will try to work cooperatively together in the first place. Prime Ministers can see all the important papers flowing through the core executive. Perhaps more important, both the civil servants in the Cabinet Secretariat and those who work in the 'Prime Ministerial' units (such as the Private Office and the Policy Unit) are primed to alert both each other and the Prime Minister as to what papers might be sensitive from the point of view of the government. On the skill and sensitivity with which this 'alerting' function is performed can depend the ultimate fate of the Prime Minister and his government.

Formal rules of business

The whole formal organization of business in the core executive is designed to ensure coordination and consistency. That is the purpose of the existence of orderly rules for the preparation and circulation of papers and files through the Cabinet system. In recent years governments have often tried to strengthen coordination by appointing a senior Cabinet minister without departmental responsibilities at the centre as an 'enforcer': in other words, with the responsibility to chase policy initiatives through to see that they do not conflict with other parts of the Government's programme, and to see that they are being implemented in a way consistent with that programme.

The Cabinet machinery is also dominated by the task of trying to manage business in an orderly way. One of the most important examples of this is the management of the government's legislative programme. The yearly policy cycle in government is heavily dominated by the cycle of legislation. New laws are one of the main ways governments try to make policy and put their stamp on affairs. There is always less parliamentary legislative time available than there are potential proposals for legislation coming out of departments. The Cabinet Committee on the Legislative Programme therefore has the particularly important job of putting the proposals in some order of priority and ensuring some balance and coherence.

Informal understandings and contacts

Beyond this formal world, coordination relies heavily on informal contacts and sources. Here again the Prime Minister is critical. More even than departmental Cabinet ministers, Prime Ministers spend most of their time talking to people: in bilateral meetings with particular officials and ministers; picking the brains of their staff who in turn are their eyes and ears in government; talking formally and informally to senior figures in their own party, including senior Cabinet ministers, in the knowledge that if the party goes down at the next general election they all go down with it; spending a large part of each day talking on the telephone; even listening to early morning radio news to try to be alerted to any banana skins that might await them for the rest of the day. Prime Ministers usually feel at a disadvantage when they contemplate the formidable civil service resources available to their department Cabinet colleagues, but there is also an advantage to their position: they are not chained to the backbreaking job of running a large specialist department and have correspondingly more freedom to range widely over the whole of government. A particularly energetic Prime Minister with ability to master detail quickly, like Mrs Thatcher (1979–90), can in this fashion intervene widely in government.

MANAGING THE PRESENTATION OF POLICY IN THE CORE EXECUTIVE

One reason policy coordination is so important in government is that it affects public presentation and perception. British politics is highly adversarial. A government always faces an official opposition in Parliament, and will have large numbers of critics of almost any policy it decides to pursue. Opponents are constantly trying to highlight inconsistencies in policy and splits within government. Few things are more damaging to the image of a government than the impression that it is disunited and not in control of all aspects of policy. Since governments are almost always disunited, and rarely in control, policy presentation is vital. Three forms of presentation are especially important.

Briefing

The most important means of presenting policy is through the mass media – newspapers and broadcasting – since it is here that electors get their first information about what government is currently up to. Briefing of journalists goes on constantly, and has always gone on. Politicians and political journalists in London inhabit the same world, mixing together both formally and socially. Politicians, whether in or out of government, are always briefing: putting their side of any argument to journalists. Since leading politicians are also almost always intensely ambitious and have large egos, this briefing about policy is usually mixed up with more personal briefings: defending their own positions and criticizing those of their opponents and rivals in their own government. In the core executive in recent years, however, this briefing process has become more organized, a bit more open and more like systematic news management. Press officers in departments, once just career civil servants, are increasingly being displaced by specially recruited 'spin doctors' – a term originating in the expression 'to put a spin' on something, meaning to manipulate the way it is perceived. This exactly expresses the role of the spin doctor, which is not just to present information, but also to take events and announcements and put on them the 'spin' most favourable to the minister and the Government. Cabinet ministers usually have their own dedicated spin doctors to manage relations with the media. The shift to more organized briefing is most obvious right at the centre of the core executive, where the Prime Minister's personal spokesman has in recent decades emerged as a distinctive public figure in his own right. (The first to become a substantial media celebrity was Bernard Ingham, 1979–90, who acquired the title of Chief Press Secretary and who spanned exactly the years of Mrs Thatcher's Prime Ministership.) In Sir Bernard's period the role of the Chief Press Secretary as the public 'voice' of the Prime Minister was permanently established. This has accompanied growing openness about the role of the Prime Minister's official spokesman. Originally, lobby briefings were totally unattributable; then they were acknowledged as coming from the Prime Minister's spokesman; then, since everyone informally knew his identity, that was acknowledged. At present, we are at a point where by clicking on the Downing Street website it is possible to read an account of the daily briefing meetings (www.number-10.gov.uk; see Documenting Politics 6.1). As the role has become more open it has also become more overtly political in a partisan sense. The best known spokesman of the Blair era was Alistair Campbell, a former journalist and long-time Labour Party supporter. He became so identified with the communication of the Prime Minister's view that following the 2001 election his role and title were redesigned in an attempt to give him a lower profile. The growing politicization of the communications function in the core executive has thus had the side effect of making its formal organization more unstable, as Prime Ministers try to shape it to their immediate concerns.

Though the Prime Minister's Official Spokesman is very important, focusing only on that role can be misleading. Modern government is far too big for briefings to be controlled by one person. This partly explains the rise of an increasingly well-resourced news-management capacity in the core executive. This news-management capacity is also increasingly linked to news

DOCUMENTING POLITICS 6.2

The dark art of the spin doctor

'A good day to bury bad news'

On 11 September 2001 a terrorist attack on the World Trade Center in New York, resulting in the loss of several thousand lives, was relayed live around the globe by television. Watching in London Jo Moore, special advisor to the Secretary of State for Transport, Local Government and the Regions, sent the following email to her colleagues: 'It is now a very good day to get out anything we want to bury. Councillors' expenses?' The suggestion was that a potentially embarrassing news item about payment of expenses to councillors in local government might safely be released because the media in the coming days would be focused on the tragedy in New York.

'Absolutely brilliant Damian'

In January 2009 Damian McBride, Prime Minister Brown's main spin doctor, had an exchange of emails with Derek Draper, who ran a pro-Labour blog, offering examples of how to 'smear' leading Conservatives with untrue, and scurrilous, allegations about their private lives. Draper replied: 'Absolutely brilliant Damian. I'll think about timing and sort out the technology.' McBride was obliged to resign in disgrace when the exchange was leaked in April 2009. Draper also resigned; a decade earlier he had been forced to resign in a scandal over claims to exercise influence for lobbyists.

■ The first email became notorious as an example of a cynically manipulative approach to news; the second was widely interpreted as symptomatic of the moral culture of news presentation in the core executive.

management inside the governing party. Modern technology, especially text retrieval via such devices as keywords, allows almost instant rebuttal of criticism. If a government is accused of a particular policy failure the retrieval system can usually locate quickly some contradictory, supporting bits of evidence. If the accusation comes from the parliamentary opposition, text searches can often locate some embarrassing contradiction between the Opposition's present stance and one it occupied in the fairly recent past.

The problem of organizing the communications function at the heart of the core executive resurrects a difficulty we examined earlier: the difficulty of separating the party political from the governmental roles of a Prime Minister. In daily business the two are usually hopelessly entangled, but governments are very sensitive to the charge that they are manipulating the news for partisan purposes (though this is exactly what all governments have to do to survive). This explains the continuing instability in the organization of the media management functions in the Prime Ministerial machine. As we saw above, Alistair Campbell tried to adopt a less publicly visible role after 2001 in the belief that he had become too visible and too identified with partisan briefing. On Mr Campbell's departure in 2003 the Prime Minister commissioned a review whose recommendations have now been implemented. Essentially these try to organize the 'governmental' and the 'partisan' communication separately. How far this separation in practice can be managed is uncertain.

Broadcasting

'Broadcasting' is used here in the general sense of positively putting abroad the Government's case, not merely broadcasting on radio or television. It means the open presentation of policy. This is particularly important when new policies are made. Governments spend a lot of time preparing those policies, but they equally spend a huge amount of time working out how to launch them in the media. All ministers are skilled in this – otherwise, they would probably not reach top office and certainly would not survive there. The most skilled is usually the Prime Minister. All modern Prime Ministers are past masters at radio and television broadcasting: they can manage the 20-second sound bite for the evening news, the extended statement commending some new initiative or the tough adversarial interview.

Defending

Mention of the adversarial interview connects to the third key aspect of presentation, because in British government policy hardly ever has a neutral, dispassionate reception. Just imagine the following. Suppose we saw a student presenting a paper to a class, and then found that everyone in the class, including the tutor, denounced the paper as worthless in the strongest possible language and impugned the motives of the

paper giver. We would certainly conclude that they were all mad or malicious. Yet that is the atmosphere in which government policy is presented. Journalists define their role as the sceptical questioning of ministers, even if they privately agree with them; and the government's political opponents will always try to put the worst possible construction on what is being done. The core executive therefore is in a kind of permanent court where it is perpetually in the dock. This means that the ability to defend effectively against ferocious criticism is at a premium. This again puts the Prime Minister at the centre of the process, and a Prime Minister who seems to be losing this capacity to defend is usually thought to be failing. This also explains why, when Parliament is sitting, Prime Minister's Question Time looms so large. Just how far success and failure at Question Time, which increasingly involves a joust with the Leader of the Opposition, actually influences the public is uncertain; but it is certain that Prime Ministers put enormous resources into preparing for the event and feel shaken if they do badly.

TENSIONS WITHIN THE CORE EXECUTIVE

The above summarizes the most important separate components of the machinery of the core executive, but it gives little sense of the powerful tensions that constantly shape the way that machinery operates in practice. There are three great sources of tension.

The tension between the formal and the informal

Although the machinery described here is complex and generates a huge amount of business (not to mention paper) it actually involves a comparatively small number of regular participants. Most of these people work in close physical proximity to each other and constantly meet both formally (in committees) and informally. The image of a village is often used to describe the atmosphere of the core executive and it is an accurate image: it catches the importance of informality and personal acquaintance, and also catches the spite and malice of village life. The result is that, outside the formal machinery, all sorts of informal groupings and contacts – cabals, bilateral meetings, casual contacts in a corridor while waiting to go into a meeting, drinks and dinners – are important in building alliances and making deals. The telephone (increasingly the mobile phone) and email are important modes of doing business informally.

Prime Ministers are particularly important in fixing the balance between the formal and the informal at the

POLITICAL ISSUES 6.1

Tinkering with the machinery of government

In June 2005 Tony Blair, then Prime Minister, changed the name of the Department of Trade and Industry to the Department for Productivity, Energy and Industry. Even in the history of relabelled and reorganized departments the new creation set a record: after a week the new Secretary of State, Alan Johnson, persuaded the Prime Minister to restore the old name. Although Mr Johnson said the change required only 'a man with a screwdriver' the true cost was probably £30,000. (The reversal was partly because industrial interests were unhappy about the disappearance of 'Trade' and partly because DPEI could too easily be vulgarly represented as the Department of the Penis.) The farcical episode illustrates something serious: the persistent inclination of all Prime Ministers to chop and change the titles and responsibilities of central departments. One reason is because titles can be symbolically useful. In 2007 the new Prime Minister, Gordon Brown, created a Department of Innovation, Universities and Skills to signal that universities should make a contribution to the national economy. It lasted two years. A second reason is that big departmental empires with impressive names can be used to reward political allies. The Department of Innovation, Universities and Skills was dismembered to aggrandize the department headed in 2009 by Lord Mandelson, who in that year was critical to the Prime Minister's retention of office. Lord Mandelson's empire, renamed in 2009 the Department of Business Innovation and Skills, had long gobbled up the old Department of Trade and Industry. All this political manoeuvring is possible because of genuine intellectual uncertainty about the principles of departmental organization, an uncertainty that goes back to a famous report, the Haldane Report, of 1918 (Ministry of Reconstruction 1918).

top. All Prime Ministers like to fix things informally. That can range from having a 'kitchen cabinet' of trusted confidants with whom they discuss things constantly off the record; regular off the record meetings with their most senior ministerial colleagues; periodic on the record meetings with senior colleagues, often to try to sort out some particular problem. ('On the record' here means that a civil servant will be present to make a note of the discussion.) The balance between the informal and formal is partly a function of Prime Ministerial temperament and partly a matter of Prime Ministerial ascendancy over colleagues, which tends to change with, for instance, the Prime Minister's perceived value in winning the next election. Broadly, the more in the ascendant a Prime Minister feels, the more he or she is likely to do business informally; the less in the ascendant, the more likely to feel obliged to go through the machinery of committees.

The tension between the departmental and the central

British government is still a government of departments. Ministers, including most Cabinet ministers, spend most of their time on departmental business. They define their current political identity largely by reference to

their departmental roles: they are the Home Secretary, for example, or the Secretary of State for Health. Most of the resources – technical expertise, staff – important to government are lodged within departments, and most of the spending is done by departments, rather than by the core executive. This imparts another powerful source of tension: between the core executive and the distinct departments. In part that tension is personal and institutional. There are some important people (the Prime Minister, the Cabinet Secretary) whose whole lives are the core executive, and there are others (for example ministers not in the Cabinet), most of whose lives are in the departments. There are institutions (notably the Cabinet Office) whose whole territory is the core executive. Departments, by contrast, have a different territory to defend. The tension also exists inside the minds of all senior ministers: the Home Secretary, or the Foreign Secretary, is constantly being pulled between the departmental territory and the territory of the core executive.

The tension between the personal and the political

The core executive is a small world, and an intensely stressful one. Part of the stress is built into the demands

101

DEBATING POLITICS 6.1

Do we have Prime Ministerial government?

ARGUMENTS THAT WE DO	ARGUMENTS THAT WE DON'T
▶ Prime Ministers command enormous powers of patronage by virtue of the huge range of appointments in their gift.	▶ The patronage powers of modern Prime Ministers are so vast that they can only allocate jobs after advice from others.
▶ Prime Ministers have a particularly important source of patronage, appointing ministers.	▶ Prime Ministers usually find that in appointing and dismissing ministers they have to pay regard to their most powerful Cabinet colleagues – who are also usually rivals.
▶ Modern elections are dominated by the Prime Minister of the day and his or her main rival, the leader of the chief opposition party.	▶ Prime Ministers who are thought unlikely to win the next election will be weak in dealing with senior colleagues and will be subjected to constant conspiracies to remove them.
▶ Prime Ministers do not have to run a large specialized department and can roam widely across the whole of government.	▶ Prime Ministers have to cover the whole span of government with staff resources that are quite small by comparison with the resources of most ministers.
▶ Prime Ministers are the single most important figure in ensuring coordination and consistency in government policy.	▶ Prime Ministers who become fascinated by their role on the European or world stage often find that some rival at home has taken over control of key parts of domestic policy.
▶ Prime Ministers are the single most important voice and symbol of their government abroad, in Europe and elsewhere.	

we have described in this chapter: the need to manage across the range of government everything from the most momentous, like a war, to the trivial but embarrassing, like a minister's private life. But stress also arises from the personalities of this small group of people who work so closely with each other. All are intensely ambitious; most have large egos; all live to work, never switching off. Most are trying to rise up the career ladder. Virtually the only two people in the core executive who are content with their present jobs are the Prime Minister and the Cabinet Secretary, who have reached the top of their respective hierarchies. Many of their immediate colleagues have their eye on the jobs of these two. Thus there is: intense competition; ferocious jealousy; non-stop plotting; constant forming and reforming of alliances behind powerful patrons; continual briefing against each other to the media; and never ending manoeuvring to catch the ear of the most senior figures.

POWER IN THE CORE EXECUTIVE: AN OVERVIEW

The concept of the core executive helps us to avoid some pitfalls in the study of Westminster government in Britain. In particular, it helps us to avoid imposing an overly rigid division between the roles of politicians and permanent officials, and it stresses the importance of central coordinating institutions and offices, like the Cabinet Office and the Prime Minister. But we should never forget a process central to the workings of the core executive: the struggle for power. The outcome of this struggle is vital for the workings of British democracy. There remains one key difference between elected politicians and the rest: the former can be held accountable to the people in free elections, even if the mechanisms of accountability are often imperfect. Traditional questions about the balance of power between ministers and officials, and of the balance between different parts of the core executive, are therefore of central importance to the workings of British democracy. There are many complex issues here, but three are especially important.

Struggles between the centre and departments

Westminster government in Britain is departmental, in the sense that the departments have a huge say in the delivery of policy, and are important concentrations of staff, expertise and money. The department is still the funnel through which most important things flow. More subtly, as we have emphasized, departments are tribes: they tend to be the institutions to which fierce loyalty is felt. The development of the concept of the 'core executive' reflects the growth of central coordinating capacities. But a constant struggle exists between the departments and the centre. On the side of the centre is the fact that it contains the most prestigious institutions in the system, notably the Treasury and the Cabinet Office. It also contains the most prestigious individuals, like the leading politicians, the Prime Minister and the Chancellor.

But its weaknesses in the struggle with departments are manifold. The 'muscle' in government – the specialized expertise and other resources – lies in the departments. The centre has a huge span of issues to cover, and its resources are thinly spread. Moreover, the 'centre' is an abstraction: in reality, most of the time it just imports all the divisions and struggles that exist elsewhere in government. In every modern government, for example, there have been powerful tensions between the Prime Minister and the Chancellor of the Exchequer – and, by extension, between the Treasury and the Office of the Prime Minister.

The power of the Prime Minister

The role of the Prime Minister was transformed during the twentieth century, but it is hard to agree on the significance of this transformation. That there has occurred a long-term growth of Prime Ministerial authority, and prominence is undeniable. The break-up of the Cabinet system into a large number of specialized committees, working groups and bilateral negotiations has made the Prime Minister, as the figure most able to operate across all these, especially important in the vital role of coordinating policy. The widened public roles of the Prime Minister, in the presentation and defence of policy, and in the diplomacy of the EU, has made it much easier for Prime Ministers to intervene at will in any area of government policy. To that extent, the hold of departmentalism has been weakened. Electoral competition has put increasing emphasis on the role of party leaders,

and when Prime Ministers are successful in this kind of personality competition – for instance, after a great election victory or when riding high in the polls – their authority over the rest of government is greatly enhanced.

A popular way in the past to summarize the consequences of these developments was to argue that we were developing Prime Ministerial government to replace Cabinet government. But this theory, though it alerted us to the growing importance of the Prime Minister, suffered from a number of defects. 'Prime Ministerial government' implied a model of executive organization, and it was not clear what this model really was. Sometimes it seemed to suggest that what was developing was a 'Presidential' system, but, since there are numerous kinds of presidency, that characterization was not illuminating. The theory of Prime Ministerial dominance also glossed over the great limits, both in resources and authority, that still hem in Prime Ministers.

These limits take many forms. The break-up of the Cabinet system into so many small parts constantly strains the ability of even the most energetic Prime Minister to keep abreast of issues. Most people the Prime Minister deals with are specializing in one policy area; the Prime Minister is trying to keep abreast of them all. This is one reason why Prime Ministers are often tripped up by surprise developments and unforeseen crises, and why they fret so much about problems of coordination and presentation. The resources available to the Prime Minister, either to analyse policy or to see it through to conclusion, are severely limited. Most of the time a Prime Minister relies on other parts of government to provide expert analysis and to execute a Prime Ministerial decision. The authority that comes from electoral success can as easily drain away with electoral failure or the threat of electoral failure. Within a year of winning a third successive general election by a large majority in 1987, Mrs Thatcher was being conspired against; by late 1990 she had been deposed.

The struggle between ministers and officials

Finally, an age-old tension still lies at the heart of British government. Departments are tribes, and the most loyal members of the tribe are the officials. They have often spent a working lifetime living with the tribe. By contrast, ministers are transients. Most politicians spend most of their working lives outside government. For instance, in the long years of Conservative rule between 1979 and 1997 – an ideal opportunity therefore to create stability – only two members of the House of Commons other than Mrs Thatcher served in government positions throughout the period (Kenneth Clarke and Malcolm

Rifkind). In Labour's long tenure between 1997 and 2010 only three figures were continuously present in Cabinet – Gordon Brown, Jack Straw and Alistair Darling – and of course none of these occupied the same position throughout. A good example of the impact of transience is provided by the case of the office of Chief Secretary to the Treasury, a Cabinet level appointment which, because it mainly involves detailed negotiations with departments about public spending plans, demands great command of complex detail. There were 14 Chief Secretaries between 1990 and 2010: the record for brevity was held by Stephen Byers, who lasted only five months from his appointment in July 1998.

The sources of the engrained tensions are obvious. The lives of politicians are dominated by a short-term institutional objective – how to ensure that their party is re-elected – and by a short-term personal objective – how to move on up the hierarchy by switching out of their present department to a higher level. Just about the only politician who wants to stay long term in the same job is the Prime Minister. A couple of senior ministers (like the Chancellor) will always be sizing up the Prime Minister's job; and below them will be the whole government of more junior ministers, extending to the most obscure junior minister in Culture, Media and Sport, all jockeying for advancement. Officials, of course, are moved by institutional and career ambitions, but these are rather different. They build their careers usually for the most part inside a single department. They have a long-term interest in the department, and they often develop strong emotional identification with that department.

Review OF CHAPTER 6

Three themes have dominated this chapter:

◖◗ The 'core executive' defines an unstable world of shifting actors, frenetic activity and unclear boundaries.

◖◗ Inside the core executive are distilled most of the great tensions at the heart of government: between elected and appointed officials; between Prime Ministers and their ministers; between specialized departments and those concerned to coordinate the totality of government policy.

◖◗ Inside the core executive coordination of policy is inseparable from the presentation of policy. 'Spin' is central to the core executive, because above all it has to manage appearances to give a picture of consistency and strategic coherence – even if there is none in reality.

FURTHER READING

ESSENTIAL

If you read only one book it should be the classic comprehensive study of the core executive by Burch and Holliday (1996); but read also their article (Burch and Holliday 2004) to update.

RECOMMENDED

Smith (2000b) reports detailed research on relations in the core executive. Marsh et al. (2001) report important work on the reshaping of the Whitehall system. Richards (2007) is a study of New Labour, the civil service and the Westminster model. The two volumes collected by Rhodes (2000) report the most ambitious modern studies of how the centre of British government is changing. Part II of Bevir and Rhodes (2010) has a very particular interpretation of things, but is fantastically interesting. Mullin (2009) is a wonderful portrait of the (fairly miserable) life of being a junior minister. Rawnsley (2010), though highly contested by many of those he writes about, gives a really vivid picture of the frenetic nature of life in the core executive.

CHAPTER 7

Departments and agencies in the Westminster system

AIMS

This chapter:

- ☐ Describes the new, more fragmented organization of government in the Westminster system

- ☐ Describes the continuing importance of civil service departments despite this fragmentation

- ☐ Outlines the origins and development of the Next Steps (Executive) Agencies

- ☐ Explains why regulation of privatized industries has become so important, and sketches its organization

- ☐ Describes the rapidly expanding world of government through regulatory agencies in Britain

- ☐ Examines how far all these developments suggest that Britain at the Westminster centre is turning into a regulatory state

THE NEW WORLD OF AGENCIES IN BRITISH GOVERNMENT

The growing acceptance of the concept of the core executive, which dominated the last chapter, was due to two developments. One had to do with the study of government at the centre in Britain; the other with the actual practice of government. The first, which we noted as our starting point for Chapter 6, was the realization that we needed a more adequate way than was offered by traditional models of minister/civil servant relationships to make sense of things right at the top of British government. The second factor was the rising demand for one of the key services fulfilled by a core executive: centrally coordinating the management and presentation of policy. And coordination and presentation have become increasingly important because of changes in the structure of British government in the last couple of decades. These changes dominate this chapter.

Over the last two decades, British government at the Westminster centre has become more fragmented. What was once the dominant form of government – the civil service department controlled by a minister in Whitehall – has been supplemented, and in some instances displaced, by new kinds of agencies. Departments do still remain important, as we shall see in the next section. But in the last couple of decades three developments have greatly altered the traditional structure and 'dispersed' the executive through a wide range of institutions. This chapter is mostly about the structures created by these changes.

The first set of changes examined here dates back to reforms begun in the 1980s. They are sometimes called the 'Next Steps' reforms after the title of the report which heralded them. The report led to the creation of a wide range of specialized agencies, either newly created or 'hived off' from the traditional civil service departments. These new executive agencies have taken over responsibility for the delivery of a large number of government services. The second momentous change also dates back to the 1980s. In that decade the Conservative Government began an ambitious programme of 'privatization': selling to private owners industries that for many decades had been publicly owned. These industries included some of the most important in the British economy. They covered, among others, telecommunications services, water supply, electricity generation, gas and electricity supply, coal mining and rail transport. The importance of these industries meant that they could not be transferred to private ownership without any safeguards over how they would be operated in private hands. Consequently, many privatizations were accompanied by the creation of a specialized agency, with legal powers, charged with regulating

IMAGE 7.1 ■ The oldest and most powerful regulatory agency?

Photo: Michael Moran

■ A major theme of this book is the rise of a special kind of public body – the specialized regulatory agency. But it is not new: the Bank of England, pictured, is one of the oldest of all agencies, founded in 1694. Since then it has been at the centre of the management of public finances and the regulation of the financial system, and since the great financial crisis of 2007–08 has become more powerful still.

the privatized industry in the public interest. The creation of these new regulatory agencies is the second great institutional change which is examined in this chapter. It created a virtually new, and very important, area of economic government.

Alongside the creation of regulatory agencies for the privatized industries there also occurred a wider change: agencies were created to regulate a wide range of markets and other social spheres. The spheres, we shall discover, were strikingly diverse: they encompassed things as different as the regulation of financial markets, food safety and human fertility. This is the third momentous change examined in this chapter.

THE DEPARTMENTAL WORLD

If the core executive is the coping stone which holds together the whole structure of government in the Westminster system, departments have been the building blocks of that system. Departments vary hugely in size, function and political weight, but taken together they are outstandingly important. The five major reasons for this importance are summarized below.

They are key to accountability

Departments remain one of the most important institutions through which attempts are made to practise the accountability which lies at the heart of the theory of British democracy. The team which forms the political head of the department – the Secretary of State and the more junior members of the ministerial team – are answerable to Parliament through the workings of the doctrine of individual ministerial responsibility. Historically, this doctrine developed when government was small and ministers could realistically hope to control all of importance that happened in their department: for example Palmerston, the greatest of nineteenth-century Foreign Secretaries, wrote by hand most of the letters going out of the Foreign Office. Now ministers would not even expect to see most that is written on their behalf. Ministerial responsibility in the literal sense of believing that ministers can be held responsible for all that is done in their name is therefore no longer a serious influence on British government. But it has turned into a living doctrine of ministerial accountability, if only in this restricted sense: both in Parliament and through the media ministers expect to have to give an account – to explain and defend – what is done by their departments. The internal life of departments at the most senior levels is heavily concerned with equipping ministers with the information to give these accounts. A further sign of the accountability functions of departments is that the senior civil servant in a department – the Permanent Secretary – is that department's 'accounting officer': responsible for accounting for the resources committed by the department.

They are key arenas of politician/civil service tension

Departments are run by a team made up of elected politicians – ministers mostly with a seat in the House of Commons – and appointed civil servants. Like most teams the departmental team tries to work together but is also often subject to great internal tensions. Because ministers expect to have to give an account of departmental policy and actions, they also expect both to be able to shape the most important decisions made within the department and to be kept informed of what is going on. The day to day life of departments, especially at the most senior levels, is dominated by making sure ministers are indeed informed and able to defend the department's position. But into this is built one of the great tensions in the Westminster system. Ministers are usually more transient than civil servants. Perhaps even more important, they have their own special priorities: above all, since they are only ministers because their party has a majority in the House of Commons they are focused on electoral success. Individually they have little loyalty to the department: their career depends on moving on, and up, as quickly as possible. Their horizons are short term. But the time scale of much that government does is long term: new ministers inherit projects that began long ago, and will be completed long after they have departed. Civil servants, by contrast, are typically deeply concerned with these long-term commitments. It has been usual until now – though as we shall see in the next section this may be changing – for civil servants to make virtually their whole career in a department. This is what gives departments the 'tribal' culture that we discussed in the last chapter. The tension between the preoccupations of civil servants, who have to live with projects in the long term and who develop emotional commitments to a department, and more transient and electorally focused ministers, makes departmental life an important arena of tension in British government. Elected, accountable ministers running departments is a key element in the theory of democratic government in Britain. The way these tensions are resolved is important well beyond the immediate preoccupations inside departments: it affects how real democracy is in Britain.

One of the most important signs of that tension in recent years has involved, not ministers and civil servants directly, but permanent civil servants and the rising number of special advisers that ministers now bring with them into departments. These advisers are usually active supporters of the governing party. Their rising number and importance is due to the feelings of politicians that, alone, they cannot exercise sufficient influence over policy and its presentation in the department. Their job therefore directly expresses the politician/bureaucrat tension, and this tension has often in recent years spilled over into acrimonious public dispute. A striking case is illustrated in Briefing 7.1.

They are key arenas for struggles over the allocation of resources

We saw in the last chapter that life in the core executive is dominated by a struggle for resources – especially for money and, in planning the Government's legislation, parliamentary time to pass laws. Departments are key institutions in this struggle. They compete with each other for money. They compete with each other for parliamentary time. And they compete with each other for jurisdiction over policy: a great deal of argument inside government concerns which department has the right to make decisions about policy. For example, who should be the lead department in managing policy over asylum seekers? The Home Office or the Foreign Office?

BRIEFING 7.1

A civil war in a department: how tensions between ministers, their advisers and civil servants can create chaos

In Documenting Politics 6.2 we saw the case of the infamous email sent by Jo Moore, an adviser in the Department of Transport, suggesting that colleagues 'bury' bad news by issuing it the day after the cataclysmic terrorist attack on the World Trade Center in New York on 11 September 2001. Moore was eventually forced to resign but the aftermath only revealed more clearly the chaotic and hate filled working relationships in the Department. In February 2002 the Department's Chief of Communications (Martin Sixsmith) was forced out, in part because supporters of Moore and Stephen Byers (the Secretary of State) believed that he had helped orchestrate the campaign against her and had briefed journalists against his minister (charges denied by Sixsmith). A farce ensued, in which Sixsmith insisted that he had not resigned and the Department (and the Prime Minister's Office) insisted he had. Leaked accounts of meetings, which had the Department's Permanent Secretary (senior civil servant) using language that would have been shocking even on the Stretford End at Manchester United, revealed that the minister and the Permanent Secretary had bad personal relations and that a complicated set of negotiations had been designed to try to secure a severance package for Sixsmith in return for a 'gagging' clause – negotiations that failed. Later in 2002 Byers himself resigned, in part because of the bad blood created by the whole affair. In 2010 he was disgraced when a 'sting' operation filmed him boasting that he operated like a cab for hire at the service of business lobbyists.

■ 'Official' accounts of working relations between ministers and civil servants paint a picture of settled constitutional understandings. But there is also a human face to department life. Members of the departmental tribe live in an intensely stressful atmosphere where work almost entirely dominates their lives. Here, differences about policy and poisonous personal relations often combine.

They are a symbol of status and prestige

Not all departments are equal. The 'pecking order' is often unclear, and it often changes, but there are great and persistent inequalities. Nobody doubts that the Treasury, though a department with a comparatively small staff, is way ahead in both influence and status of the Department for Culture, Media and Sport. This has some obvious consequences. The most important players in government – the leading politicians and the leading civil servants – measure their success by the status and prestige of their department. For civil servants this will often turn into a struggle to augment the resources and policy jurisdiction of the department. For ambitious ministers it turns into a constant struggle to move up the departmental hierarchy. The ambitious Secretary of State in a middle ranking department wants to move on to the Home Office or the Treasury. The fact that the department is a symbol of status and prestige also explains why departments are so often being remade and renamed. In recent years several

departments have in effect been created to meet the ambitions of powerful political figures. This was true of the Deputy Prime Minister under two recent Prime Ministers: both Michael Heseltine (Deputy under John Major) and John Prescott (deputy under Tony Blair) had large administrative empires created to meet their ambitions and massage their egos; while Peter Mandelson, who became Deputy Prime Minister in all but name in the closing months of Gordon Brown's Premiership, likewise had an administrative empire carved out for him.

The unstable boundaries of departments also point to one of the most enduring questions concerning departmental structure: on what principles should they be organized? At the end of the First World War – after a period of huge expansion in the scale of the state – a famous committee of enquiry recommended that departments be organized along functional lines: that is, according to the responsibilities they carried out (Ministry of Reconstruction 1918). This has never been implemented more than approximately. Departmental structures are the product often of historical accident, and the departmental 'tribes' powerfully resist reform: what they have, they defend; and what they do not have they often covet. And the ambitions of politicians, as we have just seen, constantly intervene to compromise general organizational principles.

They are a means of policy formulation and implementation

The core executive, we saw in the last chapter, is very important to policy coordination and presentation and to the making of some key areas of high strategic policy – for instance the big historical decisions such as whether Britain should replace the pound sterling by joining the eurozone. But most policy arguments and struggles in British government are departmental struggles, either within or between departments. Within departments life is dominated by providing advice about policy decisions to ministers. These ministers in turn expect their lives to be dominated by making and publicly defending policy decisions. Some of the biggest will be embodied in legislative proposals – parliamentary bills – for which the minister will have to fight for time and space in the core executive: for instance, in the Cabinet Committee on the legislative timetable which we encountered in the last chapter. But even a senior Cabinet minister would not expect to deal normally with more than one big piece of legislation per session. Daily life will be dominated by an unpredictable mixture: making and defending some decisions, ranging from those involving huge resources to those concerning individuals. Ministers will expect to advocate and defend these decisions in both Parliament and the media, and they will expect their senior civil servants to provide them with the ammunition for defence. It is a foolish, or badly served, minister who appears on *The World at One* or *Newsnight* without a briefing note from the civil service.

Policy ranges unpredictably from the minute to the grand, and the public importance attached to it can also be unpredictable. A Home Office Minister can often spend large amounts of time defending decisions affecting single individuals – such as an individual prisoner or an individual asylum seeker. Not surprisingly, ministers and civil servants often feel overloaded by the volume of decisions needing to be taken and defended. As we shall see in a moment this was one of the sources of the initiative to create Executive Agencies. But another source concerned, not the making of policy, but its implementation.

Not all departments have been historically closely involved in policy implementation: the Treasury, for

DOCUMENTING POLITICS 7.1

The creation of the Next Steps Agencies: the picture painted by the creators

The main strategic control must lie with the Minister and Permanent Secretary. But once the policy objectives and budgets within the framework are set, the management of the agency should then have as much independence as possible in deciding how these objectives are met. A crucial element in the relationship would be a formal understanding with Ministers about the handling of sensitive issues and lines of accountability in a crisis. The presumption must be that, provided management is operating within the strategic direction set by Ministers it must be left as free as possible to manage within that framework.

■ The passage here reproduces the central argument from perhaps the most important modern document about the organization of central government in Britain. It launched the 'Next Steps' agencies, whose multiplication fundamentally changed the traditional organization of the civil service. Notice a key assumption in the passage: that a consistent separation could be made between 'strategic control', which was to remain where it traditionally lay, with the minister and the most senior civil servant, and daily management which was to be done independently by the agencies. This distinction proved hard to preserve in practice.

Source: Jenkins et al. (1988:9, the original 'Next Steps' report).

example, is largely concerned with strategic policy advice and formulation. But many departments have historically been huge policy delivery institutions: for example, the Home Office in its concern with prison administration, or social security departments concerned with the administration of the whole benefit system for unemployment. A feeling that the culture and skills of the London-based civil service elite was not well suited to administering large, complex delivery systems also lay behind the great initiative which we next examine: the creation of the Executive Agencies.

THE WORLD OF THE NEW EXECUTIVE AGENCIES

The development of the new executive agencies, which date from the reforms of the Conservative Governments at the end of the twentieth century, was the most ambitious reform of the structure of central government in modern times. The question of how those fundamental institutional reforms have really changed the working of government in the Westminster system is now one of the great issues in studying British government.

The Next Steps Agencies: the context

The cryptic label 'Next Steps' Agencies dates from the title of a report on the reform of the management of central government produced in 1988 by a team headed by Sir Robin Ibbs, then head of the Efficiency Unit established in the core executive by the Prime Minister in the 1980s. As the title implies, the purpose of the report was to carry forward the revolutionary programme of the Conservatives, which by the end of the 1980s was already well on the way to privatizing most of the big publicly owned industries. As these historical origins suggest, the creation of the Agencies cannot be considered in isolation, or as only an institutional change in the form of central government. They are part of a more long drawn out process of reform in the administrative centre of the state in Britain, a process which can be dated back to the 1960s. For the 50 years after the end of the First World War the administrative centre was dominated by a model which put the civil service department, headed by a minister advised by permanent civil servants, right at the centre of the governing process. We saw in the last section that this model still remains enormously influential. But it has been increasingly challenged, on three chief grounds.

That it is uncoordinated. The rise of the core executive, described in the last chapter, represents an attempt to assert central control over the coordination, the presentation and even in some cases the making of policy. This can be seen as a reaction against the power of the departmental 'tribes' that have traditionally dominated in the Westminster system.

That it is overloaded. As we saw in the last section departments are a frenetic focus of demands for decisions about matters large and small. Ministers and their most senior civil service advisors instinctively search for some ways of 'off-loading' responsibilities, thus allowing them to concentrate on a smaller range of strategic issues.

That it lacks the necessary skills. Modern government demands high levels of managerial skills: in data analysis; in managing large scale projects, like construc-

tion projects, from start to finish; in managing huge numbers of people in complex, multilayered bureaucracies. Since the 1960s – when a report on the civil service chaired by Lord Fulton argued that the service lacked these managerial skills – there have been periodic reforms designed to remedy the perceived defects. The result has been that over a period of 30 years the perception of the skills needed to administer modern government changed hugely: just how hugely is illustrated in Documenting Politics 7.2.

The Next Steps initiative can therefore be seen as the most determined attempt yet to respond to perceived problems in the civil service as traditionally organized, notably to the problems of overload and skill deficiency.

DOCUMENTING POLITICS 7.2

How the perceived skills needed to manage modern government have changed

If you entered the civil service in, say, the 1960s (as I did) the literature would have told you that senior civil servants were policy makers. They were not expected to know the cost of the resources that they controlled or the staff who worked for them. They would not have had budgets. They would not have described themselves as managers. We now require people in public service to be good managers and good leaders of their organizations and to know how to achieve results through the people who are working for them and through the application of project management skills. (Sir Richard Wilson, Cabinet Secretary, 1999)

■ Sir Richard Wilson was the most successful civil servant of his generation, reaching the very top of the tree – Secretary to the Cabinet – in the 1990s. His recollection of how the job of managing government changed over more than 30 years is therefore authoritative. And his picture of greater demands for technical managerial skills, and more systematic managerial information, illustrates precisely the pressures for change that helped created the Next Steps Agencies.

Source: Wilson (1999).

The Next Steps Agencies: the principles

Four principles lay behind the initiative that has led to the large scale creation of executive agencies in British government.

Separating strategic policy advice and decision from delivery. As the extract from the original definitive report in Documenting Politics 7.1 shows, this was the key principle that lay behind the initiative. The attractions of this to senior civil servants and ministers are clear. The sense of being 'overloaded' arises partly from the sheer volume of demands for decisions made on departments, and partly from the way those at the top of departments often feel uncomfortable in dealing with the details of policy implementation. Politicians in particular often struggle with detail, in part because they have so many competing demands on their time, and in part because temperamentally they often have a limited attention span. Senior, highly educated civil servants are used to playing the game of policy advice in the upper reaches of departments; their training has traditionally prepared them less well to get on top of the often tedious details of policy delivery. Making a supposedly clear separation between strategic priorities (a phrase which readily trips off the tongues of senior ministers and their advisors) and daily management is thus immensely attractive.

Making the relationship between the agency and the department explicit and clear. It is one thing to say in general terms that strategic decision is to be separated from daily management; another to operate this distinction in practice. The creation of the agencies has thus been accompanied by an important innovation: laying down, usually in a written 'framework document', the details of the division of responsibility between the agency and its department (see Documenting Politics 7.3 for an example.) This marks a significant innovation in the organization of government, for hitherto the division between strategic decision and management had been 'bundled up' inside the department.

Guiding agency management by performance indicators. The era of the creation of the agencies coincided with another shift in the culture of British government: the rise of a concern with measuring the performance of government and judging the adequacy of government by the extent to which quantifiable performance targets had been met. From the start the framework of agency behaviour has been shaped by quantitative performance indicators and the targets set to reach those indicators.

Loosening the ties with traditional civil service organization. As we shall see in a moment agencies come in all shapes and sizes, and there is no one single template guiding relationships with the civil service. But

---

DOCUMENTING POLITICS 7.3

Extract from a framework agreement: the case of the National Offender Management Service

In delivering the sentences and orders of the courts effectively, the NOMS Agency will commission providers from the public, private and third sectors to:

- deliver effective punishments;
- protect the public from offenders and communities from the impact of crime;
- reduce re-offending;
- deliver the sentence plans in accordance with the court's requirements;
- take account of the needs, wishes and rights of the victims of crime;
- rehabilitate offenders and
- make the best use of resources.

■ The work of each new executive agency is governed by a 'framework agreement'. This is intended to govern the principles by which it operates – both how it treats its clients and how it deals with its 'parent' department of state. The example here comes from one of the largest and most politically sensitive of the agencies – that concerned with the management of the prison and the probation service. In its early years, despite the attempt to establish working principles in the framework agreement, the prison service agency was beset with controversy, culminating in the sacking of its head by the Home Secretary. The issue of the division of responsibilities between the Home Office and the Prison Service is also the subject documented in Documenting Politics 4.2. The delicacy of relations is indicated by the length of the document: this is only a short passage from a 45-page-long agreement.

Source: Ministry of Justice (2008).

---

because the creation of agencies in part resulted from dissatisfaction with the civil service as a manager of policy delivery, the Next Steps reforms also attempted to depart from traditional models of civil service organization. There are three particularly important signs of this. First, the heads of the new agencies have been appointed by open competition, not by internal promotion from within the civil service – though many heads are indeed drawn from the civil service. Second, there have been conscious attempts to introduce private sector working practices and management styles into the new agencies. These take a variety of forms. Market testing has become widespread. This involves measuring the efficiency of 'in-house' service provision against the terms offered in competitive tendering by private sector providers. The service can range from office cleaning to the provision of large scale IT support. Some of the changes are symbolic, but the symbols are designed to communicate a change in culture. Agencies now routinely speak of their 'customers', for instance, and try to measure customer satisfaction with their services. The overall effect of these changes has been to make relationships much more contractual in nature. The relationships between the agency and the department are rather like those of a supplier and customer, with the framework agreement and performance targets embodying the terms of the contract. Working relationships inside agencies are also heavily contractual in nature, working life being governed by the need to achieve specified performance targets. And the agency is itself increasingly involved in contractual relationships with private sector suppliers of services.

The third and final institutional change takes the logic of these developments to their fullest expression: to privatize the agency itself. The agency then becomes a private enterprise which has a contract with government to deliver services under specified conditions, for instance governing price and quality. A good example is provided by an agency which the readers of this book will probably use at some time to buy an official publication: the Stationery Office (see Documenting Politics 7.4).

Executive Agencies: scale and range

Briefing 7.2 gives some idea of the scale and variety of the Executive Agencies at creation. The history of their creation has three key features, only two of which are readily clear from the briefing box itself.

Scale. The scale of the agency creation is immense: over 140 agencies now employ over 370,000 staff. Measured by this, not unimportant, indicator, the rise of the Executive Agency is one of the most important changes to come over British Government in modern times.

Diversity. The diversity of the agencies is an obvious implication of the very scale of creation. But this diversity goes beyond the obvious – as Briefing 7.2 makes clear, we are looking here at institutions that vary hugely in size and responsibilities. Close studies of the experience of agency working suggests a deeper diversity: in the extent to which the creation of an agency really does

DOCUMENTING POLITICS 7.4

The Stationery Office as a privatized agency

ABOUT US

TSO (The Stationery Office) was created in September 1996, when most of the assets and commercial activities of Her Majesty's Stationery Office (HMSO) were sold to The Stationery Office Group Ltd (TSOL). This company demerged its operations on 31 March 1999, creating The Stationery Office Holdings Ltd and three new independent companies.

In July 1999 The Stationery Office Holdings Ltd was sold to funds managed by a leading venture capital company, Apax Partners, with additional finance provided by the Bank of Scotland. Apax Partners manages more than 5 billion euros for major institutional investors, both public and private. They own 74% of the shares of The Stationery Office Holdings Ltd, with the rest held by TSO management and staff.

■ The case of the Stationery Office is a striking example of how the changes in the structures of public administration have reshaped the line dividing the public and the private sector. Once the very epitome of a public service organization, the Office is now a privately owned company like any other, contracted with the public sector to produce official documents, and subject to frequent changes of ownership in the market for corporate control.

Source: www.tso.co.uk.

result in a change in institutional culture and working practices. For some, the effects of separation from the department have been comparatively modest. For others – obvious examples would be those that were fully privatized – the changes have been quite fundamental.

Political visibility. One of the most important sources of diversity arises from the political visibility of the functions for which the agency is responsible. Some of these agencies are not only small – they inhabit routine backwaters of British government. It takes a lot to reveal them to the public eye, and in particular for

113

BRIEFING 7.2

The variety and scale of the new executive agencies at creation

Agency	Numbers employed	Main function
Civil Service	220	Provides in-service training for civil servants
Companies House	839	Receives, stores and disseminates company reports
Wilton Park	37	Runs an upmarket conference centre chiefly for foreign policy conferences
Employment Service	28,612	Runs all high street employment services
Serious Fraud Office	149	Investigates major financial frauds
Social Security Benefits Agency	66,296	Administers all social security benefits
Social Security Child Support Agency	7,909	Administers rules involving, chiefly, obligations of non-resident spouses to contribute to upkeep of dependents
HM Prison Service	39,363	Runs prisons in England and Wales

■ These data derive from an official overview published in 1998. At the time, there were over 140 agencies employing over 370,000 staff. The examples are designed to show the diversity of the agencies. They range from tiny bodies carrying out utterly uncontroversial functions, to huge bureaucracies delivering large scale public services that constantly arouse political controversy: notice the presence of the Prison Service, a crisis in the government of which was the occasion of the issue in Documenting Politics 4.2. But notice also that size is no measure of controversy: the medium-sized Child Support Agency was constantly at the centre of controversy, principally because of its pursuit of payments from divorced parents; and the tiny Serious Fraud Office has likewise been in continuing controversy, chiefly because of the collapse of high profile trials involving financial fraud.

Source: Extracted from Annex A of *Next Steps Report 1998* at www.official-documents.co.uk.

their activities to cause problems for ministers. But others are highly visible, not only in the scale of the services they deliver, but in the potential for political problems that they create. Despite the formal separation of 'strategy' from 'daily management', political problems usually draw ministers into daily operations. In some cases this visibility and sensitivity is just engrained in the agency. The best example is what was at creation the Prison Service Agency. Everyday details of prison policy – for instance, whether particular notorious prisoners might be eligible for parole – are the subject of intense party argument and media interest. No Cabinet minister responsible for prisons can keep his or her fingers out of that aspect of daily management. One measure of this irreducible political sensitivity is that such agencies keep being renamed: the Prison Service is now part of the National Offender Management Service inside the Ministry of Justice. Some agencies just get catapulted into political visibility by a failure of service delivery, for example, or

because they become mixed up with highly contentious schemes: the Passport Agency has, after a disastrous beginning when it made a mess of issuing passports, now morphed into the Passport and Identity Service, the second half of the name indicating the controversial ambitions of the Labour Government until 2010 to create a national system of identity cards. A sure sign that an agency has not been separated from politics is a history of name changing.

REGULATORY AGENCIES AND PRIVATIZATION

Although the creation of the executive agencies was a major change in the structure of British government it was not the biggest single change in the last couple of decades of the twentieth century. That distinction belongs to the privatization programme which was carried out, principally, by the Conservative Governments in power between 1979 and 1997. In those years, and especially in a few revolutionary years of the 1980s, whole industries were sold to the private sector, mostly through flotation on the Stock Exchange. Privatization dismantled a whole range of public enterprises that had been organized in nationalized corporations (like British Steel or British Rail) or in publicly owned authorities, like those that controlled water supply. It thus *contracted* the scale of British government. But it simultaneously *expanded public authority* because it created new kinds of public agencies to regulate these privatized enterprises.

The special features of the regulatory agencies for privatized industries

The regulatory agencies for the privatized industries, though they bear some superficial resemblance to the executive agencies, differ from them in four important respects.

They are new creations. The executive agencies were carved out of civil service departments and have mostly retained close relationships with those departments. The regulatory agencies for the privatized industries are for the most part new creations. They are an important innovation in British government, for while some historical ancestors can be found in the nineteenth century they amount to a new way of governing the economy.

They regulate. Public ownership created huge organizations that produced and delivered goods and services – ranging from coal to water to rail travel. That often gave departments in the Westminster system the opportunity for direct hands-on control of large parts of the economy. The new regulatory agencies are of outstanding importance because they span equally important domains of the economy. But unlike either the old nationalized corporations or the new executive agencies they deliver no goods or services. Their importance lies in the fact that they regulate how goods or services – ranging from water to electricity to phone services – are produced or delivered. Regulation means that they literally control the rules under which markets operate. Thus they have an important say in such vital matters as: what firms can enter a market; what prices they can charge, and by how much they can increase prices; when they can cut off services to customers, for instance for non-payment of bills; and what service standards – for instance governing speed or response to customers – they must observe.

They have unusual independence. The executive agencies, we saw, have a complex relationship with civil service departments and with ministers. Although they often do have a large amount of operational independence they are constantly subject to intervention, especially if their activities prove sensitive to the careers and priorities of ministers. The regulatory agencies are not immune to this sort of intervention, but they have established a much clearer tradition of independent operation. They are usually governed by a single director general whose powers and authority are specified in statute. They have from the beginning recruited from outside the civil service and have established their own management styles, and career patterns, separate from the civil service. The individual director generals have, since they first emerged in the 1980s, established themselves as independent public figures in their own policy domains.

They are a vital form of economic government. The new regulatory agencies have only existed in their present form for a generation: the first, OFTEL, which regulated telecommunications, was only established when the old nationalized telephone service provider was privatized in 1984. But in the years since then they have emerged as major instruments for governing the economy in Britain. The privatized sector is a major part of the economy. It includes industries, like telecommunications that are at the leading edge of modern technology, are organized on a global scale, and are dominated by large multinational firms. It includes those that provide public services that are vital to the economy and everyday life, like rail services. And it includes services that we hardly think about but whose maintenance is vital to the very fabric of community life: every time we turn on a tap expecting an instantaneous flow of clean water we are drawing on the services of a regulated, privatized industry. (Not, however, in Scotland, where water privatization was never implemented.) The importance of the industries helps answer a vital question which we examine next: why were these major new public institutions created?

Why the regulatory agencies were created

At first glance it is not at all clear why regulatory agencies should have been created for the newly privatized industries. After all, we know from earlier chapters that Britain's is primarily a market economy where private ownership dominates. Large parts of the economy have historically been run by private firms and, beyond general laws such as those concerned with preventing fraud, it has not usually been thought necessary to establish special regulatory bodies for individual industries: we do not have a special regulator for the automobile production industries. The creation of important state regulatory agencies in the privatized sphere tells us a lot not just about the privatized sector, but about the nature of the governing system. Above all, it throws an important light on a key question that has to be settled in any system that, like Britain, is simultaneously democratic

BRIEFING 7.3

The new world of regulatory agencies

Name	Date established	Responsibilities
Office of Communications (Ofcom)	2003	Responsible for all broadcasting regulation hitherto carried out by a range of separate bodies
Office of Rail Regulation	Predecessor established by Railways Act of 1993; took over present role in 2006	The regulator for the economics and safety on the privatized rail system
National Lottery Commission	1999 (succeeded Oflot, established 1993)	Regulates all aspects of the national lottery from sales to proceeds distribution
Office of Gas and Electricity	Created in 2000, fusing hitherto separate authorities regulating gas Markets (OFGEM) and electricity markets	Regulates firms in energy markets
Human Fertilisation and Embryology Authority	1991	Regulates scientific research into, and use of, embryos for intervention in human fertility
Financial Services Authority	1997 (fully operational 2000)	Regulated all financial institutions for honesty and stability. Dismembered in 2010 for incompetence.
Food Standards Agency	2000	Regulates all stages of food production in the interests of public health
The Gambling Commission	2005	Regulates all commercial gambling

■ The closing decades of the twentieth century saw a major institutional innovation in British government: the rise of the special-ized regulatory agency charged with control of an industry or social domain. The dates of foundation chart the recent rise of the agencies. The agencies are commonly associated with the aftermath of the privatization programme of the Conservative govern-ments in the 1980s and 1990s, and some of the examples above are indeed charged with regulating privatized enterprises: in telecommunications, energy and rail. But some other examples show that the regulatory agency is now a standard way of exer-cising public control. In some cases the new agency replaces other public arrangements: for instance, the Food Standards Agency took over duties hitherto carried out by a central department, the old Ministry of Agriculture, Food and Fisheries.

and capitalist: how much control can the democratic state exercise over private enterprise?

There are four main reasons why it was felt neces-sary to create special regulatory agencies. All point to conditions where state intervention is needed in a market economy.

Controlling monopoly. Some of the privatized industries are near perfect examples of what is some-times called 'natural monopoly'. That is, the nature of the good supplied, and the network through which it is supplied, means that it is all but impossible for there to be competition between suppliers. The water industry is a good example. Although in principle it is possible to envisage a system of competitive supply of water, in practice no such competition exists in Britain: I have no option but to take my water from the network supplied by the privatized company that delivers water in my town. It is common ground virtually right across the political spectrum that where monopoly exists, and market competition cannot therefore control the monopolist, a potential for abuse of power exists and must be restrained by special regulation. Beyond natural monopoly there are other privatized industries where one firm is so dominant that, while there exist competitors, its weight is so great that we cannot depend on competition to restrict its power: for most of the history of the privatized telecommunications industry, for example, that has been the situation with British Telecom (BT).

Regulating franchises. In many privatized industries there is in effect a special kind of monopoly: a 'franchise' or licence granted to a firm to provide a service, usually for a fixed time period under specified conditions. This is how the train operating companies following rail privatization provide services in different regions of Britain. A franchise obviously gives special privileges to the franchisee: Virgin Rail holds the franchise to provide the west coast intercity rail link between Manchester and London, and thus has a monopoly on that line for the life of the franchise. Part of the job of regulators in the rail industry is to 'police' franchises: to award the franchise in the first place, to measure how well firms are meeting the conditions of their franchise, and to penalize them when they fail to meet service targets.

Ensuring the supply of essential services. If I take out a loan to buy a new Mercedes, find that I cannot keep up the payments, and have the car repossessed, everybody will conclude that I have been unlucky or foolish. Nobody will think that I have an entitlement to a new Mercedes. But many of the goods and services provided by the privatized industries are of a different order. They are widely perceived as essential for anyone to have a decent everyday existence in modern Britain. If I cannot pay my gas, electricity or water bills, disconnection of supply is not so obviously a solution as is repossession of my Mercedes. Apart from my own needs, how are others in my family to cook, keep warm and wash? Special rules are needed for the disconnection of these essential supplies of the sort that are not needed in repossessing luxury cars. Formulating and enforcing those special rules is an important function of a regulator. That function connects with the regulation of price, for obviously the price at which a good or service is set will affect the chances of the poorest in the community being able to meet charges.

DOCUMENTING POLITICS 7.5

Regulation on the ground: the reach of a regulatory agency

STAGECOACH/EASTBOURNE BUSES MERGER
Competition Commission invites evidence

The Office of Fair Trading (OFT) has referred the completed acquisitions of Eastbourne Buses Limited and Cavendish Motor Services Limited by Stagecoach Bus Holdings Limited to the Competition Commission (CC).

The CC has been asked to decide whether the acquisition may be expected to result in a substantial lessening of competition within any market or markets in the UK.

Prior to the acquisition, Eastbourne Buses and Cavendish Motor Services Limited provided local bus services in Eastbourne and Hailsham, while Stagecoach is one of the largest bus and coach companies in the UK, with operations in over 100 towns and cities.

The CC is expected to report by 27 October 2009.

The CC would like to hear from all interested parties, in writing, by 4 June 2009.

■ Although the privatized industries resemble conventional private sector firms in respect of ownership, their operations are very closely controlled by public regulatory bodies. This document shows just how minute is the regulatory detail: an inquiry into a merger in one small part of Sussex.

Source: http://www.competition-commission.org.uk/press_rel/2009/may/pdf/23-09.pdf.

Responding to economic crisis. In the 1980s and 1990s regulatory agencies were created to control newly privatized industries. But in the great economic crisis that began in 2007 the state was forced to move in a different direction: to take some parts of the banking industry into public ownership and to put larger parts still under public direction. A generation ago it would probably have created a nationalized corporation to run the banking industry. Now it handed over responsibility to a special regulator housed in the Treasury, UK Financial Investments (UKFI), whose purpose is to manage the

EUROPEANIZING 7.1

Europeanizing regulation: the case of competition regulation

Regulating competition is critical in a market economy, and regulating how firms do business is central to the regulation of competition. Since the UK entered the original 'Common Market' in 1973 the enforcement power of the European Commission has grown greatly. EU rules govern any activity which would disrupt competition across EU markets – which means that firms of almost any size can be affected. The Commission has proved particularly vigilant in respect of price fixing between firms; the creation of cartels (collusive relationships between firms designed to limit competition); and the creation of monopoly. The Commission's power to impose penalties is striking. In 1994 British Steel was fined £25 million for price collusion with other leading European producers; in 2009 British Telecom was fined £16.6 million because the Commission ruled that it illegally benefited from a state guarantee for its pension fund. The aggressive enforcement stance of the Commission has also encouraged more aggressive enforcement by other regulators: in 2007 British Airways was fined £270 million in a joint action by British and American competition regulators.

■ Regulating competition is a key function of the state in a market economy; and as this box makes clear, the function now has to be performed in close combination with the Commission of the EU.

government's holdings in the banking industry. The way UKFI emerged virtually overnight out of the great banking crisis of 2008 is a testimony to how far the idea of a regulatory institution as a solution to problems of economic management is now engrained in minds of those who manage the Westminster core executive.

At the back of all these reasons for creating special regulators for the privatized industries lies an important general principle: the principle of making economic power accountable. What all the particular reasons mount up to is the conclusion that in the privatized sector we have created important domains of economic power, and that democratic government has a duty to hold this power openly accountable. But of course it is not only in privatized industries that there exist important domains of economic power. Parallel to the rise of the regulatory agencies in the privatized industries there has been a wider adoption of the public regulatory agency to control economic and social life. We examine these agencies next.

GENERAL REGULATORY AGENCIES IN BRITAIN

One of the most remarkable features of government in Britain in recent decades is the rise of regulatory agencies charged with control of important domains of

economic and social life. There are four particularly important areas where we can observe the rise of the regulatory agency.

Reorganization of traditional 'inspectorates'

There is nothing new in the principle of government inspecting and controlling particular fields of social and economic activity. For instance, regulation of safety at work and regulation of the environment to control air pollution have nineteenth-century origins: the former dates back to the establishment of the Factory Inspectorate in 1833; the latter to the Alkali Inspectorate in 1863. But this was a piecemeal, fragmented system of inspection built up by a long period of gradual historical change. In recent decades we have seen these piecemeal, fragmented, state inspectorates organized into centrally coordinated agencies. Two examples are the Health and Safety Executive, which in 1974 reorganized all the nineteenth-century inspectorates concerned with health and safety at work into a single agency; and the Environment Agency, which in 1996 did the same thing for a variety of different specialized agencies concerned with the control of environmental pollution.

Transformed self-regulation

There has long been regulation of social and economic life in Britain but it has been dominated by self-regulation. Under self-regulation the state is usually a marginal influence and legal rules are rarely important.

Institutions, such as firms in markets, agree voluntarily to controls and then police their own obedience to those controls. Some of the most important areas of British life were historically governed by self-regulation: for instance, the single most important sector of the British economy, the financial markets in the City of London, was governed in this way, and self-regulation was also the manner in which sport was governed. Recent changes have dramatically altered self-regulation. Some have involved a wholesale transformation of what were once independent domains of self-regulation into domains now regulated by public agencies with statutory powers: that is the situation in the financial services industry since the establishment of the Financial Services Authority, originally backed by statutory powers in the Financial Services and Markets Act of 2000. As we shall see in a moment this domain has in recent years been subject to even more radical regulatory transformation. Some changes are less dramatic but are still significant: the founding of Sport England in 1997 meant the establishment of an important state agency to distribute substantial public funds, in a domain which traditionally was governed by pure self-regulation.

Growing regulation inside government

Regulation 'inside the state' is one of the most rapidly growing areas of regulatory activity. This is partly due to a trend which we noticed in our description of the new executive agencies: the trend towards setting targets, monitoring performance and imposing sanctions when targets are not met.

Regulating new social domains

The regulatory agency is now established as a standard response by government in Britain to the problem of controlling economic and social life. This means that when new social problems appear, or when innovation creates new social activities, it is almost instinctive to create a regulatory agency to exercise control. Three important recent examples illustrate this process.

First, the Food Standards Agency was created in 2000 as a result of a series of scandals in food safety, especially the discovery that the disastrous disease BSE had infected large parts of the national cattle herd in Britain. Although there had been hitherto some regulation of food standards, the establishment of the Agency represented a step change in the control of safety standards in agriculture, in food processing and in food retailing.

Second, the establishment of OFLOT (Office of the National Lottery) in 1993 showed another important development: new social and economic activities – in this case the establishment for the first time of a national

lottery in Britain – can now expect to be subject to specialized regulatory control. The case of OFLOT also shows how operational problems can reshape agencies: after a history of ineffectiveness OFLOT was replaced as regulator by the National Lottery Commission in 1999.

Third, the establishment of the Human Fertilisation and Embryology Authority in 1991 marks the extension of the agency idea to another important social arena: the control of scientific research and the application of that research. The Authority is concerned with regulating the conditions under which women can benefit from the new technologies of artificial reproduction. But the importance of the Authority goes beyond this particular field, important though it is to those who seek IVF (*in vitro* fertilization): it establishes the principle that scientific technologies, and especially new technologies, can only be applied when they are subject to public controls through a regulatory institution.

EXPLAINING THE RISE OF REGULATORY AGENCIES

The rise of the new regulatory agencies marks an important long-term change in the way the state operates in Britain. The change has two particularly important features. In part it signifies a retreat by the state. For about the first three-quarters of the twentieth century the state relied on steadily growing public ownership to give it control over social and economic life. That was reversed in the privatization programmes of the 1980s and 1990s. But in part it signifies an advance by the state: some domains that governed themselves by self-regulation no longer enjoy that independence, and some entirely new domains of regulation have been created. And indeed, as we saw above, even the onward march of privatization was reversed in the state takeovers of the banking industry after 2007. Many particular factors explain these transformations, but three general forces can be identified.

Crisis and scandal

Some key creations in the world of agencies have been the result of large scale breakdowns of traditional control, and these breakdowns have led to public scandal and crisis. Two of most important agencies created in recent years, the Food Standards Agency and the Financial Services Authority (FSA), owe their existence in part to these forces. The Food Standards Agency was the direct result of a great crisis of public confidence in the safety of the food we eat arising from a run of failures. These culminated in the great BSE crisis of the mid-1990s, when a public inquiry established that there

TABLE 7.1 The rise of regulation inside government

Public-sector regulation, 1976 compared with 1995

Regulators	No. of bodies, 1995 (and % change since 1976)	Estimated staffing increase 1976–95	Estimated increase in real terms spending 1976–95
Public audit bodies	4 (same)	+60%	+130%
Inspectorates and equivalents	27 (+17%)	+75%	+100%
Ombudsmen and equivalents	17 (+78%)	+150%	+200%
Central agency regulators	18 (+38%)	same	same
Funder-cum-regulators	14 (+133%)	+10%	+100%
Departmental regulators of agencies	26 (–10%)	n.a.	n.a.
Central regulators of local public bodies and the NHS	29 (+11%)	n.a.	n.a.
All regulators in government	135 (+22%)	+60%	+106%

■ This material is extracted from the standard study of 'regulation inside government', by Hood and his colleagues (1999). Their work paints a picture of long-term growth in the scale and intensity of regulation right across the public sector. The material here is a snapshot, and emphasizes the diversity of regulatory forms, the diversity of institutions covered, and the diverse ways regulation of public bodies is funded.

Source: Extracted and adapted from Hood et al. (1999: 30).

had been a total breakdown of safety regulation in farming, the spread of the disease BSE throughout the national cattle herd, the entry into the human food chain of diseased meat, and the possible infection of humans by a fatal, incurable disease. The FSA was created in 1997 after a series of scandals and collapses in the banking system. In turn it was dismembered and its powers largely transferred to the Bank of England after the failures revealed by the great financial crisis of 2007–08 (see Image 7.1).

The EU

The traditional British system of self-regulation put the law at the margins. But with Britain's increasing integration in the EU a very different regulatory culture was encountered: in both the Union itself, and in the most important members like Germany and France, law has been much more important in the regulation of social and economic life. As we saw in Chapter 5 the Union itself is a legal creation – through the treaties that marked its foundation and extension – and it is natural that it should therefore work through law; and as we also saw the ECJ, and the interpretations it delivers, are important to the way public power works. An important consequence for Britain, therefore, is that traditionally non-legal systems of self-regulation

have often had to be recast in legal language. This was a subsidiary reason for the reorganization of self-regulation in the financial markets, and it has been important in reshaping self-regulation in another important area, the regulation of professions like medicine, the law and accounting.

Power and democracy

The theory of British democracy pictures the state as an institution concerned with the control of private power, such as great private economic power. The retreat of the state from many fields of economic intervention in recent decades – a retreat most obvious in the privatization of public enterprise – raised an obvious question: how was public control now to be exercised? The regulatory agency has emerged as one answer to that question. How adequate an answer it amounts to I will now examine.

THE NEW REGULATORY STATE: ACHIEVEMENTS AND PROBLEMS

The developments described in this chapter summarize a great transformation that has come over the Westminster model of British government in the last two

POLITICAL ISSUES 7.1

A new era of privatization? The Private Finance Initiative

The Private Finance Initiative (PFI) originated in a scheme introduced by the Conservative predecessor to New Labour and, after denouncing it in Opposition, Labour in office fine tuned the scheme and adopted it enthusiastically. The PFI is basically a mixture of franchising and hire purchase. Traditionally, large public investments like hospitals and schools were paid for 'up front' from taxes. Under PFI, private consortiums contract to design, build and manage projects over periods as long as 30 years. The cash for the project is raised on the financial markets and is repaid with interest over the life of the project: hence the 'hire purchase' element. The consortium also collects fees for managing the project – hence the 'franchising' element. The initiative has been used by the Government to create a new generation of public sector projects even in such traditionally 'non-commercial' areas as schools and hospitals. But the adoption of a scheme originally created by the Conservatives has bitterly divided the Labour Movement, raising four key issues:

■ The conditions of workers. Critics in the Labour Party and the trade unions assert that profits are made by worsening the pay and conditions of those employed, by comparison with traditional pay and conditions in the public sector.

■ The economics of the projects. Although there are standard tests designed to ensure that the only projects funded are those that could not be funded more cheaply with traditional public financing, these tests are inevitably uncertain. This raises the common complaint that PFI is simply a more expensive way of funding public projects.

■ The limits to public sector efficiency. One reason trade union opposition is so intense is precisely because PFI is being used to circumvent working practices in the public sector which stand in the way of the efficient use of labour and facilities.

■ The limits of private investor support. After the 2007 financial crisis private investors became wary of commitments: in 2009 the Treasury was obliged to 'bail out' PFI schemes in waste management at a cost of over £120 million.

decades. Two key components of that model have been fundamentally changed:

● the civil service department, while remaining important, is no longer the kingpin for policy delivery;
● publicly owned industries *managed by nationalized corporations* are no longer important as a means of controlling economic life.

The changes amount to the rise of a new 'regulatory state' which is marked by three features:

● the new executive agencies are in essence contracted to deliver policy and are regulated to measure how effectively they manage delivery;
● the new privatized sector is subject to a network of specialized regulatory agencies;

● government has turned to the specialized regulatory agency to control large areas of economic and social life.

The achievements of this new regulatory state are considerable. From the point of view of the functioning of democratic government in Britain two are particularly valuable.

Transparency

The most obvious feature of the new regulatory arrangements is that they oblige increasing openness and explicitness in the way institutions are run and in how they deal with each other. This is illustrated by the way the relationship between the new executive agencies and departments is formally described in the founding 'framework document'; by the way the powers of priva-

DEBATING POLITICS 7.1

Target setting in the new regulatory state: improving or damaging democracy?

TARGET SETTING AIDS DEMOCRATIC GOVERNMENT	TARGET SETTING DAMAGES DEMOCRATIC GOVERNMENT
▶ Targets set measurable standards by which government agencies can be judged.	▶ Targets involve crude measurements which fail to capture the subtlety of social life.
▶ Targets provide standards against which public servants can be held accountable.	▶ Targets lead to 'top down' control by managers, making government excessively hierarchical.
▶ Targets make open and transparent what would otherwise not be publicly debated.	▶ Pressure to 'hit' targets encourages public servants to manipulate indicators.
▶ Performance targets are widely and successfully used in business – so why not in government?	▶ Business can use profits – the bottom line – as an authoritative target.

tized regulators are laid down in law and the obligations of regulated industries are made explicit; and by the way the new regulatory agencies like the Food Standards Agency both have their powers explicitly stated and are obliged publicly to report their proceedings and decisions. All this marks a great advance, because it strengthens a value which is central to democratic decision making: the value of transparency. It is now much easier to find out how decisions are made in the new regulatory state than under the system that preceded it; and knowing who is making decisions, and how they are being made, is a first condition for the exercise of democratic control.

A focus on performance

We have seen that the rise of the new world of regulation was accompanied by a parallel movement: an increasing emphasis on target setting and the measurement of how far targets have been achieved through measurable performance indicators. There is room for argument about the practical effect of many of these changes. It is obviously not certain, for instance, that just renaming an agency's 'clients' its 'customers' will produce more responsive service delivery. There are many examples of performance targets being manipulated (and even fraudulently falsified) both by managers in agencies and by political leaders. But the rise of target setting marks an important set of cultural changes in governing institutions. It places into the open important questions about the purpose of those institutions and creates a contin-

uing debate about whether those purposes are being realized in practice.

To set against this, the rise of the new regulatory state has created serious problems. We highlight two here.

Accountability

Much of the advance in transparency outlined above is formal in nature: that is, much more is now spelt out in documents about the powers, duties and relationships of regulators and the regulated. But that is not the same as the practical exercise of accountability and control. The creation of the executive agencies and regulatory agencies greatly increases the range and complexity of 'quasi-government' in Britain: that is, of institutions that have an ambiguous relationship with the state. This ambiguity can have serious consequences for public accountability. For example, it is recognized that traditional forms of parliamentary accountability that could be exercised over civil service departments and nationalized industries were often ineffective. But nevertheless, doctrines of accountability and responsibility did usually oblige Ministers to, for example, give an account of activities in which their departments were involved. It has been an avowed purpose of the creation of executive and regulatory agencies to 'hive off' these activities, and the result has been to make it much more difficult than hitherto to exercise parliamentary control. This is made more difficult still by the ambiguous legal status of many of the new bodies. The FSA supplies a good example. It exercised great public powers derived from the law, notably from the authority given it in the Financial Services and Markets Act of 2000. But it was not actually a public body: it was a company limited by guarantee, and it was funded by a levy on firms in the financial services industry. It is now widely accepted – even by those who ran the Authority – that this made it too accommodating to financial interests and was one of the causes of the regulatory failures that led to the financial crisis from 2007. In other words the impressive public powers of regulation in financial markets were wielded by an institution which was 'owned' by the private interests that it was designed to regulate. But the FSA only illustrates a wide pattern in Westminster government identified by Flinders (2008): the value placed on 'arms length' administration, in which administrative agencies keep at 'arms length' the democratic state.

Effectiveness

We have noted that a culture stressing the importance of effective performance is embedded in the agencies created by the new regulatory state. But how far that culture actually delivers more effective services is a separate matter. Whether we think the new regulatory state more effective than what preceded it will depend in part on our values. Those values will, for instance, help to determine whether we think regulated privatized

water companies deliver better services than the old publicly owned water authorities. In some cases the agencies have simply not been operating for sufficient time to allow us to make a realistic judgement: we do not really know even now, for instance, whether the Food Standards Agency is an improvement on what went before. The impact of food regulation on health can probably only be judged over a span of decades. But some parts of the new regulatory state have ruled over what everyone agrees is a shambolic state of affairs: most people would not contest such a judgement, for example, about the regulation of the financial services industry under the FSA between 1997 and 2007.

But a more fundamental difficulty influencing effectiveness than problems in particular sectors is the danger of 'regulatory capture'. The new regulatory state deliberately sets up relationships between regulators and regulated which are close, involving daily contact. As we saw above, in the case of the FSA the regulated actually 'owned' the regulator. There is an obvious danger in this, a danger often observed in the case of the US, from which much of the theory of the new regulatory state has been borrowed: that the regulator will grow so like the regulated that the two will simply share common interests and a common view of the world, and the independence so vital to the new regulatory agencies will be undermined.

Review OF CHAPTER 7

Four themes have dominated this chapter:

◖◗ The decline of a model of state control in which the department located in Whitehall was the central institution.

◖◗ The rise of a system of rule in which institutions 'contract' much more explicitly than in the past to deliver public services.

◖◗ The passing away of public ownership as a means of public economic control and the rise of the regulatory agency as an alternative.

◖◗ The spread of the regulatory agency model beyond the privatized sector and its rise as the characteristic institution of the new regulatory state in Britain.

FURTHER READING

ESSENTIAL

If you read only one book it should be Flinders (2008) which analyses every possible dimension of delegation in British government.

RECOMMENDED

Moran (2007) is a study of the 'regulatory state' in Britain. Hood et al. (1999) study the reorganization of inspectorates and regulators. Rhodes (1997) studies the impact of the new governance theories on the structure of government. Skelcher (1998), though now a little dated, is an exceptionally important study of quasi-government and British democracy. There are useful overview pieces on the subjects covered in this chapter by Flinders, by Moran and by James in Flinders et al. (2009).

CHAPTER 8

Representing interests in the Westminster system

CONTENTS

AIMS

This chapter:

- ☐ Describes why interest representation is of growing importance

- ☐ Distinguishes the most important forms of interest groups

- ☐ Explains what determines interest group influence in government

- ☐ Sketches some of the most important ways the world of interest representation is changing

THE RISING IMPORTANCE OF INTEREST REPRESENTATION

No government makes policy in a vacuum. One of the most important influences over what governments do comes from the wider interests in society. That is true even of the most dictatorial of governments and is truer still of governments that, like Britain's, have to function within the rules of democratic politics. These elementary points help to explain the central part played by the representation of interests in British politics.

The importance of interest representation long pre-dates the rise of democracy. Even the most traditional political institutions reflect this fact: thus the historical division of Parliament into Lords and Commons, which we discuss in the next chapter, was intended to reflect a wider social and economic division between great aristo-cratic landed interests and other forms of property.

There is thus nothing new about interest representation in politics. Its development in modern British politics has, however, been marked by four distinctive features.

Growing complexity of economic interests

'Interests' to an important extent mean economic interests. Historically, they referred overwhelmingly to particular forms of property, especially ownership of land. But the rise of a modern economy has greatly diversified the forms of material interests. Land ownership has been supplanted by more important forms of ownership, in industry and commerce, and by the great range of interests contained in the modern workforce – managers, the professions, industrial manual workers.

Growing range of campaigning groups

'Interests' always meant something more than material interests. Were we to describe interest representation in British politics in the nineteenth century, for example, our account would have to go well beyond material interests. The first half of the century was marked by a large number of campaigns – such as those against slavery – which united people who shared intensely held beliefs. Just as the complexity of a modern economy has multi-plied the range of economic interests, so the complexity and diversity of modern society has widened the range of groups mobilizing to campaign for different, intensely held preferences about moral questions. This will be an important theme later in the chapter.

Growing formal organization

Groups come in all shapes and sizes – from the biggest and more formally organized institutions, like churches or big business corporations (see Image 8.1) to those

IMAGES 8.1 and 8.2 ■ **The interest groups around the corner**

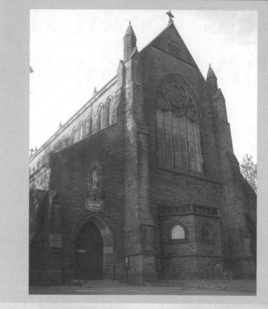

Photos: Michael Moran

■ We stressed in Chapter 1 a key feature of modern political life: that overt participation in politics is a minority interest. This gives the institutions that are the subject of this chapter a unique importance, because what we usually call interest groups are a key means of linking the state to civil society, and a key means by which millions of us, even if we do not realize it, make a contribution to the process of government. The two images make the point. They are both branches of multina-tionals: the church is Catholic, the bank originates in Hong Kong; they both have numerous 'branches' world wide. The Church lobbies constantly on policies to do with areas like education, overseas aid and public morals; the bank on a wide range of issues to do with economic policy.

that spontaneously spring up from public demonstrations. But over the long term there has been an increasing tendency for groups formally to organize, if only because the scale and diversity of modern society is marked by big, formal, social organization.

Growing involvement with government

One of the important reasons for the growth of formal organization is that groups have become more and more important to the process of government. Although the extent to which the state is willing to share control of policy with particular interests waxes and wanes, the complexity of modern government, and the need to rule by consent, means that governments rely to a huge extent on what groups tell them by way of specialized information and advice, and what groups tell their own supporters about the decisions made by government.

Interest representation in modern government, viewed in the historical long term, therefore means something more than the commonsense proposition that groups beyond the formal organization of the state are important in the governing process. It means that, in modern government, organized groups, sharing either economic interests or common moral preferences about issues, are deeply involved in the whole business of making policy and are correspondingly important in putting it into effect.

THE VARIETIES OF GROUPS

Groups span churches, professions, unions, corporations, sports clubs, so it is obvious that they are huge in number and wide in diversity. It is also obvious that we could systematically classify these groups in a whole variety of different ways. Indeed the simple language used above already classifies them just by the way they identify themselves. But it is plain that no one form of classification is definitive. We can see this by a single thought experiment of our own. How might we classify ourselves? The answer is clear: it depends on the purpose of the classification. For sporting identification someone might be an Irish, not an English, football fan; for musical purposes an opera lover and a ballet hater; for the purposes of the tax inspector, an employee rather than self-employed.

The fact that purpose determines classification explains the single most important way of classifying interest groups. 'Interest' is a word with two different meanings: it commonly refers to a material interest (the interests of firefighters or students); or it can more widely mean a preference in the sense of a taste or belief (a shared interest in soccer or opera). The commonest

IMAGE 8.3 ■ The giant firm as an organised interest

Photo: Michael Moran

■ There could hardly be anything more everyday than this image. Tesco is Britain's largest and most successful supermarket chain, and a store such as this can be found in virtually any town of any size in Britain, and increasingly in cities across the world. Yet every time we shop here, we encounter a formidable political organization. Tesco is entirely typical in having a huge range of interests to defend, and in organizing to defend them. Some of the most immediately obvious are:

- Interests in tax law, to protect both corporate profits and the incomes of senior executives.
- Interests in company law: when the photo was taken Tesco, like other large firms, was resisting changes in company law that would have reformed the rules governing the pay of senior executives which would have forced greater disclosure and more consultation with shareholders.
- Interests in farm policy: like other large supermarkets Tesco is accused by farming interests of not passing on reductions in farm gate prices.
- Interests in competition policy: Tesco and other big supermarkets have had constantly to defend themselves against official investigations on charges of uncompetitive price fixing.
- Interests in land use planning policy: supermarkets like the one pictured here occupy a large amount of space, and any new supermarket usually involves an acrimonious planning argument. In the case of the example pictured here Tesco circumvented the problem by buying an existing store from a rival chain.
- Interests in food safety policy: big supermarkets like Tesco are the key organizations in 'delivering' food safety regulation under Britain's food safety laws.
- Interests in employment policy: supermarkets are large employers of labour, especially part-time labour, and they have a keen interest in issues like minimum wage legislation.

division of groups separates them in this way: into groups that band together people who believe they share a common economic interest because of the functions they perform in the economy; and groups that join people who believe they share common preferences, whether these are profound – religious belief – or trivial, such as an interest in a sport.

Many different terms have been employed to try to catch this divide: interest/promotional groups; interest/cause groups. In this chapter we will express the distinction as one between *functional* and *preference* groups.

Functional groups

These arise out of a feature central to any modern economy, the division of labour. We can see this most obviously in the range of groups that represent professionals and other workers, but it is also central to the wide range of important groups that cater for different parts of business – whether they be the British Bankers Association or the Chemical Industries Association. All these groups reflect the occupational and industrial specialization by which our economy operates. Membership of groups might consist of individuals: doctors make up the membership of the British Medical Association. It might consist of organizations: the membership of the Chemical Industries Association consists of firms in the industry. All these groups are vital not just to the economy but to the governing process, precisely because they are the expression of the division of labour. They create and deliver goods and services. No government expects effectively to govern without at least some measure of their cooperation. But as we will see shortly, for many groups this importance goes well beyond cooperation with government; their active participation is a necessary condition of effective policy making. The language of 'function' expresses this importance: these groups represent people and institutions that perform functions vital to social and economic life.

Preference

These groups are created when people or organizations believe they are united by some set of common preferences. Two features of these groups are immediately obvious: they cut across the functional groups created by the division of labour, and unlike functional groups their range is potentially infinite. They cut across functional groups because they unite people with different functional interests: churches, for instance, contain both employers and workers. And while the range and variety of functional groups is wide, limits are set by the division of labour in the economy. By contrast, the perceived preferences that we share with others are only bounded by our imagination and the way we want to combine. We might be linked with others because of sexual preferences, a common link in recent decades expressed, for example, by the foundation of gay rights groups like Stonewall. We can be linked by religious preference – and the rise of immigration into Britain has widened the potential range beyond the Christian denominations that traditionally dominated religious preferences. And we can be linked by combinations of these preferences: gays and Christians have united, for example, in a variety of gay Christian groups.

This distinction between groups that spring from the division of labour and groups that spring from shared preferences is very helpful in ordering the complex multitudes of the group worlds. But we should not imagine that groups are sealed off into the two worlds of the functional and the preference. Functional groups often develop philosophies which unite their members: professions like doctors have elaborate ethical codes; many trade unions have been shaped by socialism or by more general ideas about fraternity. Conversely, many preference groups also have a functional life. Churches are not just groups of people sharing the same religion. They are also often large property owners, sharing interests with other property owners; and they are often large employers, sharing interests with other employers. Some of the most important examples of groups that straddle the divide are provided by those that unite people who have the shared experience of being *clients* or *customers* of functional groups. For example, suffering a long-term chronic disease or disablement often powerfully unites groups: we have in recent decades seen the rise of groups representing categories of patients (for example those suffering chronic diseases like multiple sclerosis) and groups representing those who are united by the experience of what is conventionally viewed as physical disablement.

THE MAIN FORMS OF FUNCTIONAL REPRESENTATION

The division of labour in a modern economy is complex so the range of organized functional interests is also wide and complex. But the main lines of division in Britain are nevertheless not hard to identify.

Capital

Britain's is a market economy. This means that private ownership of property is central to economic life. In particular, economic life is concentrated in a comparatively small number of big enterprises. Many of the household names that supply the goods and services that

DOCUMENTING POLITICS 8.1

A peak association as an organized interest under multilevel governance

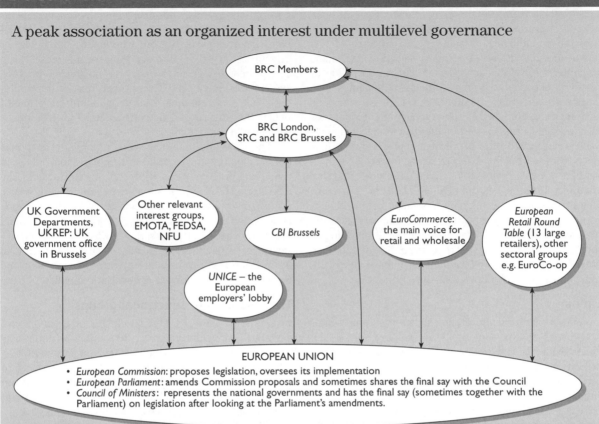

■ Peak associations developed a central role in interest representation because they offered great economies of scale and because they could claim to speak for a wide range of interests. The British Retail Consortium is a key peak association because it speaks for one of the most dynamic parts of the British economy – and of course represents firms that are part of the daily lives of us all. This figure, reproduced from the BRC website, perfectly sums up the complex institutional world in which an important peak association has to operate. It is obliged to organize at three different levels of government: BRC London works with SRC, its Scottish sister organization, whose importance derives from the devolution reforms discussed in Chapter 10; and with BRC Brussels, the Consortium's EU permanent lobbying operation. Note too how the web spins out from Brussels: back to Britain to the central departments in Westminster; to other interest groups, like farmers (the NFU); to other employer/business peak associations, such as the Confederation of British Industry (CBI Brussels); to a Europe-wide lobby for retailing (Eurocommerce); and to the European Retail Round Table, a separate organization for the biggest retailers in Europe.

Source: www.brc.org.uk.

we consume are giant multinational firms. You will almost certainly do your food shopping at the branch of the giant multinational supermarket chain pictured in Image 8.3 or at one of its few giant competitors. This book is being written with hardware (a PC) produced by a Japanese multinational (Toshiba) using software produced by an American giant (Microsoft Corporation).

These institutions are central to economic life; and to political life.

Their organized presence takes a variety of forms. Capital is organized in Britain in a number of so called 'peak organizations', like the Confederation of British Industry. In effect these are specialized lobbying organizations that exist to do little more than try to speak for business as a whole. But just as important are the 'peak' organizations that speak for particular industries and sectors. This is indeed the characteristic form of business organization, usually organized into a trade association for an industry or sector. Any industry of any importance has at least one trade association. As a single example: the Retail Consortium is vital in speaking for retailers, especially the big ones like the giant supermarket chains that dominate our high streets (see Documenting Politics 8.1). The domination of industries by a few giant firms has also made the individual big firm itself a vital institution of interest representation. It is easy to see why. In many economic sectors, only a handful of firms really matter. The structure of a retail giant like Tesco makes the task of organizing to present views to government much more straightforward than if coordination is necessary with other groups of firms. The biggest firms also have the resources – most obviously the money – to organize for this purpose. Any giant firm nowadays will therefore have a department that specializes in putting the firm's views to government.

Labour

Labour's organized importance in interest representation comes in two, sometimes overlapping, forms. The most visible is the organization of labour into trade unions, most of which are in turn affiliated to labour's own specialist lobbying 'peak' organization, the Trades Union Congress. For over a century unions, while they have risen and fallen in numbers of members and influence over government, have been an exceptionally important medium of interest representation for labour.

But overlapping with unions is a second critical set of institutions: that representing the interests of professions in British society. Professionals like doctors and lawyers resemble any other group of workers in the sense that they make a living by selling their labour. But professions are different in the way they function in the labour market, in the way they are internally organized and in their capacity to exercise influence. They are different in the labour market because the most successful professions, like doctors and lawyers, exercise a large amount of influence over entry into the occupation: one of the marks of a profession is the control exercised through qualifying examinations or by control of entry to the courses which prepare candidates for qualifying examinations. This is the key difference between, say, doctors and window cleaners: the labour market for the latter we can all freely enter if we have a ladder and a bucket of water. Professions are also distinctive in their internal organization, because they usually have their own governing institutions, setting standards of behaviour and establishing the profession's

identity, both internally and externally. And professions are different in the way they exercise influence in government precisely because so much of modern political and economic life is professionalized. If we look at big organizations in Britain, whether in the public or private sector, we will find that they are substantially run by groups of professionals: for instance, lawyers, accountants, engineers. Thus professions exercise influence not just by openly arguing about government policy; they are part of the very process by which policy is made and put into effect.

The divisions identified here are handy analytical distinctions but they should not be used too rigidly. In the real world people are not so neatly divided. The managers of big firms are more often than not also professionals, as we have noted. Nevertheless, one reason for creating the whole category of functional groups is that it identifies those with very distinctive resources – and these resources often make them vital both to interest representation within government and to the making and delivery of government policy.

The resources of functional groups

Imagine you were a Cabinet minister or a senior civil servant. Why would you ever take notice of functional groups? The answer is simple: if you systematically ignored them you would never get far in making or putting into effect public policy. The most important reason for this state of affairs is that these groups have at their disposal vital resources. Four are especially important: their place in the working of the economy; organization; expertise; and money.

Economic role. We call these groups functional precisely because they are central to the division of labour, the most important feature in a modern economy. Unless firms, workers and professionals do their job, the modern economy does not function. This gives functional groups a presumptive right to a say in making policy: that is why, for instance, no government would ever introduce a big reform of business taxation without consulting widely with firms. But economic role is the source of a deeper importance. The way firms and workers go about their daily business shapes the success or failure of government: in the end, the fate of economic policy depends on firms investing and utilizing capital, and on workers producing goods and services. Suppose, for instance, that government wishes to change tax policy so as to increase the level of investment by firms in the economy. It cannot compel firms to invest more; it can only create the circumstances that induce them to do so. For this reason it would be foolish to frame changes in tax policy without close consultation with the industries where it is hoped to promote more investment.

BRIEFING 8.1

The resources of one powerful functional group: the case of the British Medical Association

The British Medical Association is one of the best documented of powerful functional groups. Its 'functional' importance derives from the fact that its members are vital to the delivery of a key public service: health care. We have probably all encountered a member of the BMA, when visiting our local general practitioner or if we have been unfortunate enough to be in hospital.

- the Association has 140,000 members, covering 80 per cent of all UK practising doctors;
- it is simultaneously a trade union for doctors, a major publisher (the *British Medical Journal* is both an important scientific weekly and a leading journal of medical opinion) and a scientific and educational body;
- its annual income at the most recent count (2008) exceeded £87 million;
- it runs its own Parliamentary Affairs team in London (and separate teams in Scotland, Wales and Northern Ireland) providing briefing material for politicians, advising members on how to lobby public officials and coordinating BMA activities with parliamentary committees.

■ The British Medical Association is one of a family of powerful functional groups. As the details above show, this is in part because it has considerable 'muscle' – resources of money and people. But it is also because the modern state in Britain relies very heavily on professionals, like doctors, to put policies into effect: imagine the National Health Service without the cooperation of doctors.

Source: To read more about the BMA as a powerful functional group see www.bma.org.uk.

Organization. Every major functional interest is organized, whether that organization be the Trades Union Congress for union members, the Retail Consortium for big retailers, or Tesco for a single giant firm. This kind of organization is one of the keys to success in shaping policy in modern government. Organization brings a continuous presence: a perpetual nagging away at issues; a build-up of expertise about issues; a permanent capacity to argue a public position; and a place in stable networks of contacts both with government and with other functional interests.

Expertise. Organization allows expertise to be assembled and used. One of the great strengths of functional groups is that they are natural repositories of expertise, by virtue of their position in the division of labour. Governing Britain is, among other things, a highly complex business; doing it properly demands a command of great technical detail. Sometimes government itself is on top of this detail; more often than not it has to rely on functional groups. We can see this immediately if we think about some of the tasks of government. Imagine trying to do such things as devising safety standards for the pharmaceutical drugs that can be sold to

patients, the safety standards for the construction of offices, or the standards for the prudent conduct of banking business. All three involve dealing with immensely complex technical detail; and in all three cases the best informed groups are, respectively, pharmaceutical firms, architects and bankers themselves. Of course we immediately see here the dangers created: the affected interests will give advice that fits their own interests, as the bankers consistently did in the workings of regulation before the great crash from 2007.

Money. Not all functional groups are rich, but many are; we only have to think of the resources of the biggest firms to realize that. Using lots of cash is no guarantee of success in lobbying, but it helps. Money brings some obvious advantages. Organization, which we have already identified as an important independent resource, is much easier if money is available. Rich organizations can hire the best experts to consolidate their position as centres of expertise. Big firms operating in the City of London, for instance, are some of the most authoritative commentators on the British economy simply because they have the money to pay salaries commanding the full-time service of top economists. Later in this chapter we will see the rising importance of professional lobby-ists in Britain – hired guns who will lobby for any interest prepared to pay them. Usually these hired guns do not come cheap. Money can also bring some ancillary advantages. Most of the really successful functional interests in Britain have their headquarters located in central London, for an obvious reason: it is where a great deal of the policy action is located. Office premises in central London do not come cheap; nor are they cheap in Edinburgh or Cardiff, close to the devolved administrations.

Functional interests and the governing process

Enough has already been said in the last section to suggest that functional interests are absolutely central to the governing process in Britain. Indeed, this is the single most important point about this part of the world of interest representation. The great functional interests – the biggest firms, the key professions – are not just important interests trying to influence government from outside, though they may sometimes do that; they are integral to the whole process of making and putting policy into effect. This is perhaps the single most important change that has come over British government in the last century or so. If we had looked at British government in 1900 we would have found numerous important functional interests, but they were mostly organized lobbies trying to influence government from the outside. In the course of the century this changed: the greatest functional interests on the sides of capital and labour were integrated into the governing machine. They became de facto governing institutions: consulted at every turn; entitled to places on government advisory committees; and even entitled to places on public bodies concerned with the implementation of such policies as the regulation of health and safety at work, or the regulation of environmental pollution.

This connection to the governing process has, certainly, varied in strength at different moments. It was especially close at moments of great national crisis, notably in the two world wars of the twentieth century. It was also very close during the two decades after 1960, when governments of all parties usually accepted a doctrine of 'tripartism': a doctrine that the economy should be managed in a partnership between government, business and labour. It was probably least close in the last two decades of the century, during the period of Conservative rule that began with Mrs Thatcher's election victory of 1979. The Conservatives were particularly determined to push the trade unions outside the governing machine, but they also showed less interest than their predecessors in sharing policy making with

'peak' business organizations like the Confederation of British Industry and with the professions. But much of this rejection was at the 'headline' level. In the daily routines of government – the area where the functional groups have usually exercised most influence – groups remained, for all the short term ups and downs, partners in the governing process.

The reasons for this enduring presence as governing institutions arise from the hard facts about the resources of groups that we sketched above. Functional groups need government; but government needs the groups even more. Above all, groups can perform three vital services for government.

Provide advice and hard information. Almost all policy made by government in Britain – or in any other advanced industrial country for that matter – involves judgements about highly specialized matters. In many cases, this specialization is highly technical: consider the kinds of issues involved in making policy concerning health and safety in the construction industry, or the standards governing emissions of pollutants from chemical plants. The most important functional interests – big firms, trade associations, trade unions, professional institutions – are the obvious sources of specialized advice and hard data. Governments sometimes make policy without consulting the affected groups, but they usually regret the omission. Hence, the business of policy formulation involves a continuous exchange with functional interests as government tries to winkle out this advice and information.

Offer cooperation. Passing laws is one thing; actually doing the surveillance and enforcement to ensure compliance is another. Government often has few resources to put policies into effect. The life of government is made much easier if important functional groups recommend cooperation with policies. But cooperation often goes further than just commending a policy. In the case of professions, for instance, the actual job of implementing is very often delegated to the professional organizations. In the case of health care professions – the most notable examples are doctors, dentists and nurses – there are national councils (such as the General Medical Council for doctors) which are responsible for such matters as prescribing and putting into effect standards of professional education and proper conduct, under authority delegated to them by the state. This is a world of government which rarely gets onto the front page or into the battle between the front benches in Parliament – but it is part of the important everyday reality of government, and the functional interests are full scale partners in that reality.

Provide legitimacy. Legitimacy, we can recall from Chapter 1, is a vital condition of effective government.

EUROPEANIZING 8.1

Europeanizing interest representation: the case of the business lobby

We now have more than two decades' experience of the evolution of lobbying in the EU since the passage of the original legislation to complete the single market (1986) – and this legislation is agreed to have stimulated a lobbying boom in Brussels. Coen's work (1997, 1998, 1999, 2002, 2007a, 2007b) allows us to chart the development of a changing, and distinctive, lobbying system. The picture encompasses more than lobbying by business, though this is the most numerous, the best organized and the best resourced of the lobbying interests, especially in Brussels. Present estimates suggest that about 20,000 lobbyists operate in the city alone. There are over 1,400 formally organized interest groups and over 260 law firms and public affairs firms. The biggest change over time in the case of the EU is, simply, growth in scale: there was an 'explosion' (Coen's word, 2007b) in numbers in the 1990s. A second change over time is the widening range of institutions and arenas that are targeted by business lobbyists. When Coen surveyed the lobbying community in the mid-1990s he found that the Commission was the main target. But when he replicated his survey a decade later he found that, while the Commission was still the most important object of lobbying attention, there was a much wider spread of activity including, for instance, the EP.

■ In the last 25 years the rising importance of the EU as a source of decisions affecting British business has opened up a whole new world of lobbying.

Legitimate authority means that those subject to laws and institutions obey because they believe government has a right to claim obedience. If policies are not seen as legitimate, the policies are likely to fail. The extent to which citizens can be made to obey policy by force, or the threat of force, is very limited. Governments claim legitimacy by many means. One of the most important general foundations for the claim invokes the rules of democratic politics: government has the right to govern because it won that right fair and square in a free election. But the legitimacy that comes from democratic elections is itself restricted: in Britain it is almost unheard of for a government to win a clear majority of the popular vote. Labour recorded large majorities in the House of Commons in the general elections of 1997, 2001 and 2005 without ever getting close to a majority of the popular vote. The Conservative Government that introduced the 'Poll Tax' – a new form of local taxation – in the late 1980s had a huge majority in the House of Commons; the tax had to be abandoned because it produced large scale civil disobedience from those who refused to accept its legitimacy.

The rise of the great functional interests in the twentieth century was a recognition that there were limits to the legitimacy that could be gained by winning elections on votes of individual citizens organized in territorial constituencies. When policies are made in consultation with affected groups – still better if they are put into effect by those groups, as in the example of the professions given above – then the claim by government to legitimate authority is greatly strengthened. But the flow of legitimacy is not one way. There is an exchange of legitimacy between groups and government, and this helps to explain why groups so often cooperate. Being consulted, and still better being designated by government as the authority with responsibility for a policy, transforms what would just be a sectional interest into an institution with a responsibility for safeguarding the public interest: the group can see itself, and be seen, as a governing institution.

Of course things do not always run smoothly. The price of advice, cooperation and legitimacy is giving groups a share in deciding the content of policy. Often governments decide that this price is too high and make policy in defiance of functional interests. When and why this sort of exclusion happens we will examine in the next section.

The powerful and the excluded in the functional world

The world of functional representation is an unequal world. How far groups get into a position where they are accepted as natural partners in the policy-making process is determined by their resources and the skill with which they use those resources. In the case of really important groups they more often than not do not even have to shout to be heard. When government makes policy about the taxation rules to be applied to the profits of oil exploration in the North Sea, for example, it will more or less automatically consult the big oil companies; and if by some oversight it fails to do so, the companies have battalions of tax lawyers, accountants and professional lobbyists to make their views clear. The chief executives of the oil companies will never have to march in the rain behind banners denouncing the government. The same point can be made about a second important set of functional groups, the most leading professions. Indeed in the case of professions the advantage is even more marked because, as we have seen, the point about professional organization is that much of the business of governing is actually delegated to the professional organization itself.

This is not to say that big business and the most important professions automatically get their way in policy making – in a moment we will see some important mechanisms that compensate for their influence. But if the effort to influence policy by groups is like a race, then these functional groups always have a flying start; everyone else has to try extra hard to catch up.

The most powerful functional groups are identified by their wealth, expertise and efficient organization; the weakest are those that strikingly lack these attributes. Being badly organized, or not organized at all, not only contributes to weakness; it also usually tells us that such groups lack other attributes, like economic resources. The obvious way employees can try to influence government is through organizing in trade unions. But only about one-sixth of private sector workers are in unions, and even that figure is down from around a quarter in the early 1990s. (Union membership, though, is more widespread in the public sector, covering nearly 60 per cent of employees.) Many rich and powerful people decline to organize in unions, but the unorganized also include some of the poorest paid and most insecure people in the workforce: workers in low paid jobs, in part-time jobs and in jobs where the risk of being sacked is very high. Within business too there are great variations in influence. Small businesses, for example, are usually much less well organized for influencing government than are big firms. It is not difficult to see why. It is partly a matter of numbers: it is much easier to coordinate action by a half dozen big supermarket firms than by thousands of corner shops. It is partly a matter of resources: again it is easy to see why a group dominated by half a dozen giant firms would have fewer problems commanding the resources needed for effective lobbying than would one representing small shopkeepers.

But if the big battalions – big firms, big unions, prestigious professions – have a flying start in influencing policy there are lots of compensating mechanisms that ensure that they do not always win the race. Often the big, well-resourced groups are competing against each other: even within a single industry like supermarket retailing it is not automatically the case that the interests of Sainsbury and Tesco will be identical. While governments depend on the biggest groups for all the things we identified earlier – approval, expertise, and so on – they also need things that the biggest groups cannot always deliver. Above all, governments need to win the support of millions of voters. Unless they win elections politicians are out of business. This does mean that a well organized functional interest that can influence votes is doubly powerful. Thus big media corporations that own the popular press in Britain have all the usual resources of giant firms, but are also believed by politicians to be able to sway voters. Thus they are deferred to particularly obsequiously. But even the most badly organized, if they are prepared to vote, and to switch their vote, can influence policy through the ballot box. As we will see when we turn in a moment to preference groups, this consideration may be growing as an influence over policy. There is also some evidence that the ability of the unorganized spontaneously to mobilize and force governments onto the defensive is growing. Consider the case in Briefing 8.5 which documents the astonishing speed with which an apparently unorganized coalition of small farmers, road hauliers and taxi drivers almost brought the economy to a halt in the autumn of 2000 in a protest over government tax policies on vehicle fuel. Later in the chapter we will examine what episodes like this tell us about the changing world of interest representation in British politics.

THE MAIN FORMS OF PREFERENCE GROUPS

As we have already noted there is one striking difference in the way functional and preference groups are created. The variety of functional groups is wide, but the limits of the functional world are defined by the division of labour in a modern economy: there exist a finite, though very large, number of occupations and industries. In the case of preference groups, by contrast, the potential range is infinite, because we are examining here groups that

BRIEFING 8.2

The Low Pay Unit and the high pay unit: contrasting fortunes of two interest groups in Britain

The Low Pay Unit was founded in 1974. For nearly 30 years it was the main group lobbying for the interests of the most poorly paid in Britain. It operated in three important ways:

- by gathering and publicizing research about low pay and the wider issue of poverty among those in work;
- by lobbying government in Britain about the problem of low pay;
- by joining and supporting European-wide networks to lobby the institutions of the EU.

Low paid workers did not generally give active support to the Unit: the low paid tend to have poor skills at lobbying and have little money left over to contribute to political campaigns. The Unit therefore depended heavily on donations, and when in 2003 its main supporter decided to withdraw financial support, the Unit ceased to exist.

The Institute of Directors is, as the name suggests, Britain's leading organization for company directors. Membership is for individuals. At the time of writing a yearly subscription cost £307 (life membership £5,526). The Institute offers a wide range of special services to its members, such as free legal advice. It also lobbies government for those policies that its members favour; unsurprisingly, these often advocate lighter regulation of business. At the time of writing the Institute had 52,000 members and an annual income exceeding £35 million. Readers can enjoy an interactive tour of the IOD's handsome headquarters in Pall Mall (the centre of London's clubland) by visiting www.iod.co.uk.

■ It is not hard to form interest groups in Britain; there are literally tens of thousands. But running an effective group is hard work and demands both skill and financial resources. The two cases show just how different can be the resources, and the fates, of different groups.

people form because they share some preference – and the combination of human preference is infinite. Not all possible preferences are realized, of course, but even so the variety in this part of the group world is staggering. In Britain today people are organized because they share common religious beliefs, sexual preferences, sporting interests, hobbies, tastes in beer – and virtually infinite combinations and recombinations of all these. You can experience this diversity by a simple personal experiment. Do a count for yourself, and for a couple of friends or a couple of members of your family, of the preference groups to which they belong. I guarantee that even for the most solitary the total will soon reach double figures.

We were able fairly readily to classify functional groups by their place in the division of labour, but no obvious parallel way of categorizing preference groups exists. One illuminating way to think about the variety is

by reference to the way groups fit into the wider fabric of society – because this difference often has important consequences for the importance of the group to the making of policy. Viewed thus, we can see four important kinds of preference group.

Established social institutions

Some groups are, so to speak, only incidentally part of the world of interest representation. They have historically well established alternative roles which make them central to the lives of communities. Some of the best examples are the long established Christian denominations. They plainly do not exist primarily for the purpose of trying to exert influence on public policy, but equally plainly they in practice spend a great deal of effort in trying to do precisely that. Churches have views about education, about policy affecting the family, about

DOCUMENTING POLITICS 8.2

Modern campaigning by a powerful preference group: the case of the RSPCA

Our chicken challenge

Back in January 2008, we challenged all British supermarkets to be the first to only stock higher welfare chicken by 2010.

Nearly three out of four people feel supermarkets should only sell higher welfare chicken such as Freedom Food, free-range or organic.

In conjunction with Compassion in World Farming (CIWF), we are in the process of calling an industry-wide meeting, to include supermarkets, the government and the chicken industry, to discuss ways of increasing the proportion of chickens reared to higher welfare standards.

Hugh champions Freedom Food

The great chicken debate continues this year as Hugh Fearnley-Whittingstall embarks on his new mission to convince consumers to trade up to Freedom Food labelled chicken in his programme, *Chickens, Hugh and Tesco Too* – part of Channel 4's *Great British Food Fight* season.

Freedom Food is the RSPCA's higher welfare farm assurance and food labelling scheme that approves well-managed free-range, organic and indoor farms, providing they meet the strict RSPCA welfare standards.

■ The RSPCA has its origins in the nineteenth-century discovery of a new sensibility about cruelty to animals – but its concerns and campaigning techniques are strikingly modern. This extract from the Society's web pages illustrates these. It continues the Society's campaign against cruelty in battery rearing of hens. Two features are especially striking:

- lobbying is not just lobbying of government: here the targets are big corporations;
- notice the symbiosis with other media – the use of TV programmes by celebrity chefs.

Source: http://www.rspca.org.uk/servlet/Satellite? pagename=RSPCA/RSPCARedirect&pg=chickens.

foreign aid, about how and when war can be waged; and naturally they intervene in debates about these issues. There is thus virtually no area of government policy where we might not expect to find a Christian denomination trying to shape policy and to influence public opinion.

Charities

What we have called social institutions central to the fabric of everyday life overlap with the huge array of charities in the community. Indeed institutions like churches are usually registered as charities to gain the tax breaks that come with charitable status. But charities are worth separating because they often have a special importance in particular policy fields. Over 166,000 are presently registered with the Charity Commission (the main regulator), all concerned to protect or promote some value or interest. Take as an example the RSPCA, a charity founded in 1824 in response to growing sensitivity about the treatment of animals. The RSPCA is probably the best known, and best resourced, animal charity in Britain. It stands for a value now central to the life of the community – the humane treatment of animals – and devotes most of its energies to promoting that value and to the practical care of animals. But as a consequence of the commitment to these values, a large amount of energy is also devoted to trying to influence public policy: directly to persuading government and indirectly trying to shape the wider climate of public opinion (see Documenting Politics 8.2). As we will see later in this book when we consider the practical delivery of policy, charities have become increasingly important in recent decades in actually delivering public services, especially in the field of welfare.

New social movements

The huge array of charities in turn shade into something more diffuse which can be labelled 'social movements'. The best way to understand these is through examples: we can think of the women's movement, the movement for gay rights or the environmental movement as instances. They all represent loosely connected constellations of many different kinds of groups: some are formally organized nationally, others are local, informal and often short lived. Like the great charities and churches they obviously serve a wide range of social purposes. Take what is loosely called the gay rights movement. It encompasses particular charities, for instance the Terence Higgins Trust which is devoted to support for those diagnosed as HIV positive. More widely, it has been important in helping create social worlds where gay people can feel secure and free from

TABLE 8.1 The rise of a movement: the case of environmentalism (membership of selected organizations, in thousands)

	1971	2008
National Trust	278	3,560
Royal Society for the Protection of Birds	98	1,007 *
Greenpeace	–	221
Friends of the Earth	1	100
Ramblers' Association	22	170 **

* Claimed estimate by RSPB is 'over one million'.
** 2007 figure.

■ The figures show the extraordinary growth in membership of groups concerned with the environment in the closing decades of the twentieth century – a growth that continues apace. Of course membership of Greenpeace, an international campaigning group, does not have the same meaning as membership of the National Trust, an organization mostly dedicated to the preservation of ancient stately buildings and the protection of parts of the landscape. But this is precisely the character of a movement like environmentalism: it is not a single organization, but a loose and shifting network linking a wide variety of groups whose members often have very different world views and aims.

Source: Calculated from Social Trends (1999, Table 11.4) and from organization websites and annual reports.

intimidation and discrimination. Many large English cities (such as Manchester) now have informally identified 'gay villages' where gay people can live and spend leisure time in a culture which they find non-threatening. Some religious denominations often also have these social-movement-like characteristics: they provide social networks where people mix with the like-minded, and they elaborate philosophies which give moral meaning to the wider social movement. And, equally, they put a great deal of energy into trying to influence public policy: health, education and, of course, the environment are only the most obvious examples. As the example of religious denominations shows, there is in principle nothing novel about a social movement. Nevertheless, the other examples given here are of comparatively new social groupings. We shall see that they have a double importance: not only are they of growing importance in the world of interest representation, they are important in pioneering new kinds of political participation.

We commonly speak of 'new' social movements because some of the most striking are truly new, like the example from the gay community used here. But in reality these movements hark back to an older tradition of political action in Britain – a tradition where lifestyle, intellectual commitment and political action united large numbers of people. Their ancestors include, for example, the great movements against alcohol, slavery and the subjection of women that were so important in the nineteenth century.

Specialized lobbies

One important feature of the preference groups identified so far is that interest representation in the sense of arguing with, or bargaining with, government is a by-product of their larger social purposes. But just as there are groups in the functional world who exist only to lobby, so there are specialized lobbies in the preference world. Take the case of the Society for the Protection of Unborn Children. This is not, as one might imagine from the name, an organization concerned with encouraging practices that foster the health of babies in the womb, or with developing more effective antenatal care. It is an organization that was created largely in response to the changes in the law in the 1960s that allowed legal abortion in some circumstances; and it is devoted to resisting the extension of that original reform and to ensuring that such law as presently exists is enforced as strictly as possible and, as an ultimate objective, to returning the law to the state it was in before the original reforms of the 1960s.

Specialized lobbies, by their very nature, obviously devote their energies to intervening as effectively as possible in debates about public policy. It is natural to think of them as particularly important in the world of preference groups. But as this sketch of the variety of preference groups shows, they actually only form a minority of the population of the preference world.

The resources of preference groups

Because functional groups exist through their place in the division of labour it would be natural to assume that this automatically gives them access to resources superior to those of preference groups. The assumption would be wrong. There are many preference groups which can command impressive resources. Five kinds of resource are especially important.

Some are quasi-state bodies. We saw earlier that over the course of the twentieth century many functional groups became de facto governing institutions. Some preference groups have an even more impressive claim: they are so closely connected to parts of the state that they can be considered to be at least quasi-state institutions themselves. A perfect example is the Church of England. As the 'Established' Church it is actually headed by the Monarch. Anglican bishops presently sit in the House of Lords, and any leading Anglican clergyman can offer opinions about almost any aspect of public policy with the certainty of commanding a hearing and, often, extensive publicity. As a very different example, consider the National Trust. This is legally a charity, formed at the end of the nineteenth century to protect the natural beauty of our landscape and buildings. It is now a rich and well connected institution: a membership of 3.8 million brings it an annual income of more than £380 million. On its governing council sit members of some of the most socially prestigious families in the land.

Most have great cultural resources. 'Culture' here does not refer narrowly to the arts, but to the wider culture of our society. Many preference groups have important cultural resources in this latter sense: that is, they can appeal to values which are deeply held and uncontestable across the community. It is possible, for example, for governments to decline particular demands from the RSPCA, or from the National Society for the Prevention of Cruelty to Children. But in any debates about policy these groups can naturally occupy the moral high ground, and no politician could safely question their general objectives. Their opposition can damage, or their support enhance, the legitimacy of a policy; and as we know from our earlier discussions, legitimacy is a key condition of effective policy making.

Many preference groups have wealth and numbers. Some preference groups have precisely the resources that we saw conferring influence on functional groups. They are rich. Many religious denominations, and older environmental groups like the National Trust and the RSPB, have large memberships and huge incomes from subscriptions, donations and property holdings. They have the precious gift of permanent organization. For instance, while religious observance in Britain is low by international standards, nevertheless millions of Britons are available weekly in the church, the mosque or the synagogue to listen to the views of clergy. Minority religions often command particularly powerful allegiance. For instance,

issues that affect Islam became central to British foreign policy after the terrorist attacks on the New York World Trade Center on 11 September 2001. Though only two per cent of Britons profess the Islamic faith, weekly attendance at the mosque is particularly high, and thus what is said at the mosque about British government policy is a highly sensitive matter for politicians.

They deliver policy. Many preference groups also resemble functional groups in playing a central role in the delivery of public policy, and are particularly important in the delivery of welfare policy. Primary and secondary education in Britain would be utterly different without the contribution of church schools. But this role in policy delivery has grown in recent years: charities are vital to the care of the very young, the old, the sick and the long-term disabled. It is only natural that when a group delivers policy it claims, and is granted, a right to a say in how the policy is made.

They are experts. Many preference groups have expertise quite as valuable to policy makers as the expertise of big firms or professions. Governments concerned with the large issue of how to manage a sustainable environment, or with something as specific as the impact of particular farming practices on a bird species, will naturally look for expert advice to the RSPB – and indeed will not even have to look, because the Society is already geared up to supplying a constant stream of information and advocacy.

In short, the most important preference groups have exactly the same potential to participate in the governing process as we identified earlier for the key functional groups: for government they are vital sources of advice, cooperation and legitimacy.

The powerful and the excluded in the preference world

We have seen that it is wrong to think of preference groups as inevitably less powerful than their functional counterparts. But just as there is a power hierarchy in the functional world, so there is one among preference groups. This point nevertheless brings us to an important difference between the two worlds. Although short-term factors shape power in the functional world, in the long run importance depends on economic weight. For instance, 150 years ago agriculture was probably the dominant interest in government; now, with the decline in the economic importance of farming, agricultural interests, though important, no longer have that commanding position.

The leverage that preference groups can wield in government is partly a function also of these familiar factors. Groups like the National Trust and the RSPB are important because they are rich and can use their wealth

BRIEFING 8.3

The powerful and the excluded in the preference world: two examples

The Campaign to Protect Rural England (formerly the Council for the Preservation of Rural England) dates its origins back to 1926. It has more than 60,000 members organized in a network of over 200 local groups. The Campaign's aim is to protect and enhance the countryside. It now markets itself as one of Britain's leading environmental groups and appeals both to modern ideologies of environmentalism and traditional visions of rural Britain. In the most recently available yearly accounts it spent £4.7 million. Its Patron is Her Majesty the Queen.

The London Detainee Support Group was founded in 1997. It aims to alleviate poverty, sickness and distress amongst refugees, asylum seekers and others who are, or have been, detained in London and elsewhere. It spent just over £120,000 in the most recently reported financial year. It has no Patron.

■ We saw earlier that there are huge variations in the power, resources and acceptability of different 'functional' groups. The same is true for preference, campaigning groups, and the two examples document the range. The wealth and support base of the Campaign to Protect Rural England are evident; the identity of its Patron exemplifies its acceptable 'insider' status. By contrast, the London Detainee Support Group was founded at a time when both leading parties, and most newspapers, pictured the arrival of asylum seekers to Britain as a serious problem and sought various ways of containing both their numbers and their movements. It is hard to imagine the Queen agreeing to be a patron of a group designed to protect detained asylum seekers.

Sources: Charity Commission Annual Reports (www.charity-commission.gov.uk).

to buy expertise and organization. But a much more subtle process of inclusion and exclusion also affects preference groups, and this takes us back to the question of the *cultural* approval that they can command. Any minister or senior civil servant can readily argue about particular policy options with the Royal National Lifeboat Institution or the National Society for the Prevention of Cruelty to Children, but only someone insane or malign would oppose the general aims of these groups.

But by no means all groups command the same, or any, cultural approval. Even among 'approved' groups there can be striking variations in intensity of approval, and these differences are often culturally founded. For instance it is much easier for charities speaking for the blind than for the deaf to organize in Britain, because while everyone perceives the seriousness of blindness, deafness is of much lower salience and, in some circumstance, is even treated as a subject of sick humour. Even more important, some groups are so subject to hostility that they are overtly excluded from influence over policy. Historically, some forms of religious discrimination functioned in this way. In the past, it was hard to speak for and represent Catholicism and Judaism, and indeed both religions faced legal bars to participation in

political life and in the wider life of the community. In modern Britain some of the same cultural (though not legal) obstacles exist in speaking for and representing Islam. Until the late 1960s it was also virtually impossible to speak for, and represent, gay people. Anyone who did so faced possible criminal prosecution (because same sex relations between men were illegal) and certain social hostility and damage to their career. In contemporary Britain, groups that attempt to speak for, and represent, asylum seekers also face official and popular hostility (look at Briefing 8.3). At the most extreme points of hostility, to try to speak for some groups actually leads to the danger of prosecution and harassment by vigilantes, since they arouse deep popular animosity: imagine, for example, trying to organize a group that defended the views of paedophiles in Britain now.

NEW WORLDS OF INTEREST REPRESENTATION

Interest representation in what we have been calling the Westminster system remains hugely important. It shapes the patterns of inclusion and exclusion which we

BRIEFING 8.4

The world of the professional lobbyist

Professional lobbying has been a boom industry in recent years. After a number of scandals in the 1990s attempts have been made to organize self-regulatory bodies in the industry. The most important of these is via the Association of Professional Political Consultants. (Lobbyists prefer to call themselves consultants, or specialists, in political communication.) Over 80 per cent (by turnover) of Britain's political consultancies are in membership. The Association maintains a highly informative register of consultants, detailing, for instance, all the clients represented most recently by individual firms. It also promotes a code of conduct: for instance, it forbids the offer of financial inducements to promote business.

The style and scale of the work of professional lobbying is well illustrated by the account offered of its activities by Bell Pottinger Communications, one of the leading firms. (One of its partners was once an advisor to Prime Minister Margaret Thatcher). The firm:

■ advised Newport Borough Council on its campaign to achieve city status;

■ advised the Association of Friendly Societies on a campaign to secure changes in the regulations governing the operations of its members, thus strengthening their competitive position in financial services markets;

■ organized a mass campaign by the National Federation of Sub-Postmasters against threats to close small post offices;

■ advised the Guide Association on a successful campaign to scrap proposed charges to carry out security checks on volunteers working with young people – thus helping the Association save £450,000 annually.

■ This material provides both a 'bird's eye' and a 'worm's eye' view of the modern lobbying industry, from the point of view of the organization of the whole industry and of the daily business of lobbying, with examples from the website of Bell Pottinger. The material should be read with care, however. It is all from the public material provided by the industry. It says nothing of the scandals that compelled greater organization in the 1990s. The examples of work provided by Bell Pottinger also focus on the most socially acceptable groups and causes: while one might argue with particular features of the four campaigns documented, nobody would argue with the desirability of ensuring that these groups have their voices heard in policy making.

Sources: www.appc.org.uk; www.bell-pottinger.co.uk.

outlined above. It is heavily centralized on a small geographical area covered by the main political institutions of the Westminster system, notably the government departments headquartered in central London. Functional groups that have the wealth and expertise to be useful in this governing world enjoy privileged access. This Westminster world helps shape the cultural preferences and prejudices which, as we have also just seen, are so important in determining which preference groups are 'in' or 'out'.

The world of interest representation is nevertheless changing. Some of these changes are reinforcing the dominance of the powerful and privileged, and some are challenging existing hierarchies. The changes are in part traceable to wider developments which are a major theme in this book: the reshaping, and the decline, of the Westminster system of government.

Three sets of changes are particularly important: the rise of professional lobbying; the development of new forms of group mobilization, often linked to new social movements; and the 'Europeanization' of interest representation.

The rise of professional lobbying

One of the obvious features of the groups considered so far in this chapter is that, for most, interest representation is largely a by-product, albeit a vital one, of their main activities: firms need to make profits; professions need to organize their bit of the labour market; churches need to save souls. But in the last generation a different kind of figure has appeared on the interest representation stage: the professional lobbyist, a 'hired gun' available to speak on behalf of any group willing to pay. There have indeed always been well placed individuals – backbench members of Parliament, former ministers, 'fixers' in leading law firms – who would lobby on behalf of clients. But the new world of professional lobbying, which is influenced by the much more highly developed lobbying system that exists in the US, is distinctive in three ways:

● it is openly organized in firms that advertise their services, rather than being a discreet service offered by individual 'fixers';
● it is developing into an industry in its own right, with trade associations that attempt, in turn, to promote codes of professional conduct;
● the firms in the industry claim a special expertise in the act of lobbying government itself.

The grounds for this last claim to special expertise and effectiveness are various: that lobbying firms are especially well placed to obtain access to government; that they have a unique expertise in assembling a case in terms that will appeal to policy makers; and that they command the technology – for instance to produce well-directed mail shots – that will maximize the effectiveness with which a case is presented.

The rise of the special lobbying firm is due partly to a refinement of the division of labour in interest representation. The biggest and most powerful groups – giant firms, trade associations – already have specialized government relations divisions, even if they do not always call them by that name. It is quite a small step to re-creating this specialization for the whole lobbying world. Likewise, there is an obvious cross-over between the work of the professional lobbyist and some longer established firms: for instance, those that specialize in public relations, advertising and offering legal advice. There is thus a growing supply of specialized lobbyists, as entrepreneurs spot a potentially lucrative business niche. There is also a growing demand for their services. Government is a huge and complex organization. Exercising influence often depends on knowing exactly who to target. Personal contacts date very quickly, since, as in every organization, people change jobs. Groups are experts in their policy field, but they are not naturally experts in government. Professional lobbyists claim precisely this latter sort of knowledge.

The rise of the professional lobbyist is important for understanding the nuts and bolts of British government. But it has also raised issues about the workings of democratic politics. Three issues are especially sensitive.

Privilege. Professional lobbying is not cheap. It is a service therefore only available to rich groups, and in the main professional lobbyists are used by well organized functional groups, like firms and trade associations. If we make the assumption that using professional lobbyists raises the chances of success in influencing government, then we must conclude that professional lobbying is a privileged service disproportionately available to the rich.

Probity. The rise of professional lobbying has been accompanied by a number of newspaper exposures of scandals involving privileged access by special interests. Both Mr Major's Conservative Governments (1990–97) and Mr Blair's first administration (1997–2001) were damaged by such scandals. In 2010 three former members of Labour Cabinets were covertly filmed by the TV programme *Dispatches* offering to use their contacts to help business lobbyists. In Chapter 4 (see Briefing 4.2) we documented the importance of the Committee on Standards in Public Life in pressing for more openly codified standards of conduct in that area. The Committee owes its existence to scandals publicized in the early 1990s: newspapers revealed that backbench MPs in the House of Commons were covertly paid substantial sums of money by professional lobbyists for 'placing' questions to ministers. These particular instances reflect a more general problem of ethical standards. At heart, what the professional lobbyist offers is access. The lobbyist claims an expertise, not in the client's particular subject, but in government itself: how it works; who the people in government are who will really make a difference to a policy decision. Very often this knowledge itself comes from a period in public service or in political activity. Most lobbyists, if successful, are so because their previous careers equipped them with a good contacts book and with the friendship of those who have power in government. This is why probity is an important issue: it concerns the moral rightness of using privileged connections with public figures to exercise influence over policy on behalf of special interests. In other walks of life using contacts in this way would be viewed as improper. Suppose, for instance, that I were to set up a business charging to advise sixth formers applying for places at the University of Manchester; and suppose I were to claim that my years of service in the University gave me lots of contacts with admissions tutors to help applicants make their case for admission. That would be highly improper and would lead, rightly, to my dismissal from the University. Yet it is not clear how the exploitation of privileged connections by lobbyists differs from this.

Power. Issues of privilege and probity in turn imply issues to do with the exercise of power. Professional

BRIEFING 8.5

'A regular and normal part of British political life': the case of the fuel protests in 2000

In September 2000 a network of farmers and road hauliers launched a campaign of direct-action protest against diesel fuel prices. Their main tactic was to blockade oil refineries. Within days a fuel shortage paralysed distribution networks, leading to food shortages and a dramatic collapse of public support for the Government. But an attempt to widen the protests, and to organize the protestors more formally, entirely failed, and by October the protests had collapsed.

Doherty et al. (2003) explain the rise and success of the protests in terms already used in this chapter: lesson learning from other protestors, notably French farmers; the use of new technologies of communication, like mobile phones; the vulnerability of modern economies to disruptive action; the existence of numerous 'outsiders' who think 'insiders' in government are indifferent to them. They explain the collapse of the protests as the product of tactical errors and the difficulty of imposing permanent organization on spontaneously arising groups. But they emphasize that 'disruptive and confrontational protest is now a regular and normal part of British political life' (19).

■ The fuel protests were spectacular; but they are only one of dozens of examples of confrontational protest organized through loosely coordinated networks. I guarantee that a week's reading of a good newspaper will produce at least one example, local or national.

lobbying is not a charitable activity. The lobbyist serves those who can afford to pay, and those who can afford to pay are, naturally, already rich. In short, the activities of the professional lobbyist reinforce existing power imbalances in the interest group system.

To these worries, the professional lobbyist can make a number of replies. Although there is a need for professional standards, and although there are periodic lapses from the highest standards, this is nothing unique to professional lobbying. It is true of all professions, and it is particularly true of professions that have traditionally been closely connected to professional lobbying, like the law, public relations and politics itself. Lobbying has always gone on. The rise of professional lobbying makes open and organized, and therefore available for scrutiny and regulation, what was once hidden from public view. While undoubtedly professional lobbyists have to be paid, the best solution to problems of power and inequality is to encourage the growth and diversity of professional lobbying as an occupation, because with growth and diversity firms will emerge that specialize in different groups of clients and policy areas. Some lobbying firms have already been set up, for instance, with the aim of only serving clients of whose aims they approve. This is not hugely different from the way law firms, for example, specialize in different kinds of legal representation – some working in commercial law, some in human rights law. Professional lobbying is a service offered on the marketplace, and in any flourishing marketplace there will be a diversity of firms serving a diversity of clients.

New forms of group mobilization

Consider Amnesty International, a group that campaigns on behalf of prisoners of conscience, which has a large individual membership both in Britain and worldwide; or a group like Shelter, which for 40 years has campaigned on behalf of the homeless in Britain. Groups like Amnesty and Shelter illustrate what is sometimes called the 'bumble bee' problem in studying interest groups. According to the laws of aerodynamics the bumble bee should not be able to fly, but it does. Likewise, these groups should not exist, or at least not flourish. Prisoners of conscience and the homeless do not have the obvious resources – like money and organization – that support flourishing and effective groups. Yet Amnesty and Shelter exist and flourish. The campaigning group, often with a large membership, and often campaigning on

People in Politics 8.1

Three leading political entrepreneurs in the world of preference groups

Des Wilson has claims to be the founder of the modern political entrepreneur in preference groups. A campaigning journalist originally from New Zealand his CV reads like a history of modern campaigning groups: he has been both director of Shelter (the campaign for the homeless) and chairman of Friends of the Earth, the leading environmental group. But his last job was as head of corporate affairs at a leading economic interest, the British Airports Authority.

Eamonn Butler's career shows that the modern political entrepreneur need not work on the left of politics. In 1977 he co-founded the *Adam Smith Institute*, a think tank which has campaigned for more free market forces. He now directs the Institute. Under him the Institute pours out a stream of advocacy for the market, commissioning research, publishing working papers – all designed to reinforce the message that the market is best.

Jonathan Porritt's career is highly modern but he is also a familiar figure in the history of British politics: the toff with a conscience. Educated at Eton, he inherited the family baronetcy. He has been both director of Friends of the Earth and chair of the Ecology (now Green) Party. He is probably the best known face of 'green politics' in Britain. His patrician connections latterly surfaced when he became the informal 'green guru' to the Prince of Wales.

Cartoons: Shaun Steele

■ The three sketches show the diverse sources of political entrepreneurs who have done so much to revitalize issue campaigning in Britain, especially on behalf of groups who do not have the resources to defend their own interest: an immigrant, a university meritocrat, and an upper-class product of Eton.

DOCUMENTING POLITICS 8.3

Professional lobbying at the EU level: the view from the professionals

There are many interest groups and offices which are based in Brussels, playing an indispensable role in the European institutions' decision-making process ... But what kind of a future does a profession in constant evolution and of growing importance have if no training exists and there is no preparation for it? What are the social consequences?

These thoughts led in 1994 to the creation of the European Institute for Public Affairs and Lobbying, EIPAL, the first of its kind in Brussels.

The EIPAL training programme allows managers, experienced professionals, company heads and even young university graduates to gain a thorough grasp of the decision-making process at the European level and of the different methods of defending public or private group interests. The programme allows participants not only to learn the basics of the lobbying profession, but also to follow the latest developments in this sector. It also helps them discover and understand the links between the European Union and all sectors, both public and private.

Since 1994, EIPAL has trained more than 250 professionals including diplomats, civil servants, consultants, graduates, corporate and multinational executives, officials from interest groups and European federations. Experience gained over the previous thirteen sessions is our trump-card for efficiency and professionalism.

■ This extract from a very successful professional training organization for lobbyists in the EU shows how the rise of the Union is transforming the world of interest representation. The scale, diversity and complexity of policy making, especially in Brussels, means that many old British tactics simply no longer work. In particular, the informal cultivation of personal relationships by insiders is giving way to much more systematic organization of the activity of lobbying – skills which bodies like this one offer to teach.

Source: www.eipal.org.

behalf of some dispossessed group or cause, is an increasingly important part of the political system. Three connected factors lie behind this important development.

Creative leadership. In the jargon of political science this is sometimes called *political entrepreneurship*. Many groups are brought into existence by energetic and idealistic figures, prepared to commit their energy and idealism wholesale to a cause. Sometimes these individuals become well known national figures: consider the examples given in People in Politics 8.1. Sometimes the groups emerge locally, and rapidly fade away: many environmental campaigns against projects like new roads are sparked off in this way. Of course creative leadership and idealistic people have always existed. Some wider conditions must now be helping creative leaders to have an impact. The two factors considered next may provide clues.

Political skills and confidence. Organizing and acting politically in an effective way comes naturally only to a gifted few. For most of us, the ability to run things, and to make a case, depends heavily on possessing skills and confidence: for instance, the skills and confidence needed to write, address public meetings and broadcast. There is no doubt at all that formal education helps foster these, and the figures for formal education tell a straightforward story. More and more Britons are now able to raise their skill and confidence levels through extended secondary and tertiary education: 40 years ago about 5 per cent of 18–21 year olds entered universities; now about 40 per cent are in higher education.

Technology. Organizing and campaigning depend heavily on being able to communicate – with government, with supporters and with those among the public whom one wishes to persuade. We only have to contrast technologies of communication now with conditions 50 years ago to see how much easier, cheaper and quicker communication has become. Then, the telephone was a luxury available only to the minority of the population, and limited to landline systems; now almost everyone has a phone, and well over 80 per cent of people over the age of eight years have a mobile phone. Then, telephoning abroad was cumbersome and expensive; now, virtually instantaneous global communication networks can be used via the Internet. These changes in hard technology have in turn reshaped what are sometimes called 'soft' technologies – techniques of campaigning and communication. Creative political leaders have learnt how to exploit the new conditions: targeted mailshots, using databases that identify potential groups of supporters, provide an important way to raise funds quickly; confident and well educated members learn how to work the media so as to maximize reporting of their activities and

POLITICAL ISSUES 8.1

Sleaze and lobbying

The common view that British politics is marked by high standards was damaged by a series of episodes under both the Conservative Government of John Major and under the governments of New Labour 1997–2010. The episodes produced allegations that economic interests could buy special access for cash. Under Major, Conservative MPs were revealed as willing to ask 'planted' parliamentary questions for money in a 'sting' organized by a newspaper. A government minister (Neil Hamilton) resigned over revelations of his connections with the owner of Harrods and lost his seat in the 1997 general election to an 'anti-sleaze' independent, the TV journalist Martin Bell. The Conservative Cabinet minister Jonathan Aitken resigned from the government to sue *The Guardian* for libel over stories concerning his business connections; he lost and ended up in jail for committing perjury. The stream of cases led to the setting up of the Committee on Standards in Public Life in 1994 (see Briefing 4.2) and to the passage of new rules concerning the registration of interests by MPs (see Documenting Politics 9.3). The Labour Leader Tony Blair announced that in office he would run a rigorously clean administration. The promise was soon badly damaged. A sting by a newspaper led to the revelation that a special advisor in the Blair Government was boasting of his ability to gain preferential access for clients. A string of decisions – ranging from the treatment of cigarette advertising in Formula One motor racing to the awarding of government contracts – was soon suspiciously linked to donations to the Labour Party. And in 2010 three former Labour Cabinet members were covertly filmed boasting about their ability to use their contacts for business lobbying.

'Sleaze' was a journalistic coinage to express the dark, discreditable world thus revealed. The immediate rows over individuals often obscured the wider issues. These included:

- What should be the connections between public servants and private interests?
- Should the connections be declared?
- Should they involve payments? In particular, how legitimate is it for Members of the House of Commons to benefit from payment as 'consultants', for which read lobbyists, for commercial interests?
- Should they be regulated, and if so by whom? Is 'self-regulation' by bodies like the House of Commons sufficient, or is some outside regulatory body needed?

views; use of mobile phones and email networks allows rapid communication and the organization of widely spread groups without the need for traditional, formal, permanent organization in offices. (For a case study of what can be accomplished see Briefing 8.5.)

Creative leadership, the spread of political skills, and technological innovation have all helped produce a more diverse and open world of interest representation. Thus these developments help counteract the historical inequalities in the system. They have also made the interest group world more unstable: groups often rise and die with extraordinary swiftness. Briefing 8.5 not only documents the rapid emergence of an alliance that depended heavily on the mobile phone for coordination; it also documents a movement that faded away almost as quickly as it had appeared.

The Europeanization of interest representation

Interest group representation tends to follow the contours of political power. Since Britain's original entry into the (then) EEC in 1973, the EU has emerged as a powerful political presence in Britain. Naturally, interest groups have responded to this. The consequence has been a profound *Europeanization* of interest representation. This has a number of different faces.

The most obvious is the tendency of existing groups to direct some of their activities to Union institutions, especially to the Commission in Brussels. One of the simplest but most invariable rules of political life is that well organized interest groups go to where the power lies. If we came across a novel political system and wanted to find out quickly where power lay, just about

DEBATING POLITICS 8.1

Interest groups: undermining or promoting democracy in Britain?

INTEREST GROUPS UNDERMINE DEMOCRACY

▶ The most powerful and wealthy are always best organized, so strengthening inequality.

▶ Groups promote sectional interests over the common interest.

▶ Groups can challenge the authority of democratically elected governments.

▶ There is no check on the extent to which groups are themselves democratic, and indeed most are run by small minorities of members or by professional officers.

INTEREST GROUPS PROMOTE DEMOCRACY

▶ Group representation complements and extends the representation of territorially elected democratic governments.

▶ Groups use their expertise and legitimacy to support and improve the policies of elected government.

▶ Group organization is flexible and changing, allowing new and hitherto excluded interests a voice.

▶ Groups are a counterbalancing power against that of the state.

---

the quickest way to find out would be to look at where the big functional groups – business, professions, large trade unions – were directing their lobbying. And a couple of days in Brussels – or even a couple of hours on the Web navigating the sites of the big British functional groups – soon shows us that any group of weight has a big presence in that city. That presence can take a variety of forms: intensive lobbying at home – for instance of ministers – to influence how national governments behave in Union level bargaining; establishing a permanent office in Brussels; periodically hiring professional lobbyists to navigate through the complicated EU decision-making system. 'Brussels' is shorthand here for all the major institutions of the Union, but it has become universal shorthand because the single most important object of pressure is the Commission, which has its headquarters in that city. When we look at lobbying in the Commission, and in lesser institutions like the EP, we find not only British groups at work. All this British lobbying is replicated for the other member states. Another face of Europeanization has therefore been created by the unification of separate nationally organized interest groups into European-wide federations. They range from the European Fishing Tackle Trade Association to the European Federation of Pharmaceutical Industries and Associations. Tremendous obstacles often lie in the way of creating

these groups: for example, even within national associations representing firms in the chemical industry, there can be huge differences of opinion and interest; these internal differences are obviously magnified when representation becomes pan-European. But Europeanizing interest representation in this way is helped greatly by the institutions of the Union itself. The Commission in particular is committed to a style of decision making which involves close consultation with affected interests before decisions are arrived at. And where there is no obvious organized European voice for an interest, the Commission often takes an active part in promoting the creation of such a voice. Thus many of these bodies are in practice *governing* institutions at the European level: more than one hundred organizations influence, set and direct standards for products traded across the Union.

The tendency of the Union actually to promote Europeanization of representation is strengthened by the way it typically tries to implement policy. One feature of the Union we noted in Chapter 5 was that its financial and administrative resources were actually quite weak. It has neither the money nor the people to put policy into effect on the ground. It relies on nations to implement its directives, and within nations it relies particularly heavily on well organized functional groups for implementation. For example, under the rules of economic integration there are now, in most professions, well developed systems of accreditation for ensuring that professional qualifications from the different member states are mutually recognized. These systems of mutual accreditation have more often than not been negotiated between the separate national professional associations, and responsibility for their implementation is delegated to those associations. The Union has also widened the range of arenas and issues where groups can campaign. One of the most important instances of this concerns the courts. As we saw in Chapter 5 the Union, because it was created by treaties, has a well developed system of laws and entitlements whose exact interpretation is adjudicated by the European Court. In recent years the Court has been an important place where organized British groups have been able to go to test, or challenge, the validity of a policy.

INTEREST REPRESENTATION IN THE WESTMINSTER SYSTEM: CHANGE AND CONTINUITY

The Westminster system is shorthand for a highly centralized arrangement that governed Britain until recently. It was geographically centralized, dominated by institutions located in central London, mostly clustered around the Westminster Parliament. The most important of these institutions were the core executive and the civil service departments. As we have seen in Chapters 6 and 7 this system has been fragmenting. A system of interest representation grew up around this centralized system, with many of its centralized features. It too is changing, due to the fragmentation of the Westminster system. In part the changes consist of developments that are outside the range of this chapter but which will become clear later: for example we will find that the creation of newly devolved administrations in Edinburgh and Cardiff has switched important interest group activity away from the London metropolis. The traditional Westminster system of interest representation, because it was highly centralized, was also very hierarchical and unequal. It divided the interest group world pretty clearly into 'insiders' and 'outsiders'. Some of the changes sketched in this chapter have made this centralized, unequal system less so: social and cultural change have stimulated the formation of groups and equipped many of them with the resources and skills to exercise much more open pressure. But some other changes have actually made wealth and the things that go with wealth even more important in interest group mobilization. These changes are partly reflected in the rise of professional lobbyists – the expensive 'hired guns' available to those who can afford to pay.

The ambiguous nature of change is perfectly illustrated by the consequences of Europeanization. On the one hand the EU has shifted much interest group lobbying away from the world of insiders in Westminster. It has opened up new possibilities for exercising influence and created new arenas of influence, for instance in the courts. But it has also made the activity of lobbying even more complex and therefore more manipulable by those groups that can invest heavily in professional skills.

Review OF CHAPTER 8

Five themes have dominated this chapter:

◖ The diversity and complexity of worlds of interest representation that span both the functional and the world of preference groups.

◖ The weight that accrues to functional groups from their place in the wider division of labour.

◖ The importance of cultural preferences in determining the political weight of preference groups.

◖ The way social and institutional change are reshaping what was a closed, hierarchical, Westminster-focused system of interest representation.

◖ The way change is both making the new system more open, but also more vulnerable, to groups speaking for the already rich and powerful.

FURTHER READING

ESSENTIAL

If you are only going to read one book it should be Beer (1969/82), the classic study which provided the template for most later studies of groups, and which is also a great meditation on the character of British politics.

RECOMMENDED

Two exceptionally important works which have stood the test of time are Middlemas (1979) and Grant and Marsh (1977). Grant (2000) is still the best authoritative survey of the field. Jordan's chapter on lobbying in Flinders et al. (2009) helpfully updates on the specialist literature and on many of the issues to do with the control of lobbying.

CHAPTER **9**

Parliament in the Westminster system

CONTENTS

AIMS

This chapter:

- ☐ Stresses the physical presence of the Westminster Parliament as an important symbol of the system of government

- ☐ Describes the practical organization of the House of Commons

- ☐ Describes how the functions of the House are in some degree determined by this organization

- ☐ Summarizes important sources of change and stress in the place of the Commons in the Westminster system

- ☐ Describes the roles, organization and reform of the House of Lords

PARLIAMENT: DIGNITY AND EFFICIENCY

The very fact that we use the phrase 'Westminster system' to describe the most important institutions of British government conveys something of the significance of Parliament. In our everyday speech when we refer to 'Westminster' we more often than not mean the Houses of Parliament, the buildings that lie beside the Thames in the borough of Westminster. Even a first inspection of Parliament shows the importance of the famous distinction in the English Constitution made by Walter Bagehot, which we discussed in Chapter 4: between the dignified (the symbolic) and the efficient (the practical working). Parliament, we will discover, has some importance in the efficient working of the system; but it is absolutely central to the dignified, the symbolic. Indeed it provides just about the most commonly reproduced image of British government – a version of which is also reproduced here in Image 9.1. It has appeared on everything from a famous label on a sauce bottle which you can probably find in the kitchen cupboard at home (HP sauce), to cartoons, to official accounts of the British way of life. Parliament is, to state the obvious, a place, a set of buildings. The layout and form of these buildings is highly revealing about the roles of Parliament in the wider Westminster system. It will help us greatly, therefore, to begin with a quick tour of Parliament. It will have to selective, for the Palace of Westminster, to use its more formal title, is a vast, rambling collection of buildings.

A TOUR OF PARLIAMENT

If we want to tour Parliament the first thing we will discover is that we cannot do this at will. Most of the Palace of Westminster is closed off to the public. Virtually the only way to see beyond a few selected areas is to be given a tour by a Member of the House. This is not difficult: backbench MPs in the House of Commons spend a fair part of their time escorting groups of their constituents around the Palace. Our MP guide will meet us in the central lobby. This was historically a place of unregulated contact where constituents could accost members – hence the origin of the modern verb, to lobby, which we saw in the last chapter is commonly used to describe interest representation. But threats from terrorist attack in the last three decades have now turned the lobby into a meeting place where access is tightly regulated. We will only get into the lobby on evidence of a confirmed appointment with our MP guide.

IMAGE 9.1 ■ The face of the Westminster Parliament

Photo: Michael Moran

■ The photograph shows in part the single best known image in British politics: the clock tower of the Palace of Westminster, Big Ben. The clock tower is an icon of British democracy and, via the chimes broadcast to announce numerous radio and TV news bulletins, is also a powerful symbol of the London-focused system of government. But the angle of the photograph also shows the complexity of the physical and political reality of the Westminster Parliament. Big Ben seems a timeless symbol of traditional British government (though it only dates from the nineteenth century). The closer building is Portcullis House, the recently completed state-of-the-art offices provided for backbench Members of Parliament. One of the many ironies of this juxtaposition is that the completion of this enormously expensive addition to the facilities of the Westminster legislature coincided with its increasing loss of powers and functions, both downwards to devolved government, notably in Scotland, and outwards to the institutions of the EU.

Parliament is technically a bicameral legislature: it consists of the two 'chambers', the Commons and the Lords. Since our tour is swift and selective we should spend most time on the Commons, the more important of these.

It is natural to want to begin our tour with the actual chamber of the House of Commons. Since parliamentary debates were first televized in 1991 this is the arena where we are most likely to have viewed Parliament in action. What will immediately strike us if we have done a little homework is how little the Chamber, nominally the heart of Parliament, is occupied. Business is only formally conducted there for about 150 days in the parliamentary year (even this is more than was typically the case a century ago). At any one time the visitor will see remarkably few MPs actually present. Indeed the Chamber is designed on the assumption that all Members will rarely attend. On the few occasions when there is a full turnout there is standing room only for some: the long benches (rather than the specially designated desks for each member usual in other parliaments) mean that nobody is guaranteed a reserved seat. These rare occasions include: Prime Minister's Question Time, when both sides join noisily in adversarial abuse between the Prime Minister and the Leader of the Opposition; the annual Budget statement by the Chancellor of the Exchequer; and occasionally on a great national crisis, like a war or a government scandal. Unless we have turned up on one of these rare occasions we will see sparsely occupied benches.

The benches, the panelling of the Chamber, fittings such as the lighting, the high ceiling: all make the Chamber resemble an assembly hall in an ancient school, or even a church. At first glance the Chamber, like the view of the Palace of Westminster from the outside, suggests that we are looking at an ancient building dating from medieval times. In fact the shape dates from the middle of the nineteenth century. After a great fire in 1834 the present Palace of Westminster was constructed after extensive debate and an elaborate architectural competition, the Chamber only opening in 1850. The present Chamber only dates from 1950. It was rebuilt as a modified version of the original following destruction in an air raid in 1941.

At this point the shape of our tour will depend on how friendly and influential is our guide. But if a compliant MP is showing us round we can now see important parts of the Palace to which members of the public are not normally admitted unaccompanied. These are the tea rooms, the bars and the restaurants. The House of Commons resembles a large and well equipped club which keeps unusual hours – at least by the standards of most conventional work places. Until very recently it normally began business in mid-afternoon and often did not conclude until late at night. (Below I will summarize some recent reforms.) It is the custom to keep these social facilities open at least as long as the Chamber of the House is in session. Because

MPs represent territorial constituencies, only a minority of Members have their main dwelling within commuting distance of the Commons. Most live in rented flats and houses, often shared with other Members of the same Party, or alone in flats which they have been able to buy in recent years with a much disputed system of special allowances (see Political Issues 9.1). In these circumstances the social institutions like the bars and dining rooms become very important for many Members. The fact that for the most part access to these is highly restricted strengthens the atmosphere of a private club – a place where Members can eat and drink (sometimes to excess) out of the public gaze. This intense and privileged social aspect to Commons life helps explain why, despite the fact that much of the actual business of parliamentary life is tedious and tiring, MPs often become intensely attached to the place and suffer serious traumas when they lose their seat. One prominent Conservative who lost his seat in the 1997 election could not bring himself to re-enter the precincts of the House as a guest, waiting until he was eventually returned as an MP in a subsequent by-election.

Until recently our tour of this part of the Palace would have also allowed us to examine MPs' offices. Office accommodation was cramped, office sharing being the norm – indeed until a generation ago many MPs only acquired a locker on first being returned to Parliament. But now we can cross to the other side of Westminster Bridge and examine Portcullis House. This is a recently erected purpose built office accommodation for members (see Image 9.1). Its existence reflects an important development, which, we shall see later, is a source of great tension about the role of the Commons: the development of a more conventional model of professional organization. The physical impression conveyed here is deliberately different from that of the traditional Palace. It has all the trappings of the modern. The visitor enters a large atrium, like the entrance to the headquarters of a big business corporation. Suites of offices for members provide room for secretaries and research assistants, and the offices have all the facilities of state of the art IT.

Parliament consists of both the Houses of Commons and Lords, and since the former is by far the more important it is natural that on our tour it attracts most attention. But we should now retrace our steps to the lobby of the Palace of Westminster where we originally entered. Now we go down the corridor opposite to that taken to explore the Commons. We can thus explore 'the other place', as the Lords are quaintly called in formal House of Commons' language. The tour replicates the main features we noticed in the Commons: a main chamber

DOCUMENTING POLITICS 9.1

The culture of the House of Commons: the partisan battle at full pitch

Mr David Cameron (Witney) (Con): This morning the Prime Minister said that a general election would cause 'chaos'. What on earth did he mean?

Prime Minister Brown: What would cause chaos would be the election of a Conservative Government, and public spending cuts.

Mr. Cameron: So there we have it: the first admission that the Prime Minister thinks he is going to lose! I know that the Prime Minister is frightened of elections, but how can he possibly believe that in the fourth year of a Parliament, in one of the oldest democracies in the world, a general election could somehow bring chaos? Have another go at a better answer.

Prime Minister Brown: I am not going to support a programme of Conservative public spending cuts. But look here: the House has got to have some humility about what has happened in the last few days. We have got to recognise – all of us, in all parts of the House – that mistakes have been made by Members of Parliament in all parties. Having had the humility to recognise that, we also have a duty to sort the problem out. The only way to sort out the system is to go ahead and sort out the system, and that is what we are proposing to do.

Mr. Cameron: Does the Prime Minister not understand that the best way to show some humility is to ask the people who put us here? The Prime Minister is so hopelessly out of touch. How can the answer to a crisis of democracy be an unelected Prime Minister? In past months, during this economic crisis, there have been elections in India, South Africa and New Zealand. They all have new Governments with a new mandate. The United States had an election in the middle of a banking crisis. Was that chaos? Is President Obama the agent of chaos?

Prime Minister Brown: I notice that at no point does the right hon. Gentleman enter into the policy issues that are at stake here. At no point does he want to talk about what would be the effect of a Conservative Government in this country cutting public spending in schools, hospitals and public services generally, or about what they would do in leaving people on their own in this recession. Our duty is not only to clean up the system in the House of Commons – and every Member has a responsibility to work on that now – but to take this country through the difficulties of the recession, and not say to people that unemployment is a price worth paying ...

■ The dominant theme of this chapter is that the House of Commons is an institution that exists mainly to fight battles between parties. Prime Minister's Questions (normally taken weekly on Wednesdays when the Commons is in session) epitomize this partisan culture. The extract (which I have heavily edited) catches the mixture of elaborately choreographed theatre and often chaotic intervention on the issues of the day. The exchange took place in an especially fraught atmosphere: the Speaker had announced his resignation the day before.

Source: HC Debates, 20 May 2009, cols 1495–7.

fitted out in mock medieval manner; committee rooms and bars; tea rooms and places to dine. The main difference is that the Lords is physically even grander than the Commons. Indeed the main ceremonial occasion in the parliamentary year is held in the chamber of the Lords. This is the televized 'speech from the throne', when the Monarch reads a speech written by the Government of the day outlining its main legislative plans. The dignified function of the Lords has been even more prominent than the dignified function of the Commons. What the future holds for the Lords is examined near the end of this chapter.

THE HOUSE OF COMMONS: ORGANIZATION AND POWERS

The House of Commons lies at the heart of the Westminster system – indeed as we have noted it is its best known public symbol. The organization and functions of the Commons, and the way these two elements are changing, are in turn important emblems of the way the once dominant wider Westminster system of governing Britain is changing.

If we imagined designing an institution from scratch, it would be rational first to decide its functions and then to design its organization. Real world institutions are hardly ever like this, and the House of Commons is no exception. The way it is organized is a function of long-term historical evolution punctuated by dramatic changes, such as those associated with the great extensions of the franchise described in Chapter 2. Thus organization has often determined function, rather than vice versa. We can see this by describing three key influences that shape the organization of the House: the way members are selected; the connected question of the importance of political parties; and the organization of the business of the House.

Territorial representation

The Commons is made up of 650 individual members elected for separate territorial constituencies in the UK. Numbers have varied over time, though there has been a gradual tendency towards the expansion of the House – one which the coalition Government elected in May 2010 is intent on reversing. In Chapter 17 I will describe electoral systems of the UK, but the distinctive feature operating for the House of Commons should be immediately noted: constituencies are represented by a single Member, and the House is composed solely of these representatives of the individual constituencies. (We shall see very different principles at work when we turn to the elected institutions for Scotland and Wales.) This basic principle of territorial representation, and its focus on the constituencies represented by a single Member, has a number of important consequences for the way the Commons functions, but the most obvious can be simply stated: the working life of the Commons is deeply affected by the problem of how to keep these territorial representatives occupied.

Party organization

As it happens, party organization provides the most important solution to the problem identified above. The dominance of party organization is the single most important influence on both the way the House runs its business and the functions it performs. The House of

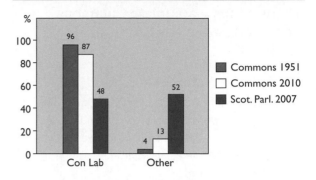

FIGURE 9.1 ■ **Party domination of the House of Commons and the Scottish Parliament compared**

Legend:
- Commons 1951
- Commons 2010
- Scot. Parl. 2007

Con Lab: 96, 87, 48
Other: 4, 13, 52

■ The bars measure percentages of the total parliamentary representation. In the middle of the twentieth century the House of Commons had no British rival as a legislature, and was virtually monopolized by the two leading parties: only just 1 per cent of seats were in other hands. By 2010 there had been an appreciable rise in rivals to Labour and the Conservatives – though, as we shall see in Chapter 17, the electoral system used for the Westminster Parliament meant that the rise did not reflect changes in the distribution of the popular vote. But one feature was virtually unchanged: the Commons was a party-dominated chamber. There were no non-party independents in 1951, and none in 2010. Under a very different, more proportional, electoral system in Scotland the two big UK parties had lost their dominant position.

Source: Figures for 1951 calculated from Butler and Butler (2000); other figures from Electoral Commission data.

Commons is a party institution. There are two key signs of this.

Affiliation of members. It is almost unknown for a Member of the Commons to be returned as an independent, that is, without the label of a political party. Indeed for most of the period of modern British politics – which we can date from 1918 – the overwhelming mass of MPs has been drawn from two parties, Conservative and Labour. The two parliaments of 2001 and 2005 were unusual in returning a single independent; the one elected in May 2010 returned to type – the single independent lost his seat. While the representation of smaller parties has grown in recent decades, partisan domination of the House, and the domination of the two main parties, remain its most striking features.

Party cohesion. Members with party affiliations dominate many modern legislatures, but the influence of party goes deeper than mere affiliation in the Commons. Party organization shapes the behaviour of Members, the

DOCUMENTING POLITICS 9.2

How whips manipulate Commons proceedings: extract from an MP's diary

May 14

Late this morning DD of the SS (David Davis of the Government Whips Office) found me and handed me a slip of paper, a little strip, no more than two inches deep and four inches wide.

'What's this?' I asked.

'It's a question for the PM,' he smirked. 'You're asking it. This afternoon.'

'But I haven't got a question down for the PM,' I protested.

'Stand up and you'll be called.'

'How do you know?'

'I know. Trust me. Just learn the question. You've got to have if off by heart, no reading, no glancing at notes. Just wait for the Speaker to say your name then spit out the question. We've put a joke in for you.'

■ The central place of whips and whipping is a sign of a theme emphasized throughout this chapter: the way the Westminster Parliament, especially the House of Commons, is driven by the partisan battle. A good whip tries to manipulate the apparently spontaneous battle in the Chamber. This extract from the diary of a Conservative backbencher under the Government of Mr Major shows a good whip at work.

Source: Brandreth (1999:96).

styles of debate and the practicalities of working. When Members of the Commons vote, they vote overwhelmingly on party lines. While this unity has declined in recent decades, partisan voting is still the overwhelming norm. This party cohesion is supported by a powerful system of internal party organization based on the 'whipping' system. The language of 'whipping' is itself an illustration of how the culture and organization of the House echo its historical evolution. The original 'whippers in' operated on the foxhunting field, whipping the hounds into line. The adoption of the language as parliamentary reflected the Commons' historical domination by upper-class representatives of rural constituencies, for whom fox hunting was part of a way of life and a natural source of everyday imagery. In modern parties, styles of whipping vary enormously, from the autocratic to the most diplomatic. But what unites them all is that the whipping system is vital to the maintenance of party unity and helps to organize the daily life of the Member of the Commons. All the parties, both in government and out, have a chief whip who leads a team of whips. The whips' key functions are to – depending on style – discipline or cajole members into public support of the party, to monitor the state of opinion within the party in Parliament, and to advise party leaders about the state of that opinion. More immediately, when Parliament is in session a key influence over individual MPs is the communication from the whips indicating when an MP has to be present for a vote in the Chamber of the Commons. So important is this last that its form of expression has entered the wider language, for instance as a 'three line whip'. (The urgency of attending to vote is indicated by underlining, three lines being a virtual command.)

The formalities of the whipping system, though important, are only the outward expression of even more profound ways in which party organization shapes the Commons. Although the physical layout of Parliament encourages a huge amount of informal contacts in those bars and tea rooms that we saw in our tour, and while there are occasional friendships across party lines, party organization is very important in shaping even this informal life. And, as we shall now see, it is also central to the conduct of parliamentary business.

The organization of Commons business

When we look at the practical details of how the Commons organizes itself, three features stand out. The first is the *organization of debate*, because the Chamber in particular is above all a debating forum. The second is the *organization of time*, because the cycle of the parliamentary year is vital to the way the House runs itself. The third is the practical *organization of daily business*, because it is here that we see vivid illustrations of the House in action. Let us examine each of these three in turn.

The organization of debate. The first, revealing clues to the organization of Commons business, we will already have gleaned from our quick tour of the Palace of Westminster. As we looked down on the Chamber of the House we will have seen a layout that is actually quite unusual among legislatures in modern democracies. The important features of physical layout to notice are: the separation of the governing party from the rest of the Commons and the physical line of division between the two halves, ensuring that they face each other across the Chamber; and the symbolic placing of the Speaker – the chair of the session – between the two. But another important physical feature only becomes clear when we look a bit more closely at the actual seating of members. If we can recognize our political personalities we will soon see that the leading members of the two main parties all occupy the front benches on either side: government ministers on one side, leaders of the main Opposition party on the other. (Hence 'backbencher' for rank and file MPs.) In other words, this is a House organized to conduct a public battle, albeit a non-violent one, between the supporters of the governing party and the rest. On the side of the Opposition this is further organized by the now long-established practice in the opposition parties of forming a 'shadow' administration: a front bench team which confronts its rivals from the Opposition benches, stretching from the Leader of the Opposition (a paid position) to that of the most obscure shadow minister of sport. If we have chanced on the House on one its big set piece occasions – such as Prime Minister's Question Time (see Documenting Politics 9.1) – we will soon see that the organization of business is dominated by a public adversarial contest between the governing party and the Opposition.

The organization of the parliamentary timetable. Our immediate first impression from the Chamber of the House that party is vital to organizing the conduct of business will be supported when we look more closely at how the Commons organizes its time. The most basic of all organizing facts – the organization of the Commons year – shows this. The governing party largely determines the organization of parliamentary time, and indeed what remains is mostly shaped by opposition reactions to the governing party and by the desire to prosecute the adversarial party battle.

The shaping influence of parliamentary time comes in two particularly important forms.

The cycle of the parliamentary year. The first is that the legislative programme of the government of the day dominates the parliamentary year. The present conventions of passing legislation through the Commons (and then through the Lords, which we examine next) reinforce this domination. Legislation must pass through a series of stages, the most important of which are a debate on the principles of the legislation (Second Reading) and a virtual line by line examination of the proposals (Committee Stage). If all stages are not concluded in both Houses in the space of a year then the legislation lapses. (This is itself a marginal relaxation, the result of a series of changes to working practices introduced in 2002. Before that, legislation not passed at the end of the parliamentary session was lost irrevo-

cably.) For over a century, therefore, the single most important influence on the organization of parliamentary business has been a virtual imperative for the governing party: to use its majority to control parliamentary time in order to see through its legislative programme.

The rhythm of the parliamentary day. Imagine that we could examine the daily diary of a Member of the Commons. What we would discover would depend greatly on the role of that MP. Members of the Government are drawn predominantly from the House of Commons, and if our MP were a minister we would find that he or she spent most of the time in his or her department rather than in the House. (If we look back at Briefing 6.1 we will find that this marks an important historical change: the nineteenth century Prime Minister Gladstone would expect to spend the largest part of his day actually in the Chamber when the House was in session.) If we examine the diary of a government backbencher – numerically the commonest form of parliamentary life – we will notice several striking features. The actual amount of time spent in the Chamber, still less speaking in the Chamber, is quite small. As we probably sensed from our opening tour, for most of the time when the Chamber is in session it is occupied by only a handful of members. A significantly larger proportion of time spent on official Commons business is devoted to hearings of House of Commons Committees. (For more details of these, see Briefing 9.2.) The extensive range of tea rooms, bars and restaurants that we saw on our tour would have alerted us to the large proportion of the working day spent in these. 'Socializing', dining, drinking and working are thus all mixed up together in the daily business of the Commons and in the daily life of the Member. Finally, we will notice that the MP whose diary we are examining spends a large amount of time on constituency business: either actually in the constituency, where most MPs have their main residence, or in his or her office dealing with issues raised by constituents. Why the organization of daily business takes this form is something we will understand as we turn to examine the functions of the Commons.

THE HOUSE OF COMMONS: FUNCTIONS

The House of Commons is part of the legislature, and if we simply looked superficially at how it spends its time daily we might decide that passing laws is indeed its main function: quantitatively, most debate and argument is about legislation, proposed or passed. But the House of Commons is misunderstood if viewed as a legislator. Virtually all legislative proposals originate from, and are shaped by, the Executive, which means the Government

BRIEFING 9.1

The stages of parliamentary legislation

The pre-parliamentary stages.

■ Most legislation has a long gestation. It may be preceded by formal consultations with affected interests in the form of Green Papers or White Papers: the former indicate the Government has a truly open mind, the latter that it is committed to proposals in outline.

■ Even in the absence of formal public consultation, there will typically be extensive consultation and debate, between central departments, between departments and organized interests, and within the department that proposes to sponsor legislation.

■ Most important legislation to be proposed by the governing party will be announced in outline in an annual Queen's Speech – an elaborate 'dignified' occasion, but one that also announces the government's legislative programme for a session.

■ The final proposal (a bill) is drafted by a team of lawyers in the Parliamentary Counsel Office of the Cabinet Office.

The parliamentary stages.

Bills go through identical stages in both Houses, though most important bills begin life in the Commons

■ First reading: a purely formal laying of the bill before the House.

■ Second reading: a wide ranging debate on the broad principles of the bill. Although focused on the proposals, the broad range of the second reading often means that debate is integrated into the partisan battle which is ever present, especially in the House of Commons.

■ Committee Stage. Most bills are considered by one of a series of Standing Committees, typically consisting of about 18 members. Though Committees are composed to reflect the partisan makeup of the wider House, smaller size, more informal procedures and a focus on detail means the process is not so shaped by the party battle.

■ Report Stage. This 'reports out' the amended bill to the wider House, at which stage Committee amendments can be overturned and new amendments inserted.

■ Third Reading. Formally a brief overview of the final product, more commonly an opportunity to resume the full partisan battle using the bill as an instrument.

The post-parliamentary stages.

■ Royal Assent: a purely formal stage of assent by the Monarch of the bill (last withheld in 1707), followed by its printing as an Act, whence it becomes the law of the land.

■ This schematic outline of the stages of parliamentary legislation actually omits two critical considerations. First, time is of the essence: each bill must complete all stages within a parliamentary year and lapses if this is not accomplished. Second, the really critical stage is often after all this: government legislation is usually successfully carried, but often fails in its objects at implementation stage: see Chapter 19.

BRIEFING 9.2

Select Committees in the House of Commons

Standing Committees are ad hoc committees constructed to conduct the 'committee stage' of legislation (see Briefing 9.1). But *Select* Committees are more permanent and attempt to expedite the business of the Commons. Their numbers and titles often vary, but they mostly come in one of three forms:

■ Those concerned with the domestic management of the House itself: for instance, the Broadcasting Committee which advises the speaker on the broadcasting of the Commons.

■ Those that are a legacy of a time when the Commons was a much more powerful controller of the Executive: the Public Accounts Committee dates from the nineteenth century and reflects the historical role of the Commons in attempting to ensure financial accountability of the Executive.

■ Those that embody the larger architecture of the government system, designed to ensure that the main functional divisions of the Executive are covered (for instance the Treasury Select Committee). This architecture was substantially redesigned in reforms introduced in 1979 by Mrs Thatcher's first Leader of the House of Commons, Norman St John Stevas.

■ The Select Committee has become more comprehensive and publicly visible in recent years.

of the day, advised by the civil service. Nor are the Commons' extensive debates on either the principles or details of legislative proposals of great significance in shaping the law: secure government majorities (which up to now have been the usual state of affairs) mean that legislative proposals are hardly ever overturned wholesale, and detailed amendments are usually the result of concessions by ministers.

The only significant departure from this pattern is Private Members' legislation. A small amount of parliamentary time is allotted for the consideration each session of a number of bills sponsored by backbench Members of Parliament. Access to this privileged time – confined to a share of about ten Friday sessions and some Wednesday morning sessions per parliamentary year – is governed by an annual ballot. Drawing a 'winning number' in the ballot can do wonders for the reputation of the individual backbencher. Some highly contentious issues which divide parties internally (such as abortion law reform) have been dealt with in this way, since 'unwhipped' votes are normal on Private Members' Bills. Nevertheless, Private Members' legislation is of marginal importance (see Briefing 9.3).

The fact that the Commons is neither a serious originator nor a shaper of legislation does not mean that the time spent on debate about legislation is pointless; only that its point must be understood within the setting of the wider functions performed by the Commons, and within the context of the dominant feature of the Commons 'culture' – the fact that it is a party dominated institution. This partisan culture both enables, and hinders, the ability of the Commons to perform key political functions. Six of these are particularly important, and are now considered. They are:

● supplying and supporting the government;
● fighting the partisan battle;
● scrutinizing legislation;
● scrutinizing the Executive;
● representing interests;
● protecting individual constituents.

Supplying and supporting the government

There is intense competition to enter the House of Commons, as we shall discover in Chapter 18. The single most important reason is that membership of the Commons is a virtual requirement for any ambitious politician who wishes to serve as a government minister. (When we turn to the Lords we shall discover an alternative route, mostly to office outside the Cabinet, which some find more congenial.) This fact defines perhaps the single most important function of the Commons in the wider Westminster system: it provides the main pool of talent from which members of the Government – and the

BRIEFING 9.3

Private Members' legislation

Most bills that pass into law by receiving the Royal Assent originate as proposals from the Executive. A small number, and a tiny proportion of the whole, originate as bills from backbench Members of Parliament. Although Private Members' legislation can originate in either House, the bulk of successful bills originate in the Commons. Formally, there are three sources of proposals for bills in the Commons, but only the third described below is of significance as a source of legislation.

- Ten minute rule bills: a Member may move a motion to seek House approval to introduce a bill. The proposer is allowed ten minutes to make a case. The motion is rarely allowed and this method is recognized, not as a serious attempt to move legislation, but as an attempt to gain publicity for an issue that concerns the Member. Nevertheless, between 1983 and 2001, 10 bills passed into law through this route.
- Ordinary presentation bills: these are laid before the House, but not debated. The proposer will have little prospect of turning the bill into legislation, but will typically use it as part of continuing a process of keeping 'alive' an issue on which the Member has legislative ambitions. Between 1983 and 2001, 39 bills passed into law through this route.
- 'Ballot bills'. Early in each session a ballot is held allocating an allotment of parliamentary time – principally on Fridays – for Private Members' bills. Up to 400 MPs typically enter the ballot. Many do not even have a particular bill in mind. Typically 20 'slots' are allocated in the ballot. Realistically, only those drawn in the top ten have any chance of turning proposals into law: in 1999–2000, for instance, only five 'ballot bills' were turned into law. A Member who draws a 'high' number in the ballot will be inundated with draft bills from pressure groups and parliamentary colleagues. This category of Private Members' legislation is associated with groundbreaking reforms, especially in the area of social reform: laws originally decriminalizing homosexuality, abortion and abolishing capital punishment originated in this route. But of the 147 ballot bills that became law between 1983 and 2001, most were on technical and uncontroversial subjects. While the leaders of the major parties – especially the governing party – often prefer to leave to Private Members' legislation highly sensitive issues that divide parties internally, this very sensitivity makes passage difficult. This is because there are so many opportunities to delay legislation when party controls are relaxed that any controversial legislation is likely to be ambushed on its passage through both Houses.

■ The most precious commodity in Parliament is time. Parliamentary time is controlled by the governing party which controls the Executive; time allocated to Private Members' bills is very limited. This makes proposals – even when they enjoy the support of a majority of Members – immensely vulnerable to delaying tactics by opponents. It is easy to 'talk out' a proposal by debating with real or specious points. A Member lucky enough to come high in the annual ballot, to maximize the chances of getting a bill into law, should choose a technical and non-controversial measure. If a contentious measure is chosen, it is only likely to succeed if it has the implicit support of the Government of the day – a feature of the famous measures of social reform like decriminalization of homosexuality.

Source: HC Information Office (2010).

rivals who would like to replace them from the Opposition front benches – are chosen. It helps to explain why, despite the development of other legislatures like the European Parliament, most ambitious British politicians still aim for a seat in the Commons. What is more, those who become ministers retain their seat in the legislature (a practice not universal in the other democracies). While the demands of ministerial office inevitably reduce their time spent at Westminster, this membership is vital in all kinds of ways. Above all, it obliges ministers to be present to defend government policy and actions against the Opposition. It means that those government backbenchers who have not been recruited to office still have a vital governing function: their votes ensure that government business carries through the Commons; their voices ensure arguments supporting the Government of the day. This last role is in turn central to a second important function that we now examine: fighting the adversarial battle between the parties.

Fighting the partisan battle

Normal people only occasionally view the House of Commons at work, and then usually on high profile occasions, like the weekly 'joust' at Prime Minister's Question Time between the Prime Minister and the official Leader of the Opposition. And normal people are often shocked at the atmosphere of debate: the point scoring and the apparent lack of interest in reasoned exchange where arguments would be conceded and modified. Were we to observe this style elsewhere – say in a university class or in a business meeting – we would undoubtedly think that these were peculiar, dysfunctional people in a peculiar, dysfunctional world. But this is to miss the point in respect of the Commons: partisan point scoring is the very essence of Commons life because it is a party dominated institution, and because the conventions of party life stress adversarial confrontation. This is not an inevitable consequence of party organization: other democracies have legislatures, with parties, where there is much more stress on consensus and accommodation of different views. But for better or worse the history and culture of the Westminster House of Commons has implanted this adversarial style. The House works best either when what it does can be easily accommodated to this style or when for some reason the style is totally suspended. Suspension is most likely to happen in two almost entirely opposite circumstances: when some great national crisis (like a war) unites all in a common purpose; or when the issues are so technical and detailed that it is hard to convert them into partisan form. We shall see later that this latter style can be observed in some of the work of Select Committees. But even in

national crisis, or when faced with a technical question, MPs usually instinctively look for a partisan 'spin' on the issue.

Scrutinizing legislation

Much the most common way of scrutinizing the details of proposed legislation is through the institution of the Committee, notably the small Standing Committee. In these Committees some of the culture of party adversarialism is modified, for reasons that are not hard to understand. Business is done less formally than in the Chamber. (On some occasions the whole House transforms itself into Committee mode as a 'Committee of the Whole House', and here too formality is diminished.) Smaller numbers, the more intimate atmosphere of a Committee Room, diminished public attention, the often grinding detail of working through the clauses of a bill: all encourage a more normal exchange of views. Committee stages like this also fulfil other purposes: for the ambitious backbencher this is an occasion to impress the whips with a grasp of detail and therefore increase the chances of promotion to the front bench. But the process is still dominated by the fact of partisan organization: the Members almost always in the end vote on party lines; the object of the exercise for the majority is to report the bill out for further progress to the statute book; and amendments will not pass unless the minister responsible for managing the bill is convinced that they are appropriate.

Scrutinizing the Executive

The more general scrutiny of the operations of the Executive has historically been an important function of Parliament. It is partly constrained, and partly enabled, by the adversarial battle across the floor of the Commons. As a general rule, the more the scrutiny of the actions of the Executive involves the high politics of the Government of the day, the more it is likely to be dominated by the pursuit of that adversarial party battle. The most extreme version of this is provided by Prime Minister's Question Time which, while nominally about holding the Prime Minister to account, is now dominated by a virtually gladiatorial, personal battle between the Prime Minister and the Leader of the Opposition. The process can, by happenstance, wring information and accounts out of the Government of the day, but this is virtually an incidental side effect. Nobody pretends that the occasion is seriously about holding the Executive to account. It is about measuring the calibre of the two gladiators. Although it is doubtful that the performance in the battle by either the Prime Minister or the Leader of the Opposition makes any significant impact on public opinion, it is intensely followed within the Commons:

EUROPEANIZING 9.1

Europeanizing the legislative process: the work of the European Scrutiny Committee

The European Scrutiny Committee assesses the legal and/or political importance of each EU document (about 1,100 per year) and decides which are debated. The Committee receives an Explanatory Memorandum on each document from the relevant Minister. All documents deemed politically or legally important are discussed in the Committee's weekly Reports.

Debates recommended by the Committee take place either in a European Committee or (more rarely) on the Floor of the House. Under the scrutiny reserve resolution passed by the House, Ministers should not agree to proposals which the Committee has not cleared or which are waiting for debate.

The Committee also monitors the activities of UK Ministers in the Council (through parliamentary questions and sometimes by questioning Ministers in person), and sometimes conducts general inquiries into legal, procedural or institutional developments in the EU. The Committee is appointed under Standing Order No. 143 and has 16 members.

■ This, in its own words, is a description of the most significant attempt by the Commons to come to terms with the fact that a flood of law and regulation now comes out of the Union, not out of the domestic legislative process. The issue is obvious: how far, given the flood of documentation, is Parliament equipped to scrutinize it?

Source: http://www.parliament.uk/parliamentary_committees/european_scrutiny.cfm.

Prime Ministers invest significant time in preparation, and the fate of the Leader of the Opposition can hang on whether Opposition backbenchers feel their Leader is doing well in the public jousting across the floor of the House. The single most important reason why Iain Duncan-Smith was deposed as Conservative Leader in 2003 was his failure to best the Prime Minister in these gladiatorial exchanges.

The further the scrutiny of the Executive gets from this adversarial struggle – which in part means the further it gets from the floor of the House – the more it indeed recognizably looks like an attempt at scrutiny: to examine the actions of the Executive; to extract information from the Executive; and to pass judgements on the Executive. The most effective instrument for all this is the House's system of specialized Select Committees. Although in composition these attempt to mimic party strength in the wider House, the culture of the Committees often suppresses much of the partisan debate and unites members in the common pursuit of scrutiny. Some of the most important of these Committees are in direct descent from an age of executive scrutiny in the nineteenth century when party ties were weaker than now and the assertiveness of back-

benchers greater. But the system was considerably strengthened by reforms at the end of the 1970s which established a stable system of Committees that, despite some changes in name and jurisdiction over time, have since then established that every significant department of state is 'shadowed' by its own Committee.

The significance of these Committees derives from three features:

● They have real power to call witnesses and demand documents both from departments of state and from a wide range of other public agencies. While officials and ministers often wriggle out of producing evidence and giving straightforward testimony, the Committees have an impressive record in this kind of scrutiny.

● The Committees represent substantial areas of specialist expertise. Although their numbers of permanent staff and specialist advisers are tiny by comparison with the resources of departments and public agencies, they nevertheless represent a considerable accumulation of information and expertise, at least by the modest historical standards of expertise available to backbenchers.

• The Committees have gone some way to solve a perennial problem in a partisan Parliament. We saw earlier that a prime function of the Commons was, simply, to provide a pool of talent for both Government Office and the Opposition Front Benches. What does an MP do who fails to make it to the front bench? For MPs of talent who either have failed to progress or whose front bench careers are over, the Committees have created an alternative Commons career. In particular, chairing a Committee offers a rewarding and often well-publicized public role.

Representing interests

Interest representation is built into the very nature of the Commons. Territorial representation is at the heart of the Member's life, and this naturally stretches to representing the economic interests of the territorial constituency. A Member for, say, a constituency with a large car plant within its boundaries becomes a natural, and legitimate, voice for the interests of the automobile industry. A more troubling link connects Members of the House to the world of functional representation described in the last chapter. Historically, Members were virtually expected to speak for functional interests: the Labour Party, for instance, began as a parliamentary group speaking for organized trade unionism. Members were not even paid a salary until 1912. In this era before the payment of a salary, a pattern developed of MPs combining their seat in the Commons with outside economic interests, either in the form of employment or property ownership. That pattern, though changing, still persists. Indeed in the last generation it has been expanded and systematized by the spread of consultancies, through which members hire their knowledge and connections to outside interests. This is a development connected to the rise of professional lobbying which we also described in the last chapter. Since the 1970s a register of interests has tried to keep track of, and to put into the public domain, all the payments received by MPs from outside interests. A series of scandals in the early 1990s, when some MPs were revealed as willing to ask parliamentary questions in return for covert payments, led to the establishment of a Committee on Standards in Public Life. On the Committee's recommendation there was established an Office of the Parliamentary Commissioner for Standards. The workings and powers of the Commissioner have been the subject of much controversy (in 2002 the incumbent Commissioner was in effect forced from her post at the end of her first period of office as a result of conflict with powerful groups of MPs). A great expenses scandal that consumed Parliament for much of 2009 has led to further reform of the regulation of standards, the details of which are in Political Issues 9.1.

These controversies touch on fundamental differences about the function of MPs in representing interests, and go well beyond issues about personal honesty or publicity of payments. MPs are now paid a handsome professional salary with liberal 'perks', such as very generous pension arrangements. This leads some to argue that paid connections with any special interests should cease and that the Member should become solely a full-time professional, representing only the interests of the territorial constituency. Others argue that this violates the historically important role of the Member of Parliament. As we shall see later, this argument connects to a fundamental uncertainty about the purpose of the modern House of Commons.

Interest representation is a central function of the Commons, but what this means for the daily behaviour of Members is plainly disputed. There is more agreement on the final function that we now examine.

Protecting individual constituents

A historically well-established function of the Member of the Commons lies in protecting individual constituents. This 'case work' aspect of the MP's role is constantly growing. As the 'back office' support has become more sophisticated, casework has become increasingly important, not least in trying to establish the Member's reputation and visibility among the constituency electorate. It comprises a range of work enormous in its variety and significance. The institution of the 'surgery', where an MP is freely available at set hours in an office in the constituency, remains central to the lives of most Members. (Indeed some Members now try to reach out further by holding regular surgeries in places like supermarkets.) This fairly unrestricted public access means that MPs hear everything, from the ravings of barely sane cranks to accounts of the most grievous miscarriages of justice. The office business of any efficient MP is dominated by chasing this casework, especially in the first instance by correspondence with the relevant public agency. Down the line, if correspondence does not produce a satisfactory resolution, lie more public means of pursuit: a request for a written parliamentary answer from a minister; raising the issue in a direct oral question to a minister on the floor of the Commons; even employing the device of an adjournment debate, when backbenchers can use a short debate to raise a particularly serious case.

At the end of this chain of mechanisms for protecting constituents lies one that dates from the founding of the Parliamentary Commissioner for Administration (the

DOCUMENTING POLITICS 9.3

Commons' resolutions on declaration of interests

RESOLUTIONS OF THE HOUSE RELATING TO THE CONDUCT OF MEMBERS' REGISTRATION AND DECLARATION OF MEMBERS' INTERESTS

Lobbying for Reward or Consideration
Resolution of 2nd May 1695
Against offering Bribes to Members

'The Offer of any Money, or other Advantage, to any Member of Parliament, for the promoting of any Matter whatsoever, depending, or to be transacted, in Parliament, is a high Crime and Misdemeanour, and tends to the Subversion of the Constitution.'

Resolution of 22nd June 1858
Rewards to Members

'It is contrary to the usage and derogatory to the dignity of this House, that any of its Members should bring forward, promote or advocate, in this House, any proceeding or measure in which he may have acted or been concerned for or in consideration of any pecuniary fee or reward.'

Resolution of 15th July 1947, amended on 6th November 1995 and 14th May 2002
Conduct of Members

'It is inconsistent with the dignity of the House, with the duty of a Member to his constituents, and with the maintenance of the privilege of freedom of speech, for any Member of this House to enter into any contractual agreement with an outside body, controlling or limiting the Member's complete independence and freedom of action in Parliament or stipulating that he shall act in any way as the representative of such outside body in regard to any matters to be transacted in Parliament; the duty of a Member being to his constituents and to the country as a whole, rather than to any particular section thereof and that in particular no Member of the House shall, in consideration of any remuneration, fee, payment, reward or benefit in kind, direct or indirect, which the Member or any member of his or her family has received, is receiving, or expects to receive advocate or initiate any cause or matter on behalf of any outside body or individual, urge any other Member of either House of Parliament, including Ministers, to do so, by means of any speech, Question, Motion, introduction of a Bill or amendment to a Motion or Bill, or any approach, whether oral or in writing, to Ministers or servants of the Crown.'

■ This text, reproduced in edited form from the Guide to MPs on completing the register of interests, contains the key Commons resolutions which guide the declaration of interests by Members. It is a long standing problem, as is plain from the date of the earliest resolution (1695).

Source: www.parliament.uk/comm/hecom.

'Ombudsman') in 1967. The Ombudsman has extensive powers of investigation in cases where a citizen's grievance is thought to be the result of abuse of administrative powers. While the report and recommendations of the Ombudsman in a finding of maladministration are not binding on a department, the weight of the report is hard for even the most arrogant of departments to ignore. The connection with the role of MPs is that the MP is the 'gatekeeper' to the Ombudsman; an investigation by the Ombudsman requires the approval of the complainant's Member of Parliament. That rule makes the backbencher important in the processing of grievances from the individual citizen. It is also an added weapon in the hands of the backbenches, since the mere threat of referral means that a department is faced at the very least with considerable potential extra work in the event of an enquiry by the Ombudsman. The Ombudsman system is part of wider mechanisms for the redress of citizen grievance – something examined more closely in Chapter 22, where we also explain more fully the idea of 'maladministration'.

THE HOUSE OF COMMONS AND THE CHANGING WESTMINSTER SYSTEM

The House of Commons is the best-known symbol of the Westminster system of government, and the pressures to which it is subject are good indicators of the strains on that system. Three issues have proved especially troublesome: legitimacy, professionalism and purpose.

Issues of legitimacy

Had we looked at the Westminster system as recently as the 1970s we would have noticed that the House of Common stood alone in one key respect: it was the only elected legislative chamber in the UK. In a system of government that claims to be democratic, and where a key mark of democratic legitimacy is popular election, that was an important mark of distinction. Now it is faced by a clutch of elected assemblies: for instance the European Parliament, directly elected since 1979; and the Scottish Parliament and Welsh Assembly since 1999. As we shall see in a moment some reform proposals would also face the Commons with a directly elected House of Lords. None of these developments have yet supplanted the legitimacy of the Commons: turnout in European elections is low and the public visibility of MEPs slight; the Scottish and Welsh Assemblies have, we shall see, had their own problems of legitimacy and popular support. But the Commons can no longer claim the special, definitive mark of democratic legitimacy in the way it once could.

Issues of professionalism

Historically the Commons was a very 'unprofessional' institution. That is, it rejected the notion that its members should be full-time, professional legislators. Paying a salary of any kind is, we saw above, barely a century-old practice; and paying a conventional professional salary is less than a generation old. Partly in conse-

---

DOCUMENTING POLITICS 9.4

Declaring interests: extracts from the Register of Interests

BRENNAN, Kevin (Cardiff West)

Gifts, benefits and hospitality (UK)

　14 February 2009, I attended the Wales v England Six Nations rugby match at the Millennium Stadium with a guest, as guests of BBC Wales. *(Registered 19 February 2009)*

　18 February 2009, I attended the Brit Awards 2009 as a guest of the BPI (British Phonographic Industry). *(Registered 19 February 2009)*

　I am a member of MP4, the Parliamentary rock group. The group has received sponsorship towards the launch of an album for charity in the form of financial assistance towards the recording costs from Ladbrokes plc and Research in Motion UK Limited. *(Registered 26 March 2009*

FABRICANT, Michael (Lichfield)

Sponsorship or financial or material support

　Provision, free of charge, of internet site detailing my work as a Member of Parliament by SolNet Systems Limited of Lichfield.

Land and Property

　House in Maine, USA, lived in by friends who maintain the property but do not pay rent.

■ The range and value of interest declared vary greatly, but these two entries from undistinguished backbenchers are typical. The full list is at http://www.publications.parliament.uk/pa/cm/cmregmem/090610/memi02.htm.

---

quence, the House historically organized itself as a kind of social institution. Its hours of work (typically beginning in mid-afternoon, usually stretching into the late evening, and often lasting overnight) were very different from those of any conventional professional body. That was in part because many members had occupations (for instance in law) that they practised earlier in the day. The odd hours of business encouraged the development of an intense social life, where the politics of the Commons were mixed up with dining, drinking, gossiping, conspiring and fornicating. Conventional office facilities were among the poorest in any legislature across the democratic world. Overwhelming domination by men reinforced the atmosphere of a club.

More conventional styles of professionalism have for at least a generation chipped away at this self-conscious 'unprofessionalism'. The salaries of members are now comparable to those of other middle-class professionals, like doctors or university professors. A declining proportion of Members try to combine being a member of the House with an outside profession. Indeed for most, politics *is* their profession; we will also notice the rise of the professional politician when we come to Chapter 18 on leadership recruitment in British government. As we saw above the 'back office' support for the member – secretaries, personal assistants, research assistants, the latest IT – has recently improved greatly. The occupations of Members before entering the House are increasingly preparations for the parliamentary life – for instance as researchers or advisers to senior politicians. The rise of Select Committees means that, outside the Chamber, much formal business is now done at conventional business hours, in morning hearings. In 2002 reforms were even introduced to reschedule the sittings of the Chamber to allow a more conventional professional timetable, with fewer late sittings. The fact that parliamentary sessions still reflect the old rhythms of political life has if anything strengthened some aspects of this professionalism. It has encouraged MPs to use the greatly improved back office facilities to pursue their 'case work' function, in turn raising their profile in the constituency. But the rise of this professionalism has itself raised important issues, and these go to the heart of the modern meaning and purpose of the Commons.

Issues of purpose

The single most important functions of the Commons are, we have seen, to provide a pool of talent for the front benches, and especially for the Government of the day; and to provide an arena where the adversarial battle between government and opposition is fought out. But this latter function in particular developed before the rise of the 'professional' ideal in the Commons – in an age when being an MP was for many a part-time occupation to be fitted in with other social roles, such as a career in business or the professions, or local prominence as a landowner. The rise of professionalism raises questions about the adversarial function, because the professional ideal stresses a very different approach to political life: an approach that emphasizes the importance of the dispassionate scrutiny of the details of government. For

the modern backbencher with no obvious hope of serving on the front bench, acting as a cheerleader for the front bench or an abuser of the Opposition often does not seem a tremendously rewarding long-term career. Hence the pressure to develop professional career patterns such as service on Select Committees. For traditionalists, however, the rise of this kind of professionalism seems a betrayal of the traditional ideal of Commons life – the triumph of an arid, bureaucratic, technical model over the notion of the House of Commons as a jousting arena where the great conflicts of national life are played out.

THE HOUSE OF LORDS: STRUCTURE, INFLUENCE, REFORM

We noted at the start of this chapter that Britain has what is technically known as a bicameral legislature, consisting of the House of Commons and the House of Lords. Bicameralism is normal among democratic nations (and some undemocratic ones). But the British version of bicameralism has three features which have shaped the modern relationship between the Commons and Lords: there is a history of tense relations between the two Houses; in modern times the House of Commons has been by far the dominant Chamber; and the tensions, combined with Commons domination, have now combined to destabilize this part of the Westminster system, to the point where the Lords has not only been radically reformed, but its very existence brought into question.

The history of a tense relationship

The House of Lords was originally the dominant Chamber in Parliament. Before the rise of industrialism it contained the greatest holders of economic power, titled aristocrats who owned landed estates. The balance shifted after the nineteenth century for two reasons: the industrial revolution meant that other kinds of wealth, notably that based on manufacturing, became more important; and the extension of the vote to, eventually, virtually the whole adult population meant that the House of Commons became the dominant voice in a system of government that claimed to be democratic. At first, however, the decline in the relative power of the Lords largely happened by custom – the Lords came to accept that there were limits to the extent to which it could obstruct decisions of the House of Commons. But the difficulty with customary understandings was that they were likely to be challenged in any crisis. That potential for crisis was engrained in the social and political nature of the House of Lords.

Timeline 9.1

The long road to Lords' reform

	DATE OF MEASURE/PROPOSAL	COMMENT
1911	Parliament Act	Lords effectively loses veto over any money bills; and veto over other legislation abolished, replaced by ability to delay Commons' legislative proposals to two years.
1949	Parliament Act	Reduces Lords' delaying power over Commons' legislative proposals to one year.
1958	Life Peerage Act	Allows addition of peers created for life to existing hereditary peers, and leads to creation of women peers for first time.
1963	Peerage Act	Allows hereditary peers to disclaim their title following campaign by heir of Lord Stansgate, who disclaims his inheritance, adopting instead the title 'Tony Benn'.
1969	Labour Government reform Bill	Agreed in Lords, but dropped after opposition in Commons from an alliance of left-wing Labour radicals and right-wing Conservative traditionalists.
1999	House of Lords Act	Abolishes hereditary entitlement to a seat in the Lords; 92 hereditary peers selected by other hereditary peers to continue sitting in House as a transitional measure.
1999	Royal (Wakeham) Commission on reform of second chamber appointed	Commission reports in 2000. Proposes largely appointed upper house, but with small minority of elected members; 15-year tenure to replace tenure of life peers; representatives of other faiths to be added to existing Anglican bishops in House. Proposals not adopted.
2001	White Paper, *The House of Lords: Completing the Reform*	Proposes a minority of elected peers (120) but 480 to be appointed. Proposals not adopted.
February 2003	Free votes in both Houses on range of options	No option on offer in Commons- secured majority. Leader of House (Robin Cook, advocate of an elected House) advises MPs to 'go home and sleep on it'.
March 2004	reform plans postponed	Secretary of State for Constitutional Affairs announces indefinite postponement of further reform in face of antireform majority in Lords.
May 2010	Conservatives obliged to commit to reform as price of securing Liberal Democrat support in Commons after general election	Con–Lib coalition agreement commits to preparation for wholly, or mostly, elected Upper House.

By the end of the nineteenth century almost the whole of the landed aristocracy supported the Conservative Party, and the Lords was a perennially Conservative institution. The first great crisis of the twentieth century therefore occurred in 1909 when a reforming Liberal Government introduced a Budget too radical for the Conservative dominated Lords. Despite a convention that the Lords did not 'block' budgets approved by the Commons, the Lords did exactly this. A profound constitutional crisis culminated in the passage of the Parliament Act of 1911: this abolished the Lords' veto over money bills and gave it only a delaying power on most other legislation.

The Labour Government elected after 1945 reduced the delaying power to, in effect, a single year, in the Parliament Act of 1949. These restrictions still left the Lords with significant influence and left ample potential for tension in the relationship between the two Chambers. The need to pass legislation through debates in the full Chamber, and through a committee stage in the Lords, gave the Lords, if it chose to threaten it, considerable control over one of the scarcest commodities in Parliament – time. In a crowded legislative timetable, even delay can kill a bill given the present convention that a proposal must pass all stages in a year.

The competition for legitimacy between Lords and Commons

While the House of Lords consisted only of hereditary peers it had very weak claims in any struggle over legitimacy with the House of Commons. For almost the whole of the twentieth century the system of government gave primary legitimacy to elected representatives such as those in the Commons. But the Life Peerages Act of 1958 subtly changed the long-term balance of advantage. The Act provided for the creation of peerages that would not be inherited – hence life peers. The creation of a large body of life peers diminished the importance of the inbuilt Conservative majority derived from hereditary peers in the Lords. Before the reforms of 1999 described below, over one-third of all peers were life peers, and active members of the House were overwhelmingly life creations.

The life peers broadly formed two groups. The first were those nominated by the leadership of the political parties, overwhelmingly Conservative and Labour. These were often distinguished former Commons members, and many became active 'working peers' for the parties in the Lords. They were particularly important in augmenting Labour support, because the Party could count on the support of few hereditaries. The second group of life peers were creations on the basis of distinguished service (in business or the professions,

for example). Many, though not all, were 'cross-benchers' declining any party allegiance. The inbuilt Conservative majority provided by hereditary peers still existed, and could occasionally be brought out to win a vote, but now the most able and industrious members of the House were increasingly the life peers. 'Lifers', by virtue of ability and achievement, were far from compliant with either the Commons or the governing party. There were numerous occasions in the 1980s and 1990s when the Lords amended legislation in defiance of majorities in the Commons, and this only reflected the tip of the iceberg of the Lords' influence: the mere threat to amend and delay legislation obliged governments with a majority in the House of Commons to pause. In part this assertiveness came from a strengthened sense of legitimacy. The life peers greatly strengthened the technical capacity and the authority of the Lords, for many of the life peers could (and can) speak with great authority on policy – indeed, typically could speak with greater technical knowledge when the issue touched their area of expertise than could most members of the Commons.

The historically tense relationship between the two Chambers, then, was based on a clash between the principles of election and the principles of inheritance. The tension was magnified because the hereditary peers, though most were inactive, nevertheless gave the Conservative Party an inbuilt majority and also created a majority which occasionally could be mobilized against radical measures. But by the last two decades of the twentieth century this tension had receded into the background. The governing party in the Commons that had most trouble with the Lords was the Conservatives in power from 1979–97. It suffered defeats in the Lords in every one of its parliamentary sessions and in some years the number of these exceeded 20. This reflected the growth of new potential sources of legitimacy that were used to challenge the right of governments to make policy on the basis of their elective majority in the Commons – and thus the growth of new sources of tension. This new claim to legitimacy derived from the claim to shape law by virtue of experience and knowledge – attributes that were often superior to that of the Commons. It also amounted to a claim to legitimacy by virtue of a principle of representation which we examined in the last chapter: by virtue of speaking on behalf of some great interests in the community, such as the professions, industry and even universities.

Reforming the Lords under New Labour

In the decades after the introduction of life peers the House of Lords became increasingly effective in three areas:

People in Politics 9.1

The importance of expertise in the House of Lords

Baroness Warnock (b. 1924, created 1985)
A Cambridge don and principal of a college, she chaired, or served on, most of the leading official committees concerned with laboratory experiments on humans and animals in the last two decades of the twentieth century, notably the Advisory Committee on Animal Experimentation and the Inquiry into Human Fertility.

Lord Soulsby of Swaffham (b. 1926, created 1990)
One of the leading academic researchers into animal diseases in Britain in the twentieth century. A distinguished research career culminated in a period as Professor of Animal Pathology, University of Cambridge, 1978–93. He chaired subcommittee 1 of the Select Committee on Science and Technology, investigating the control of infectious diseases in the UK.

Lord Wilson of Dinton (b. 1942, created 2002)
He exemplifies an important source of talent in the Lords: the senior civil servant (he ended up as Cabinet Secretary) whose public life was prolonged after formal retirement. He entered the House of Lords with an unrivalled knowledge both of the machinery of government and the personalities involved.

Cartoons: Shaun Steele

■ It is now rare for Members of the House of Commons to have any significant experience in any other occupation than politics, and the most successful have usually been full-time politicians from early adult life. But the creation of life peers after 1958 brought into the House of Lords distinguished (if usually elderly) figures from all walks of life in Britain.

- In performing a classic function of a second chamber: scrutinizing the details of legislative proposals and amending them.
- Through its own specialist committees, akin to the Select Committees of the Commons, but with members who were often genuinely authoritative experts in examining both policy problems and government actions.
- Through debates in the Chamber of the Lords. Whereas the Chamber of the Commons is dominated by the language of the adversarial party battle, debate in the Lords has been very different in style: less adversarial, more directly addressed to the problem at issue, and at least conveying a sense that the issue in question was being debated on the merits of the case. Normal members of the public would immediately find Lords' debates more appealing and recognizable than they would those in the Commons, though in recent years there has been some infection from the adversarial culture of the Commons .

This growing effectiveness did not protect the Lords from fundamental change after the return of Labour to office in 1997. Indeed it may have helped endanger the Lords by making the Lords/Commons relationship tenser. The new Labour Government was committed to the most radical programme of Lords reform ever. That commitment had two origins. First, there was an engrained historical tension between the Lords and the Labour Party because, despite the life peers, there was still a huge inbuilt Conservative Party majority in the Lords provided by the hereditary peers. Second, in its long years of opposition in the 1980s and 1990s the Labour Party became converted to the view that British political institutions generally needed reform – that they were archaic, conferred excessive power on the central executive and hampered democracy. Reform of the Lords was therefore part of a larger programme – notably the devolution reforms which we will examine in Chapter 10.

Two problems faced Labour in achieving reform, one short term and one that continues to dog all reform efforts. The short-term problem was that, if the reform was to be achieved reasonably swiftly, the majority of peers had to vote for their own extinction: the hereditary turkeys had to vote for a constitutional Christmas. This led to complex bargaining, notably with the leadership of the Conservative peers. It explains the shape of the only reform presently achieved. The House of Lords Act 1999 abolished voting rights of almost all hereditary peers. But as an interim measure, in order to put together a majority for the reform in the Lords, the initial proposals were amended to allow the retention of 92 hereditary peers. All but two of these were elected by a very special constituency – composed of fellow hereditary peers. The reform has nevertheless drastically changed the composition of the Lords: the numbers of hereditaries was cut from over 750 to 92; when one of the hereditary peers dies there is a 'by-election' to select a successor.

Reforming the Lords after 2010

All the parties publicly agreed that the 1999 reforms were only an interim solution. Yet for more than a decade reform was becalmed. The stasis arose from more than tactical problems; at root it was caused by the difficulty of agreeing a principle of representation for the House once the hereditary principle is discarded. The Blair government established a Royal Commission to examine reform options. Its report is, however, now only one of a number of reform proposals that have been debated and then forgotten. The sheer difficulty of arriving at a conclusion is the single most revealing feature of the whole process. (In the next chapter we will see a marked contrast where the fundamental changes involved in devolution to Scotland and Wales were executed with clinical swiftness after 1997.) The difficulties arise because modes of reform are connected in a complex way with different views of the proper functions of a second chamber.

The immediate difficulty involves agreeing a principle of selection by which a reformed House should be constituted. The issue is difficult because the principle of selection in turn affects the legitimacy of the institution itself. In other words, it resurrects the great historical source of tension between the Lords and Commons. Any principle of selection creates problems. A fully appointed House – an option for a long time publicly supported by Tony Blair, who was Prime Minister during the critical reform years – is widely opposed on the grounds that it puts too much power into the hands of the Government, and especially of the Prime Minister. Election on the basis of territorial constituencies – a commonly supported option – raises a key issue: how would differences between two democratically elected Houses, Commons and Lords, be resolved?

A very different principle of selection has been advocated historically, for instance by the great Conservative statesman Winston Churchill in the 1920s: that the Lords could become a chamber of 'functional' representation in which the great interests in the community – industry, commerce, labour, professions – were given a voice. As we saw in the last chapter, the idea that functional interests have a legitimate right to representation is embedded in the way the interest-group system works.

POLITICAL ISSUES 9.1

Pay and allowances in the House of Commons

In the spring and summer of 2009 Parliament was convulsed by a series of articles in the *Daily Telegraph* which drew on a CD detailing the allowances claimed by MPs. The most damaging revelations centred on housing allowances originally designed to allow MPs representing constituencies beyond Greater London to cover the cost of a second dwelling. The cases aroused huge public discontent, and were prompted by issues as various as triviality of claims (for toilet brushes), extravagance (contribution to cleaning out the moat of a stately home) and dubious legality (payment for non-existent mortgages). The publicity terminated the Parliamentary careers of more than one hundred MPs. But the longer term significance of this issue is twofold:

1. It highlighted the ambiguous conception of what it is to be an MP: is it a job or a public vocation? Until the 17th century Members were paid. From the 18th century they were not, but only because membership of the Commons allowed numerous opportunities for corruption. The cleaning up of British politics in the 19th century led to sustained pressure for payment. In 1911 for the first time an annual payment was introduced, but in introducing it the Chancellor of the Exchequer denied that it was a salary: 'it is not a salary. It is just an allowance, and I think the minimum allowance, to enable men (sic) to come here.' In the last forty years the role of the MP has been professionalized and payment has come to reflect that professionalization: pay was first linked to other 'top salaries' from 1970; a pension scheme, a normal expectation in most middle occupations, was first introduced in 1964; an office cost allowance was introduced in 1969; the additional accommodation allowance, which caused so much trouble in 2009, originated in the 1970s; a staffing allowance was introduced in 2001. The fundamental problem lies not in corruption, but in the incomplete professionalization of the MPs' role: the language of 'allowances' continued to convey Lloyd George's sense that payment was neither a conventional salary, nor a conventional expense. (Hence the widespread practice also of using the office cost allowance to employ family members.) Since most citizens have, at best, a salary and tightly monitored expenses, the revelation created public bemusement and fury.
2. It led to the end of Parliamentary self-regulation of the allowances system. Recommendations of the Committee on Standards in Public Life in autumn 2009 attempted to prohibit practices like employment of family members, and a government bill established a Parliamentary Standards Authority to administer the expenses system.

Source: House of Commons Information Service (2009), from which the quotation from Lloyd George is also drawn.

To some degree the principle has informed in an unsystematic way the selection of some life peers, who owe their peerage in part to their distinction in a profession, a trade union or in business. But there are obvious formidable problems in the way of working out this principle systematically as a means of selecting the whole Chamber: how selection in practice would be made; how the different interests would be numerically balanced; and, once again, how any clash between elected territorial representatives and representatives of functional interest would be resolved.

These difficulties in settling a principle of selection are formidable because they either implicitly or explicitly rest on competing views of the proper functions of a second chamber. There is no settled agreement about these functions, and the difficulty of arriving at an agreement is compounded by the practical evolution of the functions actually performed by the present Lords. The present House performs a variety of almost accidentally acquired functions, not all of which are easily compatible. We can see this by considering four of the most important.

169

It represents interests. The House of Lords is not a chamber of industry and the professions, but many of the life peerage creations of the past half-century and more have been designed to give a voice to leading industrialists, professionals and trade unionists. In many public debates, therefore, there are Members of the Lords who do plausibly claim to speak for particular interest groups, by virtue of their individual expertise and by virtue of their careers.

It scrutinizes legislation. Scrutinizing the details of legislation is a common function of second chambers, notably of those that, like the House of Lords, are clearly subordinate to another chamber. A large amount of parliamentary time in the Lords is indeed spent on this function, and the absence of an adversarial party culture means that attention to proposals on their technical merits is easier than in the Commons. But how much 'added value' this creates is uncertain. Members of the Lords often bring considerable expertise to bear on policy proposals. But the extensive process of consultation with interest groups which, we noted in the last chapter, accompanies policy making, means that proposals will already have been subjected to the expert scrutiny of the affected interests well before they reach the Lords. More commonly, the Lords' stages provide an opportunity for interests that have not had their way in earlier consultations to make a more public attempt at exercising influence – and, occasionally, a successful attempt to delay a measure.

It prolongs distinguished public lives. Membership of the Lords via the life peerage route has provided an extended coda to the public lives of senior public figures, notably distinguished politicians. It has become almost universal for successful Members of the Commons to have a peerage conferred on them at retirement. Since retirement from the Commons does not always come at a normal retiring age – members are at risk of losing their seat at any election – this function has often extensively prolonged the lives of public figures.

It provides a source of patronage for party leaders, especially for the governing party. Prolonging public lives is a particular aspect of a wider function that the life peerage system has made important. This function is patronage. Peerage creations are largely in the control of the parties, and are especially closely controlled by the party of government. The social prestige of a peerage means that it is often a cheap way of rewarding a party functionary: for instance, this is the route by which Lord Archer, a peer who became infamous as a convicted perjurer, arrived in the Lords. It has sometimes been used as an inducement to Members of the Commons to vacate their parliamentary seats at short notice, thus allowing some favoured candidate of

the governing party a run at the vacancy. And it has become important as a means of recruiting talent to the governing party, and indeed to the ranks of the government. While it is rare to find more than two or three Members of the Lords in the Cabinet, they are often considerable figures in the governing party: in Mr Brown's cabinet, for instance, Lord Mandelson was deputy Prime Minister in all but name, while Lord Adonis was a forceful and high profile Transport Secretary. In addition, there are some fascinating and well-paid ministerial posts below Cabinet level. Able potential ministers who cannot, or will not, run the gauntlet of democratic politics by contesting a seat in the House of Commons, can find this a painless route to ministerial office. Typically in recent years up to 20 per cent of ministers have been peers, though peers have in the main held comparatively junior posts.

In view of the considerable problems of breaking the reform deadlock after 1999, the Conservative–Liberal coalition agreement of May 2010 therefore represented a quite dramatic development. The agreement committed the new Government to establishing a committee which would bring forward, by the end of the year, a set of proposals for a wholly, or mainly, elected Upper House, with the election organized on some principle of proportional representation. Although many of the problems identified above still remain as obstacles, the coalition agreement represents here, as it does in other fields, a quite startling acceleration in the pace of constitutional innovation. It has also opened up the road for the final transformation of the Lords by, most unexpectedly, a Conservative dominated government.

THE WESTMINSTER PARLIAMENT: RENEWAL OR DECAY?

Great constitutional changes transformed the Westminster Parliament in the first quarter of the twentieth century. The power of the House of Lords was greatly reduced through the Parliament Act of 1911. The general election immediately after the First World War returned the first Commons to be elected on something close to universal suffrage. Home Rule for the Irish Free State in 1921 removed a large body of Irish Members from the Commons chamber. For virtually the rest of the twentieth century the Commons was utterly dominated by two disciplined party blocks, Conservative and Labour. The functions and power structures of Parliament were also set for many decades.

Since the 1970s, however, the Westminster Parliament has seen great changes, some swift and dramatic, some slow moving but fundamental. In the

DEBATING POLITICS 9.1

Do we need a second chamber at Westminster?

WE NEED A SECOND CHAMBER BECAUSE

▶ A check is needed on the power of the Executive in the House of Commons, where the governing party is usually in control of a majority.

▶ Modern legislation is so complex that a second chamber is needed to review the detailed implications of legislative proposals.

▶ Virtually every successful democracy in the world has a second chamber, suggesting that it is a functional necessity of good democratic government.

▶ A second chamber, however selected, will widen the range of talent that participates at the highest level of national political life.

ABOLISH THE LORDS AND WORK WITH A SINGLE COMMONS CHAMBER BECAUSE

▶ No workable principle of selection can be devised that does not either extend Executive patronage (appointment) or challenge the democratic legitimacy of the Commons (popular election).

▶ Scrutinizing the details of legislation is what a serious Committee stage in the House of Commons should already do.

▶ In the devolved Assemblies we already have elected counterweights to the House of Commons.

▶ Checking the power of the Executive majority is most effectively done through the wider groups of civil society, such as the mass media and pressure groups.

House of Commons backbenchers are more independent minded, and more willing to defy the front-bench leadership, than was the case up to the 1970s. The Commons as an institution is better equipped to scrutinize the Executive, through more effective systems of specialized committees and through the provision of better 'back office' facilities for backbenchers. Modest changes in procedure have made the Commons a more businesslike place. The life peerage reforms have revitalized the House of Lords.

This summary points to an optimistic interpretation of recent parliamentary history: it suggests that we have been living through an era of renewal. Pessimists view recent history very differently. The Westminster Parliament is now surrounded by democratic rivals, in the European and Scottish Parliaments and the Welsh Assembly. It is no longer an unchallenged democratic giant. Reform of the Lords is presently in a cul-de-sac, and such reform as has been achieved has strengthened the role of Executive patronage in its composition. The Commons is turning into an institution where backbenchers immerse themselves in the detail of policy in Select Committees, to the neglect of the Chamber as the cockpit of national debate.

As this summary shows, whether we are optimists or pessimists depends on more than the facts of what has been happening to Parliament. It also depends on our judgements about what are the proper functions of Westminster parliamentary institutions in a democratic political system.

Review OF CHAPTER 9

Three themes have dominated this chapter:

◑ The overwhelming importance of party on the functions, powers and style of the House of Commons.

◑ The way changing ideas of political life, and the changing ambitions of the party politicians, have called into question traditional ways of doing business at Westminster.

◑ The way the impasse over reform of the House of Lords has dramatized the tensions inherent in the two-Chamber Westminster system and has highlighted the tensions to which that wider Westminster system is subject.

FURTHER READING

ESSENTIAL

If you read only one book it should be Norton (2005), a comprehensive overview by the most distinguished living scholar of Parliament.

RECOMMENDED

Judge (1993) is now old, but its originality and theoretical acuteness make it still highly relevant; see also Judge (1999). Russell (2000) very helpfully sets the debates about Lords reform in longer-term, comparative perspective. Cowley (2002) is part of a growing literature on the voting behaviour of MPs, and Cowley (2005) adds a later instalment.

CHAPTER 10

The devolved systems of governance: Scotland and Wales

CONTENTS

AIMS

This chapter:

- Establishes how and why the devolution reforms that were introduced by the Labour Government in 1998 are so important

- Describes the 'roads to devolution' in Scotland and Wales

- Describes the institutions of devolution

- Describes the practical, changing experience of devolution since 1998

- 'Sets' the devolution experience into our wider understanding of the shift of the UK governing system in the direction of multilevel governance

DEVOLVED GOVERNMENT AND MULTILEVEL GOVERNANCE

A key theme of this book is the transformation of a once settled system of government in the UK. We have labelled it the Westminster system, in recognition of the extent to which its institutions and powers are heavily concentrated in a small part of central London. In this chapter we will examine one of the most important ways in which the Westminster system is being changed: by the rise of newly devolved systems of government beyond the capital city. (The two succeeding chapters extend this. In Chapter 11 we look at the devolved system in Northern Ireland. In Chapter 12 I describe how the Westminster system is also being reshaped in a less publicly noticed way: by political innovation in local and regional government.)

The reshaping, and partial dissolution, of the Westminster system has taken different forms in different parts of the UK, and the fact that the discussion here covers three separate chapters recognizes this fact. But in this chapter I consider the experience of Scotland and Wales as a piece. This is not to suggest that the Scottish and Welsh experiences are identical. On the contrary: one theme of the following pages is the dissimilarities between the two nations. Scotland and Wales nevertheless should be examined together. One obvious reason is that devolved government was introduced into the two nations at the same moment: formally, legislation passed in the Westminster Parliament in 1998 brought the devolved institutions into existence in January 1999. But an even more important reason is that a comparison of the two experiences of devolution is itself very illuminating. It illuminates, obviously, the similarities and differences in the paths to devolution taken by the two countries. It illuminates, likewise, similarities and differences in the powers with which the devolved institutions were initially endowed. But most important of all, it illuminates the practical experience of devolution; and in so doing it tells us not only about devolution in Scotland and Wales, but also about the changing nature of the wider British system. We now have more than a decade's experience of devolved government – and thus of a critical experiment for wider UK politics. Devolution is a critical experiment because on its outcome rests the fate of a single, *united* system of government in Britain. Some of devolution's supporters – for instance the Labour Party that introduced the original reforms – hope that it will succeed in stabilizing constitutional arrangements in Britain and in ending the threat of national secession in Scotland and Wales. Some other supporters – for instance many nationalists – hope that it is an inherently unstable arrangement and that it will succeed in

IMAGE 10.1 ■ The new face of devolved government

■ The face that government presents to the public is immensely important symbolically. The new devolved administrations in Edinburgh and Cardiff had the chance to shape their symbolic image. The photo shows the Scottish Parliament building. Its construction was a fiasco, but it may yet, like many public building fiascos, become an icon of Scottish government as powerful as the iconic Palace of Westminster. However, the fiasco continues: when this photo was taken in April 2010 parts of the front entrance to the building were already having to be repaired.

Photo: Michael Moran

producing an irreversible move to national independence. We are at a point where we should be able to offer at least an interim judgement on the outcome of the experiment.

SCOTLAND AND WALES: SIMILARITIES AND CONTRASTS

The immediate forces leading to the landmark devolution reforms of 1998 are similar in the cases of Wales and Scotland. But the more fundamental historical forces creating pressure for devolution are subtly different in the two countries, and these help to explain important differences in the forms taken by devolution.

Scotland and Wales both experienced the consequences of the great centralization of government that occurred over most of the twentieth century in the UK. We saw in Chapter 2 that the beginnings of modern democratic politics in Britain can conveniently be dated from 1918, the year when the First World War ended. The election fought at the end of that year was the first to be contested on something close to universal adult suffrage, and it produced a pattern of two party rivalries between the Labour and Conservative parties that domi-

Timeline 10.1

The road to devolution in Scotland

1928 National Party of Scotland founded.

1945 SNP wins Westminster seat at by-election in Motherwell; loses seat in General Election three months later.

1967 SNP wins seat in Hamilton by-election to Westminster Parliament.

1970 Conservatives commit to a measure of Scottish devolution; Labour opposes.

1973 Kilbrandon Commission on the Constitution recommends foundation of a Scottish Assembly.

1979 Labour Government Bill falls after failure to secure special majorities of 40 per cent of all Scottish electorate in referendum, a clause inserted by Labour anti-devolutionists at Westminster.

1979 Election of Mrs Thatcher begins 18 years of Conservative Government in which Conservative Party support in Scotland drains away.

1989 Campaign of mass disobedience to Westminster Parliament's poll tax (new form of local authority taxation) begins.

1989 Scottish Constitutional Convention begins extended national debate about form of devolved government.

1996 Labour commits to post-election devolution in Scotland and Wales.

1997 Labour wins landslide victory in General Election; referendum on principle of devolution and giving tax raising powers to a Scottish Parliament gives majority for both.

1998 Scotland Act puts devolution into law.

1999 First Scottish Parliament elected, first Scottish Chief Minister (Donald Dewar) appointed, first (coalition) Executive formed.

■ Devolution in Scotland did not suddenly spring on British politics in the 1990s; it was the product of a long period of evolution and struggle, dating back to the 1920s.

Sources: Adapted from Butler and Butler (2000); Cook and Stevenson (2000); www.scottishparliament.uk.

nated the system of government for half a century. That era was one of great centralization in British politics, the high point of what we have called in this text the 'Westminster system'. Although only the Conservative Party labelled itself 'Unionist' in its full, formal name, in truth both parties were unionist from the 1920s onwards: that is, they thought a political union closely controlled from the metropolitan centre was the best way to govern Britain.

The centralized Westminster system that the parties ran was subject to serious challenge from the latter part of the 1960s. At the end of that decade, as we shall see in the next chapter, there was a full-blown nationalist revolt in Northern Ireland. A nationalist party committed to full independence for Scotland (the Scottish National Party) won a seat for the first time to the Westminster Parliament in 1967; since then there has been virtually continuous Scottish nationalist representation in the

Westminster Parliament. In the 1997 general election – following which the devolution measures described below were introduced – the nationalists won six seats and over a fifth (22 per cent) of votes cast in Scotland. Plaid Cymru, the party of Welsh nationalism, also achieved a Westminster breakthrough in the 1960s, winning its first ever seat in 1966. While its advance was not as great as that of the Scottish nationalists, by the 1997 election it was able to win four seats and almost a tenth (9.9 per cent) of the Welsh vote. The result of the May 2010 general election indicated no continuing advance, but it did support the view that nationalism has now consolidated itself as a permanent political force in Westminster: the Scottish Nationalists remained at six seats, while Plaid Cymru returned three, gaining one seat.

The most obvious reason for the success of this nationalist challenge was the persistent failure of Westminster governments successfully to manage the British economy and the way Wales and Scotland bore much of the brunt of resulting economic decline. By the end of the 1970s the challenge was so strong that the Labour Government in 1979 attempted, unsuccessfully, to implement devolution in the two countries. The fall of Labour in 1979 led to 18 years of Conservative government and this intensified the consequences of centralization of power in Westminster. In this era of Conservative dominance a wide gap developed between the political colour of Westminster, which was dominated by Conservative majorities, and of Wales and Scotland, where the Conservatives lost popular support. Thus, for much of the last two decades of the twentieth century Wales and Scotland were ruled by a government that would not have been elected had the vote been in these two countries alone.

This experience connected to a wider movement for constitutional reform in the UK that influenced, but was not confined to, the Labour Party. That movement traced the wider problems of the UK to the highly centralized nature of the Westminster system. In Chapter 19 we shall see that there has been a long history of policy failure in Britain. If this failure was due to excessive centralization of institutions in London, an obvious remedy was to decentralize through devolution to political units like the separate nations of the UK. The connection between centralization and policy failure is, we should note, one that can be contested; for present purposes we only need to know that it was an argument that influenced thinking about constitutional reform.

Wales and Scotland thus share a common long-term experience – the weakening of the Westminster system of centralized rule – and they share also the short-term experience of being ruled for the closing years of the

twentieth century by a government that relied for majorities on English voters.

But there are big differences in the nature of nationalism in the two countries. The most important source of distinction lies in different conceptions of national identity. Welsh nationalism has been focused on defending and encouraging the Welsh language, and by extension defending and encouraging the cultural distinctiveness of which language is an expression. In Scotland, by contrast, the language has been a much less central issue; indeed there are only about 60,000 Gaelic speakers left in the whole country. In part this difference in cultural emphasis has also been reflected in the social bases of support for the two movements: the original core of Welsh nationalism lay in rural, Welsh-speaking communities; the rise of Scottish nationalism encompassed significant parts of urban Scotland, especially the belt that links the two most important cities, Glasgow and Edinburgh. However, as we shall see, the politics of devolved government has helped considerably to reshape these original bases of support.

The distinctions between the political cultures of Scottish and Welsh nationalism were accompanied by differences in support for devolution. Electoral support for nationalism has been higher in Scotland than in Wales, and correspondingly there has been more Scottish enthusiasm for devolution when it has been tested in referendums. A glance at Figure 10.1 shows these differences. Support has been consistently higher in Scotland than in Wales: when a referendum on proposals was held in 1979 Scotland was markedly more enthusiastic, and this pattern was repeated in the referendums which led to the devolution reforms of 1998. This higher level of Scottish enthusiasm in part reflected the already greater distinctiveness and autonomy of Scottish institutions.

A separate Scottish Office with its own administration based in Edinburgh dates from 1892; a Welsh Office with a Secretary of State for Wales in the Westminster Cabinet was only established in 1964. The differences in pre-devolution governing arrangements reflected wider differences between the two countries. Unlike Wales, Scotland has a long established, and separate, legal system; a separate and distinct education system, stretching from elementary schools to universities; and while both countries have their own mass media, Scottish newspapers are more distinctive and better established than are those in Wales. Wider patterns of popular culture mirror these differences. For instance 90 per cent of newspapers in Scotland are produced in Scotland (McGarvey and Cairney 2008:42). In professional football the most powerful Scottish teams play in their own league, while the most powerful Welsh ones –

Timeline 10.2

The road to devolution in Wales

1925 Plaid Cymru formed to campaign for Welsh independence.

1951 Appointment of Minister (outside Cabinet) for Welsh Affairs in Westminster.

1962 Formation of Welsh Language Society to campaign for the Welsh language frees Plaid Cymru to concentrate on wider political issues.

1964 First ever Secretary of State for Wales appointed by incoming Labour Government.

1966 Plaid Cymru wins first Westminster Parliamentary seat in by-election.

1970 Plaid Cymru claims 11.5 per cent of Welsh vote in general election.

1979 Only 12 per cent of the Welsh electorate (20 per cent of those voting) supports the Labour Government's devolution proposals. Return of Conservatives for 18 unbroken years of government ends this first stage of attempts to secure Welsh devolution.

1993 Welsh Language Act in law and Welsh Language Board established to foster the language.

1995 Plaid Cymru becomes Wales's second largest party, after Labour, in local government elections.

1997 Labour landslide in general election; referendum approves principle of devolution.

1998 Government of Wales Act provides for institutions of devolution.

1999 Welsh Assembly elections; Labour forms administration as largest party but without a majority of seats; Alan Michael is First Minister.

■ The devolution movement in Wales, though following a similar timeline to that in Scotland, has had to struggle against a much less receptive political environment. Note, however, the common origins of modern Scottish and Welsh separatism in the 1920s: both are in part a response to the success of Irish nationalist separatism.

Sources: Butler and Butler (2000); Cook and Stevenson (2000); www.wales.gov.uk.

Cardiff and Swansea – play in English dominated leagues. Some parts of Scotland, indeed, barely feel British in any conventional sense: any visitor to the Shetland Islands, for instance, soon feels the proximity of Norway and sees signs of a long Scandinavian presence. This is hardly surprising: a glance at an atlas will show that Lerwick, the 'capital' of the Shetland Islands, is closer to Oslo than to London.

However, as we will see later in this chapter, one consequence of the experience of devolution has prob-

ably been to narrow these differences between the two countries. The 'demonstration effect' on Wales of observing greater Scottish devolution, combined with the way the devolved institutions in Wales have helped consolidate distinctively Welsh political networks, has considerably strengthened Welsh support for more ambitious forms of devolution in the principality. This point becomes clearer when we turn, as we now do, to description of the *initial* institutions of devolution themselves; as we shall see, these have undergone a complex development since 1999, in many ways involving a convergence between the two national systems.

SCOTLAND AND WALES: THE FIRST INSTITUTIONS OF DEVOLUTION

Devolution in Scotland was introduced by the Scotland Act 1998. It provided for the election of a Scottish Parliament, with devolved powers to make laws over a wide range of policy, and for the nomination by the elected Parliament of a First Minister (formally appointed by the Queen). The First Minister in turn selects the ministers that compose the Cabinet of the Executive, again subject to agreement with the Parliament and approval of the Monarch. In parallel, the Government of Wales Act 1998 provided for the election of a Welsh Assembly. This Assembly inherited the powers exercised before devolution by the Secretary of State for Wales, though as we shall see these have expanded over time. That office of Secretary of State for Wales dated, as noted above, from 1964. The Assembly elects a First Secretary to serve as leader of a government, who in turn appoints Assembly Secretaries, who cover important policy areas like agriculture, and who constitute the Cabinet.

In chronology and bare structure the devolution arrangements in the two countries are similar. But small differences of language – a Scottish *Parliament* but a Welsh *Assembly* – hint at more substantial differences to which we shall shortly come. This has been an important part of the dynamics of the devolution experience – especially in the case of Wales.

The dynamics of the devolution experience have, however, been deeply shaped by basic institutional features that are shared by the two systems. These concern how representatives are elected and how this affects the composition of devolved administrations. The election arrangements for the Assembly and Parliament are strikingly similar, mark an important break with the prevailing arrangements for Westminster, and are thus significant not only for devolved politics but for our understanding of electoral arrangements in the UK generally. One common departure from the Westminster 'norm' is that both institutions are elected for fixed terms of four years: at the time of writing we have had elections in 1999, 2003 and 2007, and there will be a further round in 2011. By contrast the Westminster Parliament is elected for a maximum period of five years, but within that period Prime Ministers can request dissolution from the Queen virtually at their own calculation. (This is to be changed to a fixed term of five years under the plans announced by the Conservative–Liberal Democrat coali-

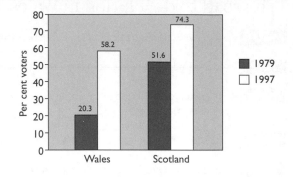

FIGURE 10.1 ■ **Popular support for devolution in referendums in Wales and Scotland (per cent voting 'yes')**

■ The electorates in Wales and Scotland have been given two opportunities to vote on devolution proposals offered by the Westminster Government: on both occasions the percentage voting 'yes' – the figures summarized here – have been higher in Scotland than in Wales. The proposals fell in 1979 through lack of popular support. The differences are also reflected in turnout: in both 1979 and 1997 turnout in Scotland was higher than in Wales.

tion in Westminster from May 2010.) The devolved arrangements therefore immediately change a critical traditional element of the rules of the game by comparison with Westminster: it is impossible for devolved administrations to try to spot the most electorally opportune moment to call an election – a key part of the traditional strategy of any governing party in Westminster. It also indicates a fundamental difference in the roles of the Prime Minister and his devolution 'counterparts', because responsibility for selecting the election date has been up to now a critical element in the 'job description' for any Westminster-system Prime Minister.

The rules of the political game by comparison with Westminster are also fundamentally changed by the mode of election to the Parliament and the Assembly. We shall see in Chapter 17 that Westminster has up to now used the 'first past the post single member constituency' system: a single member elected for each separate territorial constituency, chosen according to which candidate secures simply the largest number of votes. (The intention again in the May 2010 coalition agreement is to change this in favour of the 'alternative vote' – see Chapter 17.)

Both in Scotland and Wales the devolved system uses different, virtually identical arrangements. Each elector has two votes to cast. One of these is used to select the single representative for the territorial constituency in which the voter is registered, the winner being, Westminster fashion, the candidate who receives the largest number of popular votes. For these purposes Wales is divided into 40, and Scotland into 73, constituencies. The second vote is cast to indicate a preference from party lists of candidates grouped regionally: Wales is divided into five, Scotland into eight, regions. In Wales this method selects an additional 20, and in Scotland an additional 56, members. This 'additional member system' selects according to the proportion of votes received across whole regions. This familiar form of proportional representation is intended to redress one of the best known defects of the 'first past the post' single constituency member system: the inability of candidates from parties with minority but significant support that is widely dispersed geographically to gain representation in the elected institution.

We now have experience of three sets of elections to the Parliament and the Assembly: in 1999, 2003 and 2007. These elections have produced profoundly different outcomes from those common in the Westminster system, and these outcomes have been critical to the dynamics of devolution. Four important effects can be observed.

Simple majorities rare

Although Labour emerged from the 2003 Welsh Assembly elections with a small majority of seats, achieving this is much more difficult than in the Westminster Parliament. The very large majorities commonly enjoyed by governing parties in the Westminster Commons are virtually impossible. Scotland was ruled by coalition (between Labour and Liberal Democrats) from 1999 to 2007, and from 2007 the Scottish National Party (SNP) governed with a minority (but the largest block) of seats in the Parliament. In Wales, for a year after the first Assembly elections in 1999, Labour tried to govern alone as a minority, but was obliged in 2000 to enter a formal coalition with the Liberal Democrats. It returned to sole control of government on the back of a small majority in 2003, but in 2007, as we shall see in more detail below, it was obliged to return to coalition, this time with Plaid Cymru, the Welsh nationalists. The initial attempt to govern alone in 1999 without a working majority was a sign of the difficulty Labour found in abandoning the working assumptions about single party government formed by nearly 80 years experience of the Westminster system.

In Scotland, from the beginning Labour was obliged to be constitutionally more radical. Devolved government there, as we have seen, involved a continuous coalition between Labour and the Liberal Democrats,

stretching to the sharing of ministerial posts and the development of joint policies, until 2007, when the minority nationalist government took over. By contrast, there had not been a single formal coalition government in the Westminster Parliament since 1945, until the Conservative–Liberal Democrat coalition of 2010. Recall that in describing the Westminster Parliament we emphasized the extent to which its culture was shaped by the need to support, or to oppose, a single governing party with a majority – for instance in developing a particularly extreme form of adversarialism in political exchange. We can see immediately that the electoral arrangements for the Parliament and Assembly foster a very different culture of cross-party accommodation. The culture of the new institutions is shaped by the realization of all parties that they face a high probability of having to cooperate with a rival party, either in a formal coalition or in some more informal arrangement to support the single party in office.

A more 'proportional' allocation of seats

The additional member system achieved the objective of ensuring a closer correlation – though not an exact one – between the proportional allocation of seats for parties in the Parliament and Assembly, and their shares of the popular vote. This greater 'proportionality' also ensured that minority radical voices that would not be heard in a body elected under the first past the post system are represented under the devolved arrangements. Thus in the 2003 Scottish Parliament the radical Scottish Socialist Party returned six representatives, all elected under the additional member list rather than from territorial constituencies. The Party subsequently disintegrated as a political force under the impact of personal scandals and faction fighting, and returned nobody in 2007; but in that election the Scottish Greens returned one member, something that up to then had been beyond the capacity of Greens operating under the Westminster first past the post system. (In the May 2010 Westminster general election the Greens finally won a single seat, from Labour, in the rather bohemian constituency of Brighton Pavilion.)

Distinctive electoral calculations

The new electoral system has greatly altered the electoral calculations of the parties, probably in the direction of strengthening their official central organization. This is because election under the additional member system, by allocating seats proportional to a party's popular vote, makes one factor critical for the ambitious candidate: where he or she is in the party's ranked list of candidates. (This works in an even more imperative way in the case of European elections.)

BRIEFING 10.1

The electoral system under devolved government in Scotland and Wales

The elections to the Scottish Parliament and the Welsh Assembly are governed by essentially the same method, a mix of the 'simple majority' method that also elects MPs to the Westminster Parliament, and the 'additional member' system:

- A majority of seats (40 in Wales, 73 in Scotland) elect on a simple majority system: the single candidate with the largest number of votes is declared elected, even if that candidate wins only a minority – less than 50 per cent – of votes cast. The constituency boundaries are the same as those for elections to the Westminster Parliament.
- 20 seats in Wales, and 56 in Scotland, are held by 'additional members', hence the label. In both cases the countries are divided into regions (five in Wales, eight in Scotland) with seats divided equally between the regions.
- Voters have two votes: one for the 'single member' simple majority constituency selection, and a second cast for a party. The second vote is used to 'top up' a party's representation from candidates on a party's list, to bring the party's total representation in a region as close as possible to its proportion of the popular vote. This explains why Labour in 1999 in Wales had only one additional member, while Plaid Cymru had eight: Labour had almost achieved its full proportional allocation via those returned in single member, single majority contests in the constituencies. The system also greatly helped the Conservatives: they won no 'single member' seats in Scotland, for instance, but gained 18 members under the additional member system in 1999.

- The electoral system for devolved government marks a major innovation in the governing system. As we see at several points in the text of the chapter it has enforced a more consensual governing style, which is very different from the partisan, adversarial system that we saw in Chapter 9 and which is embedded in the Westminster system. It has also helped to widen the range of political talent recruited to political leadership.

Ambitious candidates therefore in principle have two routes into the Parliament or Assembly: via adoption as a constituency candidate or via the party list under the additional member election. In practice use of the latter has already allowed party leaderships to ensure the election of favoured candidates. The best-known example of this was the return under the list of Alan Michael, the founding First Secretary in Wales. Mr Michael was 'parachuted' in from the Westminster Government at short notice when Ron Davies, the architect of Welsh Devolution, was obliged to resign at very short notice because of private troubles. Mr Michael had a weak political base in Wales, was adopted for no territorial constituency in the Assembly and could only serve as First Secretary via election on the additional member list.

The two categories of members have also introduced an additional complicating tension, precisely between members on the list and those with a defined territorial constituency. It is not obvious how the 'surgery' work of the two categories of MPs should be divided, and Bradbury and Mitchell (2007) detect some tendency for additional member list representatives to locate their offices in territorial constituencies that are marginal – an obvious statement of intent to contest the seat at a later election. Whatever the precise calculations, the two categories of members create a tension and competition obviously entirely absent at Westminster.

A more modern parliamentary style

We saw in Chapter 9 that the Westminster House of Commons is dominated by a traditionally engrained

BRIEFING 10.2

The distinctive workings of elections under devolved government: an illustration from Wales, 2007

	Per cent of votes cast	Seats won
Conservatives: single member constituencies	22.4	5
Conservatives: additional members	21.4	7
Labour: single member constituencies	32.2	24

■ The table is illustrative only: it does not summarize the full result; it is intended to show the practical workings of the electoral system. The first and third rows give a good idea of how Assembly strengths would have been allocated were Wales to operate the Westminster first past the post system alone. These results, and those in Scotland, are virtually a natural experiment showing the impact of different electoral systems on election outcomes.

Source: Calculated from Electoral Commission data.

adversarial culture. This owes a great deal to the way the electoral system for over 90 years produced a chamber dominated by two opposing parties who only cooperated in government during the crisis of war. The cultures of the devolved Parliament and Assembly are different. For example, procedures in the two elected bodies are self-consciously 'modern', by contrast with the studied culti-vation of the ancient that we observed in the case of the Westminster Parliament. Members are allocated indi-vidual desks in the Chamber, and voting is electronic, by contrast with the Westminster practice of actually walking through separate lobbies for the purposes of counting the vote. There is also a greater attempt to at least appear to practise more open government. For instance, Westminster Cabinet Minutes are only officially made public after a gap of 30 years; minutes of the devolved government are published more or less imme-diately on the Web. How much this contributes to open government the reader can judge by looking at the extract from the minutes of the Welsh Cabinet repro-duced in Documenting Politics 10.1. As a further expres-sion of modernity both the Scottish Parliament and the Welsh Assembly have commissioned modernist designs for new buildings to house their proceedings (see Image 10.1). Both building projects were bedevilled by huge cost overruns and delays in construction, but both are iconic – striking symbolic statements of departure from the practices of the old Westminster model.

The new institutions of devolution in important ways therefore have from the beginning created a common Welsh and Scottish departure from the prevailing politics of the Westminster system. In particular, they are embedding a style of governing and political debate which differs radically from the adversarial culture of Westminster, stretching as far as the prospect of long-term coalition government; they are facilitating the representation of minority voices not capable of being heard in the House of Commons; and they are changing some of the calculations which ambitious candidates must make in trying to build a successful political career.

There nevertheless were important differences from the beginning between the two devolved systems. These in the main concerned the different powers and scope for independent action of the institutions. The evolution of the systems from the starting points in 1999 provides many clues to one of the key questions with which we opened this chapter: is the devolution settlement a means of stabilizing the UK as a political unity, or a further step on the road to its dissolution?

The single most important *original* contrast lay in the formal powers of the Scottish Parliament and the Welsh Assembly. In two critical respects the powers of the Scottish Parliament were markedly greater. First, Parliament was empowered to pass its own legislation that, having progressed through three stages, receives the Royal Assent in the manner of laws passed by the Westminster Parliament. Second, the Scottish Executive had power to vary the base rate of income tax by up to 3 pence in the pound. The Welsh Assembly, by contrast, had no power independently to pass legislation, and no tax raising authority. (This has now altered materially in respect of the first of these.)

These original formal differences are substantial and have undoubtedly produced different experiences of devolution in the two countries. But while important differences remain, what is striking is the convergence in experiences between the two countries. The original Welsh 'settlement' proved particularly unstable, and much of the development of the Welsh system has involved a movement towards a 'Scottish' model of devolved powers.

THE EXPERIENCE OF DEVOLUTION

We have seen that the first formal design of the institutions of devolution in Scotland and Wales provided a mixed picture of similarities and contrasts. The most important contrast lay in the fact that the extent of devolution in the Scottish case was self-consciously greater than is the case in Wales. Examination of the experience of devolution since the first elections in 1999 is a complicated story. Scotland and Wales have a lot in common, unsurprisingly; but they do not fit into a single uniform template that we can label 'the politics of devolution'.

We have to unravel their experiences under a list of distinct headings: sometimes the result is convergence, sometimes the persistence of difference. Here, we do it in the following terms:

● the experience of the powers of the governing systems;
● the experience of policy outcomes;
● the experience of the party systems;
● the experience of the Chief Minister in Scotland and the Welsh First Secretary;
● the experience of stability and instability;
● the experience of careers and policy networks;
● the experience of popular support for the new devolved systems;
● the experience of Europe in the workings of the new institutions.

The experience of the powers of the governing system

The most important changes here have occurred in the case of Welsh devolution, and they support the view that there is an inbuilt momentum which is expanding the range of powers and authority of devolved institutions. The disparity that we noted above between the formal powers of the Scottish Parliament and the Welsh Assembly at foundation led to pressures to expand the powers of the latter. In 2002 the Assembly Government established a commission to review Assembly Powers, and its report (the report of the Richard Commission)

proposed endowing it with powers to legislate in stipulated areas. The Westminster Government responded with proposals in-line with these recommendations, and these are now embodied in the Government of Wales Act 2006. The Act narrows further the distinction between devolution in Scotland and Wales, notably by endowing the Assembly with law-making powers in a wide range of policy fields. The evolution of powers was then given a further potentially radical turn by the outcome of the 2007 Assembly election. As a condition of entering coalition with Labour, Plaid Cymru extracted a commitment for a referendum on conferring full law-making powers for the Assembly, to be held by May 2011 (when the next Assembly elections must be held). As we shall see later, there is convincing survey evidence that this will command a popular majority. The sense that we are witnessing a convergence in the scope of the formal powers of the two system is reinforced by the Scottish experience: there is evidence that there is not a popular majority at present to push the Scottish system to the next level of power – which would be independence.

The experience of policy outcomes

As we have noted, the Scottish Parliament, by contrast with the Welsh Assembly, acquired the power to pass legislation, and it has indeed used this power to create policies that are in some respects distinctive both from the Westminster Parliament and from Wales. The examples range from the symbolic to the outstandingly important. Hunting with dogs was outlawed while the Westminster Parliament still struggled with the issue; the 'demonstration' effect of the Scottish ban probably helped facilitate the ban in England. Two other issues affect millions and involve substantial resources: the Scottish Parliament, as one of its first measures, abolished the fees for higher education imposed by the Westminster Government; and it has likewise departed in important ways from the Westminster policy of charging for care of the aged.

These differences with both Westminster and with Wales are important, but they should not be allowed to obscure the very real departures on policy that have been possible in Wales. The Assembly, though wielding no power to pass legislation, inherited the range of powers wielded by the old Welsh Office. As Briefing 10.4 shows, it is striking how wide ranging has been policy innovation in both the devolved jurisdictions. It seems that the formal differences between the powers of the Parliament and the Assembly may matter less in the actual practice of making distinctive policy. Moreover, attempts under the minority nationalist administration since 2007 to widen further the differences between Scotland and England have been frustrated by the lack of

BRIEFING 10.3

The scope and limits of devolved government in Scotland

DEVOLVED ISSUES INCLUDE:

- health
- education and training
- local government
- social work
- housing
- planning
- tourism, economic development and financial assistance to industry
- some aspects of transport, including the Scottish road network, bus policy and ports and harbours
- law and home affairs, including most aspects of criminal and civil law, the prosecution system and the courts
- the police and fire services
- the environment
- natural and built heritage
- agriculture, forestry and fishing
- sport and the arts
- statistics, public registers and records.

RESERVED (NON-DEVOLVED) ISSUES INCLUDE:

- constitutional matters
- UK foreign policy
- UK defence and national security
- fiscal, economic and monetary system
- immigration and nationality
- energy: electricity, coal, gas and nuclear energy
- common markets
- trade and industry, including competition and customer protection
- some aspects of transport, including railways, transport safety and regulation
- employment legislation
- social security
- gambling and the National Lottery
- data protection
- abortion, human fertilization and embryology, genetics and vivisection
- equal opportunities.

■ The scale of devolution reflects the strength of the movement for separation in Scotland and the pre-existing strength of Scottish institutions.

a parliamentary majority: the most high profile failure was the rejection of the nationalist administration's proposal to abolish the council charge in Scotland.

The experience of the party systems

One of the most important reasons for this convergence in the production of distinctive policy outcomes in the two devolved governments lies in the party systems. Devolution demanded great strategic choices for all the parties. They had to operate under unfamiliar electoral systems, and they had to anticipate electoral outcomes very different from those of Westminster, where the electoral system had delivered domination for Conservative and Labour since 1918. For the nationalists in Wales and Scotland the strategic dilemma was how far to work the devolved institutions, since it was plain that the central point of devolution was to draw the sting of nationalism:

to the extent that it worked it was designed to create a stable long-term alternative to independence. But the problems of the established parties, especially of Conservative and Labour, were even greater.

In Wales and Scotland the parties share a problem that, we shall see in Chapter 14, has afflicted parties across the UK: they are declining institutions, having lost their mass membership over the last generation and suffered great financial problems. (One of the contingent causes of successive scandals within Scottish Labour is due to the problem of financing the party and its activities.) In the case of the Conservatives the problem was made more acute by the virtual disappearance of the party as a significant electoral force in Wales and Scotland, and its close identification with Unionism and English domination of the UK. (It initially opposed the devolution reforms.) Thus if the strategic problem for the nationalists was how far to engage with the institutions of devolution, for the Conservatives it was how to rebuild some political presence in the devolved systems and for Labour how to differentiate the party in Wales and Scotland from that in Westminster.

It is obvious that the Labour Party was the central actor in all this, and the party with the most acute strategic problems. The origins of Labour's problems are plain. The first decade and more of devolution coincided with Labour domination of the Westminster Parliament. Labour has also been continuously in office in Wales since 1999, either as a minority administration or as part of a coalition; and until the 2007 elections was the perpetual, dominant, coalition partner in Scotland. Studies of the internal organization of the party show that comparatively little change took place in a party structure which had for decades been 'unionist' in its outlook: that is, focused above all on managing the electoral fortunes of the Party at Westminster. Labour indeed remains formally a 'unionist' party despite devolution. But the reality of everyday party life has changed: both in Scotland and Wales the Party has had considerable freedom to adopt distinctive policies (as we saw above), to design the tactics of fighting elections in the devolved institutions, and to select candidates. (The disastrous experiment of parachuting in Alan Michael as the preferred Westminster approved leader in Wales has not been repeated.) Internally, both in Wales and Scotland the parties have become less hierarchical (Shaw 2002; Laffin et al. 2007). If anything, the Welsh Labour party has shown more independence since devolution. The explanation probably lies in relatively short-term factors. Scottish Labour in the 'devolution' generation was dominated by a set of powerful personalities, of whom the most important was obviously Gordon Brown, who made their careers in Westminster. Nevertheless, even in Scotland the need to show national electorates that Labour is independent of the Party leadership in Westminster has helped to produce the record of policy innovation which we noted above. In this record of innovation the experience of First Minister has been crucial.

The experience of the chief minister

The chief minister (the First Minister in Scotland and the First Secretary in Wales) might be instinctively thought of as the equivalent of the Prime Minister in Westminster. Yet much of what we know already suggests that the roles are evolving in ways very different from the Westminster pattern. The most important source of difference arises from the limits on the authority of a chief minister in Scotland or Wales imposed by the very different patterns of party strength.

Every Prime Minister in Westminster between 1945 and 2010 has been able to run a single party government, and for almost the whole of that period has had the cushion of a large Commons majority. Managing a governing party in Westminster cannot be done in an authoritarian way, and every Prime Minister has to conciliate party rivals and party factions. Nevertheless, the two parties that alternated in government in Westminster – Labour and Conservative – generally offered a stable base of support for the Prime Minister and his or her Government.

The absence of secure majorities for the largest party in Scotland and Wales turns the chief minister in those countries into a figure who has to be much more concerned with bargaining and compromise and with 'brokering' deals in order to win support in the Assembly and Parliament. The skills to be called on are different in all three countries. The Scottish First Minister and the Welsh First Secretary are not at all in the same position. In particular, the situation facing the First Secretary has been much more fluid. The lesser powers assigned to the Assembly originally compared with those devolved to the Scottish Parliament meant that the future of devolution in Wales was much more open. The first four years of the Assembly were as much about trying to work out this future as about actually exercising the devolved powers. Was devolution in Wales to be of a significantly lesser order than in Scotland, or was it a staging post to devolution on at least a Scottish scale? The roles of the first two leaders of Welsh Government encapsulated the competing choices. The first, Alan Michael, was very close to the Westminster executive. Although a Westminster MP for a Welsh (Cardiff) seat he was a Home Office minister who was, as we saw above, parachuted at short notice into the leading role in Welsh devolution politics. Mr Michael then had rapidly to be found a seat in the new Assembly via the additional member system. His time in office was devoted to establishing and managing the existing devolution arrangements. He resigned in 2000, essentially because he could not command majorities for policies in the Assembly. His successor, Rhodri Morgan, though also a Westminster MP, was disappointed in his hopes of office at Westminster on Labour's return to power in 1997, and from the start pictured himself as intent on maximizing Welsh distinctiveness and autonomy from the Westminster system. He subsequently proved himself an adept player at the politics of coalition construction in Wales. However, the election of 2007 failed to deliver a workable majority for any party, and after complex manoeuvring Morgan was reinstalled as First Secretary in a coalition with Plaid Cymru. Morgan remained in office until December 2009, almost as long as Tony Blair

BRIEFING 10.4

The difference devolution makes: how Scotland and Wales have departed from a UK norm

SCOTLAND

- Free long-term personal care for the elderly
- Abolition of up-front tuition fees for students in higher education
- Three-year settlement for teachers pay and conditions
- Less restrictive Freedom of Information Act
- Abolition of fox hunting
- 'One stop shop' for Public Sector Ombudsman
- Abolition of ban 'promoting homosexuality' by repeal of Section 2A of the Local Government Act ('section 28' in England) before it was repealed in England.

WALES

- UK's first Children's Commissioner
- Creation of 22 Local Health Boards
- Homelessness Commission, and extending support for the homeless
- Abolition of school league tables
- Free medical prescriptions for those under 25 and over 60
- Free bus travel for pensioners before it was introduced in England
- Free school milk for those under seven
- Six weeks free home care for the elderly after discharge from hospital.

■ This table, drawn from research on devolution commissioned by the Economic and Social Research Council, shows how far there is a distinctive policy dynamic on the ground in the devolved administrations. It reinforces the argument of this chapter that devolution has created a set of distinctive political systems within the UK. Note how some innovations (for instance free bus travel) have subsequently been adopted in England; the devolved systems are thus also laboratories of policy innovation.

Source: Economic and Social Research Council (2004).

remained as Prime Minister, and was able to pick his moment of retirement. But the simple measure of longevity conceals the compromises necessary to remain in office.

The experience of First Minister in Scotland has been even more turbulent, a fact indicated by something we have already noticed: the tenure of first ministers has been more precarious. There were four in the first eight years of devolution: Labour provided the first three, but following the 2007 Assembly elections the SNP emerged as the largest single grouping. After complex interparty bargaining designed to create a coalition – now virtually a permanent outcome of all the devolution elections – the SNP failed to find a coalition partner and after that ruled as a minority administration, with Alex Salmond as First Minister.

The role of Salmond as First Minister exemplifies more general features of the office, as highlighted in a pioneering study by Lynch (2006). Salmond made most of his career at Westminster, and only returned to lead

the Nationalists in Scotland following internal party dissatisfaction with his predecessor John Swinney. Salmond's reputation meant that, rather like Rhodri Morgan in Wales, he was a dominating figure in the Executive, in the way it is difficult for even the most powerful Prime Minister to dominate. A Prime Minister in the Westminster system has to work alongside other leading officers of state, like the Foreign Secretary and the Chancellor. But prestige and authority in the devolved executives is far more concentrated in the office and person of the First Minister or First Secretary.

In summary, even after more than a decade of devolution we have to recognize that the role of the leader of devolved administrations in Wales and Scotland continues to evolve (as, of course, does the office of Prime Minister). The best summation is probably that we should not think of the First Minister/First Secretary as occupying roles analogous to that of the Westminster Prime Minister. Leaders in the devolved systems are different for three reasons. First, much of their time is spent in devising roles (and adopting policies) which distinguish them from Westminster: this is true if, like Salmond, they have a long-term aim of establishing an independent Scotland; or if, like Morgan, they were intent on showing that they are not creatures of the London based party leadership. Second, they are in some respects strikingly more dominant in the administration than is the Prime Minister, simply because their colleagues in government neither occupy great offices of state nor, typically, have the kind of high profile enjoyed by leading figures in a Westminster Cabinet. Third, however, they are weaker because they are incessantly engaged in managing either an administration without a legislative majority (the case in Scotland after 2007) or a formal coalition with a rival party (Wales). In short, instability is a fact of life under devolved government.

The experience of stability and instability

Both the Scottish and Welsh system share a very important common experience that marks them out from Westminster: it has proved much more difficult for governing parties to manage the Parliament and the Assembly than has traditionally been the case with the Westminster system. A simple index of this is the turnover of first ministers: since 1990, when Mrs Thatcher fell, there have only been four Prime Ministers in Downing Street, and of course Mrs Thatcher's was the longest peacetime occupation of Downing Street in the twentieth century, and Mr Blair's was almost as long. By contrast, as we saw above, there were four First Ministers in Scotland in the first eight years of devolution. In part the difference is just due to human misfortune: the first Scottish First Minister Donald Dewar sadly died in office. But it also reflects a more turbulent parliamentary atmosphere where it has been much more difficult than in the Westminster Parliament to create stable governing majorities. This problem was the direct cause of the downfall of Alan Michael, the first Welsh First Secretary, who resigned after suffering a motion of no confidence.

Each successive spin of the electoral wheel has reinforced the lesson that managing government instability is now a fact of life in the Welsh and Scottish systems. At the time of writing we have the experience of the third round of Assembly/Parliament elections, held in 2007. Developments in the Scottish system as a result of the 2007 elections were potentially most momentous of all, for they brought to office a party dedicated to the creation of an independent state. Following the Assembly elections of 3 May 2007 the SNP emerged as (just) the largest party, with 47 votes, a gain of 20; Labour lost 4, reducing its total to 46. These two parties now dominate Scottish parliamentary politics: the next largest group in the Scottish Parliament is the Conservatives, with 17, while the Liberal Democrats have 16 seats.

The norm in Scottish government since devolution had been coalition, a striking contrast with Westminster, where single party government was the only form of rule for over 60 years. Since devolution Labour had ruled as the main governing party in a coalition with the Liberal Democrats. It had briefly seemed after the May 2007 election that the Liberal Democrats would once again participate in government, as the partner of the SNP. (A 'rainbow' coalition of Greens, Liberal Democrats and the SNP would have commanded 65 seats, just enough to form a simple majority.) But efforts at coalition creation foundered on Lib Dem opposition to a key Nationalist commitment – to holding a referendum on independence 'with a likely date of 2010', as the SNP manifesto put it. The water was further muddied by a series of fiascos in the conduct of the election resulting in many thousands of spoilt ballots – the result, apparently, of the decision to combine Assembly with local elections, the two systems operating distinct electoral arrangements. The main lesson of the fiasco is just how far the UK has now moved from the once traditional, monolithic, first past the post, electoral system, in favour of a complex patchwork of systems operating in different national jurisdictions and at different levels. In the event Alex Salmond, the SNP leader, was voted in as first Minister on 16 May by 49 votes to 46, the Greens supporting Salmond, Labour voting against, with the Conservatives and the Liberal Democrats abstaining.

The formation of a minority government is not a first for the devolved system – there was, as we noted earlier, a brief, early and unhappy attempt in Wales – but the attempt in Scotland brings special uncertainty. Mr Salmond announced that he would seek to command majorities 'policy by policy'. The result has been government, not so much 'policy by policy' as 'crisis by crisis'. In 2008 the government nearly fell in a standoff over the budget, and only survived because none of the parties relished what would have been an inevitable – a return to the polls. One of the main potential casualties of this strategy is the very policy on which the coalition talks with the Liberal Democrats foundered – the commitment to a referendum on independence. As we shall see below, Mr Salmond almost certainly has no chance of getting legislation enabling a referendum through the Scottish Parliament.

In Wales, small shifts in the distribution of Assembly seats in 2007 were enough to destabilize the ruling Labour Adminstration. Labour lost four seats, achieving a total of 26; Plaid Cymru, the Welsh nationalist party, gained three, leaving it with 15; the Conservatives gained one, increasing to 12; while the Liberal Democrats

People in Politics 10.1

Enriching the political gene pool: how devolution expands the range of available political talent

Rhodri Morgan (1939–)

First secretary for Wales, 2000–09. Former senior civil servant, Labour MP in Westminster Parliament 1987–2001, front-bench spokesman on Welsh affairs, 1992–97. He reacted to being overlooked for Westminster office in 1997 by turning to Wales. He finally succeeded the disastrous Alan Michael in 2000, and then led a succession of coalitions and single party administrations until retirement in 2009.

Tommy Sheridan (1964–)

Member of Scottish Parliament, elected on additional member list of Scottish Socialist Party. Local councillor for Pollok, Glasgow 1992–. Elected from prison cell, serving six-month sentence for preventing a poll tax warrant sale; leader of Scottish anti-poll tax campaigns. Advocate of policies long abandoned by New Labour, such as universal provision of free school meals. But devolved careers are as precarious as any other: his career was effectively ended by a scandal over his private life and the imploding of the Scottish Socialist Party.

Martin McGuinness (1950–)

Sheridan's career shows how devolved political careers can be like shooting stars; McGuinness's that it can be a long journey from outsider to insider. Imprisoned as an IRA activist in the 1970s, by the end of the 1990s he had helped lead Sinn Féin to constitutional politics. Acknowledged to have been a highly capable Minister of Education in the first devolved Administration, after the re-establishment of devolved government he became an equally successful Deputy First Minister.

Cartoons: Shaun Steele

■ In Chapter 18 we will see that the range of political recruitment in the Westminster government is narrowing: politics is increasingly dominated by professional politicians with similar backgrounds and social experiences. These three examples show how the devolved institutions are allowing space for those who would be excluded in the Westminster system. The three cases stand for the more general widening of the pool of available political talent: for instance, the Welsh Assembly elected in 2003 was the first nationally elected institution to have a (small) majority of women members.

remained unchanged on six. Attempts to create a coalition with the Liberal Democrats, which would have given a workable majority, failed; a prospect of coalition between Plaid Cymru and the Conservatives turned out to be a briefly tantalizing fantasy. This time around the stakes had been raised in Wales, for the new Assembly inherited significantly augmented powers. It seemed until the end of June 2007 that the outcome would replicate that in Scotland – a minority administration, but in this case with Labour rather than Nationalist in composition. That would not have been unprecedented: Labour had a similar, if unhappy and brief, attempt in the first stage of devolution; and at the end of the last Assembly Labour was already ruling as a minority administration, albeit by only a small margin: it ended up with 29 seats in the 60-member assembly. But on 27 June Labour and Plaid Cymru unexpectedly announced a coalition deal. The deal was 'unexpected' not only to outsiders: it aroused serious opposition in both parties. It was opposed by leading Welsh figures such as Lord (Neil) Kinnock, former leader of the UK party. But at a special Labour party conference on 6 July 2007 it was ratified by an overwhelming majority (almost 80 per cent in favour). Although the new government was ratified by clear majorities of both the trade union and constituency sections, the majority in the latter (with 38 per cent against) was less clear cut than among the unions, indicating grass roots unease with the world of coalition. Plaid ratified the agreement on the following day, clearing the way for coalition.

The single most important feature of the deal was a commitment to a referendum to confer full law-making powers to the Welsh Assembly – a proposal for which both parties agreed to campaign. This proposal shows just how unstable is the devolution settlement in Wales – if implemented it would be the second major augmentation of Assembly powers since the original devolution act. The lesson of these tortuous exercises in majority creation and majority management is that instability is a fact of life in the devolved systems. The skill-set demanded of a First Minister or First Secretary is therefore very different from the skill-set demanded of a Westminster Prime Minister, who must build support within the relatively stable confines of the majority party in the House of Commons, whereas a leader in the devolved systems has to build support not only within the party, but in the much more uncertain lines across parties.

The experience of careers and networks

Though devolved administrations are chronically unstable, devolution itself is nevertheless established as a permanent fact of British political life. One reason we

can be reasonably confident that some form of devolved government will endure is that even after only a few years of operation highly distinctive political communities have developed around the new institutions. In Wales and Scotland distinct political careers are being made separate from those offered by the Westminster system. Although the most ambitious Welsh and Scottish politicians still gravitate towards Westminster there have been some notable cases of individuals – the best known being the founding First Minister of Scotland, Donald Dewar – abandoning a Westminster career for one in the new institutions. The simple fact of a separate career line is not in itself novel: there is a long tradition of powerful politicians establishing both a career and a power base in local government, as we shall see in the next chapter. But whereas for ambitious politicians local government careers are typically a 'jumping off' point for a Westminster career, there is no sign of this developing in the case of Wales and Scotland. In some instances politicians who felt 'blocked' at Westminster diverted to the devolved institutions: that was the case with, for instance, the second Welsh First Secretary, Rhodri Morgan. After filling Westminster front-bench duties for Labour in opposition he was passed over for office when Labour returned to government in 1997, and made a successful alternative career in Cardiff. Thus ministerial office in Cardiff and Edinburgh now offers a long-term paid alternative to a Westminster career.

Nor is this just a matter of the careers of individuals. Distinct governing networks are being created or, where they previously existed, are being strengthened. The establishment of departments with substantial policy-making authority has developed exactly the kinds of networks that exist in London. Interest representation through the kind of lobbying that we described in Chapter 8 has developed around the new institutions: consider the example of the Scottish Retail Consortium described in Documenting Politics 8.1. In this way the devolution of government institutions has been followed by the devolution of the activity of interest representation, for the very good reason that important decisions have shifted from the Westminster system to the institutions in Cardiff and Edinburgh. The devolution reforms of 1998 are therefore having effects well beyond the institutions of government; they are stretching into a wider reshaping of the nature of political action and of the way policies are made.

The experience of popular support

Devolution has therefore been 'institutionalized': that is, it is now embedded in the governing systems of both countries. But that is not the same thing as enjoying

DOCUMENTING POLITICS 10.1

A more open political culture? Publishing the minutes of the Welsh Cabinet

EXTRACT FROM MINUTES OF THE WELSH CABINET MEETING OF 5 OCTOBER 2009

Matters arising – Christmas Cards

The First Minister indicated that, although he was retiring in December, he believed it would be appropriate to send Christmas cards just before stepping down.

The Budget

The Minister for Finance and Public Service Delivery advised Cabinet that he would be tabling the draft budget report later that afternoon. He confirmed that funding had increased in 2009–10 and 2010–11, but compared with indicative plans at the Final Budget December 2008, there had been reductions in 2010–11, arising from efficiencies (£212.6 million revenue and £75 million capital) and from the effects of bringing forward Departments' capital spend into 2008–09 and 2009–10 (£119.9 million).

It was noted that near-cash reserves for 2010–11 would be around 1 per cent of the Wales Departmental Expenditure Lines (DEL) budget.

Oral Items – Swine Flu

The Minister for Health and Social Services advised Cabinet that the number of cases of swine flu was on the increase in Wales, particularly among children, although, as yet, no schools had had to close.

Cabinet Secretariat

October 2009

■ Apart from the minutes of proceedings which I have heavily edited here, I have also cut out the list of those attending: with Ministers and Officials it numbered 27 in all. In short, it is almost a public meeting, and in that sense it resembles meetings of the Westminster Cabinet. But a key difference is that we see these minutes almost immediately; in the case of Westminster we have to wait 30 years. Notice the mix of substantively important (budget, public health and swine flu) and the trivially ceremonial (Christmas cards).

Source: http://wales.gov.uk/about/cabinet/cabinetmeetings/.

deep and widespread popular support and trust. On this, the evidence is uncertain. On the one hand, over 75 per cent of those who voted in the referendum on the principle of devolution in Scotland in 1997 supported the proposal for a Scottish Parliament. But on the other hand, turnout in both Scotland and Wales was low by the historical standards of UK-wide general elections: just over 60 per cent of Scottish voters, and just over 50 per cent of Welsh voters, turned out. Even this modest level of popular engagement has proved impossible to sustain. Turnout in the 2003 elections, the second in the history of the Parliament and the Assembly, was 49 per cent in Scotland and 38 per cent in Wales – lower even than the historically low turnout in the 2001 UK general election.

The 2007 elections saw an improvement, but only a marginal one: to 51 per cent in Scotland and 43 per cent in Wales. Part of the difficulty has been – as we shall see when we come to examine participation in Chapter 13 – that the foundation of the devolved institutions coincided with an apparent UK-wide fall in commitment to established forms of political participation like voting and the rise of a more generally sceptical popular attitude to politicians and to established institutions in general. But part of the difficulty has also been specific to the new institutions. For instance, in both Scotland and Wales the impressive new modern buildings intended to symbolize the new political order were costly fiascos. These fiascos contributed to a sense that the new institutions are expensive and wasteful. In the Scottish case, the leading party – Labour – has also been dogged by a series of scandals, one of which, involving official expenses, forced the resignation of a First Minister.

These problems, however, are hardly unique to devolved politics, and there is now convincing evidence that at the very least the fact of devolution is a settled matter in the mind of the majority of the public. The evidence from Wales is particularly convincing in this respect, since as we saw above Wales was long the less enthusiastic supporter of devolution. The most ambitious study yet of Welsh public opinion was published in October 2009. The conclusions were as follows:

> Notwithstanding the emphasis that has long been placed on Wales' political divisions, the evidence … strongly supported other work on public opinion conducted over the past decade … which points to a substantial homogenisation of attitudes to devolution having occurred in the years since the 1997 referendum. For instance, when survey respondents were asked to choose their most-preferred option for how Wales should be governed from four possibilities (Independence, a Parliament with substantial law-making powers, an Assembly with only limited law-making powers, and No Devolution), the results that emerged were remarkably consistent across the five electoral regions of Wales.
>
> Independence was the least popular option in all five regions; No Devolution was the second least popular in all five regions. And the Parliament option was chosen by a plurality in all five regions.
>
> (Scully and Wyn Jones 2009:74)

The result suggests also that the outcome of the referendum on full legislative powers agreed as part of the formation of the coalition in 2007 will be positive. But the picture on popular support for an extension of the powers of the Scottish Parliament is considerably more clouded. The position of the Labour Party is especially tortuous. Under the leadership of Wendy Alexander the party announced that it would support a referendum on independence, confident that it could fight it successfully. The opinion polls indeed continued to suggest only minority support for independence, with the economic crisis having weakened further public confidence in the viability of an independently controlled Scottish economy (Curtice 2009). But following the fall of Alexander in June 2008 (from a familiar mix of a scandal over business donations and the poisonous internal politics of Scottish Labour) the Party reversed its position,

joining the other parties to vote down an SNP proposal in the Parliament in 2009.

The experience of Europe

Relations with the EU mark a common and permanent point of departure from the traditional routines of Westminster Government. We have already seen that over 30 years of membership of the EU has reshaped the Westminster system in profound ways – indeed so profoundly that we can no longer easily speak of separate British and European government. The role of the devolved governments marks a further important development in that reshaping: in effect it involves devolution of the role of the EU itself away from Westminster. Although EU relations do not formally come within the competence of the devolved administrations, in practice they are deeply involved in policy and negotiations over policy. Since the devolved administrations are responsible for implementation of much policy agreed at EU level, it has been felt sensible to involve them also in its negotiation. Both Wales and Scotland also have powerful direct incentives to lobby in Brussels because of the interests at stake. For example, Scotland is more dependent than any other part of Britain on the Union's Common Fisheries Policy, while Wales was in receipt of over £1 billion in EU funds under the Union's programme of Structural Funding in the period 2000–06. Both countries are deeply affected by the Union's Common Agricultural Policy.

The separate establishment of Brussels-based offices quickly followed devolution. Though both the Welsh and Scottish Offices in Brussels liaise with the (Westminster) Government's Permanent Representative in Brussels, they are dominated by the need to serve the devolved administrations. Both are integral parts of the devolved administrations and are designed both to provide intelligence for Ministers in Edinburgh and Cardiff and to lobby for national interests. The Scottish case shows particularly independent activism. 'Scotland House' – where the Brussels activities of the Scottish Government are sited – provides a public face for the new government in Brussels, and Scottish representatives in Brussels have made strenuous efforts to create alliances with other regional groups across the Union. Within the devolved administrations themselves there is also specialist organization designed to monitor and influence lobbying. In Wales, a European and External Affairs Division is part of the office of the First Secretary, with a dedicated European Policy Secretariat. In the Assembly itself a European and External Affairs Committee monitors the European dimension of the full range of devolved powers.

BRIEFING 10.5

Devolved Scotland in Europe

DEVOLVED SCOTLAND – KEY ISSUES:

- Fisheries: EU Common Fisheries policy vital to Scottish fishing industry
- Agriculture: reform of Common Agriculture Policy impacts on (mostly poor) Scottish farming
- Environment: EU environmental policy impacts on pollution by Scottish industry, problems of acid rain and desire to protect wilderness for tourism
- Regional policy: European Structural Funds are major source of financial support for infrastructure development (e.g. roads).

DEVOLVED SCOTLAND – THE TACTICS:

- Ministers attend some meetings of the EU Council of Ministers
- External Relations of the Executive in Edinburgh oversees Scotland's external relations with the rest of the world, including the EU
- Scotland provides eight members of the EP
- Scotland Europa, headquartered in Scotland House, an alliance of public and private bodies, promotes Scotland as a business location, speaks with a European voice for non-governmental Scottish interests.

DEVOLVED SCOTLAND – THE BIGGER PICTURE:

- Scotland looks to other small successful national economies in the EU, as a model of small nation success in the EU
- The revival of Edinburgh as a significant centre of government also recalls the historic place of Scotland as a centre of the European Enlightenment – the key intellectual movement in the making of modern European identity
- Scotland House also promotes connections with other parts of Europe with strong regional and national identities, such as Catalonia.

■ Devolution did not of itself make Europe relevant to Scotland, nor did it lead to the invention of Scottish lobbying in the EU. But the creation of the Scottish Executive gave an institutional resource for organizing a Scottish presence in Brussels; the system of devolved elections for the Parliament gave Scottish politicians an extra incentive to recognize the issues where Europe impinged on Scottish economy and society; and the sense of rediscovered national identity ('the bigger picture') led to the search for allies among other small European nations and regions.

SUMMING UP: A NEW POLITICS OF DEVOLUTION?

Breaking up the experience of devolution in the manner above gives us a good sense of how much variety there has been. There is no one single 'politics of devolution'. Nevertheless, after more than a decade of devolution, we are in a better position to try to evaluate the devolution experience. There are five areas where we can try to answer the question: does devolution constitute a truly distinctive element in British politics?

A new politics of leadership recruitment?

This is probably the domain where the new devolved systems have the strongest claim to distinctiveness. We can see two particularly important ways in which they have 'enriched' the political gene pool from which political leaders are drawn. First, they have been significantly more successful than the Westminster system in recruiting women to positions of political leadership. However, the two main legislatures created out of devolution still have different experiences. In both 2003 and 2007 a majority of returned Assembly Members in Wales were women. Scotland has been less 'successful': in

191

2007, 35 per cent of MSPs were women. A second source of recruitment distinctiveness is less commonly remarked: the new institutions have broken the increasingly strong grip which elite English universities had come to establish over the Westminster system. The break with Westminster patterns is due to a complex range of factors, but a key influence arises from the different electoral systems in operation under devolved government. The single most important consequence has been to increase central control over legislative recruitment and thus to allow central leadership to 'steer' the system in the direction of centrally approved aims, such as an increase in the recruitment of women into leadership positions. Women prosper more under devolved government not necessarily because Wales and Scotland are more 'women friendly' cultures but because leadership recruitment is more centralized. But the electoral system may also be partly responsible for one key way in which the political 'gene pool' has been reduced in size under devolution. In Scotland Members of the Parliament with experience of blue-collar or industrial work has fallen to miniscule proportions – much lower even than the diminished proportions in the Westminster Parliament. Politics under devolution is, overwhelmingly, a calling for bourgeois professionals.

But the electoral system has not only created a new politics of leadership recruitment; it has also created new patterns of elite competition. The most obvious effect of the electoral arrangements is to create, within the new legislative elites in Scotland and Wales, two 'classes' of member under the new system: those that represent territorial constituencies and those selected from the additional member list (see Bradbury and Mitchell 2007). Indeed, citizens in the devolved systems are now faced with four different kinds of legislative representative: the two created by the electoral arrangements of devolution; the representatives of the territorial constituencies of the Westminster Parliament; and the territorial representatives of the large multimember constituencies of the EP.

A new political style?

Much of the institutional substance and the symbolism of the new systems are designed to impart a sense of distinctiveness from perceived features of the Westminster system – in particular, to create a distinctive political culture for the new systems that breaks with the highly adversarial mode of party competition in the Chamber of the House of Commons. Symbolically, the freshly designed chambers for the Welsh Assembly and the Scottish Parliament departed from the physical confrontation between a governing party and an opposi-

tion in the layout of members' desks. Procedurally, the business of both institutions is more self-consciously 'businesslike': hours of work more closely resemble conventional office hours (in the process, increasing the extent to which they are 'women' or 'family' friendly). Because they are less like 'total' institutions functioning round the clock there is also less of the 'club like' atmosphere which characterizes, in particular, the House of Commons. This is reinforced by voting procedures, which have dispensed with the physical voting in opposing lobbies of the Westminster Parliament in favour of electronically registered votes cast from members' desks, thus symbolically reducing the physical 'confrontation' involved in expressing differences. But by far the most distinctive feature of the new systems is also imposed by the electoral arrangements, which over the cycle of three elections (1999, 2003 and 2007) has failed to deliver what has been the norm at Westminster: stable majorities for a single governing party. Even rule by a single party has been the exception, and when it has occurred (as presently in Scotland) it involves a party (the SNP) without a majority. The norm has been some form of cross-party coalition and, in the brief intervals of single party rule, the expectation of cross-party coalition in the near future. In short, political leaderships in the devolved systems are obliged to cooperate with each other to an unusual degree – a marked departure from the adversarial tribalism which has marked Westminster. The strength of this consensual culture should not, however, be overstated. Party competition can be vicious, and the instability of government can make it more so. In June 2008 Wendy Alexander was obliged to resign as leader of the Scottish Labour Party after a ferocious campaign against her led mostly by members of the SNP in the Scottish Parliament – a campaign in which the minority SNP administration saw an opportunity to strengthen its weak parliamentary position arising from its minority governing status.

One further critical aspect of the style of the new devolved adminstrations has yet to be subjected to close academic scrutiny. The rationale for devolution was decentralization: it was based on the analysis that the Westminster system was too centralized to deliver effective and responsive government. What is not yet clear, however, is how far this doctrine of decentralization is being practised in the devolved systems. Government in Cardiff and Edinburgh is geographically closer to citizens than is government in Westminster, but the experience of central control from Cardiff or Edinburgh is not necessarily less distant for the geographically peripheral parts of the devolved systems than was the case under the preceding system. Indeed, one aftermath of devolution, we shall see in Chapter 12, has been to strengthen moves to decentralize the Government of England, at the very moment when Wales and Scotland have been building new centralized institutions in Cardiff and Edinburgh. Niether Wales or Scotland have anything like the high profile mayoralty that now exists in London. The paradoxical effect of devolution may be eventually to produce a more decentralized system within England than exists in Wales or Scotland.

A new politics of leadership?

The constraints on political leadership have also impacted on the way government functions at the very top in the devolved systems. At least three of the last Prime Ministers in Whitehall – Thatcher, Blair and Brown – were powerful centralizers, determined to build up the capacity of the core executive to control the making and presentation of policy. This 'strong core executive' model is very different from that developing in the devolved systems. In the case of Northern Ireland the elaborate model of power sharing precludes anything like it. But in the case of Wales and Scotland too there are powerful constraints, especially on the role that can be played by the First Minister in the two systems. (Lynch 2006 is a very good summary of this.) First Ministers are, by comparison with the leader of the core executive in Westminster, much less able to intervene in the details of policy making. But above all they are constrained by the politics of government making and especially by the fact that coalitions are the norm. One of the first and most important effects of coalition making is to remove from the hands of the First Minister a key instrument of control and patronage that has normally been wielded by the Westminster Prime Minister: the ability to hire and fire is constrained by the need to accept as ministers those chosen by coalition partners.

A new politics of policy innovation?

These differences in recruitment, style and political leadership have, unsurprisingly, begun to produce systematic differences in policy outcomes. Although some of the distinctiveness lies in the detail, it is in the detail that public service provision is felt by individual citizens. Scotland and Wales, for example, have no city academies, no foundation hospitals, no school league tables and no 'beacon councils'. Even where there is some commonality – for instance in public–private partnerships or transfer of housing stock from local authority control – the scale and speed of change is markedly differently under devolution. In the case of Scotland we have also seen the abolition of upfront tuition fees for students in higher education and the institution of free long-term personal care for the elderly. In part these

differences can be traced to well established features of the political cultures of the two nations and their contrasts in this respect with England. It is hardly surprising that two national systems that entirely failed to embrace the Conservative Party at the height of its triumphs in the 1980s and 1990s should also turn away from so many of the policies pioneered by the Conservatives and subsequently embraced by New Labour. But there are also more immediate institutions of political competition at work. In the devolved systems governing majorities not only have to distinguish themselves from their opponents; they have also had to distinguish themselves from the ruling majority in Westminster. A key to Rhodri Morgan's long, if precarious, tenure as leader in Wales was his ability to distance himself from Westminster Labour by a stream of policy innovations.

A new politics of economic management?

The momentous events that have unfolded since the beginning of the great economic crisis in 2007 also have potentially great consequences for the devolution project. A key part of the case for devolution was that central control of the economy from the Westminster system was an undesirable anachronism: for nationalists, it represented English metropolitan domination over the Celtic nations of Britain; for supporters of devolution who were not of a nationalist persuasion it represented an over-centralized governing system which was vulnerable to incompetence and fiasco. The unfolding economic crisis has in some respects strengthened those arguments. The fiascos in regulation and in the practical management of the markets have been fiascos of a London controlled regulatory system and of the wider institutions of the City of London. The sheer brutality of the economic crisis is also a crisis sweeping over the Westminster system. But the outcome of the crisis has also raised questions, especially about the viability of a nationalist future. Although the crisis had a London epicentre, the collateral damage, especially to the Scottish financial system, was catastrophic: one of the biggest, and most scandalous, casualties was the Royal Bank of Scotland, a venerable Edinburgh institution. Perhaps more important, as events unfolded it became clear that in the management of the banking crisis Scottish institutions, especially the Scottish Executive, were bystanders: such power as existed to prevent a total banking collapse was lodged in the central executive in London and in the wider international networks where segments of the central executive played a part. Even the collapse of a national economy like that of Iceland did damage to the nationalist case, for a part of the Scottish argument in partic-

BRIEFING 10.6

Devolution then and now: how the world of devolved government has changed since 1998

- Cross-party consensus develops that there is no going back to the world before 1998: Conservatives abandon opposition to devolution
- New political networks of interest representation and leadership recruitment develop in Cardiff and Edinburgh
- Nationalist parties in both Cardiff and Edinburgh experience time in government
- The range of Welsh devolved powers converges on the range of Scottish powers
- Independence for Scotland re-emerges as a significant political issue
- Labour domination of Wales and Scotland is ended.

■ The single most important feature of devolution is that it is not a static political settlement: it has changed since 1998 and will continue to change.

ular had been that small nations had the ability to carve out a prosperous niche in the global economy, free of control from great metropolitan centres of power like London. Alex Salmond, the present First Minister, had indeed pointed in the past to the successes of Iceland and Ireland – two of the biggest casulties of the economic crisis – as models of success which Scotland could emulate. Since 2007 it has become harder to argue that there is a viable, separate, nationalist path to successful economic management.

DEVOLUTION: TOWARDS MULTILEVEL GOVERNANCE

Of all the subjects in this book, the future development of devolution is the most uncertain. As Debating Politics 10.1 shows, it can be interpreted as a way of stabilizing the pressures on the unity of the UK or, very differently, as a large first step to the break-up of Britain. Yet even after a comparatively few years, and even allowing for the special uncertainties in Northern Ireland which we shall describe in the next chapter, we can be sure that devolution is here to stay, and that it is producing large scale changes in the politics of the separate nations of the UK and in the Westminster system itself. Most of this chapter has been about what devolution is doing to the internal workings of these different systems. We can now stand back from the particular national effects and summarize what the changes are contributing to the

system of government as a whole. It is immediately clear that they are reinforcing a development which recurs through the pages of this book: they are a further large step in embedding multilevel governance in the UK. Their contribution may be summarized as follows:

- they are helping establish arrangements where the governing institutions are dispersed at different levels of the political system;
- authority and control over policy has to be shared between those levels;
- a premium is placed on success in coordinating the different policy processes and policy outcomes at these different levels;
- the most important actors – such as the politicians who form governments in the different systems – have to put a large amount of time and energy into calculating how different actors at different levels of the multilevel system will respond to their manoeuvres;
- those same actors must put a large amount of energy into managing their careers so as to exploit the opportunities opened up by multilevel governance, such as the opportunities created to choose a variety of paths to a political career.

We see here that the impact of devolution is part of a wider set of influences that are shaping the governing system. We have observed parallel effects arising from membership of the EU: policy-making splits between

DEBATING POLITICS 10.1

Devolution: the road to ruin or the salvation of the UK?

DEVOLUTION BEGINS THE BREAK-UP OF THE UNITED KINGDOM	DEVOLUTION IS A STABLE REFORM OF AN OVER-CENTRALIZED POLITICAL SYSTEM
▶ The devolution settlement is unstable as shown by way the original settlement has been constantly challenged.	▶ Devolution modifies the unbalanced and biased system that existed for much of the 1980s and 1990s.
▶ The existing devolution is embedding distinctive political systems in the different countries of the UK.	▶ The electoral system in the devolved governments in Wales and Scotland makes compromise between parties virtually certain; domination by a nationalist party is therefore unlikely.
▶ Devolution has opened up fundamental questions about the nature of 'England' as a political unit.	▶ Embedding distinctive political systems in the UK is far from a disaster: many successful states have this kind of variety.
▶ Devolution was created in economic good times; in hard times it will intensify struggles for resources between the constituent parts of the UK.	▶ The notion of a single, sovereign UK focused on Westminster is already an anachronism in a system of multi-tiered governance within the EU.

different institutions at different levels, in London, Brussels and other centres of EU government; resources invested in managing the coordination of policy at different levels; demands on political actors – especially those in government – to develop new diplomatic and managerial skills effectively to operate in a world of multilevel government. Thus, the government of the UK, once focused on a centralized set of institutions clustered in central London, is now being 'stretched' outwards and downwards.

Review OF CHAPTER 10

Four themes have dominated this chapter:

- Scottish and Welsh nationalism have different historical roots, cultural preoccupations and political bases.

- These differences were reflected in an initially more thoroughgoing devolved system in Scotland.

- The evolution of devolution has resulted in a convergence between the devolved systems.

- This convergence reflects that fact that the devolved system is constantly changing, and its long term impact on the unity of the United Kingdom is uncertain.

FURTHER READING

ESSENTIAL

If you only read one item it should be Jeffery's chapter on devolution in Flinders et al. (2009) which synthesizes much of Jeffery's own work and the work of an important research programme on devolution which he directed.

RECOMMENDED

Keating (2005) and McGarvey and Cairney (2008) are book length treatments of the Scottish experience. Lynch (2006) is particularly important on the role of the First Minister. For Wales, where the story is so fast moving that academic monographs are often out of date even before they appear, there is fortunately an outstanding resource, the website of the Institute of Welsh Politics at the University of Wales, Aberystwyth: http://www.aber.ac.uk/interpol/en/research/IWP/. This publishes a now long-running series of research reports monitoring the progress of devolution, not only in Wales but in the other devolved system. It should be the first point of call for anyone wanting to find out more about Wales.

CHAPTER 11

Devolved government in Northern Ireland

CONTENTS

AIMS

This chapter:

☐ Describes the history of Northern Ireland in British politics

☐ Shows how the breakdown of the old system was a sign of wider crisis in the Westminster system

☐ Gives an account of the reconstruction of the system of government before and after the Belfast Agreement

☐ Describes consociational government in Northern Ireland

☐ Shows the construction of a working devolved executive since 2007 and how this represents only a very limited move to the development of 'normal' politics

NORTHERN IRELAND IN BRITISH POLITICS

The role of Northern Ireland in British politics is the most extreme sign of a problem that goes to the heart of the nature of the UK: what should be the boundaries of that Kingdom and how can its boundaries be maintained? In 1800 an Act of Union abolished the Irish Parliament in Dublin and united the whole island of Ireland under the British Crown. In 1922 an Irish Free State came into existence with the same degree of independence enjoyed by other members of the Commonwealth like Canada and Australia. This followed a treaty that brought to an end five years of military conflict between the British state and Irish Republican nationalists. But the new Irish state only covered 26 counties with an overwhelmingly Roman Catholic population. The remaining six, in the north of the island, dominated by a Protestant population that supported continued union with the Crown, were granted a high level of devolved government within the UK. That devolution lasted 50 years. The degree of devolution was unusual in an otherwise highly centralized political system, and was the result of a great clash about the identity of the UK. The independence settlement involved partitioning the island and incorporating the six northern counties as a component part of the UK, but one with its own legislature, executive and extensive control over its own domestic affairs.

The devolved system that survived in Northern Ireland contained features that eventually led to its collapse. It was designed from the start to ensure a permanent majority for a Unionist party which, as the name suggests, stood for unity with the rest of the UK. This party also overwhelmingly drew its support from Protestant denominations in the Province. Although its numerical majority ensured perpetual rule, it reinforced this with a variety of discriminatory measures – for instance in drawing electoral boundaries – against the minority, Catholic, population. This minority population was indeed highly distinct in religious affiliation and political allegiance: it was dominated by practising Catholics, and many among this minority did not accept the legitimacy of the political settlement that had been arrived at in 1922. In this latter conviction it was supported by the new Irish State in the south, which for almost all of its history had the aspiration of a united Ireland as at least a formally expressed aim.

The Northern Ireland system collapsed in a few short years at the end of the 1960s. A movement for civil rights reform (largely aimed at removing discriminatory measures against Catholics) caused deep divisions within Unionism, between those who wanted to conciliate and those who wanted to suppress reformers. By the end of the 1960s the authorities were unable to ensure public order (and in some cases unable even to ensure that their own police force did not breach public order by attacking civil rights demonstrators). In 1969 the British Government dispatched troops to police the Province. In the Catholic community this was rapidly followed by the rise of a new kind of radical Republicanism: as a party it took the form of Sinn Féin, and as a military group it took the form of the Provisional IRA. Within three years there had been a large-scale breakdown of public security in a three-way struggle between republican paramilitaries, the British Army and Protestant Unionist paramilitaries. In 1972 the separate institutions of Northern Ireland were finally abolished, to be replaced by direct rule from the Westminster Government through a Secretary of State with a seat in the British Cabinet. For over 20 more years military struggle, rather than orthodox democracy, shaped the politics of the Province. Over 3,500 people have been killed in the conflict. The cost in wider human suffering, economic decay and social dislocation is huge and incalculable. The majority of the dead were victims of military republicanism, but many were also victims of the armed forces and of Protestant paramilitary forces. The majority too were the victims of 'sectarian' violence, that is attacks on Catholics or Protestants by those of an opposing religious and nationalist loyalty; but many were also the victims of violence within their 'own' communities.

Numerous attempts were made in these decades to construct institutions and settlements that would restore some kind of 'normal' democratic politics resembling the politics of the rest of the UK. All failed until the 1990s. From 1990 the main republican groups and the British Government began secret (and widely denied) negotiations. In December 1993 the British and Irish Governments issued a joint 'Downing Street Declaration' that was intended to reassure both nationalists and Unionists: the former by holding out the prospect of unity if a majority, both north and south, supported it; the latter by stressing, precisely, that no unity would take place without the support of a separate majority in the north. In August 1994 the Provisional IRA announced a ceasefire, followed shortly by the Unionist paramilitary groups. A difficult, prolonged series of public and private negotiations at first was brought to failure in February 1996 when the Provisional IRA spectacularly resumed bombing operations at Canary Wharf in London.

When Labour returned to office in May 1997 it reopened a new round of all-party talks and announced a deadline for the completion of negotiations of May the following year. In July 1997 the IRA renewed its ceasefire. The ensuing negotiations involved the very highest reaches of both the British and Irish Governments

(Prime Ministers), influential foreign institutions such as the EU and the US Government, and an elaborately put together collection of the many different political forces at work in the Province. That led to the Belfast Agreement, which was concluded on Good Friday 1998; hence the better-known alternative name.

We examine the content and aftermath of the Agreement in a moment. But whatever its final fate, there is no doubt that a sea change took place in the politics of Northern Ireland in the second half of the 1990s. At the very least it produced a dramatic reduction in the level of violence, though not its elimination. Four important changes lay behind this development.

Northern Ireland changed

The Northern Ireland of 1969 – when the Troubles first fully erupted – was very different from the Northern Ireland of the Good Friday Agreement nearly 30 years later. New generations of political leaders had developed: for instance the young Republicans who had fought on the streets in the early 1970s were leaders, in Sinn Féin, of a nationalist political party which could claim to be the most rapidly rising party on the whole island from the 1990s onwards. Religious observance, which was very strong by mainland British standards in the late 1960s, had declined. Nearly 30 years of reform had created policies and institutions designed rigorously to outlaw any sign of discrimination on religious or other grounds.

The Republic of Ireland changed

The hostility of a nationalist, Catholic state in the south had been overwhelmingly important in the fate of Northern Ireland for 50 years after 1922. Whether governments in Dublin were really serious about wanting a united Ireland is uncertain. But the aspiration for unity, and the fact that it was enshrined in the Republic's Constitution, was a real source of fear to Unionists. In 1973 the Republic joined the (then) EEC. Over the next quarter century Ireland was transformed: 'European' identity in substantial degree supplanted traditional Irish identity; Catholicism largely lost its popular hold; the economy boomed from the late 1980s, so that prosperity in the once impoverished Republic outstripped a Northern Ireland economy wrecked by the decades of violence; and the country became increasingly urban and self-consciously modern in its attitudes. Although the aim of a united Ireland was still in the Constitution, by the 1980s no leading politician in government seriously pursued it.

Britain changed

The Conservative Party styled itself the 'Unionist' party, but for nearly 50 years from the early 1920s all leading British politicians were Unionists, in the sense of not questioning the domination of the 'Westminster' system. By the 1990s the Conservative Party was, at first secretly and then openly, negotiating its end for Northern Ireland; and as we saw in the last chapter the 'unionism' of the Labour Party was greatly weakened during its years of opposition in 1979–97. In the year of the Belfast Agreement Britain also marked a quarter century of membership of the EU – years that had also seen a great change in the political environment of the institutions of the Westminster system.

The wider world changed

The international environment of 1998 was radically different from that of 1969, when the violent years began. The EU was now both a major institution – playing an important role in the negotiations that produced the Belfast Agreement – and an important new source of political loyalty and identity. The collapse of the Soviet bloc in the early 1990s ended the Cold War. As a result it turned American attention to managing many smaller conflicts that had been relatively neglected. That helps to explain why pressure and conciliation from the US played so large a part in brokering the Belfast Agreement.

THE BELFAST AGREEMENT AND THE PEACE PROCESS

The Belfast Agreement was designed to create peaceful devolved government in the province, replacing the direct rule from the Westminster government put in place over a quarter of a century before. In this it has had mixed success. There has been no resumption of terrorist violence on the scale that existed before the ceasefire. But the institutions created by the Belfast Agreement were from the beginning periodically interrupted by suspensions. They were suspended continually from October 2002 to May 2007. In that latter month two formerly intransigent parties – the Democratic Unionist Party and Sinn Féin – entered as the dominant partners in a fragile, but still enduring, coalition Executive. The Executive is headed by in effect a dual leadership: the First Minister is at the time of writing Peter Robinson of the DUP, and the Deputy First Minister is Martin McGuinness of Sinn Féin. The reinstatement of the Executive amounts to a big step in the 'normalization' of Northern Ireland. By 'normalization' is meant the establishment of a pattern of politics in which the bread and butter issues of economic management, social welfare and service delivery come to displace the politics of sectarian confrontation. But the process of

Timeline 11.1

The road to devolution in Northern Ireland

1920 Government of Ireland Act creates separate Northern Ireland Parliament with extensive devolved powers and creates 'Westminster' constituencies in the Province.

1922 Remainder of Ireland becomes effectively independent as the Irish Free State.

1925 Tripartite Agreement between Westminster government, government of Northern Ireland and government of Irish Free State confirms what had hitherto been provisional boundaries between North and South.

1937 New Irish Constitution contains clauses making explicit commitment to reincorporating Northern Ireland into a united Ireland.

1967 Northern Ireland Civil Rights Association established to campaign for reform of housing, employment and electoral laws.

1969 Attacks on civil rights marchers and riots in Derry and Belfast leads to despatch of British troops to Province. Split in Republican Movement leads to formation of Provisional IRA.

1971 Death of first British soldier.

1972 Paratroopers shoot 13 marchers to death on 'Bloody Sunday' in January. Northern Ireland government suspended and direct rule via Secretary of State in Westminster Cabinet introduced.

1974 Peace talks lead to formation of 'power sharing' Executive; abandoned following general strike of Protestant Ulster Workers Council.

1981 Death of IRA hunger strikers leads to riots that cause over 50 deaths.

1984 IRA bomb at Grand Hotel Brighton narrowly misses Prime Minister Thatcher and kills five people.

1993 John Hume (Social Democratic and Labour Party) and Gerry Adams (Sinn Féin) begin exploratory talks for a settlement; British government admits to several months of secret negotiation with the IRA. Downing Street Declaration jointly by British Prime Minister and Irish Taoiseach leads to opening of all-party talks.

1994 IRA declares ceasefire, quickly followed by ceasefire declaration by Unionist paramilitary groups.

1995 First official meeting between IRA and a British government minister for 23 years.

1996 IRA ends ceasefire with bombing of Canary Wharf in London, killing two. American Senator George Mitchell chairs (not quite) all-party talks: Sinn Féin excluded.

1997 Labour general election landslide; IRA and Unionist paramilitary ceasefires resumed; Sinn Féin readmitted to all party talks.

April 1998 The Belfast Agreement concluded on Good Friday after intense negotiation involving direct participation of all parties and indirect external pressure from the US government and the EU.

June 1998 Elections for Northern Ireland Assembly.

July 1998 Meeting of 'shadow' Assembly, and David Trimble (Ulster Unionist) and Seamus Mallon (SDLP) selected as First Minister Designate and Deputy First Minister Designate respectively.

Timeline 11.1 (continued)

August 1998	Bomb attack in Omagh by breakaway Irish Republican group kills 29 and injures over 200 – worst single atrocity in the history of the troubles.
September 1998	First prisoners released under the prisoner release scheme negotiated as part of the Belfast Agreement.
November 1998	Northern Ireland Act implementing Belfast Agreement receives Royal Assent.
July 1999	Collapse of attempts to progress further implementation of Belfast Agreement, principally because of differences over police reform and decommissioning of IRA weapons.
November 1999	Assembly meets and first Executive selected.
December 1999	Power devolved to Assembly and Executive.
February 2000	Westminster Secretary of State suspends devolved government because of dissatisfaction with progress of IRA weapons decommissioning.
May 2000	IRA offers concessions on inspections of its arms dumps and Assembly and Executive restored.
July 2001	David Trimble resigns as First Minister over issue of decommissioning of IRA weapons.
August 2001	Secretary of State suspends Assembly for one day – a device to allow an extra six weeks to reach agreement and reselect the First Minister and Deputy First Minister.
September 2001	Secretary of State suspends Assembly again for one day to buy more time for an agreement.
October 2001	All Ulster Unionist ministers resign from the Executive. David Trimble renominates his Ulster Unionist colleagues as ministers.
November 2001	David Trimble and Mark Durkan (SDLP) elected as Minister and Deputy respectively, following procedural manipulation to create majorities.
October 2002	Suspension of devolved government, following allegations of security breaches and alleged Sinn Féin spies in the Secretary of State's Office.
May 2003	Assembly elections, due imminently, are suspended amidst widespread belief that results would further weaken the SDLP and Ulster Unionists in favour of the more confrontational Democratic Unionist and Sinn Féin Parties.
November 2003	Assembly elections finally held; Democratic Unionists opposed to the Good Friday Agreement win largest number of seats in the Assembly; Sinn Féin displaces SDLP as largest nationalist party.
May 2005	David Trimble loses Westminster parliamentary seat.
October 2006	St Andrews Agreement paves way for restoration of devolved Executive.
May 2007	New Executive headed by First Minister from the Democratic Unionist Party and Deputy First Minister from Sinn Féin.

■ The road to the restoration of devolved government in 2007 has been long and difficult.

BRIEFING 11.1

The Belfast (Good Friday) Agreement

PRINCIPLES:

- Change in the constitutional status of Northern Ireland can only come about with the consent of a majority in the province.
- The Government of Ireland Act, claiming British jurisdiction, to be repealed.
- The Irish Government to hold a referendum to amend articles of the Republic Constitution, which claim jurisdiction over Northern Ireland.

IMPLEMENTATION – THE THREE STRANDS

Strand one: the 'north' dimension:

- A 108-member Assembly to be elected by proportional representation.
- Rules to ensure that the Assembly cannot be dominated by a simple majority.
- 'Cross community' majorities required to elect the First Minister and Deputy First Minister.
- The First Minister and Deputy First Minister to head an Executive Authority with up to ten ministers with departmental responsibilities; ministerial posts to be allocated on a proportional basis.

Strand two: the north–south dimension:

- A north–south Ministerial Council to be established under legislation at Westminster and in Dublin for consultation on matters of joint interest and to create cross-border initiatives.
- Council decisions to be made consensually.
- Annual meeting of full council and regular 'bilateral' meetings between Northern Executive Ministers and their counterparts in the Republic.

Strand three: the 'east–west' dimension:

- A British–Irish Council to be established consisting of representatives of the British and Irish Governments and devolved institutions in Northern Ireland, Scotland and Wales, the Isle of Man and the Channel Islands. Twice yearly summit meetings and more frequent meetings of particular policy sectors.
- British–Irish intergovernmental conference to be established, providing the formal machinery for cooperation and joint action at the highest levels (up to British Prime Ministers and Irish Taoiseach) of the two sovereign governments.
- European Convention on Human Rights to be incorporated into Northern Ireland Law.

- This summarizes what the parties signed up to in 1998.

normalization has been difficult, prolonged and, we shall see, quite limited.

The limitations start with the system of government established by the Belfast Agreement. It is very different from the models of devolution established in Wales and Scotland, because it is designed to manage a political culture that is still highly sectarian. Northern Ireland now has what is technically usually called a 'consociational' form of government. This means that however far Northern Ireland moves to 'normal' politics in the sense of being concerned with bread and butter issues of economic prosperity and social welfare, the fundamental constitutional structure for the Province will be anything but 'normal' by the standards of the other devolved systems. Consociationalism is a widespread device employed in societies trying to practise peaceful democratic government in conditions of extreme religious or ethnic division. It recognizes the necessity of living with these divisions and concentrates on developing rules and institutions that allow the divided communities to cooperate peacefully. It involves election procedures, rules for forming government and rules for making policy which try to maximize the range of groups included in government and which give to groups power to veto decisions, thus ensuring that any simple numerical majority cannot use that numerical dominance to impose its view on minorities.

The marks of consociationalism in the system of government created out of the Good Friday Agreement are threefold. First, the system used to elect the Northern Ireland Assembly is designed to support consociationalism. The Assembly consists of 108 members, elected for multimember constituencies. There are 18 constituencies in all, each with six members. Voting is by a variant of proportional representation, the single transferable vote (for details, see Briefing 11.2). Although this voting system has been used to elect local councils in Northern Ireland since the 1970s, its use for Assembly elections marks a sharp break, both in rules employed and the intended results, with that used for nearly a century for the dominant (Westminster) parliament. The first past the post election system for Westminster is, we shall see later, designed to produce single party majorities. The electoral systems in Wales and Scotland, as we saw in the preceding chapter, are designed to produce single party majorities if the popular vote is indeed dominated by a single party. But the system adopted in Northern Ireland is designed precisely to frustrate this outcome, regardless of the distribution of the popular vote. It is designed to avert the possibility that any one party could command sole power, in the manner usual in Westminster and possible in Cardiff and Edinburgh. The Assembly has a deliberately larger proportion of elected representatives to electors than the Westminster Parliament, to improve the chances of all shades of opinion being represented. There is an average of one elected member per 11,000 voters; the contrasting figure for the Westminster Parliament exceeds 60,000. The variant of proportional representation used in Northern Ireland is designed, by obstructing the emergence of any single majority, to compel the parties to compromise. This is reinforced by an additional measure. On election all Assembly members have to register themselves as nationalist, Unionist or 'other' – and as we shall now see this is critical to how decisions are taken within the Assembly. This is a much more

radical departure from the Westminster rules even than that adopted for the new institutions in Wales and Scotland.

Second, the composition of the Executive – in effect the Government composed of ministers – is likewise designed to reinforce consociationalism. The devolved Government is headed by a First and Deputy Minister who *jointly* head the Executive Committee. The two must stand for election jointly and, to be elected, must have cross-community support: a majority of those members who have designated themselves nationalists, a majority who have designated themselves Unionists, and a majority of the whole Assembly, must vote for their joint candidature. The individual ministries are then allotted in proportion to party size in the Assembly, the total size of the ministry being decided by the First and Deputy Minister acting jointly. As an additional incentive to consociationalism, ministers are only eligible to take office if their nominations are supported by three designated Unionists and three designated nationalists.

Third, the rules of decision within the Assembly are also designed to build consociational arrangements. Virtually all decisions require a simple majority support from both the designated Unionists and nationalists and in some important instances require a special majority of 60 per cent of those voting.

The fundamental presumption of the Belfast Agreement is that all the political parties have an obligation to work institutions that are built on consociational principles: on the principle of power and institution sharing; and on the rejection of the adversarial politics that, as we saw in Chapter 9, is the dominant feature of the Westminster Parliament.

Any normalization of Northern Irish politics has, therefore, to occur in the very 'abnormal' by Westminster standards – setting of this consociational system. It also has to be understood in the context of the complicated history of that system in the years since 1998. As we noted above, the Executive, which had first been periodically in suspension after 1998, and then totally in suspension from October 2002, was reinstated in May 2007, with a leadership that would have seemed inconceivable a few years earlier: the First Minister was Dr Ian Paisley of the Democratic Unionist Party (succeeded in June 2008 by Peter Robinson of the same party); his co-equal Deputy Leader was Martin McGuinness of Sinn Féin. In the years since then this Executive has maintained a precarious, but tenacious, existence.

Understanding how Northern Ireland has come to this fragile settlement involves understanding three linked processes: the history of the institutions themselves since the Belfast Agreement; the further integra-

BRIEFING 11.2

The single transferable vote in Northern Ireland

The single transferable vote is used as follows in Northern Ireland Assembly elections:

- The province is divided into 18 constituencies, each with six Assembly members.
- Each party puts forward a list of candidates, up to a maximum of six.
- Voters cast votes by expressing numerical preferences for as many or as few candidates as they prefer: thus, 1, 2, and so on.
- In counting, the number of ballots are counted, the total is then divided by the number of seats to be filled, and this figure, plus one, is the 'quota': the required number of votes needed for election.
- Any candidate with enough votes to reach the quota is declared elected; any unused portion of their vote ('surplus') is transferred to the voter's second preference. If unfilled seats remain after all first preferences have been allocated, the candidate with the lowest number of votes is eliminated and their votes are transferred to their voters' second preferences. The process of elimination and reallocation continues until all seats are filled.

- Devolved government is often a laboratory of innovation. Britain is often described as having a first the post election system – see Chapter 17 – but virtually its polar opposite has existed for over 30 years in local government in Northern Ireland.

tion of Sinn Féin into constitutional politics in the Province; and the reshaping of Ulster Unionism.

THE HISTORY OF THE DEVOLVED INSTITUTIONS

From the beginning the consociational institutions of devolution proved immensely fragile. Two critical issues remained to be settled in the wake of the Belfast Agreement: decommissioning the stores of weapons held by paramilitary groups; and establishing, with Sinn Féin participation, a cross-party system for governing policing in Northern Ireland. Both were critical for plain reasons: the former because, both as substance and symbol, it concerned the extent to which peaceful politics had truly been established; the latter because policing was the single most divisive issue throughout the long history of the Troubles.

Failure to reach agreement on the decommissioning of IRA weapons led almost immediately to suspension of all the institutions of devolution and the reimposition of direct rule by the Secretary of State. This was followed by a series of reinstatements, suspensions, periodic threats to withdraw from the institutions by the Ulster Unionist Party – the party of the First Minister – and a

resignation by the First Minister himself. Finally, the institutions were suspended in October 2002 in sinister and mysterious circumstances involving police raids on Sinn Féin offices in the Assembly, and counter-charges that Sinn Féin was using its position to assist IRA spying. The authoritative chronology of all this will have to wait the passage of time and the opening of archives to historians. But it is easy to see that the attempt to work the institutions was immensely complicated by the lack of trust between figures that for three decades had been adversaries.

The suspension of the devolved institutions between 2002 and 2007 looks like an interregnum – a period when the politics of the province were put into a kind of constitutional deep freeze. It was certainly a period when there was widespread pessimism about the possibility of entrenching constitutional politics. But in retrospect, we can see that it was also a period when fundamental changes took place that affected the two parties who are now the dominant actors in the Executive: Sinn Féin and the Democratic Unionist Party. Beneath the surface of immobility the tectonic plates of Ulster politics were shifting, and shifting in such a way as to result in the reinstatement of the institutions established by the Belfast Agreement. Three of these changes are critical: the fate of decommissioning; the fate of policing; and the fate of the parties that had originally dominated the negotiation and establishment of devolved government. Let us look at each in turn.

The fate of decommissioning

In September 1997, in advance of the Belfast Agreement, the British and Irish governments had established an Independent International Commission on Decommissioning (IICD) to oversee the decommissioning of paramilitary weapons. The Belfast Agreement itself committed all participants to the total disarmament of all paramilitary organizations; the parties were required to 'use any influence they may have, to achieve the decommissioning of all paramilitary weapons within two years'. What would happen if the parties failed to influence armed groups to decommission within this desired timetable was left unstated. A critical problem in the life of the Executive subsequently was the failure to meet the two-year deadline: in particular, the failure of IRA decommissioning within the timeline fuelled the already deep suspicions on the side of Unionism. The IICD is still working on the decommissioning of some weapons stocks by loyalist paramilitary groups. However, in December 1998, the Loyalist Volunteer Force (LVF) decommissioned a quantity of arms. Subsequently, the IICD reported three acts of decommissioning by the Provisional IRA: in October 2001, April 2002 and October 2003. Then, in July 2005, the Provisional IRA made a critical symbolic commitment when it issued the following statement: 'all volunteers have been instructed to assist in the development of purely political and democratic programmes through exclusively peaceful means'. In September 2005 the IICD reported that it and independent witnesses had 'determined that the IRA has met its commitment to put all its arms beyond use in a manner called for by the legislation'.

The fate of policing

The creation of community-wide trust in the police service was a major task still to be completed when the Belfast Agreement was signed. Out of the Agreement came the Patten Commission (chaired by Chris Patten, a former Conservative Cabinet Minister). The Report of the Commission in 1999 recommended important symbolic changes, such as a change in name from the Royal Ulster Constabulary to the Police Service of Northern Ireland. A significant effort was also to be made to widen the basis of police recruitment to encompass Catholics from both sides of the border, with the aim of creating a 50/50 balance in recruits between Catholics and Protestants, in a force which historically had been overwhelmingly Protestant. Above all, Patten recom-

FIGURE 11.1 ■ Support for the Good Friday Agreement in Northern Ireland and the Irish Republic (per cent voting 'yes' in referendums on acceptance)

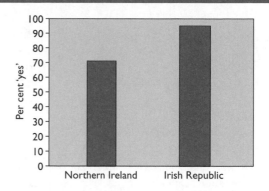

■ These figures show impressive support for the Good Friday (or Belfast) Agreement in the referendums in 1998 that followed its conclusion: 94.4 per cent voted 'yes' in the Irish Republic, and 71.1 voted 'yes' in Northern Ireland. But the bald figures hide some important features. The two populations were in effect voting on different substantive issues: in the case of the Republic, for instance, the most important was amending the Constitution to introduce clauses more conciliatory to the Unionist majority in Northern Ireland. Participation was exceptionally high (81 per cent) in the north and low (55 per cent) in the Republic, the latter indicating widespread indifference to Northern Ireland. More important still for the future of the peace process, while a large majority of voters identified as Catholic voted 'yes', voters identified as Unionists were about equally divided.

mended fundamental changes in the government of the Service, involving the creation of the Northern Ireland Policing Board, with seats allocated to the main political parties: in other words, Sinn Féin, historically an enemy of the police service, would now be bound into its government. The new service came into existence in 2001, and the main Unionist parties immediately took their place on the board, as did the Social Democratic and Labour Party. But Sinn Féin refused to join or to endorse the new Service on the grounds that the full range of Patten recommendations had not been implemented. But following the St Andrews Agreement (on which, see below) it endorsed the Service at an *Ard Fheis* (party conference) in January 2007, and Sinn Féin representatives joined the Board shortly afterwards.

The fate of the parties

The histories of decommissioning and of the reform of the police service in Northern Ireland have a common

TABLE 11.1 The rise of the DUP and Sinn Féin: the 2007 Northern Ireland Assembly election results (results for parties which gained seats)

Party	Seats	Change from 2003 (+/–)	Share of vote	Change from 2003 (+/–)
Democratic Unionists	36	+6	30.1	+4.4
Sinn Féin	28	+4	26.2	+2.6
Ulster Unionists	18	–9	14.9	–7.7
Social Democratic and Labour Party	16	–2	15.2	–1.8
Alliance Party	7	+1	5.2	+1.6
Green Party	1	+1	1.7	+1.4
Progressive Unionist Party	1	0	0.6	–0.6
Other	1	0	3.2	+0.4

■ The comparison with the 2003 results shows the continuation of a trend which was already evident in the first edition of this book, which compared 2003 with the first Assembly elections: the continuing decline of the original parties that dominated the shaping of the Belfast Agreement, and the rise of the two forces, DUP and Sinn Féin, which had been sceptical about, or even hostile to, the Agreement.

theme: they tell a story of the difficult but continuing incorporation of Sinn Féin into constitutional politics in Northern Ireland. That incorporation began back in the 1990s as the Sinn Féin leadership began to think out the implications of the failure of military attempts to expel the British government from the Province. An important clue to the shifts in political position that continued after the Belfast Agreement lies in the electoral fate of the parties. In the three Assembly elections that have taken place since the Agreement the two parties that initially dominated the Executive (providing the founding First Minister and Deputy First Minister) have been displaced as the leading electoral forces by two more–hard-line rivals. On the Unionist side the Ulster Unionist Party, whose leader David Trimble was the founding First Minister, was indeed virtually destroyed as an electoral force by the Democratic Unionist Party, which had initially denounced the terms of the Belfast Agreement. On the nationalist side the Social Democratic and Labour Party was supplanted as the primary voice of nationalism by Sinn Féin which, though it assented to the Belfast Agreement, and participated in the first Executive, gave highly qualified assent, especially, as we have seen, on the issue of policing. Table 11.1, summarizing the most recent results, for 2007, shows the domination of, respectively, the DUP and Sinn Féin.

The results of the 2007 Assembly elections were especially momentous, both because they marked a great shift in the balance of forces and because they contributed to the re-establishment of devolved government in the Province. Even in the election of 2003 (and in the general election of 2005) the two parties that represented polar opposite positions, and that had a long history of poisonous confrontation, had emerged as the largest for, respectively, the Unionist and the nationalist communities. Now in 2007 they decisively consolidated their positions as the dominant forces in the Province: the DUP gained 6 seats, to total 36; while Sinn Féin, the standard bearer of fundamentalist nationalism, increased its share of seats by 4, to 28. The two parties that had been the main architects of the original peace agreement, the UUP and the Social Democratic and Labour Party, both lost ground, the UUP disastrously: its representation was reduced by 9, to 18.

Superficially, these results must have looked like bad news for the fate of devolved government: politics in the Province was increasingly dominated by two extremely hostile adversaries. But, ironically, the results hastened an extraordinary change in the political climate. There were several reasons for this paradoxical outcome, and they are reviewed below. But a simple summary would be that the outcome shows what institutional design can achieve. The complex architecture of consociationalism, which we described above, meant that Sinn Féin and the DUP were entrapped in an institutional web that compelled them to cooperate if they were to head a devolved Executive. On 8 May 2007 the DUP leader, the Reverend Ian Paisley, was sworn in as First Minister, while Martin McGuinness of Sinn Féin, was sworn in as Deputy First Minister. In the freshly revived devolved administration the DUP now heads four ministries, while Sinn Féin controls three.

This reinstatement of devolved government under the historically unprecedented jurisdiction of two great adversaries did not, of course, happen suddenly. It was the difficult outcome of a long process of hard bargaining, the centrepiece of which was the St Andrews Agreement, to which we now turn.

THE ROLE OF THE ST ANDREWS AGREEMENT

In the development of the Peace Process, 8 May 2007 was an historic day, but it was only the culmination of six months of hard bargaining between the two major parties (the DUP and Sinn Féin) and the British and Irish Governments. The beginning of this process was marked by the publication of the St Andrews Agreement in October 2006. That Agreement was the result of three days of negotiation involving the two governments and all the parties represented in the Northern Ireland Assembly at a conference in St Andrews, in Fife. The most important product of the conference was the text of the Agreement, and the most important part of the Agreement was a 'roadmap' – a timetable – designed to culminate in the entry of the DUP and Sinn Féin as the leading parties in a restored Executive. Though bluff and counter-bluff between the DUP and Sinn Féin ensured that there was some slippage in the St Andrews timetable the stages outlined in the roadmap were all traversed. We can see from this that the critical decisions by the Sinn Féin *Ard Fheis* in January 2007 to endorse the policing system in the Province, and to take up its nominated places on the Policing Board, were a direct consequence of the St Andrews process. The Assembly elections, at which the dominance of the DUP and Sinn Féin was confirmed, were held in March 2007, and in advance of the 8th of May nominations for First Minister and Deputy First Minister the parties had already indicated their choices to fill the ministerial posts. Thus the date of the 8th of May is momentous, not because it marked a break-through, but because it signified the final success of a long period of bargaining.

The St Andrews Agreement, though much less well known than the Belfast Agreement, thus has claims to virtually equal significance. It has been sardonically described by Reg Empey, one of the two members of the Executive from the once dominant UUP, as 'the Belfast Agreement for slow learners'. It finally bound Sinn Féin into purely constitutional politics in Northern Ireland and began the process by which the DUP was committed to a shotgun marriage in the Executive with the nationalist party which it had consistently denounced. It will take the work of historians to unravel all the forces that

---

DOCUMENTING POLITICS 11.1

How the language of Northern Ireland Politics has changed: Martin McGuinness composes a poem for Ian Paisley

The lilac creature lay silent and unmoving
As the peaty water flowed over the last of the
Mohicans.Stones were the wigwam in a Donegal
river For a decimated breed of free spirits.
Tribes and shoals disappeared as we polluted and
devoured With our greed and stupidity the home
land of the brave.

■ Martin McGuinness and Ian Paisley were once sworn enemies; yet this is an extract from a poem which McGuinness composed and presented to Paisley on the latter's retirement as First Minister (McGuinness was his Deputy). Opinions can differ about its literary merits; but there is no doubting that it shows a huge cultural shift among the political elite in Northern Ireland.

Source: *The Times*, 6 June 2008.

---

produced this dramatic six months of change, and much will have to await the opening of archives and the appearance of memoirs by the leading figures. But we can even now sketch some of the forces at work.

The outcome, as we noted above, is partly a testimony to the power of institutional design. The DUP had emerged as the leading party, and therefore as the party eligible for the considerable prize of leading the Executive. But the rules of consociational government meant that this prize was not within its grasp if it could not find some way of working with Sinn Féin. Tonge (2007) has provided the most authoritative summary of the more immediate pressures that brought change about. Some of these involve the mobilization of resources by the British and Irish Governments. Thus the St Andrews Agreement included a commitment to a significant package of investment, especially in the transport infrastructure of the Province. Alongside these financial rewards went a financial threat. The salaries of Assembly members had been paid during the periods of suspension, but the British Government announced that this practice would cease if the institutions were not reinstated by the St Andrews' timetable – an obvious attempt to concentrate the minds of the politicians on the problem of reaching an agreement.

The institutional architecture of consociationalism and the rewards and threats employed by the British and Irish Governments were thus important in helping to realize the success of the St Andrews Agreement. But Tonge argues that the most important factor was movement on the part of Sinn Féin. The Belfast Agreement had continued Sinn Féin's long, but incomplete, progress to two related conclusions: that it would become a fully constitutional party and, by extension, that it must abandon its support for 'armed struggle' as a tactic to achieve the creation of an independent, united Ireland. (The Belfast Agreement allows for the possibility of unification through consent, but in such circumstances as are unlikely to be realized in the foreseeable future.) Thus processes such as decommissioning and the acceptance of the policing arrangement by Sinn Féin can be seen as the difficult, delayed, but full, acknowledgement by the dominant institution of Irish Republicanism that it would peacefully have to work a set of governing institutions within the framework of the UK. As we shall see below, this creates one of the great remaining areas of uncertainty about the robustness of the governing system created by the Belfast and St Andrews Agreements.

NORTHERN IRELAND POLITICS AND MULTILEVEL GOVERNANCE

The devolved system in Northern Ireland is simultaneously the most characteristic, and the most abnormal, symptom of a great change which has come over the system of government in Britain in the last generation, a change which provides the dominant theme for this book: the transformation of a unitary, hierarchical state into a multilayered system of devolved governance. It is the most characteristic because, for that old unitary system, it was 'the canary in the coal mine': in other words, in the second half of the 1960s it was the early sign of danger to the British constitutional settlement which had been stable since the early 1920s. This settlement was 'unionist': that is, all the leading political forces, and especially the two dominant parties, supported a political system largely controlled by the Westminster Executive. But Northern Ireland was abnormal historically, and it has remained abnormal. We have seen that the historical abnormality consisted in the way the boundaries of the British state were secured: by creating a system of Protestant and Unionist ascendancy in Northern Ireland which depended on the suppression of many of the civil rights established on the mainland.

The collapse of that system in the late 1960s created a succeeding tragic abnormality: the three decades of conflict until the Belfast Agreement which claimed the lives of over 3,500 people and caused huge social, economic and physical damage in the Province.

Violence in settling political differences is common in British political history (see Timeline 13.1), but the scale and ferocity of Northern Ireland violence was out of all proportion to anything experienced in the rest of the UK. The years since the Belfast Agreement have, as we saw above, witnessed considerable progress in establishing peaceful, constitutional government in the Province. But devolution in Northern Ireland is not like devolution in Scotland and Wales. There are three big differences which make Northern Irish devolved government anything but normal by the standards of Cardiff or Edinburgh.

First, the fundamental pattern of political loyalties is very different. Northern Ireland electoral politics remains 'confessional' – or 'sectarian', if one wishes to use a more critical term. The evolution of party loyalties since the Belfast Agreement has if anything intensified this. As we saw above, that evolution has involved the displacement of the two parties – the Ulster Unionists and the SDLP – which had partly tried to reach across the sectarian divide by the DUP and Sinn Féin, which had identified in a much more confrontational way with, respectively, the Unionist and nationalist communities. The electoral system in Northern Ireland, by allowing voters to express a set of hierarchical preferences for candidates, also allows electoral analysts to examine how far those preferences cross the historical Unionist/nationalist divide. Tonge's analysis (2007) of the pattern of transfers in the last Assembly election, of 2007, shows that there are few transfers across the divide, and even fewer between the two great antagonists, the DUP and Sinn Féin: 'over 94% of the DUP's surpluses transferred to other Unionist candidates, and, of Sinn Féin and the SDLP's surplus votes, 87% and 93% transferred to other nationalist candidates' (2007:10). Stripped of technical language this amounts to the unsurprising finding that hardly any DUP voters put Republican candidates anywhere in their list of preferences, while Sinn Féin voters likewise denied any preference for Unionists. But while unsurprising, the finding does act as a powerful corrective to the notion that in Northern Ireland we are witnessing the birth of 'normal' politics by the standards of the other devolved systems. (For more evidence of the persistence of sectarianism, see Political Issues 11.1.)

Second, the character of the Executive remains abnormal. If we think of the sets of executives with which we have now dealt – the core executive in Whitehall, the executives in Edinburgh and Cardiff and

POLITICAL ISSUES 11.1

The persistence of sectarianism in Northern Ireland

The history of the peace process since the Belfast Agreement is in part a story of a victory over sectarian conflict. Northern Ireland has the most rigorous anti-discrimination laws, for instance in employment procedures, in the UK. But it is one thing to change institutions, another to change everyday behaviour. 'Everyday' sectarianism continues to take three forms:

- A legacy of the 30 years of civil strife is that spatially the Catholic and Protestant communities are more segregated than they were even in the 1960s.
- Paramilitary groups, especially in Protestant communities, continue to exercise great power, often linked to criminal activities, especially the drug business.
- There is more overt hostility to incomers than in any other part of the UK, if those incomers are non-white or are from strikingly different cultures. The small Chinese community in Belfast has suffered years of harassment. And in June 2009 Romanian immigrants were burnt out of their homes and returned in fear to their homeland.

The high level of sectarianism is connected in part to the intensity of protestant and loyalist affiliations and in part to the sheer unfamiliarity of outsiders: between the late 1960s and the late 1990s, when much of mainland Britain became increasingly diverse ethnically, there was little incentive to migrate inwardly to Northern Ireland.

■ The peace process changed much about Northern Irish politics; but it did not fundamentally change the political culture.

that in Northern Ireland – the last is the least cohesive. We know that the power of the Prime Minister to hire and fire in Westminster is constrained by the practicalities of party politics, and is more constrained still in Cardiff and Edinburgh, usually by the fact of coalition government. Nevertheless, even coalition executives in Cardiff and Edinburgh function in a coordinated, cohesive way. But Northern Ireland is virtually a system of 'fiefdoms' for the parties that hold ministries. (At present, the DUP has five members; Sinn Féin has four; the UUP has two; and the SDLP has one.) The First Minister in Belfast has virtually no power of appointment at all. He has to be appointed in a kind of shotgun marriage with his (co-equal) Deputy from the main rival party, and Executive posts are allocated, as we have seen, in proportion to their strength in the Assembly. The strenuous efforts made by Paisley and McGuinness to present a united front of friendship after May 2007 – efforts which produced a mixture of consternation and amusement – was an attempt to cope with this chronically splintered condition. Perhaps the appearance of genial relations between the two was helped by the fact

that, uniquely in Irish politics, both were strict teetotallers.

Third, while the devolution settlements in Cardiff and Edinburgh are irreversible – the only question being how far they will develop into something more constitutionally radical still – the same cannot be said of Northern Ireland. The key to the changes which led to the reinstatement of the Executive in May 2007, and its endurance since then, is, as we have noticed above, the increasingly complete integration of Sinn Féin into constitutional politics in Northern Ireland: the two big signs of that are the final decommissioning of arms and the acceptance by Sinn Féin of the new policing regime, in the government of which it now plays a crucial part. The critical remaining uncertainty is how far Sinn Féin can carry the whole of nationalist opinion into the constitutional arena.

The splintering of dissident nationalism in the wake of Sinn Féin's embrace of constitutionalism started in the 1990s as it began its tortuous progress to constitutionalism. The greatest terrorist attack since the Belfast Agreement – the attack in Omagh on 15 August 1998

DEBATING POLITICS 11.1

Is the peace process a success?

THE PEACE PROCESS IS A SUCCESS	THE SUCCESS IS ONLY SUPERFICIAL
▶ Violent deaths from sectarianism have been massively reduced. ▶ Power sharing between former enemies is now established. ▶ A 'normal' politics of differences over social and economic issues has developed. ▶ There is extensive devolution.	▶ Sectarianism 'on the ground' is still widespread. ▶ The physical segregation of 'Loyalist' and 'Catholic' communities is greater than ever. ▶ The power sharing Executive is riddled with tensions between former sworn enemies. ▶ It has still not proved possible fully to abolish a British Cabinet appointed administration in Northern Ireland.

which killed 29 people – was the work of nationalists who rejected both the Agreement and Sinn Féin constitutionalism. There exists now a numerically small, but potentially highly destructive, set of anti-constitutional, nationalist groups that oppose Sinn Féin strategy. The murder of two British soldiers and of a police officer in March 2009 was a signal of the destructive potential of these groups, the Real IRA and the Continuity IRA. The murder of the police officer was not something that came out of the blue: it was the first success of a series of failed attempts at assassination by dissident Republican groups since the reinstatement of the devolved institutions. The unambiguous condemnation of the murders by the Deputy Minister, Martin McGuinness of Sinn Féin, shows how completely that party has been integrated into constitutional politics; but it also shows the gap which now potentially exists between this constitutionalism and those who claim to speak for the traditional aim of Irish Republicanism – the creation of a single Irish state on the island, by force if necessary.

The problem has been made more acute because Northern Ireland has yet another claim to distinctiveness: it has suffered particular severely, in terms of unemployment and the collapse of housing markets, in the great global economic crisis that began in 2007. Much of the normalization of life in the Province since 1998 has rested on Ulster's participation in the wider British economic boom, a boom that came dramatically

to an end in 2007–08. Unemployment, especially of the young, was an important contributor to the capacity of paramilitary groups to recruit in the decades after 1968, and this unemployment has now returned to the Province. At the time of writing no form of dissident Republicanism is an *electoral* threat to Sinn Féin – in the way that Sinn Féin emerged as an electoral threat to the constitutional nationalism of an earlier generation in the SDLP. But the present leadership knows that the Provisional IRA emerged as a force on the streets in the late 1960s precisely at the expense of an earlier generation of Republicans who had opted to take a constitutional route. In September 2010, indeed, one of the dissident groups – the Real IRA – issued a threat to emulate the original Provisional IRA by opening a campaign of bombing, targeted at bankers, on the British mainland.

The General Election of 2010 confirmed the reconfiguration of the party system into one dominated by the two hitherto sworn enemies, the DUP and Sinn Féin. True, the leader of the DUP, Peter Robinson, was sensationally defeated by a candidate from the cross-confessional Alliance, but this was a local earthquake explicable by scandals surrounding the Robinson family. Otherwise Sinn Féin remained the dominant nationalist force, while the UUP was extinguished as a Westminster presence: it lost its only seat, and its future probably lies in absorption into the DUP.

Review OF CHAPTER 11

Three themes have dominated this chapter:

◑ The way the Northern Irish crisis has been part of the wider crisis of the Westminster system.

◑ The way the partial resolution of that crisis has involved creating a very different kind of devolved system from that working in Scotland and Wales.

◑ The limits to the development of 'normal' politics in the Province by the standards of the rest of the UK.

FURTHER READING

ESSENTIAL

If you read nothing else, you should read O'Leary and McGarry's *Understanding Northern Ireland: Colonialism, Control and Consociation*, a third edition of a classic promised for publication in 2010.

RECOMMENDED

Adshead and Tonge (2009) very interestingly set Northern Ireland, not into UK politics, but into the wider politics of the Irish island. Tonge (2006) is a book length survey of the whole Northern Ireland experience. McKittrick and McVea (2001) is now dating, but is a classic: David McKittrick's journalistic coverage of Northern Ireland has been the best by far over the years. English (2004, 2007) are two great studies of key aspects of Irish nationalism, not confined in their range to Northern Ireland.

CHAPTER 12

The worlds of local and regional government: multilevel governance in action

CONTENTS

AIMS

This chapter:

- [ ] Describes the evolution and present organization of local government

- [ ] Describes the institutional webs – local, regional and national – within which local authorities operate

- [ ] Shows how the workings of this part of the system of government are a prime example of multilevel governance in action

LOCAL GOVERNMENT AND MULTILEVEL GOVERNANCE

When in Chapter 1 we discussed how government and the state could be defined, one feature stood out: any definition has to encompass the fact that states govern territory – an identifiable physical space. The spatial nature of government is at the heart of this chapter. As soon as we recognize the territorial face of the state we see also that government is about much more than nationally organized institutions – even institutions nationally devolved to Wales or Scotland. The local is important, both as far as governing structures and processes are concerned, and as far as the wider political life of the community is concerned.

But this recognition of the local also reveals another key aspect, not just of the character of 'local' government but of the wider system of government in Britain. Even the most superficial glance at the territorial world of government beyond national capitals like London and Edinburgh soon shows that there is no simple separation in Britain between the 'local' and the 'national' or 'central'. The territorial world, indeed, illustrates to perfection one of the key themes of this whole book: that Britain has a multilevel system of governance. This means more than the simple observation that there are indeed multiple levels at which governing institutions operate. It means that these levels interact in numerous, often complex, ways. On occasion the relations are hierarchical: national government commands, or at least seeks to command. But more commonly, networks of governing institutions are joined in more subtle ways: they are obliged to cooperate with each other, to bargain with each other, and often to try to manipulate each other. The government of a locality cannot therefore be viewed in isolation. Local governments are embedded in webs of relationships: with other local governments; with national institutions; with regional bodies. Even the most schematic outline of the local government system soon reveals this layered, multilevel character, as is shown by the simple example in Table 12.1.

That is why this chapter describes four linked aspects of the multilevel system:

- the local world of local government, which examines the institutions of local government itself;
- the national world of local government, meaning the important institutions that give local government a nationally organized presence;
- the regional world of local government, where we discuss the attempts to create, in England, a regional level of government that partly parallels the devolved worlds of government in Wales and Scotland, described in Chapter 10;
- local government and the web of governance, which refers to the extent to which local authorities are embedded in networks of quasi-government agencies, often appointed, that span policy fields like health, education, land-use planning and protection of the environment.

THE LOCAL WORLD OF LOCAL GOVERNMENT

Local government cannot be understood without knowing the long trajectory of its development. Two linked features are important: for much of the twentieth century local government was in a long decline; but in recent decades there has been a substantial process of

---

TABLE 12.1 Divided responsibilities: who keeps England clean?

	Metropolitan/London authorities			Shire/Unitary		
	Joint authorities	Metropolitan counties	London boroughs	District councils	Unitary authorities	County councils
Waste collection		●	●	●	●	
Waste disposal	●				●	●
Environmental health		●	●	●	●	●

■ Although the precise details of the division of labour in local government matters tremendously for citizens and for those who work in local government, for our purposes this matters less than the single overwhelming impression conveyed in this table: of a system which consists of a complicated series of layers of responsibilities, some very hard to disentangle. This pattern imposes the biggest single problem for local government organization: coordinating the workings of these often overlapping layers of organizations.

Source: Adapted from Local Government Association (2003b).

Timeline 12.1

Landmarks in local government history

834 Poor Law Amendment Act: establishes Boards of Guardians as special-purpose parish authorities to administer new workhouses.

835 Municipal Corporations Act: establishes directly elected boroughs in place of self-selecting medieval corporations.

888 Local Government Act: establishes 62 elected county councils, including London County Council, and 61 all-purpose country borough councils in England and Wales.

894 Local Government Act: revives parish councils and establishes 535 urban district councils, 472 rural district councils and 270 non-county borough councils.

899 London Government Act: establishes 28 metropolitan borough councils in London and the Corporation of London.

929 Local Government Act: abolishes Poor Law Guardians (set up in 1834) and transfers functions to local government.

963 London Government Act: creates 32 London boroughs and a Greater London Council.

972 Local Government Act: removes county borough councils, reduces number of county councils in England and Wales to 47, establishes six metropolitan county councils and 36 metropolitan district councils, and replaces urban and rural district councils with 334 district councils.

980 Local Government Planning and Land Act: establishes compulsory competitive tendering and urban development corporations.

982 Local Government Finance Act: establishes Audit Commission (operational 1983).

984 Rates Act: establishes system of rate-capping.

985 Local Government Act: abolishes Greater London Council and the six metropolitan councils.

reinvention and revival. These two features provide the centrepieces of what follows.

The historical decline of local government

The nineteenth century was a golden age of local government. A succession of measures reformed the system, replacing often corrupt and amateurish local bodies with professionally organized authorities and with councils elected on an increasingly wide franchise. Democratic government was pioneered at the local level. Two important Acts (in 1888 and 1894) established a structure of county and borough councils; an Act of 1899 did more or less the same job for London.

Thus by the end of the nineteenth century a structure was established that mostly lasted into the 1970s (see Timeline 12.1).

The vitality and creativity of local government in the nineteenth century made it an important source of national political leadership for the new system of government that was being created in the world's first industrial society. For instance the most important radical figure of the second half of the nineteenth century, Joseph Chamberlain, came to national prominence from a power base in local government in Birmingham. Local government pioneered provision of public services in a period when national government

Timeline 12.1 (continued)

1988 Local Government Finance Act: replaces domestic rates with Community Charge (Poll Tax).

1992 Local Government Finance Act: replaces Poll Tax with Council Tax.

1992 Local Government Act: begins further structural change; by 1998 46 new unitary authorities created in England.

1994 Local Government (Wales) Act: creates 22 unitary authorities responsible for all services in the Principality.

1998 Government of Wales Act: sets up National Assembly for Wales and establishes statutory Partnership Council between Welsh local government and the Assembly.

1999 Local Government Act: introduces 'best value' as regulator of competitive tendering.

1999 Greater London Authority: establishes directly elected Mayor and Assembly for capital, effective from 2000.

2000 Local Government Act 2000: gives local authorities power to promote the social, economic and environmental well-being of their areas and the duty to review and make new arrangements separating executive and scrutiny functions; provides for directly elected mayors.

2003 Legislation provides for referendums on issue of creating elected assemblies in selected English regions; defeated in 2004.

2004/7 Single transferable vote introduced in Scottish Local Government elections; first used in 2007.

■ There have been two great bursts of innovation in the history of local government. The first came in the later decades of the nineteenth century, when a system of local government was created to try to cope with the demands of the new society produced by the Industrial Revolution and with the emerging demands for a more democratically elected system of government. The second came in the last three decades, as governments struggled to reform the economy and the public sector in the face of a long history of economic decline.

Source: Adapted, with additions, from Local Government Association (2003a).

offered little beyond traditional functions like defence against external attack. By the start of the twentieth century virtually all the services that were later associated with the nationally organized welfare state were already being provided by many local authorities: school education; policing; public health; hospital care; road maintenance; water supply and sewage disposal; public transport; child health care and welfare; gas and electricity supplies; and public libraries. Local government not only pioneered the welfare state. It was also highly entrepreneurial, running successful businesses to supply, for example, gas and electricity. 'Municipal socialism' – providing public services at a local level –

was a common description of important local government bodies of the nineteenth century, like Birmingham City Council, even when they were run, as was Birmingham, by businessmen who were horrified by socialism.

Much of this importance in service delivery remains. Indeed, it is very likely that the typical British reader of this book mostly comes into contact with the state as a provider of public services through local councils. The one public service that visits virtually every household weekly, for instance, is the local authority run, or contracted, refuse collection service. But over the course of the twentieth century the development of local

FIGURE 12.1 ■ The reliance of local government on central government financing

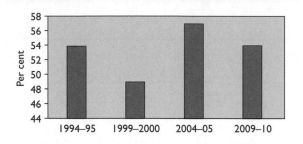

■ The figures here refer to only one part, but an important part, of spending: revenue expenditure, which excludes spending on capital projects, like investment in buildings. They also refer to England alone. But they show a stable pattern: the reliance of the locality on the centre for money. The residue of local government revenue raised is from non-domestic (business) rates and the council tax.

Source: Department of Communities and Local Government (2009).

government was essentially a history of declining importance and independence. There were a number of signs of this: money, functions, independence, stability. We now discuss each in turn.

Money. Money is often the key to power in government, and the ability to raise it is a particularly sensitive indicator of power. Over the long term local government became increasingly dependent on central government for its resources. Local authorities had historically raised money in two main ways: by charging for services and by imposing local taxes, of which the most important were those on domestic property and business property. Over the last century central government has increased its own taxation capacities, principally by drawing more and more workers into the net of income tax payers (see Chapter 20 for a longer account). By contrast, local property taxes have provided a poor yield. The three main sources of financing are:

● Central government grants, providing about a half of all revenue.
● A tax on business property, which yields about a quarter of the revenue. The rate of this tax is, however, effectively set by central government.
● A locally imposed tax on domestic property – the so-called council tax – that raises just over a fifth of revenue.

A small amount of money, covering the remainder, is also raised by charging for services at the point of consumption: for instance, parking meters or pay and display car park charges. But local government, once financially independent, now largely depends on central government for money.

Functions. Local government is still a major deliverer of services, but the range of services it truly controls has narrowed over the long term. In addition to losing much of its financial independence because it now depends on central government for money, local government was also stripped in the course of the twentieth century of many of the functions it performed. For instance local authorities lost most of their roles as providers of 'utilities' – services like gas and electricity – as long ago as the 1940s. Likewise, the establishment of the National Health Service in 1948 transferred ownership of local authority hospitals to the NHS and stripped local government of responsibilities for other health services. This loss of function has continued remorselessly. Until the 1980s local government was the dominant provider of public housing – so dominant that 'council housing' was the colloquial description of all publicly owned dwellings. But since the 1980s over one and a quarter million local authority dwellings have been sold to sitting tenants under 'right to buy' policies of successive governments. This has obviously greatly reduced the size of the housing stock administered by local government. But in addition, the remaining estates are now gradually being taken from local government control and transferred to independent trusts, often controlled by tenants. The last large service that local government controlled – primary and secondary education – is now under threat: in the last couple of decades there has been a steady transfer of control over budgets, for example, to individual schools. Both the Labour and Conservative parties would like to strip more responsibility in education away from local government.

Independence. The freedom of local authorities to act independently has also been reduced, especially in the last couple of decades. This has happened in a number of ways. As the case of the Audit Commission (Briefing 12.1) shows, central government increasingly inspects how money is spent – not surprisingly, since it provides most of that money. One reason it increasingly provides the money is that it has also, over the long term, intervened to limit the taxing freedom of local government – for instance by periodically putting ceilings, or threatening to put ceilings, on local property taxes. Central government has also tried to attach increasingly specific conditions to many of its grants, linking them to particular projects, to competitive schemes for which

BRIEFING 12.1

The rise of the Audit Commission as a control agent

The audit of local government can be traced back to 1846, when the District Audit Service was first established. But the nineteenth century notion of audit focused on establishing that money had been spent in a properly authorised way; it took little notice of the efficiency and effectiveness of spending. This narrow conception of audit lasted into the twentieth century. A sea change occurred with the founding of the Audit Commission in 1983. The rise of the Audit Commission is marked by three features:

■ The Commission is a regulatory arm of central government charged with the oversight of both local government and a range of other public bodies (see below).

•■ The Commission's functions range well beyond traditional audit, into a comprehensive responsibility to review the performance of local authorities.

■ During the 1990s the Commission's responsibilities widened to encompass other locally active bodies. It now has audit responsibility for National Health Service Authorities and hospital trusts, and is part of 'joint inspectorate' for social services with the Social Services Inspectorate.

■ In Chapter 8 we saw that there has been a major expansion in the regulatory responsibilities and resources of the state in Britain in recent decades; the rise of the Audit Commission is a sign of the rise of this 'regulatory state' in local government.

Source: www.audit-commission.gov.uk.

authorities have to 'bid', and by demanding cofinancing from private sector sources.

Stability. As we noted earlier, the great late-nineteenth-century reforms of local government lasted until well into the second half of the twentieth century. The map of local government in the early 1960s did not look very different from the map in 1900. Local government enjoyed stability and continuity. But if we look back at Timeline 12.1 for a moment, we will notice a striking feature: there is no entry for a major reform of the local government system between 1929 and 1963, when the government of London was reorganized; by contrast, the 40 years since then are littered with reorganizations. They range from major redrawing of the historic boundaries of local government (such as the reforms introduced by the Local Government Act of 1972) to the local government consequences of the Labour Government's devolution reforms in Scotland and Wales. This is symptomatic of a great change in attitude: until the 1960s local government organization (and reorganization) was 'off limits' to central government, as it was considered a settled part of the constitution; since then, virtually every government, of whatever political persuasion, has felt free to impose reorganization, sometimes of a funda-

mental nature, and sometimes involving tinkering with the system.

The reinvention of local government

All the changes summarized above amounted to the long-term decline of a particular 'model' of local government: the model that presumed that the individual local authority was a kind of miniature kingdom, able to fund its own activities, deliver the services that it chose to deliver, and deliver them without much interference from any outside agency. But the decline of this model has not extinguished the importance of local government. Rather, it has led to its reinvention. One important aspect of that reinvention is examined in a later section of this chapter, when we look at the rise of the 'national world of local government': at the increasing extent to which nationally organized local government bodies are important in, for example, lobbying over policy. But there has also been a substantial process of reinvention at the local level itself. The result has reinforced the extent to which local authorities are embedded in 'multi-level governance': part of extended networks that stretch both upwards to regional and national level and horizontally into partnerships with private sector organizations. This also anticipates a theme to which we will return later in the penultimate section of the chapter: the theme of local government and the web of governance.

The process of reinvention can be seen in four particularly important ways: the rise of the 'business-like' local authority; the acquisition of new roles by local authorities; the development of new European-focused lobbying activities; and the rise of local government as a centre of political innovation.

The business-like local authority. The business-like local authority is a phrase that summarizes important changes in the functioning and the culture of local government. This has involved local authorities working in much closer cooperation with the private sector and modelling many of their internal practices on that sector. One of the best established of the new business forms lies in the spread of contracting out. Throughout the 1980s the then Conservative Governments widened the range of compulsory competitive tendering – in effect obliging local authorities to put a range of services (from cleaning to waste disposal) out to open tender, thus inviting bids by private firms. The effect of this reform was muted in a variety of ways: many of the contracts were awarded 'in-house' to existing council departments; after 1997 the Labour Government 'fine tuned' competitive tendering to make it depend less on price competition and to remove the compulsory component. Nevertheless, the total impact has been great, even when tenders have been awarded in-house.

There is nothing in principle novel about contracting with the private sector for goods and services; it is something entirely traditional in local government. The novelty lies partly in the way the pressure of competitive tendering obliges councils to organize their own departments so as to allow effective competition with potential private sector providers. It also lies in something subtler: in the way it turns the state at the level of the local authority into a 'contracting state'. In other words, a prime responsibility of elected bodies becomes to award and monitor contracts for service delivery.

Only a small number of authorities (principally under Conservative Party control) have attempted to realize the full form of the 'contracting local authority', which would involve awarding and monitoring contracts to private firms for all major services. Nevertheless, the spread of contracting out has involved a historic reinvention: the local authority becomes responsible for ensuring the delivery of services and monitoring delivery quality, rather than doing the job directly. UK readers of this book will see a weekly example of this: the local authority is responsible for the collection of household

IMAGE 12.1 ■ The confident world of nineteenth-century local government

■ Manchester Town Hall (completed 1877) is one of the great icons of local civic pride in nineteenth-century Britain. Designed by Alfred Waterhouse after a national competition, it expressed the confidence of what was then the greatest industrial city in the world. The stylized design is medieval 'gothic', but it had a highly modern political purpose: it echoed the design of great civic buildings of independent city communities of medieval Europe and therefore emphasized Manchester's claims to a greatness independent of the capital in London. The statue in the foreground is a further expression of local pride: it depicts John Bright, a leading radical of the nineteenth century, and one identified with the economic interests of the city when it was the cotton capital of the world.

Photo: Michael Moran

waste, but will often have contracted the job to a private firm. (Try looking at the name on the refuse disposal wagon that visits your street: it will almost certainly belong to a private firm.) Nor is the shift to contracting only a matter of involving commercial firms. Many services are contracted to non-profit making bodies, such as charities – a common arrangement in the case of many social services, such as care for the elderly, for which local authorities are responsible.

BRIEFING 12.2

Reinventing public transport at local level: the case of the Manchester tram

Metrolink is the formal name given to what is colloquially called the Manchester tram system. Technically not a tram, but a form of light rail network, the first part of the Manchester network came into operation in 1992. This was a pioneering of a new kind of light rail transport, which has been followed by the development of 'supertram' networks in many other parts of the country, notably Sheffield and the West Midlands. But the pioneering aspect of Metrolink goes beyond tram technology. It also pioneered a way of joining the public and the private sectors to build and manage large, expensive, public, infrastructure projects. The infrastructure and assets (such as the tram network itself and the trams) are owned by the Greater Manchester Transport Executive, itself a consortium formed out of the local authorities in the area covered by the tram network. The first phase of the tram system was built, and operated, from 1992–97 by Manchester Metro Limited, a private consortium formed from a mix of large construction companies, builders of trams and the Greater Manchester Transport Executive itself. Later phases of the tram network have been built and operated by still more private consortia.

Technologically the 'tram' systems pioneered in Manchester are hybrids – a cross between traditional tram and rail. It is therefore fitting that they are also owned and run by hybrids – a cross between private and public organizations.

■ The case of the Manchester trams illustrates a whole series of themes from this section of the chapter: local government as a promoter of technological innovation and of innovation in public service provision; local government as a partner in investment with the private sector; and local government as the contractor in service delivery.

This 'turn' to business styles and practices has taken a particularly important form in local authorities that have suffered from troubled local economies. Here, there has been a spread of public–private partnerships, often with the aim of regenerating declining local economies and modernizing infrastructure like public transport. In some instances this has involved formally organized, large-scale, joint ventures with business, especially to fund and deliver big public investment projects. In the last couple of decades, for instance, many large English cities have built ambitious new tram networks in joint ventures with private operators, while operation of the London Underground is now a public–private partnership (though one of the two private operators went bankrupt in 2007). Briefing 12.2 illustrates a particularly important example of these ventures.

Finally, the rise of the business-like local authority has begun to affect the internal organization of authorities, especially the role of democratically elected representatives. The dominant form of organization hitherto involved committees of elected councillors covering the main functional responsibilities of local government. The Local Government Act 2000 was based on the premise that this system was cumbersome and outdated, poorly adapted to the need for swift and decisive policy making. It offered local government a choice: to move to a system of popularly elected mayors or to a 'cabinet' system with an executive leader. As we will see in a moment the first option has led to some important innovations, but most local authorities have opted for the cabinet with an executive leader – a kind of 'chair of the board' model, in part inspired by the organization of private firms.

The acquisition of new roles. As we saw in the last section, local government lost many of its important historic functions over the course of the twentieth century, especially in the second half of that century. But the reinvention of local government has involved the discovery of new roles for local authorities. The most important of these we have already touched on: the role of local government in the process of local economic development – a role that was first officially enjoined on local authorities in the Local Government Act 2000. The assumption of these new roles in economic development and regeneration was a response both to the problems of local economies and to the changed structure of the economy.

Many local communities suffered acutely from the great problems that the British economy experienced in the 1970s and 1980s. This was especially true of the areas that had been at the heart of the old Industrial Revolution – areas like South Wales and the North East of England, where industries like coal mining, ship building and steel production had been important. In these districts the British economic crisis produced the collapse of whole local economies, very high rates of unemployment, and poverty. Faced with these problems local authorities were forced into attempts at economic innovation. The problems were compounded by the wider structure of the economy, notably by the importance of mobile multinational companies to local employment. Thus local government was compelled to pursue an active policy of trying to attract, and then retain, branches of multinationals.

Some of the novel consequences of this activist role in trying to promote local economic development include: the leading position taken by local authorities in helping to raise finance for large scale projects designed to improve local public services, such as the transport case profiled in Briefing 12.2; partnerships with private developers to bring new commercial and residential developments to inner city areas; and partnerships with local business to try to create new sources of employment in depressed districts, such as that profiled in Briefing 12.3.

The rise of EU lobbying. These innovations in turn have stimulated the development of the local authority as a lobbyist, notably in lobbying for resources from central government and from the EU. In Chapter 8 we focused in the main on the lobbying activities of the private sector. But public bodies are also important lobbyists. Local government has always lobbied to try to influence other levels of government, especially central government. As we shall see later, in our discussion of the 'national world of local government' the many well organized national associations representing local authorities and those who work in local government have this kind of lobbying as one of their jobs. In recent years we have also seen the individual local authority, or the individual local authority in a consortium with a number of others, become an increasingly committed lobbyist. Probably the most important object of this activity is the EU, especially the Commission in Brussels. A large number of local authorities have now appointed staff

whose sole function is liaison with the EU; many have arrangements for representation in Brussels, either directly by their own employees or by using one of the numerous professional lobbying firms that have grown up around the institutions of the EU; and many have formed partnerships with like-minded local governments in other regions of the EU. The single most important reason for this development is that the Union, especially the Commission, is an important source of money, especially money for the kind of large scale investment in local public services – buildings, roads, public transport systems – which as we saw above have been important in the attempts to regenerate local economies.

In summary, in the last three decades local government, faced with the decline of many of its historically established functions, has undergone a substantial reinvention. This has involved:

- closer, more formally organized partnerships with business;
- shifting from direct delivery of services to contracting out those services;
- a growing role in the development of local economies;
- partly as a result of local economic initiatives, a growing involvement with the institutions and rules of the EU.

Promoting political innovation. Historically local government was one of the most innovative parts of the British system of government. In the nineteenth century it was in the vanguard of democratic reforms. It was also a leader in management practices. Many ideas to which central government only came much later – such as the importance of employing senior officers with specialized skills in areas like engineering – were pioneered by local authorities. And as we saw above, the interventionist central state of the twentieth century was prefigured in the 'gas and water socialism' of local government in the nineteenth century.

In recent years local government has rediscovered this capacity for innovation – indeed a role expressly recognized in the Local Government Act of 2000. Many large local authorities – Birmingham is a good example – have reorganized their modes of service delivery to encourage more effective local communication and responsiveness: for instance, by decentralizing their delivery operations so that offices in services like housing are much nearer to the point of delivery. Local government has also been at the forefront of attempts to combat a problem that we will discuss at greater length in Chapter 17: low electoral turnout. Nor is this pioneering role surprising. Turnout in local elections has been low, even by the standards of elections to the

BRIEFING 12.3

New roles in economic development for local government: the case of Cleethorpes

Cleethorpes is a small seaside resort on the Lincolnshire coast. Like many traditional resorts it has been hard hit by the rise of mass package tourism to sunnier parts of Europe. Yet tourism is integral to both the economic well being of the town and to the wider area: in the local government area of which Cleethorpes is a part, tourism is estimated to support more than 4,000 jobs. The efforts of the local council (North East Lincolnshire Council) illustrate both the new active roles in promoting economic development taken on by local government and the way local authorities have to work with an alphabet soup of local, national and even supranational organizations – the living embodiment of the networks of governance which we will explore more analytically later in the chapter.

The organizations include:

- the Yorkshire Tourist Board, of which the Council is a constituent member;
- Yorkshire Forward, the regional development agency, which has to fit any strategy to revive Cleethorpes into its wider responsibility for the regional development of local services;
- the Department for Culture, Media and Sport, because the efforts to promote Cleethorpes are part of the Council's wider strategy for cultural regeneration in North East Lincolnshire;
- the Commission of the EU, which is a source of funding (see below) for investing in improved tourism facilities;
- voluntary bodies, such as hoteliers' associations, whose members are targeted in attempts to improve the quality of local facilities.

The practical impact of this includes the following. The Council negotiated a grant of £140,000 from the EU to invest in improved tourism facilities and a grant of £290,000 from Yorkshire Forward, the regional development agency, to regenerate the Cleethorpes sea front. The 'on the ground' benefits include paying up to £6,000 towards the costs of new brochures for individual boarding houses, in return for investment in improved facilities, such as renovated bedrooms. The degree of EU intervention is striking: its grants even prescribe the size of double beds in guest rooms.

■ The role of local authorities in promoting local economic development is often far from glamorous, as this box shows. It involves trying to put together packages from a disparate range of organizations, in an institutional chain stretching from the immediate locality to Brussels. The Cleethorpes story, however, is only a sample; it is repeated, not only in numerous tourist resorts, but in virtually every local authority in Britain.

Sources: Wainwright (2003); North East Lincolnshire Council (2002).

devolved assemblies and the most recent figures for Westminster elections. A variety of procedural innovations have been experimented with, all designed to make the actual act of voting easier, in the hope that this will encourage electors to vote. Innovations like electronic voting through PC terminals and mobile text messaging have already been piloted in selected local authorities.

A potentially even more important innovation is the creation of elected mayors in selected local authorities, an option in the Local Government Act 2000. Only a minority of local authorities have even contemplated this

EUROPEANIZING 12.1

Europeanizing local government: reinvention at the EU level

Virtually every local authority in the UK of any size now tries to have an organized lobbying presence in Brussels. The biggest have their own separately organized offices: the Greater London Authority, for example, has established London House in Brussels. But most authorities are too tiny to run a full time operation and instead rely heavily on the European and International Unit of the Local Government Association. This is how the Unit describes its work:

> As 50 per cent of regulation affecting local government originates from EU legislation and other international agreements, the LGA's European and International Unit works with councillors and local authorities to get the best deal from the European Union and worldwide. This work involves lobbying on future legislation, highlighting problems and opportunities and promoting the skills and knowledge of local government.

■ It has long been commonplace to talk about a national world of local government, and that is a theme of this chapter. But the superficially parochial world of local government increasingly has a more international and especially a 'European World' centred on the EU.

Source: http://www.lga.gov.uk/.

innovation, and of these only a minority again have actually proceeded with the innovation. The measure requires approval in a local referendum, and two-thirds of the 30 authorities where it has been put to the vote have turned the idea down. What is more, in those authorities where it has been instituted, the impact of an elected mayor is restricted by the continuing presence of longer established forces. For instance mayors formally cannot set a budget without the support of a majority of elected authority members – which in practice often means the support of the dominant political party. However, even here, the fine detail of the procedures allows a shrewd mayor to create more freedom of manoeuvre than the letter of the rules would imply.

But the introduction of elected mayors – so far in a dozen authorities – does show how the innovation can change the balance of political forces and in turn produce policy innovations which are hard to push through in national government. The most spectacular illustration is provided in London. The first elected mayor, Ken Livingstone, ran on an independent ticket having failed to secure the nomination of the Labour Party, of which he was a long serving member. He was also a Labour Member of the Westminster Parliament. Livingstone was able to use the mayor's office, and the publicity opportunities which it creates, to build a political following in London independent of his former

party, in the process administering a number of embarrassing blows to Labour (not to mention the dismal performance of the official Labour candidate in the first mayoralty election). The new political constellation in London has led to a major policy innovation – the introduction of congestion charging as a way of managing traffic – which no other organized level of government in Britain has been able to introduce (see Briefing 12.5). So spectacular was Livingstone's political and policy success that in 2003 the Labour Party, facing the prospect of humiliation in the 2004 mayoral election, was obliged to readmit him on his own terms and adopt him as its official candidate for the mayoralty. He duly won again, running on a platform often highly critical of the Blair Government, in 2004. The Mayor's office is now recognized as a significant electoral prize, a point confirmed in 2008 when the Conservatives successfully ran one of their media stars, Boris Johnson, against Mr Livingstone.

The case of London is always special because of the scale and prominence of the capital, but established parties have been similarly undermined in the other authorities where there have been mayoral elections. Half the contests so far have been won by independents or by rebels from the established parties, such as Livingstone. A variety of eccentrics and political outsiders have defeated candidates from the official

BRIEFING 12.4

Local government as a laboratory of innovation: trialling electronic voting

As we shall see in Chapter 17, the apparent fall in turnout in national elections, notably in the 2001 general election, led to widespread official concern and an experiment with new forms of voting in an attempt to raise turnout. It was to local government that the responsible official body, the Electoral Commission, turned to conduct these experiments. In the local government elections of May 2003 the Electoral Commission launched the largest ever trial of electronic voting in Europe. Over 1.5 million voters in 18 council areas were covered. The methods trialled included:

- use of text messaging via mobile phones to vote;
- Internet voting via voter-owned PCs;
- Internet voting via specially constructed high street kiosks;
- voting via digital TVs.

■ In the nineteenth century local government was the test bed for the great political innovation of the time: widening the franchise to allow all adults to vote. In the twenty-first century it is at the centre of attempts to use the most advanced technology to combat the perceived decline in electoral turnout.

Source: www.electoralcommission.org.uk.

parties, including in one case the mascot of the local football team (a figure dressed in a monkey suit). But as the case of congestion charging shows, behind the gimmicks lies something serious: a change in the balance of political forces at local level which is weakening the old party machines and creating space for important policy innovations.

The impact of the innovation of elected local mayors is due to a variety of factors, some special to local government and some to do with the weakening relationship between voters and parties. The latter we will examine in Chapter 17. As far as local government is concerned, the innovation of the elected Mayor happened in local political systems where voter interest in traditional elections was very low. And while in Westminster elections there has been a long history of voters turning out governments, many local authorities have been dominated by a single party for decades – and even generations in a few instances. 'Mavericks' running for office therefore offer voters a way of rejecting the dominant party in their locality. That this reflects a more deep-seated rejection of the established political parties at local level seems to be suggested by the wider history of independent candidates in local government elec-

tions. Throughout the twentieth century independent candidates for council elections without a formal party affiliation declined in importance. Councils became increasingly dominated by one of the two major parties, with occasional incursions by the Liberal Democrats. But independents are once again on the rise, and they have been accompanied by the ascent of some minority parties, such as the Greens.

THE NATIONAL WORLD OF LOCAL GOVERNMENT

It is natural to identify local government with the local, but a striking and increasingly important feature is the extent to which local government has an important national presence. Look at Briefing 12.6 and you will begin to get some sense of this presence, and also an inkling both of why it exists and of why it is becoming more important.

Local government for long had national organizations – for instance, associations representing county and district councils. But the scale and coverage of national

BRIEFING 12.5

Elected mayors and policy innovation: congestion charging in London.

Managing traffic congestion is one of the most intractable problems facing government. In May 2003 the new Greater London Authority, under the leadership of Mayor Ken Livingstone, introduced a major and highly successful innovation: the introduction of a special charge on cars entering a central 'congestion' zone in the capital. Why was London able to innovate when central government – superficially much more powerful – could not nerve itself to introduce any comparable systems of charging? The answer lies in the new political system created by the reforms of London government involving a directly elected mayor and an elected Greater London authority.

■ The leading runners for the office of Mayor were political outsiders. The most spectacular outsider was the eventual electoral victor in 2000, Ken Livingstone. A maverick backbench Labour MP, Livingstone reacted to the blocking of his attempt to secure the Labour Party candidature by running as an independent.

■ The ability of a maverick candidate to succeed reflected the rise of a distinctive style of campaigning, where the organizational resources of traditional party machines could be counterbalanced by shrewd use of the mass media to generate publicity; and by the fact that at local level voters were increasingly likely to throw off their party allegiances in making their choice.

■ An innovative electoral system also had distinctive effects. In place of the first past the post system used in Westminster and most local government elections hitherto (described in Chapter 17), the Mayor was elected by the supplementary vote electoral system. This allows voters to rank two candidates in order of preference. Livingstone led on first preference votes (38.9 per cent) with Norris second – insufficient to command victory. The elimination of all other candidates and the redistribution of their voters to the top two according to expressed second-order preferences secured Livingstone his final majority of 57.9 per cent. This electoral system thus helps free voters from the crude choice between totally supporting, or totally abandoning, one party.

■ Innovation was not confined to the Mayoralty election. A London Assembly elected at the same time was chosen by the additional member system: voters had two votes, one for a 'constituency' representative and one for a party list. The party list vote was used – as in the case of the devolved assemblies in Wales and Scotland – to correct disproportionality: the Liberal Democrats and the Greens won no 'constituencies' but were each allocated four and three seats respectively to reflect their share of the list vote. Thus the electoral system again widened the range of representation beyond the two traditionally dominant parties.

■ The political system in London arising out of these arrangements has also been highly distinctive. Because politics is so focused on individual personalities, there are great incentives for leading politicians to promote policy innovations in the hope of being associated in the voters' minds with successes.

■ The robustness of the system was demonstrated in 2008. Livingstone was defeated in the Mayoral elections by the Conservative Boris Johnson, but the new Mayor has only 'tweaked' the congestion charge rules.

■ Congestion charges are not just a story about London. They show how new forms of organization at local level are creating opportunities for policy innovations too risky for Westminster government to contemplate.

BRIEFING 12.6

The national world of local government: some important associations

Association	Membership	Main functions
Local Government Association	Over 500 organizations, principally local authorities, but also including authorities responsible for fire, transport and regulation of National Parks.	Leading voice of local government in all public debates, including negotiations over resources and policy with central government, and major provider of information and lobbying services for local authorities.
Society of local authority Chief Executives and Managers (SOLACE)	Senior strategic managers working in the public sector.	Represents the views of senior managers in policy debates and provides training and consultancy services.
Public Sector People Management Association (PPMA)	Senior personnel professionals in local government and in fire, police and probation services.	Lobby to influence public policy; provides a forum for discussion of personnel function between members.
Society of Procurement Officers in Local Government (SOPO)	Over 2,900 members concerned with the procurement function in local government.	Lobby to make members voices heard in debates so as to promote better carrying out of the procurement function.
Local Government Employers (LGE)	Created by the Local Government Association as the voice of local authorities as employers.	Provide voice for local government employers and provide research and advice services to local authorities as employers.

■ The box is only a sample of the alphabet soup of nationally organized associations for local government. It nevertheless shows how dense is the national network for local government and how much institutional resource is invested in organizing local authorities as a nationally significant lobby.

organization has grown greatly. Briefing 12.6 encapsulates three forces that are impelling this creation of a nationally organized world.

The rise of local government as a nationally organized lobby

Earlier in the chapter we documented an important historical change in local authority finance: the rise of central government as by far the single most important source of money for local authorities. One obvious effect

of this development was to 'nationalize' issues of local authority finance. The financial health of an individual local authority no longer depended on how well it husbanded its own local resources, but on how well groups of local authorities did in a complex bargaining game with central government. Different groups of local authorities have different interests in this game, but all have a common interest in ensuring that in bargaining with central government the voices of local government are clearly heard. This increasingly pressing need helps to explain the comparatively recent creation (in 1997) of the single most important national organization, the Local Government Association (LGA), out of an amalgamation of three separate bodies: the associations of county councils, of district councils, and of metropolitan authorities. The LGA is not only the national voice of local government; it is also a significant provider of research and consultancy services to the organizations in its membership. This process of 'nationalizing' local government has not just been the result of initiative from local level; it has been encouraged by central government, which has an interest in bargaining with a single nationally organized representative association.

Professionalism in local government

One of the striking features of local government is the extent to which it is 'professionalized'. At the top of the official hierarchy in the Westminster system are 'generalist' civil servants offering no particular specialized professional skills. But the dominant tradition in local government has given the most prominent roles to chief officers with specialized professional qualifications: sanitary and highway engineers, chartered accountants, public health inspectors, social workers. The professional organizations of these groups of workers transcend the boundaries of individual authorities. They provide a natural way in which specialized policy issues are 'nationalized': the professions provide forums where issues can be discussed, standards worked out and the interests of the professional groups represented in both central and local government. A good example of this is provided in Briefing 12.6 by the case of the Public Sector People Management Association (formerly the Society of Personnel Officers in Local Government). This looks highly esoteric, but it goes to the heart of local government. The personnel function – the recruitment, training and management of people – is increasingly important in all organizations, and with its rising importance has gone that of the trained professional personnel officer. The example of the Society of Procurement Officers in Local Government (SOPO) is another apparently esoteric example of the same process at work. But far from being a backwater, the procurement function is vital in local government, because as a major deliverer of public services local government is also a large-scale purchaser of goods and services from the private sector. The 'procurement function' thus raises big issues about the most efficient way to buy and issues to do with professional and ethical standards among a group of professionals who have the authority to spend large sums of public money. SOPO provides both a lobbying voice for procurement professionals nationally and a series of forums where the issues facing procurement officers can be debated.

These specialized cases are samples from a wider world of national professional organization in local government, covering important occupations like social workers, housing officers, accountants and highway engineers. They form a dense, often overlapping series of networks linking the local, the regional and the national.

Local authorities as employers

Over two million people work in local government – far more than are employed by the Westminster civil service (about half a million) or by the devolved administrations in Scotland and Wales. The working conditions of these employees – their pay, hours and so on – are only marginally locally determined. Working conditions are mostly the result of national negotiations. On the side of workers, nationally organized unions representing local government employees are among the best organized group of British unions, and are a major part of the 'national world of local government'. This national union organization has been an important stimulus to the national organization of local authorities as employees – something reflected in the last example provided in Briefing 12.6. Another important stimulus has come from central government itself, on two grounds. As it is the chief financier of local government – which means the chief funder of pay, easily the biggest item in local authority spending – it naturally tries to intervene to shape the outcome of negotiations. In addition, pay and conditions obviously bear on the issue of the efficiency with which local government works – so as central government has become increasingly concerned with more efficient public sector organization, it has tried to shape pay negotiations to produce efficiencies. In some cases, settling pay has been so difficult that central government has tried to take it out of collective bargaining altogether, handing responsibility to independent review bodies to make recommendations – a solution, for instance, to the troublesome question of the pay of teachers. But this does not diminish the importance of national local authority organization, for the local authority employers are still major actors in the negotiations: in submissions to the pay review body and in arguments with central government about the precise method of funding pay awards. Even where local authorities are nominally independent negotiators, central government in Westminster often intervenes to transform the process into a national one. This was the case, for instance, with the long fire fighters' dispute that lasted from 2002–04, the first in the fire service for over a quarter of a century. Although a consortium of local authorities nominally negotiated for the employers, central government intervened both publicly and privately in the bargaining. It did this because it knew

POLITICAL ISSUES 12.1

Devolution for England?

The creation of devolved governments in Scotland, Wales and Northern Ireland has highlighted a key feature of governing arrangements in England: it remains the one part of the UK where the old Westminster style system of extreme formal centralization on London still persists. Some local elites have argued that 'devolution style' reform is now needed in England. The Labour Government, the author of the devolution reforms, tried to establish a limited system of devolution in England, but the only referendum it managed to hold, in the North East in 2004, showed little public support: on a turnout in a postal ballot of 48 per cent, only 22 per cent voted in favour and 78 per cent voted against. That effectively killed English devolution for the remainder of Labour's tenure in power at Westminster. But the issue remains alive, for three reasons. First, the Conservatives remain interested in it as part of their view that distinctive English governing arrangements need to be created in a world of devolved governments. Second, the existence of, in effect, a distinctive system of government for London makes its absence elsewhere in England anomalous. Finally, devolution of responsibility in a world of austerity government could 'off load' hard spending decisions from Westminster.

that the level of settlement would be part funded from central resources. Its intervention also reflected a determination to use the pay negotiations to introduce new, cost saving working practices into the service.

The national organization of local authorities as employers is a particularly striking instance of the 'national world of local government'. Although the issues involved are vital to the daily workings of each local authority, they are almost all debated and decided through national level institutions. And in negotiations about pay and conditions the nationally organized world of the local authority is matched by the continuous intervention of national central government itself and nationally organized trade unions. This is one particularly important area, in other words, where we just would not understand local government if we tried to make sense of it only at the level of the individual local authority.

The national world of local government is nothing new, but its rising importance reflects three themes that are central to this chapter. The first is what we earlier called the 'reinvention of local government': the extent to which local authorities realized that they had to carve out new roles by various forms of collective organization. The second is the extent to which local government in Britain has to be considered within the framework of multilevel governance, for it is in the nationally organized worlds – for example over pay negotiations – that some of the most complicated strategic games are played between the different levels. There is, for instance, now usually an annual row over the funding of a pay award for some groups of local authority workers. This row is

invariably part of the manoeuvring between local and central government over exactly how the award is to be funded.

Finally, the numerous overlapping national networks sketched here – lobbying organizations, professional institutions, employers' bodies – anticipates a theme we will encounter later: the extent to which the world of local government is, precisely, a world of networks of organizations which have to cooperate with each other. But before we turn to this theme, we will see that to the national world of local government we have to now add an increasingly important regional world.

THE REGIONAL WORLD OF LOCAL GOVERNMENT: THE FAILURE TO EMBED INSTITUTIONS

We instinctively identify local government with local authorities such as county and district councils. But there is another face of local government, the regional, and it is becoming increasingly important, especially in England. Local government has long had a regional face. The birth of the welfare state, for example, created a 'National' Health Service in which the building blocks of the national system were actually regional organizations. Likewise, both before and after water privatization the provision of this absolutely vital good has been organized partly along regional lines. This regional 'dimension' is an important contribution to what later in the chapter we will be describing as the pattern of *governance* at local

BRIEFING 12.7

Multilevel governance in action: the case of the humble wheelie bin

Virtually every British reader of this book makes a daily journey with the contents of the kitchen waste bin to the household refuse bin, typically a 'wheely bin'. That bin in turn is usually emptied fortnightly. We never think of the institutional system that disposes of our household waste, but the reality is that behind this mundane service lies a classic example of the complex, multilayered reality of multilevel governance:

- Responsibility for the weekly collection of household waste is the responsibility of the *district council.*
- Under the central government obligation to open household waste collection to competitive tendering, some district councils will have introduced a private actor – *a commercial firm* – into the process by awarding it the contract to collect waste. In this case the district authority's responsibility extends to awarding and monitoring the performance of the contracted firm.
- The waste has to be disposed of. Responsibility for the provision of waste disposal sites lies with the *county council.* Thus far, three sets of institutions – *district councils, private contractors and county councils* – are involved in emptying our wheelie bin.
- The county council in turn may contract responsibility for the management of waste sites to private firms: if you turn up at your local authority 'refuse amenity site' – the euphemism for the rubbish tip – you will almost certainly find it managed by a private firm.
- But the county council cannot simply decide arbitrarily to locate a waste disposal site where it chooses. *The Environment Agency* – central government's main agency for regulating the protection of the natural environment – licences waste disposal sites.
- In turn, the Agency cannot simply decide to locate a new site at its whim. Any proposal for a new site will enmesh all the parties in planning regulations, widening further the range of public and private actors. Location of rubbish tips provide some of the most contentious land-use planning cases.
- The Agency's system of licensing in turn involves implementing a wide range of regulations governing what waste can be tipped and what must be recycled. These regulations in turn are the result of entanglement with yet another layer of government: with the negotiations that produce *European Union* directives governing waste disposal and transportation.

■ Disposing of household waste is multilevel governance in action: we see an institutional trail stretching from the household kitchen to the European Commission headquarters in Brussels.

level: in short, it makes policy decision and delivery at local level heavily dependent on coordinating networks of organizations, including those organized at the regional level.

Since 1997 the issue of the regional organization of government has become more pressing still, as a consequence of the devolved institutions introduced by the Labour Government into Wales and Scotland – measures that we described in Chapter 10. The case for devolution rested in part on the importance of the distinctive identity of Wales and of Scotland, and partly on the argument that a decentralized system of government would be more effective and more democratically responsive than the hitherto dominant Westminster system. But these two arguments cannot be limited to the case for national devolution. If they are right, they also amount to a case for regional devolution in England. Some parts of England – such as the north-east – claim a distinct sense of regional identity. And without some form of regional devolution England, unlike Scotland and Wales, is left under the centralized Westminster system.

Yet the most striking feature of developments after 1997 was the failure to embed institutions of regional government. The Labour Government after 1997 tried to inch slowly in the direction of regionally devolved government in England. It had inherited a system of regional offices, in effect 'outposts' of the Whitehall Executive, charged with trying to manage issues at the regional level that cut across both the responsibilities of separate Whitehall departments and the limited territorial boundaries of elected local authorities. It ended up with three kinds of regional institutions, one of which has not survived:

● Government Regional Offices, originally established in 1994, charged with implementing the regional aspects of a wide range of central government policies, stretching from advisory (providing business support) to disbursing public grants.
● Regional Development Agencies, established in 1999, appointed and controlled from the centre, and charged with preparing an economic strategy for their regions.
● Regional Chambers (alternatively called Regional Assemblies), made up largely of local authority elected representatives, whose only formal function was to comment on the economic development strategy produced by the Regional Development Agencies. However, they could also be seen as a prototype for directly elected assemblies. The failure of the movement for directly elected regional government in England (see below) doomed them, however, and they were abolished in 2010.

What is most obvious about this regional structure is the extent to which the two arms that have any resources and 'clout' – the Government Regional Offices and the Regional Development Agencies – are basically part of the field administration of central Westminster government. In 2003 the Government tried to edge down the road of regional devolution when it announced referendums in three of the regions – the North East, the North West and Yorkshire and Humberside – on the issue of whether or not to create elected regional assemblies to, in effect, wield the powers now vested in the Regional Offices and the Regional Development Agencies. The delicacy with which it approached the issue of English regional devolution is shown by fact that it decided to

fund both opponents and supporters of devolution in the referendums. In the event, those in the North West and Humberside were cancelled and the ballot in the North East produced an emphatic rejection on a proposal for an elected assembly: 48 per cent of the electorate voted, and the proposal was defeated by 78 per cent to 22 per cent. The defeat in the North East, and the fiasco of the cancellation of the other proposed referenda, has killed for the foreseeable future the movement for any form of directly elected regional government in England.

This defeat is due to three factors. The first is that there are powerful entrenched interests whose very existence would be threatened by directly elected assemblies. The creation of a regional tier of elected government would almost certainly lead to an attempt to abolish one tier of local government in those parts of England where there presently exist two tiers (see below). In practice, the most endangered institutions are probably the county councils.

A second difficulty lies in identifying the governing principles for defining a region. At present the boundaries used to define the nine English regions covered by the Regional Offices and the Development Agencies are for the most part based on administrative conventions. While some regions – such as the North East – are believed to have a high sense of identity and distinctiveness, others plainly are not more than administrative inventions. The failure of the referendum in the North East was therefore a particularly severe setback. An alternative principle to that of relying on the administrative conventions of regional boundaries might be to base regional assemblies on 'city regions', on the grounds that both economic structures and a sense of identity are more easily aligned on the cities at the heart of the large urban conurbations in England, such as Manchester, Birmingham and Newcastle. Indeed there is one practical form of elected regional government of this kind already in existence, for that in reality is what the Greater London Authority amounts to (for details see Briefing 12.8). But the achievement of establishing the Authority also hints at the limits of the model for the rest of England. Whatever arguments there might be about the appropriate boundaries of Greater London, or about the division of local responsibilities within the capital, it is unarguable that London is distinctive. It has a highly distinctive economy, based in particular on the importance of finance, commerce and government itself as an employer. As a uniquely large conurbation (by English standards) it has unique resources and unique problems. How far this model might be 'transplanted' to other metropolitan areas is uncertain.

Finally, any new system of government, to be legitimate, has to arouse some public interest and support.

BRIEFING 12.8

The Greater London Authority as one model of regional government

FUNCTIONS

The Authority has key direct governing roles: it controls most aspects of public transport, most strategic planning and most provision of fire services. It has a promotional role: to attract investment to the capital and to develop London as an artistic centre.

STRUCTURES

There is an elected executive Mayor and a 25-member elected Greater London Assembly, the latter charged with the oversight of the former.

FINANCES

It receives 70 per cent of its income in grants from central government; the remainder comes as a mixture of direct charges for services and a slice of the council tax levied by its constituent boroughs.

■ The Greater London Authority is important in its own right as a key player in the government of the capital, a leading world city and one of the world's leading financial centres. But it may also be important as a possible template for further regional devolution in England.

All the evidence is that there is neither public interest in, nor enthusiasm for, regional government in the English regions: the one test, we have seen, in the referendum on the North East attracted the participation of less than half the electorate. And the fate of regional government after the formation of the Conservative–Liberal Democrat coalition in May 2010 seems to support this picture of public indifference: the coalition is intent on dismembering the regional development agencies, and the only serious dissent seems to come, ironically, from business interests normally aligned with the Conservatives.

Whatever the future of regional reform in local government, the regional face of local government brings home clearly how far the best known institutions of local government – elected local authorities – are embedded in extended networks of organizations.

LOCAL GOVERNMENT AND THE WEB OF GOVERNANCE

Local government is big business. When the state touches our lives in Britain it more often than not does it through local rather than central institutions. Local authorities in England and Wales alone employ over two million staff and account for about 25 per cent of all public spending. The range and scale of the services delivered has produced a complex and highly variegated institutional pattern. Two aspects of this complex pattern are particularly important: the pattern of organization and the pattern of governance.

The pattern of organization

There is no single pattern of local government organization, and there is no stable agreement on what a single pattern might be. The basic principles of organization are different in England and Scotland. In Scotland there is only one (unitary) level of local government, services being delivered across the country by 32 authorities. In England, by contrast, there exists no such single principle of organization. Most of the large metropolitan areas have single tier authorities. But outside these a system of two-tier authorities prevails, with divided responsibilities for district and county councils. What is more, even in areas covered by unitary authorities there are specialized bodies covering fire prevention and transport services that are in effect 'consortia' of individual local authorities. Just how complex is the resulting divisions of responsibilities we saw schematically at the very beginning of this chapter in Table 12.1.

The consequences of operating this complex system are not difficult to see. There is no 'natural' way to divide responsibilities between different local government systems, so the appropriate division of labour is a constant source of debate. Because there is no intellectually compelling way of demonstrating that one structure is better than another the choice tends to be made as a result of lobbying and struggles of interests between different groups in the local arena. This explains why the most distinctive feature of local government organization in recent decades has been its instability. The present pattern is in part the result of organizational changes introduced by the Labour Government after 1997, the most important of which was the wholesale reorganization of the local government of the capital. If the proposals to create elected regional assemblies with substantial governing powers were ever realized, it is likely that something akin to the Scottish/Welsh system of unitary authorities would have to be created. Experts on local government agree on very little, but they do agree that the simple addition of yet another layer of regional government to the existing two-tier system would be a step too far.

There is agreement on this because plainly one of the great costs imposed in a multitier system is the cost of efficiently coordinating these levels. Indeed, coordination is one of the great problems in local government. Even where there exists a unitary system there are still big problems of coordination between those authorities and the other levels of multilevel government – in the devolved institutions in Cardiff and Edinburgh, in central Westminster government, and increasingly of course in the institutions of the EU. The simple story of the 'wheely bin' told in Briefing 12.7 illustrates the reality of these issues of coordination. But this problem of coordinating the formal institutions of government is itself only part of a wider feature of local government, and perhaps its most important feature: that it is part of a broader system of governance.

The pattern of governance

In the opening chapter of this book we encountered the idea of 'government' and saw that it was closely connected with the exercise of hierarchical relations of power and authority. This notion is encapsulated in Weber's famous definition of the state (see Briefing 1.1) : 'a human community that (successfully) claims the monopoly of the legitimate use of physical force within a given territory'. But if we think about the workings of local government in Britain, this emphasis on force does

not really ring true – or at least seems only part of the picture. It is hard to imagine the delivery of the wide range of services in local government, and the coordination of the institutions of delivery, working effectively solely through hierarchy and the threat of physical sanctions. This realization explains why it is increasingly common to think of government at the local level as a series of interconnected networks that require management and coordination, rather than as a hierarchy that needs to be subject to command and control.

'Governance' is the name we commonly give to this process of network coordination. If government is, in the last resort, about using the state's monopoly of coercion, 'governance' is about recognizing the limits to what can be done with the 'monopoly of the legitimate use of physical force'. It is about seeing the everyday reality of making policy and delivering services as fundamentally a cooperative activity between institutions that somehow must live together to have a chance of achieving their objectives. Weber's picture of the state invites us to think of it as a kind of military hierarchy; 'governance' invites us to think of it as a partner in a kind of polygamous marriage, albeit an often very unhappy marriage.

A summary idea of the huge population of institutions that interact at local level is given in Table 12.2. The table conveys the often minutely complicated patterns of the divisions of responsibility at the formal level of local government organization. The most important lesson of this table derives from a simple, but profoundly important, fact: local governments operate in a definable territory, but they do not monopolize service provision in that territory. They have to work alongside institutions like universities, the health service and the machinery of justice – all delivering services in the same territory covered by local government units. The table was originally created to show the existence of a 'local state' dominated by non-elected institutions, but it serves to stress the reality of governance as a process of network coordination. It also highlights another important feature of governance at local level: not all of these networks of organizations are in the 'public sector' as conventionally defined. Some lie in a kind of indefinable 'borderland' between the private and the public: for instance, the more than 250 registered housing associations identified in Scotland alone. Some are private companies, or individual private entrepreneurs, who provide some public service under a system of 'franchises' or licences: consider in the table, for instance, the more than 2,000 registered social landlords in England.

Viewing the local as an arena of governance has a number of important implications for how we make sense of local politics and of the wider system of governance in the UK. It immediately alerts us to one of the

TABLE 12.2 Local government and the web of governance: numbers and variety of institutions operating at local level

Higher education institutions	166
Further education institutions	511
Foundation schools	877
City technology colleges	15
Training and enterprise councils (England)	72
Local enterprise councils (Scotland)	22
Career service companies (Scotland)	17
Registered social landlords (England)	2,074
Registered social landlords (Wales)	92
Registered housing associations (Scotland)	255
Registered housing associations (Northern Ireland)	40
Housing action trusts	4
Police authorities (England and Wales)	41
Joint police boards/unitary police authorities (Scotland)	8
Health authorities (England and Wales)	99
NHS trusts (England and Wales)	373
Primary care groups (England and Wales)	434
Primary care trusts (England and Wales)	40
Health boards (Scotland)	15
Special health boards (Scotland)	8
Acute NHS trusts (Scotland)	14
Primary care trusts (Scotland)	13
Integrated acute and primary care trust (Scotland)	1
Health and social services trusts (Northern Ireland)	19
Health and social services councils (Northern Ireland)	4
Health and personal social services boards (Northern Ireland)	4
Advisory committees on Justices of the Peace (UK)	119
Dartmoor Steering Group (Ministry of Defence)	1
Total	5,338

■ This table, taken from an invaluable examination of the 'local quango state' by the Select Committee on Public Administration, was intended by the Committee to illustrate the extent to which local bodies consisted of non-elected, and largely non-accountable, figures. But it also reinforces one of the main themes of this chapter: that the territorial world of local government is part of an astonishingly dense network of institutions. As we see, over 5,000 are identified in this (almost certainly incomplete) census alone.

Source: Select Committee on Public Administration (2001, Table 6).

key features of both the local and the national: the multilevel character of governing arrangements. It is at the local level that we can see this most clearly. This is not only because the local is the 'bottom' of the multilevel ladder, thus having to coordinate with institutions 'higher up' the ladder. It is because so much of the local is dominated by service delivery. It covers most of the services that as citizens we could expect to call on frequently throughout our lives: from education – the single biggest service delivered at local level – to the weekly household waste collection. In our own daily lives we constantly find that performing some service depends critically on coordinating what we do with others. Even units as small as families or student households only run efficiently if members cooperate with each other in mundane tasks like doing the washing up and emptying the waste bin.

DEBATING POLITICS 12.1

Local government: moribund or renewed?

LOCAL GOVERNMENT IS MORIBUND

- Turnout in local government elections is lower than for any other public elections and is among the lowest in Europe.
- Local authorities are run by parties that have few members and little popular support.
- Local government has lost most of its financial independence, relying on the centre for grants.
- There has been a century-long loss of functions by local authorities to central government and the private sector.

LOCAL GOVERNMENT IS BEING RENEWED

- The decline of the old parties is allowing new groups and parties to enter local government.
- Local government is a renewed source of experimentation and innovation, as illustrated by the London congestion charge.
- The decline of the central Westminster system is creating new spaces for local action.
- New functions in local economic renewal are being acquired in local government.

Magnify the task to the kind involved in delivering care for the old, education for the young or waste disposal for us all and we see immediately the immense importance of coordinating different networks of organizations. The only effective way to make policy work at the local level is to manage the governance arena: to manage, in other words, a local system where the formal institutions of local government are necessarily embedded in a dense network of both state and non-state organizations.

THE DECLINE AND RISE OF LOCAL GOVERNMENT

For most of the twentieth century local government was in decline. It relied increasingly on central government for money. Local councils were colonized by the two leading nationally organized parties, so that the turn of electoral fortunes at the local level was largely a reflection of national political trends. Over the course of the century local authorities lost many of the responsibilities which they had played a pioneering part in establishing in the latter part of the nineteenth century, such as the delivery of utilities like gas and the provision of services like health care.

Much of this decline is irreversible. For instance, there is no prospect of local government ever again becoming important in the delivery of basic utilities, and there are no signs that local government has the capacity to diminish significantly its reliance on grants from central government as a main source of revenue. But

three long-term changes are reducing the long historical subordination to Westminster government.

Devolution

Devolution has reshaped the relationship between local and central government in Wales and Scotland, and it has the potential to do it in England if elected regional government ever becomes a reality. The experience of London shows the possibilities, where the elected Mayor has become a major source of opposition to Whitehall government over issues like the funding of the London Underground system, and a source of one important policy innovation, the introduction of traffic congestion charging. The attempt under New Labour after 1997 to begin creating devolved regional government in England failed, as we saw above. But that has not solved the basic problem: after devolution English regions are now uniquely subordinated to a Westminster government, and this is unlikely to be tenable in the long run.

The decline of national parties

Party in local government is no longer just a reflection of national struggles. As the two main parties have lost their hold over the loyalties of electors, the effect has been felt most clearly at the local level. The growing diversity of the party system, with the rise of many different third parties, is more accurately reflected in the composition of local councils than in the composition of the Westminster Parliament. There now exists party representation spanning the Greens at one end to the quasi-fascist British National Party at the other. And the weakening of national party controls has, especially in mayoral elections, helped elect mavericks to office: they range from serious dissenters against the two-party system, like Ken Livingstone in London, to mavericks like the monkey-suit-wearing football mascot elected as Mayor of Hartlepool.

The shift to governance

Paradoxically, perhaps the most important reason for the revival of local government lies in the growing realization that local authorities cannot behave like little monarchies in their own territories – that they are part of the extended networks of organizations described earlier in this chapter. Local authorities have been obliged to recognize that the need to work cooperatively in these networks sets limits to authority and autonomy; but by the same token the shift to governance puts the local authority – the deliverer of major public services like education and transport – at the centre of governance networks.

Review OF CHAPTER 12

Four themes have dominated this chapter:

◖ The fall, and then the reinvention, of local government.

◖ The importance of national and regional organization of local government institutions.

◖ The growing connections between the private and the public at local level.

◖ The way local government has evolved into *governance*.

FURTHER READING

ESSENTIAL

If you read only one book it should be Bulpitt (1983). Do not be misled by the date: this is still the single most important study of the local and the central written about British politics.

RECOMMENDED

Wilson and Game (2006) are standard texts on the whole system. Stoker (2004) helpfully integrates the latest 'governance' language into the study of the subject. Two books by Rhodes (1988, 1999) are pioneering studies of the modern approaches. Pimlott and Rao (2002) are authoritative on the very important 'exceptional' case of the government of the capital city.

How citizens participate

CONTENTS

AIMS

This chapter:

- Explains the central importance of popular participation to democratic politics

- Sketches the main forms of participation in Britain

- Examines the factors that influence who participates and who does not

- Describes how patterns of participation are changing in Britain and shows how our conventional notions of what participation amounts to are being challenged

PARTICIPATION AND BRITISH DEMOCRACY

Every theory of democracy involves some notion of popular participation. The roots of the word 'democracy' itself derive from the Greek term for the people, anglicized as 'demos'. But the original history of the concept of Greek democracy shows how complicated can be the connection between participation and democracy. The theory of Greek democracy was based on the notion of direct democracy: of rule through the participation of all citizens in an open assembly taking decisions. But 'citizens' here did not mean all adults. It was actually confined to a minority of male adults: among the excluded were slaves (a large part of the population) and women (an even larger part).

Even the limited original Greek notion of direct participation has been of little importance in Britain. The dominant theories of British democracy have given a marginal role to direct participation by the mass of the people. Mass participation has mostly been confined to participation in elections for the Westminster Parliament, where all those entitled to vote can have a say in choosing governors. Obviously we could hardly expect a country of over 60 million people to organize Greek style forums where all the adult population gathered in a particular place to meet and debate. But democratic participation in Britain has been limited by more than these practical considerations.

We can see some of the limits to democratic participation in Britain if we look abroad. Some parts of the rural US, for example, have a long established system of town meetings, where communities try to recreate some of the conditions of the democratic 'forum' for all citizens. British democracy has also been more reluctant than many other democracies to use the opportunities offered by mass voting. Until recently voting in Britain mostly meant choosing on two occasions: in general elections to select representatives to the Westminster Parliament and voting to select representatives – councillors – in local government. By contrast, in the US a much wider range of selection for public office was decided by election. In addition, it has been common in the US for many important policy questions – for example concerning the setting of local and state taxes – to be the subject of popular vote (referendums). In many countries where the head of state is, unlike Britain, a president rather than a hereditary monarch, voters at large make the choice: the examples range from the US and France, where the President is a real executive head of government, to Ireland, where the President performs the symbolic roles fulfilled in Britain by the Monarch.

The formal organization of participation in Britain, therefore, has given comparatively restricted scope for mass participation. But as the chapter unfolds we will see that two important changes are coming over political participation in Britain:

- the formal opportunities to participate have been significantly widened in recent years;
- the forms and meaning of participation have changed greatly.

This second point provides a natural introduction to the next section, where we begin by looking in detail at what might be called political participation 'old style': the kind of participation that was in its heyday when the Westminster system of government was dominant and Parliament was held to be the main means of channelling the popular will.

THE RANGE OF PARTICIPATION: OLD STYLE

The evidence from the most comprehensive study of political participation in Britain now dates from the 1980s. It is therefore to some degree historically dated, but precisely for that reason it is an invaluable guide to the forms and levels of participation that were developed under the old Westminster system when it was still in fairly robust health.

As we might have expected from the theory of democracy and participation in Britain, political participation was dominated by taking part in elections, especially the infrequent general elections that cover all the UK. Other forms of participation, even very sporadic ones like signing a petition that demand little effort, were in this picture confined to a quite small minority. Democratic participation in this world was a minority sport or hobby, rather akin to train spotting, playing snooker or listening to opera. Even the numbers in Figure 13.1 almost certainly overstate the extent of participation in Britain, since they tell us about reported participation – what people in a survey told social scientists about their activity. Since participation in politics, unlike playing snooker, is in general viewed as a virtuous thing, it is almost certainly the case that reported levels exaggerate true levels. We can see this, indeed, when we cross-check against measures of actual participation. Figure 13.2 shows levels of participation in different elections across Britain; we can see that actual participation in elections is lower than people claimed to pollsters, for instance in the study by Parry and his colleagues summarized in Figure 13.1.

Not everyone participates, and not everyone participates equally. The evidence in Figure 13.1 conveys a truth, which the passage of time has not altered, namely:

FIGURE 13.1 ■ **The pattern of participation in Britain: old style (percentage of population who claimed to have engaged in different forms of participation at least once)**

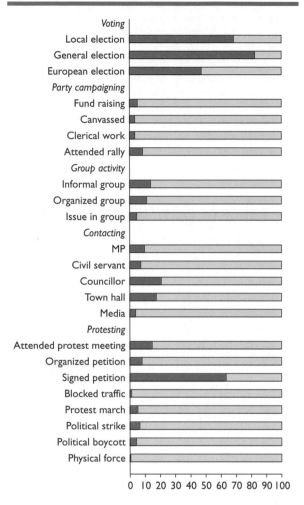

Source: Parry et al. (1992:44).

■ The figure is labelled 'participation old style' because, as we shall see later in the chapter, there is mounting evidence that some of the acts of participation performed most frequently here – such as voting – are in decline, and some new kinds of participation may not have been detected by our older notions of what constituted participation in politics. Although the publication from which the figure is drawn dates from the early 1990s, the fieldwork on which the data are based is older, dating from the 1980s. The work of Parry and his colleagues is the most thorough study of participation ever conducted in the UK, and it stands as our definitive picture of participation 'old style' – from the age when most people were still content to participate in conventional ways allotted to them by the Westminster elite, such as voting.

there exists only a tiny minority of totally committed activists for whom politics is an all-consuming activity. To some extent this is a matter of random taste: there are obsessive political activists just as there are obsessive train spotters or people with an all-consuming interest in rock climbing or rock music. This is the minority that runs political parties at local level, for instance, or that devotes all its waking hours to organizing for a particular cause, be it animal welfare or opposition to new road building. The people in this category are on the fringes of a group we will consider in Chapter 18, the full-time politicians. But just as we would find that train spotters and rock climbers are not a random sample of the population – train spotters are mostly male, rock climbers tend to be young and fit – so participation is not randomly distributed. The most important factors affecting the propensity to participate are not at all mysterious, and will be briefly summarized in what follows.

Education and class

There is a powerful link between formal education and likelihood of participating. All other things being equal, the rate of participation rises the longer an individual has spent in education. There are many possible reasons, but one of the most obvious is that formal education provides the resources and skills that make participation most effective and satisfying. In Britain participation is for the most part a cerebral activity. There are forms of participation that are far from cerebral – for instance, attacking the agents of the state or burning cars and buildings – and as we will see these can be very important in Britain. But for most people, most of the time, participation is a matter of talking, writing and organizing – skills that some people have naturally, but that are undoubtedly fostered by education.

Education is also closely associated with likelihood of participation because it in turn is associated with other important life features that help participation. The better-educated people are more likely to have white collar and professional jobs, high levels of income and high levels of consumer affluence. They have the leisure and other resources that make it easier to take part in politics. Consider, for example, how something as obvious as owning a car makes participation easier. There is thus a powerful bias in the participation system: at every level, participation rises with occupational class.

Education and class are two of the keys to variations in levels of participation in Britain, but there is still one overwhelmingly important point that we should keep in mind: high political participation is a minority activity. Although there is indeed this powerful connection

FIGURE 13.2 ■ Highs and lows in general election turnout since 1950

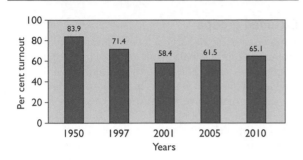

Per cent turnout

Years	1950	1997	2001	2005	2010
	83.9	71.4	58.4	61.5	65.1

Source: Calculated from standard sources.

■ The bars show the highest (1950) and the lowest (2001) turnout figures in post-war general election results before the perceived collapse in election participation in the new millennium; and indeed the figures do suggest – the last three bars are for the last three general elections – that there has indeed been a significant drop.

between education and class, nevertheless, even within the groups most likely to participate, political participation beyond the most episodic kind, like voting in a general election, is still confined to a minority. To take an example: more university professors than university porters participate intensively in politics. Professors have all the advantages: high formal education, leisure and money. But among professors themselves, still only a minority participate in politics. If we thought of politics as a hobby that consumed a fair amount of time (as distinct from the very rare act of actually voting) we would find that even among university professors it occupied a lower place than sport, opera or gardening.

Does this mean that actually participating in politics is in the end an arbitrary matter of taste, like a taste for going to the opera or to rock concerts? The answer is no, and part of the clue lies in observing the contrasts between different kinds of participation. The most obvious feature of the commonest kind of participation – voting, especially in general elections – is that the means to do it are periodically provided, and in ways that make this kind of participation easy to perform. To vote, all you have to do is take the trouble to stroll down to a polling station on election day – and as we will see recent reforms are designed to make voting easier still. But suppose you want to do something more sustained, like promote animal rights or advocate the release of political prisoners. Effectively to do this, you will need either to find a group or to found a group.

Group networks

Group participation is particularly important. Working alone – just voting or writing to your Member of Parliament – is not going to make much of a difference to what governments do. We saw in Chapter 8 that some people have the energy and skill to bring groups into life when they feel strongly about an issue. But most of us do not have the qualities to be this kind of successful political entrepreneur. We depend heavily on the prior availability of groups. Their vitality – how efficiently they are run, whether they are rising or declining – is therefore critical for whether people can realistically participate, and for whether their participation can make a difference. Imagine, for example, that you are a Muslim with strong views about how education should be organized in Britain – favouring, as many Muslims do, public financial support for Islamic schools on the same terms as are presently offered to those run by Christian denominations. If you live in Bradford or North Manchester you have a ready made network of groups – centred on the mosque and on the local community – in which to participate to help advance those views. But imagine living on Orkney, where you will be part of a tiny minority; there is no such network. You either have to participate ineffectively (say by writing to your parliamentary representative) or you have actually to build a group.

The pre-existence of strong social networks is therefore a vital influence on the opportunity to participate, and to participate in an effective way. When we turn to examine changing forms and levels of participation we will see that changes in these networks have a big influence on the way participation is itself changing in Britain.

Being lucky enough to have ready access to groups and networks therefore deeply influences what might be called the quality of political participation that citizens in Britain can enjoy. But there are also more blunt influences at work. Some factors have worked simply to exclude some groups from participation in political life. In addition, some methods of participation are symbolically excluded: in other words, are not considered compatible with participation in the normal procedure of democratic politics in Britain. These two sources of exclusion are examined next.

PARTICIPATION AND POLITICAL EXCLUSION

The rules of democratic politics in Britain provide a wide range of familiar ways of participating in politics, all of which we have seen at some stage above: they range from the one opportunity every four or five years to vote

TABLE 13.1 Politics as a hobby, compared with other hobbies

Activity	Population claiming to participate (%)
Voting in general election	82.5
Gardening	48.0
Dressmaking, needlework, knitting	22.0
Swimming	14.8
Organizing a group	11.5
Contacting MP	9.7
Darts	5.6
Taking part in a protest march	5.2
Canvassing for a party	3.5

■ The table compares what Parry and his colleagues found about frequency of political participation with frequency of participation in a range of leisure 'hobby' activities. Parry et al.'s data is from the late 1980s, that for leisure for the mid- and late 1990s. I chose one activity from each of the main Parry categories, extracted from Figure 13.1. In fact the 'test' for leisure activities is harder than for politics: Parry and his colleagues only asked if respondents had ever done any of these; the surveys of leisure require participation in the four weeks before the survey. Although voting is well ahead of leisure activities, the table puts 'old style' politics (for instance contacting an MP) in the lives of citizens into perspective: a bit more popular than darts, but less popular than dressmaking or gardening.

Sources: Parry et al. (1992:44); *Social Trends* and *Annual Abstract of Statistics*, various dates.

in a general election to the intense, all consuming commitment to political life of a tiny proportion of the population who are political activists. This model of democracy presumes that everyone who really wants to take part in politics can do so if they have a sufficiently strong inclination. It also presumes that the means of participation are sufficiently effective so that any group that has a serious interest or grievance can effectively make its voice heard.

We have already had to modify this picture by recognizing that the costs of persistent participation are higher for some groups than for others, depending in part on whether they have ready access to pre-existing social networks. But there are also significant groups in the community who are, or recently were, consciously excluded from political life. That exclusion can either take the form of open rules barring participation, or can

take the form of social pressures and a hostile climate of public opinion that all but makes participation impossible.

Excluded groups

There is a long history of overt, formal exclusion of groups and individuals from political participation in Britain. This was particularly important in the era before the development of modern institutions of democratic citizenship, like universal suffrage. The rules of exclusion included: property and gender qualifications that regulated qualification to vote; and laws forbidding the entry of many religious groups, like Jews and Catholics, into civic life. Nor was it only the avowedly religious who were excluded: only after a long struggle in the nineteenth century was it possible for atheists to sit in the House of Commons without disavowing their atheism. Achieving universal adult suffrage in 1928 – when women and men finally achieved formal equality of entitlement – was a sign that the theory of British democracy was now based on an inclusive notion of the right to take part in the political life of the community. The development of anti-discrimination legislation since the mid-1970s helped tackle some of the residual exclusions practised by institutions in politics and in the wider society. Nevertheless, in modern Britain exclusion from many forms of participation is still practised. Six grounds of exclusion are particularly important.

Age. The rules of participation openly discriminate against the young. That is because of the principle, sometimes voiced and sometimes implicit, that full participation in political life requires the maturity and experience of adulthood. Where the boundary to adulthood is set is in part conventional, depending on the assumptions of particular epochs. Until 1969, the boundary was set at 21 – the qualifying age to appear on the electoral register. The infrequency of general elections meant that this most common single act of participation could often only be first exercised by the time one was in one's mid-20s. Now the qualifying age of registration to vote, and standing for elective office, is 18. Of course as we know voting in general elections, though the commonest form of participation, is not the only one, and almost all others are in principle open to those under 18. Nevertheless, exclusion from the full rights of citizenship makes the alternative forms of participation less valuable. Many of the organized opportunities for participation for the young are viewed as pre-political: as a kind of practice for adult participation, in the form of schools councils, debating societies, the development of a citizenship curriculum in schools. Just how far the age barrier depends on conventional notions of what constitutes 'adulthood' is shown by the increasingly common

POLITICAL ISSUES 13.1

Exclusion from political participation: the case of prisoners and the vote

In 1870 all those held in prison lost the right to vote. Until recently this total prohibition held. This is internationally unusual: 17 states in western Europe allow prisoners to vote. Under the impact of rulings from the European Court of Human Rights in Strasbourg, and the incorporation into domestic law of the European Convention on Human Rights, this has now begun to change. The UK has lifted the ban on remand prisoners voting and made it easier for the unsentenced held in prison to register. But this still leaves at least 50,000 prisoners without a vote. Since 2004 the Prison Reform Trust – from whom these details are taken – has tried to challenge this following the passage of the Human Rights Act. At the time of writing the coalition government has said that it will, reluctantly, remove prohibitions.

Three issues are raised by this case:

■ What should count as an entitlement to vote: mental capacity or moral worth?

■ Is the right to vote an inalienable human right, as challenges under the Human Rights Act would suggest?

■ What are the proper boundaries of the 'people' in a democracy? If prisoners can vote, why should not those presently disqualified by age or nationality?

Source: www.prisonreformtrust.org.uk.

---

debate about the possibility of reducing the qualifying age for voting to 16.

Religion. Historically, religion was openly used to create legal barriers to participation. And as we saw in Chapter 11 the exclusion of Catholics was a central organizing principle of the state in Northern Ireland until the late 1960s. On the mainland of Britain the law now forbids the open creation of barriers on grounds of religion. (A residue of this history, however, is the prohibition against Catholics serving as Head of State, as Monarch.) Because open discrimination is illegal, there is an obvious motive to hide it, and that in turn makes estimating the extent of residual exclusion difficult. The growing indifference to organized religious practice in Britain is, in truth, probably the greatest influence in destroying these residual barriers. Such barriers to participation as are raised against religious groups probably now exist more as a by-product of wider ethnic discrimination than on grounds of religious belief. Jews, for example, are almost certainly not welcome in some local political parties, but actually attending a synagogue probably does not make the barrier to participation higher.

Ethnicity. There exist powerful barriers of exclusion against immigrants. For first-generation immigrants these barriers may exist because they lack the resources

that, as we saw earlier, are important in participation. English may not be their first language. While the economic history of migrants is highly diverse, in the first generation at least there is a necessary focus on work and economic security above participation in the wider society. Nationals of other states residing in Britain also have limited participation opportunities. But the most extreme forms of exclusion come in the case of asylum seekers and illegal immigrants. There is an increasing flow of people across borders, especially as the poorest, and those fleeing war and persecution, try to reach the comparative security and prosperity of countries like Britain. For obvious reasons (because they want to escape detection) there is an unknown, but substantial, population of illegal immigrants in Britain, whose status means that they can neither exercise formal rights to participate, like voting, nor realistically participate by other means.

Poverty. One powerful additional barrier to participation which immigrants and asylum seekers share with many of the 'native' population is poverty. As we saw earlier, participation generally is linked to the possession of economic resources. At the most extreme levels of poverty it is more than a deterrent; it is an absolute barrier. This kind of poverty is increasingly identified

Timeline 13.1

Violent political participation: as British as Barnsley bitter

715 Attacks on dissenting (non-conformist) chapels in Midlands and the north west leads to passage of first Riot Act.

739–40 Food riots in East Anglia.

763–65 Violent machine breaking by weavers in London.

780 Gordon Riots in London, with over 300 people killed in anti-Catholic demonstrations.

795 King's coach attacked in huge demonstration against war with France.

797 Naval mutinies at Spithead and the Nore.

811–12 Widespread machine breaking by gangs protesting against new technology across the midlands and north of England.

819 Reform demonstration in Manchester; 11 killed in 'Peterloo massacre'.

830–33 'Captain Swing' riots across south of England: hundreds of demonstrations, riots, machine breaking.

842 Riots and Chartist general strike in north of England.

852 Riots between Catholics and Protestants near Manchester; Catholic churches sacked.

866 Demonstrations for electoral reform lead to widespread damage to property.

886 Unemployed riot in West End of London following demonstration in Trafalgar Square.

909 Sectarian (Catholic/Protestant) riots in Liverpool.

911 Strikers shot in clashes with troops in Liverpool and in South Wales.

914 Threats of armed revolt against Irish Home Rule by Ulster Unionists, with the complicity of leading Conservatives in Britain, only averted by outbreak of First World War.

916–21 Uprising in Dublin in Easter 1916 leads to civil war ended only by the establishment of a separate Irish free state.

919 Police and strikers clash in Glasgow general strike; police strike in Liverpool is followed by riots in the city.

932 'Hunger march' on London by unemployed, followed by clashes with police; serious riot in Dartmoor prison.

936 Police and anti-fascist demonstrators clash in 'Battle of Cable Street' in London's East End.

937 113 arrested and 28 injured in illegal fascist march through East End of London.

Timeline 13.1 (continued)

1947	Anti-semitic demonstrations in Liverpool and Manchester.
1958	Race riots in London and in the Midlands.
1969	Widespread violence in Northern Ireland leads to 25-year civil war in which over 3,000 people die.
1968–71	'Angry Brigade' bombs public buildings, banks and home of Cabinet Minister before being apprehended in 1972.
1976	Disturbances at Notting Hill Carnival; Hull prison wrecked in riot.
1979	Race riots in Bristol.
1981	Race riots in London, Liverpool and Manchester leads to large scale (Scarman) public inquiry.
1984–85	Prolonged confrontations between police and mass pickets of miners in prolonged miners' strike; two people killed and over 12,000 miners arrested in course of strike.
1986	Prolonged confrontations between police and striking print workers in London; wave of riots across British prison system following prison officers' strike.
1990	Anti-Poll Tax demonstrations across Britain culminate in rioting following demonstration by 300,000 in Trafalgar Square; Strangeways Jail in Manchester wrecked in riot.
1991	Arson and looting as youths battle police in wave of summer riots in English and Welsh cities.
1994	Riots in London against Criminal Justice and Public Order Act.
1995	Race riots in Bradford and London; clashes between police and animal rights activists over exports of live animals.
1995	Anti-capitalist demonstrations in City of London cause £1 billion of damage.
2001	Race riots in Bradford.
2002	Race riots across towns of North of England.
2009	Protestors in London clash with police after storming headquarters of Royal Bank of Scotland in advance of G20 summit meeting.

■ The rules of liberal democracy stress peaceful political participation, and official versions of the British constitution stress the importance of peaceful political participation. But we have arrived at our present condition by a route that involved large scale violence both by the state and against the state. Violence and political participation are woven together in the British political tradition.

Source: Adapted, with additions, from Cook and Stevenson (1983, 2000).

with the notion of 'social exclusion'. What that idea means is that the significance of being poor extends beyond obvious material deprivation. Poverty also excludes many of the poor from meaningful participation in the life of the community. The exclusion can be extreme – as in the case of homelessness – or more subtle, as when poverty just make the daily round of life incredibly difficult: for instance, the rural poor without access to their own transport are often trapped in isolation because of poor public transport provision. It is easy to see with these examples that social exclusion and political exclusion often go together. The homeless provide the most obvious case. Until recently the homeless could not even register to vote, and the lack of a permanent abode is plainly a powerful barrier to political participation.

Deviance. British liberal democracy presumes an entitlement to participate in political life on the part of all adult citizens. The 'liberal' in the 'liberal democracy', as we saw in Chapter 1, refers in part to the toleration of a wide range of views and practices. But no liberal democracy has been able to tolerate everything, and a key issue in any such democracy is the possible range of toleration. What range of views and practices will be viewed as intolerable, and what intolerable views will result in exclusion from the participatory entitlements of citizenship? In Britain the boundaries of exclusion are drawn around both various groups and various methods of participation.

In Britain, convicted criminals who are serving jail sentences have highly curtailed citizenship entitlements: see Political Issues 13.1 for more details. Some social practices are so vilified that any attempt to participate in politics in their defence is in practice impossible. Thus, while in principle a group could form to campaign for the repeal of existing laws against paedophilia, any attempt to do so openly would soon produce intense popular hostility and, probably, police intervention. The range of people whose views and practices are labelled so deviant as to ensure their exclusion from participation in political life changes over time, as society and its cultural understandings change. For example, until the late 1960s gay people were viewed more or less as paedophiles are now. Any attempt to mobilize gays into political activity would have provoked both popular hostility and – since all male homosexual relations were criminal until 1967 – intervention by the police.

Gender. We know that historically gender was an important ground of open, legal exclusion from some important forms of participation: we only have to recall the history of the suffrage to see that. Now, the most important legacy of that history, as we will see in Chapter 18, is to be found in patterns of leadership recruitment rather than in patterns of participation. But the story is not just one of waning barriers to exclusion. Newly important immigrant groups, which themselves suffer exclusion, also have their own internal barriers which exclude women in some immigrant groups from the opportunity to take part in politics.

Participation: the excluded methods

Exclusion thus raises barriers against the participation by different social groups in British political life. But exclusion also works by establishing barriers against certain methods of political participation. Three kinds of participation have proved especially problematic, even though they have deep historical roots and are still common.

Violence. Violent protest is an important tradition in Britain. Some of the most important moments in the historical development of British politics were accompanied by, and partly caused by, violence. They include: the civil war in the seventeenth century, which led to the execution of a king and the destruction of the claims of the monarchy to exercise special, divine authority; violent public demonstrations that accompanied the campaign to change the suffrage in the nineteenth century; and an armed uprising across what was then the Irish part of the UK after 1916 which resulted, in 1922, in the foundation of a separate Irish state. Violence continues to be a tactic used by some radical groups, normally targeted against particular institutions and personalities: radical animal rights groups have, for example, targeted both firms and researchers who are believed to be involved in experiments on animals. A more pervasive form of violence, one that shades into general criminality, is a well-established pattern of racial attacks. But it is disputes about the territorial boundaries of the state that have provoked the longest violent campaigns in modern British politics. As we saw in Chapter 11, the political life of Northern Ireland since the late 1960s has been marked by persistent violent political participation. This has run the full gamut: it has included mob attacks and intimidation, for instance to force evacuation of housing; the use of the traditional tactics of terror, such as large scale bomb blasts in urban areas designed to cause both random loss of life and extensive economic damage; targeted violence against the agents of the state by both republican and Loyalist paramilitary groups; and targeted violence by the agents of the state themselves against, in particular, known republicans and parts of the wider Catholic community.

Violent forms of political participation are, therefore, an engrained part of the British political tradition. But violence is problematic since it plainly runs counter to

BRIEFING 13.1

A successful case of mass civil disobedience: the poll tax

The Community Charge (commonly known as the Poll Tax) was introduced in 1988. It replaced a system of 'rates', local authority taxes which were levied on historic rateable values attributed to owner-occupied houses. The Poll Tax, by contrast, was a fixed charge in each local authority area which was applied to all. Two features provoked widespread resistance: the spread to all of what had been a selective tax confined to houseowners; and the shift from a variable levy linked, at least notionally, to house values to a flat rate charge. Resistance was intensified by one tactical decision by the government: it introduced the charge a year earlier in Scotland (1989/90) than in England (1990/91). Scotland had already produced anti-Conservative majorities in elections. Thus the Charge was 'trialled' in uniquely hostile territory. At first opposition took the form of conventional methods, such as public demonstrations. This soon spread to passive civil disobedience: large numbers declined to pay the tax; larger numbers still simply ceased to register on the electoral register, the main source used by the authorities to track down occupants of houses. The Prime Minister, Margaret Thatcher, had identified closely with the original legislation, and pictured resistance as a challenge to established, legitimate authority. Encouraged by the Prime Minister's support, enforcement of the Charge increasingly relied on the full force of the law, notably through court orders, property seizures and prison sentences. Passive resistance soon grew to large scale organized public demonstrations and then to violent confrontations with the police, notably during a protest in London on 31 March 1990, when 300,000 took part. The resistance campaign divided the Labour Party, between those who wanted to stay within the conventional bounds of constitutional resistance favoured by the Westminster elite, and those who favoured passive, and even violent, resistance. But the consequences for the Conservative Party were greater, indeed catastrophic. As it became clear that the Poll Tax was unenforceable over large parts of the country, leading figures in the Party began to fear that the issue would cost the Party victory in the next general election. This contributed to the fall of Mrs Thatcher from office in November 1990. Her successor, John Major, appointed the man most responsible for Mrs Thatcher's fall, Michael Heseltine, as Secretary of State for Environment, with a brief to replace the Poll Tax. Its successor, the Council Tax, was rapidly introduced. The new Council Tax closely resembled the old system of rates that the Poll Tax had been designed to sweep away.

■ The history of the Poll Tax echoes features summarized in Timeline 13.1. It is in a long tradition of non-constitutional resistance to laws passed by government. The problem of how to draw the line between 'constitutional' resistance, passive civil disobedience and violent resistance has run through the history of these campaigns and deeply divided the Labour Movement in the history of the Poll Tax. The official national leadership took the position that law, once passed, had to be obeyed, until a new Labour Government could repeal it; some Labour local authorities in effect refused to enforce the Tax, joining the civil disobedience camp; and some activists allied with anti-Poll Tax campaigners from the militant left outside the Labour Party to obstruct actively the implementation of the Act, for instance by blocking court officers attempting to serve enforcement orders on Poll Tax defaulters. The Poll Tax is thus an object lesson from several points of view: for government, in illuminating the limits of enforcement when a measure is viewed as objectionable; for those who resisted, in illuminating the problem of deciding when resistance had gone beyond the pale of constitutional action; and for the Labour Party in continuing a long tradition of not knowing how to draw the line between 'constitutional' and 'unconstitutional' protest.

the expectation that politics will be pursued in a 'constitutional' way: in other words, by employing argument and the ballot box to advance policies and interests. So while violence is common, it also attracts both wide-spread disapproval and a hostile response from the agencies of the state charged with maintaining public order.

Civil disobedience. Civil disobedience consists in a refusal to obey the legal commands of the state. It is typically a tactic adopted when those commands are believed to lack moral authority. Like violence, civil disobedience has a long history in Britain. By far the most important and successful campaign of civil disobedience in recent decades was the campaign that destroyed the 'Poll Tax' (see Briefing 13.1). But civil disobedience can stretch well beyond the 'can't pay, won't pay' tactic of refusing to pay a tax. The workings of a modern economy are highly complex, easily disrupted and demand, for their effective functioning, the cooperation of large numbers of people. A wide range of tactics has been used in recent years by a variety of groups to exploit this vulnerability: blockades of the transport network; physical blockades (for example of proposed new roads) designed to prevent or delay the completion of work.

Industrial action. Industrial action is not illegal, and in most instances is not a form of political protest at all; it is just part of a normal process of bargaining between groups (workers and employers) in the modern economy. But precisely because of the nature of a modern economy, where effective working demands cooperation by many different groups, it can have a devastating effect, and therefore can be an effective weapon by disaffected groups. In the last quarter of the twentieth century many attempts were made by unions of manual workers to use the strike as a weapon of political protest. National industrial action by coal miners in 1972, 1974 and 1984–85, though in part about employment conditions, were also protests against the Government of the day.

Political violence, civil disobedience and industrial action are well-established modes of political participation. But they occupy a difficult position in democratic politics in Britain, which for so long has given a pre-eminent position to voting and assigned a kind of supreme moral as well as legal authority to the decisions taken by governments produced by voting. Challenges to government by violence, strikes or civil disobedience therefore call into question understandings central to the workings of established democratic politics. But as we will now see, changes in both institutions and in wider social values are themselves altering the relationship between political participation and democracy in Britain.

POLITICAL PARTICIPATION: NEW STYLE

We can begin our survey of change with the most commonly noticed 'headline' change in participation in recent decades. In the general election for 2001 turnout was sharply down on the average levels recorded in general elections over the years since the end of the Second World War, and this fall seemed only to confirm hints of decline which could be gleaned from general elections in the 1990s. The official response was to treat this fall as a sign of a serious problem in democratic participation in Britain and to introduce reforms designed to counter the fall. Thus we have seen experiments involving placing polling booths in more accessible places, like pubs and supermarkets, and rules easing the conditions for voting by post. Whether as a result of these innovations, or for other reasons (see Briefing 13.2), turnout increased in 2005 and May 2010; but even the May 2010 figure of just over 65 per cent was well below the highs of earlier decades.

Whether there is a serious problem of democratic participation is, however, not certain. *Patterns* and *opportunities* of participation have undoubtedly changed, but all these changes have by no means been in the single direction of weakening democratic participation, as we can now see if we survey some of the most important forms of participation.

Voting

The case of voting shows how complex is the true picture. Beyond the individual case of the spectacular fall in turnout in the general election of 2001 there is a consistent pattern of low turnout (by traditional general election standards) in the 'new' elections that were created in the closing years of the twentieth century: for instance direct elections to the EP (beginning in 1979) and elections for the Welsh and Northern Ireland Assemblies and the Scottish Parliament (from 1999). But there is nothing novel in this disparity between general election turnout and turnout elsewhere. As we saw in the last chapter there is also a long established pattern in local government of turnout that is much lower than for general elections. The 1990s were remarkable, indeed, for the way they increased opportunities to vote in a political system that had, as we noted at the start of this chapter, been very restrictive by the standards of other democracies like the US. For instance, by the end of the 1990s voters in Scotland, once restricted to voting only in local government and general elections, now were able to select the European, Westminster and Scottish Parliaments, and had been able to vote for or against the principle of devolution. The last example, of a referendum, is a striking instance of the widening range of participation.

The first major referendum in modern British politics was held in 1975, on whether the terms of membership of the EEC that had been renegotiated by the Labour Government returned in 1974 should be accepted (they were). At the time there was extensive

BRIEFING 13.2

Participation in the May 2010 general election: has the tide of decline been reversed?

Turnout in the May 2010 general election, at 65.1 per cent, was the highest since the Labour landslide year of 1997. It marked the second successive general election when turnout increased. In addition, there was anecdotal evidence of a surge of participation in the campaign itself. 'Cleggmania' – the burst of enthusiasm generated by Nick Clegg's performance in the first of the leadership debates (see Briefing 16.2) – led to turnout at some of Mr Clegg's public events that recalled an earlier era of large public attendances at speeches and rallies. In some constituencies last minute surges of voting on election day led to the polling system collapsing, with hundreds of voters turned away; at the time of writing the Electoral Commission is conducting an inquiry into what happened. But some caution is needed before we make too much of these occurrences. Beyond a few episodes of 'Cleggmania', the modern pattern of public appearances by party leaders designed to produce TV images was even more pronounced – not surprising, because none of the parties has the members any longer to turn out at election rallies. The campaign fitted the modern pattern of voters consuming events and news transmitted by the media. The 'Twitterati' – users of Twitter – remain a tiny segment of the electorate. Above all, the turnout was a recovery from the dismal levels of 2001 and 2005.

debate about the very principle of submitting a major issue to the test of a referendum, some arguing that it contradicted the responsibilities of Cabinet Government. But in the 1990s there were, as we saw in Chapters 10 and 11, referendums on devolved government proposals in Scotland and Wales, and on even bigger issues to do with government in Northern Ireland. In 2004 there were referendums in selected English regions on the principle of regional government. There has also been a spread of referendums designed to settle single issues. For instance, voters in both Edinburgh (in 2005) and Manchester (in 2008) had the opportunity to vote on a proposal to introduce a congestion charge similar to that introduced in London. In both cases they rejected the proposal. In 2004 the Blair Government reversed a long established position and promised a referendum on the terms of a new constitution for the EU, if agreed, and a referendum preceding any British adoption of the euro is also promised by all major parties. Referendums on the status of devolution are strong possibilities in both Wales and Scotland. And the constitutional changes of the Conservative–Liberal Democrat coalition in office from May 2010 involve a referendum on electoral reform. Thus only a few decades after that original referendum on our membership of the EEC referenda are an established, if sporadically employed, method of popular decision. (The Government, however, wriggled out of the commitment

to hold a referendum on the adoption of an EU constitution by insisting that the Treaty of Lisbon (2009) was not actually a constitution, when it was plain that it was so in all but name. The episode shows that the Westminster governing elite still controls the terms on which a referendum can be held.)

In the case of general elections, because we have over 90 years of experience under conditions approximating universal adult suffrage, we can discern long term trends in participation; it is precisely because the 2001 result was such a drop on the trend that it both stood out and rang alarm bells among those who think voting is important. But precisely because so many of the voting opportunities now on offer are novel it is hard to decide whether they are 'high' or 'low'. Most are low by the historic standards of general elections, though when an issue is of historical importance, as in the case of the referendum on the Belfast Agreement, the turnout can actually better general election levels.

Participation in parties

The evidence of participation provided by political parties is similarly mixed. One important measure of party participation is indeed unambiguous: the total membership of parties has fallen sharply over the last half century. (In Chapter 14 we examine the institutional significance of this fall; here we are only concerned with what it means for the bigger participa-

TABLE 13.2 Participation: the European dimension – turnout in EP elections (the UK and the average for the EU)

Date	UK turnout (% rounded)	EU average turnout (% rounded)
1979	32	63
1984	32	61
1989	36	59
1994	36	57
1999	24	50
2004	38	45
2009	34	43

■ The crisis of official participation is not confined to Britain: in every election to the EP since direct elections were first introduced in 1989 turnout has fallen. UK turnout is actually quite stable: but at a level well below the EU average. Be cautious in interpreting the European figures. The Union has changed greatly in size over time. Like all averages the figures conceal huge variations: for instance, in 2009, between Belgium, where voting is compulsory (90 per cent), and Slovakia (19 per cent).

Source: Calculated from http://www.europarl.europa.eu/elections2009.

tion picture.) Although historic measures are not totally reliable, it seems well documented that in the early 1950s the leading parties had truly mass memberships: individual membership of Conservative Party Associations in constituencies probably exceeded 2.8 million; the corresponding total for the Labour Party was probably just over 1 million. (In addition, Labour had a huge 'affiliated' membership exceeding 5 million at national level that mostly derived from the trade unions, but this just represented the size of financial subscriptions to the Party, a mechanism that is described in Chapter 14.) Both the main Party's youth wings also had large memberships, with perhaps as many as 250,000 Young Conservatives. These figures are all expressed as orders of magnitude because neither Party had exact membership records.

The figures for the early 1950s, however, probably also represented a historic high point of party membership. In other words, had we accurate figures for earlier decades for the parties as a whole we would almost certainly record lower membership levels. What is undisputed is that even by the mid-1970s this mass membership was melting away: an official inquiry into party finance put Conservative membership at about

1.5 million – in other words, a loss of more than a million in just over 20 years (Houghton 1976). By the 1990s the figures had fallen further. A membership campaign after the election of Tony Blair as Leader in 1994 produced a brief rise in individual Labour Party membership, but it has since fallen away to about 170,000. There is an even more serious crisis in the Conservative Party. Individual membership is probably at about the same level as in the Labour Party, but the age of the members is high: participation in politics through Conservative Party membership does seem to be literally dying out. There has been some compensation for the whole party system in the form of increased participation through other parties: for instance the Scottish National Party and Plaid Cymru were tiny institutions 50 years ago.

Accurate measurement of membership levels is difficult because parties are not very efficient institutions and there are almost certainly large errors in the figures they report. But the reported decline is of such an order of magnitude that we can be certain that it corresponds to real changes. Overall, there are probably about three million fewer party members in Britain than there were 50 years ago, with the two leading parties, Labour and Conservative, suffering the worst damage.

As we will see in Chapter 14, on parties and their organization, this is a serious matter for the parties. But it is less certain that it is a serious matter for the health of political participation, still less for the health of British democracy. Much depends on what participating in a party meant in the past. It is almost certainly the case that in the early 1950s membership of the Conservative Party, for instance, had more a social than a political meaning: the Party, especially through its well organized network of Conservative clubs, was a part of middle-class social life. This helps to explain the decline in membership. One undoubted reason for the fall is, for instance, the shift in occupational patterns among women. In the 1950s it was common for professional women to interrupt, or even abandon, their careers to rear children. The grassroots of the Party relied heavily on these women, who by the 1990s were typically too busy juggling careers and family to devote time to local Conservative social activities. So at least part of the change in participation through parties is a reflection of wider patterns of social life.

Membership of parties for social reasons was very important to the parties – as we will see in the next chapter these 'social members' of the Conservative Party, for example, were crucial to money raising activities. But social participation was not the same as political participation, and over time, especially in the 1990s, all the major parties have increased the opportunities for participation offered to their members. One

BRIEFING 13.3

New participation opportunities: the case of referendums

Year	Electorate	Issue	Turnout (%)
1973	Northern Ireland	Constitutional status of NI	58.1
1975	United Kingdom	UK's continued membership of the (then) EEC	63.2
1979	Scotland	Devolution for Scotland	63.8
1979	Wales	Devolution for Wales	58.3
1997	Scotland	Devolution and tax powers for Scotland	60.4
1997	Wales	Devolution for Wales	50.1
1998	Greater London	Assembly and Mayor for London	34
1998	Northern Ireland	The Belfast (Good Friday) Agreement	81
2001–	Referendums in over 30 separate local authorities	Establish elected mayors in individual local authorities	Range from 64 (Berwick-upon-Tweed) to 9.8 (Ealing)
2004	Referendum in North East on regional assembly	To decide for or against elected regional assemblies; referendums in two other regions cancelled	48 in a postal ballot (see Political Issues 12.1)
2005 and 2008	Edinburgh (2005); Manchester (2008)	To decide for or against congestion charge	Edinburgh: 61 Manchester: 53
2011	United Kingdom	To change Westminster electoral system	Not known at time of writing

■ It can seem that referenda in Britain are a bit like the proverbial London bus: you wait for ages for one, and then a bunch turn up at the same time. The table shows a small bunch in the 1970s, and then a large one after the return of Labour to office in 1997. Note the generally high level of turnout compared, for instance, with local council elections. The permanent place of the referendum in Britain is also shown by the fact that regulation of referendums is now one of the statutory tasks of the Electoral Commission established in 2000.

Source: Magee and Outhwaite (2001), with additions by author.

important example will suffice. In the 1950s both the Labour and Conservative Parties insisted on reserving the right to select the party leader to their respective parliamentary parties in Westminster – in short to an electorate composed of a few hundred, mostly elderly men. Indeed in the case of the Conservatives there was not even an open 'parliamentary' election until 1965; before that, leaders 'emerged' by a mysterious process of soundings among the parliamentary elite. Now membership of the two major parties (and most of the minor ones) gives to individual members the right to cast a vote in selecting the Leader. This illustration shows that that while the 'quantity' of participation in parties has fallen, the quality, in the sense of opportunity actually to take a meaningful part in important internal decisions, has actually become richer. Thus while there has been a substantial long term withdrawal from membership of the major political parties, the effect of this on participation is not as disastrous as the bald figures might suggest. This is in part because the fact of party membership cannot simply be equated with political participation. A much higher proportion of party members now than in the past are party members because they want to have a say in policy and party leadership, and the increasing need felt by parliamentary parties to share choices with rank and file members is a sign of this. We saw in the case of the electorate at large that opportunities to participate through elections have widened in recent years; and we can say the same thing of the internal political life of major political parties.

Group participation

In the 1990s the American political scientist Robert Putnam prompted a great debate about democracy in the US by arguing that there had occurred in the country a long term decline in the stock of what he called 'social capital'. (His most extended statement is in Putnam 2000.) One measure of social capital for Putnam was participation in associational life, and part of his argument was that figures showed a long-term decline in membership of all kinds of associations, most not directly connected with politics in any way. Hence the riveting title of his main work, *Bowling Alone*, which referred to the decline of organized club competition in (tenpin) bowling in the USA.

If a parallel decline has happened in the UK the implications for democratic participation are gloomy. Participation in nominally 'non-political' institutions, like churches, can be very beneficial for democratic participation. This is partly because even these kind of institutions intervene in political debates, giving their members a chance to have a say; and partly because participating even in non-political association can help foster the skills, and access to social networks, which allow citizens to participate more formally in politics. One institution that undoubtedly did have these beneficial effects – the political party – has lost its power to attract a mass membership. A key question for democratic participation in Britain, therefore, is whether any groups have developed to compensate for this loss.

It is easy to show that some other important institutions have to a degree shared the fate of political parties. Two obvious examples are some Christian denominations and some trade unions. It is also easy to show that other groups have in recent decades advanced in membership. Not all religious groups have declined: among the fastest growing are the evangelical churches that are popular with Afro-Caribbean immigrants and their children, and Islam and Hinduism which are strong among different groups of immigrants and their descendants from the Indian subcontinent. A Rowntree Foundation study of social capital and faith groups found that they were a powerful source of social capital (Furbey et al. 2006). In Chapter 8 we saw

striking evidence that another field of group life – those groups like the National Trust and the RSPB that cater for the growing interest in the environment – has seen huge membership growth in recent decades (see Table 8.1).

It is all too easy to swap examples of groups that have declined or advanced in membership. But deciding whether Putnam's gloomy view also applies to the UK requires a more systematic comparison over time. This makes the evidence summarized in Table 13.3 valuable. It suggests that long term, associational membership is healthy in Britain; and it also shows how important may have been immigrant groups to the renewal of associational life.

Of course counting the numbers either of organizations or their members only tells us a limited amount. Paying a subscription to the National Trust is no more significant a form of political participation than was baking the cakes for the Conservative coffee morning in the 1950s – though both activities can be important because they help fill the coffers of the organization. It is when we reflect on, and investigate, the social meaning of group membership that the connection with changes in participation becomes clearer. Here the picture is mixed. The biggest losers have probably been white manual workers and their families. The decline of trade unions has disproportionately come in traditional industries that employed manual workers; the buoyant unions are those that organize white collar and professional workers. Likewise the big decline in church membership and attendance has hit denominations that were important in the lives of manual workers: for instance, in the nonconformist denominations like Methodism. These two instances – unions and nonconformist denominations – show the subtle connection that exists between group organization and political participation (see Briefing 13.4 for more detail). Both often provided practical examples of democratic control at the lowest local level. Both offered the chance to acquire some basic skills – such as speaking in public and running meetings – that 'transfer' easily into the more formal political arena. Both provided important social networks that anyone wishing to engage in overt political activity could use. The decline of the unions and nonconformist churches has therefore made political participation by groups in the population who already suffer disadvantage more difficult. By contrast, the health of religious institutions among new communities of immigrants is important in providing a voice for those who for other reasons find conventional political participation difficult: because in the first generation they may lack fluency in English and because, as the poorest, they have least leisure to engage in politics.

TABLE 13.3 Has social capital in Britain been depleted? Associational life in a big British city: two snapshots in time of numbers of voluntary associations in Birmingham

Type of association	Number in 1970	Number in 1998
Sports	2,144	1,192
Social welfare	666	1,319
Cultural	388	507
Trade associations	176	71
Professional	165	112
Social	142	398
Churches	138	848
Forces	122	114
Youth	76	268
Technical and scientific	76	41
Educational	66	475
Trade unions	55	52
Health	50	309
Not classified	–	75
Total	4,264	5,781

■ Debates about participation in the UK have often taken a historical turn: they concern arguments about what has happened over time. The influence of the theories of social capital associated with the American political scientist Robert Putnam sharpened the arguments. Putnam showed that there had been a long-term decline in associational life in the United States (Putnam 2000). An obvious question was: had the same thing happened in the UK? The great value of the study by Maloney and his colleagues is that it allows us to compare two snapshots of the same scene – associational life in the second city, Birmingham – at two separated moments in time. What is striking is not only the continued vitality of associational life, but the way some features run counter to our conventional expectations. For instance, the UK is supposed to be a society where religion is declining in influence; yet one of the most rapidly growing categories is churches. Notice also that, contrary to some theories that society is dumbing down, there has been a huge growth in the number of associations devoted to education. One factor helping to account for these unexpected developments is the influence of mass immigration into Birmingham and other big British cities: in Britain, immigrants are usually more religious than the natives and are keener on education.

Source: Maloney et al. (2000:805).

The rise in membership of environmental groups hints at another beneficial consequence of group change for political participation. These groups too, even when they are not overtly formed to press for changes in public policy, can provide networks for those wishing to become active to change policy. For instance local Ramblers Associations – who hardly exist primarily for purposes of political participation – have been important means of allowing individuals to group together to lobby for the opening of public footpaths and more general 'rights to roam' over large parts of the countryside.

This last example illuminates an important feature of the changing relationship between group organization and political participation. All our examples so far have been of formally organized groups; but many of the groups in question shade off into more informal social movements and help to create the networks that allow these movements to operate. These movements are perhaps the single most important influence on the changing nature of political participation.

Social movements and direct action

'Social movement' is a broad and imprecise category; but this lack of precision is understandable, because we are dealing with a broad and imprecise category of social organization. We have already encountered the idea of these movements when we examined group representation, in the form, for example, of the many groups concerned with the defence of the physical environment. The new movements have considerably widened the range of public participation beyond conventional lobbying of government. They create conditions for flexible, rapid and often unpredictable mobilization of large numbers of people, often around particular issues that have appeared suddenly on the political agenda. Three examples show the possibilities:

● In the autumn of 2000 the Government was taken completely by surprise by mass blockades of fuel depots, mostly by farmers protesting against the level of fuel tax (see Briefing 8.5).
● The Countryside Alliance, a loose alliance of a very wide range of rural interests in 2005, mobilized up to 250,000 people for a protest march in London (see Image 13.1).
● An even larger series of mass demonstrations – possibly exceeding one million people in London alone – took place early in 2003 against the imminent war on Iraq (see Image 4.3). This was probably the largest single public demonstration of political protest in modern British history.

BRIEFING 13.4

The decay of two working-class networks of participation: Methodism and the miners

Methodism's founder, John Wesley, was born in 1703. Methodism began as a part of the established Church of England, attempting to reach the faithful by a more direct and colloquial style than was practised by official religion. But by the start of the nineteenth century it was a fully independent denomination, and by the start of the twentieth century it had reached its peak, with nearly a million members of Methodist congregations in the UK. A century later membership was only just over 300,000 and falling – principally because that membership is itself old. Methodism was a key institution encouraging working-class participation in politics, especially in the early decades of the history of the Labour Party. The faith was particularly strong among the manual working class created by industrialism. In an age when formal education for workers was limited, the Bible and the great hymns of Methodism were an important contribution to the literacy and general culture of workers. Methodist congregations are largely self-governing, so the life of chapels provided a training ground in politics and organizing skills. And the direct inspiration of the Bible, especially the New Testament, was an important source of the commitment to social justice in the new Labour Party. With the decay of Methodism, all this – the organizing base and the Christian inspiration – has greatly weakened. Paradoxically, the decay of British Methodism has coincided with its rise globally: there are 33 million Methodists across the globe, and prominent Methodists include George Bush (US President 2000–08) and Nelson Mandela.

The National Union of Mineworkers (NUM) was formed in 1945 by an amalgamation of the different regional parts of the Miners' Federation of Great Britain. It then had 533,000 members. Miners were the pioneers of working-class political activism. Miners' unions were the first to send their own officials into the Westminster Parliament; the acknowledged founder of the Labour Party, Keir Hardie, was a union officer in Ayrshire; and until the 1980s the Union was a powerful voice in the Labour Movement and an important means by which this group of manual workers exercised direct control in the Party, for instance by continuing to send into Parliament members who had actually worked in pits. As recently as the mid-1980s over 190,000 people worked in mining – almost all belonging to unions. By the new millennium it had only 5,000 members. The catastrophic decline is due to two linked factors: a disastrous, defeated strike in the mid-1980s, and the almost total disappearance of deep coal mining as an industry in Britain. The NUM not only provided a direct channel into politics; just as Methodism imparted political and organizing skills, running the Union at pit level was often the way future mining politicians acquired the skills needed for effective participation. All this has now disappeared.

■ The decay of Methodism and mining unionism has been catastrophic for working-class participation in politics. In some instances the impact has been redoubled because the two were historically linked: some of the greatest centres of working-class Methodism were in the coalfields, such as the now vanished coalfield communities of South Wales.

These are only the most spectacular and widely reported instances of countless demonstrations that take the form of direct action. In other words they bypass conventional lobbying of policy makers and public representatives in favour of the direct expression of, usually, hostility to some government policy. They stretch from demonstrations about the largest historical issues – such as war – to the most local, such as opposition to particular road building schemes. They also stretch across the full range of forms of participation. Most involve the peaceful, passive, mass expression of opinion, for example by marching and banner carrying. But some also involve active forms of civil disobedience: for instance, passive obstruction of large building projects like roads and airport runways by occupying the land to be built on. And on occasions, as in a series of protests against high finance and globally organized corporations, they have stretched to sabotage and other attacks on property.

A word of caution: labelling these forms of participation 'new' is potentially misleading. Though undoubtedly 'new' in the setting of modern British politics, they actually resurrect an old tradition of political participation in Britain that disappeared for much of the twentieth century. Many of the great constitutional and humanitarian reforms of the nineteenth century, such as the abolition of slavery and the extension of the franchise, were accompanied by spectacular public demonstrations, sometimes accompanied by violence and the destruction of property. The revival of direct action of this kind thus shows that while there may be a decline in some forms of participation, other forms are rising. In particular, participation that is channelled through the institutions that are most closely tied to Westminster politics – such as voting and membership of the traditionally dominant parties that fight each other in Westminster – is being displaced by this direct action. The participation that we earlier labelled 'old style' is therefore not all that old: it is mostly a characteristic of the decades in the twentieth century when the Westminster system of government was utterly dominant in the UK. And the participation that we have labelled 'new style' actually often has a long ancestry.

Many reasons help to account for the rise of direct action. One of the most obvious is, simply, the declining hold of the established political parties: 50 years ago most people who wanted to take their political views beyond the act of voting joined a political party and took it from there – and taking it from there hardly ever meant direct political action. All the parties were agreed that the point of political action was to change policy by changing government, and this meant succeeding in Westminster parliamentary elections. The fact that the politically active no longer automatically absorb themselves in party activity has opened up opportunities to bypass the party route in favour of trying to change policy by more direct means.

Numerous social changes have accelerated these developments. Many readers of this book will have direct experience of one: the creation of a mass system of higher education. In the 1960s about 5 per cent of the 18–21 age group attended university; now over 40 per cent of the same age group are in higher education. Most

IMAGE 13.1 ■ Political participation: 'new style' in action

■ The photo shows a pro-hunting demonstration against the Bill which eventually outlawed hunting with dogs in 2005. The picture shows demonstrator Daisey Crutchley, a name that might have come from a bucolic soap opera like *The Archers*. The anti-hunting demonstrators were a striking instance of the capacity of 'new style' political participation to mobilize onto the streets young demonstrators who in an earlier generation would have been indifferent to politics, or who would have been baking cakes for Conservative coffee mornings.

large British cities have areas dominated by student populations: in Manchester, for instance, there are well over 50,000 full-time students in higher education at any one time. These areas, and the universities themselves, provide ready-made networks for mobilizing people into direct participation.

But while it is possible to see the influence of this student group in mass participation in movements focused on peace, the environment and animal rights, this cannot be the whole story. For instance, while it was reported that some fox-hunting public-school boys had supported mass demonstrations by the Countryside Alliance, it is unlikely that there were many university students on their marches. To political changes, like the decline of political parties, and social changes, like the rise of mass higher education, we should add the importance of changes in technology. One historical advantage the state had over protest groups was its own well-organized communication systems. Armies and police forces usually, for instance, have their own radio communication systems. For most of the twentieth century the state in Britain was also the monopoly owner of the network for landline telephone communication. Newer technologies have tilted the balance of advantage towards citi-

DOCUMENTING POLITICS 13.1

New styles of participation: an anti-globalization movement in action

'About Us

Jubilee Research is building on the work of the hugely successful Jubilee 2000 debt cancellation campaign, and in particular its reputation for providing up-to-date, accurate research, analyses, news and data on international debt and finance ... We are not just an economic think-tank. We are a think-and-do tank. We encourage our readers to undertake advocacy and campaign action. *Jubilee Research* continues to work closely with the campaigning groups around the world which have taken over the mantle of the Jubilee 2000 campaign ... Jubilee 2000 grew from small beginnings to become an international campaign that brought great pressure to bear on G7 leaders to "cancel the unpayable debts of the poorest countries by the year 2000, under a fair and transparent process". By the end of the campaign, 24 million signatures had been gathered for the Jubilee 2000 petition, the first-ever global petition. There were Jubilee 2000 campaigns in more than 60 countries around the world.'

■ These passages are edited extracts of the main Web page of the campaigning group Jubilee Research. In Britain the group started in the run up to the millennium as Jubilee 2000, a mass campaign to persuade governments, including Britain's, to cancel the debts of poor countries. After the millennium, as the text makes clear, the campaign was converted into a wider campaign aimed at mobilizing anti-globalization groups from many sources: the radical political left, Christians and other churches. Two particularly important features should be noticed: the way the movement uses the technology of the Web to link networks of groups, partly by the simple device of providing links to other web addresses; and the way this British group is embedded in a global network of groups – once again, partly courtesy of the Web.

Source: www.jubileeresearch.org.

zens wishing to organize at short-term notice. The spread of mobile phone ownership, and of internet access, have both made important contributions, making the swift, cheap organization of new networks much easier. The rapid fall in the cost of powerful desktop computing in recent decades has also reduced the costs of organizing for participation. A PC costing less than £500 can store and process data that at the start of the 1980s could only be stored on a huge, expensive mainframe computer. In this way it is possible, for example, to store, exchange, retrieve and use the database of contacts of large numbers of supporters and potential supporters of an organization, for purposes like mailshots, circulars and newsletters. Likewise cheap, easy-to-use desktop publishing packages have transformed small group publishing, making it much easier than in the past to produce attractively laid out minority newspapers, newsletters, magazines and pamphlets. Finally, the spread of global networks linked by internet communication means that states find it hard to control and censor international communication.

FROM GROUP TO INDIVIDUAL PARTICIPATION: SUMMING UP CHANGING PATTERNS OF PARTICIPATION

Some of the social networks that were once important in encouraging political participation – like working-class Methodism – are in serious decline. Conversely, we have many new technologies that make group organization easier. These two unconnected developments may help to explain why the very latest research is telling us that participation is actually very much more common than we have conventionally assumed, but that it does not take forms that we have come to expect. Participation is happening; we have just not been looking for it in the right places. In particular, while there has been a decline in some important forms of group participation, like activism in political parties, individual acts of participation are in truth very common and may be becoming commoner. By individual acts are meant such things as signing petitions, writing letters or spontaneously attending demonstrations. For instance, a year-long study of a sample of the population conducted over 2000/2001 found that three out of four people (or 33 million adults) engaged in one or more political activities. These included: 29 million who gave money to a citizen's organization; 22 million who signed a petition; 18 million who had boycotted some products in their day-to-day shopping; and 2.5 million who had taken part in a demonstration (Pattie et al. 2003). These findings

FIGURE 13.3 ■ Political participation: new style (percentage who said they had undertaken the action in the previous 12 months)

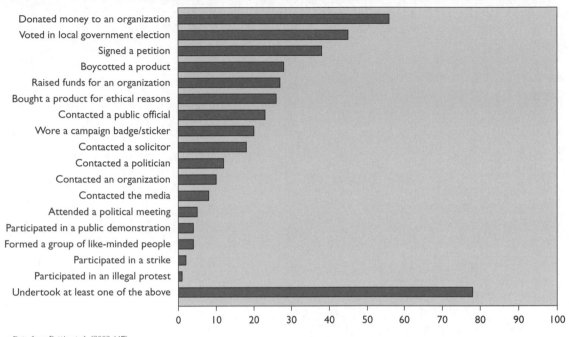

Source: Data from Pattie et al. (2003:447).

■ These figures come from a national survey dating from autumn 2000. It is instructive to compare the findings with Figure 13.1. The differences are partly due to methods of enquiry. Pattie et al. actually impose a 'harder' test because participation must have taken place within the previous 12 months. But despite this, and despite the perceived crisis of participation, the overall result actually suggests high levels of engagement. But this engagement is no longer so focused on established institutions like parties, but is highly individual: the best symbol is the figure of 26 per cent who bought a product for ethical reasons (for instance choosing a Fair Trade brand) – undoubtedly a political act, but one typically practised in the supermarket, not in any more obvious political forum.

immediately make sense of some of the features we noticed earlier in the chapter – notably the sudden rise and fall of mass demonstrations focused on single issues, whether they are fuel costs or foreign wars.

Not only does this research oblige us to be cautious about picturing ours as an age of apathy; it also calls into question our conventional notion of what constitutes political participation. A more expansive notion of participation can turn a visit to the supermarket into an act of participation: if you or I buy Fair Trade coffee in preference to Tesco own brand because we believe it offers a fairer deal to coffee farmers, then we are engaged in a political act. This is not politics as it was understood in the great days of the mass party, when participation was channelled into party membership and party activism. But it could hardly be said to be an inferior or less effective form of democratic participation. Is it less political to boycott the coffee than to brew the

coffee? Who is the more serious political activist: the boycotter of coffee products or the foot soldiers in the mass party who 40 years ago were used by the party elite to raise money by coffee mornings, stuff envelopes and get out the vote every four or five years?

PARTICIPATION AND WESTMINSTER DEMOCRACY

Political participation brings us to a paradox about the nature of the governance of Britain. We live under a system of democratic politics. At the heart of the idea of democracy – contained even in the root of the word – is the notion of popular rule. Yet genuinely popular participation in the system of government has been confined to rare moments, most obviously voting in fairly infrequent general elections. What is more, popular participation

DEBATING POLITICS 13.1

New styles of participation: damaging or benefiting democracy?

AN AGE OF APATHY IS DAMAGING BRITISH DEMOCRACY

▶ The institutions that were at the heart of the development of modern British democracy – notably the mass political parties – have lost their mass membership.

▶ 'Conventional' politics – the politics at the core of the state machine, such as voting to elect government – is what really shapes our lives and this is the kind of politics in which citizens are losing interest.

▶ Though some kinds of participation are widespread, they are typically sporadic and focused on single issues which arouse great emotional fervour and then rapidly fade away.

▶ Political participation has turned into an isolated, individual activity, rather than a sustained form of group commitment.

PARTICIPATION HAS CHANGED, NOT DECLINED, AND CHANGED FOR THE BETTER

▶ The decline of institutions like mass parties is no loss to democracy: they were just means by which metropolitan elites exploited a large rank and file to raise money and to fight elections.

▶ Much of the supposed decline in participation is due to the fact that we have not been looking in the right places – we have had too narrowly conventional a view of what 'participation' is.

▶ New technologies and new social attitudes have produced a huge growth in new kinds of participation.

▶ The new participation is much healthier for democracy than was the old, because it allows the more direct expression of citizen concerns than did hierarchical institutions like mass parties.

has been organized through institutions – like elections and the dominant political parties – focused on the political struggle in the Westminster system. Many groups were excluded from the world of Westminster politics, and many forms of participation – such as civil disobedience and industrial action – were labelled as problematic or even illegitimate.

In the domain of participation, as in other domains examined in earlier chapters, the routines of the Westminster system are now losing their importance. There has been a withdrawal of much popular participation from the established channels: the evidence includes the decline in turnout for general elections and, most striking of all, the virtual collapse in the membership of the major political parties. This is, however, not a crisis of participation, but rather a crisis in one form of participation. The opportunities to participate, even in elections, have expanded as the Westminster system has been reformed; and while

turnout in elections for the newly devolved governments is lower than has been usual for general elections, we need to bear in mind that even at these lower levels we are witnessing participation which simply did not exist a few decades ago. Moreover, new forms of participation are drawing groups into political action in fresh, and often unexpected, ways. Much of this change is renewing traditions of participation that had declined in the heyday of Westminster focused politics. The great modern campaigns, such as the campaign for the relief of third-world debt profiled in Documenting Politics 13.1, echo some of the great campaigns of the nineteenth century, like those against slavery and the evils of alcohol. There is therefore only a problem of participation in Britain if we insist on putting a special value on forms of participation that focus on Westminster and if we imply that the new patterns either are only of marginal importance or are in some way threatening to democratic government.

Review OF CHAPTER 13

Four themes have dominated this chapter:

◖◗ The restricted notions of popular participation that characterized British democracy in the era of the domination of the Westminster system.

◖◗ The numerous barriers to participation that excluded, and still partly do exclude, a wide range of social groups.

◖◗ The decline of the classic forms of mass participation that were at the heart of the Westminster system.

◖◗ The renewal of a tradition of mass political action as a result of a mix of social and cultural change.

FURTHER READING

ESSENTIAL

If you read only one book it should be Pattie et al. (2004), the authoritative guide to the 'new' political participation.

RECOMMENDED

Parry et al. (1992) is the definitive study of what in this chapter I have called participation 'old style'. Pattie et al. (2003) compress some of the main findings of their major study. Putnam (2000) created a sensation when it appeared, and while it concerned the US aroused wide interest in the UK. Hence the importance of Maloney et al. (2000), referred to in the text of this chapter, is that it suggests a considerably brighter condition for social capital than might be inferred from Putnam. Cain et al. (2003) is an important collection of comparative essays which describe the wider social forces reshaping participation and thus illuminate a key theme of this chapter – that participation has not declined, but changed. Hay (2007) also has a lot of perceptive things to say about the participation 'crisis'.

Parties and their organization

CONTENTS

AIMS

This chapter:

- Explains why party organization is important

- Introduces the historical development of party organization

- Sketches the organization of the main parties in Britain

- Shows how and why the mass party is in decline

- Describes how this decline has changed the nature of parties and how they are regulated

- Examines the argument that parties are not in decline but have evolved into new kinds of 'cartel' parties

WHY PARTIES ORGANIZE

Organized political parties are a universal feature of all modern democracies – indeed of almost all modern political systems. They have been at the centre of British politics for over two centuries, though as we will see the nature of their organization has altered greatly over that time. Parties organize because in Britain they have a central role to play in vital aspects of the system of government. If parties did not exist we would have to invent them – or invent some way of carrying out the functions for which they are organized. Four of these functions are particularly important.

Fighting elections

Competitive elections are the single most important defining feature of democracy, and in Britain the competition is overwhelmingly between parties. As we shall see when we turn to our chapter on elections, it is now rare for anyone to enter the Westminster House of Commons, or one of the new devolved assemblies, without the nomination of one of the major parties. Styles of fighting elections are changing all the time, but they still depend heavily on party organization. At local level the party is still the key unit of organization to canvass voters, distribute propaganda material and to try to persuade electors to vote on polling day. At national level, which is increasingly the most important arena for election competition, parties are the dominant unit of organization: an election campaign for the Westminster Parliament or for one of the new national assemblies introduced under devolution is largely a contest between nationally organized party machines.

Raising money

Politics costs money, and fighting elections can in particular cost large amounts: for instance, in the general election of 2001 the two big parties, Labour and Conservative, declared combined national spending of over £23 million (Fisher 2003). At the moment the figure for UK-wide spending in a general election year is effectively 'capped' at just under £20 million for a party, still a considerable sum of money. Parties use all levels of their organization to raise this money: individual members contribute subscriptions or, sometimes, larger donations; local branches of parties hold numerous money raising functions; at national level immense effort is put into cultivating rich individuals and institutions for donations. As we shall see, money raising activities have been an important catalyst in recent years for changes in party organization.

Representing interests

We saw in Chapter 8 that there exists an elaborate network of specialized interest representation in Britain, but parties are also important in interest representation, and their organization is often shaped by this fact. The clearest instance is provided by the Labour Party, which was first founded as an arm of the trade union movement, and whose internal organization, we shall see, still bears testament to these origins.

Recruiting political leadership

When I come to describe leadership recruitment in Chapter 18 we will see that the most direct (though not the only way) to the top in British politics is via membership of a political party. Above all, parties in Britain organize to provide the most important of all political leaders: those who occupy governing positions at all levels of the system of governance in Britain. Party is key to leadership recruitment in all the assemblies we have examined so far in this book: in the Westminster Parliament, in the new devolved assemblies and in the EP. And while we saw in Chapter 12 that there is some sign that the grip of party over leadership recruitment is weakening a little in the newer local government institutions – notably the new elected mayoralties – even in local government, party remains the key organizational funnel through which most potential leaders have to pass. Were we to abolish parties tomorrow we would have to find some different organizing process through which political leaders generally, and governments in particular, are selected in Britain. Parties organize, then, because if they did not we would have to invent them – or invent some other means of doing what they presently do.

THE HISTORICAL DEVELOPMENT OF PARTY ORGANIZATION

Parties have deep historical roots in British politics. Groups claiming the label 'party' were already exceptionally influential in the parliaments of the eighteenth century. But the modern history of party organization has been closely shaped by the developing history of the British system of government. The parties that grew out of the eighteenth-century Parliament were what are commonly called 'cadre' parties in their organization – meaning that they mostly consisted of a small cadre (group) of leaders at the centre. Indeed until well into the nineteenth century parties were not much more than labels worn by factions inside Parliament. They had little internal discipline, were rarely united by any coherent political principles and had only loose links with wider interests in society.

That situation was transformed by changes in the size and role of the electorate in the nineteenth century.

IMAGES 14.1 and 14.2 ■ The historical residue of the mass party

Photos: Michael Moran

■ The two photographs convey the physical face of the political party from the age of mass party organization – and show how anachronistic it now is. The first image is of a Conservative Club, the second of what was once a Liberal Club, both in a small northern industrial town. They incarnate the ambitions of parties with a mass membership, and when built they were among the most imposing buildings in the town centre. Notice the balcony feature on both, designed to allow triumphal party proclamations. The Conservative Club now functions solely as a drinking club; the Liberal Club has long been turned into a theatre – the advertisement for the latest production can be seen.

Beginning with the Great Reform Act of 1832, the size and social range of the electorate grew: before the Great Reform Act of 1832 there were just over half a million voters; by the reform of 1885, the last great extension of the nineteenth century, there were over five and a half million. In 1832, the vote was restricted mostly to a small range of property owners. Less than a century later, in 1918, after periodic relaxations of the property requirements, it was finally opened up to all adult males and most adult women. Inevitably, parties now had to organize to represent an increasingly wide range of social and economic interests.

Mass party organization was also prompted by changes in rules governing elections. Until 1872 ballots were cast in public and electors could thus be bribed or

intimidated into voting for particular candidates. The introduction of the secret ballot in that year, especially when coupled with the increase in the size of the electorate, made these weapons largely redundant. Some other way had to be found of appealing to the loyalty of large numbers of voters.

The development of the franchise throughout the nineteenth century therefore presented parties with two connected problems: how to organize an electorate which grew in size and social range; and how to attract the votes of this electorate when the secret ballot meant that it could not be directly bought or coerced. Cadre parties, made up largely of factions of Westminster parliamentarians, were useless at solving these problems. The two parties that dominated British politics from the middle of the nineteenth century until the end of the First World War in 1918 – the Liberal and Conservative Parties – both shifted from being cadre to mass parties in response to this problem. The connection between party organization and the new electorate is shown by the fact that the great spurt in party organization in the country at large happened soon after the passage of the 1867 Reform Act, the first piece of reform that not only expanded the electorate greatly but for the first time gave votes to sizeable numbers of manual workers.

Although there were differences in the organization of the Conservative and Liberal Parties, they shared important features. They both aimed to recruit a mass membership. In order to provide an incentive to members to join, they established bodies which claimed to give members a say in how the party was run, and in particular a say in the policies which the party put before electorates. They formed local organizations based on Westminster parliamentary constituencies, since the most important function of the new mass membership was to help convince electors to identify with the party, and then turn out to vote for it on election day. As a further incentive to local organization they gave these local parliamentary associations a big say – in many cases the dominant say – over who would be selected as the party's parliamentary candidate, and thus gave an early say in leadership selection to local activists. They used mass organization to raise money, both by direct subscriptions and by turning local party activists to fund raising.

By the end of the nineteenth century a model of party organization that lasted through much of the twentieth century was thus already established. The rise of the Labour Party, which displaced the Liberal Party as the main opponent of the Conservatives after the First World War, gave the mass party an extra dimension. Because the Conservatives had first existed as a parliamentary faction, and only created a mass party to solve the problems this faction faced in managing the new mass electorate, the party organization in the country had always been subordinate to the parliamentary leadership. But the Labour Party was mostly created outside Parliament and already had a fully fledged national party structure with its own constitution and conference before it became a significant parliamentary force. Labour developed a theory of party organization which, on some readings, gave it in the country, and notably in its annual party conference, the dominant voice in deciding party policy. At the party conference all the extra parliamentary interests in the party were represented: notably, the trade unions and the individual members organized into constituency Labour parties.

FIGURE 14.1 ■ **From giants to pygmies: the declining membership of the Conservative and Labour parties**

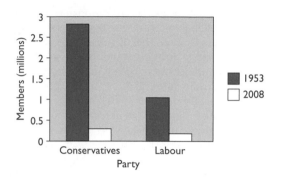

Sources: Butler and Butler (2000:141, 158); Marshall (2009).

■ Estimating the individual membership of parties is an inexact art, so the numbers on which this figure is based are approximations. But the orders of magnitude are not disputed. In the early 1950s both main parties had huge individual memberships: that is, real people who paid their own subscriptions. The Conservatives also had more than double the individual membership of the Labour Party. By 2008 (the latest date for which I could get a comparable number for both) the Conservatives were at about 250,000 and Labour at about 160,000.

Just how far this theory can be made to work, we will see, has been a long-term problem in the Labour Party.

The rise of Labour ushered in the age of the mass party, an age that lasted over half a century. The mass party flourished in a period when leaders had to reach millions of electors and when the only direct means of doing this was through personal contact. Election campaigns turned on contacting voters personally and addressing as many as possible in public meetings and by canvassing. All this demanded high numbers of volunteers. But the rise first of radio, and then in the 1950s the increasing importance of television, in contacting voters changed the styles of campaigning and made the mass party progressively less important. Leaders now began to appeal directly to voters through news and current affairs broadcasts. The mass meeting and direct canvassing of voters became just a subsidiary instrument: a means of providing 'sound bites' for radio and television. By the 1990s the mass party had even ceased to be important in reaching individual voters. Parties could do the job by centrally organized telephone canvassing. They could gauge public opinion by increasingly sophisticated polling methods. And they could try to persuade electors by expensive advertising campaigns. These developments help to explain a feature we noticed in Chapter 13: the fact that in the last 50 years total membership of parties has fallen by well over two million.

This does not mean that party organization, especially that outside Parliament, has become irrelevant. On the contrary: as we shall shortly see all the major parties have been making increasing efforts to involve their membership at large more closely in party government, especially in leadership selection. And parties have not viewed the decline in their membership with indifference: both Labour and the Conservatives have launched periodic campaigns in the last decade to recruit new members. Leaders worry about the health of the mass party because, for all the changes that have occurred in campaigning styles, it still carries out important functions. Thus while local campaigning by party members is now only marginal to results, these margins can decide elections: in the 2010 general election ten seats were won by less than 200 votes – and six were won by less than 100. It is easy to see that margins this small can be secured by superior local party organization. Constituency parties also still have a dominant say in selecting candidates for parliamentary elections (and both below and above that party members have a large say in selecting council candidates and candidates for European constituencies). Party leaders worry that if they do not have a large and local active membership it is easy for the selection process to be controlled by a small faction. And for all the changes that have come over the mass party, one factor that was critical to its birth remains as vital as ever: money. The new styles of campaigning, though no longer as demanding of people power, are even more financially demanding. The organization of individual parties reflects the legacies and problems of the age of the mass party.

THE CONSERVATIVE PARTY: ORGANIZATION AND POWER

The Conservative Party originated as a parliamentary faction and only created itself as a mass organized party to cope with the demands of fighting elections under the secret ballot and expanded suffrage in the nineteenth century. This gave the organization of the party a distinctive character. Above all, it ensured that the party in Parliament, and especially the parliamentary leadership, was the dominant component. But this by no means consigned the rest of the Party to insignificance. Above all, the parliamentary Party's control was limited by the decentralized structure of the wider party. The Party in

the constituency – the Constituency Association – was the key unit of organization in the mass party. It was impossible to join a national Conservative Party – the Conservative Party nationally was just an assembly of these different constituency organizations.

The importance of this mass organization was heightened by the fact that it was very successful. The Conservatives were easily the best organized mass political movement in twentieth-century Britain. There were around 250,000 Young Conservatives in the golden years of the early 1950s; it is possible that there are now only 5,000 of their contemporary equivalents. These figures are approximate for a reason that is itself revealing: the Party has always been haphazard about recording and retaining its members. Historically, this reflected the fact that Party organization in the country was as much social as political. The vitality and numbers derived in part from the fact that the Party was an important institution in middle-class social life. But this integration between party organization and middle-class culture made the mass party even more significant.

The decentralized nature, and the social character of the party in the country, provided the clues to how party organization in practice functioned – better clues than lie in any formal organization chart. For instance, formally the Party outside Parliament had no more than an advisory role in making policy. Thus the event called colloquially the Conservative Annual Conference was actually just an assembly of the separate autonomous constituency associations with only an advisory role on policy. In practice, relations of influence in the Party were more subtle than this simple organization model suggested. Decentralization into highly autonomous constituencies put several powerful cards into the hands of local constituency activists. It gave them a very high level of control over the selection of parliamentary candidates and therefore, in safe seats, control over who would be returned as Conservative MPs. It gave them a large say over finance in the Party, since the Party's wealth – which was great – depended heavily on the funds raised by the constituencies. When the Party had a mass of members these constituencies were formidable money raising machines. And in part because of their role in parliamentary candidate selection, local associations had a direct, if informal, line of communication with the parliamentary leadership on matters of policy and political strategy.

These generalizations are in the past tense because the Conservative Party is in a period of great change. The forces prompting this include a catastrophic fall in constituency membership; the huge defeats suffered by the Conservatives in the general elections of 1997 and 2001; and the question mark placed over Conservative

BRIEFING 14.1

Party organization under multilevel governance: the case of the Conservatives and Europe

In the age of party organization dictated hierarchically from the metropolitan centre it would be sufficient to describe UK-wide organization to picture how parties are organized. But multilevel governance has changed that. The Conservatives' difficulties with organization in the EP illustrates the point. As part of his successful campaign for the Party leadership David Cameron pledged to withdraw the group of Conservative members of the EP from the European People's Party, the block in the EP which represents most mainstream Conservative/Christian Democrat opinion. But to form an official caucus in the Parliament a group needs a minimum of 25 members. Thus since making the pledge Conservative organization at the European level has been dominated by the search for partners among like-minded parties from other EU members. The announcement in 2009 that the Conservatives now had those partners, principally Polish and Czech ones, drew furious accusations that the Party was deserting mainstream Conservative opinion in Europe; in particular it was asserted (and denied) that some of the Party's new partners had extreme nationalist, and even neo-fascist, sympathies.

■ This Briefing, and Briefing 14.3, emphasize that parties now have to organize under multilevel governance, whereas a generation ago the leadership could dictate things from a London centre.

Party organization in Wales and Scotland by the dismal results for elections to the Westminster Parliament and the development of the distinct patterns of devolved politics following the devolution reforms in those two countries. Eighteen years in government (1979–97) had led to neglect of party organization. The election of William Hague as party Leader in 1997 following the Party's landside defeat at the hands of Labour, provided the occasion for institutional reform. Plainly influenced by the example of Labour Party leaders from Kinnock to Blair in reshaping their party institutions, Hague quickly produced a series of proposals for reform. These reforms showed the impact of a new creed of managerialism in the Party. (Hague's one proper job outside politics had been a spell as a management consultant with the world's leading management consultancy, McKinsey.) An attempt was made to trim the size of some of the more unwieldy old institutions, like the Executive Council, which had a theoretical membership of nearly 1,000! A management board was established with the object of unifying what had been formally two separate institutions, the party organization controlled by the Leader and the national union of constituency associations in the country at large. An attempt was made to spell out clear lines of responsibility between the components of the party. In short, an attempt was made to replace the

decentralized, rather ramshackle, structure that had grown up since the nineteenth century.

Perhaps even more significant than the institutional changes themselves was the manner of their introduction. In an echo of a tactic used by Tony Blair when he became Leader of the Labour Party, Hague organized a plebiscite of party members through a postal ballot to give a verdict on his proposals. (They were overwhelmingly endorsed.) This attempt to draw in the wider membership was also reflected in the new rules for selecting the Leader which Hague introduced in 1998. As Timeline 14.1 shows, this continues a long established widening of the group entitled to a say in the choice of party Leader.

These reforms in part 'empower' the Party in the country more formally than in the past, but they also in part attempt to organize it on more centralized lines. This has made the position and organization of Central Office, the Party's central headquarters, more prominent and contentious. ('Central Office' is forever associated with the Party's historic, imposing headquarters in Smith Square, just round the corner from the Palace of Westminster. As a sign of the fallen fortunes of the Party, the headquarters were moved to offices over a Starbucks in Victoria Street. I retain the traditional usage here.) Central Office, like any bureaucracy, has its own distinc-

Timeline 14.1

The evolution of Conservative leadership selection methods

922–65 Conservative Leader 'emerged' by a secret, informal process of consultation involving leading Conservatives, mostly in the House of Commons. In this period every change of Conservative Leader took place while the Party held office and a name was forwarded, by the Party leadership to the Monarch, of a figure who was to be invited to form a government.

965 Leader to be elected by secret ballot of all Conservative MPs. Failure to produce majority winner (50 per cent of all votes cast and a margin of 15 per cent over second candidate) led to second ballot; if still no clear winner, then a 'run off' between the two top candidates. Leaders elected under this method were Edward Heath (1965–75), Margaret Thatcher (1975–90); John Major (1990–97); William Hague (1997–2001). All but John Major were elected while the Party was in Opposition.

975 Provision for annual re-election introduced, allowing Leader to be challenged. Procedure invoked by Margaret Thatcher in her successful challenge to Edward Heath, 1975; by Sir Anthony Meyer against Margaret Thatcher, unsuccessfully, in 1989; and by Michael Heseltine in November 1990, leading to Thatcher's displacement, but by John Major, not Heseltine.

998 William Hague introduces new rules with two provisions:
1. Annual re-election rule abolished. Provision for (maximum of one) no-confidence vote per year, to be triggered by call for ballot of Conservative MPs supported by at least 15 per cent of MPs. Passage of no-confidence vote triggers leadership election.
2. Leadership election in two stages: if more than two candidates, then MPs vote to eliminate all but the top two, the bottom candidate being eliminated in each successive round. Remaining two candidates contest for simple majority of all members of the Conservative Party in the country.

2001 Ian Duncan-Smith elected Conservative Leader by this method, following resignation of William Hague after general election defeat.

2003 Michael Howard 'crowned' as Leader, 2003: Conservative MPs agree among themselves on a single candidate, and the wider Party electorate is left merely to endorse their choice.

2005 Howard resigns after defeat in general election. David Cameron elected Leader by the Party at large mainly on strength of powerful performance in virtual 'hustings' at Party Conference.

■ The history of Conservative leadership election methods since the mid-1960s is essentially one of 'broadening the franchise' to the present point where the critical choice is formally in the hands of rank and file Conservatives in the country. The significance of starting the timeline at 1922 is the following: while before then the 'emergence' of leaders after informal consultation took place, 1922 marks the date of the beginning of formal organization by all Conservative backbench members of Parliament.

tive culture, interests and feuds, but the most distinctive feature of the national organization is the extent to which it is put at the disposal of whoever happens to be Leader of the Party at any particular moment. The Leader has the power of hiring and firing, and while this obviously cannot be done capriciously in practice the Leader does have a large say over key personnel appoint-ments. Perhaps the single most important organizational appointment made by the Leader is that of Chairman of the Party, for the Chairman can be, and in recent cases almost always has been, the main 'manager' of the Party on the Leader's behalf. As a result, the appointment of, and dismissal of, the Party Chairman has often been a public signal of internal power struggles in the Party.

The role of Central Office, and its relationship with the parliamentary leadership of the Party, depends heavily on whether the Party is in government or in opposition. Not surprisingly, when the Party was in its long occupation of government from 1979–97 it was more marginal, rising to prominence only at key moments like general elections. But the Central Office machine nevertheless has key enduring functions in the Party regardless of whether the Conservatives are in office or opposition. It is the backbone of the machine at the Leader's disposal for fighting elections. It controls an important gateway to Parliament, because eligibility for selection as a Conservative parliamentary candidate depends on being on the Central Office approved list of candidates. It is the main machine by which the Party seeks to raise funds, either from the constituency parties at large in the country, from the donations of companies or from wealthy individuals. Above all, in opposition the Central Office machine is an important means by which the Leader attempts to manage the wider Party in the country.

This brief summary highlights one overwhelmingly important contingency: the biggest single influence on the practical working of Conservative Party organization is whether the Party is in opposition or government. And this contingency makes the role of the parliamentary Party uniquely sensitive, if only because, as we saw earlier, the Party began as a parliamentary group which created its own mass organization. The whole group of Conservative MPs is commonly called 'the 1922 Committee', after a famous meeting in 1922 of all Conservative MPs led to the fall of a government. The 1922 meets weekly when Parliament is in session, and has itself a network of special committees covering some of the most important responsibilities of government. But its most important mechanisms of influence and control are informal. The number of Conservative MPs is never large: even after the great Conservative landslides of the 1980s there were less than 400; in May 2010 the Party returned as the largest party with only 306 members. These numbers mean that the parliamentary Party is a quite small tribe, albeit one often at war internally. MPs mix in the enclosed, intense, social world of the Westminster Parliament that I described in Chapter 9. The most important mechanisms of control and influence are therefore informal. The 1922 Committee has its own elected officers, the most important of whom is its Chairman. On the Chairman falls important responsibilities, mostly exercised informally: in particular, to let the Leader know the sentiments of backbenchers and especially to warn him or her of dissatisfaction on the backbenches. In extreme cases the Chairman and officers of the 1922 may have the responsibility to tell leaders that

support is so low that they should step aside. This last role has led to the development of a great legend about the role of the 'men in suits', the Committee of the 1922, in quietly telling leaders to step aside – the political equivalent of inviting a disgraced fellow officer to retire to some quiet corner with a loaded revolver. In practice leaders are so attached to office that they rarely take these gentlemanly hints: in the last 30 years Conservative leaders have only been removed after bruising conflicts (Heath in 1975, Thatcher in 1990, Duncan-Smith in 2003) or after leading the Party to electoral disaster (Major in 1997, Hague in 2001, Howard in 2005).

One reason why changes of leadership in the Party are so bloody is that traditionally Conservatives have given unusual authority to the Leader – in formal terms probably more authority than in any other democratic party in Britain. As we shall see when we turn in Chapter 18 to leadership recruitment, this formal authority has been strengthened by the leaders' prominence in the wider struggle for political leadership in Britain. This makes the changes in recent years in the method of selecting the Leader all the more important. Until the middle of the 1960s the Leader of the Party just 'emerged': when a new Leader was needed some senior older figures in Parliament informally canvassed MPs, giving special weight to the leading MPs. That secretive process, which dated from predemocratic days, became increasingly anachronistic in a democratic political system. From the mid-1960s to 1998 the Conservatives worked with the same system, subjecting it to only minor modifications. This system essentially allowed the 1922 Committee to select the Leader. In the 1990s the Conservatives' main opponents, the Labour Party, gradually widened their own 'franchise' for electing the leader to give a more direct say to individual members, as we shall see below. After William Hague's election in 1997 he moved rapidly to do the same (see Timeline 14.1 for details). In 2003 the Party, exhausted by bitter factional battles during the brief leadership of Iain Duncan-Smith (2001–03), arranged a 'coronation' in which Michael Howard emerged as the sole candidate for the leadership after negotiations within the parliamentary leadership. But when Howard resigned after the general election defeat of 2005 the new, more popular mechanism proved decisive in David Cameron's selection. Cameron, initially not the favourite, proved exceptionally skilled at communicating both with the party membership at large and with the wider electorate. At the 2005 Party Conference the contenders delivered speeches that were in effect auditions for the role of Leader; Cameron's performance was much more assured than that of his chief rival, David Davis, and from then on he was unstoppable.

THE LABOUR PARTY: ORGANIZATION AND POWER

By contrast with the Conservatives, the Labour Party first emerged in the early decades of the twentieth century as a mass organized movement in the country before Labour became a serious parliamentary force. The formal establishment of the modern party, in 1918, in fact coincided with the emergence of Labour as the Conservatives' main opponents in the general election of the same year. The constitution on which the Party settled in that year created Labour, not as a single entity, but as a federation of 'affiliated' organizations. Affiliation meant that organizations like trade unions and individual constituency parties subscribed financially to the party and enjoyed voting rights in its key national institutions in rough proportion to the size of their subscriptions. Thus Labour developed as a mass party organization before it emerged as a great parliamentary force and the voting power of the components of this organization was heavily influenced by financial 'muscle' in the Party. These historically inherited institutional features explain the key tension in the organization of the Party, a tension that has periodically threatened to pull it completely apart: the tension between a Party that is a federation of organizations in the country at large, and a parliamentary leadership that is concerned with winning majorities in Parliament and with governing when in Office.

Like the Conservatives, therefore, Labour was for much of its history a truly mass party, and the history of this mass character in part mirrored the history of Conservative development. 'Individual' membership of the Party has generally been equated with membership in the individual constituency Labour Parties. These levels of membership never matched those achieved by the Conservatives, but they have shown a similar pattern of decline: they peaked at just one million in 1952, and their recorded levels by the close of the twentieth century were below 400,000, though the true figure may now may be as low as 170,000. The only departure from this pattern occurred in the aftermath of Tony Blair's election as leader, when a national recruitment campaign produced a short lived influx of new members.

The most impressive nominal measure of mass membership historically was provided by the affiliation figures for the most historically important institutional component of the party, the trade unions. At its height at the end of the 1970s trade union affiliation to the Party was measured as the equivalent of over six and a half million members. But this was an institutional fiction, produced by a financial mechanism. The figures did not represent real people who had made a decision to link with the Labour Party. Unions created their own separate political funds, from a small additional levy added to the individual subscription of each union member. After 1946 union members had to 'opt out' of paying this levy and, since the amount is trivial, few did so. The fund could be used for a variety of purposes, but for unions affiliated to the Labour Party it financed the union's affiliation fee. The size of the subscription paid by the individual union decided the nominal number of members it had affiliated. This financial mechanism put the unions at the centre of Party organization for two reasons: historically, it made them the main sources of party finance; and since the size of affiliation fees converted into the size of the vote which a union could cast in key party bodies, it often gave them a predominant voice in any forum where decisions were made by a vote. Of these, the most important, and most contentious, was the Annual Conference.

The power of the Annual Conference of the Party was historically contested, because in the way that power was exercised lay the key to how Labour solved the tensions inherent in its organization: the tensions in a federated party where one element, the unions, provided most of the money and commanded most of the votes at the Conference; and the tensions, cutting across these, between the mass organization outside Parliament and the parliamentary leadership created by the rise of Labour as the Conservatives' main rival. Some official accounts pictured the Conference as the 'parliament of the movement', implying that it had supreme decision-making power. But this created two kinds of problem: where the use of the union 'block vote' carried decisions that overrode the votes of individual members from the constituencies; and where Conference decisions opposed the policies of the parliamentary leadership – which claimed, by virtue of fighting democratic parliamentary elections, to represent a different and wider constituency in the country at large.

Throughout much of the Party's history after 1918 these tensions were contained by a variety of means. In part they were suppressed when the Party was in government, because the parliamentary leadership then had especially strong grounds for either calling on the loyalty of the mass party or ignoring its views. The parliamentary leadership was also able, for much of its history, to create alliances with parts of the trade union leadership, thus using part of the union block voting power to carry its own views. These mechanisms broke down at the end of the 1970s when the Party lost office to the Conservatives after a difficult spell in government, 1974–79. The years in office strained relations between the unions, the parliamentary leadership and many constituency parties to breaking point. Something close to civil war broke out in the Party. The 1980s were a

BRIEFING 14.2

The block vote and the federal nature of the Labour Party

The 'block vote' is a direct outcome of the Labour Party's federal structure and has been wielded by all affiliated organizations. But historically it mattered most in the case of union votes because unions had by far the largest votes.

The 'block' originates in the case of unions from the mechanism of affiliation. All unions are permitted to establish a separate 'political fund' which is financed by a small levy on individual members. To avoid paying the levy members must 'contract out'. Few do so, and few are even aware that they are paying this supplement. This fund can be used for many political purposes. Some unions (for example the University and College Union) have a political fund, but are not affiliated to the Labour Party. But at the time of writing 15 unions are affiliated to Labour, including some of the largest like Unite and Unison. They pay affiliation fees from the Political Fund. National affiliation costs £3.00 per member. Some members 'affiliate' up to their whole membership; some up to the proportion of members who pay the political levy, or less. Thus the affiliation is not connected to the choices of real individual members. Each 'affiliation' carries one vote in, for example, voting at the Annual Conference: thus a union that pays (at current rates, a figure which has remained unchanged for some time) £300,000 annually is 'buying' 100,000 votes. With individual membership at about 170,000 this gives big unions a potentially dominant voice in votes. But a number of features moderate the impact of the union block vote:

- Even at the height of union influence in the party, the split between unions and other affiliated organizations at the Annual Conference was only 70:30.
- Unions, even at the height of their power, were divided and often 'cancelled out' the block vote of each other.
- Since reforms introduced in 1993 unions are obliged to divide their block vote at conference between each individual union delegate, who votes separately. In practice, though, most unions will vote together.
- In the electoral college for choosing the Leader of the Party unions are obliged to ballot their members and to cast their block in proportion to the choices made by the individual members.

■ The 'block vote' has commonly been pictured by opponents of the Labour Party as an undemocratic mechanism. Whether undemocratic or otherwise, it arises out of a consistent, and historically deep rooted, theory of party government.

decade of struggle, both about the content of policy and about the locus of authority in the Party. The struggle resulted in two major changes to Party organization: in the structure of party policy making and in the method of leadership selection.

The main change in the organization of policy making was first introduced in 1990. It was an attempt to 'dethrone' the Annual Conference, the formally sovereign policy-making body whose role in reality for decades had proved a source of contention. Alongside the Conference was established a series of 'Policy Forums' where larger numbers of individual party members could simply turn up and contribute to debates about policy. This was strengthened by reforms introduced in 1997, with the creation of a National Policy Forum with 175 members, hearing and considering reports from eight separate policy commissions. The whole process is in effect a rolling policy review, with the object of considering the full range of policy over the lifetime of a single Parliament. The National Policy Forum in

Timeline 14.2

The evolution of leadership selection in the Labour Party

1922–81 'Leader' means Leader of the Westminster Parliamentary Labour Party, elected at the beginning of each parliamentary session. In the rare contested elections, the winner was the candidate gaining an absolute majority of votes, if necessary through a second ballot of the best two supported candidates. First Leader elected by this method was J. Ramsay Macdonald, 1922; the last was Michael Foot, 1980.

1981–93 The 1981 special conference decides the Leader (and Deputy Leader) will be re-elected each year by the Annual Conference if the party is in opposition. The Conference to form an electoral college, with 40 per cent of votes allocated to unions, 30 per cent to the Parliamentary Party and 30 per cent to constituencies. Neil Kinnock (1983) and John Smith (1992) elected by this method.

1993 Party Conference changes balance of votes in electoral college to equal (one-third each) for union, Parliamentary Party and constituencies; and unions and constituency parties obliged to ballot individual members on their choices and divide their votes according to the expressed preferences of their members. Tony Blair (1994) elected under this method.

2007 Gordon Brown selected as Leader by a 'coronation' in which no rival offers competition.

2010 Brown resigns after May 2010 general election; Ed Miliband elected successor..

■ For most of the twentieth century both big parties gave control over leadership choice to their parliamentary representatives. Labour was the first to share control with the Party outside Parliament, but it took some years before it gave individual members a direct vote in leadership selection.

turn commends policies to the Annual Conference, which is thus often faced with a 'take it or leave it' choice. In the dying years of New Labour in office, as the leadership struggled to hold the party together, and to mobilize union support for the 2010 election, the meetings of the National Policy Forum became important events at which the parliamentary leadership and the trade union leadership tried to work out a consensus. Indeed, as the Conference has turned more and more into a stage-managed jamboree, the real hard bargaining between the different parts of Labour's federation is taking place in the Forum meetings.

The second major organizational change produced by Labour's internal turmoil in the 1980s was a transformation of the Party's method of selecting its Leader. The details of the development of Labour leadership selection methods are given in Timeline 14.2, but the direction of change can be simply summarized: for over 60 years following the rise of Labour as one of the two main parties the Westminster Parliamentary Party entirely controlled leadership selection; since the early

1980s it has had to share control over the choice with individual rank and file members and with the trade unions.

We can sum up the recent development of Labour Party organization as follows. Imagine someone who fell asleep at a Labour Party meeting in 1979 (all to easy to do) and suddenly woke up 30 or so years later. Our character would soon notice three big changes in the way the Party is run that have affected the historical building blocks of Labour Party organization:

The Parliamentary Labour Party (PLP) has simultaneously become more influential but less independent. Institutional changes in the way Party policy is formulated have allowed the parliamentary leadership increasingly to control policy debates. The Party Conference is stage managed by the parliamentary leadership: it has become a kind of annual assembly organized for publicity purposes, with carefully choreographed leadership speeches and announcements of new policy initiatives geared to provide sound bites for broadcasting. It is hard to know how enduring this ascendancy will be, because it largely dates from the 1990s. In other words, it dates from the period when all the major components of the Party decided to sink their public differences in the attempt to get back into office after the long years of Conservative ascendancy; and after 1997 it coincided with Labour's occupation of government, a condition that has always helped the ascendancy of the parliamentary leadership. But it has been buttressed by longer term changes which have, for instance, increased the control of the Leader of the Party over the Party's own central administrative machinery.

The PLP's autonomy has, however, been decreased by two long-term changes. Even at the end of the 1970s Labour MPs in safe seats virtually had a job for life, or for as long as they wished to stay in Parliament. Since then, reselection as the Party's candidate has become far from automatic, and the spread of 'one member one vote' in candidate selection has opened up the process of candidate selection to many more individual Party members in the constituencies. The numbers of 'deselected' MPs are not great, but a few examples help make all sitting MPs sensitive to this possibility and therefore careful to cultivate their local parties. The second long-term change I have already described: the PLP has lost its monopoly over the choice of Party Leader.

The trade unions' influence has declined. It is true that the electoral college mechanism for selecting the leader has given unions a secure place in selection, but in other respects organizational changes – not to mention the drift of policy itself – have left them increasingly marginalized. But this shift in organizational arrangements has only magnified the tensions at the heart of Labour's federated party structure. As institutional changes have made the block vote less effective, and the content of policy in government has often drifted completely out of control of the unions, voices have increasingly been questioning the point of continuing as major paymasters of the Party. When 'New Labour' rode high in government it could draw on substantial business finance. However, in the aftermath of the May 2010 general election the dynamics of influence are different: business support has dried up; the Party is in serious financial problems; and the unions are the only significant institutional funders.

The territorial organization, the most important aspect of which is obviously the organization in the constituencies, has become increasingly divided along national lines. One of the most important forces causing this is the devolution measures passed by the Government after 1997. The existence of new governing institutions in Wales and Scotland, and the need to fight separate elections to control those governing institutions, created quite distinct institutional forces in those

two countries and led to the increasingly separate organization of the party in those separate countries of the UK: see for example Briefing 14.3.

CHALLENGING TWO-PARTY DOMINANCE: ALTERNATIVE MODELS OF PARTY ORGANIZATION

'Third parties' used to be virtually a residual category in discussion of the British party system because the Labour and Conservative parties were so overwhelmingly important. But we have already seen that this is now far from the case. In the devolved governments 'third parties' are often no longer in third place: in Scotland the Liberal Democrats were in coalition with

IMAGE 14.3 ■ O Brother! Ed Miliband defeats his brother to become Labour Party Leader

Photo: Lefteris Pitarakis/AP/PA Photos

■ The contest for the Labour Party leadership in the summer and autumn of 2010 produced an extraordinary psychodrama: the two Miliband brothers, Ed and David, ran neck and neck in the race well ahead of the other candidates. Ed, at the beginning the underdog, finally narrowly won. The photo shows Ed (right) in a very public brotherly hug at the moment when the result was announced at the Labour Party conference in September. But if the psychodrama gripped the media and the party, the contest had wider institutional significance: Ed won because he proved more adept at courting trade union support, a key component in the federal Labour Party described in this chapter. And the protracted public contest shows how far parties have now moved from dominance by a parliamentary elite: only 30 years ago the 'franchise' would have been restricted to Labour MPs in the Westminster Parliament.

BRIEFING 14.3

Party organization under multilevel governance: devolution and the case of the Labour Party

The question of whether devolution has had an impact on the organization of the Labour Party is particularly complex, for two reasons. Historically, Labour has been a party where the 'Celtic' components, notably Welsh and Scottish, have been particularly important; and the experience of devolution so far has been almost entirely under the rule of a Labour Government in Westminster. Although Labour still has to digest the result of the 2010 general election as far as its organization is concerned, the work of Laffin et al. (2007) paints a fairly clear picture of the impact of the early years. In essence, devolution made little difference to the UK-wide party – in part because the dominant Westminster leadership, especially after Gordon Brown became Prime Minister, was itself heavily Scottish. But internally, in both Wales and Scotland, the Party changed: it was forced to become less hierarchical and to disperse power and decision making more widely.

Sources: Laffin et al. (2007); see also Hopkin (2009).

Labour from 1999 to 2007; since then the Nationalists have been the governing party. In Wales Plaid Cymru became part of the governing coalition in 2007. As we will see in Chapter 17, in elections to the Westminster Parliament the domination of Labour and Conservative has been in long-term decline.

These third parties vary in electoral significance, but that significance is often great and is almost universally growing. The Nationalists and the Liberal Democrats by now have established a secure hold within elected national assemblies and in governing institutions. Others, such as the Greens, have made periodic though unsustained breakthroughs at national level, but have a more permanent presence in local government. We shall see in the next chapter that these parties are highly varied in their ideologies. But in respect of organization they show important common features, which amount to a departure from the historically engrained nature of the two dominant parties.

The two dominant parties have been deeply marked by their Westminster parliamentary histories – by the fact that since 1918 in the case of Labour, and for much longer in the case of the Conservatives, they have been focused on the Westminster battle, and the battle in particular to occupy, and when occupying keep, office in the Westminster system. The history of, and the forces shaping, the organization in the other parties have been very different, and this is what makes them important as alternative models of party organization. These third parties have either had to create them-

selves as extra-Westminster parliamentary forces or, in the case of the Liberal Democrats, to recreate themselves as such.

The Liberal Democrats are the modern result of a fusion between two political forces of unequal weight and with different organizational histories. The Party was created in 1988 when the Liberal Party fused with the Social Democratic Party (SDP). (The original name, Social and Liberal Democrats, was changed to the Liberal Democrats a year later.) The SDP was originally the creation of a Westminster parliamentary faction. It was born in 1981 when four leading members of the Labour Party announced the formation of a new party in reaction to what they alleged was the capture of Labour by militant socialism. The Social Democrats rapidly attracted a large electoral following and a large membership. Between 1981 and 1987 they fought elections as part of an Alliance with the Liberal Party (see below). This produced disappointing results, notably in the 1987 general election, as the rapidly acquired SDP electoral support and membership almost as rapidly melted away. The disappointment of 1987 was followed by a proposal from the Liberals for a merger, a takeover in all but name. After some infighting this was accomplished, as we saw above, in 1988. The SDP brought little institutional originality to the marriage, because it was part of the old Westminster world: it was the product of a disappointed faction within the Labour Westminster parliamentary leadership. The Liberals, by contrast, had a considerably more innovative institutional history.

People in Politics 14.1

Party personalities beyond the magic circle of Labour and Conservatives

Alex Salmond (1954–)

MP for Banff and Buchan in the Westminster Parliament, 1987–; educated St Andrews University; civil servant, economist with Royal Bank of Scotland, 1980–87. Convenor (leader) of Scottish National Party, 1990–2000. Resigned as Leader in 2000, but following the fall of John Swinney in 2004 stood again for the leadership and was elected in September with a huge majority of the vote of members. Scottish First Minister, 2007–, as leader of a minority administration.

Vince Cable (1943–)

Liberal Democrat MP for Twickenham, 1997–; Deputy Leader of Liberal Democrats 2006–10; Business Secretary 2010–. Two things propelled Cable to national prominence: his success as, briefly, acting Leader of the Liberal Democrats in 2007; and, above all, his outstanding performances in the great financial crisis of 2007–08.

Nick Griffin (1959–)

Chairman of the British National Party, the main neo-fascist group in the UK. His presence here, and prominence in the party system, is a testimony to the way the old two-party system has decayed. He has a history of Holocaust denial and has been convicted on public order charges. But in 2009 he was elected a Member of the EP (along with another BNP candidate) for the multimember constituency of North West England.

Cartoons: Shaun Steele

■ The rise of third parties created some political careers which would have been difficult in the two major parties.

The Liberals were one of the two dominant parties in the UK until 1918, when they were supplanted by Labour. By the 1950s they had shrunk to parliamentary insignificance. The lowest point came in the general election of 1951, when the Party returned only six Westminster MPs with 2.5 per cent of the popular vote; but even in the 1970 general election it still returned a mere six members. Since then, as we shall see in more detail in Chapter 17, the decline of Labour and the Conservatives as electoral forces has been accompanied by a revival of the Liberal Democrats, especially in the Westminster and Scottish Parliaments.

This long, half-century road to revival has largely depended on extra-parliamentary organization, and this has been reflected in the structure of party policy making and leadership selection. The Liberal Democrats pioneered the latter through one member one vote, and they still remain distinct in this way from Labour and the Conservatives: from the former in not operating an electoral college which gives votes to constituent organizations; from the latter in not using the election in the parliamentary party as a 'filter' to select candidates to put before the membership.

On methods of internal policy-making the Party has been similarly pioneering. For instance, while devolution has in effect forced Labour and the Conservatives to develop a federal party structure to reflect the new devolved governments, the Liberals historically operated as a federation of their separate national parties. But the amalgamation with the Social Democrats reinforced their UK-wide organization, making its (UK-wide) annual assembly, for example, the sovereign policy-making body in the Party.

Organizationally, then, the Liberal Democrats represent the fusion of two very different traditions of party organization: that of a centralizing parliamentary cadre (the original Social Democrats) and that of a party re-created from the ground up after being virtually wiped out as a parliamentary force. But parliamentary organization has probably strengthened in recent years, because parliamentary representation has become stronger. As we saw in Chapter 10 the Liberal Democrats are now a major force in the Scottish Parliament and in the Welsh Assembly. There has also been a long-term rise in Westminster parliamentary representation. Although the May 2010 general election saw a fall in seats – 57 returned, against 62 in the 2005 Parliament – that still represented an advance on 1997, when only 46 Liberal Democrats were returned.

The importance of extra-parliamentary organization is even stronger in the case of nationalists. Indeed, as we also saw in Chapter 10 on devolved government, the origins of the nationalist parties are very far removed from parliamentary politics, still less from the particular politics of Westminster: in the case of Plaid Cymru the origins lie, for example, in a movement to defend the language and the traditional culture which it supports. Some, admittedly minor, elements in nationalism have even flirted with overt anti-parliamentarianism, of the sort brought to full, violent development by parts of the republican movement in Northern Ireland. The founding figures of these nationalist parties have no Westminster parliamentary pedigree, and for virtually the whole of their history their Westminster parliamentary wings have been tiny factions, nominally there to agitate for the separation of their country from the UK. The extra-parliamentary weight of the parties has been reflected in both their formal structures and in their modes of leadership selection. Whereas the two big parties, Labour and Conservative, have in recent years had to adapt to allow their extra-parliamentary wings a bigger say, the newly successful nationalist parties had their structures well established before the emergence of an established parliamentary group.

We saw in the case of the organizational history of the Labour Party that it too originated in this fashion, developing a vigorous national organization before becoming a parliamentary force. And we saw also that the Party's subsequent emergence as a force in Westminster created a powerful tension between its parliamentary and extra-parliamentary components. The creation of the Welsh Assembly and the Scottish Parliament, in which for the first time the two nationalist parties have significant representation and a genuine possibility of capturing government, means that the potential for this history of tension is being recreated within nationalism.

As we survey the parties that have emerged to challenge the domination of Conservative and Labour we move along a spectrum in which extra-parliamentary party organization is increasingly important: it is more so in the case of nationalists than in the case of the Liberal Democrats, and is more so again in the case of the Greens. This is partly, perhaps, because the Greens have yet to make the breakthrough of any significance in the Westminster Parliament (they won their first seat only in May 2010) and have only a tiny representation even under the more proportional electoral systems choosing members of the Scottish Parliament, and none in the Welsh Assembly. But it is also because the Greens have sought to develop a distinctive philosophy of organization, which emphasizes the internal control of the party by members. Two signs of this are the formal methods of policy decision and the method of leadership selection. On the former, they stress the importance of party

POLITICAL ISSUES 14.1

The problem of party funding

All three major parties have a history of difficulties over their party funding. The domicile status of one of the Conservatives' main donors, Lord Ashcroft, has long been a bone of contention. In November 2007 the General Secretary of the Labour Party, Peter Watt, had to resign because he had accepted donations amounting to £600,000 from a north-east businessman, channelled through intermediaries to protect his identity. In 2005 Michael Brown donated £2.4 million to the Liberal Democrats. He was subsequently convicted of fraud and the Party narrowly escaped having to repay the donation – a course which would have caused it great financial problems; but the refusal puts the Party, in the eyes of some critics, close to being a receiver of stolen goods. The issue, though, goes beyond high profile cases and will recur for a reason central to this chapter. The root cause is that the parties have lost the mass membership which a generation ago raised substantial sums of money and provided the free labour 'on the doorstep' to fight elections. Now, parties fight elections via expensive professionally run national campaigns and no longer have the membership to raise money. They are forced to numerous desperate stratagems – legal, quasi-legal and sometimes downright illegal – to raise the cash.

conventions involving large numbers of members as the crucial mechanism of policy choice. On the latter, until 2008 they insisted on a collective leadership rather than identifying a single figure as leader. In September 2008, however, the Party for the first time elected Caroline Lucas as its single leader, the same Caroline Lucas who became the Party's first MP in May 2010. This may be the first step on the path to a more 'conventional' party organization.

THE REGULATION OF POLITICAL PARTIES

Until the 1990s, in describing the organization of political parties, we could content ourselves largely with describing their own internal arrangements. They were essentially voluntary institutions that governed their own affairs. But the Elections and Political Parties Act 2000 greatly changed the environment in which almost all political parties operate. For the first time it created a framework of state regulation for the operation of many aspects of party life, notably to do with party finance and campaigning.

The immediate origin of the Act lies in the Fifth Report of the Committee on Standards in Public Life (see Briefing 4.2). The Committee's investigations in turn were prompted by scandals connected to the party financing in the early 1990s. However, its report covered much more than the narrow area of party financing itself, and the Act of 2000 has also been correspondingly wide. It does four particularly important things:

It sets rules for giving and accepting party donations. This is the aspect of the new regime of regulation that most directly arises from the scandals of the 1990s, when the two main parties were revealed as accepting donations from questionable sources, and suspicions existed that party policies, and government policies, were being adjusted to the interests of big donors. Now, all gifts in excess of £5,000 nationally and £1,000 locally must be declared.

It 'caps' the cost of general election campaigns. It sets the limit that can be spent on a national campaign at £30,000 per constituency, which means that parties contesting virtually all seats (as Conservative and Labour do) are limited to just under £20 million per campaign.

It establishes a wider set of rules for the registration of political parties. This is potentially the most far reaching consequence of the 2000 legislation. The Electoral Commission (see below) is a body with statutory power to register a political party – and registration is a condition of fighting elections under a party label. In considering whether to register, the Commission has to inspect and approve a party's scheme for regulating its financial affairs, such as the officers it appoints and the reporting arrangements it devises. This also extends to a system for regulating 'third parties' – in other words, registered, approved donors to parties.

It establishes a permanent, highly active regulator not only for parties, but for elections and referenda, in the form of the Electoral Commission. The Commission's statutory (legally prescribed) duties

BRIEFING 14.4

The Electoral Commission: a new regulator for political parties

The Electoral Commission, when established in 2000, was an innovation in British politics: for the first time, political parties (and the conduct of elections) were subject to a statutory regulatory body. The Commission's powers derive from the Political Parties, Elections and Referendums Act 2000 (PPERA).

The Boundary Committee for England – formerly the Local Government Commission for England – became a statutory committee of the Electoral Commission in April 2002. Thus the only statutory body hitherto concerned with the regulation of elections is now incorporated into the Commission. The Commission's main legal duties are:

- To keep a register of political parties under the 2000 Act. Without registration, an organization cannot now be named as a political party on any ballot paper (though individuals are still free to stand).
- To ensure that applicants for registration comply with the registration and financial regulatory requirements of the PPERA.
- To ensure that, once registered, parties comply with the statutory reporting requirements of the PPERA and the relevant parts of the Representation of People Act 1983.
- To regulate the conduct of any future referendums in Britain.

Beyond its strict statutory duties, the Commission is now the main institution offering guidance on the workings of the 2000 Act, and has a wider responsibility to review the functioning of competitive elections in Britain.

- The establishment of the Electoral Commission in 2000 was an epoch making event in the history of political parties in Britain. It signals a decisive change in the official view of parties: they are no longer private associations, but public bodies who must be regulated as to their organization and finances.

relate in part to the issues summarized above. In particular, it registers political parties (over 120 registered thus far) and it receives and scrutinizes reports on the sources and size of political donations. In effect it is the main scrutinizer of the financial affairs of all registered political parties. But it does much more. It is now the main public body concerned with the regulation of elections – including referendums – in the widest sense. The range of these duties is impressively wide. It includes:

- preparing and publishing a report on administration of all relevant elections, including all referendums;
- keeping under review and reporting on electoral boundaries of constituencies for both national parliaments and local government;
- reviewing and reporting on all political advertising via electronic media;

- keeping under review and reporting on the registration of political parties and their income and expenditure.

These statutory duties relate to the actual conduct of elections and of the main institutions that fight them – political parties. But the Commission also has wider responsibilities designed to improve the capacities of parties to contribute to the democratic process. These include:

- developing and administering policy development grants to political parties;
- promoting public awareness about the electoral process in Britain;
- regulating the wording of any referendum bill introduced in the UK.

THE CHANGING ORGANIZATION OF PARTIES: FROM MASS PARTIES TO CARTEL PARTIES?

Throughout the twentieth century political parties were institutions vital to British democracy. They provided one of the main mechanisms by which the people at large could express political views and, in particular, support competing political programmes. In principle they were thus a key means by which popular choices could be made between alternative policy preferences in government. They were also key institutions in the system of interest representation, because the two-party system that dominated British government after 1918 allied the two main parties to competing interests in Britain: the Labour Party to organized trade unions and a large section of the manual working class; the Conservatives to large parts of the business community and of the middle class. The parties were also important institutions of direct participation in politics because they both had a mass membership. But the nature of this mass participation showed that parties not only facilitated democratic participation – they also defined its limits. Labour and the Conservatives utterly dominated the party system and both, despite their different histories, were in turn heavily dominated by parliamentary leaderships that operated to a substantial degree independently of the party at large.

Important changes in organization, changes that now stretch back over more than three decades, are altering the structure of parties and the way they function – and in so doing are contributing to the changing character of democratic politics. The mass party is a thing of the past, as antiquated as the manual typewriter and the roneo duplicator – two technologies, incidentally, that it used very effectively. This change is partly due to changed patterns of campaigning, which now demand much less in the way of huge numbers of active supporters on the doorsteps of individual voters.

Parliamentary parties are no longer so independent of the wider party organization. This is partly because the parties that have risen to challenge the supremacy of Labour and Conservatives – such as the nationalists and the Liberal Democrats – have much stronger traditions of engagement between their parliamentary leadership and the party in the country. But as we have seen there have also been changes in the organization of Labour and the Conservatives, and these changes have given the party outside Parliament a bigger say in party government. The best 'headline' sign of the change is the way the choice of party leader is no longer the monopoly of Labour or Conservative Westminster parliamentarians.

The role of the party in interest representation has also changed. There has been a weakening of links in the case of the Conservatives and Labour between the big interests to which they were historically close: business and the trade unions. In part this separation is the work of the party leaderships, as they have calculated that they need to widen their electoral base, and to do this need to distance themselves from sectional interests. This process has been an important feature of the reshaping of the union–Party relationship in the Labour Party in recent years. In part the separation is due to organized interests. As we saw in Chapter 8 functional interests are increasingly well organized in their own specialist institutions, and close alliance with political parties increasingly looks like a very blunt instrument of interest representation. Why not cut out the middleman – the political party – and do the job directly through interest group organization?

The decline of mass membership; the increasingly distant connection with special interests; the staggering cost of the new styles of campaigning: all have combined to create serious financial problems for political parties. It was these financial problems that lay behind the scandals of the 1990s and the reforms of the legislation of 2000 described above. They thus explain the final important organizational change described in this chapter: the increasing regulation of political parties by a public body, the Electoral Commission.

The summary we have provided so far suggests that parties are declining institutions. But there is another way of reading change: that while a particular kind of mass party is in decline, this is not true of 'party' as a political phenomenon. The influential theory of the 'cartel party' suggests that we are seeing not decline, but transformation (Katz and Mair 1995). This theory suggests the following. Parties are increasingly providing functions for the state – like supplying leaders in government – rather than functions for the wider society. As state servants they are decreasingly reliant on money or membership from that wider society. They are 'cartel' parties because, like firms that can 'rig' a market by colluding in a cartel, they manipulate the political market place to protect the position of established parties against outsiders.

It is plain that the marks of 'decline' in the British mass party, notably the fall in membership, can be read as a shift to a cartel-like character. The appearance of a state regulator, in the form of the Electoral Commission, is also consistent with the cartel party thesis. The history of state funding of parties also 'fits' the thesis. State funding began in 1975 as a quite modest subsidy to opposition parties in the Westminster House of Commons, to help provide some research support. In the 1990s it was

DEBATING POLITICS 14.1

Political parties: friend or enemy of British democracy?

PARTIES ARE VITAL TO THE HEALTH OF BRITISH DEMOCRACY

- Elections are at the centre of the democratic process – and parties are the way choice is offered at elections.
- Parties remain open, voluntary bodies through which citizens can participate in politics.
- Parties have become increasingly democratic in their formal organization and increasingly transparent in their financing and regulation.
- Parties are vital institutions of democratic interest representation, complementing interest groups and catering in particular for groups that find formal interest organization difficult.

PARTIES DAMAGE THE HEALTH OF BRITISH DEMOCRACY

- The choice parties offer voters in British parliamentary elections is limited and crude and fails to allow discriminating selection.
- Parties have lost huge numbers of members in the last generation and have become moribund institutions dependent on state handouts and rich backers.
- The adversarial style practised by the main British parties produces crude, aggressive debate which alienates most citizens.
- Behind a rhetoric of common interest parties are tied to sectional interests and parliamentary factions.

first extended to the House of Lords and then, in 1999, was increased greatly in scale (by a threefold magnitude). Funding of opposition parties is plainly a significant step to transforming the party into a state institution. In the face of party funding scandals of recent years party leaders have also contemplated a significant extension of state funding to cover campaign costs, something recommended by an official report in 2007 (Philips 2007), though they have failed yet to reach cross-party agreement on this measure.

Despite this evidence, it is doubtful that the cartel party thesis fits Britain well. (It does fit parties in some other European states better.) There are two reasons for this. First, while the scale of state funding has indeed grown, the parties still rely tremendously on wider society to provide them with the funds to fight elections. Second, the evidence of party support does not support the cartel thesis, or at least suggests that, if these are cartel parties,

they are pretty hopeless at rigging the political marketplace. The history of party support, as we have seen in this chapter and will see in even more detail in Chapter 17, is a history of declining support for the dominant institutions in the 'cartel'. Outsiders – Liberal Democrats, nationalists – have long threatened to 'bust' the cartel, and in the 2010 general election all but finally did so.

One further reason the established parties are an ineffective cartel takes us back to a key theme of this book: the reality of multilevel governance. Devolution has accelerated the spatial fragmentation of the parties. The different logics of electoral competition under different electoral systems in the devolved governments, and the different pressures created by those governing systems, have all undermined the parties as 'UK' institutions. Thus not only is the mass party in decline; parties that maintain a UK-wide cohesion are also becoming increasingly hard to sustain.

Review OF CHAPTER 14

Four themes have dominated this chapter:

◖◗ Parties organize for many reasons, and these different motives often import great tension into the internal life of parties.

◖◗ The single most important long-term change to come over party organization in the last generation is the decline of the party with a mass membership.

◖◗ The party's role in interest representation has been partly supplanted by the rise of specialist pressure groups.

◖◗ Parties, once largely private associations that ran their own affairs, are being increasingly regulated by public rules.

FURTHER READING

ESSENTIAL

If you read only one item it should be the chapter by Mair on parties in Flinders et al. (2009): it has the unique merit of setting changes in British party organization in a comparative frame.

RECOMMENDED

Webb (2000) is the most important modern study of British parties, though an update is now urgently required. McKenzie (1963), the great classic study, is a 'must' for any serious beginner on the organization and history of parties. Pinto-Duschinsky (1981) is a great study of finance, with implications that go well beyond finance; and the work of Fisher (for instance 2003) always keeps the story up to date. Whiteley and Seyd (2002) are authoritative on party activism. The newly important Liberal Democrats are the subjects of a fine study by Russell and Fieldhouse (2004).

Parties and their ideologies

CONTENTS

AIMS

This chapter:

- [ ] Describes the meaning of 'ideology'

- [ ] Sketches the ideologies of the parties that have been historically dominant in British politics

- [ ] Sketches challenging and marginalized ideologies

- [ ] Summarizes the changing role of ideology in British party politics

IDEAS, IDEOLOGIES AND PARTY POLITICS

Like many key concepts in the study of politics 'ideology' has been given many different meanings. These can range from the particular to the general. 'Ideology' can be reserved for political views that are expressed as an elaborate, consciously worked out, political doctrine; or it can refer to the broad world view of a group or individual, often consisting of little more than a set of implicit assumptions. It is perfectly possible for a political party to disavow ideology in the former sense; but in the latter sense all institutions, and indeed even all individuals, operate with some kind of ideology. The meaning employed in this chapter is closer to the latter, more general, view. We are concerned to explore the broad view of the political world expressed by parties. The reason for adopting this approach is that it allows us to explore some important distinctions: notably, between parties that do indeed have an ideology which consists of an elaborate set of doctrines, and those which reject this approach to politics, operating instead with ideologies that involve only fleeting and implicit assumptions.

Just as there are different views of the meaning of 'ideology', so there are also contrasting views of the role of ideologies in political parties. A simple but helpful distinction is between the instrumental and the idealistic view of 'ideology'.

The instrumental view does not deny that parties have ideologies, but sees them primarily as instruments for other purposes – notably, in a democracy, the purpose of winning elections. We can find this view of 'ideology' both in the formal academic literature and in common everyday views of the parties in Britain. In academic studies, one of the most influential bodies of theory is derived from rational actor models. In these models parties – to be more precise, those who really control them – are thought to be primarily engaged in winning elections or, even, maximizing the vote of the party. Hence the label, because these actors have an overriding goal – vote winning – to which all other goals are subservient. (The classic study which popularized this view in political science is Downs 1957.) Thus party ideology will be adopted, modified and discarded according to its ability to win votes; it is really just part of the 'brand image' the party uses in the political marketplace. This formal academic view is often echoed in everyday 'cynical' views of parties and politicians, views suggesting that they just adopt policies without any guiding principle.

The idealistic view gives a much more powerful influence to ideology. It sees parties as shaped at least as much by the ideas of their leading members as by

■ The Labour Party's adoption of the red rose as its 'logo' was the work of Peter Mandelson who served as the Party's Director of Communications, 1985–90 – the exact period, we shall see, when the foundations of 'New Labour' were laid. Its adoption illustrates particularly well the debate about the significance of ideology in British politics. It can be viewed in diametrically opposed ways. One way sees it as a self-conscious marketing gimmick by Mandelson, the Party's genius of presentation. Red is the traditional colour of the left, and its most important symbol is the red flag which has waved above numerous demonstrations. The new logo retained the colour but absorbed it into the quintessentially English symbol of a rose. But a different view points out that the changes that occurred in the 1990s were not mere marketing developments – they did indeed coincide with substantive changes in ideology. Thus the new logo could be given an alternative interpretation, as more than a marketing device, symbolizing instead a real change in the ideological identity of the Party.

either the interests they represent or the demands of vote getting. Ideology is here pictured as part of the core identity of the party and understanding any party demands understanding both what party members themselves say are the principles of the party and what sort of view of the world we can deduce from what they say. One of the most important academic studies of British politics published in the last 50 years, Beer's *Modern British Politics* (1969/1982), is largely about the changing ideologies of the two main parties. It takes ideology seriously and assumes that understanding the parties means understanding their ideological identities. The idealistic view does not dismiss the importance of interests – including an interest in winning votes – on what parties think. But it does work on the assumption that we should take ideas in parties, and what parties say are their ideas, seriously.

CONSERVATIVES AND THEIR IDEOLOGIES

The myth of a non-ideological party

We begin with the Conservative Party for a simple reason: it has been the most important party in British politics. A simple measure of this is tenure in office. Although the Party experienced electoral hard times between 1997 and 2010, viewed over the long term the Conservatives are easily the most successful party in British politics. In the period since 1918 – the date when the modern party system first emerged – the Conservatives have been in government, either alone or as the dominant coalition partner, for over 50 years. And that reflects in turn the fact that some of the most powerful interests in British society have traditionally allied themselves with the Party: for instance, most of the business community, large and small; and the great mass of middle-class voters, especially those working in the private sector. What Conservatives believe, and what they think they believe, is of utmost importance to the study of British government and to the wider understanding of British society. Were the Conservative Party to disappear tomorrow, understanding Conservative ideology would be vital, because the Party has left indelible marks on British government and society.

The distinction between what Conservatives believe, and what they think they believe, is important, because they have a persistent self-image which dismisses the importance of ideology in the party. In political arguments they are fond of picturing themselves as the 'commonsense' Party by contrast with the impractical theorists in the Labour Party. This is more than a bluff in political argument. If we glance at Documenting Politics 15.1 we will see some examples of this from classic statements of Conservatives principles.

This self-image of the Conservatives as a 'non-ideological' Party does express important truths about the nature of Conservatism, notably the unwillingness to be drawn into elaborate, extended statements of what it stands for. But as an argument that Conservatism is a non-ideological party it is both psychologically and historically untenable. It is psychologically untenable because it implies that Conservatives are some special breed of political animal free from the commitments to ideas that mark all others in politics. In the general sense of 'ideology' that we are using, Conservatives are as governed as anyone by broad assumptions about the nature of the political world in which they operate. It is historically untenable because, as we shall discover when we turn to the reality of Conservative politics, the Party has indeed often been ideological in a more narrow sense: it has been guided by highly specific political doctrines.

The reality: the richness of Conservative ideology

The most striking feature of the Conservative Party is not that it is bereft of ideology, but that it is very rich in ideological traditions. Nor is this surprising, because the Party has been around for a very long time and, over that time, has acquired successive traditions and interests. Conservatives can trace their lineage back to seventeenth-century Britain when a 'Tory' faction emerged that defended a strong monarchy against the claims of those who wished to elevate Parliament at the expense of the Crown. 'Tory' was then an abusive term that originally referred to Irish bandits; but most modern Conservatives are happy to accept 'Tory' as a slightly slangy short label for their Party. The long history of the Party means that examining its ideologies is a bit like undertaking a piece of political archaeological research: the long history of the Party has left successive layers of ideas.

Although Conservatives can trace a line back to the seventeenth century the modern party originated in the nineteenth century from a great split over a mixture of principles and interests. In 1846 the leader of what was then known as the Tory Party, Sir Robert Peel, repealed the Corn Laws – legislation that had prevented the import of cheap corn, protecting British agriculture from competition in the process. The Corn Laws were opposed by an alliance of industrial capitalists and workers, who both wanted cheaper food; they were supported by farming interests who wanted to exclude foreign competition. In opting for repeal Peel was therefore deserting the traditional interests of the old Tory Party. But the ideological inheritance of the division in the Party that resulted was complex. The modern party was born out of the group that split from Peel, and its most important voice was Benjamin Disraeli, the dominant figure in the Party in the second half of the nineteenth century. Disraeli began fashioning a distinctive ideology for the Conservatives: by picturing them as the opponent of the new industrial society that was developing in Britain; by opposing the doctrines of free trade abroad and minimal government at home that were advocated by the new industrial interests; and by picturing the Conservatives as a Party that would unite society under the leadership of a traditional, landed, aristocratic elite, protecting the poor against the insecurity and poverty produced by industrialism.

But by the time of Disraeli's death in 1881 the Party had been transformed once again. It had now made its peace with the Industrial Revolution and was the most important party of the wealthy and powerful in Britain. It was closely identified with the great new Empire that

DOCUMENTING POLITICS 15.1

Conservatives on Conservative belief (Burke, Disraeli, Hogg, Cameron)

- Edmund Burke on the reach of the state: 'The state ought to confine itself to what regards the state, namely the exterior establishment of its religion; its magistracy; its revenue; its military force by land and sea; the corporations that owe their existence to its fiat; in a word, to everything that is *truly public and properly public* – to the public peace, to the public safety, to the public order, to the public prosperity.' (1795)

- Benjamin Disraeli on the role of the Tory Party: 'The Tory party is only in its proper position when it represents Tory principles. Then it is truly irresistible. Then it can uphold the throne, and the altar, the majesty of the empire, the liberty of the nation, and rights of the multitude.' (1862)

- Quintin Hogg on Conservative attitudes to politics: 'Conservatives do not believe that political struggle is the most important thing in life. In this they differ from Communists, Socialists, Nazis, Fascists, Social Creditors and most members of the Labour Party. The simplest among them prefer fox-hunting – the wisest religion.' (1947)

- David Cameron: 'I am a Conservative because of the values that I have believed in all my life: family, responsibility and opportunity. I am a Conservative because I believe that those values lead inexorably to a political agenda whose central mission is to give people more power and control over their lives ... because we want people to rely on their family, not the state; because you can't take responsibility for something unless you have control over it; and because true opportunity means having the freedom to achieve all you can in life.' (2009)

■ The striking feature of statements of Conservative principles is not only their variety, as illustrated here, but also how far they are the product of particular circumstances – a feature of which Conservatives themselves are proud. Edmund Burke (1729–97) is the greatest of 'British' Conservative philosophers (he was actually Irish). What is striking about his account of the state is how wide are its potential functions – peace, safety, order, prosperity. The passage was written in 1795, however, at the height of the struggle with revolutionary France. Benjamin Disraeli (1804–81) was the greatest Conservative of the next century: novelist, opportunist, statesman and creator of modern Conservatism. The passage shows Disraeli's political prescience: even before the extensions of the franchise to encompass the middle and working classes he is 'positioning' the Party as a national Party. Quintin Hogg (1906–2001) wrote his account in the most influential statement of Conservative principles produced since the end of the Second World War. Its importance is magnified by the fact that Hogg later spent over 40 years at or near the top of the Conservative Party. The passage is a reaction against nearly a decade of 'total politics' when private life had indeed been dominated by public events, notably war and the threat of war. And David Cameron's words show what happens when a practising politician tries to define Conservatism.

Sources: White (1950:81, 226, 31); Cameron quotation from http://www.telegraph.co.uk/comment/personal-view/3642528/David-Cameron-What-makes-me-Conservative.html.

Britain had acquired in Africa and India. It accepted free trade and was increasingly the natural home of the leading industrialists. Disraeli's greatest successor, the Marquess of Salisbury, fitted the old mould in coming from a traditional aristocratic family; but he had been an opponent of even the limited social reforms that the Conservatives under Disraeli had actually pursued. By the turn of the century the Party was the home of the most orthodox defenders of minimal government and free trade. Thus while Peel and his followers had split from the old Tories over exactly these issues in 1846, the inheritors of the Peel tradition in the next generation had migrated back to the Conservative Party. At the same time, the great struggles over the national identity of the UK had added another dimension to its ideology. Faced with campaigns for Home Rule in the Celtic nations – especially Ireland – it invented itself as the 'Unionist' Party, the defender of the union of the UK under the Monarchy. The 'Unionist' tradition was strengthened when many Liberals who opposed the Home Rule for Ireland policies promoted by the Liberals' greatest leader, William Gladstone, crossed over to the Conservative Party.

At the start of the twentieth century the Party stood for three broad principles:

● an economic system based on free markets;
● imperialism;
● the supremacy in the British Isles of the political institutions based in London – the Westminster Parliament and the English Crown.

Lord Salisbury, leader of the Party 1885–1902, died in 1903. Were he to be resurrected a century or so on he would be astonished, and probably appalled, at some of the ideological changes in the Party, but he would also approve some of the principles it still defends. Support for imperialism has disappeared – indeed it was Conservative Governments in the 1950s and early 1960s that dismantled much of the Empire. All that remains is a broad conviction among some Conservatives that Britain has a big role to play on the world stage – a conviction that, we shall see shortly, is important in the Party's attitude to the EU. Lord Salisbury would also be appalled at the Party's attitude to the Union. The Party still calls itself 'Unionist'. But after a rather perfunctory opposition to the Labour Government's devolution reforms it now accepts the devolved assemblies in Wales and Scotland. More important is its abandonment of Unionism in the Irish case, the great historical issue that forged Conservative identity. Until the 1960s the UUP MPs returned to the House of Commons used to vote as a block with the Conservative Party. That alliance ended a generation ago, though the general election of May 2010 was fought in a rather fragile alliance with the United Ulster Unionists, the less successful of the two main Unionist parties in the Province. Under John Major's premiership the Party in Government abandoned the claim to distinctive British sovereignty in Northern Ireland. It has also, albeit with some grumbles and hesitations, accepted the great limits on British sovereignty now in place in the peace settlement negotiated in 1998 – the details of which we examined in Chapter 11.

The one key component of Conservative ideology that Lord Salisbury would recognize is the Party's continuing defence of the free market economy. Over the century the Conservatives have nevertheless sometimes deeply qualified this defence. In the first 30 years of the twentieth century the Party was internally divided over the issue of how far it should abandon free trade, and it

DOCUMENTING POLITICS 15.2

'Circumstances produce theories': Conservatism as traditionalism and pragmatism

'The great object of our new school of statesmen ... is to form political institutions on abstract principles of theoretic science, instead of permitting them to spring from the course of events, and to be naturally created by the necessities of nations. It would appear that this scheme originated in the fallacy of supposing that theories produce circumstances, whereas the very converse of this proposition is correct and circumstances produce theories.'

(Benjamin Disraeli, 1835)

■ This passage from the greatest of nineteenth-century Conservative politicians, Benjamin Disraeli, introduces two recurrent themes in the Conservatives' own accounts of what they stand for: common-sense opposition to the fancy theorizing of their opponents (Liberals in the nineteenth century, socialists in the twentieth and twenty-first); and a pragmatic fashioning of policy to meet immediate circumstances.

Source: White (1950:36).

finally did abandon it at the start of the 1930s. After 1945, for a generation, it supported large scale nationalization and a large state-provided welfare system. But compared with its main opponent, the Labour Party, even at the height of its support for state intervention, it was still the more 'market friendly' party. In the last two decades of the twentieth century this defence of free markets became, as we shall see, much more prominent. This present state of affairs is in large part the product of a great upheaval in Conservative ideology – one that took place under the leadership of Margaret Thatcher (1975–90).

Modern Conservative ideology: the Thatcher legacy in ideology and policy

Margaret Thatcher became leader of the Conservative Party in 1975, displacing Edward Heath. Under Heath's leadership, especially in his years as Prime Minister (1970–74), the Party departed from many traditional Conservative positions.

People in Politics   15.1

Three makers of Conservative thought

Edmund Burke (1729–97)

typified the Conservative approach to political thinking in uniting a career as a practical politician with the life of a philosopher. The event that crystallized Burke's conservatism was the French Revolution (1789). His *Reflections* on the Revolution argued for a peaceful, aristocratic constitutionalism, piecemeal change and the importance of recognizing that institutions were rooted in their past and should not be radically torn from that past. Though for much of his life he was an active reformer, his reputation rests on this classic statement of Conservatism.

Earl of Salisbury (1830–1903)

was also a typical Conservative: though an intellectual by inclination he never systematized his political thought into a definitive statement. But, especially in his two longest periods as Prime Minister (1886–92 and 1895–1902), the core of the ideology that shaped Conservatism for nearly a century evolved: a vision of Britain as a world power, notably as an imperial power; a vision of a United Kingdom, under the Crown; and economic and social policies designed to unify traditional aristocratic interests with those of the growing suburban middle classes.

Friedrich von Hayek (1899–1992)

was an Austrian philosopher who spent much of his working life in Britain. Hayek disavowed Conservatism, defending a systematic philosophy defending free markets and government restricted by explicit constitutional rules. But after Mrs Thatcher became Leader (1975) the Conservative elite became much more interested in systematic doctrines, and Hayek exercised both a direct influence on Mrs Thatcher and, more indirectly, on the whole Thatcher generation that dominated the Conservative Party in the 1980s.

Cartoons: Shaun Steele

■ These three figures illustrate the variety of Conservatism, both in ideas and sources. They encompass a rigorous systematic theorist, Hayek, and in Salisbury a typical instinctive Conservative who worked his philosophy out in political practice. They also encompass an establishment figure (Salisbury was from one of England's great aristocratic families); a semi-outsider (Burke was Irish and depended all his life on aristocratic patronage); and a complete outsider (Hayek was Austrian by birth, middle European by cultural inclination, and never a Conservative).

- It abandoned any affection for the old Empire, becoming instead the leader of pro-European opinion in Britain. It successfully negotiated British membership of the then EEC in 1973, in the face of opposition from the dominant section of the Labour Party.
- It not only accepted large scale public ownership and a large scale welfare state, but actually expanded both in its period of office.
- It spent its last two years in office attempting to run a full scale system of state control of pay and prices, backed by law.
- It tried, albeit unsuccessfully, to manage the economy in partnership with the trade unions.

By contrast, by the time Mrs Thatcher was deposed as Leader and Prime Minister in 1990 the Party occupied very different positions:

- it had established the free market as the entirely dominant mechanism in fixing pay and prices;
- it had broken with the unions, reducing their power greatly by changing the law and confronting them in large scale strikes;
- it dismantled almost all the nationalized industries, selling off most state enterprise to the private sector;
- it had established itself as the most 'Eurosceptic' of all the major British political parties.

We will often encounter these revolutionary changes in policy later in this book and need not examine them in detail here. What matters is the change in ideological assumptions that made Thatcherism such a break with the past. While Thatcherism often invoked some of the Party's ideological traditions – for example support for free markets – in both its approach and the scale of the changes introduced it was novel. The novelty of Thatcherism as a Conservative ideology lay in five features.

It was self-consciously 'ideological'. Conservatism had always been ideological, but as we saw earlier the Party rarely liked to talk much about it or to expound ideas systematically, preferring to pick and mix from the various traditions as the occasion suited. Thatcherism presented itself as a self-conscious, coherent philosophy (even when in practice it was much less systematic). The most important theorist of Thatcherism among practising politicians, Sir Keith Joseph, was deeply and openly influenced by some of the great economic theorists of the free market, like the Austrian economist Friedrich von Hayek; even Thatcher herself claimed to be so influenced.

It was radical in ambitions. Before Thatcherism, Conservative leaders had normally liked to say that they

'conserved' – in other words, accepted change, but rarely initiated it. (Indeed this was one of the main reasons why Hayek rejected conservatives: he argued that they usually ended up conserving the socialism and collectivism of their opponents.) Thatcherism was not 'conservative': it set out to make fundamental changes in economy, society and government.

It radically changed the role of markets in the British economy. The single most important way Thatcherism was radical in thought and deed was that it fundamentally altered the role of the markets in the British economy. Thatcherism believed in free markets. Though many of the great reforms of the years of Thatcher's period in office were the result of on the spot tactical decisions rather than some long term strategy, nevertheless Thatcher and her supporters practised what they preached. By the time the Conservatives lost office in the 1997 general election Britain had, as a result of government reforms, a transformed role for the market compared with the situation inherited by them in 1979. It had labour markets which were among the freest from trade union restrictions in Western Europe. It had sold off about 40 per cent of what had been in public ownership at the end of the 1970s, including industries central to the old industrial economy (for instance steel) and those central to the new high technology economy (for instance telecommunications).

It radically changed the role of the state. Radicalism about markets involved withdrawing the state from some areas – but it meant radically empowering the central state in others. Thatcherism greatly centralized state authority in Britain: it used the law to subject a whole range of interests (ranging from local government, to trade unions, to universities) to central state control. It did so for a reason spelt out most compellingly by Gamble, the leading analyst of Thatcherite ideology: because remaking free markets in a radical way could only be done through a strong state which would defeat and control those who opposed free markets (see Gamble 1994).

It believed Britain's future lay with globalization. The high point of Thatcherism coincided with a surge in the integration of the global economy – and Thatcherism believed in exposing Britain to that surge. In the Thatcher years the economy of the south-east of England, especially in finance and commerce, was more closely integrated into this wider global economy, and Britain as a whole became the most important centre in the EU for inward investment by multinational companies. In this commitment lay another feature of Thatcherism that became increasingly important during the later years of her Premiership: its scepticism about the EU. Although only a tiny minority of Conservatives

BRIEFING 15.1

The contradictions of Thatcherism

'Thatcherism' is a rarity: a political creed named after a British Prime Minister. (There is no corresponding 'Blairism' or even 'Churchillism'.) But Thatcher never claimed to be a political philosopher, and so we have to infer the meaning of Thatcherism from what her governments did in office (1979–90). And what they did pointed in contradictory directions. On the one hand, they dismantled many state controls:

- sold numerous state enterprises to the private sector;
- withdrew state aid from many ailing industries;
- decisively turned away from state regulation of prices and incomes;
- obliged many institutions that remained part of the state (education, health, local government) to 'contract out' many of their functions by competition to private firms.

But in the Thatcher years, there also occurred:

- increased central control over numerous parts of the public sector, such as local government and the education system;
- more central control and direction of policing;
- the active use of the law and other kinds of central state power to curb the power of forces in wider society like the trade unions;
- the active use of state power to oblige firms to combat cartels and price fixing in the economy.

Was Thatcherism just opportunistic or incoherent? The most convincing answer, given by Gamble (1994), is that it was neither: building a free market demanded also more central control – 'a free market and a strong state'.

■ Debates about whether Thatcherism has any ideological coherence are part of a wider tradition, of debating whether Conservatism has any ideological coherence. But this particular debate is of outstanding importance, because Thatcherism reshaped all British politics, not just Conservatism.

---

advocated withdrawal from the EU, a growing majority in the Party became increasingly hostile to further European integration. This hostility was partly due to the belief that an integrated economy also meant the creation of a powerful European state which would intervene in free markets. But it also reflected a belief in the wider importance of global markets and a suspicion that the EU was designed to create a 'fortress' within which the European economy would trade with itself.

The fate of the Thatcher legacy

Mrs Thatcher was forced from office by her Party in 1990, but that made no material difference to the triumph of Thatcherite ideology in the Party for its remaining years in office to 1997. The 'remaking' of the Party after its election defeat in that year likewise showed many continuities. Indeed some elements – especially scepticism about the EU – if anything became stronger. But after David Cameron's election as Leader in 2005 there was a distinct change in language and style, an attempt to modernize the party culturally. In his acceptance speech after election as leader he immediately struck a new tone:

I said when I launched the campaign that we need to change in order to win. Now that I have won we will change. We will change the way we look. Nine out of ten Conservative MPs are white men. We need to change the scandalous under-representation of women in the Conservative Party and we will do that. We need to change the way we feel. No more grumbling about modern Britain. I live in a world as it is not how it was. Our best days lie ahead. We need to change the way we think.

Of course cultural change of this kind need not mean a radical departure from the Thatcher legacy. Indeed, we shall see that the most important part of the legacy – concerning markets and the state – was conserved by New Labour after 1997. Thus 'Cameroonian Conservatism' has been more about matching the success New Labour enjoyed for many years in speaking to the electorate in a more winning language than the Conservatives were able to enjoy.

Thatcherism transformed the dominant ideology of the Conservative Party. But its achievements were even wider: it also had profound effects on the Conservatives' main rival in the Westminster system, as we shall now see.

THE LABOUR PARTY IDEOLOGY: HISTORY, CRISIS, REMAKING

The origins of Labour's ideology

The Labour Party has always been more self-consciously at ease with ideas in politics than has its Conservative opponent. 'Intellectuals' in Britain in the twentieth century were more inclined to left-wing than to Conservative politics; and the Party itself has always contained a high proportion of 'ideas workers': teachers among local activists; university lecturers and journalists among national leaders. The Party's Conservative opponents often tried to exploit this by picturing Labour as a party of socialist dogmatism and of hare-brained professors weaving wildly impractical theories. In practice, Labour was almost as ideologically fluid as were the Conservatives before the rise of Thatcherism.

Labour was finally created as a national party in 1918, the moment being marked by the adoption of its constitution. That constitution certainly seemed to mark the Party as socialist. The famous Clause 4, which was reprinted until the 1990s on the membership cards of all Party members, committed the Party to 'common ownership of the means of production, distribution and exchange' (see Documenting Politics 15.5).

But this 'socialist' constitution was adopted at an unusual moment: a rare high point of revolutionary ferment in Britain as the shock waves of the 1917 Bolshevik Revolution in Russia swept westward across Europe. That wave soon receded, and in reality the 1918 constitution created a federation containing very different ideological traditions. The most important traditions came from the following groups.

Christian socialists, especially those brought up in highly democratic Protestant denominations like Methodism, were prominent. There is indeed a long tradition of Christian political radicalism in Britain that pre-dates Labour and which it partly inherited. In some cases this takes the form of a full blown vision, mainly derived from the New Testament, of a 'new heaven, new earth' – of a society remade in the image of a Christian community, where the equality of souls before God is matched by equality in political power and economic resources. Some of the most important figures in the Party's intellectual history, like R. H. Tawney, have been products of this tradition (see People in Politics 15.2).

Social reformers overlapped with the Christian Socialists. The single most important group in making the Labour Party were the trade unions, who were already well organized and politically influential before the Party ever appeared. Not surprisingly the trade unions had their eyes on immediate bread and butter reforms of things like working conditions. Social reformers did not want to revolutionize Britain in the manner of socialists; they wanted to use the power of the state to reform society so as to curb the effects of free markets. This tradition in the Labour Party was greatly strengthened by a historical coincidence. The great source of social reform in the early years of the twentieth century was the Liberal Party, whose government introduced reforms like old age pensions and health insurance before the First World War. But the Liberal Party was destroyed by internal divisions during the First War and Labour inherited much of its social reforming tradition and indeed some of its social reforming activists. From this group also Labour inherited a tradition of radical dissent about foreign policy. There had been an important wing of the Liberal Party that opposed imperialism at the height of empire and supported pacifist, or pacifist leaning, foreign policies. Many from this tradition of dissent migrated into Labour after the collapse of Liberalism.

Fabian reformers were small in number but disproportionately important. Indeed the 1918 'socialist' constitution was drafted by a Fabian, Sidney Webb. The Fabian Society was founded in 1884 and throughout its history has mostly been dominated by small groups of London-based intellectuals. Fabianism took its name from the Roman general Quintus Fabius Maximus (died, 203 BC) nicknamed the Delayer for his characteristic method of wearing down his opponent Hannibal by ultra-cautious military tactics involving indirect engagement, harassment and small skirmishes. (The connection shows another link in the Labour chain of historical ideas: the influence of the classics on the educated Victorian mind.) Fabian ideology was

People in Politics 15.2

Makers of Labour Party thought

Sidney Webb (1859–1947)

Began life as a radical Liberal – a characteristic of many early Labour thinkers. He helped define 'Fabianism', a doctrine that capitalism could be reshaped gradually from within by experts informed by detailed research. This gradualism deeply influenced the practice of Labour Governments. Webb also helped draft the original Clause 4 of the Labour Party Constitution (see Documenting Politics 15.5). Most of his intellectual and practical work was done in partnership with his wife, Beatrice (1858–1943).

R. H. Tawney (1880–1962)

Both an academic historian and a polemicist, he profoundly shaped 'ethical' socialism – a particularly British version rooted in religious commitment which looked back to older radical movements, such as the 'Levellers' in the seventeenth-century civil war. He stressed the importance of social and economic equality and the importance of democratizing the practice of government. The commitment of many contemporary Labour leaders to a version of Christian socialism echoes Tawney's ethical influences.

George Orwell (1903–53)

Novelist and journalist. Though long a columnist on the Labour supporting journal *Tribune* Orwell was no orthodox Labour supporter. But his writings deeply influenced Labour intellectuals in the second half of the twentieth century. Two influences are important: his widely read satires on Soviet Communism helped the Labour left line up against the Soviets in the Cold War and made it deeply hostile to violent revolution; and his explorations of English identity helped define a perceived 'British' kind of socialism.

Cartoons: Shaun Steele

■ Labour Party thought resembles that of the Conservative Party in its avoidance of systematic theory. The mix of 'practical' policy work (Webb), ethical argument (Tawney) and sharp polemic (Orwell) catches its diversity.

based on the gradual transformation of capitalism by long term reform. It blended easily with social reform, because the Fabians believed above all in the power of the state – especially of the central state machinery – to reform wider society. From the Fabians the Labour Party got its faith in central state intervention – for instance, via nationalized industries and the National Health Service, and likewise it got the metropolitan cast of mind which so dominated the Party for much of its history.

Marxist socialists were briefly important in the Party because the Party constitution was promulgated at a brief revolutionary moment in Britain – the moment at the close of the First World War when the impact of the Russian Revolution of 1917 had spread a wave of revolutionary support across Western Europe. But most of the minority of British Marxists were soon organized into separate movements, and Marxism became a minority influence in the Party.

The development and crisis of Labour ideology

We can see that from the beginning the Labour Party contained many different ideological traditions. The task of national leadership was to maintain some sort of unity between these. Great national crises often split the Party. This is what happened in the economic crisis of 1931, when Labour was in government. It led to a catastrophic general election defeat and a position of opposition and political weakness throughout the 1930s. But during and after the Second World War the different ideological traditions in the party were more or less unified around a common programme. All could sign up to the public ownership of important industries and to the creation of important institutions of the welfare state like the National Health Service (1948). But different groups signed up for different reasons: for socialists, this was a staging post to a transformed society; for social reformers part of the means by which capitalism would be controlled and humanized. Labour lost three successive general elections in the 1950s and the attempt by the Party leader, Hugh Gaitskell, to remove the 'socialist' Clause 4 of the Party constitution exposed these differences: for reformers like Gaitskell Clause 4 was an embarrassing, meaningless symbol; for socialists it was the guarantee of the Party's long term commitment to the transformation of capitalism.

Gaitskell's campaign was defeated, but in the 1980s the Party's ideology was convulsed and then transformed by a great crisis. This crisis had its origins in Labour's experience of government, especially in 1974–79. When Labour lost the general election in 1979 it had enjoyed the lion's share of government in the preceding 15 years.

But the experience satisfied none of the main ideological groups in the Party: socialist radicals saw only a failure to make any significant change in the nature of British capitalism; social reformers and Fabians saw, especially in the 1970s, a succession of failures in the task of efficiently managing and humanizing the market economy. The Party then suffered a series of electoral disasters: it lost four successive general elections (1979, 1983, 1987 and 1992) to the Conservatives; two of these (1983 and 1987) were huge parliamentary defeats, and Labour's share of the vote in 1983 was its lowest, at that point, since 1918. Labour had been defeated in a run of elections before in the 1950s, but then by a Conservative Party which won mostly by copying the Labour Party. The Conservative governments of the 1950s accepted most of the radical changes introduced by the Labour Governments of 1945–51: they accepted the welfare state, large scale public ownership and the responsibility to manage the economy so as to achieve full employment. But the victorious Conservatives of the 1980s were moved by a very different ideology – by the Thatcherism described earlier. As the Conservatives' radical policies unfolded, Labour was faced with the twin problems of how to counter them in elections and what, if anything, to do about reversing them if it was ever returned to government.

A triple crisis – of policy failure, electoral failure and the spectre of successful Thatcherism – dominated Labour ideology for the last two decades of the twentieth century. It led to the transformation of ideology and the emergence of the self-styled 'New Labour'.

New Labour: ideology remade

The Labour Party's early efforts to respond to its crises in the 1980s involved reasserting its radical socialist traditions. It fought the 1983 general election on an economic policy which advocated radical reversals of Thatcherite policies and the creation of a centrally planned, socialist economy in Britain. The greatest electoral defeat in the Party's history, in 1983, forced a rethink. The Party led by Tony Blair (1994–2007) is normally thought of as 'New Labour'. In reality the most important changes in official Labour ideology happened in the 1980s under the leadership of Neil Kinnock (1983–92), especially in the period 1985–87 when the Party established a commission on policy comprehensively to examine what it stood for.

This process produced a transformation of the ideology of the Labour Party, though this took some years to complete. Labour began by abandoning the policies influenced by the socialist traditions that had been advocated in the electoral disaster of 1983. Then, as the Conservatives' privatization programme became more

DOCUMENTING POLITICS 15.3

The predecessor of New Labour? Anthony Crosland on 'socialism'

Anthony Crosland's *The Future of Socialism* was published in 1956, and it greatly helped stimulate debates in the Labour Party about whether the Party's traditional version of socialism was now historically relevant. Crosland argued that many of Labour's traditional beliefs were outmoded: that capitalism had been transformed into a system where the profit motive was controlled by the state and the autonomy of professional managers; and that public ownership, to which the Party was attached as a mark of socialism, should actually be viewed pragmatically as one means of control among many. His arguments heralded much of the content of 'New Labour' in the 1980s and 1990s. But Crosland in *The Future of Socialism* was a figure very different from a new Labour politician in three key respects:

- *In objectives.* He argued that the Party should pursue greater equality, and in this connection argued for higher and more 'progressive' taxes and reform of institutions like the public schools and the grammar schools.

- *In values.* He favoured maximum freedom in private life, covering matters like divorce, sexual preferences and the organization of family life – all far away from New Labour's moral concerns with preserving traditional family values, and highly radical in the 1950s.

- *In style.* He thought that modern organizational politics were actually unimportant, and was thus far removed from the modern politician obsessed above all with politics: 'The time has come for a reaction: for a greater emphasis on private life, on freedom and dissent, on culture, beauty, leisure, and even frivolity. Total abstinence and a good filing-system are not now the right sign-posts to the socialist Utopia: or at least if they are, some of us will fall by the way-side.'

■ Crosland's book was the most intellectually distinguished attempt to restate socialism in the decades after the Second World War. But its importance is reinforced by Crosland's own career: he was a Labour MP and a leading figure in the Labour Cabinets of the 1960s and 1970s until his early death in 1977.

Source: Crosland (1956/64:357).

bold and sweeping in the 1980s, Labour moved through a succession of conciliatory responses. It had begun with total opposition to privatization and a commitment to renationalize what the Conservatives had sold to the private sector. It then moved to a position of abandoning a return to nationalization in favour of some notion of 'social ownership'. Next, it adopted a position of reluctant acceptance of the new status quo that the Conservatives had imposed. Finally, under the leadership of Blair it attempted to outbid the Conservatives by planning to privatize enterprises that even radical Thatcherism had not got round to, such as the country's air traffic control system.

These changes also entailed institutional and symbolic reforms. As we saw in the last chapter, a powerful historical influence on the ideology of the Labour Party had been its close links with the trade unions. Throughout the 1980s and 1990s a series of internal institutional reforms – such as in the running of the annual conference – reduced union influence in the Party. At the same time the Conservative Government's changes in the law governing industrial relations had greatly reduced the power of the unions in wider society. These changes made easier a further great adaptation by Labour: it accepted all the important changes in labour law introduced by the Conservatives that had been designed to weaken the ability of the unions to exercise power in collective bargaining. Labour also accepted much of the transformation of central state power under the Conservatives: increased controls over local government; more central control over the education system; and more centralization in the direction of parts of the

DOCUMENTING POLITICS 15.4

The parting of the ways: Neil Kinnock's 1985 conference speech

'With impossible promises you start with far fetched resolutions. They are then pickled into rigid dogma and you go through the years sticking to that, outdated, misplaced, irrelevant to the real needs. You end in the grotesque chaos of a Labour council hiring taxis to scuttle round the city to hand out redundancy notices.'

Neil Kinnock, Leader of the Labour Party, speech to Labour Party Annual Conference, 2 October 1985.

■ If there is one moment that can be said to mark the birth of New Labour it is this speech – not the election of Tony Blair as Leader in 1994. Neil Kinnock had been elected Leader in 1983 as the great hope of the Labour Left. The speech was an attack on the hard left militant faction who controlled, among other things, Liverpool City Council – the 'city' referred to in the speech. But it provoked a walk out in mid-speech by Eric Heffer, a leader of the old Left in the Party with whom Kinnock had in the past been in alliance. And the same 1985 Conference established a policy review which over the next two years abandoned most of the distinctive socialist economic policies on which the Party had fought the 1983 general election.

welfare state and of the agencies of public order, like the police.

Most of these changes had occurred in substance before Tony Blair became Leader. But after 1994 Labour also changed its symbols to match the substance of ideological change. A tiny but telling symbolic change came with the adoption of the red rose as the Party's 'logo': red is the traditional colour of left-wing socialism, but the rose is a highly traditional symbol of England. The new symbol thus cleverly fused traditional 'socialist' and 'English' symbols (see Image 15.1). The language used by the Labour Leader also stressed the importance of the market. The Party embraced another important ideological element in Thatcherism: it accepted the view that globalization of the world economy limited what any British government could do. All this culminated in a change that had been beyond Hugh Gaitskell as Leader: the removal of the old socialist Clause 4 in the party

constitution and its replacement by a 'market friendly' clause (see Documenting Politics 15.5).

Labour remade its ideology, therefore, to accommodate the Thatcher revolution. It largely accepted Thatcherism's radical departures: towards a freer market; towards a stronger central state to manage this freer market; and towards integrating Britain into a globally competitive economy. But this did not mean that Labour became simply a clone of Thatcherism. In two important areas it developed highly distinctive positions: on the constitution and on Europe.

Since the 1920s the two big parties had largely shared the same constitutional ideologies: they defended the 'Union' of the United Kingdom and they defended the supremacy of the Westminster Parliament. But in the 1990s Labour worked out radical constitutional policies, the content of which we have already summarized in earlier chapters. These included the devolution of important responsibilities to directly elected assemblies in Wales and Scotland, which were implemented after 1997 (see Chapter 10). They also included the radical (if not yet complete) reshaping of the Westminster Parliament by virtually abolishing the position of hereditary peers in the second chamber, the House of Lords. This constitutional radicalism was partly the product of the need to differentiate the Party from the Conservatives after it had accepted most of Thatcherism's economic policies. It was also partly the product of discontent in the Celtic nations with a political system that imposed Westminster governments upon them against the wishes of their own electorates: had Wales and Scotland been able to vote separately for governments after 1979 the Conservatives would never have ruled beyond England. The upshot was that New Labour rediscovered an old strand of Labour ideology: a constitutional radicalism that had been strong in the Labour movement in the early decades of the twentieth century but which disappeared when Labour rose as a party of government in Westminster. Gordon Brown's troubled Premiership (2007–10) was dominated by the catastrophic economic crisis, but it is striking that his first attempt to stamp a distinctive ideological mark on his Government was not distinctive at all: it offered constitutional reform, New Labour's big idea for over a decade, as his big idea also.

The reshaping of Labour's policy on Europe, though less historically radical, was also exceptionally important. Until the 1980s, of the two major parties Labour had been the less enthusiastic about Britain's membership of the EU. The Conservatives had negotiated British membership for 1973 and Labour only accepted this after much internal division. But from the 1980s Labour reinvented itself as a 'Europhile' Party, thus opening up a gap with the increasingly 'Eurosceptic' Conservatives. In

DOCUMENTING POLITICS 15.5

Old 'socialist' Clause 4 and New Labour's 'market friendly' Clause 4

Clause 4 of the Labour Party Constitution, 1918–1995

'To secure for the workers by hand or by brain the full fruits of their industry and the most equitable distribution thereof that may be possible, upon the basis of the common ownership of the means of production, distribution and exchange, and the best obtainable system of popular administration and control of each industry and service.'

Clause 4 of the Labour Party Constitution, 1995–

'The Labour Party is a democratic socialist party. It believes that by the strength of our common endeavour, we achieve more than we achieve alone so as to create for each of us the means to realise our full potential and for all of us a community in which power, wealth and opportunity are in the hands of the many not the few, where the rights we enjoy reflect the duties we owe, and where we live together, freely, in a spirit of solidarity, tolerance and respect.

To these ends we work for:

A dynamic economy, serving the public interest, in which the enterprise of the market and the rigour of competition are joined with the forces of partnership and co-operation to produce the wealth the nation needs and the opportunity for all to work and prosper, with a thriving private sector and high quality public services, where those undertakings essential to the common good are either owned by the public or accountable to them.'

■ The simplest contrast between the two clauses is length: the 1995 version is much wordier, even in the abbreviated version quoted here. There is a revealing reason for this. It is not necessarily that the drafters of the new clause were more verbose than the old. It reflects their attempt at a compromise between the old and the new. While the new Clause 4 abandons the old socialist rhetoric of common ownership, it still tries to gesture to traditional symbols of the party, such as solidarity and community. But it also contains radical new ideas: commending the market enterprise and competition, all viewed with hostility in the Party that felt at home with the old Clause 4.

part this change happened as the result of the long years of Thatcherite domination, because in those years the institutions of the EU often seemed to offer a source of influence which could be used by many of the groups opposing Thatcherite policies.

In the new millennium the ideological spectrum spanned by the two parties that then dominated Westminster became narrow. After more than a decade in office New Labour began to show the kind of intellectual exhaustion that afflicted the Conservatives following their long period in office between 1979 and 1997. But at the same time that the two dominant parties became increasingly indistinguishable ideologically, ideological diversity in the rest of the party universe increased, as we shall now see.

LIBERAL DEMOCRATS AND NATIONALISTS: ALTERNATIVE IDEOLOGIES

The ideology of the Liberal Democrats

The Liberal Democrats are the product of a long history, and their ideology reflects this. 'Liberal' is an echo of the historical origins of the Party: it is the descendant of the Liberal Party which before the First World War was the main party in British politics opposing the Conservatives. The Liberals were the governing party which took Britain into that War, and they emerged from it divided, and soon to be replaced as the Conservatives' main opponents by the new Labour Party. The War was catastrophic for the Liberals for reasons which still throw light on the nature of their ideology. By 1914 the Liberal Party contained two very different ideologies: a traditional radicalism which was suspicious of the state, whether it was involved in social and economic intervention at home or armed intervention abroad; and a new 'social reform' liberalism which viewed the state as an instrument for the pursuit of welfare reform at home and the defence of national interest abroad. The crises of war produced irreconcilable tensions between the two, broke the Party into pieces, and consigned it for the rest of the twentieth century to the margins of British politics – literally to the margins in most cases, since after the Second World War its small parliamentary representation tended to come from the Celtic margins of Britain.

But that history has left two marks on the modern ideology of the Party. There is still a tension between a desire to use the power of the state and a suspicion of state power. Throughout the modern history of the Party it has remained committed to its social reform tradition. Some of the most important figures in the creation of the modern welfare state were active Liberals in the period between the two great world wars. They included, for example, the economist John Maynard Keynes (1883–1946) on whose economic theories were built policies of extensive state intervention in the economy; and William Beveridge (1879–1963), who produced a famous official report (1942) on which some of the most important features of the modern welfare state were built. Indeed, since the end of the Second World War Liberals have been consistent supporters of the welfare state. The devolved government in Scotland gave the Liberals their first taste of participation in government for nearly 80 years, when they entered coalition in 1999 with Labour. They have been consistent supporters of active state intervention in Scotland.

Thus the ideology of modern Liberalism has adapted to a world of large scale state intervention in social and economic life. The modern Party is at ease with a big state. But elements of the different traditions of liberal individualism and suspicion of the state, which once dominated the Party, still also exist. The individualism is most obvious at the grass roots of the Party. Surveys show Liberal activists to be unusually strongly committed to the defence of civil liberties. The Party has long claimed to be a supporter of more decentralization in Britain. And, trying to practise what it preaches, much of the revival of the modern Party has been achieved by stressing grass roots political activity: taking the most local issues, such as the immediate quality of everyday lives, as the starting point for political campaigning. On foreign policy issues, too, the Liberal radical tradition that is pacifist by inclination has been influential: the Liberal Democrats in the Westminster Parliament opposed the commitment to war in Iraq in 2003, against majorities in both the Labour and Conservative parties.

Thus the modern Liberal Democrats simultaneously support big government in the cause of economic management and social reform, and are suspicious of big government and centralized institutions. This is obviously a complex, often contradictory, ideological inheritance. Its complexity was magnified by the history of the party system in the 1980s. At the beginning of that decade, as we saw in the preceding chapter, a group of leading members of the Labour Party (the 'gang of four') broke away from Labour to form a separate Party, the Social Democrats. The new Party principally catered to those who were enthusiastic supporters of Britain's integration into the EU (at the time official Labour was sceptical) and who opposed Labour's move in the early 1980s to a radical policy of extensive state intervention in the economy. This put the new Party very close ideologically to the Liberals. The two parties fought a number of general elections in a succession of Alliances. Following the 1987 General Election, the two fused (hence the eventual change of name to Liberal Democrats). A brief attempt to keep the Social Democrats in existence by their last leader, David Owen, soon failed. The relevance of this history to the modern Liberal Democrats is that, in the remnants of the Social Democratic Party, the Liberals incorporated a Party with a very different tradition from the old, individualistic, decentralized Liberalism. The Social Democrats were an elitist creation, the product of the ambitions and strategies of a small number of disillusioned Labour Party politicians who had made their careers in the Westminster world, and whose focus was on the politics of Westminster government. The incorporation of the Social Democrats therefore marginally strengthened the ideological elements in the Liberal Democrats favourable to strong state controls over the individualists and decentralizers; and it also strengthened those with a 'Westminster' focus over those more interested in non-metropolitan politics.

Nationalist ideologies in the UK

There are presently three important groups in the UK which advocate various degrees of nationalist separation from the present British state: Irish, Scottish and Welsh.

Irish nationalism is by far the most successful of the separatist nationalist ideologies. It had already secured one break-up of the UK (the secession of the largest part of Ireland as the Irish Free State) in 1921. Irish nationalists fought a guerrilla campaign (chiefly through the Provisional IRA) for nearly a quarter of a century after 1970 to secure integration of the six counties of Ulster into the Republic of Ireland. They

POLITICAL ISSUES 15.1

Euroscepticism: a permanent force in British party ideology?

The 2004 elections to the EP produced sensational gains for the United Kingdom Independence Party (UKIP): it won 12 of the 78 available UK seats, increasing its numbers by 10 on the previous result and pushing the Liberal Democrats into fourth place on share of the total vote.

UKIP originated in 1991 as the Anti-Federalist League, acquiring its present name in 1993. Its main aim is simply stated: to withdraw Britain from the EU, at least as presently constituted. The failure of UKIP to capitalize on its 2004 successes in the 2005 general election, and the fact that the party was mired in faction fighting and scandal after 2004, suggests that this kind of organized Euroscepticism was merely transient. But the 2009 elections to the EP demonstrate otherwise: that it is a permanent feature of British politics, a major source of division in public opinion, and a considerable problem for the three leading Westminster parties. In the June 2009 elections to the EP, UKIP marginally raised its share of the vote (up to 16.6 per cent) and its number of seats (up to 13). It once again beat the Liberal Democrats (13.3 per cent of the vote, 11 seats), but even more sensationally relegated Labour to third place (15.8 per cent) in vote share, and equalled it in number of seats. In European terms UKIP is now established as the second leading UK wide party, after the Conservatives. More important for the study of British party ideology, the results confirm that Euroscepticism is now a major ideological force. It joins the ideologies of class, nation and religion, which have helped shape the landscape of party ideas in Britain. Although the electorate in Britain has long been one of the most 'Eurosceptic' in the EU, the Westminster party elite did not reflect that popular outlook. The Liberal Democrats have long been, and remain, enthusiasts for European integration. Labour, initially hostile, became just as enthusiastic in the 1980s and 1990s. The Conservatives had led the way into Europe in the 1970s, and until the 1980s matched the two other parties in enthusiasm. In the later stages of Mrs Thatcher's premiership they edged towards a more sceptical attitude, and the rise of UKIP has compelled the party to try to stake out a more sceptical attitude still. Yet all the Westminster parties still remain on the same side of the ideological cleavage which the rise of UKIP has now exposed: by contrast with UKIP they remain committed to continuing UK membership of the Union. How long the Conservatives, in particular, can remain on the pro-EU side of the divide is now one of the major tactical issues in British politics.

accounted for the overwhelming majority of the 3,000 plus murders in the Province in those years.

The new political institutions in the north (which I described in Chapter 11) substantially weaken the sovereignty of the British state in Ulster. Nationalism there – whether committed to armed force or to peaceful means – has principally had support from sections of the Catholic community, especially from a catholic working class and a small catholic middle class principally employed in the public sector. This social base has meant that all the different nationalist factions have advocated extensive government intervention in social and economic affairs. Sinn Féin, the leading party of separatist nationalism, has often used the language of socialism. But in its participation in government following the Good Friday Agreement it has been associated with reforming rather than socialist radical policies – for example, attempting to replace selective secondary education in the province by comprehensive schooling.

Scottish nationalism is the most successful brand of nationalism on mainland Britain. Though its ideological origins looked back to a traditional rural Scotland, the SNP that now is so important in Scottish politics offers a modern vision of the country. Its aim is full independence, but one within the membership of the EU. The models it offers point to other small, successful economies in Europe (like the Dutch) and it emphasizes the 'modern' side of Scottish life, such as the country's importance as a modern European economy.

By contrast with Scottish nationalism, *Welsh nationalism* has long been, and continues to be, 'cultural' in character. Plaid Cymru, the Welsh Nationalist Party, has its roots in movements to protect and foster the Welsh language. (Scottish Nationalists have by contrast shown much less interest in Scots Gaelic.) Socially and economically it also draws on long traditions of Welsh radicalism, and has become a natural home in Wales for economic and social radicals who, for whatever reason, do not feel able to support Labour in Wales. It also draws on a tradition of radicalism in foreign affairs that has roots in the radicalism of Welsh Nonconformism. Thus Plaid Cymru, like the Liberal Democrats, opposed the 2003 Iraq war.

As we saw in Chapters 10 and 11, the environment of nationalism is changing rapidly in Britain. For the first time nationalists have participated in government; and in the new political environment the old 'British' parties, notably Labour and Conservative, are changing their strategies. Nationalist ideologies are therefore among the most fluid in modern British politics.

IDEOLOGIES OF THE MARGINALIZED: RACISTS, MARXISTS AND GREENS

The British political system, like any other, has parties which have dominated political life and others which remain at its margins in the sense that they command little popular support. But it is important not to lose sight of these marginalized groups. The 'marginal' of one decade are often central in another: a book on British politics written in the early 1960s would have treated Scottish and Welsh nationalism as little more than historical curiosities. What is more, importance lies in more than numbers. Ideologies that are marginal in the sense of enjoying little overt popular support can nevertheless have a big impact on mainstream parties: we will shortly see that this is true both of racism and Green ideology. Finally, the very fact that an ideology is marginalized may tell us something very revealing about the wider political system: we will see that this is true of the position of Marxism.

A word of caution is needed here. The ideologies discussed here are grouped together because they share a common fate – they have enjoyed little popular support. This grouping is not meant to suggest that they are morally equivalent.

Racism

Racist ideologies are based on the twin claims that some races are innately superior to others and that nations should be racially homogeneous, even if this means expelling or otherwise eliminating 'inferior' races.

Racism thus defined was a great influence in European politics in the twentieth century, and it continues to be important in many European countries. One of the big puzzles of British political history is why an important party supporting racism has never managed to establish itself in the UK: none has ever managed to gain more than a tiny minority of the popular vote. There seem to be two reasons for this. First, racist parties suffered the same handicaps as any other minority party under the long established Westminster electoral system. Second, for the past 50 years the issue most likely to gain support for racists, immigration and settlement of large numbers of people from different races and cultures, has been appropriated by the two big governing parties. Since the first appearance of overt large scale hostility to non-white immigrants in the 1950s the two governing parties have competed with each other to impose ever more strict immigration controls; in this sense they have suppressed racist parties by adopting one of their most important policies. At the same time both parties have supported the general idea that everybody already in Britain should be treated without discrimination and have put onto the statue book laws outlawing racist discrimination, and racist abuse, in the workplace and the housing market. The present main 'carrier' of racist ideology in Britain is the British National Party, which over the years has attacked a range of 'alien' targets: immigrants and their descendants from the new Commonwealth; immigrant workers more generally; and 'alien' institutions like those of the EU. After a brief moment in 2010 when it seemed that the Party might make a parliamentary breakthrough, particularly in Barking, where its leaders stood in the May general election, the BNP came a poor third, even in Barking.

Marxism

Marxism covers a broad spectrum of beliefs, all inspired originally by the work of the German revolutionary and social thinker, Karl Marx (1818–83). At its core is the argument that conflict between classes is the driving force that shapes societies. In Britain, a developed capitalist society, this means conflict between capitalists and labour, a conflict that must finally result in the transformation of society and the establishment of a socialist order where labour rules. The most striking feature of Marxist ideologies in Britain is their popular weakness. Even before the fall of Communism in the Soviet Union and eastern Europe after 1989 Britain was unusual in this respect. For most of the twentieth century countries like France and Italy had large, well supported Communist Parties based on a Marxist ideology of class conflict between an exploited mass of workers and a small elite of capitalists. The Communist Party of Great

BRIEFING 15.2

Racism: as British as roast beef and Yorkshire pudding

In twenty-first-century Britain racism is treated as a marginal, unBritish phenomenon. It is conventionally associated with small political movements that are often represented in images of thuggish skinheads, while public policy and the law have for over three decades been dedicated to its extinction in wider society. Yet racism has deep historical roots in Britain, and at various times its fundamental tenets have been widely accepted by political leaders and by established political parties. The core of racism has two components:

■ that some racially identifiable groups are genetically superior to others, for instance in intelligence;

■ that Britain should be preserved as a racially homogeneous society, notably as a homogeneous white society.

Among powerful traces of racism in the recent past are the following:

■ The belief that the British 'race' had a special civilizing mission was central to the creation and maintenance of the British Empire.

■ The belief in selective breeding to improve the racial 'stock' – technically, eugenics – was widespread among politicians of both the left and right well into the twentieth century.

■ Large scale public hostility to foreign immigrants, on the grounds that they threaten the homogeneity of society, has been historically commonplace in Britain. It spans public hostility to the Irish, to Jewish immigrants from eastern Europe and to immigrants from the so called 'new Commonwealth' countries such as Pakistan and India.

Parties such as the British National Party, which argue for the creation of a racially homogeneous Britain, are not therefore 'unBritish': they are instead systematizing, and expressing publicly, what is deep in British tradition.

■ Political ideologies are complex phenomena. They crop up in the most surprising, and often inconvenient ways, as this case of racist ideology shows.

Britain never enjoyed more than trivial popular support (except perhaps for a brief period in the Second World War when Britain allied with the Communist Soviet Union against Nazi Germany). In turn the Communists in Britain had a large number of fierce rivals in the form of tiny factions offering alternative variations on Marxist ideology. After the fall of Communism in eastern Europe the Communist Party itself fragmented into a number of even tinier factions. But Marxist ideology has been more important in Britain than formal organization or support for the Communist Party would suggest. As we saw above, it has been a minority but well established tradition in the Labour Party. Communist Party activists were important out of all proportion to their numbers in the British trade union movement. And in a more general way, Marxist ideas have been important among various

groups of British intellectuals: among many creative writers, for instance, and in the history of social science in Britain. These examples show how important it is not simply to assume that a political ideology is identical with a particular political institution. This is a point we will also notice with our next ideology.

Environmentalism

Concern with the protection of the physical environment is at least as old as the Industrial Revolution: there is a long tradition, dating from the nineteenth century, of laments about the impact of economic development on nature. In this broad sense environmental ideologies are well embedded in the main political parties. But a distinct ideology of environmentalism, with its own party – the Greens – is very new in British politics. The Green

Party was founded in 1985, as an institution with a more user friendly name than its predecessor, the Ecology Party. The most important feature of Green Party ideology is its claim to be dealing in a new kind of politics. It claims, in other words, to be about more than environmental protection. The old ideologies, according to this view, are still obsessed with economic growth. Green ideology is concerned with a wholesale reconstruction of the economy so that it can run in a way that does not depend on the continued pursuit of an economic growth that damages nature. Within Green ideology, in turn, there are varying shades of radicalism. 'Deep Greens', for example, advocate more than environmentally friendly public policy – they argue for a wholesale revolution in the nature of society's culture and institutions. This attempt to practise a 'new' politics stretches beyond policy. As we saw in the preceding chapter, Greens until 2008 rejected traditional party hierarchies, favouring collective leadership over a single Leader.

BRITISH PARTY IDEOLOGY: THE RISE AND FALL OF CONSENSUS

If we look back over half a century, there is a clear pattern to the development of party ideology in Britain. In the first half of the 1950s there were two distinct features to the pattern of ideology:

● The two leading political parties, Labour and Conservative, shared common assumptions about how the economy should be run and how the government of Britain should be organized.
● When we had described Labour and Conservative ideology we had virtually painted in the full ideological picture. Other ideologies were marginal and marginalized.

Some observers of British political history have challenged these generalizations, notably the generalization that there once existed a consensus between the two leading parties. It is undoubtedly possible to exaggerate the extent of agreement between the parties in the 1950s. For instance, while the Conservatives indeed accepted most of the reforms of the Labour governments of 1945–51 (such as the introduction of the National Health Service) they often did so reluctantly and consistently thought of themselves as the party that more instinctively understood the market economy. In the 1950s there were also deep and bitter differences over foreign policy: for instance the Labour Party strongly opposed the British Government's attempt to invade the Suez Canal in Egypt in 1956. (We might contrast this with the consensus between the Labour and Conservative leaderships over the invasion of Iraq in 2003.) In the late 1950s there also developed, partly from the socialist wing of the Labour Party, a mass movement favouring a highly radical policy – unilaterally abandoning Britain's nuclear weapons in order to set a moral example for world nuclear disarmament.

There is never complete consensus – complete agreement – in any political system, so measures of consensus are bound to be relative. And it is relative to what came later that a decade like the 1950s appears as an age of ideological consensus. Two big changes have occurred over the years. First, the old consensus about economic management between the two leading parties was destroyed. In the 1980s the Thatcherite reforms described earlier in the chapter radically broke with the established understandings about how the economy should be run. By the 1990s there had, indeed, been created a new consensus between the parties, because by now Labour had largely accepted the Thatcherite revolution: accepted large scale privatization of nationalized industries; accepted reforms in the law designed to control trade unions; and symbolically accepted the primacy of market forces in governing the economy, as illustrated by its new 'Clause 4' described earlier. But now there were new areas of dissensus. The settled agreement about how to govern the UK, which had existed since the 1920s, broke down as Labour moved to introduce its radical devolution proposals after 1997. An increasingly wide gap also opened up between the two big parties over the issue of Britain's relations with the EU – an issue of critical and growing importance as the pace of European integration increased in the 1990s, and as Britain's economy and society became increasingly entangled with that of the Union.

The decline of the old consensus therefore refers in part to what divides the two big parties in the world of Westminster government. But there is a more fundamental change still in the nature of ideological consensus. In the 1950s the two big parties dominated the political system, and consequently their ideologies were likewise dominant. Both were coalitions bringing together different ideological traditions, and the range of ideologies encompassed by those coalitions encompassed the most significant ideological traditions in Britain. Ideologies like Scottish Nationalism seemed simply to be quaint anachronisms, and ideologies like environmentalism were virtually invisible.

The situation is now very different. Not only are there vigorous and rising ideologies that challenge Labour and Conservative; ideology flourishes outside the whole party system itself. A kaleidoscope of political

DEBATING POLITICS 15.1

Ideology: fig leaf for interests or core of party identity?

IDEOLOGY IS MERELY A 'COVER' FOR THE INTERESTS THAT A PARTY REPRESENTS

- It is usually very hard to make a clear link between what parties do in British government and what they profess ideologically.
- The big parties are closely linked to economic interests and could not survive without serving those interests.
- Politicians are driven people, and what drives them is the desire to get into, and stay in, government.
- Modern politics is so dominated by marketing that deep seated beliefs are pushed to the margins of politics.

IDEOLOGY HAS AN INDEPENDENT POWER OF ITS OWN

- Leading politicians are no different from the rest of us: they need something to believe in.
- For most politically active people politics brings few material rewards, and attachment to an ideology is the only credible explanation for their activism.
- The parties do not always deliver on their promises, but what parties promise is still a remarkably good predictor of what they do in government.
- Politicians inside parties constantly fight about ideas, so the ideas must be important to them.

movements exists, often with little or no organized connections to established parties of any kinds. Two important examples, which we encountered in Chapter 8, are environmentalism and feminism. Although environmentalism is partly organized in the Green Party, it is much wider than the Greens, and takes numerous forms in a whole host of locally inspired manifestations. Partly for this reason it has also been appropriated by the big parties – if only opportunistically and rhetorically.

Feminism, meanwhile, has also influenced all the political parties, but has most of its organizational and ideological life outside the formal boundaries of party organization. The world of political ideology in Britain used to be comparatively one dimensional, capable of being summarized in the differences between Labour and Conservative. Now it is highly diverse, multidimensional and only partly incorporated inside the formally organized party system.

Review OF CHAPTER 15

Five themes have dominated this chapter.

- Ideology can either be considered as just an instrument that parties use to manage their 'brand identity' in the political market place or as a key to their essential identity.

- Party ideology in Britain is overwhelmingly shaped by the fact that two parties, Labour and Conservative, have dominated British politics for nearly a century. Understanding party ideology is to an important degree a matter of understanding the ideology of these two parties.

- Both Conservative and Labour ideologies were transformed in the last two decades of the twentieth century: the Conservative by the rise of Thatcherism; the Labour by the need to respond to the challenge of Thatcherism.

- Party ideologies once thought of as little more than historical relics, like nationalism, are growing in importance in British politics.

- The nature of political ideology in Britain is changing fundamentally. Parties are of decreasing importance in expressing ideology, as movements beyond organized parties, and often beyond formal organization at all, rise in importance.

FURTHER READING

ESSENTIAL

If you read only one book it should be Beer (1969/82). Although it was written in the age of two-party domination, and the analysis shows this, both for its exploration of the historical roots of British political ideology, and as a masterclass in how to analyse ideology, it is essential reading.

RECOMMENDED

The most important work on the ideology of modern Conservatism is Gamble (1994). Gamble (1974) ranges back in the history of Conservative ideology. Furious historical debates on the character of Labour ideology are best explored via Howell (1980). A pithy statement of the character of New Labour is Coates (2000b).

CHAPTER 16

How political communication happens

CONTENTS

AIMS

This chapter:

- Sketches the main forms of political communication

- Describes the main forms of mass political communication in the printed word and in broadcasting

- Describes the regulation of political communication and the main issues this creates

- Summarizes what we presently know about the impact of bias in mass political communication

- Summarizes how new technologies are affecting political communication in Britain

POLITICAL COMMUNICATION AND BRITISH DEMOCRACY: THE FORMS AND SIGNIFICANCE OF COMMUNICATION

Political communication is vital to the workings of any system of government, but it is particularly important in a country like Britain – a democratic political system attempting to govern a territory with a large population (just over 60 million people). We only have to reflect for a moment on the simple fact of the size of population to see that communication between governors and governed is not something that will happen automatically; it has to be organized. This chapter is about how it is organized.

Faced with the phrase 'political communication' most of us will instinctively think of the world of party communication in the mass media – of debates on television between party leaders or news reporting in national papers. But that is only a part of political communication. There are actually four overlapping forms of communication that have to happen if democratic government is to be conducted at all effectively.

Communication from the people to the government. There are many theories of democracy but all at root involve the assumption that the people's voice is heard and that government listens. Most theories of democracy assume that the people 'speak' decisively at election time. But as we shall see there are numerous other opportunities for government in Britain to 'listen' to the people.

Communication from the government to the people. A first condition of effectively conducting the business of government is that the people at large actually know what it wants to do and what it requires them to do. So government has to put a large amount of energy into communicating with the people. Take something that is part of the daily life of every motorist: obeying the speed limit. Obedience depends critically on something elementary: knowing what the limit is. Thus an elaborate network of road signs throughout the country alerts motorists to this (see Image 16.1).

Communication from the political parties to the electorate. This overlaps with the second form of communication above, because parties in office often deliberately mix up the wider job of communicating with citizens for the purpose of governing with the narrower job of communicating their own partisan message. But of course all political parties, in office or out of it, also have to both get their message across and persuade voters that their message is convincing enough to merit support at elections. This kind of communication is therefore vital to democratic political competition.

Communication between the people. It is important not to identify political communication only with what we might call 'vertical' communication – messages going up and down between political leaders and the people. Citizens also communicate with each other about politicians and about government in a whole host of ways – and, when we turn near the end of this chapter to look at new technologies of communication, we will find that this sort of communication may be becoming more important. How does each of these forms of communication happen?

From people to government

Elections. In most theories of democracy 'the people speak' at elections. Winning parties, for example, will claim that their votes give them a mandate to do what is in their 'manifesto', the document typically prepared by all parties at election time summarizing the programme they propose for government. The assumption is that a vote for a party is also an expression of support for the party's programme. In fact there is plenty of survey evidence that this is not so: often voters are unaware of the small print (or even the large print) in a party manifesto. And even when they are, a single vote can hardly be taken as assent to a whole complex programme: an elector may vote for a party because he or she strongly approves of its policy on taxation in spite of the fact that he or she disagrees with its policy on control of immigration. Elections are therefore an important form of upward political communication, but are also a highly imperfect form.

Polling. These imperfections help to explain why many other ways of detecting the popular voice have developed. Over a period of more than 60 years scientifically drawn surveys have evolved into a method of continuously monitoring the views of the population on almost every conceivable political issue, from judgements about personalities to views about the most complex policy problems.

Focus groups. One of the drawbacks of polling by mass surveys is that they usually only gather a view hastily expressed to a stranger who puts a series of quick questions. (Questions about political issues are often mixed up with quite unrelated questions of market research for products, giving an even more fragmented character to responses.) There is rarely opportunity to express more complex views and judgements, and it is consequently not possible to be confident that conventional polling tells us much about the deeply held views of the people at large. Focus groups are an attempt to remedy this problem. They literally 'focus' on a narrow range of issues or personalities. The groups are encouraged to discuss in depth their views and feelings about a

Timeline 16.1

The development of mass political communication in Britain

1702 First daily paper, *Daily Courant*.

1814 Steam presses first used to print *The Times*, greatly increasing speed of newspaper production.

1837 Invention of electric telegraph allows rapid news gathering.

1855 Repeal of stamp duty allows development of cheap popular press.

1896 *Daily Mail*, first mass circulation newspaper, founded.

1922 Radio broadcasting begun by privately owned British Broadcasting Company.

1926 British Broadcasting Corporation established as public monopoly for radio broadcasting.

1936 First regular television service.

1953 Press Council established as self-regulatory body controlled by newspaper industry to adjudicate on complaints against newspapers.

1955 First commercial television stations begin broadcasting in competition with BBC.

1973 First commercial radio stations begin broadcasting in competition with the BBC.

1986 News International moves operations for its major titles (*The Times*, *The Sun*, *etc.*) to new site at Wapping. Breaks power of print unions, fully adopts technology of photocomposition.

1989 First satellite TV transmissions begin in Britain from Rupert Murdoch-owned Sky TV.

1991 Press Complaints Commission replaces Press Council (see 1953 above) in attempt to make self-regulation by newspaper industry more effective.

2004 OFCOM (Office of Communications) established as single regulator for all broadcasting media.

2008 US survey finds Internet now most important source of news, with particular predominance among younger adults.

2010 In general election campaign Conservatives commit to abolish OFCOM in its present form.

Source: Adapted, with additions, from Cook and Stevenson (1983, 2000).

whole variety of matters – ranging again from their reaction to personalities to their feelings about policies. Focus groups originally developed in commercial marketing but are now (see Briefing 16.1) a key method of 'listening' used by the political parties.

An elaboration of the focus group approach, less tied to marketing, occurs in various forms of organized 'deliberation'. These are attempts at enriching the quality of popular reflection. Typically a cross-section of the population is assembled as a kind of 'jury' to deliberate on an important issue demanding government decision. It hears evidence, for instance from expert witnesses, and engages in extended discussion of the issue in question. At the end of the process, it is hypothesized that the views formed better reflect the true quality of popular opinion than, for instance, do instantaneous responses to conventional opinion surveys. Government is increasing the use of these jury like mechanisms, for instance to try to gauge popular opinion about issues such as how access to health care should be rationed.

Elections, sample surveys, focus groups and deliberative juries have this in common: the terms on which the communication takes place tend to be set by political leaders who are in the position to ask the questions and raise the issues. Indeed focus groups, which look at first glance like the most serious attempt to listen to the people, originated as a market research technique designed to help firms design and sell products more effectively. But there are other, more direct and less controlled forms of upward communication.

Written direct communication. These can range from individual letters to organized petitions that attract millions of signatures. For instance every Member of the House of Commons has a large postbag, particularly from constituents, on every conceivable matter. Politicians seem to attach particular weight to these individual communications, presumably on the grounds that anyone prepared to take the trouble to write has strong feelings on a subject. The spread of the Web has supplemented 'snail' mail communication with email: virtually every Member of Parliament can now be emailed, though how far the messages are read and digested depends on the efficiency of the Member's office.

Direct action. Communication does not have to be in writing. It can take the form of a physical presence, peaceful or otherwise. Marches, blockades, gathering in large public assemblies: all are established and normally peaceful ways in which groups of citizens make their views known. But direct action need not only be peaceful. Sometimes public demonstrations that start out as peaceful direct action can turn into violent confrontation, for instance with the police. And some groups decide from the outset that direct action of a violent sort is the only effective way of communicating. Some militant groups have combined written with violent communication, by mailing letter bombs to public figures. The Provisional IRA strategy of 'the Armalite and the ballot box' that was practised in Northern Ireland also joins the peaceful and violent in communication (the Armalite is a sniper's gun).

From government to people

In a democracy communications by government to people very often have a partisan purpose: the governing party wants to impress its record on voters. But there is much more to it than this. British governments address three very important forms of communication to the people.

Commands. Government has equipped itself with a vast array of powers over all our lives, and these powers are embodied in law and backed by powerful resources, such as the police force. But a command is of little use if it is not communicated. We live our lives surrounded by these communicated commands from the state. Just consider something as trivial as getting into the car to drive to the supermarket. Our journey will be shaped by commands: road signs that dictate the maximum speed at which we can drive over different stretches of road; traffic lights that forbid us to progress if they show red; national billboard advertising campaigns, especially at periods like Christmas, reminding us of the penalties of driving after consuming alcohol.

Information. Over the last century government in Britain has vastly expanded the range of services and benefits that it delivers to the population. The entitlements to these services are often governed by complex rules and there is no need to assume that we will be familiar with these. So government puts considerable resources into trying to communicate this information throughout the community. The annual figure is certainly over £300 million, but actually nobody knows quite how much is spent. We do, know, however, that the scale of the effort is growing. Take one fairly narrow measure of effort: between 1998 and 2008 the number of press officers employed by departments of the Westminster Executive alone grew from 216 to 373 – and that in a period when whole new systems of government, were of course, created in Scotland, Wales and Northern Ireland (House of Lords 2008: para. 133). A ten-minute trip to the nearest post office will illustrate what is going on: you will find a rack of leaflets and brochures covering everything from details of the savings scheme offered by government to information about housing benefit entitlements.

Advice and warnings. If you are a smoker, look at your cigarette packet now. You will see on it the following stark warning: 'Smoking Kills'. This is an example of a very common communication that government addresses in countless numbers to millions of citizens: warnings about what it is unsafe to consume or advice about what is the best style of life. As we have all become increasingly sensitive to risk in modern life, this form of advice and warning has become more common. The example of warnings on cigarette packets is particularly relevant. The National Health Service, we shall see in a later chapter, is one of the biggest of all public spending programmes, and government has developed an

BRIEFING 16.1

How focus groups work

For over half a century political parties have used their own private polls to try to 'listen' to the electorate. The poll asking questions of a representative sample of the population is a powerful and efficient way of tracking opinion. But it has some obvious defects: it provides only a superficial snapshot of opinion and is hard to use to explore deeper feelings about either policies or people. The 'focus group' originated in marketing as a way of exploring views more deeply.

■ A focus group will typically involve six to ten participants. A 'moderator' will guide the discussion, encouraging discussion between members. This group communication is a key distinction between the focus group and the conventional survey, where an interviewer poses questions.

■ Parties present a variety of features to focus groups for discussion: they can 'trial' hypothetical policies, in the manner of a manufacturer trialling new brands; they can explore the 'image' of their leaders; and they can likewise explore the images associated with the party in general.

Focus groups communicate much more subtle information about popular views than do conventional surveys. But they also present problems:

■ They are an expensive way of gathering information, and since the groups are tiny there is every possibility that they are an inaccurate guide to what people at large think.

■ Their origins in market research make some defenders of democracy uneasy, since they seem to suggest that leaders should shape policies and personalities as if they were 'brands' in the market place. This seems the very opposite of 'conviction' politics.

■ Political communication flows in all directions in a modern democracy. Focus groups are one of the most sophisticated means of channelling communication between leaders and people. For a defence of this method in democratic politics see Documenting Politics 16.1.

increasing interest in communicating advice about healthy lifestyles in the attempt to contain the demand on health spending.

From political parties to the electorate

Communications from government to the people are often semi-concealed efforts by parties to get messages across to the electorate: announcements of new welfare programmes, for instance, are implicitly boasts about the achievement of the governing party. But parties also have to put huge resources into communicating more openly with electors. Small, poorly supported parties have to do this in traditional ways long established in Britain: holding public meetings and demonstrations, or 'canvassing' voters on their doorsteps. Well-supported, rich parties do this also, but most of their effort to

communicate with their electorate consists of sophisticated political marketing: the conscious design of 'packages' of policy and personalities to appeal to groups of electors, and the conscious selling of those packages. Marketing like this involves the use of techniques of communication often borrowed from commercial market research and selling. Parties intensively survey the electorate and use focus groups of the sort described above to explore what policies will have most appeal to which groups. Like advertisers marketing a commercial good, groups are often 'targeted', with the message adapted to the target. A party may want to send a message to its 'core' support – those who can be expected to be more or less automatically sympathetic. Very often, however, parties can take their core support for granted, so packages are put together and marketed to 'swing' voters,

IMAGE 16.1 ■ Government communicates with the people

Photo: Michael Moran

■ Government communication is all around us, as this typical example from one of the most common – road signs – shows. It combines information, advice (the symbol is an 'ice warning' sign) and command (the numbers are the speed limit backed by the power of the law).

who can be detached from other parties. Election victory, as we will see in our next chapter on voting, can turn on the votes of relatively small numbers of these 'swing' voters.

In marketing their packages parties have learnt to use the most advanced forms of communication technology. Large advertising budgets mean that, especially at times of elections, many of the conventional tools of marketing, like billboard campaigns, are used intensively. As we saw in Chapter 14 the two main parties can spend nationally just under £20 million in a general election year. A combination of sophisticated surveys and modern means of electronically storing data mean that parties can also target particular groups of voters with 'mail shots' – letters and leaflets designed to communicate with special groups of voters. The existence of rich collections of data about particular groups in the electorate, coupled with the fact that virtually every household in the country now has a telephone, means that parties can inexpensively contact large numbers of key

voters by ringing intensively from a single call centre. This sort of rapid, intense, phone polling can be used quickly to test voter reaction to particular packages and to try to stimulate support among them. The Internet has given parties an extra set of instruments. All the parties have their own websites and increasing numbers of individual MPs also have their own web pages.

The single most important feature of the communication between parties and the people is that it is a highly self-conscious activity, best summed up in the idea of marketing. We will see in the next section why this gives the mass media such an important part in communication.

From people to people

As we have noted, political communication is not all 'vertical' – up and down between people and government. Communication can also be 'horizontal': between people. Survey researchers long ago discovered, for example, that we get a large part of our information and opinions from each other: for instance, by talking to friends and family. Consider Figure 16.1 for example, which reports what people told researchers about their sources of political information. One of the most important (75 per cent) was indeed 'friends and family'. This means that the kind of community in which people live has a big effect on the form of political communication. Imagine living as part of a big family in an isolated fishing community, for instance, and contrast that with living alone in a bedsit in a big city: the communication possibilities are plainly very different in the two. This kind of people to people communication can be tremendously important in either reinforcing or subverting messages that politicians are trying to put across. Since most people do not take an intense interest in politics, information picked up in 'non-political' ways – listening to family at the meal table or to friends in the pub – can be very important, but obviously is not subject to much control. So surveys repeatedly show that large numbers of people simply do not have correct information: they put leading politicians in the wrong parties and ascribe the 'wrong' policies to parties. Half an hour listening to people talk about politics in virtually any bar in Britain will also show that people communicate a whole folklore about politics to each other: gossip and rumour, some true, some untrue, about the private lives of: political leaders; conspiracies by government, and about government; disasters to which government has supposedly not owned up.

In recent years new technology has helped this 'people to people' communication: the spread of unregulated Internet news sites and the possibilities offered by mobile phones to allow rapid, easy communication

DOCUMENTING POLITICS 16.1

A defence of modern political marketing

'The public want leaders who lead, they want governments that tough it out. But they also want to be heard. Of course, governing with principles and yet in a continuous dialogue with voters is complicated. But modern politics is complicated. The electorate is more demanding and is right to be so. It is up to us to meet the new challenge. I do not just see focus groups and market research as campaigning tools; increasingly I see them as an important part of the democratic process: part of a necessary dialogue between politicians and people, part of a new approach to politics.'

■ Philip Gould is the most successful 'marketer' in modern British politics, the key influence on the 'relaunch' of the Labour Party as 'New Labour'. This extract from the most considered statement of his philosophy shows how self-conscious has been the adoption of the newest marketing techniques.

Source: Gould (1998: 328).

between demonstrating groups are only two obvious examples. We will look at the significance of these new forms of communication later in the chapter.

POLITICAL COMMUNICATION AND THE MASS MEDIA

The most important feature of political communication in modern British politics is that it does not just happen; it is *managed* by politicians in and out of government to try to have the maximum effect. Of course politicians cannot manage all communications. Events – disasters, mistakes, scandals – get in the way of control. But one of the biggest obstacles to management is that the politicians do not effectively control the most important institutions of mass communication: newspapers, television and radio. (This is a contrast with many other national political systems: even in some democratic political systems on continental Europe it is common for individual television

and radio stations to be under the control of particular political parties.)

Television, newspapers and radio are vital to political communication: that much is clear from Figure 16.1. They are vital precisely because much important communication has to be on a mass scale. With a population of over 60 million, and an electorate of over 44 million, politicians can hardly expect to communicate by direct face to face contact: contrast the situation before the first great electoral reform, of 1832, when there were only just over half a million voters in all. But these institutions of mass communication cannot be considered as a single group. There are big differences in how they operate and in the relations they have with politicians. The most important divide is between newspapers, on the one hand, and radio and television on the other.

The newspaper industry and political communication

National newspaper readership in Britain is high by international standards, though it is declining. Although there is a separate, highly distinctive press in both Scotland and Northern Ireland, in England and Wales the newspaper industry is dominated by papers edited from London. These nationally circulating newspapers have a number of important characteristics that affect their political roles.

Papers are business enterprises. All the papers have to survive in an atmosphere of intense competition, both for readers and – just as important – advertising revenue. In addition, most of the newspapers are themselves now no longer independent enterprises; they are part of larger corporations, many of which are multinational in scale and operating across a whole range of industries. For instance the most successful tabloid of recent decades (*The Sun*) and one of the most prestigious broadsheets (*The Times*) are both controlled by News International, a worldwide organized corporation with interests across all media – print, broadcasting and film. Lord Beaverbrook, a newspaper magnate famous in the first half of the twentieth century, once claimed that he ran newspapers purely for propaganda. But whatever the propaganda ambitions of modern newspaper tycoons, in the end they have to be worked around running papers as profitable enterprises.

Papers are partisan. We will shortly see that there are detailed rules intended to ensure 'balance' in television and radio broadcasting. No such rules exist for newspapers. No political party owns a newspaper, but most papers have a long-term sympathy with one of the two major parties. Because papers are business enterprises, and because they are nowadays often part of large business corporations, there has been a tendency for

305

FIGURE 16.1 ■ Where people get their information

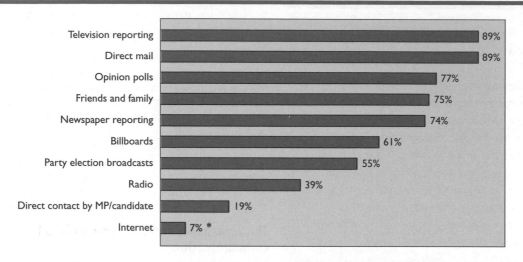

* Of course more reent data would most probably show a much greater figure for this category

Source: Data from MORI/Electoral Commission Phase 2 survey, 9–18 June 2001 reported in Lilleker et al. (2003:29) and MORI website.

■ The figure draws on survey research done by the polling organization MORI for the Electoral Commission and shows the commonest sources of information cited by the public about election issues. It shows that while the organized mass media, especially television, are very important, 'face to face communication' with friends and family is also very important.

papers to be partisan in favour of the Conservative Party. But this is hardly an iron rule. *The Sun*, for long a supporter of the Conservative Party, deserted it for Labour in the general elections between 1997 and 2007; then it reverted to the Conservatives for the election of 2010 as it sensed that they would be the winners. One reason for desertion is precisely that papers are businesses operating in a competitive world; they will not want to be too closely attached to a party if large numbers of their readers are deserting that party. They also do not want to fall out too seriously with a party if it is likely to form the next government, precisely because they have other economic interests to defend. For instance, the big business corporations that typically own newspapers in Britain often also have commercial interests in broadcasting – interests that are affected by regulations made by government.

Papers are competitive. Even when papers incline to a political party – as the Daily Telegraph, for example, has usually faithfully done to the Conservative Party – the parties cannot control what the papers publish. Papers will routinely report both news and comments that are damaging to 'their' party. One reason they do this is that a force stronger even than partisan loyalty drives them: competition. Journalists compete for

stories; newspapers compete to be first with news. The competition is especially intense in the mass market for 'tabloid' newspapers. As a glance at any issue of *The Sun* or the *Daily Star* will show, these papers are neither produced nor read primarily for their political content. They are dominated by sport, show business, scandal and 'human interest' stories; politics is incidental. Political reporting just has to fit around the competitive reporting of other parts of life. If a damaging political scandal sells papers it will be reported regardless.

Papers are weakly regulated. We will shortly see that there are powerful legal controls governing both entry into television and radio broadcasting and regulating the content of what is broadcast. These controls are absent in the case of newspapers. There is no obligation to provide 'balance' in a story. The only formal regulatory body is the Press Complaints Commission, a 'self-regulatory' body controlled by the industry itself and with no power beyond administering admonitions to offenders. A more powerful control, true, is provided by the libel laws in Britain, which on occasion have meant that juries have awarded huge damages to individuals judged to have been libelled by stories in newspapers. All national newspapers have teams of lawyers on duty that read content before publication to warn of possible libel, and rich and powerful people can use the threat of libel to prevent publication of stories. But even this is not a very powerful restriction on political reporting. Most of the really big libel awards have been about non-political stories (such as those concerning the private lives of show business stars). The two most spectacular political libel cases in recent years (involving the Conservative politicians Jeffrey Archer and Jonathan Aitken) both eventually resulted in Archer and Aitken serving jail sentences for perjury. And the competitive pressure to publish is a powerful force countering the inhibiting fear of a libel suit.

There is a second sense in which the weak regulation of newspapers is important: the regulation of entry. If you or I decide to broadcast our own radio station without a licence, technically a quite simple matter, we will be closed down and prosecuted. (From January 2004 the issue of licences became the responsibility of a regulatory agency, the Office of Communications – see Timeline 16.1.) But no licence is needed to publish a newspaper or magazine. There are indeed powerful barriers to entry, but they are mostly economic: establishing and running a national newspaper, for instance, demands the investment of tens of millions of pounds before any income is received. That explains why in the last 20 years only two new nationally circulated daily newspapers (the *Independent* and the *Daily Star*) have appeared and survived – and these two are among the weakest on the national scene. But entry at a lower level – for instance through a weekly with a low circulation aimed at a target audience – is much easier. Every conceivable shade of political opinion has its own weekly paper, most with tiny circulations. More important, there are well established magazines of opinion and comment which, while having small circulations, are read by the most active and politically committed: the joint circulation of *Prospect* and of the *New Statesman* is below 50,000, but readership of the most interested and committed gives these magazines an importance beyond what the mere figures would suggest. Some small circulation independent magazines have had effects well beyond their small proportions. The satirical fortnightly *Private Eye*, for example, has often printed stories which the national press has been too timid to publish for fear of libel, but which have subsequently been widely publicized.

Broadcasting and political communication

When we turn from newspapers to broadcasting we see immediately several important contrasts.

A mixed economy. Newspapers are commercial enterprises. The economic structure of broadcasting is more complex. The longest established broadcaster, the

British Broadcasting Corporation (BBC) is a publicly owned corporation. Its biggest single source of finance is the licence fee, a state-imposed levy that every household in possession of a television must pay. The Corporation's output of programmes is huge: two national 'terrestrial' television channels; a growing number of specialist channels that can be received by non-terrestrial satellite-based communication; dedicated specialist channels for Wales, Scotland and Northern Ireland; regional divisions producing news and specialist interest programmes for their region; five national radio stations and a range of digital specialist stations; and 37 local radio stations. The Corporation's role in political communication is immense, and understanding that role depends in part on understanding the history of the 'mixed economy' of broadcasting.

The Corporation originated as a commercial company to exploit the new technology of wireless in the 1920s, but it became a nationalized corporation in 1926. It had a complete legal monopoly of all broadcasting for the first 30 years of its history, and of radio for over 40 years: the first commercial television broadcasts only came in 1955 and commercial radio was only allowed in 1973. For much of its history it had a powerful 'public service broadcasting' culture. It produced its programmes 'in-house' rather than buying in from other providers. It relied overwhelmingly for its income on the licence fee. It not only rejected commercial advertising but also took strenuous steps to ensure that no commercial advertising appeared accidentally in its broadcasts. It operated on the principle that its role was to broadcast programmes which would be freely available to anyone with a receiver. Since radio receivers soon fell to a price that almost everyone could afford, BBC programmes soon approximated what in Chapter 19 we will call a 'public good': a free service available virtually to all on demand.

There has in recent years been some relaxation of this public service culture. Programmes are increasingly 'bought in' from programme makers in the marketplace, and the selling of BBC products is an increasingly important source of revenue. But the public service broadcasting culture nevertheless largely shapes how the BBC reports politics. The content and style of reporting resembles more the 'broadsheet' than the tabloid press. While news reporting includes a diet of human interest and celebrity stories, it is dominated by reporting of public events. There are elaborate rules designed to ensure balance in reporting, especially balance in reporting the debates between the main political parties. On important national occasions – a public disaster or a general election – the BBC's self-image as a provider of a public service for the whole nation shapes how it reports events. Much of this has to do with the Corporation's

BRIEFING 16.2

Political Communication in the May 2010 general election

Five years is a long time in the history of modern communications. The general election of May 2010 was fought in a very different media environment from that of May 2005. In 2005 Youtube and Facebook has only just been created (February 2005 and February 2004). Twitter and the 'Twitterati' who use it had not been heard of: it was launched in August 2006. Expectations of the impact of the new digital media on the campaign were thus high. But the biggest impact was something different, and quite traditional. A form invented in the US over 50 years earlier – debates between leading contenders broadcast mostly on terrestrial television – were the mass communication events of the campaign. There were three debates between the main party leaders (Brown, Cameron and Clegg). After the first the Twitterati, and more importantly the wider audience as revealed in polls, judged Clegg a clear winner. He was transformed from a marginal figure in the national campaign to its main media phenomenon. A surge of approval of Clegg, and of support for the Liberal Democrats, forced the two main parties to rethink their campaign tactics. The surge largely receded (see Briefing 17.5 for a summary). But a very traditional form of television communication had by then transformed the conduct of the 2010 campaign. The experience should remind us that the political impact of media is usually entirely different from our initial expectations of what will happen.

history, and in particular the fact that for much of the twentieth century, including the critical years of the Second World War, it did indeed have a monopoly in broadcasting to, and on behalf of, Britain.

There is a mixed economy of broadcasting because alongside the BBC there has grown up, since the foundation of the original commercial television stations in the middle of the 1950s, a large and diverse commercial sector. This includes three national commercial television services (though the first of these is composed of a federation of stations licensed for different regions of the UK); an increasingly important commercial sector which broadcasts programmes via satellite that can reach across many different national boundaries; a growing number of national radio stations mostly specializing in offering one kind of output, such as light classical music; and over 250 local stations which mostly specialize in various styles of pop music mixed with short news broadcasts usually dominated by local information. Although regulation has meant that much of the 'public service' culture is important in the commercial sector, these stations are nevertheless very different from the BBC. Commercially they resemble more the newspaper industry. They are often part-owned by large corporations where commercial broadcasting is only part of the business; in many cases these corporations are also major owners of newspapers; and like newspapers they are competitive, because they survive in the main on the

income from commercial advertising and – increasingly in the case of television – from subscriptions paid by viewers. Because they have to survive by commercial competition, they often specialize to attract particular audiences. Since the audience for serious, large-scale reporting of public events is neither large nor lucrative this means that much of the commercial sector barely reports politics – something that will be obvious to any reader who is a regular listener to the local pop music commercial station.

Broadcasting is impartial. Newspapers, we saw, make no bones about bias: most have an open commitment to one or other political party, and most write major news stories around their partisan commitments. Broadcasting aspires to be impartial in two senses. First, no broadcasting channel admits to supporting either a particular political party or a particular political outlook. (This singles out Britain from other countries: in the USA commercial stations often have a marked political bias; and across mainland Europe, even when publicly owned, they are often controlled by a political party.) Second, in the actual broadcasting of news and current affairs, all follow rules designed to ensure neutral reporting of events and balanced reporting of different viewpoints. How far this aspiration is achieved is something we will examine shortly.

Broadcasting is regulated. The aspiration to impartiality is a direct result of probably the single most impor-

BRIEFING 16.3

A single regulator for the broadcasting communications' industries

We have seen that there is a 'mixed economy' of broadcasting in Britain: a mix of private and public ownership which, combined with the development of new broadcasting technologies, also developed a very mixed system of regulation. Until 2003 there were six important regulators for broadcasting: the Broadcasting Standards Commission; the Independent Television Commission; OFTEL, the telecommunications regulator; the Radio Authority; the Radiocommunications Agency; and the Board of Governors of the BBC. The Broadcasting Act of 2003 changed all that. It established a single independent Office of Communications (OFCOM), run by a board with the legal powers replacing all but one of these regulators. (The exception concerns the BBC, details of which are given later in this chapter.) OFCOM is an independent regulatory commission with powers that run across the whole range of broadcasting. It also now wields powers hitherto exercised by regulators covering other important parts of the communications industries, such as OFTEL, the regulator for telecommunications. This 'stretch' reflects in part the way new technologies, like the Internet, are breaking down the traditional distinctions between different communications markets, such as those covered by broadcasting and telephone technologies. The establishment of OFCOM as a single regulator also, however, puts pressure on two other parts of the regulatory system described in this chapter: on the system of self-regulation in the print industry, controlled as it is by the industry itself; and on the BBC's own independent regulation, because while OFCOM regulates some aspects of the BBC, key areas are controlled by the BBC Trust – for details see Briefing 16.4. This is generally a very unstable institutional world: the Conservatives entered the 2010 general election campaign committed to abolishing, or at least drastically diminishing the role of, OFCOM.

■ The regulation of broadcasting in Britain is in flux, and the Office of Communications is a sign of this. New electronic media disseminated via the Web are a major unregulated area: see Political Issues 16.1.

tant contrast between newspapers and broadcasters: public bodies regulate the latter. Regulation comes in two forms. First, commercial broadcasters can only legally broadcast on receiving a licence. Whereas anybody with the resources can launch a newspaper, only somebody with a legal licence can launch a broadcasting service. This control over entry has many causes, but originally technology was very important: some controls were deemed necessary over the access to a limited range of broadcasting frequencies. (Technology is in turn undermining this control over entry, as we will see below.) This regulation of entry in turn leads to the second form of regulation. The licence is granted by a public body, from 2004 the new Office of Communications described in Briefing 16.3. It is for a fixed period; is usually granted after a competition between several proposers of new services; is based on a prospectus supplied by applicants, in effect a picture of the kind of service they propose to offer; and continuation of the licence is conditional on observing regulations – some of which are designed to ensure political impartiality.

The contrast sketched here between the two wings of mass communication – a largely unregulated press and a historically closely regulated world of television and radio – corresponds to two sets of problems created by the system of mass communications in government. These are the problem of regulation and the problem of bias.

POLITICAL COMMUNICATION: THE PROBLEM OF REGULATION

There are problems of regulation in both newspapers and broadcasting, but they are different. In newspapers, as we have seen, beyond the wider law of the land there

BRIEFING 16.4

Regulating the BBC

The BBC operates under a Royal Charter. Each issue of the Charter is for a limited period of ten years: the present charter dates from 2006. The last renegotiation of the Charter was an occasion for a major institutional change in the way the Corporation is regulated. Hitherto at the heart of its independent system of regulation lay a board of 12 governors. Now the role of governors in ensuring accountability has been taken over by a trust. However, it is unclear how far this institutional change is matched by a real change in power relationships; some trustees were governors of the Corporation. However, the invention of the trust has been important in keeping the BBC substantially independent of the main broadcasting regulator, OFCOM. It is, in short, a significant political institution. It may even outlast OFCOM.

■ The first Director General of the BBC, Lord Reith, established the Corporation as an independent institution. All subsequent institutional developments in the Corporation's governance must be seen as part of the endeavour to retain this independence in the face of changes in broadcasting technology, economic structure and cultural setting.

is no specialized public regulation. There is only self-regulation in the form of the Press Complaints Commission. The Commission originated in 1953 in the Press Council, and its present form dates from reorganization at the start of the 1990s that was designed to make self-regulation more effective than hitherto. The main role of the Commission is to adjudicate on complaints about press coverage received from members of the public, against a standard of a voluntary code of conduct by which all members agree to be bound. It is this voluntary character which has proved the most controversial aspect of press regulation. The sanctions of the Commission amount to admonition. The most severe penalty is to oblige an offending publication prominently to publish a critical Commission judgement. Precisely because newspapers are commercial enterprises that are highly competitive, the temptation to breach any code in the search for an exclusive story has often proved great. The political effect is twofold. First, there is now a long established debate about whether the law should step in to replace voluntary regulation. Second, many of the problems of the voluntary code have involved figures that are part of the state. One of the most sensitive issues in press regulation concerns how far newspapers can claim that it is in the public interest to report on the private lives of public figures, especially if the reporting is salacious. Reporting about leading members of the royal family and leading politicians in these terms has proved problematic in recent years.

Press regulation is a highly sensitive issue in part because the wrong sort of regulation could threaten the freedom of the press to report on events and people – and press freedom is one of the defining features of democracy. This sensitive issue also arises in the case of broadcasting. As we have seen, public regulation both of access to broadcasting bands and of what is broadcast has been an established feature since the first technology – radio – became popular in the 1920s.

The regulation of broadcasting is faced by two diametrically opposed problems: that it may be too effective and that it may be of declining effectiveness. The first exists because there is a difficult line to walk, between regulation and control of what broadcasters do, by the state. There have been times in the history of the BBC when it has clearly taken the side of government in disputes with sections of the community: thus in 1926 the BBC explicitly supported the Government against the trade unions who called a general strike in that year. All politicians try to pressure broadcasters about both the content and style of programmes. The fact that Government exercises control over the issue of commercial licences, and that it also controls the level of the licence fee and thus the income of the BBC, means that, when a governing party puts pressure on, that pressure is not innocent: the broadcasters cannot help but be aware of the sanctions that lie behind it.

By contrast, technological change in recent years has actually reduced the ability of governments to regulate some broadcasting services. The most obvious example

BRIEFING 16.5

The system of press self-regulation in Britain

Self-regulation is what the modern newspaper industry has so far offered as a compromise between the need for regulation and the fear of subjecting the press to state controls. Efforts at independent self-regulation go back over 50 years, but the present system, organized by the Press Complaints Commission (PCC), dates from the early 1990s.

■ The Press Complaints Commission is a permanent body funded by the newspaper industry. It administers a Code of Conduct originally drawn up by the industry in 1991, and subsequently amended over 30 times.

■ Any member of the public can complain in writing to the Commission that a publication has breached the Code. The Commission tries to produce conciliation before issuing a judgement: it advises all complainants in the first instance to seek an agreement with the editor of the offending publication; if it takes up the complaint it tries to secure an agreed settlement between the editor and the complainant; and only then, if the Code has been breached, does it issue a judgement against the publication.

■ The Commission's only sanction is publicity: an offending publication is obliged to publish the Commission's judgement, giving it 'due prominence'.

The industry argues not only that self-regulation protects a free press from the dangers of state control, but also that the Commission's procedures are fast and cheap, since they avoid the courts. Criticism of the Commission focus on three arguments: that it is reactive, only responding when it receives complaints; that it has no effective sanctions against powerful newspapers; and that its most powerful members are editors of the leading national newspapers – typically the most serious offenders against the Code.

■ By contrast with the regulation of broadcasting, the regulation of the print media has hitherto been conducted by the industry itself, through systems of self-regulation. Outside the special circumstances of war, the only enduring special legal restraints have been provided by the courts, in the form of libel laws. Following the passage of the Human Rights Act in 1998, a number of attempts have been made to establish a law of privacy, which would set legal limits to the right of the press to report on private individuals; but they have so far had very limited success with the courts.

Source: Details of PCC organization and workings can be found at pcc.org.uk.

is the growth of satellite broadcasting channels which can easily broadcast across national boundaries and therefore reach subscribers without the authority of national government. Across the world this has had many beneficial effects, not least because it poses problems for dictatorships in controlling what their populations view and listen to. But it also means that the long-term ability of regulation to impose public interest regulation – for instance in the interests of public decency or political balance – is weakened. Technological change in broadcasting is creating, for the moment only at the fringes, a sector that resembles the press in its freedom from regulation.

Regulation is typically conceived to be a problem because it is widely believed that the content of the mass media matters. Thus there is a connection between the problem of regulation and the second problem we have identified: the problem of bias.

POLITICAL COMMUNICATION: THE PROBLEM OF BIAS

There is no doubt that politicians in and out of government are convinced that the media do matter in shaping the opinions of citizens. That is why they spend an immense amount of time alternately criticizing and cultivating the media. Both commercial broadcasters and the BBC are the frequent and common object of complaints that their reporting is biased, and these complaints come at various times from virtually all political parties, and with great frequency from the Labour and Conservative parties. And whereas politicians complain about bias among broadcasters, they positively encourage it among newspapers. The party leaderships put a lot of time and effort into cultivating the owners of the leading national newspapers and their editors. They do this in the hope that newspapers will actively support them, especially at election times. The quickest way to be invited for tea at 10 Downing Street is to buy a national tabloid.

All these complaints and efforts at cultivation only make sense on two assumptions: that media bias does indeed exist; and that it has some effect on the way political judgements are formed. In the case of newspapers there is, as we have already seen, no argument about the existence of bias. The issue of whether there is bias in broadcasting is more complicated. Regulation itself is designed to prevent biased reporting of one party over another. This is reinforced by the professional assumptions of many broadcasters, who conceive of their role in precisely these neutral terms. But bias can operate in more subtle ways than open partisanship, and it is likely that these more subtle biases in broadcasting do shape reporting. One important way this can happen is in the way issues are 'framed': in other words, in the way they are presented as policy problems in political reporting. The technologies and production values of broadcasting can be important in this respect, even when everyone concerned is trying hard to be impartial. Television provides some obvious examples. The visual character of the medium puts a premium on reporting which can be supported by images: this gives a powerful implicit bias to the reporting of politics in terms of personality because political leaders obviously provide ready pictures. And most television reporting, especially news reporting, has to be done in a very short time: even the debate of a complex political issue will typically be compressed into a few minutes. In these circumstances, subtlety, uncertainty and ambiguity are casualties; all those involved in the debate are forced, if they are not to be lost in the shouting, to take up clearly defined, simply expressed positions.

Bias both open and subtle therefore exists. Whether it has any effect is one of the most debated issues in research on political communication. Three common views about the effects of this media bias illustrate the variety of possibilities.

The manipulative view

This view gives great power to the media. It stresses the persistent bias in the printed media, and the more subtle biases in broadcasting, coupled with the fact that in Britain broadcasting is consumed on a huge scale: the British are among the most avid TV watchers in Europe, for instance, and are also great national newspaper readers. The constant stream of biased material, coupled with the fact that the mass media are a critical channel through which most of us receive political news and comment, surely could not but shape political views and choices. Politicians are a good sign of the power of this view. As we have seen they endlessly cultivate newspaper editors and owners, so they obviously believe in the manipulative view. They have powerful incentives to form a correct view of the effects of the media on political opinion – their jobs depend on getting that view right.

The reinforcement view

The reinforcement view accepts that bias exists but gives a more modest role to the manipulative power of the media. It partly rests on a large body of evidence, some of it from social psychology experiments, which show that people come to the media with well formed views, that these views help them filter out biases that do not correspond to their own, and that they mostly pay attention to biases that do indeed correspond to their own. Newspapers are very biased but most of us spend no more than a few minutes a day reading them, and most of us read them for sport and show-business gossip rather than for politics. What could be more reasonable than to expect us to be shaped by communicating with friends and family – who plainly matter more to us than does the *Daily Mail*?

We might summarily say that the manipulative view sees the media as exploiting us all and the reinforcement view sees us all as exploiting the media. One of the difficulties in resolving these competing accounts is that it is hard to isolate media effects from other forces that shape our views: adults consuming newspapers and television already obviously have been subject to decades of other influences; and even in the short term we consume the mass media alongside a range of other influences that might be shaping what we believe. We could only disentangle media effects, if they exist, by very carefully designed research. This research has indeed now begun to uncover media effects and lies behind the third view described here: I call it the 'marginal but critical view'.

Marginal but critical

Most of us do choose to consume newspapers and broadcasting that fit our existing views, and most of us reject

POLITICAL ISSUES 16.1

Regulating the Internet

An important theme of this chapter is the rise of new electronic media at the expense, often, of established print and broadcasting media. We have also seen that newspapers and broadcasting have established institutions of regulation. The rapid rise of the Internet has outpaced systems of control and regulation, and the issue of whether it should be regulated, and if so how, is an increasingly salient one in media policy. There are three key points at issue:

■ What should be regulated? Although there are some thoroughgoing libertarians who conceive of the Internet as an entirely uncontrolled space, there is undoubtedly a predominant view that a range of illegal and morally objectionable material should be suppressed and its disseminators prosecuted. For most, child pornography is well beyond the pale of acceptability. But the traditional media are subject to much closer regulatory control: the broadcasting media, we have seen, are regulated as to the political impartiality of what they produce. How far this kind of control should spread to the Internet is much more contentious.

■ Is regulation practical? The possession and circulation of material such as child pornography is already subject to the sanctions of the criminal law. But the sources of Internet material are so huge, diverse and global that controls are often impossible. In respect of more overtly political matter, for instance, a 20-minute Google search will almost always unearth what has been suppressed in the traditional print and broadcasting media on such grounds as national security, due legal process or libel.

■ Who should regulate? We have seen in this chapter that the print media are largely governed by self-regulation, while broadcasting is mostly subject to a public agency, OFCOM. Such regulation as presently exists for the Internet is self-regulatory in nature: the Internet Watch Foundation (see http://www.iwf.org.uk) works with Internet Service Providers in 34 countries to try to locate, and have removed, illegal material. Its main focus, however, is on the relatively uncontentious task of suppressing child pornography. The obvious public candidate to be a regulator is OFCOM, but it is unclear whether it has the desire or the resources to do such a job; and it certainly presently lacks the statutory authority to do so.

Source: Royal (2009).

---

hostile media. A strong Labour Party supporter will use the *Daily Mail* for nothing more than wrapping fish and chips. Professors spend more time listening to Radio 3 than to Radio 1, and this affects the way they receive news, since the style of news broadcasts varies even between different BBC radio stations. But a minority of people do systematically use media biased against their own views. Labour supporters might read the *Daily Mail* because they like its show business coverage, or just because through historical accident it is the paper that has long been bought in the family. (Remember that for most people choosing which newspaper to buy is a trivial act of consumption, probably about as engaging as the choice of brand of hair shampoo.) A Liberal Democrat

tabloid reader has no choice but to read a hostile paper: no national tabloid supports the Party. People who consume media biased against their views are a very interesting group, because if they change their views over time that does suggest that something more influential than mere 'reinforcement' is going on. And indeed there is evidence that this is so: if we track the views of this minority in the population they do seem to modify their views and loyalties to fit with the biases of the media they consume. There is thus some 'manipulation', but only of a minority.

Media bias may therefore have only a marginal effect – but at the margins it can be critical. Take the particular case of effects on voting, the reason politi-

EUROPEANIZING 16.1

Europeanizing the media: the EU *Media* programme

If you watch films at one of the many arthouse movie complexes that now exist in British cities you may have wondered about the montage of European arthouse cinema locations that usually precedes the main feature. This is a small everyday example of an ambitious EU programme to Europeanize the audio-visual industries in Britain and across the Union. The latest is *Media 2007*, a programme that runs from 2007–13. It is the fourth such programme; the first began in 1991. Each successive programme has been financed more ambitiously. The first three were funded in total by an equivalent of just over 700 million euros. The budget for *Media 2007* alone is 755 million euros. The programme spends money in five main areas: training professionals in the audio-visual industries; developing production projects; distributing films and audio-visual programmes; promoting films and audio-visual programmes; and promoting film festivals. *Media 2007* resembles many other EU 'europeanizing' projects in combining economic, ideological and cultural aims to provide financial support for an emergent European film industry notionally capable of competing with the giant corporate enterprises that sustain the American domination of world audio-visual markets. It is intended, in this way, to sustain a key cultural arena, film, against the perceived threat of Americanization; and it is designed to foster cross-national cooperation between audio-visual professionals from EU member states. As a mark of the last, funding depends critically on assembling teams, projects or events that contribute to the creation of an EU-wide audio-visual culture.

■ The construction of the EU is a political project. As such, it has to reach out to areas of economic competition and cultural identity which do not have immediate, obvious, political relevance: the case of the audio-visual industries is a perfect example of this.

Source: http://ec.europa.eu/information_society/media/overview/2007/index.

---

cians so assiduously cultivate owners and journalists. At the 2010 general election, ten seats were won by a margin of less than 200 votes – indeed six were won by less than 100 votes. Changing the votes of a tiny proportion of the population can have a big effect on outcomes: in six general elections since the Second World War the party that formed a government had a majority over all other parties of less than 30; and in the 2010 election the Conservatives were obliged to enter a coalition with the Liberal Democrats because they won 305 seats – only 21 short of a formal majority. In other words, winning a few of the most marginal seats determined which party entered office. The claim by *The Sun* newspaper after the general election of 1992 that 'it was the Sun wot won it' is now part of the folklore of British politics. This is probably an exaggeration. But if the 'marginal' effect argument is correct, *The Sun* can claim a big part of the credit, because the Conservatives' majority over other parties in that election was only 21 seats.

This discussion of bias, insofar as it has concerned newspapers, has concentrated on the effects of what might be called 'partisan' bias: that is, the effect newspapers have on party loyalties and voting. But there are other forms of political bias, and they are growing in importance. For instance, the newspaper industry in Britain in the last three decades has become increasingly 'metropolitan' – London focused – in its operations. Newspapers have tended to scale down, or even close, their regional reporting operations and to centralize in London. This has had a paradoxical effect. It has made the cultures of the leading newspapers more London focused than in the past; yet as we have seen time and again in this book the wider shape of both society and the governing system is producing challenges to the old system of centralization based in London. This lack of 'fit' between more decentralized social and political networks and the cultural centralization of newspapers may help to explain why newspaper readership is in long term decline. New forms of communication, based on innovations in electronic technology, are displacing the metropolitan focused press in political communication and in other forms of communication.

BRIEFING 16.6

Internet access in the UK: the political implications of variations

The spread of Internet usage continues, but it is now plain that behind this lies an important story. There are huge age variations in usage, as 2009 data show: from virtually universal among the 16–24 age group to around a third of those aged over 65. There are also huge variations in usage by levels of education: among those with a degree, 95 per cent lived in a house with Internet access; among those with no qualifications the comparable figure was 52 per cent. That latter variation is also a class-related variation. As government and parties resort increasingly to the Internet for communication these variations acquire political significance.

Source: Office for National Statistics (2009).

NEW FORMS OF COMMUNICATION: THE ELECTRONIC REVOLUTION AND COMMUNICATION

Technological change and political communication are bound together and always have been. *Mass* communication of the kind that we now take for granted is itself the product of earlier technical revolutions. The mass circulation newspaper delivered to millions of breakfast tables daily only became possible in the late nineteenth century with the invention of telegraphic communication that allowed rapid news gathering and power driven printing presses that allowed print runs of millions to be produced in a few hours. Radio and television are of course the product of twentieth-century technologies. So it is not surprising that political communication is continually reshaped by new technologies. That it is indeed reshaped, and will continue to be reshaped, is just about the only thing of which we can be sure. The case of earlier technologies suggests, for instance, that we do not accurately appreciate the political implications of technologies like the World Wide Web, which has only been accessible to wider populations since the mid-1990s. For instance, at the dawn of both radio and television neither was conceived primarily for what they have become: technologies for mass popular communication. Almost certainly, therefore, we do not now at all understand the implications of the latest technological changes.

We can nevertheless make some educated guesses, and these guesses suggest four kinds of effect: on regulation; on parties and voters; on 'horizontal' communication, people to people; and on surveillance of people by the state.

Undermining regulation

Technical change is undermining the ability of government to regulate access to, and the content of, mass communication. The most obvious example of that is broadcasting. For most of the twentieth century the state in Britain controlled what the people could hear and see, by its control of licences giving access to the airwaves. The growth of satellite-based broadcasting has destroyed the monopoly of government-based regulation in Britain. Internet based communication is weakening it even further. The rapid spread of Internet access has created a system of mass communication that is very weakly regulated. Individual access requires only a personal computer that is constantly falling in price and a telephone connection; or indeed a handheld mobile like a Blackberry. Control of the content of sites on the Web varies from weak to non-existent. The implications are most profound for dictatorships that depend heavily for control of mass communication to determine what their peoples hear about politics. But even in democracies the effects are profound. The sort of state monopoly of broadcasting which was the norm in Britain for most of the twentieth century is now impossible to maintain. Technical change is also making regulation through censorship more difficult. One sign is the difficulty of operating traditional state controls over pornography in the world of the globally organized websites and satellite television broadcasting. A more obviously political example is the difficulty of censoring material on the grounds of national security: in a number of recent cases bans on the publication of books held to be damaging to the security services have been circumvented by simply posting the material on a website available to millions.

Websites may also be undermining the ability of the rich and influential in Britain to use the libel laws to control their privacy: the sort of allegations which no national newspaper will dare to print frequently turn up on the Web.

Parties and voters

In the second half of the twentieth century technology had already revolutionized the way parties communicated with voters, especially at elections. Traditional methods like mass meetings addressed by powerful orators, and face-to-face mass canvassing, became less and less important. Direct appeals via television, and manipulated contacts through organized 'photo opportunities' – staged meetings with selected members of the public that were then televized – replaced these direct personal contacts. The development of cheap and powerful computers is probably the next great stage in this evolution. At this early stage much of what is going on is passive rather than active. Parties are using the new technologies to make material quickly and easily available. As we noted earlier, all the main parties have websites, and the same is now true of an increasing number of MPs. All this is 'passive' in the sense that it simply tries to use the new technologies to communicate material that would have been less efficiently transmitted by older methods, such as 'snail mail'. But more active strategies are also developing. Large amounts of data about targeted groups of voters can now be retrieved and used rapidly; hence mail shots to these targeted groups, with the content aligned to what the parties know to be the preoccupations of particular groups. Even backbench MPs can now do this, such are the facilities offered by a cheap laptop or desktop. I guarantee that if you write to your own MP about an issue – say third-world debt – you will receive regular messages updating you on what the MP and the party are doing about it. Targeted telephone canvassing of voters, using computer assisted dialling for speed, is now also common. Technology is bringing down the cost of frequent mass communication: the most obvious case is the use of standardized email lists by the parties to pump out messages to the growing numbers of voters on email, and the use of text messages to mobile phone users.

People to people

All our examples of the impact of the new technology so far have been 'vertical' – up and down between leaders and people. But the potential of the new technologies to affect 'horizontal' communication between the people at large is particularly intriguing. We touched on this in Chapter 9 when we examined interest mobilization. Until recently this kind of communication, for instance to organize mass protests, was cumbersome and traditional: it relied heavily on word of mouth and the distribution of written material, the latter often expensive and difficult to print and distribute. But many British protest groups are now part of loosely coordinated networks that regularly organize demonstrations on big international issues, like the trading policies of the rich nations and the treatment of the debts of third-world countries. Communication through these networks via the technologies of email and interactive websites is now cheap and can be accomplished almost instantaneously. Even the adaptation of older technologies helps. The most obvious case is the spread of mobile telephone ownership. Until recently in public demonstrations the police had a distinct advantage because, unlike demonstrators, they had their own mobile radiotelephone communication system. In recent years the fact that demonstrators can use mobile phones to communicate rapidly with each other has altered the balance of advantage. The speed with which technologies are spreading means that we are probably only barely appreciating the importance of these technologies in allowing 'people to people' communication: in the mid-1990s about 15 per cent of British homes had a mobile phone owner; now virtually every adult, and many children, has one.

Surveillance of the people

The extent to which government operates surveillance over us is one of the most tense and difficult questions in democracy. This is what is best conceived of as 'unobtrusive communication': we communicate information about ourselves without ever realizing or intending to do so. Surveillance is needed, long established and accepted. The creation of an organized system of policing in the early part of the nineteenth century was exactly such a system, designed to provide security in the new cities of the Industrial Revolution. Over time surveillance has involved the adaptation of each new technology: thus the bobby pounding his beat became the bobby on the bicycle, then in the police car and, most recently, in the control room at the football match watching different parts of the ground on banks of television monitors. The new technologies are vastly expanding the possibilities for unobtrusive surveillance. Take an example given earlier: the use of speed cameras to detect motorists who break the law. So far these have been inefficient and slow to communicate and process information. The newest generation of digital cameras allows both much more reliable and comprehensive surveillance and, by link with a central national computer, much more rapid detection. (In the old technology, for instance, the cameras were often not functioning and the film had to be manually loaded and

DEBATING POLITICS 16.1

Modern technologies of communication: friend or foe of democracy in Britain?

MODERN TECHNOLOGIES OF COMMUNICATION MAKE DEMOCRACY HEALTHIER BECAUSE	MODERN TECHNOLOGIES OF COMMUNICATION ENDANGER DEMOCRACY BECAUSE
▶ They cut the costs of political mobilization and organization.	▶ They encourage a 'marketing' mentality on the part of political leaders.
▶ They undermine the monopolies over mass communication traditionally organized by the state.	▶ They give the state new means of surveillance over the population and thus strengthen hierarchical control.
▶ They promote communication between, and organization of, large numbers of physically dispersed citizens.	▶ They allow the combination and storage of masses of information about private citizens.
▶ They promote open debate and can allow electronic referenda giving all a potential voice in policy making.	▶ They discourage the face to face communication and debate which has traditionally been central to democratic life.

unloaded.) New technologies of surveillance can also be a counter to the new opportunities offered to the people at large: for instance, unless emails are encrypted (coded) it is technically a straightforward matter for authorities (either within firms or within the state) to monitor their content.

Much of the discussion of the political impact of new technologies is premised on the view that in reshaping communication it will also reshape democracy. Some accounts stress the dangers to British democracy, for instance through the new opportunities opened up to political parties to manipulate us with their sophisticated marketing and the opportunities opened up to the state to spy on us. Some, by contrast, stress the way democracy could be extended. For example, a standard justification for electing a House of Commons periodically to pass laws on our behalf is that it would never be possible to gather together over 40 million electors to choose directly what policies they prefer. But we are now almost at the point where every voter has access – for instance through a telephone keypad – to the means to register electronically their policy preferences. In principle we

could realize the dream of direct democracy, cutting out the 'middle men' (and women) in the House of Commons.

We do not know whether these visions will be realized. The one lesson from the recent history of mass communication technology is that we almost certainly do not understand the implications of present technological change for political communication. At the dawn of 'wireless' and television hardly anybody predicted the two great uses of these technologies for mass entertainment and political communication. Technologies can develop and be discarded with great speed. In the 1980s 'citizens band radio' – a system of short-wave radio communication – was briefly supposed to transform our lives. The mobile phone made it redundant. As a child in a remote west of Ireland village in the early 1960s I witnessed the widespread use of the telegraph – a system of communication based on landline wires and a special code, the so-called 'Morse code' devised by an American, Samuel Morse, in the nineteenth century. It is unlikely that any reader of this book has seen the system outside a museum.

Review OF CHAPTER 16

Four themes have dominated this chapter:

◖▶ The 'flows' of political communication are wide-ranging and complicated.

◖▶ Mass communications via newspapers and broadcasting raise very different issues for politics and politicians.

◖▶ Media bias is probably of critical importance in political communication, but critical only at the margins.

◖▶ Technology has always reshaped political communication, and the only thing we can say with certainty about the potential impact of the latest technologies is that we almost certainly do not at all understand what their long-term effects will be.

FURTHER READING

ESSENTIAL

If you read only one book for this chapter it should be Kuhn (2007), a comprehensive survey for the UK.

RECOMMENDED

Street (2001), though not confined to the UK, is all the more valuable for its wider range and link to themes of democratic politics. Seymour-Ure (1996) is the best historical overview of the development of the mass media system. Bartle and Griffiths (2001) is a collection focused on change. Mughan (2000) examines the connection between media effects and governing styles. The complex and difficult issue of media effects, on which this chapter draws, has been explored in several landmark papers by Newton and Brymin (2001) and Brymin and Newton (2003).

How elections are decided

CONTENTS

AIMS

This chapter:

■ Summarizes the roles of elections in the system of government, especially their relevance to the functioning of democratic government

■ Describes elections, electioneering and the campaigning strategies of the parties

■ Describes the factors that influence the choices electors make and summarizes how they are changing

■ Explains how election outcomes happen in Britain, especially how the rules of the electoral system shape these

ELECTIONS AND BRITISH DEMOCRACY

Elections are central to the theory and practice of democracy in Britain. As we saw in our chapter on how citizens participate in politics, going to vote is just about the most widespread act of participation. And while most of this chapter is about general elections – the UK-wide elections that happen, at a minimum, once every five years – many citizens have opportunities to participate in other elections; and these opportunities have grown in recent years. They are:

● Elections in local government. In London the range of these has now grown to encompass the direct election of a London-wide assembly and Mayor, the innovation of which has spread to some other local authorities.
● Elections to national assemblies in Scotland, Wales and Northern Ireland, which occur every four years.
● Elections to the EP, which occur every five years.
● Outside government itself elections by secret ballot have become increasingly common: for instance the reforms of trade union law in the 1980s greatly increased the use of secret ballots in choosing trade union officials and in opting for industrial action.

We live, therefore, in a voting 'culture'. Most of the elections summarized above have been discussed in earlier chapters. Partly for this reason the focus here is on general elections. But general elections also deserve a separate chapter for a number of additional reasons:

● Despite the introduction of elections in other arenas, like the Scottish Parliament and the EP, general elections still remain those which are most likely to bring citizens to the polling booth. Although, as we will see, turnout in general elections has on occasion fallen, it is still much higher than in any other elections in the UK.
● Despite the devolution of power downwards within Britain, and the transfer of power upwards to European institutions, the Westminster Parliament remains exceptionally significant. On the outcome of Westminster elections turns the identity of which party will control central government in Whitehall.
● Elections generally, and general elections in particular, are central to the theory and practice of British democracy. There are many theories of democracy, but all assign some important place to choice by the people at large through competitive election. There are also many different views about how British

democracy actually functions: they range from the view that Britain is, by world standards, a highly democratic country to the view that democracy in this country is a sham. But all these views turn in part on judgements about the effectiveness of general elections as a means of giving the people a voice in government.

Thus if we want to form a view about British democracy we had better first understand the workings of general elections.

Elections are about choice, but that simple statement conceals a powerful tension, one which runs underneath this chapter and surfaces at the end. We make choices all the time, notably as consumers in markets. One obvious way to think about electoral choice is therefore in the language of consumerism. That is an increasingly popular mode of thought, both among politicians and electoral analysts: among politicians as they use marketing techniques to sell the party brand; among analysts as they picture the voter as a calculating shopper in the political marketplace. But there is a very different way of thinking about voting. The history of struggle for the vote in Britain was not often expressed in the language of the market. When the suffragettes demanded votes for women they did not demand the right to shop alongside men in the electoral marketplace; they demanded the vote as an expression of human equality and common citizenship. The 'brands' in the market – the parties – continue to move us to depths of feeling that Tesco or Sainsbury cannot evoke: whether to feelings of loyalty or fury. When we vote are we shoppers or citizens? And are the changes coming over voting behaviour changing the balance between citizenship and shopping? We return to these questions at the end of the chapter.

ELECTION RULES AND ELECTION OUTCOMES

The rules governing the conduct of general elections in Britain were historically one of the flashpoints in the struggle to widen democracy in Britain. As we saw in Chapter 2 one of the most enduring political struggles for most of the nineteenth century and the early decades of the twentieth century concerned election rules. The most important points of struggle included the following. Who should be entitled to vote? How should voting be conducted – in secrecy or in public? What kind of inducements, if any, should politicians be allowed to offer voters to secure their votes?

One result of this long struggle is that elections in Britain, and particularly general elections, are now

BRIEFING 17.1

Registering and voting: easing the rules, combating fraud

Voting is voluntary in the UK and for nearly a century we have had 'universal suffrage' – the presumption that virtually all adults have an entitlement to vote. But exercising that entitlement traditionally was closely connected to the historical notion of the link between voting and representation – a territorial link, since the vote was cast for the representation of a locality. This imposed two restrictions:

- To register, voters had to establish permanent residence in a parliamentary constituency on a fixed registration date. This effectively ruled out registration by groups like the homeless.
- To vote, electors had to present themselves in person to a particular 'polling station', between fixed hours, on election day. Voting by proxy (for instance by post) was only allowed in exceptional circumstances. This made voting often very difficult for the mobile – frequent house movers, those forced unexpectedly to travel on election day.

There is a long-term trend in favour of easing both registering and voting rules, particularly as concern has grown about falling electoral turnout. They include the following:

- The voting innovations we described in Chapters 12 and 13: they include making postal voting available virtually on demand, introducing experiments in proxy electronic voting (e.g. via the Web), extending voting hours, and placing polling stations in more accessible places, like supermarkets.
- The Representation of the People Act 2000 eased the rules for electoral registration. In place of evidence of permanent residence, certain groups can make a 'declaration of local connection' – allowing groups like the homeless, remand prisoners and those in mental hospitals (other than the criminally insane) to be placed on the electoral register.
- The Act also provided for 'rolling registration': in place of once a year registration it is possible to apply at any time of the year – enabling those who move to a new district to register in their new place of residence, for instance; and application immediately on reaching the qualifying age. On the latter there is some evidence that the 2010 leadership debates led to a surge in this kind of registration.
- The more liberal laws on postal voting led to a surge in electoral fraud in the 2005 general election; the Electoral Administration Act 2006 is an attempt to tighten the conditions under which a postal vote can be obtained.

■ The long struggle to establish universal suffrage left a legacy of assumptions about the vote even when the struggle was won. One of the most important and subtle was that voters had to claim their entitlement to vote – a residue of the age when voting was a privilege of the few. Efforts actively to encourage voting, and to remove institutional obstacles, in part reflect fears about falling turnout, but also a change in assumption – to an assumption that voting is a right whose exercise should be actively encouraged. However, efforts to make voting easier have also made vote fraud easier.

Source: www.electoralcommission.org.uk.

conducted under elaborate rules, the most important of which are contained in statute law. (It is actually fairly unusual for political life in Britain to be so regulated by law.) Four particularly important sets of rules concern: eligibility to vote; the calling of elections; the conduct of elections; and the outcome of elections.

Eligibility to vote

The great struggles of the nineteenth century were partly about removing property ownership (of various levels) as a condition of entitlement to vote. We now speak of having a universal franchise, but that does not mean everyone is entitled to vote. Property qualifications have disappeared but the law still retains other important qualifications.

The clearest of these is age. As we noted in Chapter 2 the qualifying age was set at 18 in 1969. Strictly, this is the qualifying age for admission to the electoral register, a roll of names of all those entitled to vote. This exposes another important qualification: entitlement to vote in a general election is only an entitlement to vote in the constituency (one of the territorial divisions of the UK) where the individual citizen is entered on the electoral register. Failure to register disbars an individual from voting. This is not a formality. There are many reasons for failure to register, but the most important are connected in some way or another with the way people are housed. Until recently the homeless could not register, and although this restriction has now been eased it is certainly the case that the homeless will include few voters. Beyond the homeless, it is known that many of the very poorest – who often of course have precarious housing conditions – also do not register. The short lived Community Charge (Poll Tax), since it was levied on all those listed on the electoral register, also led to large numbers of deregistrations, and it is probable that many of those have not returned. (The Charge was first introduced in Scotland in 1989, and in England and Wales in 1990. Its abolition was announced in 1991 and was finally replaced in 1993.) At the end of the 1990s Weir and Beetham (1999:41) estimated that as many as 3.5 million voters were disfranchised at any one time. A more recent Electoral Commission study indicates that the magnitude of this problem remains unchanged: around 8 per cent of the eligible population (3.5 million) remains unregistered, and the figure is over double that for members of ethnic minorities and the population of London (Electoral Commission 2005).

Until recently, even for those registered, casting a vote could often be difficult. Voting could – except in unusual circumstances like illness – only be done in person, at a particular location (a polling station, usually a local public building like a school), for particular candidates in a particular parliamentary constituency. The apparent fall in turnout in some recent general elections – which we examine below – has led to experiments designed to ease these restrictions. For instance, it is now comparatively easy to vote by post, the opening times of polling booths have been extended, and experi-

IMAGE 17.1 ■ We have ways of making you vote

Photo: Michael Moran

■ We have seen at several points in this chapter and earlier that there is now widespread 'official' concern about electoral turnout and that a new agency – the Electoral Commission – has been created to regulate elections and parties. The image unites the two features: it shows a billboard campaign by the Commission to boost voter registration. The photograph was taken in Northern Ireland, where voter registration and participation is especially sensitive.

ments have been attempted in locating booths at more accessible locations, like supermarkets.

The timing of elections

Unlike many countries (and unlike the EP and new assemblies created by devolution) there has up to now been no fixed minimum term for the life of the House of Commons. (The coalition Government that took office in May 2010 committed itself to introducing legislation for a fixed term of five years.) The law stipulates that the life of a particular Parliament shall not exceed five years. The five-year maximum is a fairly firm constitutional convention of the kind we discussed in Chapter 4. In principle a government with a simple majority in Parliament could by a change in statute extend the period beyond five years. In practice the only time in modern British history when this has happened has been with all-party agreement in the great national crisis of the Second World War. (An election would normally have been due by 1940 but was delayed until the end of the War in 1945.) But there has up to now been no legal minimum life: the House of Commons elected in 2005 ran its full length, until May 2010; conversely, there were two general elections (February and October) in 1974.

BRIEFING 17.2

The rules on limits to campaign spending

Election	Regulated period (ends with the date of the poll)	Determination of spending limit
Westminster	365 days	£30,000 per constituency contested
Scottish Parliament	4 months	£12,000 per constituency contested plus £80,000 per region contested
National Assembly for Wales	4 months	£10,000 per constituency contested plus £40,000 per region contested
Northern Ireland Assembly	4 months	£17,000 per constituency contested
European Parliament	4 months	For each region contested, £45,000 multiplied by the number of MEPs returned for that region

■ Limits on campaign expenditure by individual candidates in constituencies have long been in place, but in the age of expensive national campaigns constituency spending became a small part of the total. The new limits introduced by the Political Parties and Referendums Act of 2000, and administered by the Electoral Commission, are an attempt to 'cap' total spending in the wake of widespread concerns about both the cost of election campaigning and related worries about the lengths to which the big parties were prepared to go to fund their expensive campaign habits. It is an illustration of the effort to get spending under control that the limits set did not change between the first and second editions of this book.

Source: www.electoralcommissio.org.uk.

Formally an election is called when the Monarch agrees to a request from the Prime Minister for a dissolution of Parliament. In practice, there is not a single instance in modern British politics of monarchs declining such a request (though we do not know, since the archives are not always available, how far a monarch might have demurred or even dissuaded a Prime Minister). Prime ministers have in effect decided when general elections are held; indeed deciding when to 'go to the country' has been among the single most important decisions that prime ministers make, though of course they would be foolish to make the decision without getting the best advice possible. It is rare for a Prime Minister to let a Parliament run its full legal life. They have occasionally asked for a dissolution because their government could no longer command a working majority in the House of Commons: that was the case with Prime Minister Callaghan in 1979. But, more commonly, they calculate what is the most favourable circumstance for fighting an election which will return

their party with a majority large enough to form a government. Among the most important skills needed by a Prime Minister are those that lead to shrewd choices of election dates. Thus the intention of the 2010 coalition government to introduce fixed terms is not only a major constitutional innovation; it amounts also to a significant restriction on the freedom of manoeuvre of a Prime Minister.

The conduct of elections

The details of the conduct of elections are elaborately prescribed. They begin with precise rules governing the nomination of candidates, whose papers must be filed by a specified date and supported by prescribed numbers of nominees from registered electors. Likewise all candidates must post a non-trivial deposit (£500) which is not returned if the candidate fails to secure 5 per cent of the votes cast. Over the course of the campaign, spending by individual candidates is also subject to strict and in the main rigidly enforced limits. The conduct of the ballot on election day is also closely regulated. Balloting is secret and anonymous. Precautions are taken to ensure that no individual's ballot paper can be identified. Once the polls close, arrangements are made to ensure that counting is efficient and honest. Independent officials – returning officers, mostly local government officials – organize the counting. Candidates are allowed scrutineers who observe the process, and who can – for instance if the result is very close – demand a recount to ensure that the outcome is not produced by counting error. These detailed – and important – legal safeguards reflect the historical struggle to create fair elections in Britain: as we noticed in Chapter 14, until 1872 balloting was open and therefore subject to bribery, intimidation and social pressure. Although there is a folklore of electoral fraud, especially in Northern Ireland, it is probably the case that the formal conduct of elections in Britain is free of any serious corruption, though there have been some significant cases of electoral fraud in recent years in local elections (see Briefing 17.4).

But the fact that the law governing the conduct of elections has largely been shaped by nineteenth-century problems has left it struggling to regulate the changed conditions surrounding election campaigns. The two most obvious instances are the national financing of elections (as distinct from financing in separate constituencies) and the national reporting of elections in the broadcasting media that became so important in the second half of the twentieth century. We look at each of these in turn.

Finance

The stringent restrictions on spending by individual candidates were until recently not matched by limits on a much more important source of spending: that by parties nationally in their campaigns. The expense of modern campaigning means that all the parties, and particularly the Labour and Conservative Parties, devote enormous energies to money raising, and their efforts have raised serious issues about the way rich interests can exercise influence over government. Following a series of scandals about sources of funding, and a set of recommendations for change by the Committee on Standards in Public Life, new statutory ceilings have now been set, administered by an institution we encountered in Chapter 14: the Electoral Commission. The short term impact of these limits is slight, since they have been set by reference to amounts spent in the most recent general election campaign, and thus still allow the parties to commit historically substantial amounts of money – and commit the parties to raising that money. But they are part of an important trend: the growing degree to which party organization and party competi-

tion are being governed by legal codes administered by the Electoral Commission.

Reporting

The framework of the law governing election campaigns was established before the advent of the most important forms of mass communication, notably television. For the first 40 years of mass broadcasting following the establishment of the original BBC in the 1920s the Corporation interpreted its duty of impartial reporting to mean that the actual conduct of campaigns should not be reported. Election broadcasting was confined to 'party political broadcasts' prepared by the parties, entitlement to air time being approximately proportionate to the number of candidates fielded. The rules governing party political broadcasts still exist, but from the late 1950s the restrictions on news coverage of elections were removed. General elections now attract saturation coverage in the broadcast media, but are still surrounded by rules concerning the balance of attention given, for instance, to separate candidates in individual constituencies.

The outcome of elections

General elections are presently fought in 650 constituencies. (The major parties feel obliged to fight in virtually all constituencies even when they patently have no hope of victory. By convention the Speaker of the House of Commons is not challenged, though in 2010 he was indeed unsuccessfully challenged by a candidate from UKIP, the main 'Eurosceptic' party.) But 'winning a general election' is the outcome of a complicated, in effect two-stage, counting process. Within each constituency, for general elections up to and including that of May 2010, the UK still determines the single winner by a 'simple majority' or 'first past the post' system: the candidate declared elected is the one who secures the largest number of votes. The Conservative–Liberal Coalition of May 2010 drastically changed the terms of debate about the electoral system: the Coalition Agreement committed to holding a referendum on the introduction of the alternative vote system. Although this is the least radical step to proportional representation (PR) (see Briefing 17.3 for a summary of the systems), in the eyes of the Liberal Democrats it is the first step to the introduction of a more thoroughgoing system of PR.

Beyond the outcome in a single constituency, 'victory' in a general election is decided, not by the letter of the law, but by conventional understandings – widely shared understandings, but nevertheless, like all understandings, sometimes unclear at the margins. The clearest and commonest case of victory is when a single

BRIEFING 17.3

Types of electoral systems in the UK

Title	How it works	Where used
Simple plurality, single member ('first past the post').	One representative per constituency; victor is candidate with largest number of votes.	Westminster Parliament; most local elections, though other systems spreading (Greater London Assembly, Scotland).
Supplementary	One representative elected. Voters vote.have two votes, ranking candidates in order of preference. If one candidate fails to win 50 per cent of first preference votes, all but top two are eliminated. Any second preference votes for top two, cast by voters for eliminated candidates, are distributed accordingly. Winner is candidate with most votes.	Mayor of Greater London.
Additional member system.	Electors have two votes. Proportion of seats allocated to single-member constituency contests settled by simple plurality (see above). Second vote is cast for a party list of candidates; remaining seats allocated according to share of votes cast, 'topping up' any seats won within constituencies so as to ensure share of all representatives is as close as possible to proportional share of popular vote.	Scottish Parliament; Welsh Assembly; Greater London Assembly.
Single transferable vote (STV).	Constituencies have multiple members (up to five). Voters 'rank' their preferred candidates in numerical order. A 'quota' of votes necessary for election is calculated, based on a division of total votes by number of seats. Successful candidates' surplus votes are allocated to the second choice candidate of their supporters. At each successive stage, if nobody has reached the quota, the bottom candidate is eliminated until all the seats in the constituency have been filled.	All elections in Northern Ireland; Scottish local elections.
Regional party list.	Electors vote for a party in constituencies covering large regions with multiple members. Seats awarded to parties in proportion to their share of the popular vote; parties rank their candidates in advance, thus determining the likelihood of a candidate actually being allocated a seat.	Elections to EP.
Alternative vote system.	Constituency boundaries unchanged; voters 'rank' candidates; candidate receiving 50 per cent of first place votes is elected; if no candidate receives this, second choices of lowest ranked candidate are redistributed; and redistributions continue until one candidate has 50 per cent of preferences.	The alternative preferred in the programme of the coalition Government in office from May 2010.

■ Britain is sometimes summarily described as the home of the 'simple majority' or 'first past the post' electoral system. It is not. And after the deal that produced a government in May 2010 'first past the post' may be consigned to history.

TABLE 17.1 Proportionality and disproportionality in Westminster parliamentary elections: examples from the general election of May 2010

Party	Popular vote (%)	Westminster Commons seats (%)
Conservative	36.1	46.0
Labour	29.0	39.0
Liberal Democrats	23.0	9.0
Scottish National Party	1.7	1.0
Plaid Cymru	0.6	0.5

■ 'Proportionality' – the extent to which seat allocation mirrors popular vote distribution – is not the only test of an electoral system, but it is an important one. And after the deal that led to the formation of the new Government in May 2010 it is right at the centre of political debate. Notice that it does not always work against small parties: nationalists in Scotland and Wales, with geographically concentrated support, more or less hold their own; it is minority parties with dispersed support, like the Liberal Democrats, who are 'punished' by the system.

party ends up with a workable majority of the 650 seats in the House of Commons over all other parties. Here is an obvious case where conventional understandings give only a partial guide. Mr Blair had clearly won the general elections of 1997 and 2001, with majorities over all other parties of 240 and 195 respectively. But parties have continued in government even when not commanding a majority, by creating an informal alliance with another party sufficient to command a majority in the Commons. And in May 2010, because the Conservatives, the largest party, fell short of a majority in the Commons, we saw the first formal coalition (Conservative–Liberal) since 1945. Even that coalition was not a foregone conclusion; it was arithmetically possible (and briefly seemed politically possible) for Labour to continue in office by stitching together a coalition of a number of parties. Thus, emerging as a winner with a 'workable majority' can depend on something other than simple arithmetic. It can mean something that can only be tested by practice: does it 'work' in the sense of allowing a government to carry on its everyday business, get important legislation passed and survive any motions of no-confidence? A majority that at the moment of a general election looks perfectly workable may over time degenerate into something very fragile. The Conservatives emerged from the

general election of 1992 with a majority of 21 over all other parties, in normal circumstances workable enough to form a government. But deaths and resignations over the life of the 1992 Parliament meant that the Party had to defend a succession of seats in by-elections (one off elections to fill a single parliamentary seat). It failed to retain a single one, and in the meantime became increasingly bitterly divided over the issue of relations with the EU. The upshot was that in the closing months of the Parliament the Government was often only able to continue in office with the tacit support of minority groups like the Ulster Unionists.

The lesson of this is that rules governing the outcomes of general elections are not hard and fast. (And as we saw earlier this is even truer in the very different electoral systems that now operate in elections to the Scottish Parliament and the Welsh Assembly.) Nevertheless, it will be obvious that the outcome of a general election is crucially determined by what the election produces in terms of parliamentary seats. That outcome is a complicated product of the interaction between the behaviour of millions of individual electors and the way the electoral system results in their views being counted. Later in the chapter we will look at each of these factors in turn; but first, we need to complete our account of the actual business of fighting elections by looking at the campaigns themselves – at electioneering, in other words.

FIGHTING ELECTIONS

The day of a general election in Britain – by convention always a Thursday – is the culmination of an intense period of open electioneering usually lasting by convention around four weeks. It follows the acceptance by the Monarch of the existing Prime Minister's request for a dissolution of Parliament. This period is frenzied, intense, often hysterical and sometimes fun, for the candidates, for their active supporters, and for the voters at large who are the object of all the frenzy. In this period virtually every parliamentary candidate, and certainly every leading figure in the major parties, spends each waking hour consumed by the elections – and, as polling day nears, usually cuts down on even the fairly small amount of sleep which leading politicians normally allow themselves. Ministers of the existing Government remain in office but attend only to the most pressing business themselves; much of the running of government is left in the hands of civil servants.

Although electioneering is conducted in a frenzy it is not completely chaotic. There are clear patterns, and these patterns are changing systematically over time.

Four long term changes of particular importance concern the length of campaigns, the role of manifestos, the significance of national campaigning relative to campaigning in separate parliamentary constituencies, and the changing role of electronic media. We examine each in turn here.

Length of campaigns

The formal length of general election campaigns (the gap between dissolving Parliament and election day) has not changed since the end of the First World War. But electioneering is not confined to these campaigns, and the extent and depth of campaigning has extended over time. In an important sense, electioneering is now continuous. As soon as one election is over parties start to prepare for the next. All the major parties now invest continuously in tracking the demands and perceptions of voters. They closely monitor published polling results and commission a continuous stream of private polling. In recent years all the major parties have invested in focus groups, of the sort that we described in the last chapter on political communication. This adaptation of a commercial marketing technique is designed to allow parties to acquire a more subtle picture of how electors view the parties and the political world generally. Thus, in the sense of continuously probing what the electorate feels, and in adapting their message to the findings, parties can now be said to be in continuous electioneering mode. This has been accentuated by the proliferation of elections. Local, devolved assembly and European parliamentary elections are important in their own right but are also now integrated into the permanent campaigning mode of the parties.

Role of manifestos

As electioneering has spread beyond the formal election campaign, so the shape and functions of manifestos has changed. Formally, manifestos are the documents issued early in a campaign which outline authoritatively what the different parties stand for. But hardly anybody reads them. This is sensible, because they are not intended to be read; they are intended to be reported and culled selectively by the Party's campaigners during the campaign. Nobody pretends that many voters read manifestos, still less make up their minds about voting after reading them. But manifestos are nevertheless important. They form the heart of the theory of the mandate: the theory that support in a general election means that voters have assented to what a party stands for and, therefore, that a winning party has the legitimate right to put into effect any commitments in the manifesto. Detailed research indicates, indeed, that parties in practice take mandates seriously: a large amount of comparative evidence indicates that the content of election manifestos is a surprisingly good guide to what parties actually do in government (Klingemann et al. 1994). So they form a kind of contract with the electorate, even if most of those involved – electors – never bother to read it.

Just as electioneering generally has now spilled beyond the formal campaign, manifesto making has expanded. The major parties typically prepare a 'pre-manifesto' a couple of years before an anticipated election – an outline draft in other words. The technique partly markets the party, by highlighting its main commitments without the clutter of detail, and partly tests commitments in the political marketplace: any that look unpromising can be quietly dropped in the final version. Parties have also elaborated the idea of the manifesto as a contract by culling the main manifesto for what are believed to be a few of the most attractive commitments and issuing them as separate highlighted pledges: for instance, in the 1997 general election campaign the victorious Labour Party gained extensive publicity for ten pledges which it extracted from the larger manifesto and 'marketed' as the Party's 'contract with the people'. The parties now typically respond to the realization that voters do not read manifestos by publishing something that follows the 1997 innovation – a short set of headline 'promises', of varying degrees of vagueness.

IMAGE 17.2 ■ The stressful business of electioneering

Photo: Jeff Overs/BBC/PA Wire

■ The big media innovation of the May 2010 general election was the US-style televized debates between the candidates of the three leading parties. The first debate undoubtedly transformed the fortunes of Nick Clegg, Leader of the Liberal Democrats, if not of his party. The image here catches the immense stress felt by the leaders: Mr Clegg and Mr Brown are both anxiously hopping on one leg as they consult their briefing notes in a moment of respite; Mr Cameron seems to have been distracted by something on the ceiling.

DOCUMENTING POLITICS 17.1

Electioneering fever, old and new

The *Daily Mirror* reports on Prime Minister Attlee's style of campaigning across the country, 1951:

'While his wife drives, Mr Attlee puts on his glasses, rests on a brown and green folk-weave cushion, and does newspaper crosswords ... If their car is held up at a level crossing Mrs Attlee gets out her knitting ... Like a good wife, before they set out every morning, Mrs Attlee puts a crease in her husband's trousers with a portable electric iron.'

Prime Minister John Major on his victorious general election campaign of 1992:

'My election schedule ... had been agreed before the campaign began. The aim was to shuttle me across the country, with the twin intentions of highlighting our predetermined themes and visiting constituencies ... I woke each morning at about 6.30, usually to find an already alert Sarah Hogg waiting edgily for me to approve a statement for that morning's press conference. Then I would scan documents briefing me on live issues of the day, gather up ministers due to appear with me, and head off over to Central Office for the daily press conference.'

■ The big contrast between these two campaigns 40 years apart is not how hard the two prime ministers worked. Attlee had an exhausting schedule of public meetings. Nor is it a contrast in efficiency: John Major's account in his autobiography emphasizes the chaos of campaigning. It is a contrast between Attlee's style, involving little administrative support and attempting to reach as many voters as possible in mass meetings; and the style a generation later which is geared to creating photo and broadcasting opportunities.

Sources: Daily Mirror, quoted in Harris (1982:491); Major (1999:298–9).

Rising importance of the national campaign

Historically, election campaigning in Britain developed primarily as a struggle in individual constituencies. But now all the important action takes place at a national level. The daily rhythm of campaigning is largely dictated by the schedules of nationwide broadcasting, television and radio, and of national newspapers. The parties typically host daily early morning press conferences designed to put a 'spin' on particular issues, sometimes chosen as part of an overall strategy, sometimes picked up at short notice to exploit a weakness in a rival party. Rapid transport – flying, or racing around the motorway system in 'battle buses' – means that most leading figures can combine a presence in London for press conferences with extensive touring. But touring, although it looks superficially like old fashioned 'meet the people' campaigning, is largely designed with the media, especially television, in mind. A set speech in the open air, a visit to a workplace or a home, or a 'walkabout' in a shopping centre: all have the same purpose. This is to create a reporting opportunity: a good photo and story for newspapers, a 30-second slot in the evening TV and radio news.

At the centre of this style of campaigning will be the individual party leaders themselves, who are the leaders because they are specially gifted at this kind of activity. Most normal people, faced with meeting a succession of total strangers, would be tongue tied. But good politicians are expert at converting casual acquaintances with total strangers into a 30-second exchange suitable for a television broadcast. They are also skilled at: summing up their party policy or denouncing their opponents', in a short sound bite suitable for radio and TV; at surviving hostile questioning by reporters; or, now virtually mandatory in general elections, at fielding questioning from 'cross-sections' of the public in TV forums. The general election of 2010 introduced another important innovation: television debates between the leaders of the three main parties at Westminster – which, the evidence suggests, did indeed significantly affect the outcome, at least to the extent of raising the profile of the Liberal Democrat Leader, Nick Clegg (see Image 17.2). There is a film clip dating from about 1950 of Clement Attlee, the Prime Minister and Leader of the Labour Party. A reporter asks Attlee if he has a message for the electorate. Attlee, famously monosyllabic, replies simply 'no'. A party leader who conducted himself in this way now would soon be replaced.

Rise of electronic campaigning

As the above suggests, there is increasing use of the most modern technology in election campaigning. Not only do parties now rely heavily on television and mass

BRIEFING 17.4

Is the system of electoral administration broken?

The administration of elections superficially looks like one of the most mundane topics in British politics. But the ability to conduct elections efficiently and honestly lies at the heart of democracy. Thus it was particularly ominous when, in May 2005, a judge in Birmingham found that there had been significant electoral fraud in the June 2004 local elections in the city. More important, he denounced the newly introduced system designed to make postal voting easier as leading to 'massive, systematic and organised fraud'. The system, he remarked, 'would disgrace a banana republic'. The case led to claims that the more liberal rules, introduced to make voting easier and thus to raise turnout, had exposed the system to widespread fraud. In two reports, based largely on analysis of Crown Prosecution Files, the Electoral Commission concluded that there was no convincing evidence of significant levels of fraud but conceded that there was a need for more systematic and comprehensive data on the matter. In a wider report on the system of electoral administration published in August 2008, however, the Commission did conclude that the system was experiencing great strains. The inquiry was prompted by widespread voter confusion in Scotland in the local and Scottish Parliamentary elections of 2007. The confusion seemed to have to do with the fact that electors were required to vote under two different electoral systems, for local government and Parliament, on the same occasion. The report indeed traces the strains in the system of administration to rapid changes in the character of electoral rules and electoral participation in Britain, changes examined more widely in this chapter and in Chapter 13.

Source: Electoral Commission (2007, 2008, 2009).

advertising to reach voters. They also increasingly use electronic technology to contact groups of particular 'target' voters – groups who might vote for the party, but whose support needs to be courted. Modern computing technology, allied to the use of social survey databases, allows parties quickly to identify these target groups, and the technology also makes it easy to send 'personalized' letters to them from the party leader in mail shots. Modern telephone technology, coupled with the fact that phone ownership is now almost universal, means that target voters can also be contacted personally. During elections the big parties now run what are in effect call centres to do this. Finally, the use of websites and email is becoming increasingly common – a mode of communication which we examined in the last chapter.

In summary, election campaigning in Britain is turning away from attempts to reach voters en masse in public places, such as in election rallies, and relying more and more on attempts to contact targeted voters directly and privately. A century ago a visitor to Britain during an election campaign who had no English would nevertheless soon realize that something momentous was going on: there would be numerous very public activities, like parades, rallies, mass meetings and impromptu open air speeches. A visitor now who had no English might well miss the campaign altogether: campaigning, though more frenzied than ever, is much more targeted and delivered by mass communication and modern electronic technology.

A great deal of debate has taken place about how far campaigns actually influence election outcomes. This issue is bound up with what we examine next in looking at what determines election results.

GOING TO THE POLLS

As voters we have to take two separate decisions: whether to vote; and, if we decide to turn out, who to support. We know a great deal about how voters make the second decision and rather less, as we will see in this section, about the first.

Deciding to vote

If voting were considered strictly in terms of its costs and benefits almost none of us would bother to turn out.

Since the reforms of the nineteenth century we cannot any longer obtain a bribe. The chances of our single vote determining the result are virtually nil: even the smallest majority in the 2010 general election was four (Fermanagh and South Tyrone) and the next most marginal was won by a majority of 42 (Hampstead and Kilburn). Thus even a group (of friends or a family) let alone one individual could not realistically think that their votes alone would decide a result. Yet tens of millions continue to turn out.

What we must conclude from these figures is that voting is about something more compex for the individual voter than the cost of voting and the benefit of winning. It is about an affirmation of some kind of identity. Since our sense of identity is formed by our own complex life histories, and our understanding of those life histories, we each turn up in the polling booth with histories that give us very different identities to affirm. For a quite small minority, those who are deeply committed supporters of a particular party, the vote is an opportunity to affirm their partisan identity and they will do it regardless of the likely outcome. These partisans would vote even if they suspected that they were the only supporter in the constituency; indeed that might be an added incentive to vote, since the affirmation of identity would be especially visible. For a larger group of voters the identity that is affirmed is an identity as citizens exercising their lawful entitlement to cast a ballot. Few people would actually use the formal language of citizenship, but the sense, however weak, that we have a duty to use our ballot is what carries large numbers of people with no great interest in politics to the polling station. And once there the actual choice can involve affirming all kinds of contingent identities, from the deepest – such as a lifelong loyalty to a party – to the most immediate – such as dislike of the personality of the Prime Minister of the day, or even dislike of a physical trait, such as the PM's tone of voice. (Worries that voters found Mrs Thatcher's tone too strident in the 1980s led to coaching designed to move her voice down the register.)

Deciding not to vote

We saw earlier that there are millions of potential voters who are disqualified because they do not register as voters. But there are also millions who, properly registered, decide not to vote. For much of the twentieth century these non-voters were a fairly small minority of the population at general elections. What is more, the little we knew about them suggested that they were 'sporadic' non-voters: in other words, they formed a floating group who shifted from voting to non-voting at different elections, rather than forming a distinct group who had withdrawn long term from electoral participation. (They were, however, a large majority in elections in local government, as we saw in Chapter 12.) It seems, however, that there is occurring a long term decline in voter turnout in Westminster general elections. Some of the reforms in voting procedure – such as making postal voting easier – are designed to try to reverse this trend. It also seems that non-voting is no longer 'sporadic'. It is consistent with other evidence we have discussed in earlier chapters. Voting in general elections is associated with support for one of the old established political parties, notably Labour and Conservative; and we have seen that there has been a long term withdrawal of active support for these parties. The rise of non-voting in general elections, though it is too recent a phenomenon for us to understand fully, may therefore indicate a permanent withdrawal on the part of large numbers of people from the kind of politics conventionally associated with competition between political parties for votes for the Westminster Parliament. There was some recovery in turnout levels in 2005 and 2010 compared with the low of 2001, but not sufficient to reach even the lowest turnout levels of previous decades. As we will see in a moment this is also consistent with evidence that the strength of identification with the parties among the electorate is declining.

AT THE POLLS: CASTING A VOTE

The evidence of turnout at elections suggests that voters are changing in their behaviour and loyalties, and this suggestion is strengthened when we look at how electors actually cast their votes. There seems to be growing volatility in voter behaviour. However, this volatility is relative; in other words, it shows up against the background of well known, long established, stable trends in behaviour. The best way to understand the new volatility is to begin first with a sketch of these old established patterns.

Party voting

If we wanted to predict how a group of voters are likely to cast their ballot in a forthcoming election, and we were allowed to have only one piece of information about them, one of the most useful bits of information to have would be how they voted last time. Voters do change, but the majority still have fairly settled loyalties to parties. Nor is that surprising when we consider both that voting is about affirming identity and that in most other areas of life – even trivial ones like the beer we consume – we tend to settle for particular brands.

FIGURE 17.1 ■ The decline of attachment to a party

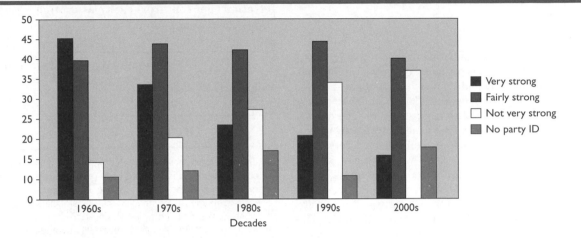

Source: Pattie and Johnston (2009:466).

■ Pattie and Johnston's summary of the history of party attachment in the last generation has one 'stand out' feature: notice that nearly 45 per cent of the electorate in the 1960s said they 'very strongly' supported a political party; the comparable figure for the new millennium is below 15 per cent.

But the way this party-link works, and the way it is changing, also provides an important clue to the way the landscape of voting is changing. Perhaps the most important reason why voters are so often willing to vote time after time for a party is that they have tended to organize their political loyalties through the psychological mechanism of party identification. Students of electoral behaviour explore this by examining responses to questions that ask voters if they feel attached to a party, and if so, how strongly they feel attached. A minority have a very strong identification, and these are a bedrock of support that a party can rely upon even in bad times. But even quite weak identification can help a party: if we only weakly identify ourselves as Scottish Nationalist or as Conservative, that nevertheless makes us a bit more receptive to the party's claims, and a bit more sceptical about those of its opponents.

How party identification is formed has been the subject of intense investigation and debate – hardly surprising, since we are talking here about a quite complex mental process. One of the most important features is what is sometimes called the 'cohort' effect: different generations of voters, with common experiences, often show distinct patterns of identification. The most famous example is the generation that entered the electorate in the years up to 1945, containing large numbers of Labour loyalists, and contributing to the

Labour Party's landslide victory in 1945. This was a highly distinctive cohort marked by the experience of economic depression in the 1930s and the common struggle in the Second World War.

The changing nature of party identification is one of the important clues to electoral change in Britain. The most important change is summarized in Figure 17.1. The changes summarized there are subtle, but consistent: there is occurring a long waning in the strength of party identification. Moreover this is consistent with patterns of voting, which involves a long term decline in support for the two historically dominant parties: in the 1950 general election Labour and Conservative combined received just short of 90 per cent of the vote; in the May 2010 election the comparable figure was 55 per cent, and this was consistent with levels in recent elections.

We have already now identified three key features of electoral change in Britain:

● in Westminster elections there has occurred a fall in turnout from historic highs, and in the new elected bodies created by devolution turnout is even lower;
● identification with political parties, especially with the two main parties, is weakening;
● votes for the two historically dominant parties, Labour and Conservative, are declining.

There are many reasons for these changes, but one probable source is the changed nature of class relations in Britain.

Class

The two-party (Conservative/Labour) system dominated British elections for half a century after the First World War and reached its peak at just about the mid-point of the twentieth century. This system was closely bound to the wider British class structure. There was a historically high level of 'class solidarity' among voters: middle-class voters, however defined, were very likely to vote Conservative, and working-class voters, however defined, were likely to vote Labour. A generation ago a leading textbook on parties and elections stated: 'class is the basis of British party politics; all else is embellishment and detail' (Pulzer 1967:98). The 'embellishment and detail' have in the intervening decades become increasingly important, as we shall shortly see, but class location still remains a very important influence over how people vote. 'Class' is itself a complex concept, but in the context of voting behaviour it usually means occupational class: the location in the class hierarchy identified by occupation. It traditionally referred to the divide between manual and non-manual workers, but as the divisions in the labour force have become more complex and subtle, that simple divide is no longer quite so revealing. But it is still not difficult to see why some measure of occupational class would be electorally significant: it is important to our perceptions of our economic interests and our judgement about which party would most likely defend those interests. As Table 17.2 illustrates, even in an election (2010) which broke with many historical patterns, class nevertheless remains a bedrock of the vote for the two numerically strongest parties, Conservative and Labour.

The connection between class and voting is changing over time, but why it is changing is a matter of some debate. The simplest indisputable reason is that one class that was at the heart of the old class-based voting system has declined greatly in numerical importance. These are male manual workers and their families, especially those employed in the old important industries of the Industrial Revolution: over the course of the twentieth century they moved from being a majority to a minority of the electorate, and a minority which continues to decline in numbers. The symbol of the change is the virtual disappearance of deep coal mining as an occupation in the last two decades, and the consequent disappearance of one of the most powerful and best organized parts of this old working class. The Labour Party, that depended so heavily on the support of this old working class, has had

TABLE 17.2 Class and voting in the May 2010 election (per cent from each class voting Conservative or Labour)

	Social Class AB	Social Class DE
Conservative	36	28
Labour	29	44

■ The table should be interpreted with care: it is a highly selective snapshot. It is designed, however, to show that at the class extremes there remain striking differences in voting behaviour: AB and DE are standard measures of class based on occupation, the first indicating those at the top, the latter those at the bottom. The figures report what voters told pollsters about how they voted in May 2010.

Source: Calculated from IPSOS MORI data reported in *The Observer*, 9 May 2010, p. 25.

to adapt its appeal beyond this working-class heartland. But it may be more than a matter of changing numbers. The culture of classes has altered greatly in the last half century. This is partly a matter of superficial changes in styles of dress, entertainment and accent – but superficial changes that may nevertheless be symbolic for class identity. More systematically documented are changes in really significant material circumstances. The rise of car ownership has shrunk the proportion of the population that now depends solely on public transport – in other words on a good provided or regulated by the state. The rise of home ownership, and the decline of 'social' housing such as that rented from local authorities, is another important long term change – again involving a decline in a key good provided or regulated by the state. This is not only breaking up the cohesion of groups such as manual workers, it may also be elevating in importance the feature of sectoral location The changing role of class in voting is important but subtle. Perhaps the best summary is that *occupational class* – class defined by the job of the main 'breadwinner' in a household – has become less important, though as Table 17.2 shows this is a relative judgement. But as we shall now see sectoral location, which is also often shaped by economic position, is also important.

Sector

All economies are divided into sectors: the publicly owned and privately owned sectors, for example, or the manufacturing and service sectors. As far as voting behaviour is concerned, the public/private divide is particularly important. Even taking into account other influences on the vote, like occupational class, private sector workers have long been more likely to vote Conservative, and public sector workers more likely to vote for the Labour Party. We could interpret this difference in terms of a rational calculation of interests: especially after the rise of Mrs Thatcher and her radical economic ideas in the Conservative Party, Conservatives were viewed as more likely to defend the interests of private sector employees than of public sector ones. Or we could interpret the difference in identity terms: that in important parts of public sector employment, like health and education, there are distinctive cultures which are more likely to favour the values of the Labour Party than of the Conservative Party. The example of employment is only one instance of the influence of sector on the vote. Housing tenure – especially whether we own, or rent publicly owned houses – and the extent of reliance on public transport can all affect the kind of calculations we make as voters about where our economic interests lie.

Territory

The influence of territory on the vote is marked, and also seems to be explicable in terms of an 'identity' interpretation of voting. In some cases these territorial variations are striking and could not be explained by, for instance, variations in the class composition of particular parts of Britain. The most vivid example was provided by the 1997 general election result. That was the culmination of a period of nearly two decades when the electorates of Wales and Scotland became increasingly alienated from rule by Conservative dominated governments in Westminster. The culmination of this alienation was the failure of the Conservatives to return a single MP in the two Celtic countries. In one part of the UK, Northern Ireland, the pattern of voting is shaped by identities which are virtually unique in Britain: the competing parties are distinctive to the province, and are expressions of national and religious identity, Irish and British, Catholic and Protestant. And territory can provide striking divergences from UK-wide trends: in the May 2010 general election, where Labour lost votes over the UK as a whole, it actually increased its vote in Scotland relative to the performance in 2005.

Religion

Religion used to be a powerful influence on voting across the whole of the UK: broadly, Anglicans were disproportionately Conservative; Nonconformist Protestants and Catholics voted for non-Conservative Parties – in the nineteenth century for the Liberal Party and then increasingly for the Labour Party. The waning of organized Christian religion in the second half of the twentieth century in Britain has left only a faint echo of this once powerful divide. Indeed, as far as the institutions of religion themselves are concerned, the social thinking of the Church of England became hostile to the sort of Conservatism represented by the governments that ruled between 1979 and 1997. But religion has reappeared in another form to which we now turn.

Ethnicity

Ethnic identity – the identification with some racial, national or culturally distinctive group – was always important: Irish Catholicism in all parts of the UK, for example, tended to be hostile to Conservatism, probably because it was associated with defence of the Union against, among others, Irish nationalists. Successive waves of immigrants over a period of more than a century have reinforced ethnicity as an influence on the vote. The most important present influence is among immigrants from the 'new Commonwealth' – the former colonial possessions of the Indian subcontinent and the West Indies – and their descendants. There are two striking features of voting among the most recent waves of ethnic minorities, at least those that originated from the 'new Commonwealth'. One is that there is markedly strong support for the Labour Party – marked even when we try to take into account long term social features, like class location, and short term features such as the overall strength of parties at particular moments. However we do the arithmetic new Commonwealth immigrants and their descendants are Labour voters. But the second feature is that black and ethnic minority voters participate in voting much less than the population as a whole. An Electoral Commission study suggests that this is due to a variety of causes. Factors such as language often hinder registration – an essential condition, as we saw earlier, of actually casting a vote. But there is also evidence that for many black and ethnic minority voters there is a feeling that the parties do not stand for the policies they would like to support (Electoral Commission 2002a).

Gender

There have long been marked gender variations in voting, though they have changed over time. Good evidence about individual patterns of voting behaviour has only become available since the rise of systematic mass surveying in the last generation. It nevertheless seems to be the case that, for at least a generation after adult women first received the vote in 1918, women

TABLE 17.3 The gender gap in May 2010: percentage of men and women reporting voting Conservative in May 2010 general election

	18–24 years	25–34 years	35–54 years	55+
Men	35	40	34	39
Women	25	27	35	44

■ It was long a truism that women were more favourably inclined to the Conservative Party than were men. That 'gender gap' began to disappear in the 1980s and 1990s. The table of reported voting in May 2010 suggests that a new gender gap may be opening up: only among the very oldest age groups are women now more inclined than men to vote Conservative, and among younger voters it is men who are more favourable to the Conservative Party.

Source: Calculated from IPSOS MORI data reported in *The Observer*, 9 May 2010, p. 25.

disproportionately supported the Conservative Party. That pattern persisted into the age when we have fairly good survey-based evidence about voting behaviour. But the special Conservative gender lead has been fading away in recent decades, and was almost indistinct in May 2010 (see Table 17.3). The reasons for this are many, but probably the most important is that the life experiences of women and men are becoming more alike.

THE OUTCOME: WINNING AND LOSING ELECTIONS

So far we have acquired what might be called a 'voter's eye' view of elections: a view of the influences that shape the individual voting decision. But parties are interested in a bigger picture: how do all these separate votes add up to an election outcome? This section is about this bigger picture. What determines the rise and fall of a party's election fortunes? We can divide the determining factors into three: what might be called the long waves of change in wider society; the short term intervention of critical historical events; and the policy performance of governing parties and their opponents. We summarize each in turn.

The long waves of change

If we look back at the development of British society over a long period – say over the last 60 or so years – we will see that there exist some clear long term changes, often taking place quite slowly, which fundamentally alter the social structure. These alterations in turn affect electoral fortunes. We have already discussed these in some detail in our 'voter's eye' picture of voting, so we can summarize them briefly.

Easily the most important is long term alteration in the class structure. In 1950 – when Labour and Conservative electoral dominance was at a peak – these two dominant parties had their roots firmly in occupational classes. That was especially true of the Labour Party. Since then the size of the manual working class has shrunk. Were Labour to rely on its old manual working 'heartland' it would never win elections, and those occasions in recent decades when it has performed disastrously – for instance in the 1980s – were marked by such a reliance. Nor have shifts in the occupational class structure only affected the fortunes of the Labour Party. The growing size of the middle class in the public sector – among teachers and health care workers, for instance – has worked against the Conservatives.

The second big long term change concerns gender. For a generation after women were enfranchised, as we noted above, the female vote favoured the Conservatives: at any given point in the class structure, for instance, women were more likely than men to vote Conservative. This persistent gender gap has disappeared, to the disadvantage of the Conservatives. Many possible reasons explain this, all connected to long term social change. Women now go out to paid work in much larger proportions than half a century ago: they made up just over 29 per cent of the workforce near the start of the twentieth century (1911) and just over 44 per cent by the end of the century (1998) (Gallie 2000:292). From a point where they barely entered higher education they now outnumber men. In short, the job and educational experiences of women are no longer as different from those of men as they once were, and in consequence their electoral behaviour is changing from the historical pattern.

A final long term change concerns the electoral impact of the Christian religion. Even though church attendance for most of the twentieth century was declining, religion still exercised a strong cultural influence, so that, for instance, the working-class vote that the Conservatives gained was an echo of working-class Anglicanism (the Protestantism of the state church). Much of Labour's working-class support echoed earlier Nonconformist and Catholic connections. The influence of Christian religion on election outcomes has faded to a distant echo. (However, in the case of non-Christian religions, notably Islam and Hinduism, there is a different story.)

POLITICAL ISSUES 17.1

Votes at 16

The qualifying age for voting was reduced to 18 (from 21) in the Representation of the People Act of 1969. The 'Votes at Sixteen Campaign' advocates a further reduction in the qualifying age. It argues the case partly on grounds of consistency – at age 16 young people have many of the obligations of citizenship, such as liability for tax, and therefore should have its entitlements. It also argues on moral grounds, claiming that the exclusion of those under 18 is similar to earlier historical exclusions, such as those barring women and the working class. The campaign now has a wide support base, ranging from established political parties (the Liberal Democrats and the Greens) to important groups in civil society, such as Barnardo's and the YMCA. In a potentially important breakthrough the Scottish Parliament voted unanimously in 2009 to enfrancise 16–17 year olds in elections to new Health Boards which will be popularly elected across Scotland.

For more on the campaign visit www.votesat16.org.uk.

The outcome of elections is therefore in part the result of long-term, slow changes like those sketched above. The composition of the electorate gradually alters by the succession of generations. At one end large numbers of people leave through the graveyard and crematorium. If they disproportionately represent a particular social formation – say manual workers or practising Anglicans – that can materially affect the chances of a party winning an election. At the other end, large numbers join as they reach the age of 18. These figures are so large that they can dwarf more short term swings in opinion. Around half a million new voters a year join as they reach the qualifying age to register; the number obviously varies with the birth rate 18 years before. Likewise a roughly similar number leave through death (and a smaller number through such factors as emigration). The 'turnover' in the electorate over a five-year life of a Parliament, therefore, is around 2.5 million. These changes often lie behind historic election upheavals: Labour's landslide victory in 1945, for example, owed a lot to the fact that war had postponed the election, and since the previous one in 1935 there had been a massive change in the composition of the electorate.

But if long term social change were the only important determinant of election outcomes, we would expect parties to rise and fall slowly. They do not; they often have dramatic changes in electoral fortunes because of the intervention of great historical events.

Critical historical events

Consider three general election results from the twentieth century: the result in 1918, the first occasion when the Labour Party decisively displaced the old Liberal Party as the main alternative to Conservatism in Britain; the 1945 result, which produced a huge Labour majority, broke a Conservative hold on government which had been almost continuous for nearly 30 years, and led to major reforms in economic policy and in the creation of the welfare state; and the 1979 result, which led to an unbroken 18 years of Conservative government, radical changes in economic policy like the huge privatization programme, and the forcing of the Labour Party to recast most of its social and economic policies. All these results were critical in the exact meaning of that word: they were great turning points in electoral history and in the history of policy. They represented decisive breaks with the past, and while they were connected to long term social change they were also a response to great historical turmoil: to the great stresses of the First World War (1918); to the equally great events of the Second World War (1945); and to the deep British economic crisis of the 1970s (1979). Thus the three most significant election results of the twentieth century were due to great historical dramas, not only to long term social change. A party can be destroyed as a major national electoral force as a result of a historical crisis, as was the Liberal Party in 1918; or it can be so badly damaged that it only recovers electorally after a long and painful transformation of its organization, policy and ideology, as was Labour's experience after 1979.

Policy performance

This leads to an obvious conclusion: parties cannot rely on the long tide of social change to carry them to office;

but equally, they do not have to submit to fate. In the 1960s there was a widely held theory that the Conservatives were doomed to permanent opposition because of the graveyard effect: Conservative voters were older than average, so they were disproportionately dying off. Yet between 1970 and 1997 the Conservatives were the governing party for all but five years. Many short term factors can affect a party's electoral fortunes, such as the skill of its leaders in marketing policy and the internal unity of the party. But in the last generation one overwhelmingly important influence has become clear: the electors' perceptions of policy performance, especially economic policy performance. As the word 'perception' indicates, the connection between the judgements voters make, the state of the economy, and the government's contribution to the state of the economy, is complex. For voters, a powerful influence is their sense of the way the economy is affecting their fortunes: do they, for instance, feel optimistic about their prospects over the coming months? It is possible for governing parties to do a lot about shaping perception: they can manipulate tax and spending policies to put money into the pockets of voters; they can use allies in the press, when they have them, to 'spin' a picture of an economy in prosperity. But no amount of spin can detach the perceptions of voters from the underlying experience of policy performance. Labour lost office in the critical election of 1979 because, either through bad luck or bad judgement, it ran the country when the economy was marked by very high inflation, successive currency crises and hugely disruptive industrial disputes.

But perception and performance are linked in complex ways. The Conservatives suffered the landslide defeat in 1997 despite four years of economic growth. What seems to have done for them was a single policy disaster: the deeply humiliating episode of 'Black Wednesday' on 16 September 1992. On that day, after a public humiliation at the hands of currency speculators, the Conservative Chancellor of the Exchequer was obliged to suspend Britain's membership of the European Exchange Rate Mechanism, then central to monetary management in the EU. Before that episode voters' perceptions – as reported in polls – had generally pictured the Conservatives as more competent economic managers than Labour; after it, Labour was consistently seen as more competent.

The equivalent for New Labour may have been 'Black Friday' on 14 September 2007, when for the first time since the middle of the nineteenth century panicky depositors queued up to withdraw their savings from a regulated bank, Northern Rock. The symbolic significance of this single regulatory failure was reinforced by the fact that it was the first great public sign of the

ensuing great recession. But while the 2010 general election undoubtedly produced a momentous outcome – a hung Parliament and the first coalition Government since 1945 – it is too soon to know whether it is a critical election in the sense of producing a long term shift in the loyalties of substantial proportions of the electorate.

WINNING AND LOSING: THE PARLIAMENTARY RESULT

It is one thing to win the popular vote; it is another to convert those votes into seats won in Parliament. The connection between popular votes and seats differs in the various election systems now working in Britain: our chapters on Wales, Scotland and Northern Ireland have described their systems, so here we focus on the Westminster Parliament in so-called general elections.

We have already described the bare bones of the system for electing the Westminster House of Commons. But although there are mechanics to election systems, the effect of election rules on parliamentary majorities is not mechanical. The rules combine both with the perceptions of voters and the distribution of voters to shape outcomes.

The system for producing parliamentary representation at Westminster has, to recall, two features:

● It is based on separate territorial constituencies with single member representatives. The size of the popular vote within each separate constituency is critical. There is no provision – as there is in the arrangements for the Welsh and Scottish Assemblies – for taking some account of the wider popular vote in calculating numbers of legislative representatives.
● Within constituencies the 'simple majority' rule prevailed up to and including the May 2010 election. This is a winner takes all system, in which the candidate with the largest vote, irrespective of whether it is actually a majority of all votes cast, is declared elected.

These features produce a number of well known effects. There is a systematic exaggeration of the movements in the popular vote at the parliamentary level. The Labour Party's share of the popular vote between 1992 and 1997 rose from 34.4 to 43.2 per cent; its share of Westminster seats rose from 41.6 to 63.4 per cent. Similar features could be observed in the more recent elections. In May 2010, the Conservatives won the largest share of the popular vote (36 per cent) but 46 per cent of the seats at Westminster; the Liberal Democrats won 23 per cent of the popular vote and 9 per cent of the seats. This is

BRIEFING 17.5

Winning and losing in May 2010

The General Election of May 2010 may be the last where we can say that the electoral system, rather than the popular vote, determined who 'won' in parliamentary terms. The coalition government formed after the election is committed to a referendum on the introduction of a new electoral system designed more accurately to reflect the popular vote in parliamentary seats; how much more accurately only time can tell. But the most important features of May 2010 have recurred throughout this chapter: the popular votes and the parliamentary allocation were significantly out of kilter; and quite small changes in the popular vote in a minority of key constituencies were critical to the parliamentary outcome. The Liberal Democrats, despite falling away in parliamentary terms, were the most spectacular short term winners because they entered government for the first time in 65 years; whether this proves a long term win again only time can tell.

precisely the result of the 'winner takes all' character of the counting system: a Party can lose its constituency majorities, and therefore its seats, on fairly modest swings of support. For the same reason the system has a tendency to exaggerate the majority of the largest winning party, a feature well illustrated in Table 17.1.

The system also tends to under-represent – relative to their popular vote – minority parties whose support is geographically dispersed rather than concentrated. For much of the period since the end of the Second World War the Liberal Party (and their successors the Liberal Democrats) have suffered in this way. Again this effect is produced by the combination of a simple majority rule and the counting of votes in separate territorial constituencies. But the big parties can also be penalized in parts of the UK where their vote sinks to the level of a small minority: that is how the Conservatives in Scotland failed in 1997 to return a single MP to the Westminster Parliament despite securing over 17 per cent of the popular vote; and in 2001 they secured only one seat with 16 per cent of the vote.

There now seems to be a growing tendency for some voters and the parties to learn strategically from these features of the electoral system: in other words, they adapt their behaviour to exploit its features. Among some voters the concept of the 'wasted vote' has long existed: the notion that it is pointless to vote for the party they would ideally prefer because it is unlikely ever to win. This is only a step away from a consciously strategic vote: supporting the candidate nearest the preferences of the voter who has the most realistic chance of winning. The result is a tendency for minority parties in separate constituencies to be squeezed out. The Liberal Democrats seem to be particular benefici-

aries: in constituencies where Labour has traditionally done badly, with large Conservative majorities, strategic Labour voters switch to the Liberal Democrats; and, vice versa, where Conservatives are weak in strong Labour constituencies, strategic Conservative voters switch to the Liberal Democrats.

The rational strategy for the two leading parties is to exploit this by pacts with the Liberal Democrats in individual constituencies. But there are huge obstacles to this, not least the problem of persuading local activists to give up their chance of even a hopeless contest. Nevertheless, the parties as organizations have begun to adapt. The Liberal Democrats' adaptation is simplest: they concentrate resources in constituencies where they are already in second place. On the part of Conservative and Labour the expectation that virtually all parliamentary constituencies will be fought, inhibits this. Nevertheless, both parties now concentrate their national resources on groups of target winnable constituencies, leaving 'hopeless' constituencies relatively neglected.

ELECTORS AND DEMOCRACY IN BRITAIN: CITIZENS OR SHOPPERS?

Competitive elections are central to British democracy. Historically, the struggle to establish democratic politics in Britain was dominated by the struggle to create a democratic franchise – to create an electorate that included virtually the whole adult population. In recent decades the democratic significance of elections in Britain has grown, if only because the range of electoral opportunities has widened. As recently as 30 years ago

DEBATING POLITICS 17.1

Elections: sham or key to democracy?

ELECTIONS PROMOTE EFFECTIVE DEMOCRACY	ELECTIONS FAIL TO PROMOTE EFFECTIVE DEMOCRACY
▶ Voting remains one of the commonest forms of political participation.	▶ Though common, voting is declining in popularity.
▶ Voting outcomes make a difference: parties seriously try to implement their manifestos.	▶ The mandate to implement a manifesto is a fiction: voters hardly ever read manifestos and are forced to accept party policies as a 'job lot'.
▶ The 'voting culture' is strengthening in Britain because of widened opportunities to vote.	▶ New campaign techniques mean that election campaigns are really extended exercises in marketing and manipulation.
▶ Voting is among the simplest and least costly forms of participation; reforms like electronic voting and easier postal voting are making it even simpler and cheaper.	▶ Nobody's single vote alone determines an electoral outcome, so the very act of voting is based on a fiction.

voters had only two opportunities to cast their vote: in local council and Westminster Parliament elections. But in the intervening three decades significant new voting opportunities have been created, and more will probably be created in the future. The opportunities include: the widened use of referendums to settle particular policy choices; new electoral opportunities in local government, notably to choose mayors; new electoral opportunities in the form of choices for membership of the devolved Assemblies; and the opportunity to elect members of the EP. At the same time what was once a highly uniform electoral system, dominated by the first past the post method of selection, is now much more varied in the electoral systems used in different elections. All these developments can be seen as an expansion of the citizenship possibilities of voting.

But the contribution of elections to democratic politics in Britain has also become more problematic. This partly reflects some healthy developments in British democracy. In particular, the growth of mass group campaigning means that citizens no longer rely so much on voting every three or four years to make their voices heard. But the power of elections to mobilize citizens democratically also seems to be waning. The new electoral opportunities are typically grasped by only a

minority of voters. The poll that historically had shown great effectiveness in mobilizing voters – the UK-wide general election – has significantly lost its drawing power.

The changing characteristics of elections and the electorate in British democracy have also influenced the way voting behaviour is analysed. In the 1960s and 1970s electoral analysts tended to view the voter as a social animal: as one moved by collective identities and group solidarity. Identification with party was pictured as a critical psychological mechanism shaping the vote and consciousness of class interest as a critical source of group solidarity. These two features lay at the heart of the first great study of voting behaviour in Britain (Butler and Stokes 1974). But the waning of party identification and the weakening of class identity has helped shift the focus of electoral analysis to the individual voter as a calculating animal. This shift has also been encouraged by fashions in political science, notably the rise of 'rational actor' models of behaviour – models that idealize political men and women as moved in their behaviour by close cost–benefit calculations of the consequences of choice. Thus the voter, once rooted in loyalty to class and party, now turns into a kind of 'shopper' in the electoral marketplace (see for instance Clarke et al. 2004).

Review OF CHAPTER 17

Four themes have dominated this chapter:

- The UK-wide general election is the 'kingpin' of the British system of elections, but it has been joined over recent decades by a variety of other electoral opportunities.

- Although the franchise is formally virtually universal, allowing all adults to vote, in practice many are excluded from voting, and many more have withdrawn.

- A wide range of social and economic factors help to explain the pattern of electoral choice, but long term change seems to be weakening what was once the overwhelming influence of occupational class on voting.

- In consequence, voting is becoming less an affirmation of citizenship and more a form of political shopping.

FURTHER READING

ESSENTIAL

If you read only one book it should be Denver (2006), which is authoritative and incorporates the primary data from the 2005 general election. It is wonderfully clear – ideal for the beginner.

RECOMMENDED

Butler and Stokes (1974) was the first great study of voting behaviour and set the intellectual agenda for decades. Clarke et al. (2004) introduce both evidence and political science models, in a subject which has been more subject to political science professionalization than most. Farrell (2001) is best on electoral systems. Johnston and Pattie (2006) is the definitive study on place and vote by the two leading electoral geographers in the UK; while their chapter on voting in Flinders et al. (2009) is an up to date overview which stresses long term change and the importance of place and space.

CHAPTER 18

How leaders are selected

CONTENTS

AIMS

This chapter:

■ Explains the connections between leadership recruitment and the theory of British democracy

■ Shows that for elected office the political party remains the all-important gateway to the top

■ Describes how elective office is being increasingly dominated by career politicians

■ Summarizes how two alternative methods to election – bureaucratic selection and patronage – work in Britain

■ Assesses how far leadership selection is done by merit and discusses how far it should be meritocratic

LEADERSHIP RECRUITMENT AND BRITISH DEMOCRACY

Choosing and dismissing political leaders is one of the keys to any successful system of government, and countries that, like Britain, claim to be democratic set themselves exacting standards. Choosing and dismissing political leaders is in modern Britain a largely peaceful business, though Northern Ireland is a partial exception to this generalization. Managing peaceful selection and dismissal of leaders is a great achievement, and just how great can be seen by glancing at less fortunate countries. Over large parts of the world, as the morning news bulletins will usually confirm, people regularly lose their lives and are driven from their homes because they live in countries which are unable to choose and dismiss political leaders peacefully. But we take peaceful choice and dismissal for granted in Britain and demand more: that the people at large should determine who become their leaders; and that all of us, as citizens, should have a fair chance of realizing an ambition to reach the top in politics. No actual democracy fully meets these stiff standards, and there are often good reasons why they are not met. But we should keep the ideal claims of democracy in mind in assessing leadership recruitment in Britain, and we will return to them at the close of this chapter. Some, though not all, theories of democracy entail views about the social structure of political leadership. In other words, it is thought to be a problem if, for example, formally democratic methods lead always to the selection of leaders from among those who are already rich and powerful. That is why the last main substantive section of this chapter looks at the social structure of leadership in Britain.

There is no single path to the top in Britain, no more than in any complex system of government. Indeed one of the things we will discover is that over time the routes to the top seem to be becoming more diverse. But there are three main paths and they are each examined in this chapter.

Competitive election

The best known is the method that is characteristically associated with democratic choice: selection for top positions as a result of competitive election. That is the route that the most publicly prominent political leaders – like the Prime Minister and other members of the Cabinet – have to follow, though as we shall see the mechanism of election is mediated in a number of important ways.

Bureaucratic selection

'Bureaucracy' is a word with unfavourable connotations for many: it conjures up images of rigid, inflexible offi-cialdom. But bureaucratic selection in its precise form has accompanied the development of democratic and accountable government in Britain. Bureaucratic selection means selection and promotion by merit or ability – as measured, for example, by success in a range of standard tests. It is an important method of selection in numerous large organizations in Britain, in both the public and private sector. It was developed in the second half of the nineteenth century as the characteristic method of selecting and promoting one key political group in Britain: the higher civil service that advises ministers on the making and implementation of policy. It remains, we shall see, an important route to the top, and possibly one that is growing in importance.

Patronage

This, we shall see, is one of the most important paths to the top in Britain, and also one of the most controversial. It is perfectly possible to achieve positions of great influence in British government without ever having contested an election, or passed any qualifying selection test, by virtue of being chosen by a powerful patron. It is plain why this is also controversial: it is hard to fit with our notions of democratic selection.

Election, bureaucratic selection and patronage are the three main routes to the top in Britain. Notice some that are, by omission, assumed to be unimportant: buying office and inheriting office. Buying office is openly prohibited, and while there are often allegations that large donations to political parties are suspiciously connected to some appointments, it is probable that purchase of office is rare. This is historically fairly novel. As recently as the early nineteenth century public office – for instance in the armed forces – could be openly bought, and it was widely assumed that the purchaser could expect a return on the investment. In other words, purchase and the corrupt enjoyment of office were directly connected. Until the secret ballot was introduced in 1872, bribing electors was a useful additional tactic in winning a parliamentary seat. The inheritance of office has taken longer to die out. Indeed, it still exists in a residual form: in the hereditary monarchy and even in the presence of a small group of hereditary peers in the House of Lords. (See the discussion of Lords reform in Chapter 9.)

ELECTIONS AND LEADERSHIP RECRUITMENT

Suppose you were asked by an ambitious young person for advice about starting off on a successful career as an elected politician. What is the best advice to give? The answer is actually fairly straightforward: get a university

People in Politics 18.1

Patronage: how to get to the top without fighting elections

Baroness Ashton (1956–)

Few members of the public will have heard of her, but she is one of the most powerful people in Europe. She was successfully nominated in 2009 by Gordon Brown for the new post of High Representative of the European Union (in effect the foreign minister of the EU). She has never fought an election: she has worked, successively, for a pressure group, a consultancy and a quango. She was made a life peer in 1999 and held various junior ministerial jobs. She made the jump into the big time when Gordon Brown nominated her as the successor to Peter Mandelson as a member of the European Commission in 2008.

Lord Ashcroft (1946–)

He has not only never fought an election, but his status as a British resident is subject to uncertainty and dispute. Yet he is a vice chairman of the Conservative Party, advises the leadership and has accompanied the Party's foreign affairs spokesman (William Hague) on trips abroad. The clue to his status can be described in one word: money. He is one of Britain's richest men and has contributed generously to the Conservative cause. He was made a life peer in 2000 on the nomination of the then Leader of the Conservative Party, William Hague. His position shows how cash strapped political parties are extending patronage to the wealthy.

Alistair Campbell (1957–)

Educated at Cambridge University; journalist 1980–1994, culminating as political editor, *Daily Mirror*; Press Secretary to the Leader of the Opposition, 1994–97; Prime Minister's Official Spokesman, 1997–2001; Director of Communications Strategy, 2001–03. Recruited by Tony Blair when he became Leader of the Opposition, Campbell was probably the Prime Minister's closest advisor, 1997–2003 and one of the most powerful people in government. Although holding no official position, he remained influential with the Labour Party leadership at least up to the 2010 general election campaign.

Cartoons: Shaun Steele

■ None of these people has fought a parliamentary election. There are many different non-elected routes to the top, but all have this in common: it helps to have a powerful patron.

education; join a political party as soon as possible; forget any career other than politics; and get elected into office – preferably in the Westminster House of Commons – as young as possible.

We can put flesh on this general advice by considering the examples of the two most successful elected politicians in Britain in recent years. Gordon Brown enjoyed 13 years at the top of British government, first as a uniquely long serving Chancellor of the Exchequer, 1997–2007, and then as Prime Minister, 2007–10. He was displaced as Prime Minister in May 2010 by David Cameron, the Leader of the Conservative Party.

At first glance these two look opposites. Brown was from modest lower-middle-class origins: the son of a Church of Scotland minister, he was educated at state schools and at the University of Edinburgh. Cameron, his Conservative rival, is authentically blue-blooded (he can even claim a distant relationship to the Royal Family). Moreover, he was educated at Eton, the most socially exclusive of English public schools, and at the elite University of Oxford.

In fact the two have a huge amount in common and their commonalities provide clues to how to get to the top in Britain. Both have the formal mark of the modern middle-class professional: a university education. Even more important, both have been virtually nothing in their adult lives but professional politicians. Although Brown was briefly a university teacher and television researcher, these were just waiting rooms before he entered full-time politics as a member of the House of Commons. Cameron had a period in public relations when the Conservatives lost office in the 1990s, but he was already working for the Conservatives at the age of 22. Both men secured an essential condition to rise in metropolitan politics: a safe seat in the House of Commons in their thirties (Brown was 32, Cameron was 35). In short, both have been little but professional politicians since leaving university – indeed Brown began a bit sooner, because he was a prominent student politician.

Of all the different advice the examples of Brown and Cameron would suggest to the politically ambitious, one is overwhelmingly important: join a political party. In the electoral route to the top in Britain parties provide the only realistic pathway. Until recently, the advice could have been even more exact: join the Labour or Conservative parties. As we know from our discussion of devolved government and local government, these two parties do not quite monopolize leadership as much as they once did. Indeed if the Conservative–Liberal coalition of May 2010 is the wave of the future the ambitious might seriously consider joining the Liberal Democrats: a higher proportion of Liberal Democrat MPS than Conservative MPs are in government office in the coali-

tion. But wherever we look for the obvious sources of political leadership that are the result of election – in the Westminster Parliament, in the Welsh Assembly, in the Scottish Parliament – we find them dominated by people with party labels. And although we will see later that a few of the top positions – for example in the Cabinet in Westminster – are occupied by people who have ascended by other means, like patronage, most of the top positions are dominated by people who began their ascent by winning elections under party colours. This is why, in examining paths to the top, we have to start with election to Parliament.

Pathways to the Westminster Parliament

As we saw in earlier chapters there is considerable doubt whether individual backbench members of the Westminster Parliament exercise any significant influence over how Britain is governed. But these doubts do not deter large numbers of aspirants wanting to become MPs, and the single most important reason is that further success in political life is heavily dependent on being a Member of Parliament – indeed of the House of Commons. The very top of the political ladder – the Cabinet – is dominated by MPs; it is now over a century since a Prime Minister was drawn from beyond the House of Commons (Lord Salisbury, Prime Minister 1885–86, 1886–92, 1895–1902). Serving in the Scottish Executive and the Welsh Cabinet also demands election to the Parliament and Assembly respectively.

It is here that the importance of party starts, for it is virtually impossible to enter either the House of Commons, or their Scottish and Welsh counterparts, without possessing a party label. And while voters are increasingly volatile in the choices they make, in practice a party's nomination for a seat is in the overwhelming majority of cases a guarantee of a seat in the Commons: in the two Westminster parliaments of 2001–10 there was a solitary independent, and he lost his seat in May 2010.

This makes the nomination and selection process, especially in the Labour and Conservative parties, a critical first step in making a political career. Both major parties operate with a centrally approved list of candidates. This list acts as a filter allowing the party nationally to rule out undesirables – whether on grounds of ideology or personal character. But the really important choices for the Westminster Parliament are still made by the parties in the individual constituencies. The party activists make these choices. There are some variations in method between the parties, but in most cases a shortlist of possible candidates is made, usually by some executive committee of the constituency party. Those on the shortlist are then usually presented to an open meeting

POLITICAL ISSUES 18.1

It's posh at the top

For a generation, being well connected seemed to be a hindrance to rising in British politics. After the old Etonian Sir Alec Douglas-Home stepped aside as Conservative Leader in 1965, the Party chose a selection of leaders of modest origins who had risen in the usual meritocratic way: of the next six all but one were state school educated; the exception, Duncan-Smith, had been to a minor public school. All were born to families of modest means. The election of David Cameron (Eton and Oxford University) as Leader of the Conservative Party in 2005, and the emergence of George Osborne (St Pauls and Oxford) as Shadow Chancellor, apparently reverses that trend. Several other prominent Conservatives, such as Boris Johnson, Mayor of London, are also old Etonians. There were 20 old Etonians in the 2010 Parliament, an increase of five over the 2005 Parliament. The Leader of the Liberal Democrats, Nick Clegg, is the son of a rich banker, and was educated at Westminster, after Eton possibly Britain's leading public school. The question is: why is democratic politics apparently producing upper-class leaders? There are three different possible answers:

- It isn't. Politics is still a predominantly middle-class trade dominated by bright scholarship types primarily educated in the state sector or in minor public schools. The emergence of Cameron, Osborne and Clegg is just coincidence.

- Political leadership, like leadership in all other organizations, is increasingly demanding and performance driven, but leading public schools like Eton and Westminster have reorganized themselves in the last generation to train their pupils to compete in this performance driven world.

- Britain has become increasingly unequal in the last three decades (see Chapter 2), so it is not surprising that the rich and well connected are once again coming to dominate political leadership.

of members of the constituency party. Nominees normally deliver a short speech and answer questions. The process puts a high premium on two things: public presentation and back stage manoeuvring. On the day, it advantages those who have the ability to speak convincingly and to respond at short notice and at short length. But the nomination is very often sewn up before the big day, because the other quality that can clinch things is the ability to find supporters and patrons, especially in the leading members of the party. Even though there is now a strong expectation that anyone with parliamentary ambitions will first fight a hopeless seat, nevertheless parties with no chance of winning often find it difficult to find a reasonably competent candidate. In these cases a novice can still turn up and win on the day with a good public performance without having powerful connections. But in safe seats the big day is always preceded by lots of lobbying and making of connections.

This account holds in broad outline for how candidate selection to the Westminster Parliament works, but in recent years there have developed subtle but important differences between the parties. In particular, candi-

date selection in the Labour Party is more under central control than in the Conservative Party, where local activists jealously guard their traditional control of the process. In 2002 the Labour Government passed legislation allowing the imposition of women-only shortlists (previous attempts had been ruled contrary to anti-discrimination legislation). This is a sign of a wider interest among the national Labour leadership in 'engineering' candidate selection. The purpose of this engineering has been various. As the 2002 legislation shows, one important aim has been to alter the gender make up of the candidates' group and thus of Labour MPs – an aim shared with the Conservative leadership, but much more effectively accomplished because of greater central control over the process. In other instances Labour has successfully engineered selection to head off the likelihood of adoption of potentially embarrassing or ideologically troublesome candidates, and to ensure the selection of candidates favoured by the national leadership.

Getting a safe seat in the House of Commons – the prerequisite for a political career at the apex of British

BRIEFING 18.1

Women-only shortlists

All the leading parties are committed to increasing the proportion of women parliamentary candidates, especially in winnable seats. Promotion, mentoring and training have all been tried, with modest results. The Conservative Party, since David Cameron became Leader, has committed itself to the creation of a single 'priority' list of women candidates from whom constituency parties can choose and to ensuring that shortlists contain a 50/50 gender balance. But the Labour Party is the only leading party to try to change things by women-only shortlists, which of course guarantee the selection of women as parliamentary candidates. An earlier attempt in the 1990s by the Party to introduce women-only shortlists was struck down after a successful challenge in the courts, the argument being that the practice breached anti-discrimination law. The Sex Discrimination (Election Candidates) Act 2002 removed this obstacle. It allows parties to introduce women-only shortlists, special gender awareness training for party selection committees and women-only training for potential women candidates and women's networks; its provisions have now been extended to 2030. The measure has often encountered strong local resistance, partly on the grounds that it prevents the selection of the best candidate on merit, partly on the grounds that it allows the national party to intervene in what should be a local selection process.

■ The case of women-only shortlists is important in its own right, but it also encapsulates a wider issue in selection for political office: how far should selection be made by some criteria of individual merit, irrespective of class, gender or ethnicity, and how far is the job of political selection to promote the political representation of some social groups?

Source: Kelly and White (2009).

politics – therefore demands persistence: willingness to fight a hopeless seat first; and spending time cultivating local supporters or a powerful patron at the top of the Party. It is best to start young, because, as we shall now see, entering the Commons before the age of 40 at a minimum is important to making it to the top in politics.

Pathways to the front bench

The 'front bench' is where the members of the government, and their 'shadows' on the opposition benches, face each other in the Westminster Parliament; it has become a widely used shorthand symbol for the Westminster parliamentary leadership of the parties. The most important frontbenchers of all are the (usually 20 or so) members of the House of the Commons who are in the Cabinet. In addition, government appoints up to an additional 80 ministers of various ranks. (As we will see below a small number of Cabinet members and other ministers are drawn from the House of Lords.) Getting into government, and finally into the Cabinet, is for most MPs the whole point of a political career. Increasingly it is precisely that – a career. In the fairly recent past there

were many MPs who combined being a Member of Parliament with other careers – for example in business and the law. But the most successful politicians now – like Cameron and Brown – have been full time politicians for almost all their adult lives.

In fact once a politician has managed to get into the Commons, the odds on getting a front-bench position shorten dramatically. Even a government with a large parliamentary presence – as Labour had for 13 years after 1997 – had to fill around one hundred jobs. So even if the selection were random the odds– with over 400 Labour MPs – would have been close to four to one. But it is not random. A sizeable minority is already ruled out of selection by a mixture of considerations: their private lives are too chaotic, for instance through drinking or shady business dealings, to risk entrusting them with a job; they have been tried in the past and found too incompetent; they are too old (it is now rare for any member of the Commons to be appointed to a first time job after their mid-50s); they have powerful enemies at the top of the party, either because of their political views or because of some personal feud.

DOCUMENTING POLITICS 18.1

The reality of political leadership: life as a junior minister

4 November 1999

To bed at 1.30 a.m., up at 5.45. My existence is now almost entirely pointless. This week I have ... replied to two adjournment debates, made speeches to the British Geological Society, the Institute of Waste Management and the Association of Residential Management Agents ... I have worked my way through red boxes piled with letters to sign and papers, almost all of which are marked 'To See' rather than 'To Decide.'

■ Chris Mullin's diary of his life as the most junior of ministers is a corrective to any belief in the glamour of political leadership: it chronicles days of tedium and ineffectiveness.

Source: Mullin (2009:43–4).

A prime minister forming a government therefore has even fewer options than the bare arithmetic of parliamentary numbers suggests. But other considerations also restrict choice. As we will see in a moment, at the level of the most important part of the front bench – the Cabinet and the Shadow Cabinet – at least party leaders work from close personal knowledge. But in filling the most junior ranks a prime minister will have to rely on others for advice and talent spotting. The whips – who maintain discipline in the parliamentary parties and generally manage them – are very important in talent spotting. Many a successful career is started by catching a whip's ear through a good speech in the chamber, a useful intervention in a committee or a favour done – for instance, by asking a helpful parliamentary question to a minister.

Apart from being hemmed in by lack of direct knowledge of many of the more junior candidates prime ministers also have to 'balance' their selection. They cannot appoint on simple competence alone. Increasingly the make-up of governments is scrutinized, and criticized, for its gender and ethnic balance, the balance between different regions of the Kingdom, and the balance between different factions in the Party. Balancing factions is also linked to appeasing powerful rivals to the

party leader. Ambitious junior MPs get ahead by acquiring a powerful patron – hitching their careers to a leading figure in the Cabinet, for instance. Since these powerful figures are always on the look out for supporters – either to boost their status generally or with an eye to a future contest for the party leadership – the network of patron and client is very important in all the parliamentary parties.

The outcome of the May 2010 election imposed an entirely novel set of constraints on the Prime Minister: in the kind of coalition constructed then the PM has to reserve an allocation of seats around the Cabinet table, and in the junior ranks, for the coalition partner. We do not know exactly how David Cameron allocated the roles to the five Liberal Democrats in his new Cabinet, but we can be certain that he will have done so by bargaining with Nick Clegg, the Leader of the Liberal Democrats – who had himself to be given the title of Deputy Prime Minister as part of the coalition bargain.

One lesson of this is that the business of picking frontbenchers is a business full of chance and personal considerations, heavily shaped by the intense political life of the quite small communities that compose parliamentary parties. This mix of chance and personality is even more important in the bigger promotion: to the Cabinet.

Pathways to the top: entering the Cabinet

A minority of Cabinet members are drawn from the House of Lords, but most come from the ruling party in the Commons (or as in May 2010 from all partners in the coalition) and it is very rare for someone to be promoted directly to the Cabinet from the backbenches. In the promotion from a junior ministerial job many factors are at work. Since the Cabinet is a small group the Prime Minister will be able to rely heavily on direct knowledge of individuals, rather than, as in the case of the many junior posts in government, having to take advice from whips or from powerful Cabinet colleagues pushing the claims of their clients. Getting into a Cabinet, and staying there, depends on a mixture of competence and luck. But the competence needed to be a Cabinet minister is fairly specialized, and we got a glimpse of it in our account in Chapter 6 of life in the core Executive. Almost everyone around a Cabinet table will be pretty intelligent, but brains are not the most important qualification for the job. Those who get right to the top will have enormous stamina, self-belief and ambition. Physically, the life of a Cabinet minister is punishing. The working day is spent in a hectic round of meetings, private and public. Paperwork – contained in the 'red boxes' into which by tradition civil servants put the papers to be read by ministers – is heavy and usually has to be dealt with in the late evening or early morning. A Cabinet minister constantly has to perform in a very wide range of settings: in official meetings, from Cabinet committee downwards, where the department's interests and values have to be promoted, often in fierce competition from equally self-confident and ambitious Cabinet colleagues; in debates and questions in the House of Commons, where the Minister is constantly attacked by the Opposition, and often from the government side; and, increasingly important, on television and radio where interviewers now commonly see their job as cross-examining ministers in as aggressive a manner as possible.

A Cabinet minister will thus often start the day at the crack of dawn trying to catch up with paperwork while being driven to the office in the ministerial car; will have not a moment of free time during the day, moving rapidly between high level appointments, most of which involve intense argument; will often have an official dinner or reception with a set-piece speech to make, in the evening; and can end up at 11 o'clock, while the rest of us are sipping our bed time cocoa, being aggressively cross-examined by Jeremy Paxman on *Newsnight*. The Minister may then have to work for a couple of hours on ministerial papers at home to prepare for the next day's round. Any weakness – a shred of self-doubt, a physical illness – will soon be magnified by this life. To enter and survive in the Cabinet, it helps to be clever; but it is essential to be hugely self-confident, limitlessly ambitious and have the physical stamina of a brewery dray horse.

Even all this is not enough: plenty of politicians with these qualities never get off the backbenches or do not survive a Cabinet reshuffle. By the time the very top is reached in politics chance plays an important role. Prime ministers choose Cabinets not just by the personal qualities of colleagues, but on a host of other grounds: they need to balance the different factions in their party, and increasingly to seek some balance on lines of gender and region; they want to have their own allies in Cabinet, but also have to give jobs to powerful rivals, many of whom are potential candidates for the job of prime minister itself. Once in, a Cabinet career can be destroyed by ill-luck: the career of Chris Smith, who served four years in the first Labour Cabinet from 1997 before disappearing into the obscurity of the backbenches and then the even greater obscurity of the House of Lords, never recovered from his department's responsibility for the disastrous Millennium Dome project in London, even though he only inherited the project.

Personal foibles also often destroy careers. Top politicians tend to be extrovert risk takers, and are likely to get into more scrapes than, say, the average timid university professor. In recent times Cabinet resigna-

IMAGE 18.1 ■ An iconic political leader

■ This famous statue of Churchill, an icon of the most iconic political leaders, also perhaps explains why we no longer commemorate leaders so readily by public statuary: located in Parliament Square in Westminster it is often vandalized during political demonstrations.

tions have more often happened because of these personal scrapes than policy failure. They include resignations for having a pregnant mistress; making love to a mistress while wearing a Chelsea football kit (allegedly); taking a huge secret loan from a colleague to buy a house; being robbed on a London common while allegedly cruising for gay sex: all despite the fact that not a single one of these activities (not even wearing a Chelsea kit in bed) is illegal.

Pathways to the top: becoming Prime Minister

Prime ministers require in abundance all the qualities demanded of Cabinet ministers, and an even more generous helping of luck to get to the top job. In the

Westminster system for over a century now they have had to be leader of one of the two main parties, and for over 90 years the job has alternated between the leader of the Labour and Conservative parties. Though these are no longer as dominant as in the past, as the general election result of 2010 attests, the best advice for the ambitious youngster wanting to end up as Prime Minister is probably still to join either Labour or the Conservatives.

The 'job description' for a Prime Minister is daunting. A necessary, but not sufficient condition, in modern times has been to achieve leadership of either the Conservative or Labour parties – and as we will see in the next section doing that demands the support of an increasingly wide range of interests in their party. Prime ministers often get the job while their party is already in government. This was the case for example with Harold Macmillan (1957), James Callaghan (1976), John Major (1990) and Gordon Brown (2007). But to hold onto the office they have both to win general elections and to convince their party that they can continue winning. This last condition is critical. Mrs Thatcher, for instance, led the Conservative Party to victory in every general election she fought (1979, 1983, 1987). Yet three years after winning a landslide for the Conservatives in 1987 she was deposed by MPs who feared that she would not be able to repeat the trick a fourth time. Brown spent his brief period in office the subject of virtually permanent conspiracies to replace him, because it became clear almost as soon as he entered Number 10 that he could not deliver electoral victory; and indeed he resigned shortly after Labour's defeat in May 2010.

Once in the job, the qualities demanded are a magnified version of those required of a Cabinet minister. Most of the problems a Prime Minister deals with are insoluble. He or she has simultaneously to be able to think and argue about issues of great complexity; be skilled at personal relations, handling others with huge egos, like Cabinet colleagues and other foreign political leaders; be able to take life and death decisions, and then move on quickly (every British Prime Minister since 1979 has had to fight a war somewhere); be good at every imaginable form of public presentation, from the set-piece speech to an aggressive interview at the hands of a TV or radio journalist. A Prime Minister who cannot excel at all this on a limited amount of sleep is lost. Surrounded by supporters and courtiers, the Prime Minister is nevertheless also subject to a barrage of criticism. Several close Cabinet colleagues will usually think they could do the job better and will be waiting for an opportunity to depose their leader. The job is all consuming, usually demanding attention for at least 18 hours a day, seven days a week (look back at Briefing 6.1, p. 95). And finally,

every bit of private life is increasingly scrutinized. Where prime ministers spend their holidays is argued over in the newspapers, and the immediate family dragged into the spotlight. Being Prime Minister is hard. Being the spouse or the child of a Prime Minister can be a nightmare: every personal foible, or even something as trivial as dress style, is jeered at by journalists and political opponents.

Even for the most ambitious, self-confident, tough and able politician, walking into 10 Downing Street as Prime Minister also demands a large helping of luck. Every British Prime Minister since 1979 bar Gordon Brown has arrived unexpectedly, helped by chance. Margaret Thatcher quite unexpectedly became Conservative leader in 1975 (the precondition of becoming Prime Minister four years later) ahead of several better placed candidates, after her predecessor Ted Heath was destroyed by electoral failure. John Major emerged from obscurity in 1990, helped mostly by feuding at the top of the Government that removed more likely successors to Thatcher. Tony Blair became Labour Leader (and inherited Labour's electoral triumph in 1997) because of the early death from a heart attack of his predecessor John Smith in 1994. David Cameron became Prime Minister in 2010 because he had quite unexpectedly emerged as a dark horse to win the race for the Conservative leadership nearly five years before. The one thing we can be sure of in speculating about future prime ministers is that, if we try to guess who the next one will be, still less the next but one, we will almost certainly guess wrong.

ELECTIVE PATHS TO LEADERSHIP: CHANGING TRENDS

We now have a snapshot of the elected paths to the top in British politics, at least in the Westminster system. But these paths naturally change all the time. Three changes are particularly important, especially the first since it is indeed modifying the significance of the Westminster route.

The widening range of routes to the top

Until very recently getting to the top in British politics meant one thing: getting to the top in the Westminster system. This monopoly of political leadership is now being broken. The alternative of a political career in the EP, though it does not compare in visibility with membership of the House of Commons, is increasingly attractive. It cannot lead to government position, but the pay and conditions are at least as good as Westminster, the opportunities to fiddle expenses much greater, the

BRIEFING 18.2

The importance of luck: how prime ministers got to the top, 1945–2010

PRIME MINISTER	CRITICAL EVENT THAT LED TO NO. 10
Clement Attlee (1945–51)	Originally became leader in the 1930s when huge electoral defeats removed stronger Labour leadership candidates from Parliament.
Winston Churchill (1951–55)	Outsider for most of the 1930s, became Prime Minister and Leader of the Conservatives because of the great war crisis of 1940.
Anthony Eden (1955–57)	A rare case of the 'heir apparent' succeeding to the job; resigned in ignominy.
Harold Macmillan (1957–63)	Emerged from an informal process of consultation when the expected successor, R. A. Butler, was found to have too many enemies at the top.
Alec Douglas-Home (1963–64)	Emerged as unexpected winner from a mysterious and secretive process to choose the leader of the ruling Conservative Party.
Harold Wilson (1964–70)	Leader of ruling Labour Party, from 1963, elected when the Party's leader, Hugh Gaitskell, died unexpectedly after an apparently routine operation.
Edward Heath (1970–74)	Won leadership of Conservative Party in 1965 in first open election for office; led victorious Conservatives to unexpected victory in 1970 general election.
Harold Wilson (1974–76)	Unexpectedly returned to office in general election of February 1974.
James Callaghan (1976–79)	Won election for leadership of Labour Party after sudden, unexpected resignation of Harold Wilson.
Margaret Thatcher (1979–90)	Won general election as leader of Conservatives in 1979; elected as Conservative leader in 1975 as 'dark horse' candidate.
John Major (1990–97)	Elected as Conservative leader and Prime Minister after Thatcher was deposed by backbenchers; 'dark horse' who came through the field late in the day.
Tony Blair (1997–2007)	In 1992 was a middle ranking member of the Shadow Cabinet. Labour's unexpected loss of 1992 general election led to resignation of Neil Kinnock as Leader; in 1994, his successor John Smith died of a heart attack. Blair inherited a virtually impregnable Labour lead in the polls.
Gordon Brown (2007–10)	Another rare example of heir succeeding; like Eden departed in ignominy after short tenure.
David Cameron (2010–)	Prime Minister as result of winning Conservative leadership unexpectedly as a dark horse in 2005.

■ Politics is often now spoken of as a career, and it is indeed becoming more professionalized. But right at the top, luck (including other people's bad luck) plays a huge role in deciding who gets into 10 Downing Street as Prime Minister.

burden of constituency casework lighter, and the scrutiny powers of the EP are steadily growing. Membership of the European Commission (there is one British member) is highly influential and very well rewarded. It is in practice in the gift of the British Government and is often occupied by those who fail to make it to the very top at Westminster, a consolation prize for missing out on ministerial office. It probably should therefore be considered part of the 'patronage' route to office examined below (see also People in Politics 18.1).

More significant alternatives still have been opened up by the devolution measures introduced by the Government after 1997. The Scottish Parliament and Executive, and the Welsh Assembly and Cabinet, now offer alternative careers to anything available in the Westminster system, both as parliamentarians and as ministers. An equally significant development, as we saw in earlier chapters, is that both these systems of government have broken the hold enjoyed for nearly a century in Westminster by Labour and Conservative: both have operated coalitions, and the electoral systems at work in Wales and Scotland suggest that coalition will be common in future. Finally, the introduction of directly elected mayors may diversify routes to the top even more: the two mayors of London elected so far (Ken Livingstone and Boris Johnson) have made significant extra-Westminster careers out of the post.

These diversified electoral routes to the top are also exerting complex effects on the role of political parties in leadership selection. As we noted, in Wales and Scotland they are destroying the two-party Conservative/Labour domination that has marked Westminster for over 80 years. The pattern in the admittedly still small number of communities that have opted for an elected mayor also suggests that the elective mayoralty may become a career route which offers a real alternative to the monopoly of the established parties: non-party 'mavericks' seem to have a better chance of success than in the Westminster Parliament. But conversely, the election systems used in the EP, and in the devolved national institutions, strengthen national party control over the chances of election, weaken constituency influence, and thus diminish the chances of returning members prepared to act independently of the party.

The widening range of selectors

An increasingly wide range of people are becoming involved in picking political leaders in Britain. The most important change we documented in Chapter 14: choosing the individual political leaders in the Westminster system. As we saw in that chapter Labour first involved members in leadership elections in the early 1980s, the Conservatives late in the 1990s. The Liberals pioneered the widening of this franchise, electing David Steel through an electoral college representing all constituency associations as long ago as 1977. Now all three of these parties give a big say to individual members through secret ballot.

Professionalization

The third and final trend is affecting all politicians, but especially those at the top of the Westminster and the devolved systems. Professionalization means that politicians who want to get to the top have to treat it as a life-time career. The most successful (like the present Prime Minister) have really never had another serious job: they enter Parliament young and their pre-Parliament job is either just to mark time or is directly linked to politics – for example, as a political adviser or researcher. A route that existed a generation ago in both the Conservative and Labour parties (carving out a successful career in business or in trade unionism before entering Parliament) has now almost disappeared. As a reflection of this shift, the real pay of politicians has been rising over the years. MPs, for instance, were only first paid in 1911, an annual salary of £400; now the pay of a back-bencher matches that of a well paid professional, has numerous 'perks' for expenses and a generous, non-contributory pension scheme. The professionalization of politics does not mean that politicians rely on their political income alone. The pay of an MP compares well with that of a university professor or a general medical practitioner, but has nothing like the job security of these professions: redundancy and obscurity beckon at every general election. MPs supplement their salaries by lucrative short-term work: directorships and consultancies, where the MP is in effect a lobbyist for an economic interest; journalism; and speaking engagements, where the rewards for good speakers can be high. But this kind of work is very different from the kind of independent career common a generation ago; it is an extension of political professionalism.

LEADERSHIP RECRUITMENT: THE BUREAUCRATIC PATH

The higher ranks of the civil service, in the Westminster and the devolved systems, exert great influence over policy. Top civil servants do not enjoy the public recognition of politicians, but for a clever, ambitious, twenty something, a career in the civil service is probably a more certain route to power and influence than running for elected office, with all the unpredictability described above. It also offers much more job security and, at the

IMAGE 18.2 ■ A very civil partnership at the top: Cameron and Clegg in 2010

Photo: PA Photos

■ The photo shows a historic occasion: the first Westminster coalition since 1945. Much was made of the socially elitist character of the new leadership: both the Prime Minister (David Cameron) and the Deputy Prime Minister (Nick Clegg) are from families made wealthy from City of London connections; both went to elite public schools (Eton and Westminster) and elite universities (Oxford and Cambridge.) But there is another similarity which has been just as important in this chapter: both are professional politicians who have known nothing of life outside the world of professional politics and public relations.

very top (for example the head of a civil service department), the financial rewards are better than those at the top in politics. In the most prestigious departments, such as the Treasury, exercising significant influence over policy need not indeed wait until the top has been reached. The Treasury is small and collegial in its working methods, and officials at formally junior levels often have access to the most important policy making discussions.

Although changes are constantly taking place in the formal structure of the civil service, the bureaucratic route to influence has not fundamentally altered since the civil service was reorganized in the second half of the nineteenth century. These original reforms were designed to eliminate selection and promotion by personal connection and political favouritism. Under various guises since then the service has had a 'fast stream', recruits who normally enter in their early twenties and who are marked out for rapid promotion to the top. Most of those in the fast stream can expect by their fifties to be at a level where they are playing a large part in advising ministers and directing the implementation of policy – both activities that confer great influence. A minority can expect to become permanent secretaries – the highest grade – heading a department and acting as the main adviser and close confidant of ministers. They always exit from these posts at age 60, when they can then expect to have an active retirement supplementing a generous pension with lucrative company directorships or membership of quangos, exploiting the expertise and contacts built up during their working lives.

BRIEFING 18.3

The bureaucratic path

'Fast stream' appointments to the civil service are the most desirable: they give early access to roles in providing policy advice to ministers and mark appointees out for rapid promotion, culminating in the most senior posts. Entrants are mostly new, or nearly new, graduates. The selection procedure is a refined version of 'bureaucratic' selection according to criteria which attempt to select impersonally – by marks of ability, independent of any considerations of background or connection. There are four stages:

■ first: a qualifying test which anyone can complete online;

■ second: a series of 'e-tray' exercises;

■ third, candidates who meet a qualifying standard are shortlisted for a one-day set of exercises and interviews at the Fast Stream Assessment Centre;

■ fourth: the successful candidates who wish to be considered for work in Parliament, the Diplomatic Service or in a European Service Fast Stream must pass a final selection board; applicants for posts in central departments only have to submit a departmental assignment form online.

■ The Civil Service Selection Board procedure, notably the third stage above, used to be caricatured as the 'country house weekend' method, in which it was often argued that candidates were being chosen by the social graces they displayed during the period of the selection exercise. Whether true or not, the Civil Service over the years has tried hard to move as close as possible to a 'bureaucratic', impersonal model of selection.

Source: http://www.civilservice.gov.uk/Assets/CSFS.

This is an attractive route to the top, avoiding many of the stresses and uncertainties of the elected route. Competition, especially to enter the fast stream, is intense; but the gate of entry is so narrow that, once in, competition is much less intense. Fast stream applicants are virtually guaranteed a long career of rising influence. Most successful applicants will have done well in formal education: until recently Oxford and Cambridge graduates dominated those recruited, and graduates of the leading universities are still disproportionately represented. Nor is this surprising because the selection process advantages the academically gifted. The first stage and second stages involve a battery of written tests; the third and final stage a series of interviews and role playing exercises, all of which are suited to the quick witted, the socially confident and those educated at elite universities where education still relies heavily on small group discussions.

The method of recruitment reminds us that the civil service is a bureaucracy, because this kind of formally impersonal selection by some measure of ability is one of the classic marks of a bureaucracy. Promotion too

depends heavily on these qualities. Top civil servants have to be able to do three things to a high standard: master the essence of a subject quickly, because they are generalists offering ministers advice about a wide range of issues; write quickly, clearly and concisely because a large part of the job is writing briefing papers for ministers who want rapid, easy to assimilate documents; and have the confidence and ability to put views across orally, since much of a civil servant's life is spent in meetings, formal and informal.

These skills are akin to those of a lawyer, a journalist or possibly a university teacher. They are different, for instance, from the skills often required in business, such as the ability to sell or to manage practically complex projects. The kind of skills needed to work in the Prime Minister's private office are very different from those required in managing a large scale building project like constructing a new hospital or a bridge. Whether civil servants need these latter skills is at the heart of the long debate about the competence of higher civil servants discussed in Chapter 7. The 'hiving off' of agencies, described in that chapter following the Next Steps

Initiative, was in part an attempt to value these latter skills more highly. Daily management of the prison service, or of the benefit system, does demand the ability to manage administrative operations of high social and technical complexity. Indeed the creation of the Next Steps agencies has also involved some direct recruitment of top managers from the private sector, and indeed more recently there have been a few cases where permanent secretaries of civil service departments have been recruited from outside.

As we saw in Chapter 7 the wisdom of creating agencies in this fashion is the subject of debate. But leaving aside these debates, the separation between department and agency has had one possibly unintended effect: it has actually made more valuable the traditional skills of the civil servant, for it has removed from departments the very tasks – managing delivery of administratively and technically complex policies – that stretched traditionally skilled civil servants. As the higher civil service specializes more and more in policy advice and strategic thinking, the traditional skills – intelligent quick wit, the ability to write and speak fluently – become even more important. The traditional bureaucratic route to the top thus remains largely unaltered.

LEADERSHIP RECRUITMENT: PATRONAGE AND NETWORKING

'Patronage' means selection for a position because one is a client, a favourite or a political ally of those who have the position in their gift. It can be contrasted with selection by some formal measures of ability (the method used for civil service entry) or competitive election. It has always been important in Britain and is becoming more so, for three reasons. First, at the very heart of the constitution the reform of the House of Lords has now virtually abolished one old way of getting to the top – inheritance of an aristocratic title. Although the reform of the House of Lords is not complete, entry now is largely an act of patronage, principally by the leaders of the three major political parties in the Westminster system. Second, government both nationally and locally has increasingly resorted to a wide range of specialized agencies to carry out its functions. Some idea of the scale of this can be gained by looking at Table 18.1 below. Third, government increasingly relies on task forces and advisory groups to help it formulate policy, and membership of these task forces, often put together at short notice, is another important 'patronage' route to positions of influence.

Agencies, task forces and advisory groups of the sort covered in Table 18.1 are staffed by official

TABLE 18.1 The scale of patronage in British government (numbers of appointments available, 2001–03)

Parliament (the reformed House of Lords, including hereditaries, law lords, archbishops and bishops)	690
Board members of executive and advisory non-departmental bodies, public corporations, etc. (central and devolved government)	21,901
Task forces, ad hoc advisory bodies, policy reviews	1,895
The courts (the judiciary throughout the UK; lay JPs, etc., except for district court service in Scotland)	29,338
Members of Non Departmental Public Bodies tribunals (not of social security and employment tribunals, etc.)	11,572
NHS (health authorities, primary care trusts, NHS trusts, other NHS bodies, commissions and tribunals)	4,591
Local public spending bodies (registered social landlords, training and enterprise bodies, board members of higher and further education institutions)	47,647
Local partnerships (statutory and on local authority initiative)* (est.)	75,000
Prison service (members of boards of visitors)	2,002
School governors**	381,500

* members are elected to a few neighbourhood regeneration boards alongside appointed and co-opted members;
** includes parent governors who are elected to governing bodies alongside other categories of members.

■ The table is taken from a series of investigations by the House of Commons Select Committee on Public Administration into the scale of appointed office in British government: into 'patronage', as used in this chapter. Not all these offices by any means are in the gift of the Westminster Executive, never mind the Prime Minister. Not all are equally important, as will be obvious. But they emphasize that the 'patronage' route to office is important whether we think of the importance of the jobs in question or of the sheer scale of the appointment system.

Source: Select Committee on Public Administration (2003: Table 1).

BRIEFING 18.4

A limited reform of the patronage system: the Office of the Commissioner for Public Appointments

The Commissioner for Public Appointments was established in 1995 following recommendations of the Committee on Standards in Public Life. Appointment by the Crown is intended to signal independence of the Executive. The Commissioner is responsible for public appointments in England and Wales; there are separate Commissioners for Scotland and Northern Ireland. The Commissioner monitors, advises and reports on public appointments in health bodies, non-departmental public bodies (examples range from the Arts Council to the British Potato Council), public corporations, nationalized industries and the utility regulators. The Commissioner's jurisdiction covers over 11,000 public appointments. The Commissioner works mainly through a Code of Practice which stipulates a set of principles (such as appointment on merit and openness in the appointment process).

■ The establishment of a Commissioner for Public Appointments was a response to the growth of patronage as a method of recruitment to public office, and is in effect an attempt to 'bureaucratize' the process: to subject it to formal, standard procedures. The effect has been greatly to increase the openness of patronage appointments. But there remain two important restrictions as the examples in Table 18.1 show: (i) at the very top the most politically sensitive appointments are exempted from this process; (ii) quantitatively, although the Commissioner covers a huge number of posts, the sheer scale of the patronage state shows that even this large number constitutes only a minority of patronage appointments.

Source: http://www.publicappointmentscommissioner.org/.

appointment. 'Official appointment' here covers many forms. The most sensitive top positions – appointing the chair of a major public body such as that of the BBC Trust – rests heavily on personal knowledge among small groups of top people. Boastful self-promotion; getting a track record by already serving on successful bodies; being personally known to the right people; making the right political alliances: all are important. But as the range of bodies to be filled has increased vastly, government has had to systematize the process. Dissatisfaction with the lack of transparency in the appointment process led the Committee on Standards in Public Life to recommend new procedures and safeguards in the middle of the 1990s. The result is summarized in Briefing 18.4: the creation of the Office of the Commissioner for Public Appointments. But this formality, while it has modified the workings of patronage, has not abolished it. For the most senior (and often lucrative) posts the creation of shortlists is now often largely in the hands of professional 'headhunters': specialist recruiters who rely heavily on word of mouth and recommendations from existing holders of elite positions to rustle up candidates for a shortlist.

Patronage of the kind described here is fairly straightforward to chart because it ends up in formal appointment to top positions. There is, though, another route to the top that is more elusive, but nevertheless important. In summary it can be called 'networking': individuals exploit their personal skills, social contacts and organizational location to gain access to the very top of government. Among the most effective networkers are 'fixers': figures who specialize in helping people at the top when they are, literally, in a fix, either because of a private or public problem. Lawyers tend to be among the most common fixers. Ministers' lives mostly consist of one crisis after another, and they constantly need people who can help them to respond. If there has been some catastrophic scandal or other policy failure in their department they often need a 'safe pair of hands' to chair an ad hoc committee of inquiry; if there is a delicate bit of negotiation they need someone reliable to have a quiet word in the right place; if they are in some personal difficulty they will need confidential advice about how to handle the problem if it becomes public, or even how to avoid the law. Since fixers often have to be found in a hurry, being well placed in easily accessible networks is a key to benefiting from this kind of patronage.

TABLE 18.2 Political leadership, 1910 and 2010

	Schooling	University	Gender
Prime Minister 1910 (Asquith)	State	Oxford	Male
Prime Minister 2010 (Cameron)	Fee paying	Oxford	Male
Chancellor of the Exchequer 1910 (Lloyd George)	State	None	Male
Chancellor of the Exchequer 2010 (Osborne)	Fee paying	Oxford	Male
Foreign Secretary 1910 (Grey)	Fee Paying	Oxford	Male
Foreign Secretary 2010 (Hague)	State	Oxford	Male

■ Analyses of the changing composition of the political class as a whole over the course of a century show some well documented changes, referred to in the text, such as the decline of aristocratic representation. But when we look right at the very top of the political tree the most striking feature is continuity: notably in the dominance of elite universities and in gender.

Sources: Calculated from *Who's Who* and from Butler and Butler (2000).

THE CHANGING SOCIAL STRUCTURE OF POLITICAL LEADERSHIP

The traditional structure

Some systems of government in the past have occasionally selected political leaders by lottery, thus ensuring that they are a random sample of the people. But political leaders in Britain are anything but a microcosm of the population. Everything we have seen in this chapter shows that only those with unusual tastes and energy are likely to persist in the struggle to the top. It is hardly surprising, therefore, that when we look at the social characteristics of leaders they are also unrepresentative of the wider population. In both the colloquial and statistical sense of the word they are not 'normal' people.

We can best understand the present by starting with a quick glance at the past. Until the middle of the nineteenth century there were two routes to the top in Britain: birth, since the country was ruled mostly by a hereditary aristocracy, and patronage, since an alternative route for the ambitious was to attach themselves to an aristocratic patron. Some of the most distinguished figures in the country's political history, such as the great Conservative philosopher and politician Edmund Burke (1729–97), relied on aristocratic patronage. The reforms of the senior civil service from the middle of the nineteenth century removed patronage from selection and opened up a bureaucratic route to the top for those who could satisfy the measures of ability used by the service in selection and promotion. The widening of the franchise in the second half of the century, coupled with the introduction of the secret ballot, meant that increasingly the route to the top lay through successfully winning elections to the House of Commons. But as we now know, this newly created electorate largely voted for parties, not individuals. This meant that the leading parties were key institutions in shaping the social structure of political leadership. The Liberal Party, the Conservatives' main rival until 1918, played an important part in modestly widening the social range of leadership recruitment: on the eve of the First World War, for instance, the Liberal Prime Minister was of modest lower-middle-class origins, having made his way via university scholarships and a successful legal career; his Chancellor of the Exchequer (who became Prime Minister in 1916) was from a poor rural Welsh family, having made his way by qualifying as a country solicitor and then forging a reputation in radical Welsh politics.

The more socially inclusive nature of political leadership was accentuated by the rise after the First World War of the Labour Party as the main opponent of the Conservatives. For instance, Labour's first nationally recognized leader (Keir Hardie, 1856–1915) began his working life as a miner; the first Labour Prime Minister (Ramsay MacDonald 1866–1937) was born illegitimate into poverty.

Looking back over the whole span of the first half of the twentieth century two trends in the social composition of the political leadership can be seen:

- for the first time in the political history of Britain a significant section of political leadership had been born in families of manual workers;
- there was a steady decline in the once utterly dominant position of the aristocracy.

355

The changing structure

The striking feature of long term developments since then is the continued decline, to the virtual point of extinction, of aristocratic influence – but also the decline of manual workers as a source of political leaders. All the main parties now look remarkably alike in the social composition of their leadership: aristocratic 'grandees' are a curiosity in the Conservative Party; working-class self-made politicians are a curiosity in the Labour Party. With the decline of aristocrats and working-class recruits the social range of political leadership has become narrower: political leadership in both parties is dominated overwhelmingly by those from middle-class families and by those who, insofar as they have ever had a job beyond politics, have pursued middle-class occupations.

The most important cause of this is something we have already noticed: the steady professionalization of politics. Politics is turning into a middle-class professional occupation like any other: quite well rewarded, demanding the skills acquired in a long formal education and full time in its demands. Even a generation ago really rich men could combine managing their wealth with a political career, and trade unionists could make a career as union officials and then enter Parliament in late middle age. But as we have seen, successful political careers now demand early and total dedication. The most successful will now only have had a brief career before entering Parliament, and that usually related to their long-term political ambitions.

Professionalization therefore has the consequence of narrowing the social-class range of political leadership. But some other common signs of professionalization are helping to widen that social range in other ways. The most important of these concerns the gender make-up of the political class. In professions at large the proportion of women has been rising, though often quite slowly. This is partly due to the persistence of factors that obstruct the recruitment and promotion of women, and partly due to the fact that, since, at the top, professions often reflect patterns of recruitment of 30 years earlier, it is taking some time for occupations to reflect the more recent advances made by women in the education system. These factors also operate in politics. One of the key first steps for an ambitious politician – being adopted as a party's candidate in a winnable seat – is still sometimes difficult for a woman because local parties are simply reluctant to select a woman candidate. (This is the origin of Labour's decision to in some instances impose women only short-lists at candidate selection stage.) Probably more serious handicaps to the ascent of women in political life are the tensions between family and motherhood, and career, created by the uniquely demanding nature of political life. Even something as mundane as the working hours of the

TABLE 18.3 The rise of the professional politician: the case of the Westminster Parliament elected in May 2010

	Labour	Conservative	Liberal Democrat
Public school educated	15%	54%	40%
University educated	86%	95%	88%
Educated at Oxbridge	20%	38%	28%
Total numbers surveyed	242	283	55

■ The table should be interpreted with caution. The research by the Sutton Trust did not manage to collate information about all MPs returned in May 2010. Nevertheless, some patterns are clear. The case of the MPs elected to the Westminster Parliament shows that some of the historical differences between the parties are still faintly present: a higher proportion of Conservative MPs are still public school educated and have attended the two elite universities of Oxford and Cambridge. But the most striking feature of the profile of the MPs from the three leading parties is their similarity: they are university educated professionals.

Source: Collated from Sutton Trust (2010).

House of Commons – until very recently stretching into the late evenings as a matter of routine – create difficulties for women. But just as the gender make-up of other professions is changing, so there is some evidence that women are now becoming commoner at the top in politics, as we can see from Table 18.4.

Widening the social range in other senses is much more problematic. Religious and racial minorities have long faced barriers to advancement. At various times in the nineteenth century Catholics, Jews and atheists were all openly barred from the House of Commons. Now there are no formal barriers to ethnic minorities but powerful, subtler barriers exist. Anti-Semitism and anti-Catholicism undoubtedly exist in some constituency parties, but are probably residual and declining, and are never openly acknowledged. Newer minorities resulting from more recent waves of immigration – particularly those descended from immigrants from former imperial territories in the Caribbean and the Indian subcontinent – are disproportionately under-represented at all levels

TABLE 18.4 The gender dimension of political leadership: percentage of women in selected 'top jobs', 2003–10

	2003	2004	2005	2006	2007/08
Members of Parliament	18.1	18.1	19.7	19.5	21.5*
The Cabinet	23.8	27.3	27.3	34.8	17.3*
Members of the House of Lords	16.5	17.7	18.4	18.9	19.7
Members of the Scottish Parliament	39.5	39.5	39.5	38.8	34.1
Members of the National Assembly for Wales	50.0	50.0	50.0	51.7	46.7
Local authority council leaders	—	16.6	16.2	13.8	14.3
UK Members of the European Parliament	24.1	24.4	24.4	25.6	25.6

* data for May 2010.

■ The ascent of women is erratic; and only one of the institutions surveyed here has ever managed to mirror their proportion in the wider population.

Source: Equality and Human Rights Commission (2008:5).

of the political class. Only in 2002 did we see the first member of the Cabinet from these groups: Paul Boateng, the child of an immigrant from Ghana, reached Tony Blair's Cabinet as Chief Secretary to the Treasury. There have been some well-publicized cases of crude discrimination on race grounds by the parties, and this probably reflects more deep-seated, subtle, discriminatory practices. But there are also powerful economic forces at work. Communities descended from poor migrants are still themselves disproportionately among the poorest. The rare success of Paul Boateng helps make the point, for he is the son of professional parents. We have already seen that, by contrast with the position half a century ago, it is now much more difficult for the very poorest to rise to positions of political leadership. The Labour Party – the main channel of ascent – has increasingly professionalized its methods of selection. Perhaps the most striking feature of political leadership in Britain at the start of the new millennium is the absence of leaders drawn from the very poorest in our society. Black, brown or white: they are all equally absent. In at least one important sense, this has made leadership selection less democratic. An important historical definition of democracy – dating from the Greek political philosopher Aristotle – pictured it as rule by the poorest. The poorest in Britain never get close to political leadership.

Is recruitment meritocratic?

The increasingly professionalized nature of leadership selection is, we have seen, partly due to the rise of a 'meritocratic' theory of leadership selection: to the notion that selection and promotion should depend on displaying 'merit' in the sense of ability measured by standards such as success in formal education. That selection and promotion should be by merit is now a deeply engrained value in British society. This does not mean that it is always practised. In business, for instance, the route to the top for those from families who own a big share of a firm is much easier than for those who simply display ability. But the attachment to the value of merit is now so strong that even in cases where nepotism determines promotion, public justification will usually at least mention merit. In other parts of our society – for instance recruitment of students to university – any apparent departure from strict meritocratic rules becomes a public scandal. This public attachment to the idea that we should be a meritocracy has probably become stronger, even over the last half century.

Meritocratic selection does not abolish social exclusion. On the contrary: it can produce elites which are even more socially exclusive than those produced by other methods. For example, the abolition of patronage in civil service recruitment in Britain in the nineteenth century actually made the service more socially exclusive. There was no longer a place for the poor clients of rich aristocrats. The method of selection itself – largely by written examinations modelled on the syllabus of the ancient universities – virtually guaranteed domination of the service by those who had a privileged public school and university education.

DEBATING POLITICS 18.1

Meritocracy: curse or blessing?

MERITOCRACY IS THE BEST METHOD OF SELECTING LEADERS IN BRITAIN

- Selection by merit involves open rules equally known to all competitors.
- Selection by merit involves choosing the most technically able people to fill positions of authority, and therefore is the best way of choosing competent government.
- Selection by merit ensures that able people without connections or wealth will have the chance to rise to the top.
- Meritocratic selection is 'blind' to the numerous grounds on which prejudice is now exercised in Britain: gender, race or religion. It therefore greatly increases the fairness of selection processes.

MERITOCRACY IS A DANGER TO BRITISH DEMOCRACY

- 'Merit' usually means academic prowess, and ruling in a democracy demands a wide range of less easily measured talents.
- A meritocratic hierarchy is still a hierarchy, like one based on wealth or inheritance.
- Because meritocratic tests so often select the academically gifted, meritocratic selection is socially unequal, because academic success is distributed in a socially unequal way.
- Democratic leadership should be representative of all the people and not just the most meritocratically gifted; a meritocratic elite is still an elite.

Beyond the senior civil service, almost all the routes to the top examined in this chapter depart from formal notions of merit, though it is routine to invoke ability as the grounds for any selection or promotion. Ability is needed at the top, we have seen, but it is not primarily the sort of academically produced ability usually displayed in meritocratic selection. The qualities demanded are stamina, toughness and self-confidence. Making alliances, and cultivating powerful patrons, matters hugely. There has indeed been some growth of meritocratic influence, and this has largely served to narrow the social range of political leadership: as politics has become more like a professional occupation where good formal education is demanded, those from both the very poor and the traditional aristocracy have been excluded.

But these meritocratic influences, though they help to shape the general conditions of political selection, have to compete with non-meritocratic influences. Democratic selection is not meritocratic selection: the characteristic way of winning in democracy is through election, not according to ability. More practically,

recently in Britain there have been powerful expectations that recruitment should take into account not just achievement but what is sometimes called 'ascription': in other words, we should be concerned with the ascribed characteristics of our leaders, like their gender or their ethnicity. This is what lies behind such initiatives as all-women shortlists in selecting parliamentary candidates in some constituencies. This is a conscious departure from meritocracy in the interests of producing political leadership that is more socially representative of groups in the population. But this in turn produces its own complications. Because most successful politicians now also have high formal education, and because participation in higher education has been particularly low among women from the families of unskilled manual workers and from some ethnic groups, consciously discriminating in favour of women actually reinforces the long-term trend to middle-class domination of politics. Of course in principle this problem can be solved, for instance by targeting selection on women precisely from these deprived groups.

Review OF CHAPTER 18

Five themes dominate this chapter:

◖▶ The importance of party in controlling the path to the top of elected office in the Westminster system.

◖▶ The continuing domination of the two-party system as a route to the top in the Westminster system; as well as the challenge to two-party domination, especially in the new devolved systems of government.

◖▶ The importance of a bureaucratic route that is organized on formally meritocratic principles; as well as a very different system of patronage and networking, as alternative routes to the top for unelected leaders.

◖▶ The rise of the professional politician is having the effect of narrowing the social range of those recruited into politics.

◖▶ The virtually total exclusion from elite positions of those drawn from the poorest and the dispossessed in Britain.

FURTHER READING

ESSENTIAL
The study of elites has gone out of fashion in political science. The best starting point is by a journalist, and focuses on the rulers of finance – but it is riveting (Peston 2008).

RECOMMENDED
Guttsman (1963) was a pioneering study, still unrivalled for its historical depth. Norris and Lovenduski (1995) and Lovenduski and Norris (2003) are essential on dimensions neglected in earlier work, notably gender. Mackay's chapter in Flinders et al. (2009) is about more than Britain but is an excellent up to date primer on gender politics. Theakston (1999) examines leadership in a key arena, while Leach and Wilson (2000) look at local leadership. Hennessy (2001) surveys the apex – the office of Prime Minister – for the post-war period.

CHAPTER 19

Understanding policy under multilevel governance

CONTENTS

AIMS

This chapter:

- Describes the special nature of policy making as a process and explains how the shift to governance in Britain is obliging us to change our understandings

- Summarizes important analytical frameworks as a means of understanding that process

- Introduces the notion of multilevel governance as a means of understanding the British policy process

- Shows that what is not decided can be even more important than the policy decisions actually taken

- Examines how far the British policy-making system is uniquely prone to failure and fiasco

UNDERSTANDING POLICY

At numerous points in this book we have examined the substance of policy decisions in Britain. In Chapters 20 to 22 we will be looking in more detail at separate important policy domains where government makes decisions – in other words, yet again at the substance of policy. This chapter has a different purpose: it is to help us make a wider sense of policy making by alerting us to the vocabularies that can be used in studying the policy process. The importance of this general understanding is underlined by a word in the very title of this book: 'governance'. The word, we know, signals a shift in the nature of the governing process in Britain: a shift from reliance on institutional hierarchies to more dispersed networks that have to be coordinated if policy is to be made and implemented effectively. Consequently, this chapter, while it does not deal in the kind of institutional description central to other parts of the book, is nevertheless very important: it helps us to stand back from the institutional detail to consider the very character of policy making in twenty-first-century Britain. That consideration needs to begin at the most obvious point: by asking what it means when we speak of policy making as a process.

Policy as a process

To most of us, the policy that government pursues shows itself as a set of separate authoritative decisions: the Chancellor delivers his annual budget; the Secretary of State responsible for the universities announces a new initiative to widen the social range of students recruited to higher education. Then everyone moves on to a different set of concerns and a new set of decisions. The reality of policy in modern government is actually very different, and the difference is well caught in the image of policy as a process. This image conveys the two most important characteristics of the policies that all systems of government in Britain make and try to put into practice:

- policy is not the product of a single decision but is the result of a continuous set of linked decisions;
- different policies are not independent of each other, but constantly interact with other policies, sometimes beneficially and sometimes harmfully.

The first of these insights tells us to think of policy in government as forming a continuing stream. There is thus rarely a moment when policy is 'made' in the sense of being finally concluded, whatever the publicity of ministerial announcements might suggest. This is not something we would ourselves intuitively anticipate,

FIGURE 19.1 ■ Policy as a never-ending stream

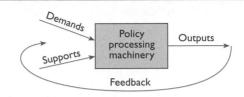

■ The figure schematically reproduces one of the commonest images of the policy process, sometimes called a 'systems' image. It has two great merits: it shows that the production of policy is shaped by both demands and supports, such as money and people; and it brings home the continuous nature of policy making by showing that policy 'outputs' feed back to introduce later 'inputs'.

because in our private lives we constantly do make these kinds of final decisions, from the trivial to the important: we can clearly say that the decision to go to one movie rather than another, or even to go to one university rather than another, is made and concluded at a particular moment. But the decisions of government are rarely like that. The moment when a minister announces a new policy is often only the moment when the real work starts. Because decisions in government usually involve large number of people, and large numbers of institutions, they only happen when those people and those institutions start to get involved. Suppose, for instance, that the Government announces a decision to recruit 5,000 extra new teachers over a fixed period – say within the next 12 months. That decision in turn involves the cooperation of a whole range of institutions and of private citizens. Among institutions, both the Department for Children, Schools and Families (the name at the time of writing for the main department concerned with schools) and the Treasury will have to be involved, the former as the department with obvious responsibility for school education, the latter as the department that tries to control the purse strings of government. Among individuals, the success of the policy will require the voluntary choices of 5,000 students not presently intending to enter the teaching profession to do so.

The simple insight that policy is a continuing process – a never ending stream – means that, while politicians in making policy announcements often separate those announcements from actual delivery, in practice there is no clear line of separation. Policy making and policy implementation are intimately bound together.

The second insight offered by the image of process – that policies across government are interconnected – has even more profound implications. The most obvious form of connection is through money. Government always has finite resources at its command. As we will see in the next chapter, in Britain these are huge by the standards of private citizens and even by the standards of other big organizations, like business corporations. But they are still finite, so each policy commitment that involves spending money – and most do – involves choices that affect other policy areas: £500 million spent on building new schools is £500 million not available for new defence equipment. But the interconnections go well beyond money. Pursuing one policy often complicates the pursuit of others. For instance, if government pursues a policy of restricting new house building in the south east of England in order to protect the rural environment, the resulting shortage helps push up house prices. In turn expensive housing makes it difficult to attract workers to public sector jobs like teaching and nursing in the south east – thus frustrating an entirely different public aim of ensuring adequate staffing for public services.

Theory and making sense of policy

The two features of policy just identified – that it comes in a continuing stream where making and delivery are inseparable, and that there are complicated connections between different policy areas – pose huge problems for government in producing effective policy. They also create problems for those who study policy. This is one reason why so much thought and argument has gone into trying theoretically to understand the nature of the policy process in the governance of Britain.

Why do we need to think theoretically about policy at all? A commonsense alternative would seem to be just directly to observe examples of policy in government and draw conclusions from these case studies. But this commonsense approach has a number of limitations. In the absence of theory, what would guide our selection of these cases; or, indeed, guide our selection generally of what aspects of the huge canvas of British government on which to focus? Some kind of theory is therefore important, above all in indicating to us what are the key policy processes to observe. Even when we have settled this difficult question, 'commonsense' observation of what we think of as 'the facts' of particular cases will not be enough. Even a single policy case in government will present us with a huge amount of material. Imagine writing an account, for example, of the history of British attitudes towards the euro (the single European currency) and trying to draw conclusions about the policy process from that account. Even if we admit to no

---

DOCUMENTING POLITICS 19.1

The limits of rational analysis: Tony Blair on 'judgement' about risk in the decision to go to war on Iraq

'As I sometimes say to people, this isn't about a lie or a conspiracy or a deceit or a deception, it is a decision, and the decision I had to take was, given Saddam's history, given his use of chemical weapons, given the over 1 million people whose deaths he had caused, given ten years of breaking UN Resolutions, could we take the risk of this man reconstituting his weapons programmes, or is that a risk it would be irresponsible to take? I formed the judgment, and it is a judgment in the end. It is a decision. I had to take the decision, and I believed, and in the end so did the Cabinet, so did Parliament incidentally, that we were right not to run that risk, but you are completely right, in the end, what this is all about are the risks.'

■ Virtually every problem faced by a Prime Minister is either insoluble or soluble only with the greatest difficulty. Here is Tony Blair on the most momentous decision of his premiership: the decision to join the US in making war in Iraq in 2003. The statement is from his oral evidence to the Chilcot (Iraq) Inquiry, 29 January 2010.

Source: http://www.iraqinquiry.org.uk/transcripts/oralevidence-bydate/100129.aspx.

---

theory in writing the account, in practice we are going to have to make a whole set of general assumptions in selecting what aspects of the case to highlight – general assumptions which in turn will, without our even realizing it, imply views about the nature of the policy process. For example, if we write the history of a British decision on the euro in terms of the struggles between leading figures in government – say the Prime Minister and the Chancellor – we are implicitly committing ourselves to the view that policy is the product of human choice and human personality, rather than, for instance, more impersonal forces like economic interests. It is far better to have these assumptions out in the open in the form of some general theoretical statements.

But even if we accept the argument for theory, we are still left with numerous problems. 'Theory' in the study of politics is very different from theory in the natural sciences. In the most highly developed natural sciences theories both guide, and are refined by, observations made under controlled conditions in laboratories. Typically, they take the form of generalizations about the relations between various forces or elements. Statements about these relations then produce predictions whose accuracy in turn can be measured either in laboratory experiments or by observation of the natural world.

It is obvious that things are very different in the study of policy. We do not study our subject under laboratory conditions, and even if we could devise laboratory experiments they would not be very interesting: we want to understand how British politics functions in the here and now, not how it might operate if we made a whole set of assumptions that produced a simplified 'model' of politics. Observation and generalization have to take place under the messy circumstances of observing everyday reality where the relationships between forces at any one moment will be both highly complicated and difficult to disentangle. One result is that notions of what 'theory' amounts to in the study of politics are much less narrow than in the natural sciences. As we will see in some of the examples that follow, predictive theory as used in the natural sciences is rare. Theory is more often a looser framework, a set of assumptions about the world of policy, or even just a helpful image of the policy process – all designed to help us organize in some systematic way the otherwise impossible diversity that we can observe in the political world. This is why in the next section we examine only different 'images' of the policy process, because they rarely amount to anything that would be recognized as 'theory' by the standards of the laboratory sciences.

IMAGES OF THE POLICY PROCESS

A rational and comprehensive image

Suppose we have to make a big decision in our private life, such as buying a house. Most of us will attempt to do this in a fairly systematic way: forming a picture of the house we really want, given what we can afford, and then viewing as many possibilities as time and energy allows, before making an offer for the one that most meets our demands. We attempt, in short, to make a rational choice: to match our final selection to our wishes and resources. And we attempt to make the choice after as comprehensive a scan as possible of the housing market in the area where we expect to live. This simple example encapsulates the essence of the rational and comprehensive image of policy choice. One of the commonest ambitions of governments is to produce policy that is likewise the result of such a rational and comprehensive analysis of the available evidence and the available options. In presenting this image of the policy process, policymakers are working according to one of the oldest theories of the policy process, though they rarely acknowledge, or perhaps even realize, this fact. This is a *prescriptive* theory. In other words, it says what should happen, not necessarily what does; and what should happen is exactly that policy production should be 'rational and comprehensive'. It should be the result of a clear picture of the objectives of policy; it should involve a full (comprehensive) analysis of the available options; and it should result in the choice of the option that most effectively realizes the objectives.

Attractive as this theory looks, it rarely matches what happens or what can happen. We can see this even in our private life. Numerous house buyers start out trying to use a rational–comprehensive method, but notoriously they often then make a choice on some unanticipated instinctive ground: for instance, just because they like the garden or the fitted kitchen. And the bigger the choice the less likely are we to do it 'rationally'. Few people select a marriage partner rationally and comprehensively; they just stumble in and out of love, and we would think anyone who tried to make a 'rational and comprehensive' choice here a pretty odd and cold fish.

If even making single choices in private life is hard to make rationally and comprehensively, how much more difficult is it to make in government. Take again the choice of whether Britain should 'join the eurozone' – replace our domestic currency with the euro and therefore become a partner in the European Monetary Union (EMU) with our fellow member states in the EU. The core of the rational and comprehensive approach is that there exists a clear objective to which the means are adapted. But it is impossible to formulate a single list of objectives for the decision on joining the euro. A Cabinet faced with the decision has to consider party, nation, special interests like business and labour – all with differing objectives, often conflicting. Individual members of the Cabinet, being only human, will also be calculating what the episode will do to their own careers. The comprehensive evaluation of evidence is impossible. Some relevant evidence – for example about the state of the economy – may be fairly precisely measurable. Other evidence – for instance about the state of the public's emotional attachment to the pound sterling as a symbol of British identity – may be highly intangible. And beyond all this there is the problem of trying to predict a highly uncertain future if Britain goes in or stays out.

DOCUMENTING POLITICS 19.2

The rational–comprehensive model encounters politics: Michael Heseltine's experience with MINIS

The Management Information System for Ministers (MINIS) 'was designed to give Ministers a thorough understanding of what each activity of the Department cost by defining each task in detail and allocating the costs of the civil servants involved'. Heseltine presented a slide show on the system to Cabinet members and their Permanent Secretaries in 1981. The Prime Minister asked John Nott, Secretary of State for Defence, what he thought. He replied:

> 'Prime Minister, at the Ministry of Defence I am trying to come to terms with an overspend of billions of pounds. Is it seriously suggested that I should spend my time grubbing around, saving ha'pennies?'

Heseltine continues: 'The row that followed marked the end of any prospect of MINIS being adopted in Whitehall.'

■ Michael Heseltine was a leading member of Conservative Cabinets in the 1980s and 1990s. He was an advocate of rational planning models influenced by his business experience. He introduced MINIS into every department he headed, but could never convince the rest of the Government to follow suit.

Source: Heseltine (2000:190–3).

An image of incrementalism

These problems lie behind the rise of an image that has challenged that of the rational and comprehensive: incrementalism. The *incrementalist* image of the policy process says we should recognize all the limits – technical and emotional – to rational decision, and recognize that in practice most policies are made piecemeal – incrementally – and amount to 'muddling through', in a famous phrase used by one of the originators of incrementalist theory, Charles Lindblom (1959). Governments hardly ever have the resources or the time to engage in rational–comprehensive analysis, so they

typically do what we all do in our private lives: just plump for the nearest available short-term choice. A more analytical way of putting this is to say that policymakers typically 'satisfice' rather than 'maximize': they cannot spend time fully analysing all the evidence and options, so they do what they can given available resources and time – both of which are often in short supply. They are like the typical car buyer who, deciding that life is too short systematically to compare and test drive ten models, buys by a single rule of thumb: because the manufacturer has a reputation for reliability, or because there is a once and for all special offer on a particular model.

It cannot be disputed that 'muddling through' accurately describes the reality of most policy processes, just as it accurately describes much of our own private decision making. But the rational–comprehensive image still offers a serious challenge: since it is prescriptive rather than descriptive it asks us how far we should accept the muddling through character of real policy making. As the frequent resort to the imagery of rational decision making in official accounts shows, it remains a powerful ideal in the minds of most modern policymakers. Incrementalism in government is particularly dangerous because of the sheer scale and diversity of government. If every bit of government is taking decisions incrementally, how can there ever be any coherence and consistency in what government does?

Rational choice institutionalism: model building

The great power of the incrementalist model is that it seems accurately to describe so much of the messy reality of government. But what if we approached the problem of theoretical understanding by a very different route: by self-consciously building a deliberately simplified model of the policy process? The 'model' here is obviously not a simplified physical representation of reality, of the sort for example commonly used in engineering design. It is a kind of mental experiment. This approach is the nearest we have in the social sciences to the controlled experimental conditions of the laboratory in the natural sciences. It is widely used, for example, in the study of economic behaviour. Economists build theories of how economies work by starting with a set of assumptions that simplify human behaviour and motivation. They then make deductions about how economic actors – either individuals or institutions like firms – would behave in different circumstances if they were so motivated. For example, in elementary economic theory it is common to assume that firms attempt to maximize profits at the expense of anything else. Nobody believes that real firms are driven just by this imperative. But the

BRIEFING 19.1

The science of muddling through

'The science of muddling through' is a classic article which influentially put the case for 'incrementalism' as both a way of understanding, and as a way of making, policy. Incrementalism proved especially popular among British policymakers because its central tenets appealed to the traditional culture of the policy-making elite. It stressed:

- ■ our limited knowledge about the future
- ■ our limited ability to store, recall and analyse our present knowledge;
- ■ the dangers of making large scale changes;
- ■ the importance of 'muddling through' by making incremental changes which could then be assessed before further change was introduced.

■ It is doubtful if many senior British politicians or civil servants have ever read Lindblom's classic paper but it precisely systematized their suspicion of rational models of policy making and their preference for making policy through piecemeal bargaining.

Source: Lindblom (1959).

assumption that firms do want to maximize profits allows the economist to explore what this would mean in different market conditions: for example, what would happen when there are only a few powerful firms in the market, as in the market for automobiles, or when there are numerous small competitors, as in the market for second-hand books?

One of the most productive sources of models of the policy process comes from *rational choice institutionalism*. It is called 'rational choice' because it is a close relative of the models built by economists, where rationality means the assumption that people are self-interested, have a few, clearly realized values that they want to maximize (like profits), and shape their behaviour to realize those objectives. 'Institutionalism' recognizes that the choices are being made here in a world where institutions shape behaviour. It is possible to define institutions in many different ways but a straightforward one is to picture the organizations that shape all our lives as institutions. It is then easy to see how a rationally self-interested individual would have to adapt to the way these institutions impinge on our lives. Imagine a student, for instance, who has a rational set of goals that include maximizing the amount of free time available, while minimizing the amount of trouble encountered from teachers. Working out a strategy to achieve these twin aims will involve working within the rules and culture of a particular institution, the college: for example, knowing exactly what the attendance

rules are and manipulating those rules. (If the rules say that students are reported after two consecutive absences, the rational student misses only alternate lessons.)

Rational choice institutionalism: builds models of the policy process by beginning with a small number of simplified assumptions about what motivates actors who contribute to policy; identifies the main incentives, opportunities and obstacles that exist in any particular institutional setting, such as the core Executive in Britain; and then works out what are the most effective strategies for rationally self-interested actors in the light of those incentives, opportunities and obstacles.

Obviously a key question in this sort of model building is: what can we assume are the motives that drive self-interested actors? Early rational choice models assigned fairly simple values: for instance, politicians wanted to maximize votes; bureaucrats like senior civil servants in Britain wanted to maximize the budgets of their departments, because maximizing budgets was presumed to be a sign of maximizing prestige and power. But later versions applied to policy in Britain have assigned more complex values (see Figure 19.2). One variation is to see senior bureaucrats as actors who want to maximize job satisfaction: they want to retain in their own hands intellectually pleasurable and prestigious activities, like advising ministers on policy; but they want to shift less prestigious and less intellectually pleasurable roles (like the stressful job of actually delivering

FIGURE 19.2 ■ Dunleavy's illustrations of different bureau budgets

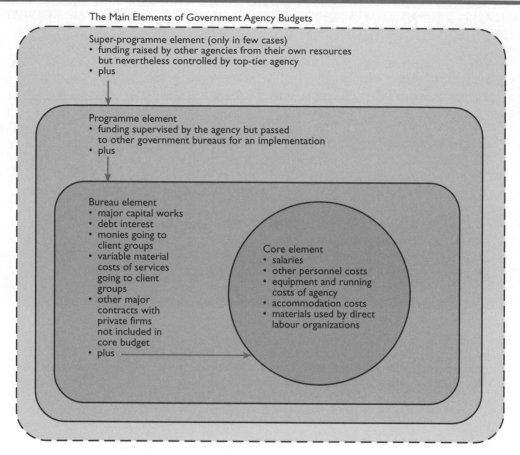

The Main Elements of Government Agency Budgets

Super-programme element (only in few cases)
• funding raised by other agencies from their own resources
  but nevertheless controlled by top-tier agency
• plus

Programme element
• funding supervised by the agency but passed
  to other government bureaus for an implementation
• plus

Bureau element
• major capital works
• debt interest
• monies going to
  client groups
• variable material
  costs of services
  going to client
  groups
• other major
  contracts with
  private firms
  not included in
  core budget
• plus

Core element
• salaries
• other personnel costs
• equipment and running
  costs of agency
• accommodation costs
• materials used by direct
  labour organizations

Source: Updated version supplied by Dunleavy in 2004 based on a diagram originally published in Dunleavy (1991:182).

■ Dunleavy's version of rational choice institutionalism gives this theoretical approach greatly added power. He retains many of the basic assumptions of the rational choice model, notably that actors try to calculate and if possible to maximize some preference. But hitherto the dominant assumptions had been fairly simple: for instance that actors in institutions would want to maximize institutional budgets. Dunleavy's apparently elementary point in this diagram – that there are different kinds of budget in any institution – immediately opens up huge possibilities: different actors at different levels of an institution will have different strategies for different kinds of budget. And Dunleavy goes further. He argues that many key actors – like senior civil servants – want to maximize not money but work satisfaction: for instance they will want to control congenial roles, like offering policy advice to ministers, and to 'hive off' difficult and tedious roles, like complex management tasks.

policy) onto other shoulders. This simple model proves to have remarkable predictive power: it would predict, for example, that senior civil servants would support a policy of 'hiving off' responsibility for actually delivering difficult policies (for example the daily running of prisons) onto specialized agencies; and that, as we saw in Chapter 7, is exactly what has been happening in the 'next steps' reforms that were introduced from the 1990s.

Images of networks and governance

The twin theories of incrementalism and rational comprehensiveness are attempts to understand the intellectual process by which policy is made – how far it involves, or should involve, the careful evaluation of all possible choices in the light of all possible information. Models of rational choice institutionalism involve working out how rationally self-interested actors play the games of real-

FIGURE 19.3 ■ An example of a policy network: Reid's version of the tobacco policy network

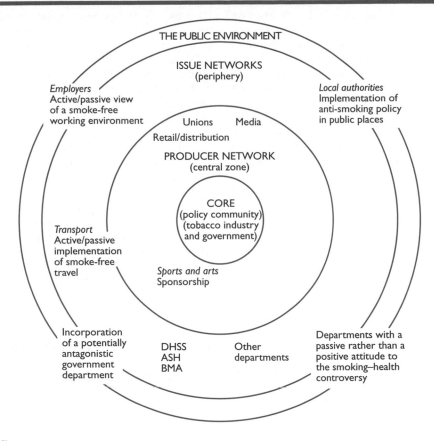

Source: Reid (1992:129).

■ Most representations of policy networks picture them as rather like wiring diagrams, with all the parts interconnected. Reid's representation of the tobacco policy network as a series of zones brings out something that can be lost in the 'wiring diagram' approach: that different parts of policy networks specialize in different things; that they vary in their centrality to the policy process; and that they vary in the amount of power exercised over the actual production of policy.

izing their self-interest within the boundaries set by the institutions inside which they have to work. Our final images of the policy process offer us an overview of the whole experience of making policy, and they have proved in recent years unusually influential among both policy makers and those who study policy. These images are usually summed up under the label 'governance'.

The popularity of governance imagery arises from changes that are taking place in the nature of modern government and society. These changes have greatly complicated the way policies can be made and put into effect. In the past taking decisions by government was often a tightly knit, hierarchically organized affair. Putting those decisions into effect was typically done

bureaucratically. 'Bureaucratic' here is used technically and neutrally, not as the pejorative term common in everyday speech, where bureaucracy is associated with slowness and rigidity in taking decisions. It simply means that government is carried out by officials organized in hierarchical institutions where everyone has a defined task and a clearly identified place in the hierarchy. Matching this is a hierarchical theory of how government itself works: the democratically elected Government of the day decides policies, which are then carried out by bureaucracies, like government departments, issuing orders putting policy into effect.

In practice hardly anything of the sort happens in government, and the history of British government has

367

for decades been one precisely of policy failure: instead of policy being smoothly and efficiently put into effect there has often been resistance and policy fiasco. (We examine some of the most spectacular of these failures later in this chapter.) The governance approach springs from an attempt to work out why policy failures happen. The essence of the governance answer is that it is no longer possible, if it ever was, to make and implement policy as if all that mattered was the issuing of orders, even when those orders come from a government that claims the authority of democratic legitimacy. Policy also has to be sensibly designed, and it has to take into account the views of those who share responsibility for putting it into effect. Policy has to be made and implemented, not in simple hierarchies like an old fashioned army, but in organizations that are connected in complex ways that make them dependent on each other.

Thus, when we look at the structure of modern government in a country like Britain, we see, not simple hierarchies, but a pattern consisting of *networks* of mutually dependent organizations. Effective policy making is about steering these networks. This becomes most obvious when we look at the attempts made to put policy into effect. Take the example of a Chancellor of the Exchequer making policies that are designed to affect the level of investment in the economy, or to raise the productivity with which labour is used. These policies, if they work, only do so when an extended chain of organizations – stretching down to individual firms – actually respond appropriately: the Chancellor can change the tax rules so as to make investment more attractive, though in the end individual firms have to do the investing; and a Chancellor can introduce schemes for the better training of workers to make them more skilful and potentially productive, though firms have to employ and use those workers so as to take advantage of their skills. When governments make policy, to be effective they cannot do so by issuing orders; their task is to participate in, and to try to manage, networks of organizations. Making effective policy is about bargaining, negotiation and compromise; about recognizing the nature of the networks in different policy areas; and about responding sensitively to the powerful organizations in those networks.

All this is summed up in the very language that shifts from 'government' to 'governance', a tiny symbolic shift with huge implications. 'Government' suggests a clear line between government and the rest of society, with government the independent source of authoritative orders. 'Governance' suggests that the act of governing in a modern industrial society like Britain usually crosses the conventional line separating government from the rest of society. 'Governance' is not confined to the conventional institutions of government, like central departments of Whitehall, but is a collaborative act that takes place in the extended networks that can be found in any policy area. What we usually think of as government is embedded in those networks. When we study policy making, therefore, we have to bear in mind a key question which is also central to the problems faced in making effective policy: since policies are made and implemented through separate, complex networks that only sometimes overlap, how can the workings of these networks be coordinated? Linking up separate networks is, in the governance approach, one of the key functions of government departments, and one of the key roles of people like senior politicians and civil servants.

One reason for the growing popularity of the image of governance is that it seems to chime with the reality of the changing nature of government in Britain. A generation ago we would usually analyse policy making in Britain in terms of a centre in London making policies for everywhere else. Now, the only sensible way of picturing policy making is through images of multilevel governance involving extended networks.

THE MULTILEVEL GOVERNANCE OF POLICY

The rise of multilevel governance in Britain

The rise of multilevel governance is connected to institutional changes which are coming over the British system of government, all of which we have already encountered in various forms in earlier chapters. The most important are, in summary, as follows.

The rise of the EU. The rising importance of the institutions of the EU, especially of the Commission and its policy-making world in Brussels, has been documented at many points in previous chapters. There is almost nothing done by way of policy making and implementation that does not have to take account of an EU dimension, something we saw clearly in Chapters 5 and 6.

The growing importance of international organizations. In many areas of policy Britain now subscribes to agreements that restrict the ability of British governments independently to make policy. For instance, as part of our membership of the EU we are bound by the agreements negotiated on our behalf by the Union in the World Trade Organization (WTO), the leading international organization that negotiates trading rules between nations. But this is only the most visible example. Virtually every internationally traded good or service – from air transport to computer software to telephone traffic – is governed by internationally negoti-

TABLE 19.1 The web of multilevel and multi-agency governance: examples

	Public	Mixed public/private	Private
Global	World Trade Organization	International Air Transport Association	Pharmaceutical Manufacturers' Association
Regional European	European Commission	European Telecommunications Standards Institute	Confederation of Food and Drink Industries of the EU
UK-wide	Core Executive departments	Privatized rail industry	Confederation of British Industry
Devolved national	Scottish Executive	Scottish Enterprise	Scottish Retail consortium
Regional	Government regional offices	North West Development Agency	North West Regional Office of the Confederation of British Industry
Local	Local authorities	Greater Manchester Passenger Transport Executive	Local chamber of commerce

■ The box simply tabulates the main levels at which institutions that can have a hand in policy operate, and creates a very simple classification according to how far they are private or public bodies. It illustrates the potential range and complexity of institutional actors in multilevel and multi-agency governance.

ated standards, more often than not settled between nominally private bodies, like firms and trade associations.

Territorial devolution in the UK. The devolution of policy authority to the new assemblies and executives in Wales and Scotland by the Labour Government in its legislation of 1998, has, as we saw in Chapter 10, created critical new levels of policy making.

Institutional devolution in the UK. All the above examples involve different territorial levels, above (the EU) or below (devolved government in Scotland) the level of government in Westminster. But there is also 'devolution' in another dimension: privatization, and the creation of agencies of the kind described in Chapter 7, shift parts of the policy making out to institutions beyond the core Executive, and even beyond the whole of the Westminster system.

There is nothing new in having different levels of government in Britain: the distinction between central and local government is precisely such an arrangement; and from 1922 to 1972 Northern Ireland had extensively devolved government, most issues of policing, welfare and economic policy being controlled by a government and a parliament within the province. But the new world of multilevel governance is novel in scale. Instead of operating at the margins of a fundamentally centralized

system it is now a defining feature of how policy is made and executed. The list of levels summarized above shows that we now have something more than the simple hierarchy of central and local government, or piecemeal devolution to particular parts of the UK. The range and importance of institutions involved, like the EU; the fact that multilevel arrangements are now connected to thoroughgoing constitutional reform, as in the measures of territorial devolution: these features show that a multilevel system is now a defining feature of the system of government in Britain.

British government was until recently thought of as 'unitary', involving a concentration of authority in one single centre, within Westminster; the new multilevel system has replaced that. The scale of multilevel governance shapes the whole nature of policy making in Britain. Now, policy cannot be made at the centre but is a matter of negotiation and coordination between the levels. The levels in the multilevel system are not independent of each other. To the contrary: they both have to share authority and to make decisions in the knowledge that decisions made at one level of government can produce effects through the rest of the system. Multilevel governance is therefore changing the very nature of the problems that the British system faces. What these problems are we now examine.

Policy problems of multilevel governance

Multilevel governance spread because the old, centralized, hierarchical system created numerous policy failures. But the multilevel policy system is creating its own special problems. The rise of multilevel governance is profoundly changing the political 'game' in Britain; policymakers have to learn new ways of solving problems that the new game produces. In summary, they are problems of authority; of resources; of 'turf'; and of coordination.

Authority. The formal distribution of authority in the old unitary system was simple. Parliament was supreme: 'Parliament can make or unmake any law whatsoever', in the words of a famous constitutional authority on the old unitary system of government (see Chapter 4, p. 50). Now authority is distributed in a complicated way across many levels. Short of actually withdrawing from the EU, British government now has no option but to share authority over numerous important policy domains with the institutions of the Union. And 'below' the level of government in Westminster and Whitehall, there are now three directly elected popular assemblies – in Scotland, Wales and Northern Ireland – which not only have allocated to them the authority to make policies directly on a wide range of issues but also can claim the authority which goes with direct election. Elected mayors in cities like London are also now a growing source of authority over policy. Authority can no longer be exercised by Westminster; it has to be negotiated, and negotiated in a multilevel system where there is increasing diversity in decision-making arrangements and policy preferences. If we think back to Chapter 1 we can see that this wider distribution of authority also has consequences for legitimacy. Authority is important to any system of government because it is the most effective and economical system of rule: if authority is recognized, then it is voluntarily obeyed. But in the new multilevel system there is increasingly no one, obvious source of authority; the locus of authority at any particular moment has to be negotiated.

Resources. The problem of authority is compounded by the problem of resources. The independent resource raising power of government beyond Westminster is still small. The EU cannot tax citizens or institutions directly; the resources at its disposal have to come from the member states. Within the UK only the Scottish Assembly presently has independent tax raising power, and this is comparatively marginal: it can raise or lower the standard rate of income tax by three pence in the pound, but has so far not used the power. In other words, a separation is growing up between the place where resources are raised and the place where policies that demand resources are decided. That is not in itself novel in Britain. In the old unitary state it was common for Westminster government to pass laws that imposed obli-

gations on local government, without providing the money to meet those obligations. But in the new system of multilevel governance the relationships are often reversed: the policy commitments are being made beyond Westminster. 'Above' Westminster lies the EU, into which of course the UK Government directs substantial influence but which produces an important flow of authoritative decisions that have to be incorporated into UK law and policy. Below it, especially in Scotland, lies a new system of government which is producing policies that not only differ from those coming out of Westminster but which have very different spending consequences from Westminster policies. As we saw in Chapter 10, though there are formal differences in the status of the Scottish Parliament and the Welsh Assembly, in practice the impact of devolution has been remarkably similar. Control of a block grant from the Westminster Government to administer a very wide range of domestic policy has allowed the devolved governments to make decisions, especially in the sphere of welfare policy, which are making Scotland and Wales increasingly different from England.

Turf. 'Turf' is a political image imported from America (and originally an image transferred from land distribution struggles). Struggles over 'turf' are struggles between institutions in government for control over areas of policy. Recall our image in Chapter 6 of central government departments in Whitehall as competing tribes. One of the main things the tribes struggle over is the right to have a say in particular policy issues, because this is a sign of departmental prestige, and because the first condition of having a real influence over policy is that the department's right to a say in policy debates should be recognized. Inside any system of government 'turf battles' command the time of most of the important people, whether they are politicians or civil servants.

The newly created systems of government under devolution have their own internal turf battles, often of a complexity and bitterness unknown even in the Westminster system. For instance, as we saw in Chapter 11, the whole system of devolved government in Northern Ireland is organized around a very delicate allocation of responsibilities and jobs in the Executive between representatives of the different communities. More generally, since these systems are still being built, they are also still working out understandings about turf allocation. London provides striking examples: under Mayor Ken Livingstone for control over the management of the London Underground rail network; and under Mayor Boris Johnson for control over policing in the capital.

But the turf issue is not confined to the internal organization of the different levels in the multilevel system; it goes to the very heart of managing the rela-

DOCUMENTING POLITICS 19.3

The 'concordat' as an attempt to solve problems of coordination and 'turf' in multi-level governance: extract from the Scottish Concordat on Procurement

Scottish Concordat on Procurement

'CONCORDAT ON CO-ORDINATION OF EU, INTERNATIONAL AND POLICY ISSUES ON PUBLIC PROCUREMENT ...

3.1 Relations with the EU on public procurement policy and the development of EC legislation and international agreements in this field are the responsibility of the United Kingdom, as member state, Parliament and Government. The development and application of public procurement policy in Scotland, however, is a devolved matter. The UK Government therefore wishes to involve the Scottish Executive as directly and fully as possible in decision-making on EU and international public procurement matters.

3.2 To ensure that non-devolved matters which may affect devolved areas and devolved matters which may affect non-devolved areas are considered fully, Ministers and officials of the Scottish Executive and the UK Government will maintain close working relationships and will inform each other at an early stage of any relevant proposals or other developments on procurement policy and legislation, including litigation and infraction cases of potentially wider significance.

3.3 Given the common aim of achieving value for money, normally through competition and having due regard to propriety, regularity and the costs of acquisition, the Scottish Executive will seek to ensure that the policy and legal framework for public procurement in Scotland complies appropriately with the UK's EU and international obligations and will not prejudice the UK's objective of seeking EU and international measures which are effective in opening procurement markets while not imposing any unnecessary burdens or constraints on purchasers or suppliers ...'

■ 'Procurement' is shorthand for purchasing decisions by government. As the biggest customer in Britain, purchasing world wide, government has to work out rules that satisfy all levels of government: local, the devolved administrations (the focus of this box), the EU and global organizations governing world trade, like the WTO, with whom Britain has agreements. Concordats were developed particularly rapidly to try to manage multilevel government after the devolution reforms of 1999. This document illustrates well their reach and their complexity: less than a quarter of the document is reproduced here. The dense prose is worth sampling, because it gives a direct sense of the daily reality of policy making in multilevel governance.

Source: www.hm-treasury.gov.uk.

tionships between the institutions of multilevel government. In laws, treaties and concordats we can read the formal description of how turf is allocated – the description of the formal division of legal rights and responsibilities between different levels of government. Just how elaborate these can be is illustrated in Documenting Politics 19.3. But famously in government the letter of the law settles nothing, especially in allocations of turf. Struggles for jurisdiction over policy are built into the very nature of the multilevel system.

Coordination. Coordination of policy making and policy delivery is a problem in any organization, even in the simplest: think of the number of times even among your friends and your family you have failed to coordinate properly, missing appointments, duplicating tasks or failing to sort out who was responsible for what tasks, so that in the end nobody did them. If this kind of coordination problem litters even our simple daily lives, it is easy to imagine that it is even more acute in modern government: big organizations with lots of internal divisions charged with complicated tasks that involve the cooperation of lots of different people and institutions over long periods of time. If a group of students in a flat cannot sort out who is responsible for doing the shopping, how much less likely is it that big government will be able to sort out the exact responsibility for the delivery of urban renewal or education policy?

This is to emphasize that the existence of coordination problems in multilevel governance is nothing new. But for a multilevel system the problem is more acute for the most obvious of reasons: the essence of multilevel governance is not just that the governing process is divided between different levels, but that it has to involve constant bargaining over how policy is to be made and put into effect. It also in many cases deliberately builds in the possibility of producing policies that are inconsistent with each other – something that the older unitary system always sought hard to avoid. For example, in the old unitary system before devolution of authority to Scotland there existed a powerful principle in welfare policy, sometimes called 'universalism': the principle that the entitlements and obligations of citizens should be the same right across Britain. But by devolving responsibility for making important decisions about welfare policy to the Scottish and Welsh devolved governments this principle has been modified. We have already seen some important results: student fees in higher education have been abolished in Scotland while remaining in force in England and Wales; and charges for long term residential care (for example of the very old) had been abolished in Scotland while remaining in force across the border. It is important to realize that the new multilevel governance entirely changes the character of coordination problems. For example, if we discovered that students from Lancashire were obliged to pay fees while those from Yorkshire were exempt, we would immediately identify this as a breach of the principle of universal entitlements and a serious policy coordination problem; but the growth of differences of this kind between Scotland and England has to be accepted as a normal consequence of the new system of government.

The issues raised by the development of multilevel governance in Britain are partly technical: any big, complex organization has to work hard at transmitting information and orders from one part to another, and has to work hard at trying to make sure that decisions made by different bits of the organization are consistent with each other. But the issues now go well beyond technicalities. Problems of authority, coordination, control over resources and battles for turf show that the new system is fundamentally altering the relations of power within the British system. The rise of multilevel governance in Britain involves the transformation of an old Westminster-focused unitary system of government, where power was heavily concentrated in a small number of institutions and people at the centre in London, into a semi-federal system of government, where power and

authority are distributed at many different levels, all of which have to invest a great deal of effort in communicating with, and bargaining with, each other.

POSITIVE DECISIONS, NEGATIVE DECISIONS AND NON-DECISIONS

Our discussion of the policy process in Britain has thus far had an important but unacknowledged bias: we have discussed only cases where government actually takes decisions. But just as important are the decisions that government, for one reason or another, neglects to take. This is what we now examine.

Power, decision and non-decision

It is natural to be interested in what government actually does – in the great debates that take place, in the policies that arise from these debates, and in the sometimes dramatic choices that follow, like a decision to go to war. The great drama of historical events provides the stuff of politics. When we look back at Mrs Thatcher's Premiership we soon fix on the great drama of the Falklands War of 1982. We likewise think of the Iraq War of 2003 as a key episode in the Blair Premiership. The defining event of the Brown Premiership was the great financial crisis of 2007–08. But this focus on the things that happen can blind us to something that is equally important: the things that do not happen, either because it never occurred to anyone to do them, or because the likelihood of their happening has been suppressed. Power in government obviously partly consists in the ability to make things happen: to pass new laws or commit to a military campaign. But power can just as certainly come from the ability to suppress decisions.

The way we usually express this is through the image of an 'agenda' in government. The metaphor of an agenda is approximate but helps make the point more concrete. Imagine a committee meeting. Like most committees it will have its particular agenda – a list of items of business, usually in printed form, about which there will be discussion and decision. Influence in the committee partly consists in the ability to decide what decisions are made on each agenda item. But it is easy to see that even more influence could arise from the ability to make sure that issues for decision inconvenient to a powerful member never actually appear as an agenda item at all – and therefore never have to be defended. The metaphor of an 'agenda' in government is approximate because British government is too varied and complicated to work from a single committee-like agenda. But government at any one time will have its metaphorical agenda: policy issues that are thought to be

BRIEFING 19.2

Positive decisions, negative decisions and non-decisions: the case of fuel taxes

Positive decision: At the time of writing the duty on road fuel is just 54 pence a litre. In normal circumstances it is uprated periodically, and in the 1990s an 'escalator' was introduced by the Treasury ensuring that the levels were increased automatically; the increase due in 2008 was delayed because of the financial crisis.

Negative decision: The duty on 'red diesel' is much lower than for other road fuels: the latest available figures showed it at only 3 pence a litre. Red diesel is ordinary dyed diesel, only available to farmers for use on their vehicles in connection with farm work. It arises from a 'negative decision': to exempt this class of fuel from the levied duties described under 'positive decision' above, and in particular to exempt it from the 'escalator' clause introduced in the 1990s.

Non-decision: Aircraft fuel presently attracts no national fuel duties. The decision dates from the 1944 Chicago Convention. Signatories (of whom Britain is one) are legally bound to exempt aircraft fuel (and some other goods and services used by airlines) from national duties.

■ The distinction between positive, negative and non-decisions is helpful in making sense of why some issues are decided after intense public argument, and why others just seem to 'happen'. But the decision is not hard and fast: even the case of the exemption of aircraft fuel from taxation was the result of a negative decision made long ago, and it is increasingly being challenged, notably by those who argue that air traffic is environmentally damaging.

in need of attention and policy options from which a choice has to be made. Getting something on the agenda of government ensures that it will at least be debated; conversely, keeping it off the agenda means no debate, let alone decision – and no necessity for the interests that benefit from inaction to defend themselves.

There are two ways in which the agenda of policy debate and decision is shaped: by 'negative decisions' and by 'non-decisions'. They can be hard to distinguish at the edges but nevertheless are worth separating, especially because negative decisions are the easier to identify.

Negative decisions and the policy agenda

A negative decision happens when some group is sufficiently powerful to manipulate either the content of policy or the terms of political debate to ensure that a decision harmful to its interests is suppressed. In a democratic political system with an inquisitive press that can be a hard trick to pull off. It can usually only be achieved by some group which is especially well placed within the higher reaches of government. The best way to understand how it works is to consider two examples.

Taxation of the monarchy. Although many powerful institutions and individuals hire experts to minimize their tax liabilities, or even to ensure that they pay no tax at all, only one individual – the Monarch – has enjoyed exemption from the obligation to pay taxes on private income. It has not even been necessary to hire a smart firm of tax accountants to minimize tax liabilities, as other rich people do. This exemption dated from the 1930s, when taxes on income first began to become substantial. It was renewed in 1953 by a truly negative decision: not to extend obligation to pay tax on income to the new Monarch when the present Queen succeeded her father. It lasted until the early 1990s. The result was that the Queen and her advisors did not have to do what all other taxpayers were obliged to do: give an account to the Inland Revenue of income and pay the bill levied. The Queen did not get the kind of letter received by other people (see p. 10).

Farmers and planning law. As anyone who has tried to build a porch on the front of their house knows, there are rigorous laws restricting the alterations we can make to our houses, and even more rigorous laws restricting our entitlement to put up new buildings.

These planning laws are justified on a number of grounds: safety, public health and aesthetics. However, many farm buildings are exempt from these planning regulations. The result is that in erecting new buildings that have agricultural purposes farmers do not, unlike other builders, have to engage in open argument in defence of their proposals.

The point of these examples is not to debate whether the negative decisions are right or wrong; readers can work out their own views. It is to show that decisions not to do some things can be just as important in shaping policy as positive decisions favouring a particular course of action. The examples also give us some idea of the conditions under which a 'negative decision' can shape policy. Producing a negative decision demands that the interest or group whom it favours already be powerfully placed: the Monarchy in the middle of the twentieth century had uniquely good relations with government and was surrounded with such a mystique that it was widely agreed that the Monarch should be exempt from many of the rules that governed her subjects.

Negative decisions are not only most likely to favour the already privileged and powerful; they reinforce existing power and privilege. Once the negative decision has been made, the privileged interest no longer has to do what other groups find necessary: mobilize its resources in defence of its interests in open political argument. In some cases – like farmers' exemption from some planning laws – the exemption is publicly known but is just conventionally accepted as part of the natural order of things. In others, like royal exemption from taxes, it was for long not known to the wider public at all.

Exercising power through negative decision is probably becoming harder to achieve. The Monarch's exemption from income tax, for example, was abandoned in 1993, at a time when the funding of the Monarchy in general was coming under increased public scrutiny. Why it is becoming harder connects to wider questions about the changing nature of democracy in Britain, and we look at those in our final chapter.

Non-decisions and the policy agenda

Non-decisions are difficult to study. A negative decision, as we saw above, involves a choice at some moment not to do something, and even if the choice is kept secret – as in the case of the Monarch's tax paying obligations – historians usually eventually track it down. But a non-decision does not involve a choice to suppress a particular policy option; it consists of a persistent bias in the way both debates and institutions are organized such that some policy choices never get considered at all –

usually because it never occurs to anyone that they are viable options.

This is what gives non-decision its elusive quality. By the definition of non-decision given above there is literally an infinite number of non-decisions 'not taken' at any one time – since the range of options not considered is numberless. More concretely, we could easily conjure up possible policy options that are never considered because they seem self-evidently absurd. For example: during the last century donkeys, which were once widely employed in farm work, have been made redundant by technological change. Were I to suggest that we should have a national policy for retraining donkeys to do alternative work, backed up with unemployment benefits for donkeys, I would be dismissed as absurdly eccentric. The failure to consider such absurd options tells us nothing about the connection between power, policy and non-decision. But we have to be careful in using the 'absurdity' criterion, because what just seems absurd in one historical setting will be revealed as the exercise of power in another. For instance, had we lived at the start of the eighteenth century the notion that there should be policies backed by law prohibiting cruelty to donkeys would have seemed as absurd as paying unemployment benefit to animals. But now we see that failure to consider the possibility of anti-cruelty laws reflected a particularly brutal aspect of power: wielding dominion over helpless creatures in the animal world.

The example of historical change gives us some idea of how to explore the way non-decisions shape policy. Looking back at what was considered absurd, and what sensible, about the protection of animal rights is an exercise in comparison between our own times and some time in the past. Comparisons of this kind can alert us to which non-decisions to look out for. They can alert us to non-decisions that reflect power differences, as distinct from options that are not considered because they are truly absurd. Comparison is the key to understanding how non-decisions shape policy. Briefing 19.3 shows some of the most important forms of comparison that can illuminate non-decisions.

POLICY SUCCESS AND POLICY FAILURE IN BRITAIN

Government, we now know from all earlier chapters, is a huge presence in all our lives: it follows us from the cradle to the grave. Naturally a vital question is therefore: what makes government a success or a failure? There is increasing interest in exploring this question through examination of policy: why do some policies succeed and some fail? Most attention is focused on

How to identify non-decisions

The number of non-decisions is potentially infinite. We can decide which are revealing about power and the policy process by three approaches:

- By comparing across a single policy domain: that is how in Briefing 19.2 above we can see that the absence of duty on aircraft fuel is a key non-decision.
- By comparing across countries. The non-decision discussed in the text, to exempt the Monarchy from income tax, would have been immediately evident had we compared across Western Europe, where it is usual for monarchies to pay taxes.
- By comparing across time. Looking at the past identifies what were non-decisions then: for instance we see immediately that cruelty to animals was shaped by non-decision in early nineteenth-century Britain. By showing us how important issues have been shaped by non-decision in the past it can make us sensitive to the possibility that the same is happening in our own time.

■ Because non-decisions are by definition limitless, we need some strategies to help us identify those that matter.

policy failure. There are good reasons for this: if we can isolate why some policies spectacularly fail, then in principle we can improve the chances of success by not repeating those mistakes; and policy failures in recent decades have inflicted huge costs and a great deal of human harm.

The idea of policy 'failure'

The notion of policy 'failure' is not straightforward. In our private lives 'failure' is often easy to identify. But things are more complicated in government, where the aims of policy are often unclear and the measurement of the impact of policy decision is often extremely difficult. Consider for a moment an episode that many of us experience in our private lives: taking a driving test. When we take the test we can easily identify success or failure because the aim (to pass) is unambiguous and the measurement of success straightforward (the decision of the examiner). But government hardly ever takes this straightforward kind of test; indeed since identifiable failure in government is usually punished by public criticism and even loss of office, governments have a strong incentive to 'fudge' the aims of policy and the way success will be measured. But often they do not have to fudge: ambiguity and uncertainty are built in. Consider an example of a great historic decision, our entry into the original EEC (Common Market) in 1973. Depending on your point of view this either remedied an earlier policy

catastrophe (the failure to join the original Common Market at its foundation in 1957) or was itself a disaster because it led to the loss of Britain's historical sovereignty. And even measuring the 'impact' of our 1973 entry is very hard: separating out the impact of 'Europe' from all the other forces working on British government in the intervening years is a tall order.

The identification of 'failure' will therefore often be uncertain and controversial. Nevertheless there are some important episodes in British government in recent decades which hardly anybody would dispute have amounted to catastrophes. They are also very important for a straightforward reason: they have been identified as catastrophes because the costs they impose (either in money, disruption or loss of life) are very large. In other words, they reveal the importance of trying to avoid failure in government, because the scale of modern government means that failure can have huge consequences. Government ministers who make a mess of their private lives mostly damage only themselves and their families; a minister who makes a mess of economic policy damages millions of people.

Just how catastrophic policy failure can be is illustrated by some of the most spectacular instances in British government in recent decades. Public housing provides one well-documented example. In the 1950s and 1960s local and central government demolished millions of modest terraced houses that were

BRIEFING 19.4

The main kinds of policy fiasco in Britain

Type of fiasco	Why a fiasco?	Example
Icon	Projects are designed by politicians to create an 'icon' – a prestige project.	Millennium Dome; 2012 London Olympics.
Great Leap Forward	Named after disastrous 'Great Leap Forward' of Chinese dictator Mao Zedong. Policy tries to short circuit careful,tedious preparation to achieve a revolutionary breakthrough.	Rail privatization.
Confrontation	Power of state and control of Parliament used to 'steamroller' through radical change without consultation.	The Community Charge ('Poll Tax').
Club	Policies are made by insiders in a cosy club without systematic evaluation or investigation.	Banking regulation: collapse of Barings Bank in City of London 1995 and near collapse of whole banking system after 2007.
'Capture'	Policy dominated by one set of interests who have captured the policy-making process to the exclusion of the wider public interest.	BSE ('mad cow' disease).

■ There are many different ways of making policy fiascos; my simple classification tries to enumerate them.

Source: Adapted from Moran (2001).

condemned as slums and replaced them with high-rise flats. The new estates cost billions. Many were structurally unsound. Most were very unpopular with their residents, and many were social failures, becoming centres of crime, unemployment and despair. A huge number had to be demolished in turn and replaced with 'low rise' – replicas of the very terraced dwellings they had originally displaced (Dunleavy 1981 is a classic study of this catastrophe).

Almost any attempt to travel by train in modern Britain provides another example of failure. Rail privatization was introduced by the Conservative Government in the middle of the 1990s. It took a poorly functioning national rail system and turned it into a catastrophe. Train reliability declined at one period to a point when there was effectively no reliable timetabled rail service over large parts of the country. The operator of the track established at privatization, Railtrack, subsequently went bankrupt. Some other catastrophic policy failures are, mercifully, more short lived, but their costs are huge. For instance, the Millennium Dome, a specially constructed building in east London, to be Britain's commemoration of the year 2000, ended up costing the taxpayer £750 million and remained empty for several years, an embarrassment to all connected with it (see Image 19.1).

Thus we see that policy failure can destroy whole communities, can irreparably damage national systems of communication, and can land the taxpayer with huge bills.

IMAGE 19.1 ■ The face of a policy fiasco: the Millennium Dome

Photo: Michael Moran

■ The modern history of British government is littered with policy fiascos. The strange tent-like structure photographed here across a dreary urban landscape pictures one of the most farcical: the Millennium Dome. Planned as Britain's showcase symbol of the new millennium in 2000, it was a farrago almost from the start: poor project planning, poor cost controls, ludicrously over optimistic business projections and even a chaotic opening night. It cost in the end over £750 million of public money. It is now sponsored by a mobile phone company and hosts music concerts for groups like Boyzone.

Explaining policy failure

Why do these failures happen? There are, broadly, three competing explanations.

Fatalism. One obvious possibility is that failure is just inevitable because neither institutions nor people are perfect. There are plenty of examples from the past of disasters: industrial and traffic accidents that killed hundreds; military catastrophes that resulted in the death of hundreds of thousands, even millions; failure to protect the physical environment that resulted in fatal pollution and epidemics. This is often the view that is implicit in official inquiries into disasters: we can learn from disasters, but since the world is an uncertain and dangerous place we must expect disasters to occur in the future.

The risk society. Fatalism argues that catastrophes are nothing new. By contrast, the risk society account argues that we are living in novel historical conditions that greatly increase the chances of policy catastrophes, and that these catastrophes in turn inflict harm on large numbers of people. Ours is a risk society because this kind of risk of catastrophic harm is a dominant feature

both of government and of the lives of us all. The scale and geographical reach of modern technologies mean that when they fail they inflict catastrophic harm on large numbers of people who cannot, separately, do anything to protect themselves. The most obvious example is the threat from safety failures in nuclear power plants: the 'meltdown' at the Chernobyl nuclear power reactor in the old Soviet Union in 1986 spread radiation across wide parts of Europe. But the risk society is not only about the objective existence of risk; it is also about perceptions of risk. Rising levels of education, the spread of different forms of reporting in a wide range of mass media, and the increasing willingness of citizens to organize in defence of their interests means that there is growing sensitivity to risk and growing willingness to organize in response to the prospect of risk. Thus governments find themselves in a difficult position: they are increasingly likely to fail catastrophically in making policy; but they face increasing demands from their citizens to protect against the consequences of failure.

A British disease. Arguments that policy failure is just inevitable given the complexity of modern govern-

POLITICAL ISSUES 19.1

BSE: Mad Cow Disease as a policy fiasco

Bovine Spongiform Encephalopathy (BSE), more popularly known as Mad Cow Disease, was first recognized as a problem in the 1980s. The disease destroyed cattle brains, causing them to stagger crazily – hence the vulgar popular name. For long, most scientific and official opinion minimized the importance of the disease, first picturing it as marginal to the cattle population, then as confined to cattle. By the mid-1980s it was clear that a huge proportion of the national herd was stricken; soon after, the responsible ministry admitted that it could 'jump' the species barrier – could potentially infect those who consumed beef from affected cattle. Though never conclusively demonstrated, there is a strong suspicion that consuming infected beef is a source of the human variant of the disease, CJD. An official inquiry, in its final report and in 17 volumes of evidence, traced the history of BSE, the way it grew out of industrialized intensive farming, and the way the meat in turn entered the human food chain. The 'facts' are therefore very well known. But the issue illuminates the diversity of theoretical themes that run through this chapter.

■ The failure to recognize and contain the disease is one of the most spectacular instances of the policy failure for which British government is so well known.

■ Despite the magnitude of the catastrophe not a single minister or official resigned or was punished for the failures, despite the fact that the report of the official inquiry documented a long history of official conceal- ment. Perhaps the most notorious stunt involved a minister publicly feeding a beefburger to his daughter to demonstrate food safety.

■ BSE illustrates one of the major recurrent issues in modern policy making, discussed in the accompanying section of this chapter: the central place of 'risk' in our modern experiences with big organizations. BSE grew out of many of the features that make society a 'risk society'. It involved processes and technologies unknown to lay people; it imposed risk collectively throughout society; and it involved the exercise of power by strong coalitions of organizations in government and in the food and agricultural industries.

To read more of the evidence on BSE, see www.bseinquiry.gov.uk.

ment, or is the product of a risk society, obviously assert that failure in Britain is not due to particular British conditions. But while all countries experience policy catastrophes, not all suffer the same levels and kinds of catastrophe: only Britain made a complete mess of running its rail network; and only Britain built the Millennium Dome. The suspicion is obvious: policy failure is a British disease. If the British are uniquely prone to policy failure, it could be due to a variety of factors. One is technical incompetence. Getting policy right in modern government demands a very high level of technical skill – stretching from a mastery of scientific and financial information in making a policy decision, to competence in managing complex projects to conclu- sion. Politicians hardly ever have these skills; and the tradition of the gifted amateur 'generalist' in the civil

service for a long time undervalued them among perma- nent officials. A second culprit might be overcentraliza- tion of the machinery of policy making. Before the devolution measures introduced by Labour after 1997 the UK had one of the most centralized systems of government among democratic countries. Centralization guarantees that one catastrophic policy decision at the centre – such as rail privatization – sends its effects widely across the whole of society. The new systems of multilevel governance discussed earlier, for all the new problems they bring, may therefore be a way of reducing the likelihood of catastrophic policy failure.

A final source of policy failure may be secrecy. One way we try to avoid making wrong decisions in our everyday lives is by consulting and debating. Organizations that allow open criticism and scrutiny also

DEBATING POLITICS 19.1

Policy failures: are the British uniquely incompetent?

BRITAIN IS UNIQUELY PRONE TO MASSIVE POLICY FAILURE

▶ The history of national decline in the twentieth century, especially of economic decline, is testimony to policy failure.

▶ Huge misjudgements were made about matters of high policy, such as the decision to stand aside from the early stages of European unification in the 1950s.

▶ From high rise housing to the Concorde airliner to the Millennium Dome: virtually any policy area produces an example of a catastrophic project.

▶ Excessive centralization, excessive secrecy and weak management skills locked Britain into a cycle of failed decisions, preventing the learning from failure.

THERE IS NOTHING UNIQUE ABOUT THE BRITISH EXPERIENCE

▶ Fiascos are inevitable given the scale and complexity of modern government.

▶ 'Failure' is often a contested judgement: it is not obvious that 'high politics' such as attitudes to European unification can be judged a failure.

▶ Numerous examples can be found abroad of great policy fiascos: indeed one commonly cited British fiasco – the decision to build the Concorde airliner – was shared with the French.

▶ British policy performance, especially in economic policy, actually compares well with our big European neighbours, over the last three decades.

raise the chances of learning from failure. But there is a long tradition of secrecy and concealment in British government. This culture of secrecy was strengthened in the twentieth century by the impact of war and the threat of war. In Chapters 21 and 22 we will explore further what the rise of national security did to the secrecy with which many parts of British government operate.

Review OF CHAPTER 19

Five themes have dominated this chapter:

- ◖▶ 'Policy' in British government is rarely the result of one single decision; it is part of a continuous stream of choices.

- ◖▶ A central problem of British policy making, therefore, is the problem of managing this continuous stream of choice so as to ensure some consistency in policy.

- ◖▶ Problems of coordination have become more urgent with the rise of multilevel governance in Britain.

- ◖▶ The visible face of policy choice is complemented by two other faces: of negative decisions and non-decisions, both of which exert great influence over the policies pursued by British government.

- ◖▶ The search for policy success is imperative, because the costs of failure, human and financial, can be huge.

FURTHER READING

ESSENTIAL

If you read only one book it should be Rhodes (1997), still the outstanding study of the UK policy process.

RECOMMENDED

Moran et al. (2008) provides a sampling of the weird world of academic policy analysis; Hill (2009), now in its fifth edition, is especially strong on theory and on the delivery of social policy. Parsons (1995) is comprehensive on theories of the policy process. The idea of non-decisions and negative decisions is still best described for the beginner by Lukes (2004). Moran (2001) introduces the debate about British policy failures. Hood et al. (2001) introduce the idea of risk and policy, and provide some good, concrete case studies.

Raising and allocating resources

CONTENTS

AIMS

This chapter:

- Explains why government seeks to influence the way resources are allocated

- Describes how British government raises and spends the key resource – money

- Examines the impact of spending and other forms of influence over resource allocation on social and economic inequality, emphasizing the issues of definition and measurement raised in the study of policy impact

THE BRITISH STATE AND THE ALLOCATION OF RESOURCES

In preceding chapters we examined competing accounts of how policy decisions are actually made – or avoided – in government. That examination was important because, as we saw, the mechanism or process of decision can have a large bearing on what is done. The most obvious instances concern negative and non-decisions, which can be critical to what government does and what it decides it is not able to do. Process is therefore important because it helps settle the content of policy. But we need to go beyond this – to look directly at the content of what government does, because this shapes lives. Traditionally government exercised power of life and death over all who lived in its territory, but the range of responsibilities that it acknowledged was comparatively limited. In the main it claimed to defend territory against external aggression and to maintain law and order internally. But throughout the course of the twentieth century British government expanded its responsibilities widely beyond these traditional areas. In particular, it took on increasing responsibility for the regulation of economic life and for ensuring the provision of a wide range of welfare services – like health care and education – for citizens. It became, in short, critical to the allocation of resources. The subject of resource allocation is the concern of this chapter.

The new responsibilities for resource allocation were often prompted by a common purpose: to intervene so as to reshape the way resources were allocated by the economic system itself. This economic system was for the most part run according to the principles of supply and demand in the market. Government intervened, and continues to intervene, because while the principles of market capitalism are widely accepted in Britain, there are believed to be a number of important instances where it produces unacceptable outcomes.

In part intervention is justified by a long established argument: that there exist a category of goods and services, commonly known as 'public goods', that would not be provided at all, or would be insufficiently provided, if market mechanisms were left to do the job. We can see why this might be so if we consider the essential defining feature of a public good: that if supplied at all it is necessarily supplied to everybody. Expressed technically, this is to say that the good is always *jointly consumed* and *non-excludable*. A classic example is the clean air produced by environmental controls such as those regulating emissions from factories: everybody breathes the same air and nobody can be excluded from breathing it. Other examples include street facilities like lighting and pavements, or public parks. If we relied on

IMAGE 20.1 ■ Ambitious commitments of public resources are nothing new: the example of reservoirs

Photo: Michael Moran

■ The reservoir pictured in Longendale, Derbyshire, is part of a chain constructed by local government in the nineteenth century to provide water for Manchester, then the greatest industrial city in the world. They were the most ambitious programme of reservoir construction in the world of their time. At the bottom of the photo can be seen a mark of another, later, huge scheme of public works: the pylons and wires of the electrification schemes that brought the electricity supply to virtually the whole of Britain in the 1930s.

the market to supply these goods they would either not be supplied at all, or supplied insufficiently, or the mechanism for demanding payment would become impossibly complicated. Imagine waking up one morning and finding that the supply of clean air was now a commercial concern and that we would be charged according to how much we consumed – as we are charged according to how much beer we consume in a pub. The attempt to measure the comparative air consumption of different citizens would involve absurdities like implanting a measurement instrument in the lungs of everybody. That helps to explain why the state provides clean air free at the point of consumption, but does not provide beer free at the point of consumption. Notice the good is not 'free' but 'free at the point of consumption'. Any good or service has to be paid for. A distinguishing feature of a public good is that its supply involves using the coercive power of the state. In the case of clean air, the state passes and enforces laws regulating emissions; in the case of street lighting the state uses its coercive power to tax and then allocates the money to the cost of lighting.

'Public goods' cover some of the services traditionally provided by government: for instance, the defence against invasion from abroad provided by the armed services is available to all alike. But the growth of state responsibilities over the last century reflected more than the belief that there was a special category of public goods that should be provided by the state. It also arose from the belief that, even when markets could allocate resources, they had unacceptable distributive consequences: that they produced levels of inequality which were too extreme and that these inequalities needed to be moderated by state intervention to reallocate some of the wealth created by market mechanisms. Thus the state became committed to more than the provision of some services; it also became committed to the allocation, and thus to the redistribution, of resources. This was a great historical change. Before the rise of democracy, government was usually conceived – at least by those with power – as a means of defending inequality, not with its moderation.

Even putting the issues in the simple terms used here exposes some of the debates to which state intervention has given rise. How 'public' are 'public goods' in reality? How true is it that, for instance, national defence could not be supplied commercially? History contains numerous examples of mercenary armies who supplied defence, and offence, for payment. In Britain today the private security industry provides many services, from patrolling individual neighbourhoods to transporting money. Thus it is not even certain that the most traditionally established state functions should indeed be publicly provided. But it is when we move beyond the sphere of public goods to resource redistribution that arguments become really intense. The use of the state to redistribute presumes that governments, if they intervene, really do produce more equality of outcome than markets can achieve – a debatable assumption that has, indeed, been widely debated. Even if that presumption is accepted there are a host of other areas of argument. What price do we pay by restricting markets in the name of more equality? Do we sacrifice efficiency and liberty in the process – and if we do, how big a sacrifice should we make? Given that very few people support the aim of using the state to achieve complete equality, what level of inequality is acceptable?

These are the issues that lie at the heart of this chapter, which is built around three blocks: how the state raises resources; how it allocates resources; and what impact allocation has on the distribution of resources.

Notice in passing the significance here of the word 'resources'. It marks an important limit to the concerns of this chapter. The state also plays an important part in the allocation of values other than material ones. Historically, the British state prescribed, for instance, the religious values that could be tolerated: at various times it sought to prohibit, or put barriers in the way of, creeds like Judaism, Catholicism and Quakerism, and in the way of belief systems like atheism. The rise of doctrines of religious toleration meant that the state withdrew from these attempts, though the fact that the Monarch is the Head of the Established Church in England and Wales signifies a residue of that desire to allocate 'spiritual' values. In recent decades the state has also tried to use the law to promote some values at the expense of others: thus anti-discrimination and anti-racism legislation seeks to prohibit some doctrines and practices defined as racist or discriminatory, and to promote other values, like toleration and respect for others of different ethnic or religious persuasions.

HOW THE BRITISH STATE RAISES RESOURCES

Although huge in scale and complex in structure, government can still be pictured as resembling a household: like a household, it receives income and is committed to spending. Indeed, study of the domestic economy of government was one of the earliest areas of specialized scholarship in the study of the state. But because government in Britain is large and complex its sources of 'income' are much more diverse than those of any domestic household.

Traditionally governments have been able to raise resources in five ways, and all are still used by British government. They are discussed here in ascending order of importance.

By fiat money

'Fiat money' refers to the state's monopoly of the right to create money, in the most immediate instance literally by printing and minting. This is obviously one source of revenue raising that is not open to us as private citizens; if we try it the state prosecutes us for forgery. The presence of the Monarch's head on coin and notes is a symbol of the state's monopoly of the right to create 'legal tender'. This partly explains why the proposal to adopt in Britain the single European currency (the euro) is so controversial. If adopted, the traditional right to create fiat money would have to be shared with all the other partners in the federal European Central Bank. Historically the creation of fiat money was vital to raising resources and the state imposed draconian punishments on those who forged or minted illegally. It remains symbolically significant of

Timeline 20.1

The tide of privatization floods in – and then recedes?

1981 British Aerospace 1; Cable and Wireless 1.

1982 Britoil 1; Amersham International.

1983 Associated British Ports 1; British Petroleum; Cable and Wireless 2.

1984 British Telecom 1; Associated British Ports 2; Enterprise Oil; Jaguar Cars.

1985 British Aerospace 2; Britoil 2; Cable and Wireless 3.

1986 British Gas.

1987 British Airways; Rolls Royce; British Airports Authority; British Petroleum; Royal Ordnance.

1988 British Steel.

1989 10 regional water companies.

1990 12 regional electricity companies.

1991 Electricity generating companies 1; Scottish Electricity; British Telecom 2.

1992 Property Services Agency; Northern Ireland electricity generation.

1993 British Telecom 3.

1994 Coal industry; London Buses.

1995 Electricity generating companies 2.

1996 British Rail; British Energy; HMSO (Stationery Office).

2001 National Air Traffic Services.

2002 Defence Evaluation and Research Agency.

2008 State forced to 'nationalize' a number of failing banks and to take large holdings in others.

■ The British privatization programme was the most ambitious and extensive in the advanced industrial world. Privatized enterprises ranged from huge utilities which had to be privatized in stages (the numbers against instances like British Telecom indicate this) to small 'core' parts of the Government, like the Stationery Office. But a key date to focus on in the timeline is the entry for 2008: in the great banking crisis of that year the state was forced to take over a large part of the banking system. After more than a quarter of a century of privatization public ownership reappeared as a major feature of public policy.

Source: HM Treasury.

state power, but has been outstripped by other ways of raising resources.

By income from assets

British government has historically been a large property owner and this property, like any other asset, can generate income. Much of the property was acquired in the distant past: for instance, government receives income from licences issued to companies extracting oil from the North Sea because exploitable minerals were historically the property of the Crown. With the growth of industrialism the state acquired some lucrative new assets. Thus until near the end of the twentieth century the provision of telecommunications' services was a lucrative state monopoly; and until recently the monopoly enjoyed by the Royal Mail was also profitable. In principle the state can acquire fresh resources by confiscating the assets of private citizens or associations. Since Henry VIII dissolved the monasteries and distributed their property in the Reformation this has been recognized as a significant way for the state to acquire assets. But in a democracy this confiscation, especially without generous compensation, is not easy to carry through on a large scale.

By sale of assets

Historically governments often 'sold the family silver' when short of cash. In the last couple of decades of the twentieth century, however, government in Britain sold assets on a huge scale through the privatization programme, as Timeline 20.1 shows. But of course there is an obvious limit to how far revenue can be raised by selling assets: there comes a point where there is nothing of significance left to sell. Though the state in Britain has not yet reached that point, the high water mark of 'selling the family silver' was reached in the years covered by Timeline 20.1. But the timeline also shows that the great financial crisis after 2007 may have stopped the high tide of privatization: the state was forced to take into public ownership a huge part of the banking system.

By borrowing

Historically governments often borrowed on a large scale, and we shall see in a moment that this is also true of modern British government. Government can usually borrow on better terms than we can as private individuals. It can often borrow more cheaply than us, for instance by appealing to the patriotism of private citizens to subscribe to national savings. In the great world wars of the twentieth century government raised large amounts by this kind of patriotic appeal. Government can also often borrow for much longer than can private

citizens. Loans stretching over 50 years have not been unknown, whereas even the longest house mortgage term for private citizens is usually 30 years. If repayment becomes a problem, government can also default on its debts. Defaulting can have adverse consequences on future ability to borrow, but states do default and they can get away with it. If you or I default on our building society mortgage, in the end our house will be repossessed or we will be made bankrupt. It is hard to repossess assets from a state and virtually impossible to make a state bankrupt in the way private citizens or firms can be made bankrupt. An additional attraction of borrowing is that, when borrowing for a long period, governments can often spend the money more or less immediately and leave the problem of paying the debt to successors in the distant future. For democratic governments needing to work to quite short general election cycles of four or five years this is obviously an attractive option.

Borrowing is now integral to revenue raising by government, and in recent decades the means of borrowing have been transformed by the development of more ingenious methods. Simple appeals to small savers to lend cheaply – either because of patriotism or because of the greater security of the state as a creditor – are decreasingly important. There are now huge and sophisticated markets in government debt where financial institutions trade blocks of government bonds that vary in terms like the rate of return and the date of redemption. In this way government does what no private individual could ever do: it perpetually extends, redeems and renews its debt from generation to generation.

By taxation

Governments have always taxed, and indeed disaffection with taxes has been one of the great dangers to rulers. Some of the greatest revolutions in history, like the French Revolution, can be traced to tax revolts. And closer to home a huge revolt against a new form of local taxation in Britain in the late 1980s – the Community Charge or 'Poll Tax' – led to its abandonment and contributed to the fall from office of the then Prime Minister, Mrs Thatcher.

In the twentieth century taxation became the most important source of income for British governments, and it remains of primary importance. This happened because government developed powerful administrative techniques for levying taxes in ways that were hard to avoid. We can see the power of taxation by considering the main ways taxes are levied in Britain. Taxation comes from four main sources.

● Direct taxes on individuals' incomes, of which the most important source is the regular (usually weekly

FIGURE 20.1 ■ The scale of government borrowing declined historically ...

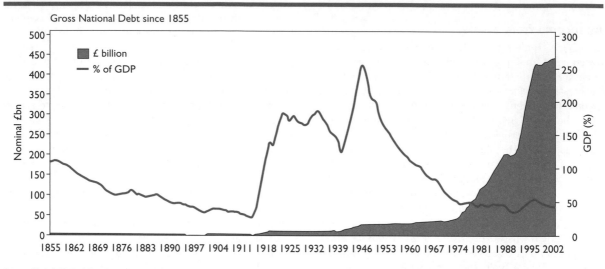

Gross National Debt since 1855

Source: National Debt Office (www.dmo.gov.uk).

or monthly) deduction of tax at source on the incomes of the employed, usually called Pay As You Earn (PAYE).

● Direct taxes on the assets of individuals. Among the most important of these are various kinds of 'death duties' – taxes on the assets which individuals leave at death, and which in principle are targeted at the rich.

● Direct taxes on institutions, of which the most important are various taxes levied on business firms. For instance, the tax bill paid by the Royal Bank of Scotland (RBS) in 2004, after a bumper profits result, was in excess of £2 billion; but just how uncertain this can be is shown by the fact that RBS was the most costly rescue to the public purse in the 2007–08 financial crisis. The cost wiped out the benefits of the tax receipts.

● Taxes on goods and services, of which the most important is Value Added Tax (VAT). VAT is experienced by most of us as a tax on sales: the cost of the PC on which this book was written had 17.5 per cent added to it by VAT. VAT was instituted in Britain in 1973 and it replaced a variety of older sales taxes. It has proved to be a highly effective way of raising resources, and Chancellor George Osborne turned to it again in his crisis budget of 2010, when he raised the VAT rate to 20 per cent. But the principle of taxing a good or service was well established before VAT: historically, duties on goods like alcohol and tobacco were an important source of Crown revenue, and they remain important in contributing to the public coffers.

FIGURE 20.2 ■ But rose dramatically in and during the post-2007 recession

Net debt

Source: Office for National Statistics 2009.

■ The two figures help to put the state's finances into historical context. Figure 20.1 shows that, though the nominal cash value of the debt grew over the twentieth century, as a percentage of Gross Domestic Product (a conventional measure of total national output), it fell over the second half of the century. But Figure 20.2 shows that it began to grow after the turn of the millennium, and accelerated after the great financial crisis of 2007.

The importance of taxation dates from the middle decades of the twentieth century. Two administrative innovations already mentioned in passing explain why it became the centrepiece of resource raising.

The first innovation was developed in the Second World War in order to raise the huge resources needed to fight that War. It was the system of Pay As You Earn (PAYE) referred to above. The great administrative advance of PAYE was that, through its deduction of fixed amounts from the pay packet received by workers, it made taxation a routine and eventually almost universal experience for everyone in work. With rising incomes it meant that virtually everyone in work was drawn into the tax net and the state was provided with a hugely efficient source of tax revenue: there were less than 4 million income taxpayers at the end of the 1930s, compared with over 29 million now. In effect employers did the collecting by direct deduction from wages and then simply transferred the money to the state, to the department of the Inland Revenue.

The second administrative invention, VAT, is more recent. It was introduced, as we saw above, in 1973. Although not in principle a new tax – in essence VAT is experienced by most of us as a sales tax, and taxes on the sale of goods have a long history – it is a uniquely thorough and subtle tax that is proving a hugely productive source of revenue. It is by far the most lucrative of the many levies collected by Customs and Excise, yielding over £78 billion in the financial year 2008–09 (the most recent financial year for which figures are available).

The importance of VAT is also indicative of an important shift in the balance of taxation in recent decades: a shift away from taxes on income to taxes on sales, good and services. One of the most important reasons for this is that governments have come to believe that there is significant resistance to income tax and that this resistance can be electorally damaging. Taxes taken from income are highly visible: every time employees look at a pay slip they see the size of the tax deduction. Taxes like VAT, or duties on goods like tobacco, by contrast, are partly concealed in the overall cost of a good or service. In addition, there is evidence that taxes on consumption are less 'progressive' than income tax. By 'progressive' here I mean to describe, not make a value judgement. It is common to distinguish between 'progressive' and 'regressive' taxes. A 'progressive' tax extracts proportionately more from those with higher income; a 'regressive' tax extracts more from lower income groups. In principle income tax rates rise as income increases, and are therefore progressive. VAT is levied irrespective of income, and this is also true of an important category of taxes that more directly tax consumption: special duties paid on individual goods. The best-documented example is the duty on cigarettes.

FIGURE 20.3 ■ The spread of the income tax net

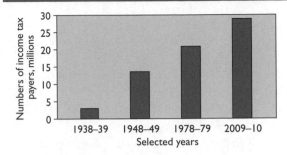

Source: Calculated from HM Revenue and Customs data.

■ The figures from the selected years show the number of income tax payers over a period of more than 70 years. The jump in the decade after 1938 illustrates the importance of the introduction of PAYE. Overall, the figures show that paying income tax has been transformed from an experience of a fairly wealthy minority to one experienced by virtually every adult.

Smoking is now disproportionately concentrated among the poor; thus raising money through duty on cigarettes is a 'regressive' rather than a 'progressive' way to raise resources. The shift to indirect taxation is therefore in part a response to the influence of organized interests: taxpayers, especially higher rate taxpayers, are better organized and more vocal than are the poor.

One of the main reasons why both PAYE and VAT are so important to revenue raising is that they are hard to escape. But the ability of individuals and institutions to escape the tax net is nevertheless a key problem for British government. Escape comes in two main forms, conventionally labelled tax evasion and tax avoidance. Evasion refers to illegal escape: businesses can falsify their books, thus escaping VAT and other tax obligations; workers can operate in the 'black economy', taking payment in cash without declaring it to the authorities. These problems explain why government has a big apparatus of tax surveillance: VAT inspectors raid firms; the Inland Revenue conducts spot checks on individual tax returns. It is hard to know how big is the loss of revenue by evasion, since the whole point of the operation is concealment. In some cases an additional reason for concealment is that the source of income may itself be also criminal: drug dealers prefer cash not only because they want to avoid paying income tax, but also because they want to conceal the very source of their revenue.

We use 'tax avoidance', by contrast, to summarize legal ways to minimize our tax liabilities. Most taxpayers practise tax avoidance. When the Inland Revenue agrees

EUROPEANIZING 20.1

Europeanizing public spending: the impact of the Maastricht criteria

Britain is of course not a member of the eurozone – it has opted not to replace sterling with the euro. But public spending levels still have to be set within European boundaries. One of the most important formal limits is set by the Maastricht Treaty 1992, of which the UK is a signatory. Article 104 of the Treaty obliges member states to avoid excessive budgetary deficits. The Protocol on the Excessive Deficit Procedure, annexed to the Maastricht Treaty, defines two criteria and reference values for compliance. These are a deficit to Gross Domestic Product (GDP) ratio of 3 per cent, and a debt to GDP ratio of 60 per cent. But general government net borrowing in 2008/09, the latest year for which definitive figures are available, showed that it was equivalent to 7.1 per cent of GDP, over twice the 'Maastricht' limit. The breach is only tolerable because it is substantially due to the impact of the financial crisis of 2007–08, which has affected public finances across the Union. But it undoubtedly is an influence on government determination to cut the deficit in the medium term.

to treat the cost of my annual purchases of academic books as an allowance against my tax bill, I am engaged in tax avoidance. This unsophisticated avoidance is dwarfed by the modern tax planning industry, run mostly by multinational firms of lawyers and accountants, who specialize in devising means for big corporations and the very rich to plan their affairs so as legally to minimize their tax losses. Thus while inheritance tax is incurred presently on estates valued at £350,000 or more, a quite modest threshold in the age of house price inflation, it is a very foolish or unlucky rich person whose estate pays duty on death: a good accountant will devise a trust to escape the liability. Likewise big multinational corporations are skilled in channelling their revenue through tax havens and shelters: for an illustration, see Political Issues 20.1.

Revenue raising by government is among the most technically complex areas of public life but as this summary shows it is also one of the most intensely political: success in revenue raising is vital for the effectiveness, and indeed the very stability, of government; and the struggles over where to lay the burden of revenue raising involve great clashes between different economic interests.

HOW THE BRITISH STATE ALLOCATES RESOURCES

In the previous section we looked at the 'income' side of the domestic economy of government; now it is time to look at the outgoings. The rise of the state in Britain as a large-scale allocator of resources has taken the form of two very different kinds of spending programmes. The state can use the money it gathers in to fund services that it directly delivers. This is the characteristic feature of such important services as health care and schools education in Britain. It is natural instinctively to equate spending on direct provision with the state as an allocator of resources. But this is only half the picture and, quantitatively, the less important half. Another large chunk of spending is accounted for by what are normally labelled 'income transfers'. Here government acts as a channel taking money out of the pocket of some groups – for instance wage earning employees – and putting it into the pockets of other groups: for instance the unemployed or pensioners. But the government is not a passive channel through which resources pass. Actually getting hold of the money, and then distributing it, requires large and expensive administrative machines. For instance, HM Revenue and Customs, the collector of taxes on income, employs nearly 89,000 staff. And the detailed rules of transfer – the entitlements that govern who gets what – are obviously critical to how the money is allocated upon transfer. As we will see in the next section, the way the resources for income transfer are raised, and the way they are distributed, are not just administrative technicalities; they go to the heart of how we view the purpose of government in Britain today.

Income transfers of the kind described here are obviously a very different way of allocating income from that operated by the market. Indeed, historically they were conceived as an alternative when the market 'failed': as 'income support', in circumstances when individuals could not command an income, or a living income, by sale of their labour. Thus the earliest large programmes of income transfer provided pensions for the old and benefits for the sick; both groups, for different reasons, being unable to command wages in the free labour market.

The scale of resource allocation by British government is huge; it makes the state the biggest spender by far in British society. Understanding the history and recent composition of resource allocation is therefore vital, not just for the particular purpose of making sense of public spending but to understand the changing role of the state in Britain. Three features of resource allocation stand out.

Public spending has risen greatly over the long term

In Chapter 1 we saw this trend illustrated. Over the course of the twentieth century there was a huge rise in the proportion of national wealth that was taken, and allocated, by the state. And as that figure showed, the two major boosts to spending occurred in the two great world wars that the British state fought during the century. Indeed it was the demand for spending – to fund the wars and the greatly expanded welfare programmes – which prompted great administrative inventions like PAYE.

Total spending was stable for about 30 years from the middle of the 1970s

In the early 1970s a long period of sustained economic growth that had stretched back to the Second World War ended in Britain. At the same time political parties, both of the Left and Right, began to argue that the growth in state spending had to be stopped. The Conservatives who came to office in 1979 had the ambition of reducing the proportion of national income spent publicly (though note that in a growing economy this does not necessarily mean that total public spending has to decline). That ambition was very hard to realize, for reasons that we discuss below. But undoubtedly this new hostility to taxing and spending produced a new era of constraint on public spending, by contrast with the long history of growth over almost the whole of the preceding decades of the twentieth century.

The great economic crisis after 2007 has produced a new era of public indebtedness

As Figures 20.1 and 20.2 show, there has been a renewed surge in the scale of public debt, and this is largely traceable to the economic crisis which began in 2007. The sources of this new era of indebtedness are threefold. First, in order to prevent the collapse of the banking system the government was forced to 'bail out' failed

FIGURE 20.4 ■ The spending priorities of a modern state: examples of the relative importance of spending in different departments

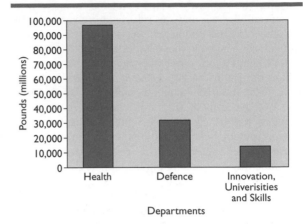

Notes: Figures relate to planned outturn for 2010–11. Health figures are for England.
Source: Calculated from Treasury statistics.

■ Behind the huge totals for public spending lies a complex pattern. These three sample figures just illustrate the pattern: a historically recent function – health protection – dominates, dwarfing a traditional function, defence. The figure for innovation, universities and skills reflects the modern state's increasing concern with the 'knowledge base' of the economy.

banks, like the Royal Bank of Scotland. It was also forced to guarantee on an even larger scale the present bad debts of big banks, involving a long term commitment whose scale cannot be exactly known, but which is huge. Second, as a result of the recession – the economy actually shrank and did not begin even a small expansion until the end of 2009 – the income of government, from tax revenues, shrank. Finally, the obligations of government under existing income transfer programmes – notably support for those out of work – rose as unemployment grew. In short, a recession is very bad news for the 'household budget' of the state.

The impact of the great economic crisis also illustrates another more long term feature: the composition of public spending has changed over time. The kinds of measures we have been using above are handy, but crude, summaries: they just measure the total volume of resources allocated by the state. Some of these changes have to do with great historical events. As Figure 1.1 (p. 12) showed, both world wars gave a huge boost to spending, but obviously that military related spending declined radically when the great wars ended. Some changes have to do with the cycle of the economy. Two very good instances are provided by spending to 'service' public debt and spending on benefits for the unemployed. When the economy is booming, especially when unemployment is low, government budgets are often in surplus: the demand on spending for unemployment benefit is lowered; and tax returns are boosted by the expansion in the number of tax paying wage earners. Conversely, economic recession usually puts pressure on governments to borrow. Thus when unemployment was falling rapidly in the late 1990s it was possible for the Chancellor of the Exchequer actually to repay significant parts of the 'capital' on the public debt, because the Treasury was getting a double benefit: falling demand for unemployment benefit, and rising tax revenues from those in work. After 2007 the reverse happened in a dramatic way: the scale of public debt, both existing and projected, rose dramatically.

Even totals of public spending that are stable over time can nevertheless conceal big changes in the composition of spending. Not all changes are due to big historical events, like war, or the cycle of the economy. They are due to political choices made by governments, and these choices are naturally influenced by the power of different groups of interests in society. Part of the reason why in the 1980s and 1990s politicians of most parties became hostile to increased public spending was that they were listening to powerful groups of taxpayers who wanted their tax bills reduced. But the ambition actually significantly to reduce the overall level of spending was very hard to achieve. Most public spending is due to commitments that are hard to abandon, especially in the short term. A good example is the whole range of 'income transfers' that lie at the heart of the welfare state: these arise from legal entitlements to a range of benefits (child benefit, old age pensions, benefits for the disabled, unemployment benefit) that have to be paid out as a matter of law. Only changes in the rules can cut or abolish these. Such changes take time and naturally will be resisted by any threatened group powerful enough to organize effectively. Another example was the way the power of bankers operated after 2007, when the state was persuaded to commit huge sums of taxpayers money to underwrite the biggest banks.

These factors throw a lot of light on the changing composition of public spending. To cut spending, governments have to cut commitments, and they will naturally look for the 'softest' targets: at spending on those social groups who are poorly organized politically or who happen not to be obvious supporters of the party that is in power. Thus over the years of Conservative rule up to 1997, while there was little change in the total levels of spending, some programmes were severely cut: for instance, investment on public housing was sharply

FIGURE 20.5 ■ The difference a crisis makes: the impact of the financial crisis on levels of public spending

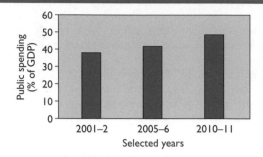

Note: Figure for 2010–11 is planned expenditure.
Source: Calculated from HM Treasury figures.

■ The figures extract from Treasury sources the proportion of GDP accounted for by Total Managed Public Expenditure, a standard measure; compare this with Figure 1.1 (p. 12) which gives a historical run. The really dramatic change is the effect on the public finances of the great banking crisis of 2007–08: the cost of the bank bail out and the cost of the recession in decreasing tax revenue, a smaller economy and spending on the unemployed.

reduced, a change confirmed by the policies of the Labour Governments after 1997.

For the 30 years up to the financial crisis of 2007–08 struggles over public spending were essentially struggles for a share of a 'cake' of more or less fixed size (by contrast with the era before that, when the cake grew in size over the decades). A critical factor, then, has been the relative effectiveness of different social interests in protecting their share of the cake. This is only part of the larger political struggle of public spending, because obviously there is a similar struggle on the taxation side, as different groups try to minimize the amount they have to contribute to the public purse. As we saw earlier, over recent years there has been a shift from direct taxes on income, to indirect taxes, like VAT, and the effect of this has been generally 'regressive': that is, it has meant that the poorest have paid an increasing share of the total tax bill.

There is therefore a close and delicate connection between the politics of resource allocation in government and the way the wider political system is itself organized. It is obvious that some groups are well placed to defend their interests in the struggle of taxing and spending and others have little or no means of their own. We need only look back to Chapter 8 at our discussion of the way interests are represented to see how and why these differences exist. This does not mean that those

BRIEFING 20.1

The new fiscal crisis of the British state

Figures 20.1 and 20.2 summarize the dimensions of the new fiscal crisis of the state. They show that while public sector debt was stable or declining for most of the second half of the twentieth century, it accelerated dramatically under the impact of economic recession and the banking crisis after 2007. That the problem is great is not disputed by any serious commentator. But the scale of the crisis is a matter of argument: the arguments turn on how far it is possible to rein back the scale of debt without significantly cutting provision of public services; and how far the UK deficit is large by international standards – an argument bedevilled by the difficulty of agreeing standards of comparison between different national economies.

without resources of their own cannot have a voice. Take the example of those suffering severe intellectual disabilities. They will often find it very hard to organize politically. But as the existence of groups speaking and lobbying on their behalf, like MENCAP, shows they need not be without a voice. How effective that voice can be raises questions that are central to the nature of democracy in Britain. As we will see in our concluding chapter, one optimistic view of democracy says that there are a wide range of different resources open to different groups, and that these can partly balance each other out. The arguments about this difficult matter we will examine there. But the issue shows that the whole area of public taxing and spending is far more than technical; it goes to the heart of the nature of democracy in Britain. Who pays, and who benefits, from public spending are therefore two key tests of the character of democratic politics in Britain.

There is also another sense in which the technical details about resource allocation are of importance: they are relevant to large questions about the social impact of government in Britain. This is examined in the next section.

THE IMPACT OF THE BRITISH STATE ON THE ALLOCATION OF RESOURCES: EVIDENCE AND DEBATES

Until the start of the twentieth century government within Britain was mostly concerned with what we would now think of as narrow concerns. These were chiefly to do with maintaining public order, especially with protecting property and people. The biggest single change that occurred in the twentieth century was that

this narrow range of concerns widened greatly. The first half of the century saw the development of a welfare state. This involved the creation of a range of institutions and programmes where the state took responsibility for ensuring widespread access to services like health care, education and income support for groups like the old and unemployed – a mix, in other words, of spending on direct provision and on income transfer.

Behind the rise of the welfare state lay the idea, which we have already encountered, that government needed to reallocate resources in such a way as to modify the kinds of allocations that would happen if the economic marketplace alone were allowed to do the job. This idea has provoked some of the most important debates about British government. In essence: can the state, or should the state, seek to modify the market as a mechanism of resource allocation? And if it should, how radical should that modification be? One highly controversial but influential view – which lay behind the attempt made in the last couple of decades to cut back public spending – was that the attempt to modify the effects of the market had gone too far: for instance that it required such high levels of taxation that it was undermining efficiency in markets and therefore weakening the economy's ability to produce the wealth needed for reallocation in the first place. These views were originally associated with radical supporters of the free market, though they ended up being subscribed to even by the Labour governments that were in power between 1997 and 2010. An equally radical argument has come from some of the socialist Left: that when we look closely at the efforts by the state to redistribute resources we find that it largely fails to modify the unequal distributions produced by the market.

These debates are both politically contentious and intellectually complex. They are contentious and complex because they simultaneously raise three different sets of questions about the state and the allocation of resources:

● Who pays for state activity? Since the state only allocates resources after first raising them (through taxation for example) any view about allocation has to depend in part on evidence about which social groups are paying in the first place.
● Who is receiving the benefits of allocation? The theory of the welfare state was that those who for various reasons were badly placed to benefit from the market should receive the bulk of resources. But is this true?
● What is the impact of allocation? This question raises some of the most difficult questions of all about the links between state activity and social and economic inequality. For instance, even if resources do go to the poorest, do these resources significantly moderate inequality?

Who pays?

Earlier in the chapter we got a picture of the main sources of government revenue, but this only gives us a very indirect idea of the identity of the payers. Until the twentieth century there was a well-established view on this matter. It was that taxation should be regressive: that is, every attempt should be made to ensure that the cost of government was borne by the poor rather than by the rich. This was because property was thought to be the foundation of the social order; it was therefore dangerous for government to tax it. But for over a hundred years the dominant view has been that taxation should be progressive: more simply, the rich should pay more to the upkeep of government than should the poor. Many of the formal rules of income and property taxation are designed with this in mind: the most obvious instance is provided by the rules for taxation of income, where the very lowest paid are exempted from taxation and the proportionate tax levy is supposed to rise with income.

The formal principle that contribution to the cost of government should be on a progressive basis does actually very roughly correspond to the reality of the main sources of government income. Income tax is the most important source of revenue, and liability to pay rises with income. But the 'progressive' nature of contributions is only rough and ready, for a variety of reasons that we have already encountered in passing. The formal rules of progressive taxation are often easily avoided. As we saw above, there is a large industry of tax advice which is designed to ensure that the wealthiest individuals and institutions can do exactly this: in the jargon of the accountant, 'tax efficient' organization of both individual and corporate income considerably cuts tax liabil-

ities. In addition, the sheer size of the state's appetite for money in the age of big government has forced it to widen the tax net socially. At the end of the 1930s, for example, only a minority of the wealthiest earners paid any tax at all; now, as we saw earlier, the vast majority of wage earners have to pay (see Figure 20.3).

There has also been, as we saw above, a powerful trend shifting the bias of taxation from the progressive to the regressive in recent decades. This is due to the perception (right or wrong) that the limits of direct taxation on incomes have been reached. The result is a long-term shift to indirect taxes. The most obvious sign is the long term growing importance of VAT and of special duties on targeted goods, of which the best known are cigarettes. Some of these taxes (like excise duty on cigarettes) are direct taxes on consumption; and VAT has many of the features of a consumption tax since the cost is in the end passed on in the final price of the good. Consumption taxes need not be regressive. Indeed, one of the few historical exceptions to the principle that the poor should pay more than the rich in tax lay in so-called 'sumptuary taxation': the special taxation of luxury goods. Some of this principle is retained in elements of indirect taxation: food is exempt from VAT partly because it is obviously a necessity rather than any kind of luxury, while the taxation of tobacco and alcohol, though partly done to deter consumption on health grounds, also reflects the assumption that these are dispensable luxuries. Nevertheless, the bias of indirect taxation is regressive rather than progressive.

The way the costs of government are distributed cannot therefore be reduced to any simple sum. The most important reason for this is that there is a continuing struggle over who should bear these costs, and the losers and winners in this struggle form a complicated, and shifting, pattern. Much the same can now be said about the other side of the balance sheet: who benefits from what government provides.

Who benefits?

We can identify four important kinds of goods and services that are provided by government. The importance of these variants is that each have different distributional profiles.

Pure public goods. The first are close to being pure public goods in the sense identified at the beginning of this chapter. Many of the 'benefits' of government spending are indivisible: once provided they are automatically available to all, are equally consumed by all and are equally worthwhile to all. Some of the classic traditional functions of government fall into this category, and they are further examined in the next chapter when we turn to the state and the maintenance of security: protection against

People in Politics 20.1

Three who shaped our attitudes to public spending

Karl Marx (1818–83)

German philosopher and revolutionary, and founder of one of the most successful political creeds of the twentieth century. Marxism enjoyed little popular appeal in Britain, despite the fact that his most important work used Britain as a key case. But Marx's picture of the market economy as a generator of inequality and misery deeply influenced many on the Left, strengthening the commitment to high public spending to combat market inequality.

John Maynard Keynes (1883–1946)

The most famous British economist of the twentieth century, he deeply influenced attitudes to public spending right across the political spectrum. Though an advocate of balanced budgets, Keynes popularized the idea that markets were not self-regulating, that active government economic management was needed, and that part of this would involve high levels of public spending. He supported the Liberal Party, but his influence transcended party politics.

Milton Friedman (1912–2006)

American economist, the most famous critic of high levels of public spending in the last quarter of the twentieth century. He argued that free markets were almost always superior to public provision and that a large public sector was a threat to liberty. His ideas, summarized in his book *Capitalism and Freedom*, deeply influenced the Thatcherite reformers who governed Britain after 1979.

Cartoons: Shaun Steele

banditry and thuggery is equally valuable to you and to me. An even better example is the one we discussed at the start of this chapter: clean air. The Clean Air Act of 1956 introduced and policed more stringent restrictions over such emissions as fuel burning in fires in domestic homes. The Act is partly responsible for the fact that British cities are no longer afflicted by the 'smogs' which had hitherto caused the deaths of significant numbers of people and produced discomfort and filth for many more. The clean air resulting from the legislation is probably as close as we could find in the real world to the 'ideal' public good proposed in the models of economists: it is indivisible, in the sense that once available its consumption cannot be restricted to some members of the community, and therefore cannot be assigned to particular groups; and it is jointly and equally consumed by all. But pure public goods are not the only kind of output of government.

Universally available free services. A second important kind of benefit has a more complex distribution. There is an important class of goods provided by government which is available freely and with little or no formality, but which is known to be unequally consumed by the population at large. One example is the free public library service. The free public library movement has its origins in the nineteenth century and, especially before the rise of mass education, was an important route to self-education for many. Public libraries still provide important benefits available equally to all in the community, and using them involves the minimum of formalities: if you wish to join your local library you will have to do no more than provide a local address to be granted borrowing rights. But in fact libraries are only used by a minority, and this minority is not a microcosm of the population at large – as a glance at Figure 20.6 shows.

Public services allocated by 'gatekeepers'. The issue of the unequal consumption of the goods provided by government is central to this third category of benefits. Many of the services to which government commits large-scale resources are only available to those who can persuade a figure controlling access to the service to make it available. A good example is hospital care, which is available free but not to all of us on demand. Except in special circumstances, like an emergency, none of us can turn up at a hospital and demand care. We have to be referred after consultation by our general practitioner, who makes a professional judgement as to whether we need to be seen and treated in a hospital. The general practitioner, in other words, is the gatekeeper to some of the most important parts of the National Health Service. Obviously how the gatekeeper makes the judgement critically influences how the resource is allocated. General practitioners do not make capricious judgements in deciding which patients to refer to hospitals, but they do make a discretionary judge-

FIGURE 20.6 ■ Class variations in the use of a public service: libraries

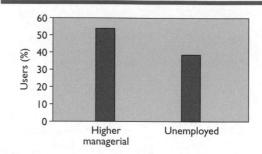

Source: Calculated from *Social Trends* (2008, Figure 13.6).

■ The higher of the two charts is for 'higher managerial and professional'; the lower for 'never worked and long term unemployed'. The figures are based on reported use of a public library in the 12 months prior to interview.

ment, and that discretion decides who gets to consume the resources of the hospital.

A striking example of the importance of gatekeeping is provided in Figure 20.7. It shows vividly for one important domain of public sector provision that expansion can actually redistribute resources away from the poor to the rich. During the 1990s the British Government vastly increased the scale of provision in higher education, leading to a great increase in the proportion of 18–21 year olds who entered colleges and universities. Though students in England and Wales pay fees these nowhere near cover the cost; higher education is heavily subsidized by the state and is indeed one part of the welfare state that has expanded greatly in the last two decades. Higher education is, as many readers of this book will have experienced, only available to those admitted to a college or university. In a case like this, the critical questions are: what rules do the gatekeepers to heavily subsidized higher education use to regulate entry, and what are the distributional consequences of the way the rules are applied? The evidence here is overwhelming: spending on higher education distributes public resources disproportionately to those from middle and upper income families; those from families in the very lowest income groups are very weakly represented in higher education. This is not mainly because universities are biased against particular categories of applicants (though there is some evidence that universities that interview do fall victim to unconscious discriminatory practices). It is because the commonest rule that is applied – success in public examinations – produces a socially biased entry, simply because success in these

FIGURE 20.7 ■ How the welfare state can benefit the better off: the case of higher education, percentage participating in higher education, drawn from families of selected social classes

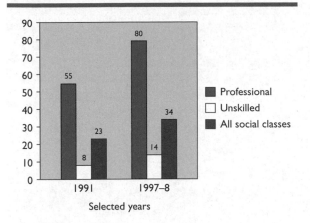

Source: Calculated from *Social Trends* (1999:61).

■ In the early 1990s there took place the greatest expansion of numbers in higher education for a generation. The 'participation rate' – the percentage of the age group normally in higher education – jumped dramatically, as the chart above shows. It was common to justify this great expansion as part of a programme to expand social opportunity, but as the figures show the expansion mostly benefited students from better-off families. The figures measure the proportion from families where the main earner was either a professional or an unskilled manual worker. By the end of the period the proportion of students from the homes of unskilled manual workers had risen modestly; for the children of professionals, when the normal exceptions are taken into account, higher education was now virtually guaranteed. If we looked at the most socially exclusive and prestigious universities – like Oxford, Cambridge, Manchester or LSE – we would find the disparities even more striking.

examinations is closely correlated with the class background of candidates. As a consequence, public spending on higher education is 'regressive' rather than progressive: it disproportionately benefits students from better-off families. The expansion of provision in the 1990s therefore involved a significant increase in regressive redistribution: from the poor to the children of the middle and upper income group families. (This is simply an observation about the evidence. It does not necessarily mean that subsidy to higher education is undesirable, nor that the 1990s expansion was wrong. Justification is possible on a variety of grounds, ranging from the need to educate the most able to the desir-

ability of supporting intellectual activity for its own sake, in the same way as opera is publicly subsidized as a 'useless' but valued art.)

Targeted public services. The case of higher education might be thought of as an unintended, or at least unstated, case of spending that allocates resources unequally. But the fourth area where government commits resources involves programmes that are openly targeted at particular groups. Distribution, in other words, is intended to be unequal, and not to be freely available to all. Some of the most important programmes in the welfare state are of this kind. The 'income transfers' that were discussed earlier provide some of the best examples: they are designed to support those who can no longer work, like the old, the unemployed or the physically disabled.

This simple fourfold classification of the different kinds of goods that are allocated by government leads to an obvious conclusion: it is not easy to draw up a balance sheet of who benefits most from the resources allocated by government. In our first case of pure public goods – such as the resources allocated to police clean air legislation – we should probably say that everyone in the community benefits more or less equally. But our second case of goods universally available free of charge – public libraries – unequal allocation is created by different rates of consumption. In our third case – goods available only after a decision by a 'gatekeeper' – the crucial issue is which rules, consciously or unconsciously, the gatekeeper applies. And in the case of some of the resource transfers designed to maintain incomes of groups like the sick and the otherwise unemployable, we can say that much of the allocation that is taking place is progressive – deliberately favouring the poorest in the community.

One helpful way to think about all this is to see government as a machine for transferring resources between different groups in the community. These groups can take a wide variety of forms: they could be the rich and the poor, those in work and those unemployed, the young and the old, the sick and the healthy. For example: when you and I reach old age we hope to draw a state pension which has partly been funded by our own contributions during our working lives, but which will also rely on the taxes of those younger than us who are still in work; and if you or I are unfortunate enough to become seriously ill, we expect to be treated virtually free of charge by the National Health Service, funded by the taxes of the healthy who are in work. (Most of the money spent by the Health Service is spent on patients in the last couple of years of their lives.) Wider arguments about the benefits of government spending, therefore, are also arguments about how that

BRIEFING 20.2

Osborne's axe: public spending cuts after 2010

The Comprehensive Spending Review is part of a regular, five-year planning cycle to determine public spending in the Westminster system. The results of the Review announced on 20 October 2010 are much more momentous than usual. They attempt to reverse nearly two decades of growth in public spending, and attempt the deepest cuts in spending made by any post-war British government. The planned cuts are intended to take £81 billion off the spending budget over four years. Average departmental budgets are planned to fall by 19 per cent. £7 billion is intended to be cut from the welfare budget, encompassing cuts in incapacity benefit, housing benefits and tax credits. The state pension age is planned to rise, as is the contribution made by employees to public sector pension provision.

Three questions remain disputed about these hugely ambitious proposals. First, why are they necessary? The government blames them on the profligacy of its predecessor; others blame them on an economic crisis induced by financial market excesses.

Second, can they be achieved? The history of post-war budgeting is littered with ambitious cuts programmes that were never fully realized. Third, in so far as they are realized, who will bear the biggest burden? The government claims that the wealthiest will contribute most (see HM Treasury 2010). Critics will claim that it is the poorest on benefit who will suffer most. In all the polemical exchanges about burdens the student of public spending will find in the work of the Institute for Fiscal Studies (for instance, Institute for Fiscal Studies 2010) the best informed and most dispassionate analysis.

transfer machine is working: is it really seriously shifting resources from the poor to the rich, for example, or is it mostly transferring resources, regardless of wealth, between groups like the presently sick and the presently healthy (in the case of health care spending) or between different generations (the case of old age pensions)?

What is the impact of spending?

All we have discussed so far is about the way resources are allocated. But in our own lives, when we lay out money we usually ask a further question, especially if we have spent a large amount: did the money provide what we expected? The same kinds of questions are asked about government, usually in the language of impact: do particular spending programmes achieve what they set out to do? Often a further question, sometimes not voiced, lies behind this: could the objectives have been achieved by a more cost effective alternative? These two questions are actually hard to disentangle, as we will now see.

Researchers who specialize in studying particularly expensive areas – like health and defence – can provide long lists of wasteful, failed spending programmes: for instance, expensive weapons systems that end up vastly

over their budget and are delivered several years late. These are in effect studies of policy impact – and studies that conclude that the impact was at best a wasteful commitment of public resources. So it would be no surprise to find that public spending commonly did not achieve the objectives for which it was intended. The more difficult questions are: how frequent is this, and how far do these failures mean that we should doubt the ability of government to achieve the intended impact of spending programmes?

These questions are hard to answer. Asking whether a particular public spending programme has achieved its objectives assumes that we have a straightforward, measurable view of those objectives. But the reality is less clear-cut. Would we, for instance, measure the success of a programme to cut youth unemployment straightforwardly by its impact on measured levels of youth unemployment – or also by its impact on the electoral popularity of the government that introduced the programme? Because government is a complicated business some programmes may actually have very different, and even contradictory, objectives: in pursuing housing policy, for example, government simultaneously usually wants to ensure cheap, affordable housing in the south

POLITICAL ISSUES 20.1

Tax avoidance and the globally organized firm

We have seen in this chapter that over the course of the twentieth century various forms of taxation became the most important source of income for the state. Virtually everyone tries to avoid these taxes – tax avoidance being the practice of organizing financial affairs legally to reduce the amount of tax one is obliged to pay. (Tax evasion is the illegal evasion of tax obligations.) For the rich and powerful a large industry of tax accountancy has developed which takes legal tax avoidance to a high art. Most of the best known corporate names operating in Britain – Virgin, News Corporation (the vehicle for Rupert Murdoch's media empire), Microsoft – practise 'tax efficiency', which is the worldwide organization of their financial resources so as to minimize their tax bills to the British state. Murdoch's enterprises paid hardly any UK tax in the 1990s because they successfully practised tax efficiency. The commonest way to practise this is to create special trusts registered in 'tax havens' – jurisdictions which impose little or no taxation on trusts – through which profits are 'booked'. The transaction is purely a bookkeeping arrangement which legally avoids UK corporate tax. Well known 'havens' include the Isle of Man, Guernsey and Bermuda. But being tax efficient within the law is a highly complex business – hence only those with the wealth to hire very skilled lawyers and tax accountants can realistically practise it. The phenomenon is worldwide, but Britain occupies an especially central place because most of the leading tax havens are Crown dependencies. Estimates of the amounts saved by corporate tax efficiency reach as high as £85 billion annually – nearly twice the annual cost of the NHS. Tax avoidance is quite legal, but raises four important issues:

- It raises issues of fairness in the distribution of tax burdens, since loss of tax revenue to the financially mobile means that extra taxes have to be levied on those who do not have the ability to organize their financial affairs globally.
- Since corporate avoidance is very common, it raises the issue of whether, in a world of global accounting, British corporate tax rates may not be too high.
- It raises an issue at the heart of the operation of the global economy: whether national governments such as the British any longer have the capacity effectively to control the largest global corporations.
- It raises the issue of whether it is now compatible with solving the fiscal crisis of the British state – see Europeanizing 20.1. After the global financial crisis of 2007–08 there were calls for closer international control of tax havens.

Source: Sikka (2002).

east, but also to ensure that house prices do not fall in the south east.

Even where we are clear about the objectives of a programme, we also face the problem of deciding whether observed effects are actually due to the programme that interests us. Did youth unemployment fall because of a special programme – or because of some other improvement in the wider economy? Studying government cannot be like the studies of nature conducted in laboratories: we can never run controlled experiments in which we isolate the factors that interest

us to observe their effects 'uncontaminated' by other forces. We can therefore never be sure that some other forces are not at work. The case of government spending on health provides a good, well-documented example. Since the establishment of the National Health Service in 1948 the health of the people has, by any measure, improved immensely: we live longer and our lives are freer of all kinds of pain and disability than the lives of the generations who lived before the establishment of the NHS. Yet the connection between all this and spending on health is uncertain. Some significant

DEBATING POLITICS 20.1

The welfare state: success or failure?

THE WELFARE STATE IS A SUCCESS IN REDISTRIBUTING RESOURCES	THE WELFARE STATE IS A FAILURE IN REDISTRIBUTING RESOURCES
▶ Most of the essentials of a good life, from education to health, are paid for by the welfare state.	▶ Some of the most important beneficiaries of the welfare state are drawn from the prosperous and well organized.
▶ Inequalities produced by markets would be much greater were it not for the way the welfare state modifies the impact of markets.	▶ Welfare state redistribution has failed to stem rising inequality in the last three decades.
▶ Welfare state services are vital for the most vulnerable, like children and the disabled.	▶ The welfare state produces large bureaucracies and hard to fathom rules about entitlements, consuming scare resources in paying for welfare professionals.
▶ The commitment to redistribution by the welfare state expresses our obligations to each other as members of the community.	▶ The welfare state encourages a culture of dependence and undermines personal initiative and enterprise.

improvements in health have to do with lifestyle changes: for instance, with better diet, more exercise, better control of pollution of the physical environment. To take this last example: the comparatively modest cost of clean air legislation may be far more cost effective in curing chest diseases like bronchitis than much larger health spending on respiratory care. And at this point in the debate the problem of identifying the objectives of a programme re-enters. The NHS, a huge, diverse and historically long established service, has had many different objectives ascribed to it. A common view is that it should be seen as having quite modest aims: not to make the population more healthy, but as a kind of national repair service, patching us up when we fall sick. On this last view, to measure how far spending is meeting objectives means looking, not at measures of the overall health of the population, but at how quickly and effectively 'patching up' is being done: for instance, at how quickly the sick get medical attention or at how successful doctors are in 'patching up' – for instance at success rates of hospital operations measured by indicators like the survival rate of patients. The one thing we cannot do is run a controlled experiment in which we 'simulate' the health history of the British people over the last 50 years with a different kind of health service, or no health service at all, to observe what difference the NHS has made. The measurement of impact is therefore a special case of an issue that we discussed in the preceding chapter: the care we have to take in arriving at

a judgement about the success or failure of a policy. And indeed it is a special case of an issue that we discussed in Chapter 1: to what extent can we, in the manner of a natural scientist, understand the flow of cause and effect in political life?

The case of health care also highlights another important feature of the measurement of the impact of resource allocation. Spending on the National Health Service is one of the largest programmes in what for shorthand we call the welfare state. Other large programmes have cropped up in this chapter: income transfer programmes such as old age pensions; programmes of large scale subsidy of services, such as that for higher education; programmes that provide free services available on demand to all (public libraries). All these, we have seen, have different patterns of usage – and therefore different potential impact. Debates about access to, and the impact of, the care provided by the National Health Service encapsulate the wider arguments about what impact we expect from the welfare state. Is it fundamentally about moderating the inequalities created by other social forces, such as the workings of the market? In that case we would judge it by how far its impact consisted in giving preferential care to the poorest in the community. Alternatively, is it fundamentally about providing a kind of public good similar to the clean air we all of us, rich and poor, can breathe? In that case we judge it by the quality of the service it provides for the whole community and by the impact it has on the health of all, rich and poor alike.

Review OF CHAPTER 20

Four themes have dominated this chapter:

◑ The state raises resources in many ways but taxation is the most important.

◑ Within taxation, government has a particularly important choice to make: whether to tax income or to tax sales, service or consumption, using methods like VAT and excise duties. In recent decades it has shifted towards the latter, though income taxes remain the single most important source of revenue.

◑ The way the state allocates resources has produced an extended debate about the vast scale of public spending in Britain, both about its purposes and about how far those purposes have been, or could be, realized.

◑ These debates also connect to wider debates about British society: notably about how social and economic equality can or should be promoted in a market economy.

FURTHER READING

ESSENTIAL
The range of this chapter is wide so it is not easy to fix on a single study, but if you are going to read only one book, a wonderful study of the key place of taxation in resource raising is Steinmo (1993). It has the added merit of dealing with Britain alongside other leading nations.

RECOMMENDED
Gamble (2009) has a lot to say about the impact of the great financial crisis, with the added merit that it sets the UK in a global context. Thain and Wright (1995) remains the best modern study of the public spending policy process, but Chapter 7 of Grant (2002), though short, is outstanding for the beginner. Goodin and Le Grand (1987) though now obviously dated is still the best introduction to the vexed question of whether the provision of public goods contributes to equality.

The state, public order and security

CONTENTS

AIMS

This chapter:

■ Explains the central role of the state in the maintenance of public order

■ Summarizes the roles of the agencies and institutions in Britain concerned with the maintenance of public order

■ Sketches the issues of efficiency and impartiality raised by the workings of these agencies and institutions

■ Shows the development of recent attempts to cope with problems of efficiency and impartiality

IMAGES 21.1 to 21.3 ■ The new technology of surveillance

Photo: Michael Moran

■ Closed-circuit television cameras are everywhere: in supermarkets; guarding public spaces even in wild parts of Britain – the photo was taken at over 600 metres above sea level in the Derbyshire moorlands; and guarding whole townscapes – the third photo was taken in Belfast, where much of the new technology of surveillance was pioneered.

THE STATE AND PUBLIC ORDER

In our everyday lives most of us look to the state for protection and security. If our flat is burgled, or we are threatened or physically assaulted, we expect the institutions of the state to act: we demand that the police catch the villains and that the courts punish them. If burglary or physical assault is at all common we complain that these institutions are not doing their job.

This everyday expectation springs from a key function of the state in Britain, and in many other societies: preserving public order and protecting the lives and property of all who live within the state's boundaries. Indeed most definitions of the nature of the state – such as those we examined in Chapter 1 – spring from the view that the preservation of order and security in society is one of its fundamental purposes. There we found (Briefing 1.1) one of the most influential of all definitions of the nature of the state, offered by Max Weber: that it is 'a human community that (successfully) claims the *monopoly of the legitimate use of physical force* within a given territory'.

In Britain, in order to carry out the functions of preserving order and security we have a set of institutions which enjoy great power and which consume substantial resources in money and people. Some, like the judiciary, are historically ancient, tracing their origins to medieval times. Some, like a professionally organized police force, only date from the first part of the nineteenth century: the Metropolitan Police in London from the Metropolitan Police Act of 1829, and police forces elsewhere from the obligation in the Municipal

Corporations Act 1835 requiring all boroughs to appoint a force of constables. Some, like MI6, the branch of the security services which spies abroad for the British state, are largely the product of the great world wars that the state fought in the twentieth century.

When we experience threat or loss, the duty of the state usually seems straightforward. If we are attacked on the street we feel rage and outrage, we want the police to appear rapidly, to catch the assailants and to bring them before the court for punishment. But in the wider organization of British society and government the great power and resources given to the agents of public order raise issues that go the heart of the nature of democratic government. They are a main concern of this and the next chapter. Three are especially important.

Public order and liberty

Since we live under a system of government that claims both to be democratic and to respect the liberties and rights of all, the great power and resources given to the agents of public order should be used in conformity with principles of democracy and liberty. But behind this simple claim lie complex and troubling issues. Observing the rules of democratic government implies, at a minimum, that institutions like the police and the security services will be subject to control by the democratically elected government. But even if this is achieved that meets only the condition of democratic accountability – of control by, for instance, elected politicians. It does not in itself meet the condition that the agents responsible for securing public order and security will respect the liberties and rights of citizens.

401

BRIEFING 21.1

Criminal justice under multilevel governance

We sometimes loosely speak of 'British justice'. But the systems of criminal justice differ markedly in different UK jurisdictions and have become more different in a post-devolution world.

CRIMINAL JUSTICE IN ENGLAND AND WALES

If the police charge someone with a criminal offence, they pass information about the case on to the Crown Prosecution Service (CPS). The CPS will prosecute in court if it believes there is enough evidence to prove that there is guilt and if it thinks it is in the public's interest to do so.

The least serious crimes are called 'summary' offences, and trials in those cases can only be held in a Magistrates Court. More serious crimes such as murder, manslaughter and robbery are called 'indictable-only' offences, and trials in those cases must be held in Crown Court with a judge and jury.

Criminal trials

Criminal trials usually take place in open court – which means that members of the press and public are allowed to hear and see what is happening.

Criminal juries

Jury members are chosen at random from the Electoral Register and attend court for two weeks or for the whole of the trial. In each case, the judge will make decisions about the laws involved, sum up the case for the jury and then either release or pronounce sentence. The jury is independent of the judge and the court. Its 12 members are responsible for deciding what is true and what is not from the information provided to them in court.

CRIMINAL JUSTICE IN SCOTLAND

There are two types of criminal procedure in Scotland: 'solemn' and 'summary'.

Solemn cases

Solemn procedures are for the most serious cases, involving a trial before a judge or sheriff, and with a jury. A Scottish jury is made up of 15 people and they can decide on a verdict when eight or more of them agree.

Three verdicts are available to them: 'guilty', 'not guilty' or 'not proven'.

Summary cases

Summary procedures are used for less serious offences. They involve a trial by a sheriff without a jury, or a magistrate who may hear the case with two other magistrates.

CRIMINAL JUSTICE IN NORTHERN IRELAND

The justice system in Northern Ireland has been deeply marked by the history of sectarian conflict and remains in flux even now. Presently the Northern Ireland Office deals with criminal law, the police and the penal system, and the Public Prosecution Service is responsible for all criminal cases.

■ There is no single system for the administration of the justice system in the UK; and even within a single jurisdiction, like England, different branches of the state have to be coordinated.

Source: Adapted from http://www.direct.gov.uk/en/CrimeJusticeAndTheLaw/Thejudicialsystem/DG_4003098.

Democratically elected governments are quite capable of ignoring these. The maintenance of public order has to take place within a set of restraints additional to those of democratic control: it has to be limited by respect for the rights and liberties of all of us, whether we are the victims of crime or are those who commit it. But agreeing what rights we should have against agencies like the police and the security services is not at all straightforward. Enforcing those rights is also difficult. Maintaining public order usually demands that we allow a large amount of discretion in daily operations. It is not practical continually to look over the shoulder of the policeman on the beat or to try to prescribe in detail rules for all security circumstances. We have to trust agents of public order to respond appropriately as situations arise. But how far they can or should be trusted is one of the big problems that has to be solved in maintaining public order while at the same time preserving liberties. These issues recur in this chapter, and are also a main focus of Chapter 22. They have become even more sensitive since the terrorist attack on New York in September 2001, which dramatized the fact that states live in a new and dangerous environment of terrorist aggression.

Public order and efficiency

Providing public order involves delivering a very special kind of public service because, as we saw above, it has historically been the core function of the state. But nevertheless, functions like policing are, viewed another way, just public services – like health, education or rubbish disposal. Just as we can try to measure the efficiency of health care or education provision, so we can try to measure the efficiency of the agencies of public order and, if they do not seem to be performing satisfactorily, debate how to organize them better. This raises issues which have cropped up in different policy domains in earlier chapters: for instance how far the state should itself directly 'deliver' the service of public security and how far it should contract out to private firms.

The relationship between 'external' and 'internal' security

Traditionally the state operated with a clear distinction between the domains of 'internal' and 'external' security. We expected the armed forces to protect us from external threats, mostly from other (hostile) nations; and we expected agencies like the police to provide defence against internal threats. We did not normally expect to see the army involved in policing on the streets of our cities. This division between the internal and the external is now increasingly difficult to maintain. For 30 years from the late 1960s the army was chiefly respon-sible for trying to maintain order on the streets of Northern Ireland, in cooperation with security services and the civilian police. 'External' threats now often come, not from other nation states, but from secretive, loosely organized terrorist networks who try to operate freely across national boundaries. Countering those threats demands close cooperation between all the agencies of public order in Britain, and with agencies in other states. As we shall see, combating terrorism is an exercise in multilevel, indeed multidimensional, governance.

The issues raised here are wide-ranging and complicated, and recur in this and the following chapter. They will also be important in our review, in the final chapter, of the nature of democratic government in Britain. In the sections that follow, merely for ease of description, we condense them into two: the efficiency with which institutions and agencies operate; and the extent to which they are even-handed and impartial in the way they treat citizens.

COURTS, JUDGES AND PUBLIC ORDER

We saw in Chapter 1 that the exercise of authority in British government is in the main what Max Weber classified as 'rational–legal': that is, the claims for obedience that public bodies make on citizens rest on their decisions being made in conformity with agreed rules governing the powers of public agencies. The most important source of rational–legal authority is the law, and this is why judges and the courts are so important to the state's function in maintaining order. Five particularly important roles for the courts should be highlighted.

Symbolizing the law

Laws are among the most important expressions of state power, and thus both courts and judges are among its most visible public symbols. In the language of Walter Bagehot (see Documenting Politics 4.1) the courts perform important 'dignified' functions. Many apparently trivial aspects of the courts and judges, especially of the highest courts, are designed for symbolic effect: the historical practice of wearing arcane outfits (wigs, gowns); the use of a specialized language and procedures; the construction of impressive buildings to house courts – all these perform the function of 'dignifying' the power of the state expressed in law.

Applying the law

This emphasis on 'dignity' and symbols is designed to assist the courts in performing important 'efficient' roles, to use again the language of Bagehot. In this respect the most important function of the courts is to apply the law: to convert the often general language of a statute passed by Parliament into an application in a particular circumstance, deciding whether the state's authority has been defied and, if so, what sanctions should be imposed. A good deal of what courts do consists of fairly straightforward application of the law. Over time there have developed standards of applicable evidence in deciding a verdict, a long history of cases (which can be invoked as precedents to guide both verdict and sentence) and 'tariffs' which give guidance as to sentencing for particular categories of offence. This role of applying the law is particularly prominent in the lowest levels of courts, where magistrates – lay people who devote only part of the time to the role – hear cases on a wide range of offences considered to be of a relatively minor order of seriousness. But courts are far more than institutions for mechanically applying the law, and this gives to the remaining roles considered here a special importance, and a special political significance.

Interpreting the law

We noted earlier in this chapter that maintaining public order usually involves giving discretion to the agents of the state. The discretion to interpret statute is vital in the courts. No statute passed by Parliament can cover every eventuality, and for the most part statutes are very general in the language they use. Application of the law therefore in practice commonly demands interpretation. Indeed, this is the most creative role played by the courts, and especially by the highest courts. Historically this role was performed by the most senior judges, the Law Lords – so called because they sat as members of the House of Lords. But in 2009 a momentous change was introduced by the creation of a 'Supreme Court' which replaced the Law Lords (see Briefing 21.2). Not only does it separate the most senior level of the judiciary from the legislature; it also implicitly recognizes something that will have been clear to us from Chapter 4 – that there is now developing in the UK a written constitution which demands judicial interpretation and review. The most important role of the Court is to hear appeals on points of law: in other words, precisely on whether the law has been properly interpreted and applied. The importance of interpretation immediately highlights the political sensitivity of judging as an activity, since it plainly raises the issue of how far interpretation is guided by ideological preferences, open or implicit. This is an issue we directly address later in discussing the impartiality of the courts. But it is also an issue in the way judges perform two other important roles that we now discuss.

Making the law

In the modern democratic state law is typically thought of as arising from legislation – from the law making activity of a specialized institution, a legislature. Law making in this explicit way is becoming more important, as is shown by the historical increase in the volume of laws passed by parliaments both in Westminster and in Scotland. In addition, the EU has emerged as an important source of law, through its directives and regulations. But historically things were very different. Until well into the nineteenth century the volume of laws passed by Parliament was small, and most law was the product of the 'common law'. The common law refers to a wide range of practices, including the historically established customs of the courts, covering both procedures and the rules of evidence, and the legal reasoning courts employ. A particularly important source of common law lies in judicial decisions on important cases. They become a source of authoritative precedents, guiding courts in the way they reason about later cases. When elected legislatures such as the Westminster Parliament were not highly active, passing by modern standards comparatively few statutes, judge-made common law was the most important source of law. Even today, the common law remains an important point of reference for courts, because of the binding power of precedents in particular cases, and because it provides a framework of customary assumptions about legal reasoning. It will also be plain that judge-made common law shades into the interpretation of existing statutes that we discussed above.

Reviewing the application of the law

Judicial review has in the past been of most importance in systems of government that have a written constitution (such as the US or the Federal Republic of Germany). In those systems an important function of the higher level courts is to review the decisions of public bodies when there is a challenge to a decision on the grounds that it breaches the constitution. The doctrine of parliamentary sovereignty, discussed in Chapter 4, limited the role of judicial review in the UK, since that doctrine assigned to Parliament the power to make laws free of the restraints of a written constitution. Nevertheless, judicial review was still historically important. Judges retained and used the power to strike down decisions of public bodies, including decisions of ministers of the Crown, on the grounds of 'ultra vires': that the decision was made without the sanction of law. Since the original decisions were almost invariably made in the belief that they were indeed sanctioned by some existing statute, it is easy to see that judicial review of this kind was really a species of interpretation – courts taking a

BRIEFING 21.2

The new Supreme Court of the United Kingdom: the sign of a new constitutional settlement

The Supreme Court was established in 2009, replacing the 'Law Lords' as the highest court in the UK. Notice the range of its jurisdiction – it reaches into the different system described in Briefing 21.1. It consists of 12 judges.

- it hears appeals on 'arguable points of law' from all the UK in civil cases, and additionally from England and Wales, and Northern Ireland, in criminal cases;
- it hears cases on devolution matters under the Scotland Act 1998, the Northern Ireland Act 1988 and the Government of Wales Act 2006.

The language used by the Court to describe itself is illuminating about the new constitutional settlement in Britain. It says of the Court's location that it: 'is highly symbolic of the United Kingdom's separation of powers, balancing judiciary and legislature across the open space of Parliament Square, with the other two sides occupied by the executive (the Treasury building) and the church (Westminster Abbey)'.

■ The new Supreme Court emphasizes two major features in this book: we are coming ever closer to a system with a codified, written constitution; and the newly developing system involves the coordination of many different levels and branches of government.

Source: http://www.supremecourt.gov.uk/.

---

different view of the meaning of the law from that taken by the offending public body.

The scale and scope of judicial review has grown greatly in recent decades. This is due to three influences:

- It is a natural result of parliamentary activism: the growing volume of legislation means that there are many more points where the powers of public bodies depend on (contestable) interpretations of the meaning of the law in statutes enacted by Parliament. This has become even more significant with the passage of ambitious and far reaching statutes such as the Human Rights Act (discussed in the next chapter) that confer on citizens rights against the power of the state.
- There has been a huge expansion in the volume and range of what is usually called administrative law, administered by a quasi-judicial system of tribunals. (These are described in the next chapter.) This area of law covers matters of tremendously complex detail, ranging from entitlements to the services of the welfare state to entitlements to migrate into the UK. The complexity of the issues is reflected in the complexity of the rules and therefore there is

constant pressure on the higher courts to arbitrate on the contested meaning of the administrative rules implemented by the tribunal system.

- Membership of the EU has begun to introduce some elements of a superior written constitution. British government, and the courts, are bound in various ways by the Treaties creating the Union, such as the Maastricht Treaty of 1992 and the Lisbon Treaty of 2009; by the regulations that the Commission of the EU is empowered to make; and by the directives which are made by, in the last analysis, the Council of Ministers and the EP. That is why the ECJ has on occasions enforced judgements in advance of what would be claimable through domestically made UK law. The best known examples concern issues of equal pay between men and women, where the ECJ enabled employees to enforce rights against employers that went further than the Equal Pay Act 1970 and the Sex Discrimination Act 1975 (Bradley 2000:43).

As we have seen, the role of the courts in review has now been institutionalized in the form of the new Supreme Court, and as we see from Briefing 21.2 the Court itself acts with a model of the constitution involving a separation of powers between the executive, the legislative and the judicial.

The wide range of judicial functions summarized here has raised in especially serious form the two major issues which we identified near the start of this chapter: those of impartiality and efficiency.

Impartiality and the courts

The traditional image of Justice pictures her as a blindfold figure balancing truth in a pair of scales, to symbolize the even-handed character of the courts in weighing evidence. This claim to 'blindness' is also central to the claim of the modern state to base its authority on rational legal grounds – on impersonal rules that apply to all. But it is well documented that in the past justice was far from 'blind': for instance, it protected the rights of particular kinds of property, and until well into the twentieth century was hostile to some kinds of organized interests, notably trade unions.

Accusations that the modern judicial system fails the test of impartiality rest on two grounds. First, the social world of the law and the courts remains highly exclusive. The world of the lay magistrate; the world of the organized legal professions, like solicitors and barristers; the world of the judiciary itself: all show significant social biases, with a wide range of groups – women, members of ethnic minorities, those born to working-class families – strikingly underrepresented. A second ground for accusations of partiality concerns the institutional structure of the judicial system, notably organization at the highest levels. Unlike many other democratic states the UK has not until recently had a separately organized Ministry of Justice or a distinct Supreme Court. The head of the judiciary, and the main 'manager' of the court system, was the Lord Chancellor, a political appointee who combined a role as a member of the Cabinet – and therefore partisan political commitments – with a judicial role and a role in making key appointments in the judicial system. The most supreme court, the Law Lords, not only included the Lord Chancellor, but was composed of judges who also sat as members of the legislature in the House of Lords. These institutional connections tied the leading members of the judiciary to the Government, not in any partisan sense, but in the sense that it led them to share some of the preoccupations of the governing elite in Whitehall. These included a shared predisposition to favour particular values, such as a preference for secrecy about the policy-making process. The replacement for the Lord Chancellor's Department – presently labelled the Ministry of Justice – is likewise headed by a partisan politician, a member of the Cabinet. But as we have seen above, an effort is now being made to institutionalize a separation between the judicial and legislative functions in the form of the new Supreme Court. Nevertheless, issues of social and ideological bias remain, as Briefing 21.3 makes clear.

The argument that the impartiality of the judicial system is compromised, either by the social makeup of the judiciary or because of institutional connections with the executive and the legislature, is strongly disputed. But as we shall see shortly it has seriously influenced important reforms in the administration of justice in recent decades. Before turning to these reforms let us briefly examine the second theme, of efficiency.

Efficiency and the courts

That the system of justice is slow and inefficient is a long established belief: it is, for instance, the dominant theme of one of the great English novels of the nineteenth century, Dickens's *Bleak House* (1852), where the suit of *Jarndyce vs Jarndyce* makes a tortuously slow and ruinous progress. In recent years, however, the pressure for efficiency has become more intense as the New Public Management has penetrated the administration of justice. As we shall see below, similar influences are at work in other parts of the system for the maintenance of public order, notably in the police and prison services. Since 1995 the administration of the court system in England and Wales has been 'hived off' to an executive (Next Steps) agency, the Courts Service, which employs over 9,000 people. (We discussed the general organization of Next Steps agencies in Chapter 7.) In the devolved system of the administration of justice, the Scottish Court Service is also an executive agency. Its relations with its governing department, the Ministry of Justice, are ruled by a framework agreement and by negotiated performance targets. It also publishes a charter for users of court services describing the standards it expects to reach in delivering its services to clients. (For extracts from a typical framework agreement for an agency see Documenting Politics 7.3 which details an example that affects prisons.)

Reforming the institutions of the justice system

Arguments about impartiality, and pressures for greater efficiency, have been important in producing reforms in the administration of justice. Under the Conservative Government before 1997 many changes were introduced by Lord Chancellor Mackay, 1987–97. They accelerated under New Labour in 1997–2010. Reforms have been introduced which were designed to make appointments at all levels of the legal system, from lay magistrates upwards, more transparent in the appointment procedure and more inclusive in the social range of those appointed.

BRIEFING 21.3

Judicial bias: fact or fiction?

The modern debate about whether judicial bias was a problem was begun in the 1970s by Griffith (1977). He argued that judges exhibited persistent class bias by virtue of their elite social origins, their training and the culture of legal institutions. Since the 1970s these allegations about class bias have been added to by arguments that the judiciary at all levels shows distinct gender and ethnic bias. Regardless of whether or not these arguments are sustainable, it is undoubtedly the case that they have produced institutional responses intended to guard against bias. Two important examples are:

- The Judicial Appointments Board was established in 1979 to advise the then Lord Chancellor on training at all levels of the judiciary, from magistrates to Lords of Appeal. Over the years it developed extensive training programmes that go well beyond technical legal training: for instance, courses aimed at sensitizing the judiciary to a wide range of issues to do with gender and ethnicity;
- The Commission for Judicial Appointments was established in 2001 to review appointments of judges and Queen's Counsel (the most senior barristers) and to investigate complaints about the operation of those procedures.

The debate about social bias in the judiciary has been reopened by the composition of the Supreme Court established in 2009: the 12 judges are overwhelmingly male (one woman) and overwhelmingly the product of education at expensive fee paying schools and elite universities.

■ Arguments about judicial bias are particularly damaging in a system of government that relies heavily on the exercise of rational–legal authority, since the key claims are that authority is exercised impartially and within openly stated rules. The reforms summarized are part of a continually developing programme to try to demonstrate that rational–legal authority exists.

Sources: www.ja-comm.gsi.gov.uk.

But the most important reforms have involved changes in institutional structure. The Lord Chancellor's Department was abolished, to be succeeded in 2003 by a Department for Constitutional Affairs. Though there was a brief interregnum when the formal title of Lord Chancellor persisted, all this was superseded by a Ministry of Justice, created in 2007. These changes may be best interpreted as an effort to modernize the administration of justice by making it look more like the administration of any other government service. But the Ministry was carved out of part of the Home Office and the shortlived Department of Constitutional Affairs. There is absolutely no guarantee that this institutional structure will endure. As we know (see Political Issues 6.1) Prime Ministers obsessively tinker with the machinery of government – the short life of the Department of Constitutional Affairs being one symptom of that obsession. Nevertheless, the creation of the Ministry, and the creation of the Supreme Court, do show that there is occurring a fundamental reform of the system for the administration of justice in the UK.

THE POLICE AND PUBLIC ORDER

Most of us obey the law most of the time quite voluntarily, but professionally organized police forces are nevertheless in the front line defending public order. Maintaining public order through policing is nothing new in Britain, but modern policing was created in the nineteenth century. The Industrial Revolution, alongside its amazing technical and social advances, also brought huge social problems. The scale of cities, coupled with poverty, lack of education and lack of even rudimentary social services, helped make crime rife. As we noted in the opening section of the chapter, most of the institutions that we now think of as traditional to British policing were created in this period, notably in the

Metropolitan Police Act of 1829 and the Metropolitan Corporations Act of 1835. So rapid and complete was the development that by the start of the twentieth century the uniformed British 'bobby' was perhaps the most important authority figure representing the power of the state that people came across in their daily lives. The connection with state power was emphasized by the particular status of the police officer. Although the organization of police forces was highly decentralized, the individual police officer was an officer of the Crown, bound by an oath to preserve the Queen or King's peace. This connection with state power is still represented symbolically by the design of the police officer's badge which most uniformed officers have on their helmet. Next time you see a police officer have a look (but not too obvious a look) at that badge: you will see that it contains a reference ('EII R') to the officer's role as a direct servant of the Monarch.

The historical origins of policing have affected present organization and have helped to shape the pressures for changes in that organization. The police services in the UK were historically one of the most decentralized parts of the public sector. The territorial organization of police forces – into forces largely based on county boundaries headed by a Chief Constable – has been the dominant 'building block' of organization. These forces have had their own separate governing systems, in the past closely tied to local government; their own budgets; and, below the most senior levels, police officers generally made their whole careers in a single force. The contrast with a European neighbour like France, where policing has historically been closely controlled by the central government in Paris, is striking. Even now, a separate police authority governs each of the regular police forces. Outside London, the authorities comprise local councillors and magistrates; under the provisions of the Police and Magistrates' Courts Act 1994, the police authorities also include independent members. This system is under the overall supervision of the Home Office, but as this formulation shows there is plenty of room for manoeuvre in settling the balance of influence between centre and locality. London, as the largest and most complex police jurisdiction, has special arrangements. The government of policing in the capital was reformed as part of the changes of the government of London introduced in 1999 (see Chapter 12). The Greater London Authority Act of that year also created a Metropolitan Police Authority.

Although the historical imprint of decentralization is deep, in recent decades the balance of influence has swung in favour of the Home Office. The reasons for this take us back to the twin themes that we saw were important in the organization of the judicial system: the search

for efficiency and the pressure to demonstrate impartiality.

The efficiency of policing

The efficiency of public services has been a dominant theme of political debates for many decades. As Documenting Politics 21.1 shows, many of the key features of the 'New Public Management' – notably concern with developing performance measurements – have reached into the police service, particularly through Home Office initiatives. In addition, there have been changes in the style of some traditional Home Office means of inspection, designed to squeeze more efficiency out of individual forces. Thus for over a century there has existed the Home Office based HM Inspector of Constabulary, but only in the last couple of decades have inspectors' reports focused systematically and critically on the performance of individual forces measured by such indicators as clear up rates of crimes.

The drive to organize policing more efficiently has had a number of important results. It has helped accelerate a trend that we noted above: growing central control over what used to be a highly decentralized police service. One reason for this connection with centralization is that gauging and increasing efficiency involves developing common standards and targets: if we are to compare the efficiency of police forces in Manchester and London we plainly need some standardized measures to make the comparison. The search for greater efficiency has also made the police a much more consciously *managed* service. Police operations are now organized around achieving a whole series of performance targets: for instance, detection and 'clear up' rates for offences like burglary. Promotion within the police depends much more than in the past on acquiring management skills. As a result far more resources than in the past are invested in the training of individual officers, not only in policing skills but also in general management skills, like control of budgets. The search for efficiency has also made policing a much more overtly political matter than in the past. This may seem an odd consequence, for we might expect the pursuit of efficiency to make policing more technical and organized around neutral 'management' issues. But much of the drive for more efficiency comes from the rising political sensitivity of policing. As a result, national politicians now openly compete for votes by promising to organize the police more efficiently than their party rivals. What is more, the issue of control over policing has become a much more overtly partisan issue. After the election of Boris Johnson as Conservative Mayor of London in 2008 the control of London's policing became so intensely political that it contributed to the resignation of the

People in Politics 21.1

Guardians of public order

Sir William Blackstone (1723–80)

Educated Charterhouse public school, University of Oxford, fellow of All Souls College 1744. Professor of Civil Law, 1753. Though a judge of the Court of Common Pleas from 1770, he was mostly an academic lawyer whose *Commentaries*, first published in 1765, became the most authoritative source in the eighteenth and nineteenth centuries for the content of the 'common law' in an age when Parliament passed few laws.

Sir Robert Peel (1788–1850)

Educated Eton public school and University of Oxford. Though chiefly known as the dominant figure in British politics from the 1830s until his death, associated with the repeal of the Corn Laws and the resulting division of the Conservative Party, one of his most significant acts was to reorganize the way London was policed, creating in 1829 a new Metropolitan police force – 'bobbies' and 'peelers' echo his importance.

Cartoons: Shaun Steele

Lord Denning (1899–1999)

Educated University of Oxford, Law Lord, 1957, Master of the Rolls, 1962–82. Probably the best known judicial figure of the twentieth century, his tenure as Master of the Rolls allowed him to make many landmark judgements. His interventionist approach – 'The judge should make the law correspond with the justice that the case requires' – was applauded by some and denounced by others as a usurpation of Parliament.

■ These are three key figures in the history of law. The differences over the centuries are great. But note one striking commonality: all were educated at the elite University of Oxford.

DOCUMENTING POLITICS 21.1

The New Public Management comes to policing

The Policing Performance Assessment Framework (PPAF)

'*Background*

The Policing Performance Assessment Framework is a joint initiative of the Home Office, the Association of Chief Police Officers and the Association of Police Authorities.

Improved police performance is central to the Government's vision of better public services. Until the Policing Performance Assessment Framework, the police service had lagged behind many other public services in terms of the extent, robustness and transparency of the framework for assessing its performance.

Features

The Policing Performance Assessment Framework is about "policing" as a whole and is designed to reflect the breadth of modern policing. It is about the contribution of local communities and other organisations as well as the police service itself.

In addition to focussing on operational effectiveness, the Policing Performance Assessment Framework will provide measures of public satisfaction and overall trust and confidence in the police, as well as measures that put performance into context in terms of efficiency and organisational capability. In line with the Government's desire to enhance policing accountability at a local level, performance against both national and local priorities will be fully reflected in the assessment framework.'

■ A major theme of this chapter is that the delivery of public order is a service in many ways like the wider range of services delivered by government. The New Public Management in recent years has increasingly tried to measure the effectiveness of service delivery and to provide quantitative indicators against which service deliverers can be measured. The feature here illustrates how this is increasingly being applied to the delivery of policing.

Source: Extracts from www.homeoffice.gov.uk/police reform.

Commissioner (head) of the Metropolitan force; and nationally the Conservative Party is committed to the creation of elected commissioners who would exercise control over chief constables and their forces.

The search for efficiency has been intensified by two other connected developments that transcend the influence of the New Public Management. Social and economic changes in the last generation have greatly increased the social sensitivity of policing and therefore made more complex the task of the police in doing their job. The example of traffic offences shows the implications of change. Before the rise of mass car ownership, for most middle-class citizens the police officer was mainly a distant and fairly benign figure. The increasing regulation of the conditions under which we can drive vehicles – covering such sensitive issues as the narcotics and stimulants we may not consume before driving, the

speed at which we drive – has drawn into the law-enforcement net millions of these citizens. The change highlights the delicate balance between surveillance and voluntary obedience to the law. Technological developments – ranging from the breathalyser to speed cameras – are designed to ensure more efficient surveillance. For the most part, however, the police have no alternative but to rely on voluntary compliance. No matter how large a police force, and no matter how impressive its resources of surveillance, it could never hope to monitor the behaviour of millions of inhabitants of big cities. The police already have difficulties 'clearing up' house burglaries; if most of us practised theft as a way of life they would be overwhelmed. We often see the limits of policing when large groups in the community lose confidence in the police or decide that they just will not obey a law.

EUROPEANIZING 21.1

The uncertain Europeanizing of policing: the case of EUROPOL

The extent to which the EU should have jurisdiction over policing has proved a fraught issue, principally because policing is at the heart of the traditional functions of the nation state. The main EU agency at present is Europol. Though its establishment was part of the Maastricht Treaty on European Union of 1992, the Europol Convention did not come into effect until 1998, following ratification by all member states. Europol commenced full operations in July 1999. The Agency is located in The Hague (the Netherlands). Europol's mandate is wide: it covers drug trafficking, illicit immigration, terrorism, trafficking in humans, forgery and money laundering. However, its executive authority is slight, and it mainly acts as an information exchange and as a source of expertise and advice to national forces.

■ Even the 'core' domestic functions of the state, like policing, are not immune from Europeanization, albeit at a slow and irregular rate, as this example shows.

Source: www.europol.eu.

The second influence making more complex the search for efficient policing is the growing realization that effective policing is bound up with the effective management of multi-level government. Europeanizing Policing (21.1) shows the growth, admittedly presently small, of one important dimension of multilevel governance: the Europeanization of the policing function, as a result of our membership of the EU.

The impartiality of policing

It is fundamental to the theory of good policing in a democracy like Britain that the police should be, above all, even handed in the way they carry out their tasks. The perception of impartiality is also vital for effective policing: in the end the enforcement of the law depends on popular willingness to obey voluntarily, and that willingness will not be forthcoming if the police are seen as hostile or biased. As we saw in our discussion of Northern Ireland in Chapter 11 the impartiality of policing has been – and remains – a particularly difficult issue in that province. But it has also become increasingly clear that it is an issue in the rest of Britain. A number of scandalous cases have established that there have been spectacular instances of the police not acting in an even handed manner: in the next chapter, the Stephen Lawrence case provides one of our three boxes documenting scandalous breakdowns in the way public bodies have treated private citizens (see Briefing 22.6). Much more difficult than establishing that there are

these scandalous instances is working out how to organize policing so that they do not recur – that impartiality is assured. Discretion is engrained in policing. In enforcing the law police officers necessarily have to make thousands of decisions daily, often instantaneously and often under great stress and danger. The mechanisms for redress of complaints and grievances that are discussed in the next chapter are not themselves sufficient – indeed they exist, on the assumption that there will be lapses, to remedy the results of those lapses. Many standard means to ensure impartial treatment are just not practical in the case of policing. For instance anonymity is now widely used to guard against (often unconscious) bias in areas like examination grading. But 'anonymized policing' does not make sense.

Faced with scandalous cases police forces have tried to restore the reputation for impartiality in three broad ways:

- by trying to recruit more officers from groups in the community who have particularly suffered in the past from partial policing, such as various ethnic minorities and groups like gay people;
- by appointing senior officers with the special role of monitoring police behaviour, such as officers with responsibility for relations with ethnic minorities;
- by changing police education and training to make officers more aware of the problems of partial policing.

411

In the next chapter we will be setting these developments into the wider context of the relations between the state and the citizen in Britain. But as we shall now see, many of these problems recur in other agencies charged with the maintenance of public order.

PRISONS AND PUBLIC ORDER

The prison service has a unique importance in the government of public order in Britain. We turn to prisons for the maintenance of order more readily than almost any other country in Europe. The total prison population exceeds 80,000 and has grown steadily in recent years. Historically the prison system was also, much more than the police service, a centrally controlled organization, in the case of England and Wales from within the Home Office. This historical centralization partly explains why the prison service is a uniquely politically sensitive area of the system for the maintenance of public order. There is no such thing as a 'non-political' area of prison management or administration. Even the most everyday matters of daily life – such as the kind of accommodation or food provided for prisoners – are grist for political struggle: good food and better class accommodation are often cited as signs that prison is failing because it is insufficiently punishing; bad food and accommodation are as equally cited as failure because they are seen as part of a system which fails to deal with prisoners humanely. Thus the prison service is politically sensitive from the biggest issues of policy – such as the rights of prisoners – to the most routine and daily, such as the kind of food served. The twin issues that have so far guided us in examining the institutions for the maintenance of public order – efficiency and impartiality – are more contested here than perhaps in any other public service.

We have indeed already seen just how difficult and politically sensitive the management of prisons can be. The prison service was part of the very first wave of Next Steps agencies, a testimony in part to the need for any Home Secretary to provide some distance between the Office and the daily management of the system. Indeed the Service has now been incorporated into a National Offender Management Agency which seeks to integrate both the prison and probation services. The original attempt to create a Next Steps agency in respect of prisons produced one of the great constitutional crises of the 1990s, with accusations that, whatever the formal relationship between the Prison Service as an executive agency and the Home Office, the Home Secretary had, faced with politically embarrassing escapes by prisoners, exceeded his formal powers in securing the dismissal of a

prison governor (see Documenting Politics 4.2). The affair shows just how difficult can be the issues of efficiency and impartiality.

Efficiency and the prison service

The Prison Service historically was a part of the public sector very far removed from the kind of pressures for efficiency associated with New Public Management. The system was highly centralized in a command structure controlled from the Home Office. Individual prisons were often 'total institutions', segregated from wider society. Indeed, many virtually had their own independent domestic economy, with their own farms and workshops. The workforce of the prison service – prison officers – was well organized into a powerful, militant trade union with a high level of control over daily operational life in prisons.

In short, this was a very 'traditional' part of the public sector, and it is therefore not surprising that the rise of the culture of the New Public Management has forced some particularly radical changes in the way the Service operates. Three are particularly important.

Hiving off. As we have seen, the Service was one of earliest candidates for being hived off into a separate executive agency, with the aim of developing a relationship focused on the achievement of performance targets, and it is now part of the National Offender Management Agency.

New styles of inspection. A characteristic feature of the New Public Management – the more aggressive and adversarial inspection of the institutions of service delivery – has also developed in the Prison Service. This is a quite novel development in the case of prisons. The HM Inspectorate of Prisons was only established in 1980. It inspects prisons, reporting to the Secretary of State on the treatment of prisoners and conditions in institutions. The style of successive inspectors has been consistently adversarial and critical. They have commonly used their power to arrive unannounced and to offer highly critical verdicts on conditions in individual prisons. As a result they have had tense relations not only with those who work in the Service, but with successive Secretaries of State who have found the reports politically embarrassing. Nevertheless, the institution of critical inspection is now built into the system.

Privatization to cut union power. Determined attempts have been made to change working practices. As we have noted, the organization of this part of the public sector was very 'command like', and was marked by a high level of militant trade union organization in the form of the Prison Officers' Association. Under the impact of the New Public Management this has produced successive efforts to change working practices in the

BRIEFING 21.4

The Prison Service and the New Public Management: the case of prison privatization

The Victorian Era was a great period of both prison reform and prison construction. The state systematically organized for the first time the incarceration of offenders in a nationally organized public service. But like most other state services, in the closing decades of the twentieth century the traditional organization of the Prison Service was challenged by the model of privatization. Presently there are 11 private prisons, falling into two categories:

- 'Management only' prisons, where the prisons are managed by contracted private sector firms but were built by traditional procurement methods. Although only two prisons are 'management only' this is an obvious model of privatization for the large stock of prisons inherited from the Victorian era.
- 'Design, Construct, Manage and Finance' (DCMF) prisons, which are built and managed under the Private Finance Initiative – an increasingly popular method of organizing public services, in which the capital for service provision is privately raised and a long term contract for service delivery is awarded to the service provider.

Since 1992 not a single prison has been built from public money.

■ The most radical manifestation of the New Public Management is privatization: the transfer of ownership or functions from public organizations to private firms. Here, we see that it has even arrived in the prison service.

search for efficiency. The most radical of these efforts have involved attempts to depart entirely from the old command system by the privatization of parts of the Service: Briefing 21.4 shows the presently limited creation of private prisons contracted to deliver services. It exemplifies the attempt to shift to a performance-focused Service based on contracted commitments from providers. But this is only part of the story, because there has also developed an increasing reliance on private delivery in the 'public' part of the Service – for instance, through the use of private security firms to manage the transfer of prisoners between different parts of the justice system.

Impartiality and the prison service

We have noted in the case of other institutions designed to ensure public order, such as the police and the courts, that impartiality in the way clients are treated is a core value about which there is widespread agreement – the arguments are about whether impartiality is actually practised. The agreement reflects the fact that Britain claims to be governed by a system where the rule of law is a paramount value. It is a foundation of the claim to rational–legal authority made by a state like the British state. The 'clients' of the courts and the police are, however, citizens with all the full rights of citizenship until found guilty of some offence. It is obvious that the main 'clients' of the prison service are different: they are both coerced clients and are subject to varying degrees of control designed to modify their behaviour. The only remotely comparable group are those among the mentally ill who have been subjected to compulsory detention orders. And indeed in the case of one particularly difficult category of prisoner – the criminally insane – there is necessarily a link with those parts of the public service concerned with management of extreme mental illness. Prisoners therefore manifestly do not have exactly the same presumed rights as other citizens. At the same time, prisoners are even more vulnerable than the free population. Prisons contain disproportionate numbers of the mentally ill and of those without basic life skills such as literacy. The fact that the suicide rate for prisoners greatly exceeds that for the general population is a summary indicator of this vulnerability. The recent history of the prison service has exposed some scandalous examples of partiality, ranging from straightforward bullying and brutality to systematic racism among some prison officers. These examples have undermined the credibility of the traditional safeguard offered by the service to ensure impartiality. This traditional safeguard might best be summed up as self-regulation: relying on the internal control systems of prisons. In their place we are seeing the development of externally organized systems of inspection and investigation. The issues reported on by the Prisons Inspectorate, though focused on efficiency in service delivery, have also often been central to issues of impartiality. Thus evidence of bullying – one theme of some of the reports – plainly bears on this issue. But the efficient daily organization of the system, which is a main concern of the Inspectorate, also bears on impartiality. For instance, evidence that prisons are so badly run that basic hygiene, cleanliness and freedom from infestation by vermin cannot be guaranteed, plainly bears on issues of how prisoners are treated. A second external mechanism has now been created in the form of the Prisons and Probation Ombudsman. All prisoners, sentenced or on remand, can complain about virtually any aspect of their treatment by the Prison or the National Probation Service. Complaints are only considered after the exhaustion of the Service's own internal complaints procedures; the Ombudsman, if the complaint is considered and found to have substance, can issue a full report recommending to the Service remedial action.

We shall consider at the conclusion of this chapter, and in Chapter 22, how far such changes in formal organization effectively solve problems of partiality.

THE ARMED SERVICES AND PUBLIC ORDER

The conventional phrase 'the armed services' refers to the army, navy and air force. It conveys also an important conventional implication which the passage of time has made less true: that we can draw a clear line between services which are armed, for the purpose of defending the country against external threats, and forces such as the police which historically were unarmed and concerned to maintain order domestically. The conventional division has partly been undermined by the increasingly common practice of arming the police, albeit only in explicitly prescribed circumstances; and also by the increasing extent to which the armed services have been drawn into public order roles within Britain. The use of the armed services in these domestic roles still only takes place in crises, but these crises are becoming more common. They mainly reflect a develop-

ment mentioned at the start of this chapter: the fact that the conventional divide between internal and external threats to order is breaking down, principally under the threat of terrorism.

There are three sets of circumstances where branches of the armed services have been involved in maintaining order internally:

- *Where the civilian forces cannot keep the peace.* The single most important recent instance of this concerns the history of public order in Northern Ireland. For nearly 30 years after 1969 the army was the key agency in policing the province.
- *Where the provision of emergency services by normal service providers is disrupted.* The most important examples in recent years have occurred in industrial disputes: in 1977 and 2003, when the fire services took industrial action, sections of the army were drafted in to provide emergency cover.
- *In planning against the threat of international terrorism.* While the army has now substantially withdrawn from an active policing role in Northern Ireland, this function is becoming increasingly important, notably since the terrorist attacks in New York in September 2001. Briefing 21.5 shows a characteristic feature of modern planning against terrorist attacks: it is a multilevel and multi-agency operation, and as such involves the armed services coordinating with a wide range of other public institutions.

There is no doubt that the threat of terrorist attacks is drawing the armed services into new roles in the maintenance of public order. Here once again the performance of these roles raises linked issues to do with efficiency and impartiality. In the case of the armed forces the efficiency and impartiality issues are so closely linked that they should be discussed together. They are linked because at root they concern the suitability of armed services trained to combat external threat to the task of securing order in a domestic civil arena. The arguments have crystallized in a number of highly contentious cases, notably during the army's long service in policing Northern Ireland. Briefing 21.6 summarizes the most serious and the most long drawn out of these: the claim that on 'Bloody Sunday' in January 1972 in Derry armed paratroopers illegitimately opened fire on unarmed civilian demonstrators. In addition, the history of policing in Northern Ireland by the army was bedevilled by claims that there were problematic connections between the army and branches of the security services operating covertly. There are thus important overlaps between the role of the armed services and the security services. Indeed

BRIEFING 21.5

Combating terrorism: an exercise in multilevel and multidimensional governance

The threat of terrorism, a threat that obeys no departmental or geographical boundaries, compels coordination between agencies at the same, and at many different, levels of government.

- The Home Office is the 'lead' domestic department. The Home Secretary chairs the Cabinet committees on terrorism and related issues. The Home Secretary is also responsible for counter-terrorist policy and legislation, the police and the security and intelligence operations of the Security Service (MI5).

- The Foreign and Commonwealth Office is the 'lead' department in liaising with foreign governments and with international organizations to combat terrorism.

- The separate area-based police forces, under their Chief Constables, are responsible for operational decisions, such as investigating terrorism as a criminal offence. The Commander of the (London) Metropolitan Anti-Terrorist Branch is appointed by the Association of Chief Police Officers (ACPO) as national coordinator for investigating acts of terrorism.

- The armed forces have specialist equipment and expertise – for instance in bomb detection and disposal. They are involved at the request of a police force, a request channelled through the Home Office to the Ministry of Defence.

- Immigration and Customs Officers have important anti-terrorist functions in their roles in the area of border control.

- The Security Service (MI5) is the main gatherer of intelligence within the UK about terrorist and potential terrorist groups, gathering intelligence by a wide range of methods, including covert surveillance. It reports to the Home Office.

- The Secret Intelligence Service (MI6) collects intelligence overseas for the British Government and reports to the Foreign and Commonwealth Office.

- The Cabinet Office is the location of the Director of Security and Intelligence, a civil servant of Permanent Secretary rank (the highest) charged with overall coordination of the government's anti-terrorist machinery. The coordinator also oversees the work of the Civil Contingencies Secretariat in the Cabinet Office, which plans for a wide range of disasters, natural and terrorist produced.

- Local authorities have a key role in planning for emergencies, including terrorist emergencies, and in dealing with the consequences for emergencies.

- The emergency services (police, fire, ambulance) have a lead role in responding to any terrorist attack.

■ This formal summary of the way responding to terrorism draws in agencies at all levels of government gives a sense of how multilevel governance is central to the management of any terrorist threat. But behind the formal demarcations lies an even more difficult reality: of competition for jurisdiction ('turf') between competing agencies and of the sheer difficulty of deciding how to divide up the complex job of combating terrorism.

BRIEFING 21.6

The Saville Inquiry and the problems of using the armed forces to suppress civil disturbance

The Bloody Sunday Inquiry (often called the Saville Inquiry, after its chairman, Lord Saville) was established in 1998 to inquire into 'the events of Sunday 30th of January 1972 which led to loss of life in connection with the procession on that day, taking account of any new information relevant to the events of that day'. On that day members of the Paratroop Regiment, charged with maintaining order, shot and killed 13 members of the public in Derry, Northern Ireland. The Inquiry was established to discover the truth of claims and counter-claims – that there was a plot to shoot civilians in the security services, or alternatively that the paratroopers shot in response to fire from IRA paramilitaries. The Inquiry took over 1,700 witness statements and cost over £100 million – possibly as much as £150 million. But when it finally reported in June 2010 it produced unambiguous conclusions that were immediately accepted by the Government: that the civilians shot had all been unarmed.

■ Use of the armed forces to keep the peace is not unknown in Britain, but has usually been confined to individual, critical instances. But maintaining public order in Northern Ireland meant using troops for a whole generation often, as in the case here, with catastrophic consequences.

Source: www.bloody-sunday-inquiry.org.

one important component of the security services is the Defence Intelligence Staff, an integral part of the Ministry of Defence. It is to the security services that we now turn.

THE SECURITY SERVICES AND PUBLIC ORDER

Britain has a long history of security services: Queen Elizabeth the First (reigned 1558–1603) had, for example, a 'spymaster' who ran a large network of informers. But the present history of the security services largely dates from the twentieth century, a century dominated first by two global wars (1914–18 and 1939–45) and then a 'Cold War' between two superpowers, the US and the Soviet Union, with the UK an ally of the former. The arms of the security services are all twentieth-century creations. The Secret Intelligence Service (MI6) and the Security Service (MI5) both originated in 1909 in a period when there were fears of a German invasion. Their later separation is the origin of the conventional distinction between the roles of the two agencies: MI6 is concerned with gathering intelligence abroad relevant to British national security; MI5 with gathering domestic intelli-

gence. MI5 therefore has an explicit, historically established role in the maintenance of public order domestically.

Even at the height of the Cold War this distinction between the functions of the two agencies could not always be maintained, since governments and security services often took the view that domestic 'subversion' and foreign threats were connected. The end of the Cold War in the 1980s, followed by the collapse of the Soviet Union in 1991, led to the development of a new security doctrine: that the threat from a single foreign superpower had been superseded by the more diffuse threat from networks of terrorism. In this new doctrine the distinction between foreign and domestic security intelligence became even more occluded than was the case in the Cold War. The potential link between the two is now recognized in the existence within the Cabinet Office of the Joint Intelligence Organization. The head of the Organization chairs a Joint Intelligence Committee and acts as a coordinator of all state intelligence, national and foreign. In 2005, in the wake of an official inquiry into the quality of intelligence in advance of the Iraq War, there was created within the Committee a professional head of intelligence analysis.

The two most important secret intelligence services – MI5 and MI6 – were created in response to threats to

FIGURE 21.1 ■ Structure of the security services: ministerial responsibilities

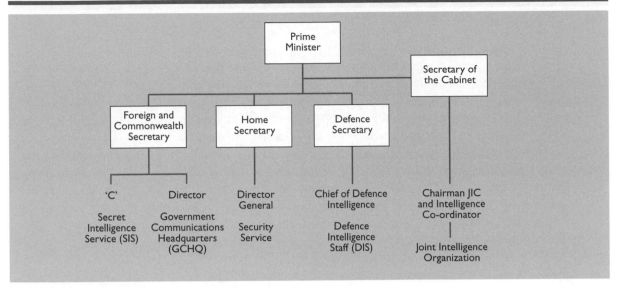

Source: Stationery Office (2001a:15).

■ The diagram shows the official representation of the hierarchy of ministerial control over the security services. The reality, as the continuing revelations about the role of intelligence in the decision to invade Iraq in 20003 show, is often chaotic, with no clear line of division between the political masters and the intelligence staff.

national security in the early years of the twentieth century. It is not surprising, therefore, that for much of their history operations were conducted with a degree of secrecy and lack of open democratic accountability unmatched by any other public service. Whatever the historical justifications for this secrecy, it created serious long-term problems in assessing and defending the impartiality and efficiency of the security services. It was commonly alleged, for instance, that MI5 persistently identified those on the Left of politics as potential threats to public order and subjected them to surveillance. Likewise, in some of the great industrial disputes of recent decades, notably the great miners' dispute of 1984–85, MI5 spied on some of the strikers and officials of the union. In the absence of an open account and defence of the agency's operations it was hard either to estimate the extent of this partiality or to hear a reasoned defence of the operations.

Secrecy also inhibited any systematic estimation of the efficiency of intelligence gathering operations. It is hard to apply the performance measurement techniques of the New Public Management to intelligence gathering, since so much is concerned with long term collation of information, much is covert, and success often consists in averting threats which are never made public. Nevertheless, the secrecy with which the system oper-

ated meant that even the most rudimentary scrutiny, for instance of the disposal of public funds, was impossible: the budget for the security services is bundled into a single request for total resources. A number of scandals suggested that the services were poor at recruiting competent and reliable people. For instance, during the Cold War there were a number of spectacular instances of SIS being penetrated by foreign agents, in some cases to a very high level. In part these difficulties lay in recruitment practices. In place of the conventional meritocratic methods employed throughout the rest of the civil service – described in Chapter 18 – the security services preferred to recruit by personal recommendation, often from tutors at a small number of elite universities. The result was a Service with a strikingly narrow social range. All the Services now profess a desire to recruit more diversely, all have websites that publicize activities to potential recruits, and even MI6 has abandoned its traditional use of 'talent spotting' by university tutors.

These difficulties in assessing efficiency and impartiality are part of the reason for a series of institutional changes dating from the late 1980s and 1990s. The Security Services Acts of 1989 and 1996 gave an openly acknowledged statutory foundation to the Security Service, under the political supervision of the Home

POLITICAL ISSUES 21.1

Identity Cards

There is nothing new about identity cards: they were introduced as compulsory items in the Second World War and remained until 1952, when the government abolished the requirement to carry them in the face of widespread public disregard of the obligation to produce a card. A number of other member states of the EU also have ID cards. The Labour Governments in office after 1997 made several attempts to mount a scheme of ID cards, culminating in 2009 in a proposal to introduce a national identity register in 2011–12. In 2009 a scheme for voluntary acquisition of cards was also 'trialled' in Manchester. Labour argued that the scheme was necessary for security reasons. Critics, who included every other political party represented in the Westminster Parliament, opposed it on the grounds that the creation of a national register was an intrusion by the state into liberty and privacy. In addition, many critics, notably researchers at the London School of Economics, argued that the eventual cost of the scheme could be up to £20 billion; the government estimated it at £5 billion. Had Labour won the 2010 election it had intended a Commons vote on making acquisition of the cards compulsory.

Labour's scheme for identity cards has not survived, but the issues which gave rise to it, and which made it such a contentious issue, remain. On the one hand, the arms of the state responsible for internal security continue to search for new ways of checking and surveillance in a world of continuing terrorist threats. On the other hand, there exists powerful resistance, not only to cards but to other modes of surveillance, on civil liberties grounds. In addition, the technology of the scheme involves complex and expensive investment in IT systems – a field where British government has a long history of expensive fiascos. Thus Labour's particular proposals have not been realized, but the identity card issue nevertheless is an important symptom of the tensions between security and civil liberties, and the state's difficulty in exploiting new technology.

Secretary. The Intelligence Services Act of 1994 performed a similar function for the Secret Intelligence Service under the political supervision of the Foreign Secretary. Attempts were also made to subject the operations of the services to more formal scrutiny. In 1994 there was established the Intelligence and Security Committee of the House of Commons. The Committee is a cross-party mixture of senior backbenchers from both Houses of Parliament appointed by the Prime Minister in consultation with the Leader of the Opposition. It scrutinizes the Services, delivers private ad hoc reports to the Prime Minister and lays suitably censored reports before the House of Commons. It is an advance on what existed previously by way of parliamentary scrutiny, but plainly does not operate remotely like other Select Committees of Parliament. The Regulation of Investigatory Powers Act 2000 created three new public officers. The Intelligence Services Commissioner reviews all warrants issued by the different Secretaries of State authorizing surveillance by the Services. The Interception Commissioner does likewise in respect of warrants to intercept messages or mail. The Investigatory Powers Tribunal hears complaints about the activities of the Security Services, notably in respect of warrants and intercepts.

Recent developments in the government of the Security Services show two features, and both reflect general themes of this chapter. The first is the increasing extent to which the maintenance of public order involves the attempt to coordinate the activities of a wide range of public agencies at multiple levels. The effect in the case of the security services has been to diminish the traditional, conventional distinction between conducting surveillance operations abroad and at home. The second development is the rise of more formal ways of subjecting the services to public accountability. This parallels the development of more formally organized systems of inspection and complaint in other domains, such as the Prison Service. In Chapter 22 we will look more closely at the wider significance of this shift to formality – and at its effectiveness.

DEBATING POLITICS 21.1

Secrecy and national security: necessary defence or danger to democratic politics?

SPECIAL LEVELS OF SECRECY ARE NEEDED IN ANY MATTER OF NATIONAL SECURITY	EXCESSIVE SECRECY SURROUNDS SECURITY OPERATIONS
▶ We live in a threatening world where foreign powers and terrorist networks operate secretly.	▶ The secrecy culture is an outdated legacy of the cloak and dagger atmosphere of the early twentieth century.
▶ Confidential reporting to groups like ministers and senior backbenchers can adequately ensure accountability.	▶ Ministers, and even civil servants, are too much at the mercy of what the security services decide to divulge.
▶ Public reporting can endanger the operations, and even the lives, of members of the security services.	▶ The security services of other states operate as effectively with much higher levels of accountability and publicity.
▶ Effective recruitment and promotion policies in the security services can ensure that they are staffed by those who respect democratic and constitutional government.	▶ The recruitment and promotion policies of the security services have too often promoted incompetents and even traitors in the service of foreign powers.

PUBLIC ORDER, EFFICIENCY AND ACCOUNTABILITY

The agencies and institutions described in this chapter lie at the heart of state power in Britain, because they are concerned with what might be called the core functions of the state: exercising its claimed monopoly of the legitimate means of coercion in order to maintain public order. But special as these institutions are, we can still ask of them questions that we now routinely raise about other providers of public services. In particular, we can ask how efficiently they do their allotted jobs. As we have seen, the pressures and demands of the New Public Management have begun to penetrate even the most secretive security agencies of the state. Some other institutions of public order, like the prisons, have been at the forefront of the changes, such as hiving off, privatization and the development of performance targets.

As we will see in the next chapter, many of the issues raised by the workings of the agencies examined in this chapter are only particular examples of those created by the exercise of authority by all public bodies over citizens and clients. The police, judges, prisons, security services: all have power to shape our lives and all have discretion in the way they exercise that power. But so do many other public bodies, notably institutions of the welfare state. In this chapter, therefore, we have been examining just one special set of cases concerning the relationship between the state and the citizen in Britain. But it nevertheless *is* a special set. The institutions examined in this chapter are special because they are able to employ the coercive resources of the state, often to inflict physical sanctions on us and to deprive us of our liberty. Some are also special because – like the security services – they have been able to make special claims to secrecy in their operations on grounds of national security in a threatening world. Attempting to ensure that the great power physically to coerce, and to operate secretively, is compatible with the impartial treatment of citizens, is a difficult business. There is a pattern to developments in the different services described in this chapter: there has been a growth of formal mechanisms of inspection and account giving. The same pattern, we shall see in the next chapter, is observable in the wider relations between the state and the citizen. The adequacy of that response is also examined in the next chapter.

Review OF CHAPTER 21

Four themes have dominated this chapter.

◗ Agencies like the police and security services, and institutions like the courts, are central to the exercise of state power in Britain.

◗ Issues of efficiency and impartiality are often enmeshed in examining the operations of these institutions.

◗ The most recent threats to public order, notably from terrorism, are demanding a much more conscious organization of multilevel and multidimensional governance.

◗ There has been a growth of more formal means of accountability and inspection.

FURTHER READING

ESSENTIAL

If you read only one item for this chapter it should be Aldrich's chapter in Flinders et al. (2009). It cannot cover the whole range of institutions but it is outstanding on the shaping influence of security issues on the state.

RECOMMENDED

Reiner (2010) is authoritative and up to date on policing. Johnston (1999) is also useful on the subject. Griffith (1977) began a prolonged debate about the impartiality of the judiciary, one which has deeply affected many of the changes described in this chapter. Le Seuer (2004) examines more of the most recent changes. Hood et al (1999, ch. 6) is a rare 'political' analysis of the prison service.

The state and the citizen

CONTENTS

AIMS

This chapter:

- [ ] Sketches the main issues arising in relations between state agencies and private citizens

- [ ] Examines some of the most important institutions concerned with control of state power over individuals

- [ ] Examines the wider social and cultural constraints on these powers and evaluates how effectively they operate

BRIEFING 22.1

The abuse of state power, scandal 1: the case of Munchausen's syndrome by proxy

In 2002 and 2003 the courts overturned a series of convictions against mothers who had been sentenced to long terms of imprisonment for murdering their babies. The cases involved a series of miscarriages of justice. The convictions were based on a scientific theory associated with one particularly prestigious medical expert, who claimed to be able to detect a syndrome labelled Munchausen's syndrome by proxy, which disposed a mother to infanticide. It became clear from the judgements overturning the convictions that this theory was seriously flawed science. But the scandal turned out to be much greater even than these headline cases suggested. It transpired that many thousands of babies had been removed from mothers, often just after birth, and put into care and permanent adoption, in the name of this theory. Moreover, these decisions had been taken after secret discussions and decisions by a mix of social workers, medical professionals and children's courts, from which the parents had been excluded, and the proceedings of which the press were forbidden to report, on pain of incurring contempt of court proceedings. But the problem of assigning culpability has proved intractable: a decision by the General Medical Council to strike one of the medical professionals involved from its register of qualified practitioners was struck down on appeal by the courts.

■ In the last three decades numerous institutions have been created to protect the rights of citizens against powerful institutions. The crucial question, however, is how far these formal protections work. Three scandalous cases are summarized in this chapter. They are chosen to illustrate very different domains of government. At the heart of the scandal reported here lies a key feature of the modern welfare state: its necessarily heavy reliance on the discretionary judgement of professionals.

CITIZENS, THE STATE AND BRITISH DEMOCRACY

In the last chapter we concentrated on the organization of a fundamental function of any state: maintaining internal public order and external security. We also concentrated chiefly on how the various arms of the state are organized and on the operational issues – like efficiency – that are raised by the way they work. This chapter looks more closely at issues touched on only briefly in Chapter 21: at issues of accountability and liberty. As we did see in the last chapter the special powers conferred on the arms of the state concerned with preserving order – especially powers to engage in surveillance, to exercise physical force in the last resort, and to imprison – all raise sensitive questions about public accountability and the rights of us all against the state. But these are only the most extreme instances. Making all the operations of the state accountable – not just those parts that have coercive power – is at the heart of the theory of democracy in Britain.

All states have great power over the lives of those who live in their territory. But over the course of the twentieth century Britain, like many other states, added to these traditional powers of compulsion huge powers in other social domains. As we saw in Chapter 20 the state allocates enormous resources to different social groups. Through devices like taxation and the distribution of social welfare it takes money from some in the community and gives it to others. It compels us from the cradle to the grave: when we are born our parents are obliged to register us with a public official; and when we die there is an obligation likewise for our death to be registered. Between the cradle and the grave the state constantly intervenes in our lives: it obliges us to spend our childhood being educated; and when we go to work it takes a large proportion of the income of most of us through taxation. Throughout our lives it constantly collects information about us and uses it to make policies. It has a huge say over what can and cannot be done to our physical environment: planning law stretches from the most minor matters – for instance whether we can build an extension to our house – to the most important, such as whether a nuclear power station can be built on our doorstep. The state has also become increasingly important in deciding who can live in Britain, and on what terms: asylum and immigration law has become one of the most difficult and contentious areas of public policy in recent decades.

The state in Britain has to provide a moral justification for the exercise of these great powers. We saw in Chapter 1 that the heart of this moral justification can be summed up in the claim that Britain is a *liberal democracy*. If Britain is a properly functioning liberal democracy, then the exercise of state power over the individual citizen should be fully guided by a number of principles.

Liberties should be protected. The 'liberal' in liberal democracy means that citizens are entitled to a range of freedoms (for instance freedom of expression, organization, conscience) and that the exercise of state power should be governed by openly understood rules. These rules should set clearly the boundaries of state power over all of us as individuals, and they should be applied impartially between all of us. As we shall see some of these expectations have now also been embodied in a key law, the Human Rights Act.

Democratic control should be practised. Democracy refers to many features, which we have examined in earlier chapters: for instance, how adequate is the electoral system in allowing the people at large a voice in deciding who shall govern? But in relation to the state and the citizen it means that the exercise of state power over the individual citizen should be open and accountable. This means that when the state exercises power over us (whether it be in the form of a police officer questioning us about an offence or in the form of a tax inspector assessing our income tax obligations) that power should be subject to democratic checks. Institutions like the police and the Inland Revenue should be effectively under the control of elected representatives.

But being answerable to elected representatives is not enough. What guarantee could we have that the elected in turn will respect liberty and legal restraints? That is why the exercise of great public power over individual citizens has to be surrounded by a range of rights of individual appeal and redress. If we feel that individual decisions that affect us are improper – are not sanctioned by the law – we should find it easy to appeal against them; the appeal system should work impartially between us and the state; and if the appeal is upheld there should be swift and effective redress.

One of the most important ways these notions have been expressed in practice in Britain lies in the provision of safeguards against *maladministration*. This may summarily be defined as the excessive or incompetent use of administrative powers – 'administrative' being used in a wide possible sense to encompass the powers of all public agents, including such powers as those to

IMAGE 22. 1 ■ The new face of the law: the Supreme Court

Photo: Fiona Hanson/PA Images

■ The new Supreme Court is possibly the most important institutional innovation in the years between the first and second edition of this book (see also Briefing 21.2). The photo shows the new justices outside their building. Notice the ethnic and gender makeup of the Court. The justices are also striking educationally: they are overwhelmingly the product of private schooling and elite universities.

police. But when the notion is unpacked it turns out to be highly complex, and this complexity means that the processes by which safeguards operate are also necessarily complex. 'Maladministration' combines a number of disparate notions encompassing moral expectations about the exercise of public power coupled with expectations about its technical quality. The following definition, the standard in the work of public law, shows this. The notions encompassed are:

corruption, bias, unfair discrimination, harshness, misleading a member of the public as to his [sic] rights, failing to notify him properly of his rights or to explain the reasons for a decision, general high-handedness, using powers for a wrong purpose, failing to consider relevant materials, taking irrelevant material into account, losing or failing to reply to correspondence, delaying unreasonably before making a tax refund or presenting a tax demand or dealing with an application for a grant or a licence.
(Smith and Brazier 1998:641)

The statements of the democratic and liberal safeguards against maladministration are ideals. It would be amazing – a counsel of perfection – if in every case they were observed to the full in Britain. But they provide the standard against which to judge the state, and against which the state should judge itself in the way it deals with citizens. But there is another extension to these principles that we should also bear in mind. The use of 'citizen' here is fairly novel in discussing these matters in Britain. Traditionally we were 'subjects' of the Crown, and a subtle but important shift in understanding lies behind the change in vocabulary. The language of the 'subject' dated from a pre-democratic era when such rights as we had were privileges granted us by the monarch. The increasingly common use of 'citizens' reflects the fact that in a system of government that claims to be democratic, where the Monarch occupies mostly a symbolic role, we are much more than subjects. However, the language of the 'subject' has buried in it an assumption that the state, through the Crown, has special entitlements in its dealing with us all, and these assumptions often shape arguments about how far the powers of the state should be restrained. The assumptions are particularly important when the boundaries of citizenship start to run out. Who exactly is a 'citizen' is often unclear. The problem is particularly acute in dealings between the British state and those who are not legally British, or whose British status is uncertain. The most troubling problems concern the treatment of those who wish to come to live and work in Britain, either as permanent immigrants or as temporary refugees. How the state treats these vulnerable groups who have few of the formal rights of the settled population is one of the greatest tests of liberal democracy in Britain. We will see later how these difficult issues work in practice.

This chapter focuses in the main on the important issue of the direct protection that exists for individuals against the power of the state. I will spend some time on institutions and procedures that attract relatively little 'headline' attention because they nevertheless lie at the heart of attempts to safeguard the citizen against state power. Tribunals are a striking instance of this. They are easy to picture as inhabiting a backwater of dry legal technicalities. Certainly anyone who spent a day observing tribunal proceedings would not have an exciting experience. Yet the adequacy of the tribunal system critically affects the defence of citizens' rights against the state. It is to tribunals that citizens – and non-citizens who wish to live in Britain – look for defence against excessive use of the great administrative powers of the modern state, and it is in the tribunals that the state in turn tries to defend the extent of its powers.

Formal institutions and procedures are therefore important – but they are not the whole story. Many of the wider mechanisms and institutions of accountability we have discussed in earlier chapters also, if they operate effectively, work to create a climate where individual rights are respected. They thus provide protection of a more indirect kind. Thus if Parliament, the media and the wider institutions of society like pressure groups, scrutinize and control the state effectively, it is the more likely that individual citizens will be respected when they encounter the power of the state. Our discussion of the role of the House of Commons in Chapter 9 can be taken as a twin of this chapter, for much that goes on in the Chamber and in committees is designed to make executive power in Britain more accountable. Later I will directly address the contribution of wider social institutions like the media and pressure groups to the defence of citizens against the abuse of public power. The detailed examination begins, however, with two critical sets of institutions: Administrative Tribunals and the Ombudsman system.

THE TRIBUNAL SYSTEM

To examine the Tribunal system (for an overview, see Briefing 22.2) is to appreciate immediately the complexity of the exercise of state power in Britain. Tribunals are essentially adjudicatory bodies: that is, they resolve, or attempt to resolve, disputes concerning the application of the law. These disputes can involve two separate categories of parties: they can concern disputes between two private parties; or they can concern disputes between a private party and a public body, normally in the latter case involving an appeal by a private individual or group against an administrative decision by a public agency. Among the most important of the former is, for instance, the system of tribunals concerned with adjudication of employment law – covering issues as various as appointment, promotion and dismissal. Some of the busiest tribunals are

BRIEFING 22.2

Revolutionizing the system of Tribunals

One of the marks of the New Public Administration is almost incessant change in administrative arrangements. The Tribunal system is experiencing exactly this kind of permanent revolution. Following the Tribunals, Courts and Enforcement Act 2007 a new administrative structure is being created intended to incorporate all tribunals into one hierarchical system. First Tier Tribunals are essentially the first port of call by an aggrieved citizen: they cover the kind of tribunals illustrated in Briefing 22.4. They are grouped into a series of 'Chambers': for instance, the Tax Chamber and the Social Entitlement Chamber. Upper Tribunals hear appeals from decisions of First Tier Tribunals and are judicial bodies, in their powers, their procedures and their personnel – they are headed by judges. The full change will take several years to effect and will mark the attempted development of a system of administrative law.

■ The Tribunal System administers what is in effect a system of administrative law – law governing the powers of administrative bodies. Though they commonly attempt to conduct business in a more informal way than a court, they typically have the authority, and the evidential standards, of courts.

Source: http://www.tribunals.gov.uk/.

concerned with this latter form of adjudication, but for present purposes our interest lies in the part of the Tribunal system concerned with adjudicating on decisions made by public agencies.

Tribunals of this latter kind developed in response to the growth of the interventionist state in the twentieth century to regulate the great power which the decisions of the servants of that state could have over the lives of individuals. These shaping decisions are potentially very great indeed: they range from decisions over entitlement to a wide range of monetary benefits, to entitlement to the very right to settle in the country. In his classic study of the administrative system in Britain, Robson (1928/1947) showed that the Tribunal system developed as an alternative to challenges through the court system for a variety of reasons:

● the size of the interventionist state, and the volume of adjudications to which its decisions gave rise, would have overwhelmed the traditional courts had appeals against administrative decisions been channelled only through these courts;
● the Tribunals were supposed to be more approachable to private citizens than were the courts: conducting their affairs in a language closer to the everyday than the specialized jargon of the law; conducting their proceedings without the 'dignified' features of the courts, such as the special uniforms of

barristers and judges; and conducting their hearings not in court settings but in ordinary offices;
● Tribunals were supposed to offer a less expensive form of adjudication, for instance by making it more realistic than in the courts for individuals to present their own cases and by offering speedier forms of adjudication.

These are the aspirations that lie behind the Tribunal system. Realizing them has, unsurprisingly, proved more difficult than expressing them. In their beginnings, Tribunals displayed many of the traditional features of the wider administrative system, notably an inclination towards secrecy in dealing with clients. The report of the Committee on Administrative Tribunals (Franks 1957) made a series of what now seem very modest proposals: that Tribunal hearings be in public; that the parties should know in advance the cases they had to meet; that hearings should no longer be held on government premises; that reasons should be given for Tribunal decisions; and that there should be rights of appeal against those decisions. These features are now a commonplace of most of the Tribunal system (though we shall see that in the highly contested area of appeals by refugees and asylum seekers the state is making efforts to limit the range of appeal). Tribunals are normally chaired by an expert in the policy area involved in the appeal, commonly an individual with legal training; but in a

BRIEFING 22.3

Calling rational–legal authority to account: appealing against Her Majesty's Revenue and Customs

In Documenting Politics 1.2 we saw an example of the attempted exercise of rational–legal authority: a tax demand received by me. What happens if I dispute this exercise of rational legal authority, and if the Revenue and I cannot settle the dispute between ourselves? Under the new Tribunals system one of the 'First Tier' sets of tribunals covers all tax matters, and I can appeal to the Tribunal. But the process is daunting. I must first complete a five-page notice of appeal form; my notice then goes through a complex filtering process which may result in an appeal being heard, or not (the process is described in a closely printed 12-page booklet); if the appeal is held I must appear on the due date. If I wish to dispute the Tribunal decision I can appeal to an Upper Tribunal. But I must apply to the Upper Tribunal to do so (mastering another form and an accompanying explanatory form). My application must include a description of the decision of the Tribunal to which it relates, identify the alleged error or errors in the decision and state the result I am seeking.

■ The Tribunal system is formally designed to allow the citizen without legal resources to challenge rational legal authority; in practice, as this example shows, the process is daunting for anyone but a well informed professional.

Source: http://www.tribunals.gov.uk/tax/.

further attempt to distance their proceedings from the formalities of court procedure two lay members normally sit alongside the Chair.

The effective working of the Tribunal system is vital to the exercise of state authority in Britain, and Briefing 22.3 illustrates why. It picks up a trail that was originally laid down in Chapter 1. There we saw that the most important foundation of authority in Britain is what Max Weber called 'rational–legal authority' – obedience resting on the claim that decisions have been made under the authority of laws legitimately passed and correctly observed. Documenting Politics 1.2 showed an illustration of this in action: a tax demand. Briefing 22.3 shows what a taxpayer who wants to challenge the demand can do, illustrating the quite complex trail of the appeal process. The feature is only intended to be illustrative of the wider adjudicatory character of the Tribunal system, but it shows why Tribunals are so central to the effective exercise of rational legal authority, for on their efficient and impartial workings rests any guarantee that state authority in Britain does indeed have credible rational–legal legitimacy. But it also shows the problems that the individual citizen faces in calling rational–legal authority to account: even the abbreviated description in Briefing 22.3 shows that a private citizen faces high hurdles in managing an appeal against the tax authorities.

In accomplishing the hard task of helping to create legitimate rational–legal authority, Tribunals face three main issues: securing efficiency, impartiality and informality. Each are dealt with in turn here.

Efficiency

Tribunals only work as institutions for safeguarding the rights of individuals if they operate both efficiently and speedily. This is because many of the decisions appealed involve substantial deprivation of claimed entitlements. These claimed entitlements could be financial, most obviously to the wide range of benefits allocated by the welfare state. They can be literally matters of life and death, such as the claimed entitlements by asylum seekers to refuge in Britain from what they argue are murderous home regimes, a staple of the immigration appeals system. Getting the decision right, and getting it right quickly, are essential. In this search for efficiency the Tribunal system has now encountered the influence of something we have seen several times in the pages of this book – the philosophy of the New Public Management and its efforts to redesign institutions in the language of efficiency. There have consequently been two major upheavals in the Tribunal System in the new millennium alone. It was concerns about efficiency which led to the Leggatt Review of the Tribunal system, whose report in turn produced the greatest reforms of the system since the aftermath of the Franks Report of 1957 (Leggatt 2001). The reforms in effect tried to bring the world of the New Public Management to Tribunals. They established (in 2006) a unified Tribunals Service as an Executive Agency of the Ministry of Justice – one of those agencies created as a result of the Next Steps programme. As a result, the strategic aims are couched in the efficiency language of the New Public Management: for instance, raising customer service and standards.

The establishment of the Service has now led to another upheaval. The Tribunals, Courts and Enforcement Act 2007 creates two new tiers of Tribunal; a First Tier Tribunal and an Upper Tribunal. Most of the existing tribunal jurisdictions are incorporated into the First Tier, which in turn is organized into a number of 'Chambers' made up of groups of similar jurisdictions (for instance all tribunals concerned with tax issues). The Upper Tribunal is effectively the main channel of appeal against decisions made by First Tier Tribunals; appeals against decisions of the Upper Tribunal can be made to the Court of Appeal, but only on points of law, not on the substance of the decision. The two important features to note about this new system are:

- A patchwork of Tribunals that was assembled in an ad hoc way over the twentieth century is being rationalized into a single hierarchy.
- This is producing clarity in organization, but the clarity is being compromised by another feature of the New Public Management: incessant institutional change in the search for more efficiency. Recall that we are now on our second major set of changes since 2001, when Leggatt was published; before that the last major change dated back to the publication of Franks more than 40 years earlier in 1957.

Impartiality

The detailed work of Tribunals can be highly technical, but the issues that they deal with are often politically and personally fraught. It is hard to disengage them from partisan political debate. This constantly creates problems in operating the Tribunal system in an even-handed manner. There are particular problems in deciding whether all classes of complainants about administrative decisions should be treated equally. An especially problematic area is created by the distinction between those who are full subjects of the state and those who are not. Embedded in our thinking about the way the state should behave is the assumption that it is relations between the state and British subjects that should be closely controlled, rather than relations between the British state and those who cannot presently claim British nationality. This is why the part of the Tribunal system that deals with appeals against decisions in respect of immigration is particularly troublesome. The issue of immigration – notably in recent years applications to enter by refugees – has become politically highly contentious, and the individuals concerned are usually neither British nationals nor British residents. A particularly controversial change was enacted in the Asylum and Immigration Act of 2004. The Act abolished an existing two-tier system of appeals against decisions of immigration officers in applications for asylum and, most controversially, removed the safeguard of judicial review of the most important asylum decisions. In other words, it subjected the Tribunal system covering issues of immigration and asylum to a lower level of safeguards than applies to Tribunals that deal with residents of the UK. The change dramatizes the question of who should have safeguards against the exercise of state power in Britain, and on what terms. From one point of view it is a serious departure from a key principle that should inform the operation of the Tribunal system: impartiality and even-handedness in the treatment of all who resort to it. From another point of view, it not only recognizes the peculiar difficulties of implementing immigration policy, but recognizes also that different standards of safeguards necessarily apply to British subjects and to foreigners.

Informality

One of the important historical justifications for the Tribunal system was that it created a more informally organized alternative to the procedures and styles of argument characteristic of the courts. This was supposed to make hearings more accessible to normal people and therefore more open to effective participation by those without legal training. In some degree this aim has been achieved, in the sense that the style and setting of the typical First Tier Tribunal is less surrounded by formality and a specialized legal language than we expect to find in a Court. However, the very endurance and success of the Tribunal system has made it difficult, whatever efforts are made to simplify language and relax style of proceedings, to depart from the specialized world of the law. The Tribunals are at the heart of a system of administrative law. Their style of reasoning is therefore inevitably coloured by the legal cast of mind, and success in hearings can depend on understanding a dauntingly complex body both of existing regulations and preceding adjudications. Although individuals can indeed present their own cases, the prudent citizen knows that effective presentation of a case is most likely if there is access to professional help – which more often than not means hiring a lawyer.

One special kind of Tribunal has emphatically not

BRIEFING 22.4

The extraordinary range of the tribunal system

Asylum and Immigration Tribunal	Hears appeals against decisions made by the Home Secretary and his officials in asylum, immigration and nationality matters.
Criminal Injuries Compensation Tribunal	Hears appeals against review decisions of the Criminal Injuries Compensation Authority (CICA) on claims for compensation.
Gender Recognition Panel	Assesses applications from transsexual people for legal recognition of the gender in which they now live.
Mental Health Tribunal	Hears applications and references for people detained under the Mental Health Act 1983 (as amended by the Mental Health Act 2007).
Social Security and Child Support Tribunal	Deals with disputes about (among others) income support, retirement pensions, child support, tax credits, statutory sick pay and housing benefit.
Tax Tribunal	Hears appeals against decisions relating to tax made by Her Majesty´s Revenue and Customs (HMRC).
War Pensions and Armed Forces Compensation	Hears appeals from ex-servicemen or women who have had their claims for a War Pension rejected by the Secretary of State for Defence.

■ This tiny sample from a large population nevertheless conveys something of the incredible variety of tribunal work – and therefore of the impact of the state on the lives of citizens. It ranges from the most immediately monetary (war pensions) to huge issues of personal identity (gender recognition).

Source: Compiled from http://www.tribunals.gov.uk/.

conformed to a model of speed or informality. These are special Tribunals of Inquiry established under a variety of pieces of legislation stretching back to the Tribunals of Inquiry (Evidence) Act of 1921. They are 'one off' Tribunals established to examine particular issues. They have ranged diversely across cases of corruption, large disasters and failures of regulation. Some have produced notoriously lengthy proceedings, with huge costs incurred in hiring lawyers. Among the most famous, or notorious, are the inquiry into the building of a nuclear reactor (Sizewell B) in 1985, which lasted 340 days; and the Saville (Bloody Sunday) Inquiry which began sitting in 1998, cost over £150 million, and did not report until 2010 (see Briefing 21.6). Faced with these delays, especially in the planning of large scale infrastructure projects, the Government in 2009 announced the creation of an Infrastructure Planning Commission to make decisions on such projects. The nominated list was very wide: railways, large wind farms, power stations, reservoirs,

harbours, airports and sewage treatment works. The object was to circumvent the long delays in the old system, delays of the kind that afflicted the Sizewell B inquiry. But the uncertainty and complexity of all this is shown by the fact that the coalition Government in office from May 2010 announced that it would abolish the new Commission. It cannot, however, abolish the major policy problems which the Commission was designed to solve.

OMBUDSMEN: ORGANIZED MEANS OF REDRESS

We have already encountered the Ombudsman (in Chapter 9 on the role of Parliament in the Westminster system) when we described the Parliamentary Commissioner for Administration. It was appropriate that the Parliamentary Ombudsman was there allotted an especially prominent role, for he is a pioneering

BRIEFING 22.5

The onward march of the Ombudsmen: examples

- *Estate Agents Ombudsman* covers all the large chains of agents and deals with complaints from private individuals as sellers or buyers. Disputes over surveys and lettings are excluded.
- *Legal Services Ombudsman* investigates all complaints against legal professionals in England and Wales, providing the relevant professional body has first considered the complaint.
- *Local Government Ombudsmen:* three cover England, Wales and Scotland, investigating complaints against most councils. Some key areas, such as internal running of schools, are excluded.
- *Northern Ireland Ombudsman* has a very wide ranging remit to investigate complaints in virtually any part of the public sector in the Province.
- *Independent Police Complaints Commission* investigates complaints about the conduct of police officers in England and Wales, and prescribes the disciplinary outcomes when complaints are upheld.
- *Scottish Legal Services Ombudsman* covers for Scotland broadly the area covered for England and Wales by the *Legal Services Ombudsman*.
- *Scottish Public Services Ombudsman* considers complaints covering virtually the whole of the public sector in Scotland, analogous to the wide remit of the *Northern Ireland Ombudsman*.
- *Prisons and Probations Ombudsman* investigates complaints about virtually any aspect of the Prison Service and the National Probation Service in England and Wales from all prisoners, sentenced and on remand.
- *Northern Ireland Police Ombudsman* investigates complaints against police officers, a uniquely sensitive role given the policing history of the Province.
- *Parliamentary Ombudsman* investigates complaints passed on by Members of the Westminster Parliament.
- *Welsh Administration Ombudsman* investigates complaints of maladministration against the National Assembly and a wide range of Welsh public bodies.
- *Pensions Ombudsman* considers complaints by individuals against most parts of the private and public pensions industry.
- *Telecommunications Ombudsman* has been established by the private telecommunications industry to consider complaints against member companies.

■ There are now so many Ombudsmen that there exists a British and Irish Association of Ombudsmen, from whom the information in the box is drawn.

Source: Compiled from www.bioa.org.uk.

figure. (Many Ombudsmen are women, but one of the quirks of the institution is that the original title has stuck.) The Parliamentary Commissioner for Administration has turned out to be an institutional innovation that has spread widely through British government and British society. As Briefing 22.5 shows, the very title itself is now used in many different settings, and the basic device is common even when some alternative title is used.

The world of British government now is very different from the world of 1967, when the original Ombudsman was created. It is therefore not surprising that as the original innovation has spread it has partly replicated, and partly altered, the terms of that original innovation.

Four important features of the original Ombudsman reform have been widely copied.

Reactive style

All Ombudsmen are essentially reactive. They do not expect to intervene in the operation of institutions to improve their workings from the point of view of how citizens are treated. Nor do they expect actively to monitor the performance of institutions in the way they treat citizens. Of course their decisions can and do have a wider impact than the substantive case in question, since decisions upholding complaints can both create precedents and can highlight wider features of administrative systems that need to be reformed. But fundamentally the Ombudsman system depends on waiting for a complaint and then trying to put it right.

Conciliatory style

All Ombudsmen practise a conciliatory adjudicatory style. That is, a critical judgement is a very last resort. In some cases the complaint indeed only reaches the Ombudsman after earlier attempts to conciliate between the complainant and the offending public office have been exhausted. The Parliamentary Ombudsman described in Chapter 9 exemplifies this, for a complaint will only be referred after a Member of Parliament has exhausted other means of seeking redress. But even beyond this, when Ombudsmen are involved, they will first attempt to agree a voluntary settlement between complainant and the offending institution before moving to the point of issuing a critical judgement.

Recommendation over prescription

One of the features of the original Parliamentary Ombudsman scheme was that the Ombudsman could only recommend, not enforce, remedies to redress grievances if a complainant has been the victim of maladministration. The capacity to cause public embarrassment to ministers and civil servants; the sense of obligation among ministers and civil servants: these are the resources upon which the Parliamentary Ombudsman must in the end rely. This reliance on voluntary compliance has persisted in the numerous Ombudsmen schemes subsequently created. Curiously, private sector Ombudsmen sometimes have more teeth in this respect, if only because when a firm signs up to membership of an Ombudsman scheme it also often signs up to a willingness to abide by the decisions of the Ombudsman. In the public sector the only case of an Ombudsman with significant power to enforce decisions is the Police Ombudsman for Northern Ireland – a very special case given the turbulent policing history of the Province and frequent allegations that police forces have abused their power.

Informality over law

Although the original Ombudsman has often been hard to reach, since access is via the gatekeeper Member of Parliament, once access is gained the Ombudsman's services are available without the need for the formality or the expense of the law or lawyers. Successor Ombudsmen have followed this style. Indeed in the private sector Ombudsman schemes have commonly been developed to support systems of self-regulation that are designed to avert regulation via the law, and access to the Ombudsman is available directly to any member of the public with a complaint.

There is therefore continuity in the Ombudsman system in the more than 40 years that have elapsed since the original innovation of 1967. But since the shape and the social context of British government is very different from 1967 it is not surprising to see changes also in the way the Ombudsman system has evolved. Three developments are particularly noteworthy.

Devolution has reshaped institutions

Devolution is one important reason for the proliferation of the Ombudsman as an institution. A glance at Briefing 22.5 will show how many of the new Ombudsmen are the product of devolved government in Scotland, Wales and Northern Ireland. It is also striking that the 'devolved' Ombudsmen are often more formidable institutional creations than the original Parliamentary Commissioner for Administration, having a much wider jurisdiction across the public sector than had the original Parliamentary Commissioner.

Multilevel governance has reshaped Ombudsman institutions

The public sector of the 1960s, when the original Commissioner appeared, was structurally a fairly simple affair, dominated by the Executive in Whitehall. The spread of Ombudsmen across public bodies – into local government, the health service, the agents of law enforcement – is in part a recognition of the importance of a wide network of agencies to the making and implementation of policy and of the need to create some means to redress grievances when things go wrong with policy delivery in these networks.

The shifting public/private divide has reshaped Ombudsman institutions

A glance at Briefing 22.5 shows a remarkable feature of the development of the Ombudsman system in recent years. Ombudsmen are no longer specialized figures designed to deal with redress of grievances against public sector bodies; they exist right across British society. Indeed the list in the box is selective, since it largely concerns those figures that have 'badged' themselves with the Ombudsman label; as we saw in the last chapter there are many 'redress of grievance' institutions that are not formally labelled 'Ombudsman'. One reason for the rise of the Ombudsman institution is a change in

BRIEFING 22.6

The abuse of state power, scandal 2: the Stephen Lawrence Case

In July 1997 the then Home Secretary appointed an inquiry into the conduct of the investigation by the Metropolitan Police of the murder of a black teenager, Stephen Lawrence, following extensive public disquiet about the case. The inquiry, chaired by Sir William MacPherson, reported in February 1999. The report found that there had been numerous errors by the police in the conduct of the investigation. But its most important finding was that many of these errors were not the result of simple human failings or administrative incompetence, but were due to an institutional culture in the Metropolitan Police which systematically discriminated against members of the public on grounds of race. It made 70 recommendations, covering both the organization of the Metropolitan Police and policing in general. The aim was to combat *institutional racism* which, the Report argued, was embedded in the Met. It defined institutional racism thus: 'The collective failure of an organisation to provide an appropriate and professional service to people because of their colour, culture, or ethnic origin. It can be seen or detected in processes, attitudes and behaviour which amount to discrimination through unwitting prejudice, ignorance, and racist stereotyping which disadvantage minority ethnic people.'

■ The importance of the scandal of the conduct of the investigation into Stephen Lawrence's murder was twofold: it was part of a long history of difficulties in relations between the police and ethnic minorities; and the MacPherson Report argued that the problems were engrained in the police as an institution – hence the scandal of institutional racism.

Source: MacPherson (1999: para. 6.34).

the notion of what can be considered 'private' as distinct from 'public'. In Briefing 22.5, the final entry, for example, summarizes the Telecommunications Ombudsman, established by the privately owned telecommunications industries. But these industries are themselves the product of privatization measures dating from the 1980s when industries that had long been publicly owned were transferred to private ownership. As we saw in Chapter 7, these privatized industries are typically subjected to public regulation. In other words, they are presumed to have various kinds of public obligations because they exercise great potential power over consumers.

The example of the Telecommunications Ombudsman highlights a more general feature of the development of the Ombudsman as an institution designed to secure redress of grievances. The state in Britain has in recent years retreated on many fronts, notably in the scale of public ownership. But as we saw in Chapter 7, the range of regulatory duties undertaken by the state has actually widened greatly. That expansion of regulation partly reflects the blurring of the divide between the public and private, and in particular the growing concern with regulating private, as much as public, institutions.

Many private sector Ombudsmen schemes are designed to protect private institutions against the threat of direct public regulation. Ombudsmen are created either to meet criticism in the wake of scandals that reveal the abuse of private power over consumers, or more generally are intended to strengthen the institutions of self-regulation. A good example of the former is the creation of the Pensions Ombudsman for an industry with a long history of marketing scandals; good examples of the latter are the Legal Services Ombudsman and the Estate Agents Ombudsman.

Arguments about the worth and effectiveness of 'private' Ombudsman schemes are very like those invoked about the effectiveness or otherwise of public sector Ombudsmen ever since the first appearance of the original Parliamentary Commissioner for Administration in 1967. The symbolism of the Ombudsman is very powerful. It borrows an institution from the Swedish system of government, a system with an open administrative culture and an egalitarian culture in wider society, where public servants expect to have to give a very full account of their actions. In some cases, as we can see from the first entry in Briefing 22.5, the very title Ombudsman is borrowed to give added symbolic weight

DOCUMENTING POLITICS 22.1

So what do you do all day? The working life of the Parliamentary Ombudsman – in her own words

Example 1. The Ombudsman found that the Benefits Agency and the Independent Tribunal Service had made serious mistakes which caused a long delay to a woman's appeal against a refusal of attendance allowance. An ex-gratia payment was made by the Independent Tribunal Service and the Benefits Agency agreed to consider further compensatory payments if it were shown that the woman's health had been affected.

Example 2. The Ombudsman found that Customs and Excise had made mistakes when measuring and recording the length of a fishing boat, with the result that the boat needed more safety equipment than the owner had been led to suppose. Customs paid £12,000 to the owner of the boat in recompense.

Example 3. Delay by the Ministry of Agriculture, Fisheries and Food in informing a farmer of the result of his application for the sheep annual premium quota led the farmer to incur additional costs. After the Ombudsman's investigation the Ministry agreed to pay 191 farmers compensation totalling nearly £70,000.

Example 4. A man complained that the Inland Revenue had mishandled the tax affairs of a business in which he had been a partner. Following the Ombudsman's intervention, the Revenue took action to offset nearly £19,000 against the PAYE debt of the former partnership.'

■ These examples, provided by the Ombudsman, show a slice of the working year, in the Ombudsman's own words; the Annual Report updates these instances with further cases studies.

Source: www.ombudsman.org.uk.

to quite limited schemes for handling complaints. Debates about the effectiveness of this symbolically significant figure turn on how far the characteristic styles of British Ombudsmen are up to the job of redressing grievances: styles that are reactive, conciliatory, permissive and informal. However, the Ombudsman institution is now embedded across British society, in private and public institutions. In multilevel governance it is taking increasingly diverse forms, departing in many ways from the single, simple template of the original Parliamentary Commissioner for Administration.

CREATING RIGHTS

In the Tribunal system and in the spreading institutions of the Ombudsmen we see attempts to create organized means of regulating relations between the state and the citizen, and to provide organized means of defending the citizen against the abuse of public power. In recent years a new and, for the UK, constitutionally novel solution has been attempted to the problem of safeguarding citizens' rights: the creation of rights embodied in law.

As we have noted on several occasions in these pages, the dominant constitutional tradition pictured a monarchy with 'subjects', where claims against public power were privileges granted by monarchical government. These claims were not trivial. Historically they included, for example, such long-standing legal claims as those contained in the Habeas Corpus Act of 1679. The title literally translates from the Latin 'you have the body'. In substance, it meant that in England (though not elsewhere in the Kingdom) those detained by Crown servants – such as police officers – could apply to the courts to test the right of the Crown to detain them. In practice, the law limited the time span when institutions like the police could detain individuals without bringing a charge to be tested in court.

Though often providing substantial protection against the abuse of power by public institutions, the protections traditionally afforded had a number of important limitations:

● their jurisdiction was often limited: Habeas Corpus, for example, was a protection extended only by the English courts;
● they were an incomplete net of protections, built up piecemeal historically, from a mix of individual statutes and the judgements and conventions of the common law (see pp. 403–4 for the significance of the common law);
● the doctrine of the supremacy of the Westminster Parliament meant that any particular protection could

BRIEFING 22.7

The Human Rights Act

The Human Rights Act 1998 does the following:.

■ It makes enforceable in domestic law the rights contained in the European Convention on Human Rights, an international agreement to which the British Government was a signatory, but whose provisions could hitherto only be enforced by the expensive and time consuming procedure of taking a case to the European Court of Human Rights.

■ It makes it unlawful for a public body to violate Convention rights; if possible all UK law should be consistent with Convention rights; and it provides for the enforcement of those rights through a domestic court or a tribunal.

■ The Convention guarantees 16 basic human rights. Some of these are uncontentious in a British setting, such as the prohibition of slavery. Some are uncontentious in general terms but their application is highly contested: some anti-abortion groups contend that abortion violates the right to life. Some are uncontentious, but British governments have engaged in the prohibited practices in the recent past: for instance torture was practised on some detainees in Northern Ireland.

■ The Act is also part of the process of the 'Europeanizing' of human rights: see Europeanizing 22.1.

■ The Human Rights Act is a great innovation in a system of government where historically we were 'subjects' of the Crown rather than citizens with rights. But it has not overturned the old practices totally. The Scottish Parliament and the Welsh Assembly must both be bound in all their decisions by the Act. But the Westminster Parliament still retains the sovereign power to claim exemptions from the Act and to pass laws in violation of its provisions. Following the terrorist attack in New York in September 2001 the Government passed anti-terrorist laws which involved an explicit departure from some of the Act's safeguards, such as right to liberty and fair trial.

be suspended by a countermanding item of legislation – as happened, for example, to Habeas Corpus in time of war, and as happened to a wide range of protections during nearly 30 years of the struggles with paramilitary forces in Northern Ireland from the early 1970s.

Two broad areas of change illustrate the developments that have been taking place. The first concerns the collection, holding and transmission of information, especially electronically collected and stored information; and the second concerns the broader regime of human rights.

Two pieces of legislation, and one important institutional innovation, mark the attempt to subject the use of information to closer legal control: the Data Protection Act, passed 1998 and in force from 2000, and the Freedom of Information Act 2000. The Data Protection Act principally gives rights to access data held both by private and public institutions about individuals, and to have mistakes in that data corrected. The information

can range from the data about individuals' financial affairs, commonly held by private institutions such as credit rating agencies, to information such as character references, for instance those held by universities about students or by employers about their employees. But the Act also for the first time subjects the rapidly spreading technology of surveillance by closed-circuit television (CCTV) to legal control. In enforcing both the sections of the Act concerning the holding of data about individuals, and in respect of the regulation of CCTV, the Information Commissioner, an official established under the Act, is a key figure. For instance, the Commissioner is responsible for the creation and maintenance of a code of conduct governing the use of CCTV by those who establish and operate these surveillance systems in public places. The Commissioner is also responsible for the implementation of some important EU regulations governing access to telecommunications traffic. For instance the Telecommunications Regulation of the European Commission of 1999 gives effect to a directive dating from 1997 guaranteeing a

EUROPEANIZING 22.1

Europeanizing human rights

The Human Rights Act (see Briefing 22.7) represents a considerable potential 'Europeanization' of the human rights regime in the UK. The Act incorporates, as we saw there, the European Convention on Human Rights into British law. Britain has been a comparative latecomer. The Convention on Human Rights is an international treaty which was first negotiated in 1950 and entered into force for signatories in 1953. A Court of Human Rights (not to be confused with the EU's own European Court of Justice) was established in 1959, located in Strasbourg. The court has a pan-European jurisdiction; adherence to its rulings is via signature of the international treaty outlining the Human Rights Convention originally drawn up in 1950. Forty-seven European states with a combined population in excess of 800 million are now signatories to the convention and are formally committed to enforce the Court's judgments domestically. In over one hundred cases the Court has found against the British Government. But there are limits to the extent to which this potential for Europeanization is being realized. Decisions of the Court depend for enforcement on domestic implementation. One of the most high profile cases concerns the rights of prisoners to vote. In 2005 the Court ruled against the British Government ban on the prisoner vote; yet that ban has still to be lifted. However, the Coalition Government may reluctantly do so.

Source: European Court of Human Rights (2009).

'right to privacy' in respect of the telecommunications traffic of individuals.

The Data Protection Act is in essence intended to provide entitlements to individuals in respect of personal data held about them by institutions. The Freedom of Information Act 2000 is best conceived of as providing access, not to data about individuals, but to a wide range of documentation held by public authorities, for instance about the processes by which policy has been made. Thus it is not directly addressed to the question of redress of instances of grievances created by maladministration, but can be conceived of as one more attempt to create a more open and accountable culture of policy making, thus reducing the likelihood of the abuse of official power. The rights under the Act entitle, in principle, anyone to request access to documents and records held by public authorities. Requests must be specific enough to make it clear what is being sought. In other words, it is not possible simply to carry out 'fishing expeditions' for information. Refusal to supply information can in the last resort be appealed to the Information Commissioner who has power to investigate and adjudicate.

We shall see that there are different views of the significance of these measures, but at the very least they amount to important symbolic statements about the rights of citizens to have access to information. The significance of the Human Rights Act 1998 is greater still.

Formally the Act might be thought to advance little in the way of creating rights, for it only made enforceable in domestic law the rights contained in the European Convention on Human Rights. The UK had been a signatory since the original Convention of 1950 and thus bound itself to observe the judgements of the European Court of Human Rights, sitting in Strasbourg. (The Court should not be confused with the European Court of Justice, the judicial body concerned with the interpretation of the law of the EU, an institution described in Chapters 4 and 5.) Indeed in the near half-century between the signing of the Convention and the passage of the Human Rights Act the Court made a number of judgements that compelled important changes in law and policy. These included changing the law on contempt of court in 1979, when the *Sunday Times* successfully challenged its use to try to prevent the paper publishing details of a scandal concerning birth defects caused by a drug prescribed to expectant mothers; the abolition of corporal punishment in UK state schools following a successful challenge that the practice infringed parents' rights concerning their children's education; and a judgement in 1995 which ruled that British soldiers used unreasonable force in shooting to death three suspected IRA terrorists in Gibraltar. (See Pyper, 1998 and 2002, from where these examples are drawn.)

Before the passage of the Human Rights Act, however, the enforcement of rights under the Convention was both a protracted and expensive process. The Court of Human Rights could only be invoked at the end of domestic judicial process, and domestic law was not made by reference to the provisions of the Convention. As Briefing 22.7 summarizes, the Act attempts precisely to remedy this. Courts can make a declaration of incompatibility between a law and the Convention. The Act makes it unlawful for a public body to violate Convention rights; makes the Convention in effect enforceable in any domestic judicial arena, meaning that enforcement need not depend on the time consuming and expensive route of appeal to Strasbourg; and is designed to ensure that both legislative proposals and administrative practice are shaped around the provisions of the Act.

The Data Protection Act, the Freedom of Information Act and the Human Rights Act are all comparatively recent creations. Since their avowed purpose is to alter the culture of the state, we should not expect their impact to be short term. It is therefore difficult to arrive at any firm view of their wider importance in regulating the relations between the state and the citizen in Britain. Two contrasting interpretations might be considered. An optimistic interpretation – optimistic from the point of view of those who wish to entrench constitutional safeguards against state power – would note the timing of this legislation. It was passed as part of a wider raft of constitutional change, examined earlier in this book: the most notable examples are the devolution reforms and the reform of the Second Chamber. In other words, whatever particular limitations exist on the range of rights practically enforceable under these laws, they can be viewed as part of a systematic modernization of the constitution in the UK. The package of modernization has both reduced the powers of the traditionally dominant Whitehall Executive and opened the operations of public bodies to greater scrutiny and explicit control. Devolution has also widened the range and variety of controls: the devolved Scottish system, for example, has its own freedom of information regime.

A pessimistic interpretation of what rights' reform amounts to stresses two points. First, these rights are anything but entrenched constitutional safeguards. They are surrounded by numerous exemptions. More important, the Whitehall Executive still has the power to suspend them on foot of wider considerations, such as public security: measures passed to counter terrorism in the wake of the attack on the World Trade Center in September 2001 do precisely this in respect of some of the safeguards in the Human Rights Act. But a second ground for pessimism is even more fundamental, because it concerns the wider setting in which these formal rights have been enacted. Pessimism here begins with the incontrovertible observation that formal rights enshrined in statute mean very little without the existence of wider social and cultural safeguards for the citizen in dealing with public power. From this point of view, all measures like the Data Protection Act do is marginally rein in new forms of surveillance created by new technologies, such as visual surveillance and technologies that allow centralized storage and onward passage of personal information. The Human Rights Act likewise, on this pessimistic view, is marginal in a world where the threats of terrorism and the desire to control the movement of immigrants across borders are pressing the state in the direction of increasing controls over personal freedoms and personal privacy.

Thus, whether we take a pessimistic or an optimistic view of the recent spate of rights creation depends on much more than an inspection of the content of those rights. It depends also on how we view the wider social and cultural context regulating the relations between state and the citizen. It is exactly this setting that we next examine.

SOCIAL AND CULTURAL INSTITUTIONS OF CONTROL

We have seen that an important trend in the regulation of the relations between the state and the citizen is the growing turn to the creation of formal safeguards. This formality encompasses the institutions of the Tribunal system, the march of the Ombudsmen and the creation of a legally enforceable human rights regime. The effectiveness of these formal safeguards, however, depends on the existence of wider social and cultural forces that constrain government. Three are particularly important: self-regulation; media scrutiny; and pressure groups in wider civil society.

Self-regulation

Relying on public servants and public institutions to observe self-imposed restraints on the exercise of their powers was traditionally the most important means of regulating relations between the state and the citizen. In their landmark study of systems of internal control in the public sector, Hood and his colleagues (1999) identified this method as 'collegial': it depended on the capacity of equals within the administrative system to both check themselves and to check each other. In an important sense, self-regulation has to remain a key mechanism of control because discretion is inevitable in the administrative process. That discretion applies whether it is

BRIEFING 22.8

The abuse of state power, scandal 3: the Equitable Life Affair

Not all scandals involve obvious physical harm. The Equitable Life Assurance Company closed to new business in December 2000, and many thousands of existing policy holders saw their savings and pensions reduced drastically in value. An Ombudsman's report on the affair concluded that there had been such a degree of failure by responsible public regulators that the dereliction amounted to maladministration (see p. 423 for a definition of this). The scandal of maladministration was then compounded by the response of the Government to the Ombudsman's findings, and to the recommendations that the state should compensate Equitable Life policy holders: the responsible department (the Treasury) first delayed responses, then argued at length with the Ombudsman's findings, and then declined to implement the scheme of compensation recommended by the Ombudsman. The resistance to accepting the Ombudsman's findings and recommendations was so strong that it survived not only a lengthy response from the Ombudsman, but two highly critical reports from the House of Commons' Select Committee on Public Administration. The public grounds for the government's resistance were tortuously procedural; the substantive reason seems to have been the embarrassment of losing face in admitting maladministration on the part of powerful agencies in the Executive, the cost of an appropriate compensation scheme and the fear of creating precedents for compensation in subsequent cases of regulatory failure. The episode shows the limits of the Ombudsman's capacity to secure redress, even when the scale of regulatory failure is admitted to be great, and even when the Ombudsman is publicly supported by reports from a major House of Commons Select Committee. It also shows the capacity for delay: almost nine years after the original failure the Public Administration Committee could report that there was not even a timetable for the payment of the limited compensation on offer. Above all, it shows the power biases in the system. Equitable policy holders were neither poor nor inarticulate; they were a well informed middle-class lobby group. Yet even they were unable to make headway; the conclusion must be that poor, badly resourced groups who suffer maladministration are even more helpless. In 2010, the new Coalition finally announced a settlement.

■ Our first two scandals of the abuse of public power concerned relations between welfare state professionals and families, and between the police and ethnic minorities. The Equitable Life affair concerned the abuse of power by institutions right at the heart of the core Executive in Britain.

Source: Public Administration Committee (2008 and 2009).

exercised by the police officer reacting to a problem on the beat or by the official in the benefit agency deciding whether a client's circumstances amount to grounds for entitlement. Much of the training of public servants consists not just of acquiring techniques or formal knowledge of rules, but in absorbing the more informal codes of the organization – whether the organization be a police force or an Executive Agency. Yet numerous developments summarized in this and the preceding chapter show decreasing confidence in the effectiveness of self-regulation. The spread of inspectorates, varieties of Ombudsmen and the creation of formal entitlements

in law all show that, however important self-regulation, it is decreasingly relied on to provide safeguards.

Media scrutiny

The mass media are important in regulating the relations between the state and the citizen for both particular and general reasons. Some of the most important individual scandals of abuse of public power have either been revealed, or pursued in detail, by the media. We saw in the last section, for instance, that the campaign to uncover the failings in drug safety revealed by the Thalidomide scandal by the *Sunday Times* led to the

DOCUMENTING POLITICS 22.2

The seven principles of public life, according to the Committee on Standards in Public Life

The Seven Principles of Public Life

Selflessness

Holders of public office should act solely in terms of the public interest. They should not so do in order to gain financial or other material benefits for themselves, their family or their friends.

Integrity

Holders of public office should not place themselves under any financial or other obligation to outside individuals or organisations that might seek to influence them in the performance of their official duties.

Objectivity

In carrying out public business, including making public appointments, awarding contracts, or recommending individuals for rewards and benefits, holders of public office should make choices on merit.

Accountability

Holders of public office are accountable for their decisions and actions to the public and must submit themselves to whatever scrutiny is appropriate to their office.

Openness

Holders of public office should be as open as possible about all the decisions and actions that they take. They should give reasons for their decisions and restrict information only when the wider public interest clearly demands.

Honesty

Holders of public office have a duty to declare any private interests relating to their public duties and to take steps to resolve any conflicts arising in a way that protects the public interest.

Leadership

Holders of public office should promote and support these principles by leadership and example.

■ We encountered the Committee on Standards in Public Life in Briefing 4.2, noting the way it was shifting constitutional understandings from informal understandings to explicit codes. One of the Committee's first actions, however, was to try to strengthen self-regulation as a mechanism of restraint by enunciating these seven principles of public life. The principles are always reprinted on the inside cover of the Committee's separate reports. Optimists will see the spelling out of the principles as an advance in the self-restraint with which all those in public life exercise authority and influence; pessimists might wonder why such self-evident principles of good conduct ever needed to be spelled out in the first place.

Source: The statement of the seven principles can be found in all the Committee's reports and on its website at www.public-standards.gov.uk.

important judgements by the European Court of Human Rights in 1974, but this was only one episode in a long campaign by the paper to reveal the chain of incompetence and failures in safety regulation which inflicted birth defects on new born children. Another important European Court of Human Rights Judgement referred to above – the judgement that unreasonable force had been used to kill suspected IRA terrorists in Gibraltar – was also greatly assisted by investigative journalism, notably by television journalists. These particular instances are important in their own right, since they concern scandals where public power inflicted suffering on individuals. But they also connect to the second, general reason why media scrutiny is important. The presence of a scrutinizing mass media creates a wider climate where public institutions know that their actions may well be the subject of investigative reporting. The demonstration effect of particular investigations – the way they show to public servants the possibilities of media scrutiny and exposure – can plainly be important in fostering a culture of restraint in the exercise of power. Some of the legislation passed in recent years has strengthened the hands of the investigative media. For instance, revelations of widespread abuse of the system of parliamentary allowances in 2009 by the *Daily Telegraph* was only possible because the paper was able to draw on data released under the Freedom of Information Act about expenses claims made by individual members of the House of Commons (see Rayner 2009).

Just as we can be pessimistic or optimistic about the worth of creating a formal regime of human rights, so we can be pessimistic or optimistic about the effectiveness of media scrutiny in supporting that regime. Whether we are optimistic or pessimistic depends quite heavily on the time frame we use to examine the media. If we looked back a half-century or so to the mid-1950s it would be hard to argue against the view that media scrutiny has grown in volume and effectiveness since that time. Then, for example, there was only one licensed broadcaster – the BBC – and its coverage of politics was highly deferential to those in power. Investigative journalism in both the print and electronic media is now much greater than in the 1950s. On the other hand, much of this investigative culture was created in the 1960s, when small magazines like *Private Eye* pioneered investigative practices. Since then both the economics and institutions of journalism have become weighed against scrutiny. Investigation is both expensive and often demands willingness to pursue a story for a long period of time. Increasing competition for an audience – in the case of newspapers for an audience in long-term decline – has produced pressure to cut expensive activities and to produce 'news' – literally, a constant stream of fresh stories. At the popular end of the market, in both print and broadcast journalism, reporting is increasingly dominated by non-political material: sport, celebrity gossip, horoscopes, sexual peccadilloes of royal and sporting nonentities.

Pressure groups

We saw in Chapter 8 that pressure group formation has been particularly rapid in recent years, and in Briefing 4.1 we saw examples of groups – *UnLock Democracy* and *Liberty* – that are concerned with issues central to this chapter. Briefing 22.9, a case study of the Refugee Council, shows the importance of organization in defending weak groups. Indeed the organized defence

of the interests of the citizen against state power is, when we consider it in the light of group organization, not at all confined to what we might conventionally call 'civil liberties' groups. We know from our examination of the Tribunal System, for example, that one of the most vexatious areas of state–citizen relations is created by decisions about entitlements to the money and services allocated by the welfare state. Thus the wide range of advocacy groups that seek to represent potential benefit claimants – encompassing, for instance, the low paid, the disabled, the unemployed – are inevitably drawn into the domain of the regulation of state–citizen relations. Nevertheless, the example of the Refugee Council is particularly instructive because it is a sign of the increasing tendency to try to defend the rights of individuals by organized advocacy, standing alongside the groups already profiled in Chapter 4, such as Liberty. The Refugee Council, as a member organization, is the tip of the organizational iceberg, consisting as it does of over 180 constituent bodies. We can also see organizations at work that exemplify the workings of multilevel governance in this area: Amnesty, the organization founded in 1961 to campaign for prisoners of conscience across the globe, periodically issues critical reports on British domestic policy. An equally striking area of institutional growth involves organizations that campaign to protect another marginalized and stigmatized group, prisoners. While prison reform movements are among the longest established groups in the British pressure group universe, with a continuous history going back to the nineteenth century, there has been a steady multiplication of groups in recent years, often dedicated to the defence of particular categories, such as women prisoners. The Penal Affairs Consortium, a member organization that tries to create a unified voice for those concerned with penal policy, presently has over 40 organizations in its membership.

What sense can we make of the increasing tendency for the defence of individuals against public power to take this organized form? Just as we could arrive at competing pessimistic or optimistic interpretations in the case of the media, the same is true here. It is possible to see these developments as a response to a threatening change in the character of the state in the last 30 years: a shift to more authoritarian treatment of marginalized social groups. (This theory of a new authoritarianism is examined more closely in our concluding chapter.) Two of the groups identified here could be invoked to support this argument. British penal policy has turned in a markedly punitive direction, with an increasing resort to incarceration in prison and increasing use by politicians of the language of retribution. In the case of refugees, a

BRIEFING 22.9

The Refugee Council and the defence of the rights of refugees

The treatment of refugees and asylum seekers is a particularly sensitive indicator of how public power is exercised over individuals. Many protections against public power in Britain are tied to nationality. Thus refugees and asylum seekers occupy a particularly vulnerable position. The status of asylum seekers and refugees became a key issue in British politics from the end of the 1990s, but refugees have long come to Britain and long aroused hostility. At the end of the seventeenth century Huguenots, a French Protestant sect, settled in London following Catholic persecution. At the end of the nineteenth century east European Jewish refugees fled persecution, many settling in Britain. In 1935–50 over 250,000 east European refugees settled in Britain. In 1956, 15,000 Hungarian refugees came here after the failed uprising against Communism. From the 1990s, wars in the Balkans, in the Middle East and in central Asia created millions of new refugees.

The Refugee Council thus deals with issues of long standing. It is an independent charity created in 1981 by the amalgamation of two organizations that had themselves originated out of the great refugee wave of 1935–50. It is a member organization: that is, composed not of individuals, but of nearly 180 separate organizations, many community based refugee support groups. It provides both practical support services for individuals and is also an advocacy organization for the voice of refugees in policy debates. It has a complex relationship with government. As one of the largest refugee support groups (alongside the British Red Cross) it is often used by government to establish support schemes for refugee groups, for instance for the Kosovan refugees who fled war and terror in the 1990s. But as government policy increasingly turned to restrictions over the entitlements of refugees (for instance by trying to eliminate any entitlement to welfare benefits) the Council increasingly turned to criticism of policy and defence of refugee claims against public agencies.

■ There are now numerous organizations concerned with the liberties of citizens in the face of public power. The Refugee Council occupies a particularly sensitive area because of the vulnerable status of refugees and asylum seekers.

Source: www.refugeecouncil.org.

long history of hostility and suspicion culminated from the 1990s in increasingly active public policies designed to control entry, to limit entitlements to public services and to hunt down illegal entrants. The turn to organization in this setting can be seen as an attempt to protect vulnerable groups against increasingly hostile public power.

But the growth of these organizations has not taken place in isolation. As we noted in Chapter 8 there has been a wider growth in pressure group organization. In Chapters 13 and 16 I described some of the institutional, technological and cultural changes that underpin this growth. New forms of political mobilization have occurred because of a variety of developments: the success of some groups has encouraged others to learn the lesson that well organized groups can have an effect

on public policy; new technologies of communication, such as mobile telephony and the Web, have cut the costs of organization and communication in creating networks of activists; and cultural trends, such as rising levels of formal education, have increased the size of the pool of those with the skills to organize politically and to advocate causes. On this account, the rise of formal organizations designed to defend individuals against public power, including the most vulnerable and marginalized individuals like prisoners and refugees, is a sign that we have in Britain a healthy wider culture and society that is increasingly able to scrutinize the power wielded by public servants. Thus public servants in Britain, on this account, actually operate in a wider civil society that creates organizations well able to scrutinize and check.

DEBATING POLITICS 22.1

Scandals in the exercise of public power: optimism or pessimism?

SCANDALS SUCH AS THOSE DOCUMENTED IN THE BOXES OF THIS CHAPTER MAKE US PESSIMISTIC ABOUT THE RIGHTS OF CITIZENS

- ▶ They cover a wide range of institutions and thus suggest that abuse of power is engrained in British government.
- ▶ They involve abuse at the expense of a wide range of social groups: business people, young members of ethnic minorities, parents in families.
- ▶ Their revelation and correction has typically come, not through the formal mechanisms of redress, but as the result of public campaigns prompted by extreme scandal.
- ▶ Redress and public apology have typically been delayed and grudging.

SCANDALS SUCH AS THOSE DOCUMENTED IN THE BOXES OF THIS CHAPTER GIVE GROUNDS FOR OPTIMISM ABOUT THE RIGHTS OF CITIZENS

- ▶ They show that open scrutiny and reform are possible, albeit after a hard struggle.
- ▶ Many arise from attitudes and practices which are being eliminated within government; they predate the new culture of the Human Rights Act.
- ▶ They are revealed as scandals precisely because citizens are no longer prepared to put up with arbitrary and discriminating behaviour by public servants.
- ▶ Cases such as the Stephen Lawrence case have prompted large scale reform of both practices and means of redress.

THE STATE MODERNIZED OR AUTHORITARIAN?

The preceding two chapters paint a picture of a consistent pattern of change. This pattern takes three forms. First, institutions have become more formally organized and entitlements have been increasingly codified. We can see this, for example, in the growth of more formally organized systems to ensure accountability and review of institutions as varied as the police and prison services, and the intelligence services. We can see it in the spread of the institution of the Ombudsman. We can see it in the increasingly explicit codification of entitlements and obligations, culminating in large-scale codifications such as the Human Rights Act.

Second, the institutional architecture has become more diverse and complex, principally through the reshaping influence of the world of multilevel governance. This is partly visible in the immediate impact of the institutions of the EU and the institutions of devolution. But it is also visible in the increasing recognition by policy makers that shaping policy in the areas of order

and security is a matter of effectively securing multilevel, multi-agency coordination: the key example here is provided in Briefing 21.5 on multi-agency efforts to cope with terrorism.

Third, the domains examined in these two chapters have become more contentious and volatile. Part of the function of the three boxes in this chapter that summarize recent scandals in the abuse of public power is to show that formal safeguards can coexist with great abuse. But the boxes also show how scandal and intense controversy have become central features of the regulation of relations between the state and the citizen. The frequent references to decisions about asylum and immigration in this chapter show how sensitive this area in particular has become, dramatizing the issue of what constitute proper rights and safeguards, and highlighting the problem of which socially or legally defined groups should be entitled to which safeguards.

We have seen at several points in these two chapters that developments can be interpreted in contrasting ways. One way to see the growth of institutional safeguards, the increasing codification of entitlements, and the growing contestation of the use of power by public bodies, is to view these as part of a highly desirable modernization of key parts of the constitution. They all amount to the creation of more robust institutional safeguards for citizens and the emergence of a more assertive wider culture replacing the deference of the past. They are, in short, part of a passage from the status of 'subject' to the status of 'citizen'. Different views of the changes can still be held by 'modernizers', some viewing them as extensive, some as still modest; but the changes are in the right direction, and the differences are about how much further we need to go.

But we have also encountered an altogether more pessimistic view of what has been happening, one that stresses the great surveillance resources of the state and the way it treats the most vulnerable, such as would be immigrants who do not have the resources of the native population. On this view, the recurrence of the scandals illustrated in some of the boxes of this chapter is not an unfortunate blemish in an otherwise improving picture. It is consistent with the growth of public power and with an increasingly authoritarian exercise of public power, especially over the most vulnerable and stigmatized: ethnic minorities, prisoners, asylum seekers, the poorest benefit claimants. The spread of institutions like the Ombudsman, and the codification of rights in laws like the Human Rights Act, are on this view symbolic measures designed to manage expectations: in the language of Bagehot, they are part of the 'dignified' rather than the 'efficient' machinery of the Constitution.

As will be obvious from this summary of contrasting views, how we view the present relations between the state and the citizen depends on more than how we evaluate specialized institutional safeguards and procedures. It depends also on our wider view of how democracy in Britain works. That wider view is the subject of our next, concluding, chapter.

Review OF CHAPTER 22

Four themes have dominated this chapter:

◐ The growth of institutional and procedural safeguards against some forms of maladministration.

◐ The recurrence of scandalous examples of the abuse of public power.

◐ The problem of deciding how far safeguards should extend impartially, and in particular the problem of safe-guarding the rights not only of nationals and residents, but of those who wish to enter Britain as immigrants, especially as refugees.

◐ The problematic nature of our understanding of institutional and procedural change, notably how far to read it as democratic modernization or as a strengthening of authoritarian controls.

FURTHER READING

ESSENTIAL

If you read only one book it should be Gearty (2007), which is not only rich in detail but has the added merits of including considerable theoretical and comparative material.

RECOMMENDED

For many years 'Democratic Audit', operating from the University of Essex, has been publishing audits of democracy and rights in Britain (and elsewhere). Its continuing work is always worth tracking down: see in particular Beetham et al. (2002). Unfortunately the available material on its site on the UK now stops at the 2005 general election, but check for updates: Google Democratic Audit. Moran (2007), Chapter 3, is a handy summary on the robustness, or otherwise, of the system of self-regulation. Senvirante (2002) is comprehensive and up to date on Ombudsmen, and has the added strength of some comparative material. Jowell and Cooper (2003) describe the latest important human rights developments. Jowell and Oliver (2007) have several chapters relevant to the themes discussed here. Bogdanor (2009) is illuminating on the connection between the Human Rights regime and constitutional change.

CHAPTER 23

Understanding the British state: theories and evidence

CONTENTS

AIMS

This chapter:

- Looks back at the previous chapters, extracting the main lines of change in British government and politics

- Discusses competing views about what these changes imply for the wider system of government

- Discusses competing theories of how best to make sense of change

- Examines how the great economic crisis which began in 2007 affects the likely future of the British state and how the unprecedented outcome of the May 2010 general election changed the rules of the game of governance

TRANSFORMATION AND CONTINUITY IN BRITISH GOVERNMENT

Imagine studying British government a generation or so ago – say at the moment in 1964 when the election of a new Labour administration under Harold Wilson as Prime Minister had produced the first change in partisan control of the Westminster government for 13 years. With the benefit of hindsight we can see that this moment also marked a turning point – the beginning of a long period of change in both the system of government and in the wider political system. The new era of change had comparatively little to do with the Government that was elected in 1964. Rather, the change in the partisan colour of government in that year was itself a symptom of deeper changes in wider society and in the links between society and politics. We can identify six important changes, and four lines of continuity, if we glance back over the succeeding decades.

The rise of multilevel and multi-agency governance

In part this change is institutional and in part it is a change in the mindset of those involved in making policy. The institutional changes that have cropped up in many of the chapters of this book are part of the story. The two most dramatic are the increasing intersection between all levels of government in Britain and the governing institutions of the EU, notably the European Commission in Brussels; and the formalization of domestic multilevel governance which has taken place as a result of the devolution measures introduced from 1999. But just as important as the objective institutional change is the rising consciousness that government is a multi-agency matter: it involves coordinating the activities of a wide range of agencies distributed both horizontally and vertically across society. 'Joined up government', a slogan used by Labour administrations after 1997, is sometimes derided as a gimmick, but it expresses well this change in mindset. An institutional expression of this change is the growing resources put into the coordination of policy initiatives, notably from the heart of the core Executive. It is one of the most important reasons for a development we identified in Chapter 6: the increasing resources allocated to the institutions immediately surrounding the office of Prime Minister. This stress on coordination highlights an important point: we should not necessarily equate the rise of multilevel and multi-agency governance with greater decentralization. The change in mindset often only makes actors in the core Executive more sensitive than in the past of the need for central control over agencies in the name of policy coordination.

The Europeanization of British politics

Suppose someone had emigrated from Britain in 1964 to a country where British politics was rarely reported, and that he or she returned a generation later. He or she would probably find Europeanization the most remarkably changed feature of British politics. In 1964 we were not even members of the (then) EEC. Part of the change, as we saw above, lies in the intersection with multilevel governance. But Europeanization, as we have seen in numerous chapters, has deeply inserted itself into the wider workings of society and politics: into electoral competition, both because of the advent of direct elections to the European Parliament and because divisions over strategic choices in Europe have become critical lines of cleavage in and between the leading political parties; into strategies pursued by the institutions of devolved, local and regional government, because the EU is a major funder of public investment schemes; into key areas of economic policy, like competition policy, because the European Commission has a major say in domestic mergers and competition regulation; into the strategies pursued by interests groups large and small, since virtually all treat the EU as a level at which they can seek to shape policy outcomes.

The reshaped public sector

The reshaping of the public sector has involved a complex evolution since 1964, and events since the onset of the great economic crisis in 2007 have made the evolution more complex still. Three rather different changes can be observed. In some areas the public sector has simply shrunk, often to the point of disappearance: if we look back at Timeline 20.1 we can see this change summarized in the great privatization programmes; these transferred the biggest nationalized corporations, and most important public utilities, to private ownership. The second change has been subtler. It has reshaped the boundary separating the public and the private, so that the boundary itself is more complicated and unclear. The 'reshaping' here has altered our view of where the public sector ends and the private begins. Chapter 7 provided some very striking examples of this reshaping, showing how nominally 'private' institutions and activities were increasingly subject to regulation by public agencies. (For some examples look back at Briefing 7.3.) The third change has both further blurred the boundaries of the public and the private, and has led to massive state involvement in *new* areas of economic life. The most obvious sign is the wholesale nationalization of large parts of the banking system in the wake of the great financial crisis of 2007–08.

The reshaped world of interest representation

If we looked back to 1964 we would see that many of the present institutional giants of interest representation did not even exist: the Confederation of British Industry was only founded a year later, in 1965. Some of the most important features of the modern world of interest representation also either did not exist or were only present in embryonic form. While giant firms certainly operated a generation ago, and advocated their own special interests, the importance of the giant multinational firm, which we stressed in Chapter 8, has grown greatly. Many of the firms that are now classic examples of the giant firms that are also interest lobbyists – like the great supermarket chains, such as Tesco (see Image 8.3) – either did not exist or were small in scale, as recently as the 1960s. There has also been a large growth in the membership and resources of large, permanently organized campaigning groups, encompassing causes as diverse as civil liberties at home, the rights of prisoners of conscience abroad, and the protection of the environment. In Chapters 4, 21 and 22 we saw how the first of these two sets of issues – broadly constitutional in nature – have increasingly been the subject of well-organized group campaigning. And in Chapter 8 (see Table 8.1) we saw the transformed membership resources of some important environmental campaigning groups.

In the 1960s we were just beginning to experience something that has now become common to interest group organization: the rapid growth of mass, single-issue campaigning groups. In the middle of the 1960s the first great example of these – the campaign for unilateral nuclear disarmament by Britain, CND – was just starting to decline (see Parkin 1968). As we saw, notably in Chapter 13, organizing this kind of mass, single-issue campaigning group has become much commoner, and much easier, in recent years (see for example, Briefing 13.1). Alongside this growing popularization of interest representation has gone a very different trend: growing professionalization, marked by the appearance in recent years of an increasingly well organized corps of professional lobbyists, hired guns who will speak for any interest with the money to pay them. Finally, the strategies of interest representation are being adapted to the demands of multilevel governance, notably by targeting policy makers in such European institutions as the Commission in Brussels and the newly devolved administrations in Edinburgh and Cardiff.

Reshaped participation

Some accounts of changing patterns of participation paint a picture of decline over the last generation, but this is only part of the picture. What is undoubtedly correct is that the shape of participation has altered dramatically in the last generation. Many of the key forms of participation of the 1960s are either of little, or declining, importance. The most dramatic fall concerns membership of, and activism in, the political parties. In Chapter 14 we painted a picture of institutions whose membership was shrinking, and whose local political and social life was in widespread decay. There has been marginal compensation in the rise of some third parties, such as the nationalists and the Greens, but the two giants of the 1960s, Labour and Conservative, are strikingly weaker. An even gloomier picture for the big parties emerges if we look at the participation of young people: the youth wings of the parties, and the student wings of the parties, have suffered a particularly serious decline. Students – a much larger group in the population now than in the 1960s – rarely participate in politics via membership of the Conservative or Labour parties, or indeed via any of the political parties.

A second fall in 'official' participation concerns voting. In recent years, voting, especially in general elections to the Westminster Parliament, has fallen sharply. (There had been some recovery in the 2005 and May 2010 elections, but even the higher May 2010 turnout did not bring the level anywhere near the highs of earlier decades.) 'Official' political participation is less widespread than even minority hobbies (see Table 13.1). But we can draw a very different, less pessimistic, picture of what has happened to participation. The opportunities to participate have widened. There are more opportunities to vote, in referenda and in competitive elections, and there are more routes to political office than existed in the days when the Westminster Parliament was virtually the only path to significant high office. Most important of all, there has been an explosion of new kinds of participation, notably in permanently organized campaigning groups, and in single-issue groups that come and go with great speed. This is why we should speak of the reshaping, rather than the decline, of participation.

The codified constitution

The constitution of a generation ago was still a thing of understandings and conventions – a mostly unwritten patchwork. The intervening generation has seen a growing codification: this means the increasing tendency systematically to write down constitutional understandings, often in the form of laws. In part this is an aspect of 'Europeanization', because the British system of government has been drawn into other European systems where written constitutional rules are the norm. One big sign of the change, which we have come across in several

Timeline 23.1

A chronicle of political events in Britain, 1964–2010

1964 Labour Party returned to office for the first time in 13 years with tiny Commons majority.

1965 Labour Government publishes *National Plan*, attempt to emulate French style of planning and French record of economic success.

1966 Labour wins general election with landslide Commons majority of almost 100 over other parties.

1967 Pound sterling devalued following currency crisis; *National Plan* effectively abandoned in ensuing economic crisis.

1968 Civil rights marches in Northern Ireland show first sign of a generation of civil unrest in the Province.

1969 *In Place of Strife*, Labour Government White Paper proposals on trade union reform abandoned in face of trade union opposition. Troops committed to policing streets in Northern Ireland following riots and attacks on Catholics.

1970 Edward Heath returned unexpectedly as Conservative Prime Minister in general election.

1971 Negotiations begin to prepare way for UK entry into EEC.

1972 Direct rule from Westminster imposed in Northern Ireland, beginning a history of direct rule which has lasted, with brief interruptions, for more than 30 years. Conservative Government abandons free market policies, introducing statutory pay and prices policies.

1973 UK formally becomes member of the EEC. 'Six Day War' in the Middle East leads to huge rise in oil prices and beginning of severe recession in Britain and in other advanced industrial nations. Prolonged dispute with miners over challenge to statutory pay policy leads to widespread social and economic disruption and imposition of a 'three day working week' on industry and many public services, and severe restrictions over use of energy.

1974 Conservatives expelled from office in February general election; second general election in October fails to give Labour Government a clear majority.

1975 Year of unprecedented pay and price inflation approaching annual rates of 30 per cent.

1976 Following sterling crisis Labour Government forced to seek financial support from International Monetary Fund in return for cuts in public spending plans.

1977 Clashes between police and mass picketing in dispute at Grunwick printers.

1978 'Winter of discontent' sees widespread public sector strikes, disruption of essential services and violent clashes between strikers and police.

1979 Margaret Thatcher returned as Prime Minister of Conservative Government in general election.

1980 British and world recession following sharp rise in oil prices in preceding year.

1981 Widespread riots in London (Brixton) and in other cities.

1982 Argentine invasion of British possession in South Atlantic, the Falkland Islands, followed by short victorious military campaign to regain possession.

1983 Conservatives win landslide victory in general election.

1984 IRA bomb in Grand Hotel, Brighton, during Conservative Party conference kills five, injures many more and narrowly misses killing the Prime Minister.

1985 Miners concede defeat in year-long strike aimed at challenging government authority to make coal policy.

1986 Single European Act passed, committing the UK to further progress of European integration. Michael Heseltine resigns from Cabinet, beginning train of events that will bring down Mrs Thatcher.

Timeline 23.1

1987 Rupert Murdoch moves printing of his national newspaper titles such as *The Times* and *The Sun* from Fleet Street to Wapping, breaking power of print unions after long conflict. In general election Margaret Thatcher returned for third term as Prime Minister.

1988 Section 28 of Local Government Act forbids local authorities from 'promoting' homosexuality in schools.

1989 Nigel Lawson resigns as Chancellor of the Exchequer, signalling first public sign of infighting in the Thatcher Cabinet.

1990 Thatcher resigns as Prime Minister and Leader of the Conservative Party following failure to win required majority in first ballot of leadership challenge by Michael Heseltine. John Major becomes Conservative Leader and Prime Minister.

1991 Introduction of 'council tax' to replace 'poll tax', failure of which had helped to depose Thatcher.

1992 On 'Black Wednesday', 16 September, government forced to take sterling out of European Exchange Rate Mechanism, destroying public faith in Conservative economic competence for over a decade.

1993 British Government admits to holding secret talks with Provisional IRA.

1994 IRA declares first ceasefire in Northern Ireland. Tony Blair elected as Leader of Labour Party.

1995 In British Rail privatization Conservative Government introduces last and most controversial of the large privatization schemes.

1996 IRA bomb Canary Wharf in London, ending first ceasefire on British mainland.

1997 Labour Government returned to power with landslide Commons majority under Tony Blair.

1998 Signing of 'Belfast Agreement' on Good Friday begins attempted 'peace process' in Northern Ireland.

1999 New devolved administrations established in Scotland and Wales.

2000 Euro introduced for daily transactions in most member states of the EU, with Britain as the most significant 'opt out'.

2001 Labour returned for second term of office under Tony Blair with another landslide majority.

2002 Labour Government commits British troops to campaign in Afghanistan to remove Taliban government following attack on New York and Washington by terrorist guided aircraft in September 2001.

2003 Government fights war in Iraq alongside the US.

2004 Labour Party convulsed by divisions over the Iraq war.

2005 New Labour wins third successive general election with reduced majority.

2007 Gordon Brown succeeds Tony Blair as Prime Minister in uncontested succession. Scottish Nationalists form first nationalist government in a devolved administration.

2008 Great Crash threatens stability of the whole banking system.

2009 Widespread scandal over misappropriation of expenses engulfs all parties in Westminster Parliament.

2010 May 2010 General Election gives no party an overall majority in the House of Commons and compels formation of first formal coalition since 1945.

■ The text of this chapter stresses continuity and change over the last generation. This timeline only selects key events for each year of the last 40. Not all readers will agree with my selection of highlights. It would be an illuminating exercise for students to create their own timeline.

chapters (especially Chapter 5) is the importance of the European Court of Justice as a kind of 'supreme court', the arbiter of the meaning of the treaties, directives and regulations of the EU. In Chapters 21 and 22 we also saw a long-term tendency to try to create formally organized institutional safeguards – like Ombudsmen – and a tendency to write down safeguards in forms like the Human Rights Act. And in Chapter 4 we saw many signs of the growth of codification, such as that arising out of the work of the Committee on Standards in Public Life (see for example, Briefing 4.2).

Great changes have therefore come over British politics in recent decades. But the story is not only about change. If we scan over a generation there are also striking continuities. Some political worlds have shown great persistence. Four are sketched here.

The world of Westminster

Much has changed in the world of Westminster politics in the last generation, but there are also remarkable continuities. The House of Commons remains one of the most important centres of public political life – if anything, perhaps strengthened by the broadcasting of debates and their consequential use as clips in news broadcasts. For the most ambitious political aspirants a seat in the House of Commons still remains a highly desirable prize, both for its own sake and because it is a virtual precondition of winning more glittering prizes, such as a seat in the Westminster Cabinet. Commanding the House of Commons in debates, and in the jousts of Prime Minister's Question Time, remains a key to the exercise of Prime Ministerial authority. A generation ago a political fan who wanted to 'rubberneck' the leading figures in British political life only had to hang round the Palace of Westminster for a few days; the same holds true today. For the most important part of the political class in Britain political life still means Westminster life.

The world of the core Executive

A major theme of Chapter 6 was the way the core Executive is changing, but as in the world of Westminster the continuities are also striking. A generation ago, for the most ambitious politicians, the Cabinet was the pinnacle of a political career, and a small number of key offices of state (Prime Minister, Chancellor, Foreign Secretary) the very summit of that pinnacle. That is still true: in these offices we still find the 'big hitters' in politics. The increased use of the concept of the 'core Executive' in many ways only recognizes what was already a reality a generation ago: that at the heart of British government were a few hundred people working in central departments grouped around Whitehall in London, encompassing elected politicians, permanent

IMAGE 23.1 ■ The symbol of statehood: the passport

■ A British passport, the opening pages of which are reproduced here, has powerful symbolic and practical importance. Symbolically, it defines identity in a world where every piece of territory is claimed by some state. Look closely at the second page: you will see that the designation 'United Kingdom of Great Britain and Northern Ireland' is reproduced in all the languages of member states of the European Union. (The passport was issued before the enlargement of the Union in 2004). Practically, the passport confers the right to enter a wealthy part of the world. Its value is reflected in the fact that it is stolen, forged and even killed for in impoverished parts of the globe.

civil servants and more temporary advisors and aides. That is still substantially the case.

The world of liberal democracy

The two worlds of continuity identified so far are elitist worlds populated by a small group of the political class. The world of liberal democracy is different. It refers to the wider popular foundations of the system of government. A generation ago Britain claimed to be a liberal democracy, in the senses identified in Chapter 1: that is, it claimed to combine the protection of liberal freedoms (such as freedom of conscience, speech, assembly) with control over, and selection of, government by the people at large. This is still the version of British politics to which virtually anyone in Britain who argues and thinks about the system of government aspires. Those who defend our governing arrangements argue that, whatever particular blemishes may exist on the liberal democratic record, ours is fundamentally a liberal democracy. Critics of this account argue a variety of cases: for instance that the 'blemishes' are so great as seriously to compromise liberal and democratic claims; or even that the claim to abide by these standards, even imperfectly, is unsustainable. But both critics and defenders agree on liberal democracy as the critical measure by which we should judge the system of government – an agreement that also united critics and defenders a generation ago. A small minority of authoritarians of a variety of persuasions dissent from this liberal democratic consensus, as did a small minority a generation ago.

The world of the UK

One surprising continuity should be highlighted – at least it is surprising if we look back at the pessimistic, often crisis laden atmosphere, of British politics that was common about 30 years ago: the UK endures. The 1970s were a decade of particularly severe economic failure and political turmoil. By the end of the decade 'the break-up of Britain' – the title of a highly influential book by Nairn (1981) – seemed a possibility. That 'break-up' might have come in a variety of forms: from the challenge of separate nationalisms; or, as seemed possible on occasions in the 1970s, from a wider crisis of governability produced by economic failure and the inability of government to manage the demands of powerfully organized competing interests (see for instance King 1976). It has been a major theme of this book that the nature of UK government has indeed been transformed in recent decades, notably by the impact of membership of the EU and by the institutional reforms introduced after the return to power of the Labour Party in 1997. But there has been no breakdown of the UK. The Westminster system remains the single most important concentration of resources and authority in British politics. Actors from that system – notably from the core Executive – are the most important British players in the politics of policy in the institutions of the EU. Indeed involvement with the Union has given new roles to key actors: to the Prime Minister, for example, as a leading figure in the high diplomacy of the Union. In the 1980s and 1990s the Westminster Government proved highly effective at confronting institutions and interests – like the trade unions – against whom it had seemed ineffective during the 1970s. And in the case of Northern Ireland – the most radical challenge to the unity of the UK – that challenge has been repulsed: as we saw in Chapter 11 the most important part of Irish republicanism, in Sinn Féin, has now opted for constitutional politics within the framework of the UK. There nevertheless remain two great uncertainties about the future. One we have already discussed, especially in Chapter 10: it remains uncertain how far the devolution settlements in Scotland and Wales are stable and enduring arrangements, or are only staging posts on the road to full independence – and thus the break-up of the UK. The second we will discuss later in this chapter. The stability of the Westminster system rested heavily on the long economic boom that lasted from 1992 to 2007. That boom has been succeeded by a slump even greater than that which so threatened the viability of the governing system in the 1970s and early 1980s.

UNDERSTANDING CHANGE AND CONTINUITY

The forms of development in British politics are many and varied, as even the simple sketches provided above show. How do we make sense of them? In other words, how do we step back from the bare institutional detail and provide a general interpretation of the forces shaping government? Many possibilities exist, but three are especially important, both because they have been prominent in academic debates and have influenced practical political perceptions.

The network state

We began this book with Max Weber's account of the nature of authority, and notably with the different grounds on which it could be exercised: charisma, tradition or the claim to legitimacy by virtue of rational legality. The last, we saw, was the commonest grounds on which the state could claim to exercise authority in Britain: by virtue of the fact that the decisions and commands of public servants were in accordance with powers conferred by laws legitimately passed. Charisma, the claim to some divine anointment; tradition, the claim to authority by virtue of linkage to a long line of historically established custom: these are now only residually present, reflected in various antiquated ceremonies associated with a monarchy which exercises hardly any real power.

There is no doubt that rational legality is the commonest basis for claimed authority in Britain, though traces of charisma and tradition may be more deeply buried in our unconscious when we are faced with authority than we actually realize. But what each of these pictures of authority share, in any case, is a fundamentally hierarchical vision of how government should work, and does work: the state, through its public servants, tells us what to do, and we obey, if we acknowledge authority. But these conceptions of authority were formulated a century ago, and they were shaped by experience of the nineteenth-century state (Weber was born in 1864). Can they adequately reflect the complexity of modern government? We do not expect

BRIEFING 23.1

Castells on the network state

'The network state is a state characterised by the sharing of authority (that is, in the last resort, the capacity to impose legitimized violence) along a network. A network by definition, has nodes, not a centre. Nodes may be of different sizes, and may be linked by asymmetrical relationships in the network. Not only do national governments still concentrate much decision-making capacity, but there are important differences of power between nation-states, although the hierarchy of power varies in different dimensions: Germany is the hegemonic economic power, but Britain and France hold far greater military power, and at least equal technological capacity. <indent>However, regardless of these asymmetries, the various nodes of the European network are interdependent on each other, so that no node, even the most powerful, can ignore the others, even the smallest in the decision-making process. If some political nodes do so, the whole political system is called into question. This is the difference between a political network and a centred political structure. Amongst the responses of political systems to the challenge of globalisation, the European Union may be the clearest manifestation to date of this emerging form of state, probably characteristic of the Information Age.'

■ Castells (see also Castells 2000) is the foremost theorist of the network state and the network society. Here he gives it a distinctly 'European' cast.

Source: Castells (2001).

nineteenth-century technologies, like the steam engine, to power a modern economy. Why should we expect nineteenth-century ideas to power government? We do not expect social institutions like firms or universities to be organized on the same principles as governed their workings in the nineteenth century. Why should we therefore expect government to be organized by nineteenth-century principles?

It is exactly these thoughts that lie behind the title of this book, notably the reference to 'governance'. In the twenty-first century British government cannot be described with a nineteenth-century language. 'Governance' in the title is a modest recognition of the way policies and politics take place in a world of multi-level institutions and agencies. But there is an account that goes well beyond this modest linguistic shift. It can be summarily described as the theory of the network state.

At the heart of the idea of the network state is the proposition that we no longer live in a world of stable hierarchies and that government cannot any longer be conducted in a hierarchical fashion, even where those hierarchies claim the legitimacy of rational–legal authority. We live instead in a world of networks: links of institutions and people that are highly dispersed, are not necessarily hierarchical, and which cross the conven-

tional public/private boundary. For government to be effective it is no longer sufficient for it to invoke authority, rational–legal or otherwise. It must mobilize and coordinate the actors in numerous different networks to address issues and problems.

Part of the power of the network theory of the state is that it offers us both description and prescription: it suggests that the world is changing in particular ways, and that as a result the practice of making and putting into effect policy has to change, if policy is to be at all effective. Many of the features that are central to this book fit the network theory. Three are especially important.

First, the major theme of the development of multi-level and multi-agency systems, notably in the policy world, obviously chimes with the 'network' vision. The 'stretching' of policy making to span both the European and the devolved worlds plainly also fits the vision of a networked state.

Second, a large number of the wider political changes that have figured in these pages make sense when viewed through the vision of the network state. In the preceding section we summarized, for instance, the transformation of participation that has taken place in the last generation. That transformation has created a less hierarchical, more difficult to control, world. In place of the small number of political parties that 'funnelled' most participation through their mass memberships a generation ago, there is now a more dispersed and chaotic world: a huge diversity of groups organizing different people with specialized, different interests and preferences – spontaneously created groups with mass memberships, often created extremely rapidly around single issues. Behind these developments in turn lie cultural and technical developments that have undermined hierarchical control: a better educated and more self-confident citizenry which no longer takes its political cues from a London-based elite; and technologies of communication that can no longer be monopolized by the institutions of the state.

Third, theories of the network state help to explain failure in government and offer the prospect of avoiding it in future. We have seen at a number of points in this text that fiascos and failures are a common experience of British government (see especially Chapter 19). One of the most distinguished exponents of the network account, Rhodes (1997), has argued that fiasco and failure are the product of an inability to recognize the reality of networks: that government cannot any longer be carried on by the tools given us by a Weberian hierarchical theory of the nature of the state. Trying to use these tools is like attempting to steer a modern car with the skills of a nineteenth-century train driver. Disaster is inevitable unless some more subtle form of coordination and manoeuvre is adopted.

The network vision plainly alerts us to important features of multilevel governance in Britain. But should we subscribe to it fully? We might have reservations on three grounds.

The first lies in the claim to novelty. Recall that in the hands of writers like Rhodes this is an important part of the argument: modern society, and modern government, creates new levels of complexity that make old-fashioned hierarchies ineffective. The new governance has to be about managing dispersed institutional networks and seeking coordination across the old-fashioned public/private divide. But if we look at the past of government in Britain we can see numerous examples of precisely this kind of arrangement. Some examples will help illustrate the point.

● We know from Chapters 21 and 22 that traditionally the relations between the state and the citizen in Britain were heavily reliant on voluntary coordination. This part of the constitution was strikingly lacking in codification, depending on understandings by a wide range of parties that were rarely written down. If anything, the developments described in those two chapters seem to move us away from models of coor-

dination to more exact specification of the relationships between citizens and public institutions.

● Many of the key 'multilevel' relationships in government in the past were highly voluntary in nature. For instance, until the 1980s local authorities in Britain had a high level of autonomy and the central state had to rely on voluntary cooperation for the delivery of services. In other words, the centre truly had to try to coordinate networks of dispersed institutions. If anything, this declined from the 1980s as the central state intervened directly to control the actions of local government – a development described in Chapter 12.

● In the recent past central government relied on informal and voluntary agreements with many institutions and agencies to deliver services or to ensure regulation. Two very good examples are provided by universities, which were substantially independent of the central education ministry until the 1980s; and the City of London, which ruled itself through a complex network of private firms, semi-public agencies like the Bank of England, and the informal guidance of agencies from the core Executive, like the Treasury. Here again, since the 1980s there has been a move to more directive, legally based modes of control and regulation. In the wake of the Financial Crash of 2008, indeed, the state has moved more tightly to control financial markets.

Second, as some of the examples given above show, it may be a little sweeping to adopt the language of networks because there seems to be life in the old 'state' yet. The shape of state power in Britain is certainly changing. The old highly centralized, London-focused model has been greatly altered in recent decades. Many services that were delivered by state institutions are now delivered otherwise, either by private firms or – as in the case of a large amount of what used to be 'council' housing – by the voluntary sector. But as we saw in Chapter 20 the state is still a massively important institution in raising and allocating economic resources. It wields highly traditional forms of state power, the power to compel citizens to pay a variety of taxes, on pain of prosecution, confiscation and, in the last resort, imprisonment. In some areas of national life – such as in controlling who may enter and work in the country – the state is strengthening both its powers and its surveillance resources.

Third, it may be premature to write off forms of legitimacy based on Weberian models of authority. One reason may be that a 'network' state itself raises serious problems of accountability. It deliberately tries to blur the divide between the public and private, and to work through complex networks of institutions where coordination is valued over clear specification of hierarchical relationships. But one merit of hierarchy is that it identifies lines of responsibility: an aggrieved citizen has some notion of where the buck stops. That helps to explain developments described in Chapters 21 and 22 which are otherwise puzzling if we are indeed moving into a world of self-organizing networks: the increased tendency to try to lay out more exactly the terms of rational–legal authority, by codifying more explicitly the powers of public servants and the rights of citizens, and by putting on a more formal basis the means by which aggrieved citizens may seek redress. These developments show the tenacity of the rational–legal model of authority. They show that a reaction to failures of the model – for instance, when public servants use their discretion to abuse their powers – is to try to strengthen the rational–legal model by specifying it more exactly and making stronger the institutions that can pursue cases where it is abused.

The regulatory state

The theory of the regulatory state is a relative of the network state theory, but it emphasizes different forces. There are also strikingly varied accounts of what the regulatory state amounts to, and these variations catch some of the contradictory developments in British government over recent years.

The essential idea of the regulatory state is well conveyed in the name, notably in the idea of the state as a 'regulator'. A regulator in any system – it could be as simple as that providing domestic central heating, or as complex as the computer based navigation for a large ship – essentially balances the system: it receives information from the environment and adjusts system performance in the light of that information and in the light of the preset aims of the system. For a simple domestic central heating system that means turning a boiler on and off in the light of a preset temperature target and what sensors indicate about the ambient temperature; for a complex navigation system it means adjusting the direction of the vessel in the light of information received and processed about a wide range of factors, from likely obstacles to ambient weather conditions. Transferred to government, this language pictures the regulatory state as a kind of pilot for society, not actually supplying the motive power but providing overall guidance about direction. A famous American image expresses this as a state that is not 'rowing' but 'steering' (Osborne and Gaebler 1992:35).

This picture of the regulatory state is actually as old as political philosophy. In the *Republic* of Plato, one of the first great texts of political philosophy, written in Greece over 300 years before the birth of Christ, there is an explicit identification of leadership in government with the role of a pilot. This early identification tells us something potentially significant about the democratic character of the idea of the regulatory state, for the *Republic* is a consciously anti-democratic work. If we move from ancient Greece to our own times, we shall also find that the idea of government as the act of piloting has often been associated with authoritarian, not democratic, politics: Mao Zedong one of the most brutal dictators of the twentieth century (ruled China, 1949–76), was known periodically as 'the Great Helmsman'. And when we interrogate the idea applied to Britain, we shall find that in some accounts it actually has anti-democratic undertones.

The vision of the regulatory state in Britain begins with two key recent British experiences: a great economic crisis in the 1970s and the policy response which that produced; and the by now long history of the country's membership of the EU. The great economic crisis of the 1970s produced, at the end of the decade, the return of a Conservative administration led by Margaret Thatcher as Prime Minister. Throughout Thatcher's long tenure (1979–90) the state withdrew from many areas of economic control. In particular, it 'privatized' many important industries (such as telecommunications and steel) and many providers of utilities like water, electricity and gas. In many cases these had been in public ownership and control for over a century. The state also sought to guide the economy according to free market principles. It thus tried to adopt a key notion of the regulatory state: that government would set the overall direction of economic life, providing the key background conditions for markets to operate, but allowing the wider institutions of civil society to do the 'rowing' – that is, actually to produce goods and services for offer in the marketplace. It also moved in the direction of more regulation in a more immediate institutional way. For many of the privatized industries it developed specialized regulatory bodies whose purpose was to steer the privatized sector in certain key directions, such as free and fair competition. We discussed the growth of these regulatory agencies, together with examples, in Chapter 7 (notably Briefing 7.3). Though the most revolutionary changes happened in the Thatcher decade of the 1980s, they were confirmed by her successors. Thatcher's immediate successor as Prime Minister, John Major, continued the privatization programme; and the Blair governments after 1997 established many new regulatory agencies, such as the Food Standards Agency and the Financial Services Authority.

This account of the growth of the regulatory state in Britain therefore traces it to the response to a long history of British economic decline, and in particular to

BRIEFING 23.2

Majone on the regulatory state as an alternative model of democracy

'Independent regulatory bodies, like independent central banks, courts of law, administrative tribunals or the European Commission, belong to the genus 'non-majoritarian institutions', that is, public institutions which, by design, are not directly accountable either to voters or to elected officials. The growing importance of such institutions in all democratic countries shows that for many purposes reliance upon qualities such as expertise, professional discretion, policy consistency, fairness or independence of judgement is considered to be more important than reliance on direct political accountability ... non-majoritarian decision-making mechanisms are more suitable for complex, plural societies than are mechanisms that concentrate power in the hands of the political majority.'

■ Majone offers two especially important perspectives on the regulatory state. His stress on the importance of the 'EU' connection we have already encountered. The second is his direct challenge to 'majoritarian' democracy on the grounds that it is too crude to work in 'complex, plural societies'. Britain is a complex plural society which has up to now relied heavily precisely on majoritarianism – most obviously in the convention that control of a majority in elected assemblies confers the legitimate right to make policy.

Source: Majone (1996:286).

the severe crisis of the 1970s. It identifies it as part of a new consensus in politics, uniting both the major Westminster governing parties. But the British experience, though special in the severity of the economic crisis that brought it about, is not unique. The crisis of the 1970s was part of a wider change in international conditions that created economic difficulties across the advanced industrial world. Many countries responded by trying to withdraw the state from areas of economic control and by trying to adopt a more regulatory mode – more 'steering' and less 'rowing'. (Recall that this original image actually came from a study of American government.) This wider significance of the regulatory state is at the heart of the most important and academically influential version of the theory, that offered by the Italian social scientist Majone. One great strength of Majone's account is that it ties British to European developments.

Majone (1996) argues that the developments that produced the British crisis of the 1970s were part of a wider crisis, one that threatened what he calls the Keynesian Welfare State. The Keynesian Welfare State was an ambitious form of state intervention that developed across numerous advanced industrial nations after the Second World War, especially in Western Europe. It combined a large welfare state with a commitment to

close control of the economy, including large-scale public ownership. In the 1970s this kind of ambitious state found it increasingly hard to deliver aims like low inflation and full employment. Britain's problems, though extreme, were thus only part of this wider crisis. The regulatory 'turn' involves, as in the British case, withdrawing from direct ownership and control, and relying much more on 'steering'. But this regulatory turn has been strengthened in Western Europe by the rise of the EU as an actor in economic life. The EU, Majone argues, is necessarily a regulatory state. It just does not have the resources to act as an interventionist state. It has a tiny independent budget of its own and a tiny bureaucracy – both not much more impressive than the resources of a large British local authority. It cannot directly control the vast economy of the Union. It must do the best it can by laying down broad rules and relying on others to implement them. It expresses this reliance in the doctrine of subsidiarity: the doctrine that power and control should be exercised at the lowest possible feasible level of a governing system. In practice this means that responsibility for implementing the rules lies with national and subnational institutions, and often with private institutions, such as professional regulatory bodies. Since these lower level bodies have to implement rules, it is also only sensible that they should have a large say in their formation. The regulatory state is therefore a state where private interests have a big say in what broad policies are decided, since they often have the responsibility for carrying them out.

The accounts of the regulatory state summarized here share some common features: they offer a fundamentally benign view of this state, picturing it as a way of standing back from, and empowering, civil society. Difficulties immediately arise, however, in picturing the regulatory state as a 'light touch' steering state. It is true that, in such programmes as privatization, there has been significant retreat from the dominant forms of twentieth-century state intervention. But we saw in Chapter 7 that this is far from the whole story: the age of the regulatory state over the last couple of decades has seen greatly widened legal regulation, usually through agencies empowered by statute. The story cannot just be about shifting from rowing to steering, but of the state acquiring new means of control over areas of civil society, like sport and financial regulation, which hitherto largely operated independently.

One way of solving this puzzle – that the age of steering is also apparently an age of increasing control – looks to the authoritarian strand in regulation that spans, as we saw above, Plato's 'pilot' and Mao's 'Great Helmsman'. My (2007) account of the regulatory state recognizes this strand and paints the British regulatory state in a threatening and interventionist light. Here the state is using regulation not just as a response to residual problems of control left behind by privatization, but as a way of fundamentally reshaping civil society. This reshaping is taking place in the name of a variety of projects of wholesale social transformation: making the economy competitive in an age of global markets; intervening in the life styles of the population to manage their health; promoting and controlling education and scientific research.

It is obvious that one of the strengths of the regulatory-state theory is that it offers a number of different perspectives on the meaning of change in British politics. It can draw together the impact of the Thatcher revolution in economic policy and the long-term consequences of our membership of the EU. But that diversity is also a weakness. Whatever the difficulties of the theory of the network state it offers a fairly clear set of propositions that we can test against the evidence. What, by contrast, are we to make of theories of the regulatory state that do not seem to agree on whether regulation means retreat or advance, more liberal freedoms or more authoritarian controls?

One intriguing feature of the 'authoritarian' account of the regulatory state is that it connects to the third and final theory examined here: a theory that we are witnessing the rise of an authoritarian state in Britain.

An authoritarian state

The two theories we have so far examined are chiefly academic in origin and circulation. They are in the main too technical to have attracted much attention in the world of practical political argument. Our third theory is especially interesting because it has crossed these two worlds: originating in both academic and polemical accounts of what is happening to British politics, it is now widely invoked, especially by radical critics of what has happened to government in the last couple of decades.

The theory of the rise of a new authoritarianism sprang from attempts to make sense of the Thatcher revolution in policy and organization of the 1980s: the destruction of trade union power; the more active use of policing to combat industrial militancy; the onset of a new age of foreign wars, beginning with the victorious campaign to expel Argentinian invaders from the Falklands in 1982; the growth of central controls over formerly locally controlled services, be they policing or schooling.

Some of these changes could be assimilated to the theory of a 'free market and strong state' developed by Gamble (1994). This argued that free market forces in a society with strong institutions of collectivism like trade unions demanded powerful central state controls. These controls were needed both to impose the reforms in the first place and then continually to police an economy where actors had incentives to try to subvert competitive forces in order to gain advantages in markets. But while Gamble's theory opened up the possibility that the new 'free market strong state' order might be authoritarian, it did not necessarily entail authoritarianism. It is easy to imagine that a strong central state could be combined with the preservation of both democratic practices and liberal freedoms – something that seems to approximate to Gamble's own view. Faced with the Thatcher revolution in the 1980s Hall and Jacques (1983) offered a much darker picture of a new authoritarianism – an authoritarianism which not only policed in the name of the free market but summoned up old forms of repression, such as imperialism and racism (see Briefing 23.3).

This account was published at the height of the Thatcher revolution in the 1980s. Since then, radical critics have been able to accumulate continuing signs of this authoritarian 'turn' in British political life. Three pieces of evidence supporting this authoritarian account are: the new cross-party consensus; the impact of international events; and the development of surveillance technology. We examine each in turn.

The new cross-party consensus. When Hall and Jacques produced their original account, the

BRIEFING 23.3

Hall and Jacques on the authoritarian state

'The historic mission of Thatcherism has not been to win this or that election – astute as it has been at mastering the ebb and flow of the opinion polls. It is much more ambitious than that ... a new public philosophy has been constructed in the open affirmation of "free market values" – the market as the measure of everything – and reactionary "Victorian" social values – patriarchalism, racism and imperialist nostalgia. The whole shift towards a more authoritarian type of regime has been grounded in the search for "Order" and the cry for "Law" which arises among many ordinary people in times of crisis and upheaval.'

■ Hall and Jacques originally set out to understand Thatcherism at the height of its success. But their theory of a new authoritarianism has been echoed in many later radical accounts, including critical radical accounts of New Labour.

Source: Hall and Jacques (1983:10–11).

Conservatives under Thatcher were pioneers of a new kind of politics. The Labour Party in Opposition was then opposed to much of what the Conservatives were attempting. But in the 1990s 'New Labour' accepted most of the Conservative reforms, and indeed in some areas sought to 'outbid' the Conservatives. Apart from accepting most of the Conservatives' reforms designed to strengthen market forces, New Labour was particularly enthusiastic about three key areas of change. First, it strenuously pursued the agenda of more centralized and more thorough policing. Second, it sought to introduce reforms that tried to police more closely the behaviour of the unemployed, making entitlements to benefits conditional on willingness to be subjected to periodic assessments and to acceptance of offers of employment. Third, despite introducing the Human Rights Act, it tried to restrict the range of some traditional liberties, such as rights to jury trials and defences against imprisonment without trial.   Thus, what were in the 1980s highly contested measures associated with the Conservatives are now supported and promoted by the majority of the governing class. One reason for this change we now examine: the impact of international events.

The impact of international events. The collapse of the main perceived threat to British security, the Soviet Union, occurred in 1991. But far from removing the sense of threat, it actually produced in many ways a more threatening and unstable world. British government lives in an era of small – and sometimes not so small – wars: two wars against Iraq (1990 and 2003); in the Balkans (1999); in Afghanistan, from 2002. In the twentieth century, war, because of the way it was accompanied by external threats to home security, was often accompanied by the curtailment of civil liberties. A perceived, new, threatening force is provided by international terrorism, the defining moment being the successful attack on the World Trade Center in New York, and on the Pentagon in Washington, on 11 September 2001. Most democratic states curtailed civil liberties in the wake of that attack, taking power, for example, to imprison suspected terrorists without trial. These responses have been strengthened by subsequent events: by bomb attacks in London on 7 July 2005 which killed 52 people; by other attacks which fortunately did not result in loss of life; and by many security alerts. At a Downing Street press conference just under a month after the attacks (held on 5 August 2005) Prime Minister Blair identified the change as a transformation in the rules of the game: 'If people want to come here, either fleeing persecution, or seeking a better life, they play by our rules and our way of life. If they don't, they are going to have to go because they are threatening our people and way of life. Coming to Britain is not a right. And even when people come here, staying here carries with it a duty.'

The development of surveillance technology. The new era of small wars also gave a considerable impetus to another feature emphasized by those who believe we are entering an age of authoritarianism: the use by states of technologies of surveillance. States have often wanted closely to monitor the lives of their subjects, but primitive technologies set a limit to monitoring – and thus to control. If the state does not know what we are doing it is hard for it to punish us for doing it. Some of the possibilities of the new surveillance technologies have cropped up in the pages of these texts: notably, the way a combination of huge computing power and digital technologies of observation mean that our daily movements, transactions and communications can now be recorded, stored, easily retrieved and passed between private and public agencies ranging from the police to credit rating firms.

The theory of a new authoritarianism therefore begins with fairly limited historical observations of the revolution in British government introduced by the Conservatives in the 1980s, as they tried to cope with the aftermath of the British economic crisis. But the power of this theory is greatly strengthened by the way it seems to fit with so many wider developments; a state struggling with the perceived threat of terrorism; an era of small wars often connected to the fight against terrorism; a consensus about the need for closer social control of the poor that unites large sections of the political class; new technologies that make surveillance and control ambitions more realizable than in the past.

There are two rather different grounds for scepticism in the face of this theory of a new authoritarianism. One partly accepts the argument that there has been a diminution of liberty; the other argues that this account entirely misreads what has been happening to British government and politics in the last couple of decades.

Partially accepting the theory of the new authoritarianism account begins by admitting that restrictions on liberties have indeed grown, and are likely to continue to grow. That can be coupled with the argument that this is a necessary evil to avert a greater one – destruction of life, and even of our free institutions, by supporters of political violence. But the restrictions, viewed in the round of British political life, are still marginal if worrying. Most people, most of the time, retain wide liberties – of speech, conscience, assembly. Virtually every conceivable body of opinion is still able to organize and campaign. Ninety-nine per cent of the population still speak, think and organize without any restriction; and the one per cent that expresses views deeply repugnant to those of the majority still have quite ample freedoms to speak and organize. No system of liberal democratic government is perfect, but this does not seem a bad record in a dangerous world of terrorist threats. This, then, is an argument that there are indeed some worrying signs of a growth of authoritarianism but that so far their impact has been marginal.

A more thoroughgoing rejection of the theory of authoritarianism would argue that, far from growing authoritarianism, the range of liberty has widened in recent decades, and the state's coercive power has been more tightly controlled. Three pieces of evidence can be produced in support of this view.

The first is the evidence that state coercion is actually in retreat, not advancing. Suppose we compare the

coercive activities of the British state now with its activities 30 years ago, before the onset of the new age of authoritarianism. We can see three areas where state coercion has declined:

- Coercion by the police and the armed forces in Northern Ireland has greatly receded. Mass internment without trial; almost daily shootings on the streets; massive undercover surveillance of the population: all these commonplace 1970s signs of state coercion have been eliminated. Since the signing of the Good Friday Agreement in 1998, indeed, the greatest coercion in the Province comes from sections of nationalist and paramilitary loyalists, often to support criminal enterprises such as drug dealing. The coercive arms of the state – notably the police – are mostly engaged in trying to prevent this private enterprise coercion.

- State coercion of important minorities conventionally labelled 'deviant' has greatly declined. The most striking example concerns gay men. Many British cities now have openly run 'gay villages'; as recently as the 1970s – and indeed for part of the 1980s – significant police resources went into the surveillance and attempted prosecution of gay people for allegedly breaching rules that same sex relations could only be practised in private.

- Coercion of ethnic minorities was widespread in the 1970s and 1980s, notably in police harassment of young black people using 'stop and search' laws. As we saw in our sketch of some scandals of recent years (see Chapter 22) there is still argument about the extent of institutional racism in police forces. Periodic journalistic exposes still uncover examples of crude police racism and brutality against black people. But the arguments about institutional racism, and concerted official police campaigns to extinguish both conscious and unconscious racism, have greatly changed the climate of policing. It would be very hard to argue, whatever level of harassment now exists, that it is not significantly lower than was the case 30 years ago.

The second ground for scepticism about the 'new age of authoritarianism' thesis is that there has been a rise in legal and institutional safeguards against the arbitrary exercise of state power. Chapters 21 and 22 painted a picture of great institutional and legal change in recent years. These involved building institutions concerned with the redress of grievances. The original creation of the Parliamentary Ombudsman in 1967 was the start of a movement of widespread institutional reform that has spread across the public sector. This movement has also

People in Politics 23.1

Public intellectuals in political life

Michael Oakeshott (1901–90)

Though he wrote comparatively little and avoided public engagement Oakeshott had a deep effect on public life in Britain. He professed a profoundly sceptical conservatism in elegant English prose and thus exerted a great effect over the minds of many practising Conservatives. Curiously, his influence did not extend to the greatest modern Conservative leader: Margaret Thatcher was instinctively a reformer of the kind Oakeshott disavowed.

Anthony Crosland (1918–77)

A quintessential public intellectual. His *The Future of Socialism* (1956) was the key restatement of 'revisionist' democratic socialism (see Documenting Politics 15.3). For over 20 years following its publication Crosland remained the most prominent Labour Party intellectual, but he was also a leading figure in successive Labour Governments and a Cabinet member, 1965–70 and 1974–77. He died suddenly while holding office as Foreign Secretary.

Eric Hobsbawm (1917–),

A refugee from German Nazism in the 1930s, and is best known as one of the most distinguished social historians of the last century. But Hobsbawm also made a long journey from classical Marxism to more revisionist views characteristic of many public intellectuals. His 1978 Marx Memorial lecture, 'The Forward March of Labour Halted', although delivered in the spirit of revising Marx, anticipated many of the key conclusions of New Labour in Britain.

Cartoons: Shaun Steele

■ Possibly the greatest public intellectual of the last century was J. M. Keynes (profiled in People in Politics 20.1). He defined the importance of the public intellectual in a famous passage: 'The ideas of economists and political philosophers, both when they are right and when they are wrong, are more powerful than is commonly understood ... Madmen in authority, who hear voices in the air, are distilling their frenzy from some academic scribbler of a few years back' (Keynes 1936, ch. 4). These three profiles show that 'academic scribbling' can take many different forms.

increasingly involved, as we saw in Chapter 22, the transformation of informal codes into statutes, and therefore the embedding of many safeguards for citizens in the law. The culmination of this movement was the passage of the Human Rights Act (see Briefing 22.7). The exemptions from some of the safeguards of that Act operated by the Government in respect of its anti-terrorism measures amount to serious breaches of its safeguards. But the passage of the Act, and the fact that most of its measures remain unbreached, amounts to a great advance in safeguarding liberties.

A final ground for scepticism about the authoritarianism thesis is that we have seen the rise of citizen activism. The Human Rights Act did not appear unexpectedly. It was the product of profound changes in the British political culture that have made many old forms of coercion untenable. In some instances these changes have taken the form of the development of groups that campaign against the coercive exercise of state power, advocating the case for stigmatized groups, like asylum seekers. These advocacy groups are often weak and poorly resourced, but their emergence represents an increase, not a decrease, in resistance to state authoritarianism. More generally, in a number of chapters (notably 8 and 13) we have seen that the picture of the British as politically apathetic is inaccurate. The biggest falls have been in 'officially' approved forms of participation, like voting, and in membership of the characteristic organization of the political class that still dominates Westminster government – the big political party. But there has been an explosion of single-issue groups, and of more long term campaigning movements, such as those concerned with the environment. When the state tried to realize authoritarian ambitions it faces a better-organized and less deferential civil society than was the case even 30 years ago.

BRITISH POLITICS AFTER THE END OF THE GREAT STABILITY

'The Great Stability' (sometimes 'the Great Moderation') is the name increasingly given to the period of economic history between 1992–2007. In the countries of the advanced capitalist world it was the first sustained period of economic expansion since the 1960s. Britain shared this apparently benign period. By the new millennium the then Chancellor of the Exchequer, Gordon Brown, was able to boast that the country had undergone the longest uninterrupted period of economic growth since records began. Alongside economic growth went other benign features: from 1997 recorded unemployment fell to a point where the economy could be said

to have full employment; inflation, which in the last great boom in the capitalist world between the 1940s and the 1960s had been a serious problem, was controlled at low levels. The period was one of 'Great Stability' because at the macro-economic level (the level of the whole economy) governments seemed able to combine continuous economic growth with stable control over features such as the price level and the level of unemployment.

Some dissenters argued that in the case of the UK this apparent golden age was an illusion, created by the short term impact of expanded public spending, a consumer boom funded by huge levels of personal debt, and an unsustainable house price boom funded likewise by imprudent mortgage lending (see for example Elliott and Atkinson 2007). Whether the Great Stability was an illusion or not will be hotly debated for years to come, but three observations are incontrovertible: illusion or not, it stabilized not only British politics but the British political settlement in the 1990s and the beginning of the new millennium; it ended in a spectacular crash in 2007–08; and its end has left large question marks against the stability of the UK as a political system. Let us look at each of these in turn.

The stable political settlement

If we look back a quarter of a century or so at how observers then pictured the future of Britain what is striking is their pessimism. The prevailing images were of Britain in decline; of the likely break-up of the UK; of a society and a politics divided against itself in ferocious, destructive, sectional struggles (see Nairn 1981; Beer 1982; Moran 1985; Gamble 1994). Yet none of these apocalyptic outcomes came to pass. In the 1990s great strides were made in settling the most violent of all issues, that of Northern Ireland, and a devolved constitutional settlement, albeit a changing one, was worked out for Wales and Scotland. A key reason for this was that the new era of economic stability underpinned a new era of political stability.

The British economy, having performed poorly for a century up to the 1970s, and spectacularly badly during that decade, performed unusually well between the early 1990s and 2007. We enjoyed the longest uninterrupted period of economic growth since at least 1870. The rates of economic growth – the commonest measure of national economic success – were not as high as those recorded at the peaks of economic growth a half-century ago in the 1950s, but there was a critical difference: in the 1950s Britain was an international laggard, her economy pulled along by the superior performance of miracle economies like the German and the Japanese; now, Britain at least matched, and often outpaced, the performance of the other leading industrial nations. The

POLITICAL ISSUES 23.1

Exporting the British model

Should the British model of government be exported? Historically the answer given was a resounding 'yes'. Empire was used to export not only the general idea of a British style democracy, but even the particular forms of Westminster – leading to the notion of the Westminster Parliament as 'the mother of Parliaments'. The elites who ruled Commonwealth nations following decolonization in the 1950s and 1960s were very often educated at elite British universities, like Cambridge, Oxford and the London School of Economics, and initially ran Westminster style governing systems. Disillusionment with 'export' set in with the collapse of most of these Westminster style democracies into dictatorships, and with the collapse of confidence within Britain, in the face of imperial dissolution and economic crisis. But the idea of 'export' has revived in the last two decades. Two kinds of exports have been especially important:

- British institutions have tried to encourage international emulation of the British privatization revolution. Firms from the City of London have been in the forefront selling British privatization expertise.

- Through its influence in institutions like the World Bank Britain has supported the doctrine that aid to poor countries should be contingent on adopting 'good governance': in practice this means a stress on eliminating corruption from the administration of government.

Three important issues are raised by this new export trade:

- Is there 'a' British model to be exported? The merits of the British privatization programme, and the associated drive for deregulated markets, are deeply contested within Britain. They have become more contested still since the onset of the great economic crisis after 2007.

- The older attempts at export – for instance of the model of 'Westminster democracy' – failed in part because they were not adapted to the cultural and social settings to which they were transplanted. Opponents of the new export models argue likewise that mass privatization and free markets are entirely inappropriate to societies where poverty has prevented the development of any sophisticated infrastructure of services.

- The export of models is not always a voluntary exercise: in a deeply unequal world countries may be given no choice. In the case of good governance, receiving aid is contingent on adopting a foreign model; in the extreme case, like Iraq in 2003, an attempt is made to impose a democratic model by force, backed by American military power with British partnership.

consequences of a long economic boom were both psychological and material. Whatever the real origins of the boom, political leaders in the Westminster system believed that the transformation was due to revolutionary changes in policy introduced in the 1980s and 1990s. As late as 2007, when Tony Blair was still Prime Minister and David Cameron was the new, reforming leader of the Conservative Party, they shared the view that the original Thatcherite reforms have made Britain a model economy that our European neighbours should emulate. When Gordon Brown became Prime Minister in 2007 almost his first act was to organize a photoshoot in Downing Street with Mrs Thatcher. The Conservative

leadership, meanwhile, presumed that economic growth would continue, and argued mainly about how to allocate the growth dividend between increased spending and reduced taxes.

The Great Crash

The economic catastrophe that is the Great Crash of 2007–08 can be summarized thus. It began as a crisis of confidence in parts of the American financial system which had pioneered loans to high risk borrowers, especially in the housing market. It rapidly showed up in the UK in September–October 2007 in the first public 'run' on a bank (Northern Rock) since the middle of the nineteenth century, as depositors queued outside bank branches to withdraw their money. The state was forced to take Northern Rock into public ownership and to guarantee all deposits (up to a maximum of £50,000) in all British banks. But this proved merely a foretaste of catastrophe. In autumn 2008 the whole US financial system came close to collapse, and the same fate was only averted in Britain by hugely expensive state guarantees, the nationalization of several large institutions and a virtual state takeover of nearly all the largest banks. The financial crisis was rapidly transmitted to the rest of the economy: property prices first stalled and then began to fall rapidly; consumer confidence plummeted, leading to a crisis of demand across the retail sector and key industries, like car manufacturing. Unemployment began to rise rapidly.

The dreadful economic consequences of the Great Crash are thus obvious. But it also had political consequences, of which the following should be highlighted.

It turned financial market regulation into a political issue once more. For a quarter of a century the notion that financial markets should be subject to light touch regulation, and should be kept free from political control (for which read: free from democratic politics), dominated the minds of market actors and public policy makers. After the crisis all but the most zealous of free market advocates came to the view that a considerable increase in political control over financial markets was needed. After almost a generation when leading politicians of all main parties had celebrated the City of London as an emblem of British economic success that should be left to get on with its own business, both government and opposition now pledged to tighten legal controls.

It nationalized whole parts of the financial system. This was perhaps the most dramatic effect because it happened with such speed, usually under the threat of the collapse of leading financial institutions. In Britain the first great event of the crisis occurred in September 2007 when the Treasury was obliged to take into public ownership a failing bank, Northern Rock. Thus it reversed one of the defining features of the Thatcherite consensus to which New Labour also subscribed: that as much as possible of economic activity should be privatized.

It made politicians managers of the financial system. The wave of nationalization was itself the sign of a wider shift: a huge increase in the importance of politicians in financial management. The ferocity of the crisis sucked politicians into the detail of managing markets: brokering mergers and takeovers to rescue failing institutions; extending the guarantees of protection to depositors in retail banks against the threat of collapse, to the point where the state was guaranteeing virtually

IMAGE 23.2 ■ The British state: coercion and symbolic attachment

■ In Chapter 1 we described Max Weber's famous definition of the state as a coercive institution, but we also saw that it ran on the power of symbolic attachment. The final image in this book sums up the two sides of the British state. The photo was taken after an emergency at Buckingham Palace. The Guards in the background symbolize the state, and are of course a well known tourist attraction in London. The police officer with the submachine gun represents the face the state shows when it is threatened.

all deposits in the system; using treasury and central bank resources to supply the financial markets with liquidity to try to keep trading going.

It ended the ideological dominance of the 'Anglo-American model' of capitalism. The notion that the UK was, with the US, a model of capitalism that should be exported to other systems, especially across the EU, was one which leading British politicians, inside and outside government, espoused in the era of the 'Great Stability' (see Political Issues 23.1). After 2007–08 the idea that the future rested with British-style lightly regulated financial markets where virtually all assets were turned into tradeable securities was little heard of again.

British politics after the Great Crash

We have seen that the Great Stability helped rescue the UK. Its passing away, and the catastrophic manner of its demise, plainly revives the question of whether the UK can survive. In its struggle to stabilize the devolution settlement Mr Brown's Government argued that the financial crisis, and its management, vindicated the Westminster model. As we noted in Chapter 10, the crisis did indeed raise questions about the viability of inde-

DEBATING POLITICS 23.1

The future of British democracy: pessimism or optimism?

THE FUTURE OF BRITISH DEMOCRACY IS SECURE	THE FUTURE OF BRITISH DEMOCRACY IS UNDER THREAT
▶ Democratic government has shown an impressive ability to solve problems and learn from mistakes. ▶ The vast majority of Britons support democratic freedoms. ▶ The legal safeguards for democratic liberties have been strengthened in recent years. ▶ In wider society people are smarter and more confident than in the past in exercising their rights of democratic citizenship.	▶ A world of terrorist threats is producing great pressure to curb democratic liberties, in Britain and elsewhere. ▶ The state is continually increasing its control and surveillance capacities. ▶ Although only a minority, those who reject democratic politics are vociferous, active and well organized. ▶ Most people across the globe do not live under stable democratic government. Why should Britain remain an exception?

pendent small nations: the very exemplars to which the Scottish Nationalists, in particular, pointed were among the most spectacular victims of the crash. Ireland and Iceland arc two obvious examples. It was also indeed the case that the management of the crisis, insofar as it was a British affair, was an affair of the Wesminster system: indeed, largely of the core Executive and a segment of the London based business elite. Institutions beyond this privileged circle participated mostly as victims suffering collateral damage: the most spectacular participant and victim was the Royal Bank of Scotland, a venerable Scottish institution all but destroyed and put under the control of an elite of London financiers and Treasury officials.

But rapid footwork on the part of the core Executive could not conceal a key fact: the political failures that contributed to the Great Crash were failures primarily of the Westminster system. The system of regulation, especially the regulation of the financial system, which was weighed in the balance and found wanting in 2007–08, was a metropolitan creation. It was formed of institutions like the Bank of England, which were quintessential examples of the institutions that had dominated metropolitan politics. The key regulator, the Financial Services Authority (FSA), was in every sense of the word a London based body: not only headquartered in London, but tied into the networks of the core Executive and the City of London. Indeed, it is now common ground that the root of regulatory failures lay in the excessively close

relationship between the FSA and the interests in the City which it was supposed to control. Above all, the castastrophic crisis that flooded over the economy after 2007 was also a catastrophic crisis for the system of economic management practised by the Westminster core Executive. There exists, as we saw in Chapter 20, a great fiscal crisis of the state as a result of the costs of financial rescue and the losses of economic recession (see especially Briefing 20.1). The consensus that bound together all the leading Westminster politicians for 15 years about the best way to run the British economy has been found wanting.

The resilience of democratic political systems is great, since their open and liberal character maximizes the chance of learning from failure. But the scale of failure since 2007 means that learning will have to be fast and great. The last consensus was a result of such learning, mostly under the political leadership of Mrs Thatcher. Whether the present crisis will produce a figure of comparable substantive and symbolic importance we do not yet know.

THE FUTURE OF BRITISH POLITICS

The likelihood that the economic crisis can produce a leader of the stature of Margaret Thatcher is now bound up with the aftermath of the May 2010 general election. Whatever its long term consequences we can already say that the result is epochal. It brought to an end an epoch of single party government in the UK; the last coalition was formed in the great crisis of world war and ended when the war ended in 1945. The failure of the Conservatives to win a majority of seats in the House of Commons radically changed the rules of the game. A party system built on adversarialism – on the presumption that the point of party life in the House of Commons is to oppose other parties – now has to work with a coalition of two of the three main parties. In a few days after the result became known on the morning of Friday 7 May all the party leaders had to learn fast how to go about the job of constructing a coalition. David Cameron, as Prime Minister heading a coalition, faced a set of tasks which no Prime Minister had faced in over 60 years: he not only had to manage his own Conservative Party colleagues; he also had to manage the Liberals in Parliament. Moreover, not only did he have to make a Cabinet and a Government under the constraint of ensuring Liberal representation, and the agreement of Nick Clegg, the Liberal Democrats Leader; he knew that in any future reconstruction of the coalition he could only dismiss Liberal Democrat ministers with the agreement of Clegg.

These novel features of style and party management are, though, only a small part of the potentially far reaching consequences of 6 May. The coalition agreement, the full details of which were published just a fortnight after the general election, commited to a wide range of institutional reforms. (The full document, covering the whole programme of government, indeed runs to 36 pages.) Out of a long list of institutional reforms, four had the potential radically to change the Westminster system. They were:

● a commitment to introduce fixed-term, five-year parliaments;
● a referendum on the introduction of the alternative vote to replace the existing 'first past the post' electoral system for elections to the Westminster Parliament;

● a provision for recall of MPs between general elections on the strength of support from 10 per cent of constituents;
● a committee to bring forward proposals for a mainly, or wholly, elected Upper House.

Each of these has the potential radically to change the way the system works. Fixed term parliaments will eliminate a key function – and a key source of power – of prime ministers: the power to choose the most advantageous date in the parliamentary cycle on which to call an election. The alternative vote referendum was the Liberal Democrat's main price for participation in the coalition, because they believe it an essential step to the introduction of more comprehensive systems of proportional representation (PR) – and on PR, the Party believes, depends its prospects as a player in future governments. 'Recall' has the potential to change the relationship between MPs and constituents. Finally, an elected Upper House will introduce a rival assembly to the House of Commons, able to claim some of the legitimacy that comes from popular election.

The sum total of these reforms would be to change significantly the distribution of power within the Westminster system. The shadow of Mrs Thatcher – most assertive of peace time Prime Ministers – has often cast itself over the pages of this book. Thatcher was able to survive as a powerful, decisive figure who overrode opposition because she controlled the Executive, and through the Executive, Parliament. That control actually rested on a narrow electoral base; she accumulated huge majorities in the Commons on the basis of minority electoral support, and moreover electoral support concentrated in the south east of England. A reformed Westminster system may well produce leaders with the impact of Thatcher; but they will have to operate in a very different manner from her, and under constraints that she would have found intolerable.

Review OF CHAPTER 23

This chapter has:

◖◗ Reviewed important interpretations of the changing nature of British government.

◖◗ Sketched the most important long term changes that are coming over the system.

◖◗ Described the great economic crisis of 2007–08 and its consequences for the system of government.

◖◗ Examined the impact of the first coalition government since 1945 on governance in the Westminster system.

FURTHER READING

For this final chapter I have not made the usual division between 'essential' and 'recommended' reading. Making sense of the future of British politics demands continual attention to the everyday conduct of the political system. But Flinders et al. (2009) contains the most comprehensive, and up to date, collection that examines many of the themes examined in this chapter. If the coalition established in May 2010 endures, then its programme will be of momentous significance for the Westminster system. An outline of the programme can be downloaded at http://www.direct.gov.uk/en/Nl1/Newsroom/DG_187877.

Bibliography

Adshead, M. and Tonge, J. (2009). *Politics in Ireland: convergence and divergence in a two-polity island.* Basingstoke: Palgrave Macmillan.

Alford, B. (1996). *Britain in the World Economy Since 1880.* London: Longman.

Almond. G. and Verba, S. (1963). *The Civic Culture.* Boston, MA: Little, Brown.

—— eds. (1980). *The Civic Culture Revisited.* Boston, MA: Little, Brown.

Atkinson, A.B. (2000). 'Distribution of income and wealth' in A.H. Halsey and J. Webb, eds, *Twentieth-Century British Social Trends.* Basingstoke: Palgrave Macmillan, pp. 348–81.

Bagehot, W. (1867/1963), *The English Constitution.* London: Watts.

Bartle, J. and Griffiths, D. eds, (2001). *Political Communications Transformed: from Morrison to Mandelson.* Basingstoke: Palgrave Macmillan.

Beer, S. (1969/82). *Modern British Politics: a study of parties and pressure groups.* London: Faber & Faber.

—— (1982). *Britain Against Itself.* London: Faber.

Beetham, D., Byrne, I., Noan, P. and Weir, S. (2002). *Democracy Under Blair: a democratic audit of the United Kingdom.* London: Politico's.

Bevir, M. and Rhodes, R. (2003). *Interpreting British Governance.* London: Routledge.

—— (2006). *Governance Stories.* London: Routledge.

—— (2010). *The State as Cultural Practice.* Oxford: Oxford University Press.

Bogdanor, V. (1999). *Devolution in the United Kingdom.* Oxford: Oxford University Press.

—— (2009). *The New British Constitution.* Oxford: Hart.

Bradbury, J. and Mitchell, J. (2007). 'The constituency work of members of the Scottish Parliament and National Assembly for Wales: approaches, relationships and rules', *Regional & Federal Studies*, 17:1, 117–45.

Bradley, A. (2000). 'The sovereignty of Parliament', in J. Jowell and D. Oliver, eds, *The Changing Constitution*, 4th edn. Oxford: Oxford University Press, pp. 23–58.

Brandreth, G. (1999). *Breaking the Cone: Westminster diaries, 1992–1997.* London: Phoenix.

Brazier, R. (1999). *Constitutional Practice: the foundations of British government.* 3rd edn. Oxford: Oxford University Press.

Bromley, C., Curtice, J. and Seyd, B. (2001). 'Political engagement, trust and constitutional reform' in A. Park, J. Curtice, K. Thomson, L. Jarvis, and C. Bromley, eds, *British Social Attitudes: the 18th Report. Public policy, social ties.* London: Sage, pp. 199–225.

Brymin, M. and Newton, K. (2003). 'The national press and voting turnout: British General Elections of 1992 and 1997', *Political Communication*, 20:1, 59–77.

BSE Inquiry (2000). *The Inquiry into BSE and Variant CJD in the United Kingdom, Volume 1, Findings and Conclusions.* www.bseinquiry.gov.uk.

Bulmer, S. and Burch. M. (2000). 'The Europeanisation of British central government' in R. Rhodes, ed., *Transforming British Government, volume 1, Changing Institutions.* Basingstoke: Palgrave Macmillan, pp 46–62.

—— (2009). *The Europeanisation of Whitehall: UK central government and the European Union.* Manchester: Manchester University Press.

Bulmer, S., Burch, M., Carter, C., Hogwood, P., and Scott, A. (2002). *British Devolution and European Policy-Making: transforming Britain into multi-level governance.* Basingstoke: Palgrave Macmillan.

Bulpitt, J. (1983). *Territory and Power in the United Kingdom.* Manchester: Manchester University Press.

Burch, M. and Holliday, I (1996). *The British Cabinet System.* London: Prentice Hall.

—— (2004). 'The Blair Government and the Core Executive', *Government and Opposition*, 39:1, 1–21.

Butler, D. and Stokes, D. (1974). *Political Change in Britain.* London: Macmillan.

Butler, D. and Butler, G. (2000). *Twentieth Century British Political Facts*, 8th edn, Basingstoke: Palgrave Macmillan.

Butler, R. (2004). *Review of Intelligence on Weapons of Mass Destruction: report of a committee of privy counsellors. Chairman: The Rt Hon Lord Butler of Brockwell.* HC898, 2003–4. Also accessible at http://www.butlerreview.org.uk.

Cain, B., Dalton, R., Scarrow, S., eds, (2003). *Democracy Transformed? Expanding political opportunities in advanced industrial democracies.* Oxford: Oxford University Press.

Castells, M. (2000). *The Rise of the Network Society.* Malden, MA: Blackwell.

—— (2001). 'European unification in the age of the network state'. www.opendemocracy.net/debates/article-3-51-347.asp.

Clark, T. and Dilnot, A. (2002). *Long-Term Trends in British Taxation and Spending.* London: Institute of Fiscal Studies, Briefing note 25. www.ifs.org.uk/public/bn25pdf.

Clarke, H., Sanders, D., Stewart, M. and Whiteley, P. (2004). *Political Choice in Britain.* Oxford: Oxford University Press.

Coates, D. (2000a). *Models of Capitalism: Growth and stagnation in the modern era.* Cambridge: Polity.

—— (2000b). 'The character of New Labour' in Coates, D. and Lawler, P., eds, *New Labour in Power.* Manchester: Manchester University Press, pp. 1–15.

Coen, D. (1997). 'The evolution of the large firm as a political actor in the European Union'. *Journal of European Public Policy*, 4/1: 91–108.

—— (1998). 'The European Business Interest and the Nation State: large firm lobbying in the European Union and member states'. *Journal of Public Policy*, 18/1: 75–100.

—— (1999). 'The impact of US lobbying practice on the European business-government relationship'. *California Management Review*, 41/4: 27–44.

—— (2002). 'Business Interests and Integration' in R. Bulme, D. Chambre and V. Wright, eds, *Collective Action in the European Union*. Paris: Science-Po Press, pp. 255–72.

—— (2007a). 'Empirical and theoretical studies in EU lobbying'. *Journal of European Public Policy*, 14/3, 333–45.

—— (2007b). *Lobbying in the European Union*. Brussels: European Parliament, PE 393.266. www.library.ep.ec.

Cohen, N. (2003). *Pretty Straight Guys*. London: Faber.

Colley, L. (1996). *Britons: forging the nation 1707–1837*. London: Verso.

Collier, P. (2008). *The Bottom Billion: why the poorest countries are failing and what can be done about it*. Oxford: Oxford University Press.

Committee on Standards in Public Life (2008). *Survey of Public Attitudes Towards Conduct in Public Life 2008*. London: Committee on Standards in Public Life.

Conservative Party (2004). 'European Constitution: bad for Britain'. www.conservatives.com.campaigns.display.

Cook, C. and Stevenson, J. (1983). *The Longman Handbook of Modern British History, 1714–1980*. London: Longman.

—— (2000) *The Longman Companion to Britain Since 1945*, 2nd edn. London: Longman.

Cowley, P. (2002). *Revolts and Rebellions: parliamentary voting under Blair*. London: Politico's.

—— (2005). *The Rebels*. London: Politico's.

Crick, B. (1998). *Advisory Group on Citizenship: education for citizenship and the teaching of democracy in schools. Final report*. London: Qualifications and Curriculum Authority.

—— (2000). *In Defence of Politics*. 5th edn. London: Continuum.

Criddle, B. (2002). 'MPs and candidates' in D. Butler and D. Kavanagh, *The British General Election of 2001*. Basingstoke: Palgrave Macmillan, pp. 182–207.

Crosland, C. A. R. (1956/64). *The Future of Socialism*. London: Jonathan Cape.

Curtice J. (2009). 'Public attitudes and elections' in P. Cairney, ed., *Scotland Devolution Monitoring Report 2009*. London: University College Constitution Unit, pp. 17–29.

Customs and Excise (2003). *Annual Report 2002–3*. www.hmce.gov.uk/reports/ann/2002-3-stats.

Dahl, R. (1984). *Modern Political Analysis*, 4th edn. Englewood Cliffs, NJ: Prentice Hall.

Day, J. (2002). 'Blair doubles the cost of spin', *The Guardian*, 25 July.

Denver, D. (2006). *Elections and Voters in Britain*. 2nd edn. Basingstoke: Palgrave Macmillan

Department for Local Government, Transport and the Regions (2002). *Local Government Financial Statistics*. London: DLTR.

Department of Communities and Local Government (2009). *Local Government Finance: Key Facts*. London: Department of Communities and Local Government.

Doherty, B., Paterson, M., Plows, A. Wall, D. (2003). 'Explaining the fuel protests', *British Journal of Politics and International Relations*, 5:1, 1–23.

Downs, A. (1957). *An Economic Theory of Democracy*. London: Harper-Collins.

Dryzek, J. and Dunleavy, P. (2009). *Theories of the Democratic State*. Basingstoke: Palgrave Macmillan.

Dunleavy, P. (1981). *The Politics of Mass Housing 1945–75*. Oxford: Clarendon Press.

—— (1991). *Democracy, Bureaucracy and Public Choice*. London: Harvester Wheatsheaf.

Easton, D. (1965). *A Systems Analysis of Political Life*. New York: Wiley.

Economic and Social Research Council (2004). *Delivering Public Policy After Devolution: Diverging from Westminster*. Devolution and Constitutional Change Research Programme. Birmingham: University of Birmingham.

Electoral Commission (2002c). 'The electoral commission's youth campaign'. www.electoralcommission.org.uk.

—— (2002a). *Voter Engagement among Black and Ethnic Minority Communities*. London: Electoral Commission.

—— (2002b). *Modernising Elections*. London: Electoral Commission.

—— (2004). *Delivering Democracy: the future of postal voting*. London: Electoral Commission.

—— (2005). *Understanding Electoral Registration: the extent and nature of non-registration in Britain*. London: Electoral Commission.

—— (2007). *Allegations of Electoral Malpractice in England and Wales 2000–2006*. London: Electoral Commission.

—— (2008). *Electoral Administration in the United Kingdom*. London: Electoral Commission.

—— (2009). *Allegations of Electoral Malpractice at the*

May 2008 Elections in England and Wales. London: Electoral Commission.

Elliott, L. and Atkinson, D. (2007). *Fantasy Island: waking up to the incredible economic, political and social illusions of the Blair legacy*. London: Constable.

English, R. (2004). *Armed Struggle: the history of the IRA*. London: Pan.

—— (2007). *Irish Freedom: a history of Irish nationalism*. London: Pan.

Equality and Human Rights Commission (2008). *Sex and Power Report 2008*. London: Equality and Human Rights Commission.

Esping-Andersen, G. (1990). *The Three Worlds of Welfare Capitalism*. Princton, NJ: Princeton University Press.

European Court of Human Rights (2009). *The European Court of Human Rights: some facts and figures 1959–2009*. http://www.echr.coe.int/NR/rdonlyres/65172 EB7-DE1C-4BB8-93B1-B28676C2C844/0/FactsAnd FiguresEN.pdf.

Farrell, D. (2001). *Electoral Systems: a comparative introduction*. Basingstoke: Palgrave Macmillan.

Fisher, J. (2003). 'Party finance: new rules, same old story?', *Politics Review*, April, 30–33.

Flinders, M. (2008). *Delegated Governance and the British State: walking without order*. Oxford: Oxford University Press.

Flinders, M. Gamble, A., Hay, C. and Kenny, M. (2009). eds, *The Oxford Handbook of British Politics*. Oxford: Oxford University Press.

Foreign and Commonwealth Office (2003). *Annual Report*. (London: FCO.)

Franks, Sir O. (1957). *Report of the Committee on Administrative Tribunals and Enquiries*, London: HMSO, cmnd. 218.

Furbey, R., Dinham, A., Farnell, R., Finneron, D. and Wilkinson, G. (2006). *Faith as Social Capital: connecting or dividing?* Bristol: Policy Press.

Furlong, P. and Marsh, D. (2010). 'A skin not a sweater: ontology and epistemology in political science', in D. Marsh and G. Stoker, eds, *Theory and Methods in Political Science*, 3rd edn. Basingstoke: Palgrave Macmillan, pp. 184–211.

Gallie, D. (2000). 'The labour force' in A. H. Halsey and J. Webb, eds, *Twentieth Century British Social Trends*, Basingstoke, Palgrave Macmillan: 281–323.

Gamble, A. (1974). *The Conservative Nation*. London: Routledge.

—— (1981/1994). *Britain in decline: economic policy, political strategy and the British state*, 4th edn. London: Macmillan.

—— (1994). *The Free Market and the Strong State: the politics of Thatcherism*, 2nd edn. London: Macmillan.

—— (2003). *Between Europe and America: the future of British politics*. Basingstoke: Palgrave Macmillan.

—— (2009). *The Spectre at the Feast: capitalist crisis and the politics of recession*. Basingstoke: Palgrave Macmillan.

Gearty, C. (2007). *Civil Liberties*. Oxford: Oxford University Press.

George, S. (1998). *An Awkward Partner: Britain in the European Community*. Oxford: Oxford University Press.

Goodin, R. and Le Grand, J. (1987). *Not Only the Poor: the middle classes and the welfare state*. London: Allen & Unwin.

Gould, P. (1998). *The Unfinished Revolution: how the modernisers saved the Labour Party*. London: Abacus.

Grant, W. (2000). *Pressure Groups and British Politics*. Basingstoke: Palgrave Macmillan.

—— (2002). *Economic Policy in Britain*. Basingstoke: Palgrave Macmillan.

Grant, W. and Marsh, D. (1977). *The Confederation of British Industry*. London: Hodder & Stoughton.

Griffith, J. (1977). *The Politics of the Judiciary*. London: Fontana.

Guttsman, W.L. (1963). *The British Political Elite*. London: Macgibbon & Kee.

Hall, P. (1999). 'Social capital in Britain', *British Journal of Political Science*, 29:3, 417–61.

Hall, S. and Jacques, M. eds, (1983). *The Politics of Thatcherism*. London: Lawrence & Wishart.

Halsey, A. H. and Webb, J. eds, (2000). *Twentieth-Century British Social Trends*. Basingstoke: Palgrave Macmillan.

Harris, K. (1982). *Attlee*. London: Weidenfeld & Nicolson.

Harrison, B. (1996). *The Transformation of British Politics, 1860–1995*. Oxford: Oxford University Press.

Haubrich, D. (2003). 'Anti-terror laws and civil liberties', *Government and Opposition*, 38:1, 3–28.

Hay, C. (2007). *Why We Hate Politics*. Oxford: Polity.

Hazell, R. (2003). *The State of the Nations 2003: the third year of devolution in the United Kingdom*, Exeter: Imprint Academic.

HC Information Office (2010). *Private Members' Bills Procedures*. London: HC Information Office.; http://www.parliament.uk/documents/commons-information-office/l02.pdf.

Heath, A. and C. Payne, (2000). 'Social mobility' in A. H. Halsey and J. Webb, eds, *Twentieth Century British Social Trends*, Basingstoke: Palgrave Macmillan, pp. 254–80.

Heath, A., Jowell, R. and Curtice, J. (2001). *The Rise of New Labour: party policies and voter choices*. Oxford: Oxford University Press.

Henke, D. (2008). 'Long hours and obsession with minutiae. No 10's private man.' *The Guardian*, 25 June, p. 12.

Hennessy, P. (2001). *The Prime Minister: the office and its holders since 1945*. London: Penguin.

Heseltine, M. (2000). *Life in the Jungle: my autobiography*. London: Hodder & Stoughton.

Hill, M. (2009). *The Public Policy Process*. London: Longman.

Hills, J, Sefton, T. and Stewart, K. (eds) (2009). *Towards a More Equal Society? Poverty, inequality and policy since 1997*. Bristol: The Policy Press.

Hirst, P. Thompson, G. and Bromley, S. (2009). *Globalization in Question*, 3rd edn. Oxford: Polity.

HM Treasury (2004). *Economic Data and Tools*. www.hm-treasury.gov.uk.

Hobsbawm, E. (1962/97). *The Age of Revolution*. London: Abacus.

Hood, C., Rothstein, H. and Baldwin, R. (2001). *Government of Risk: understanding risk regulatory regimes*. Oxford: Oxford University Press.

Hood, C., Scott, C., James, O., Jones, G. and Travers, T. (1999). *Regulation Inside Government: waste-watchers, quality police, and sleaze-busters*. Oxford: Oxford University Press.

Hopkin, J. (2009). 'Party Matters: devolution and party change in the UK and Spain', *Party Politics*: 15(2): 179–99.

Houghton, Lord D. (1976). *Report of the Committee on Financial Aid to Political Parties*. London: HMSO, Cmd. 6601.

House of Commons Information Service (2009). *Members' Pay, Pensions and Allowances*. London: House of Commons, FS No. M6, Ed. 3.11

House of Lords (2008). Communications Committee – *First Report Government Communications*. http://www.publications.parliament.uk/pa/ld200809/ldselect/ldcomuni/7/702.htm.

Howell, D. (1980). *British Social Democracy: a study in development and decay*. 2nd edn. New York: St Martin's Press.

Hutton, B. 2004. *Report of the Inquiry into the Circumstances Surrounding the Death of Dr. David Kelly*. London: The Stationery Office, HC 247.

Inland Revenue (2004). *Tax Receipts and Taxpayers*. www.inlandrevenue.gov.uk/stats/tax_receipts/g_t01_1.htm.

Jenkins, K. Caines, K., and Jackson, A. (1988). *Improving Management in Government: the next steps*. London: Her Majesty's Stationery Office.

Johnston, L. (1999). *Policing in Britain*. London: Longman.

Johnston, R. and Pattie, C. (2006). *Putting Voters in their Place: geography and elections in Great Britain*. Oxford: Oxford University Press.

Jones, B. (2004). 'Is Tony a Tory?', *Politics Review, September, 20–3*.

Jowell, J. and Cooper, J. eds, (2003). *Delivering Rights: how the Human Rights Act is working and for whom*. Oxford: Hart.

Jowell, J. and Oliver, D. (2007). *The Changing Constitution*, 6th edn. Oxford: Oxford University Press.

Judge, D. (1993). *The Parliamentary State*. London: Sage.

——— (1999). *Representation: theory and practice in Britain*. London: Routledge.

Judt, T. (2007). *Postwar: A history of Europe since 1945*. London: Pimlico.

Katz, R. and Mair, P. (1995). 'Changing models of party organization and party democracy: the emergence of the cartel party.' *Party Politics*, 1:1, 5–28.

Kavanagh, D. and Seldon, A. (1999). *The Power Behind the Prime Minister: the hidden influence of Number Ten*. London: Harper Collins.

Keating, M. (2005). *The Government of Scotland: public policy making after devolution*. Edinburgh: Edinburgh University Press.

Kelly, R. (1999). 'Power in the Conservative Party: the Hague effect', *Politics Review*, February, 28–30.

——— (2001) 'Farewell conference, hello forum: Labour and Tory policy-making', *Politics Review*, September, 30–33.

Kelly, R. and White, I. (2009). *All Women Shortlists*. London: House of Commons Library. http://www.parliament.uk/commons/lib/research/briefings/snpc-05057.pdf.

Kennedy, P. (1989). *The Rise and Fall of the Great Powers*. London: Fontana.

Keynes, J.M. (1936). *The General Theory of Employment, Interest and Money*. London: Macmillan.

King, A., ed. (1976). *Why is Britain Becoming Harder to Govern?* London: British Broadcasting Corporation.

King, A. (2007). *The British Constitution*. Oxford: Oxford University Press.

Klingemann, H-D, Hofferbert, R. and Budge, I. (1994). *Parties, Policy and Democracy*. Boulder, CO: Westview.

Kuhn, R. (2007). *Politics and the Media in Britain*. Basingstoke: Palgrave Macmillan.

Laffin, M., Shaw, E. and Taylor, G. (2007). 'The new sub-national politics of the British Labour Party', *Party Politics*, 13:1, 88–108.

Laswell, H.D. (1950). *Politics: who gets what, when, how?* New York: Smith.

Lilleker, D., Negrine, R. and Stanyer, J. (2003). 'Britain's political communication problems', *Politics Review*, February: 29–31.

Lindblom, C. (1959). 'The science of muddling through', *Public Administration Review*, 19:1, 79–88.

Leach, S. and Wilson, D. (2000). *Local Political Leadership*. Bristol: Policy Press.

Leggatt, A. (2001). *Review of Tribunals: one service, one system*. www.tribunals-review.org.uk.

Le Seuer, A., ed., (2004). *Building the UK's New Supreme Court*. Oxford: Oxford University Press.

Local Government Association (2003a). *Fact Sheet: dates in English and Welsh local government history*. London: Local Government Association

—— (2003b). *Local Government Structures*. London: Local Government Association.

—— (2003c). *Our Work*. www.lga.gov.uk.

Lovenduski, J. and Norris, P. (2003). 'Westminster Women: the politics of presence', *Political Studies,* 51:1, 84–102.

Low, S. (1904). *The Governance of England*. London: Fisher Unwin.

Lukes, S. (2004). *Power.* Basingstoke: Palgrave Macmillan.

Lynch, P. (2006). 'Governing Devolution: understanding the office of first ministers in Scotland and Wales', *Parliamentary Affairs ,* 59: 3, 420–436

McGarvey, N. and Cairney, P. (2008). *Scottish Politics: an introduction*. Basingstoke: Palgrave Macmillan.

McKay, W. (2004). *Erskine May Parliamentary Practice, 23rd edn*. London: Parliamentary Bookshop.

McKenzie, R. (1963). *British Political Parties*, 2nd edn. London: Heinemann.

McKittrick, D. and McVea, D. (2001). *Making Sense of the Troubles*. London: Penguin.

Macpherson, C.B. (1971). *The Real World of Democracy*. Oxford: Oxford University Press.

MacPherson, Sir W. (1999). *The Stephen Lawrence Inquiry: report of an inquiry by Sir William MacPherson of Cluny*. London: HMSO, cm 4262–1.

Magee, E. and Outhwaite, M. (2001). 'Referendums and initiatives', *Politics Review,* February: 26–8.

Majone, G. (1996). *Regulating Europe*. London: Routledge.

Major, J. (1999). *John Major: the Autobiography*. London: Harper Collins.

Maloney, W., Smith, G., and Stoker, G. (2000). 'Social capital and urban governance: adding a more contextualised "top down" perspective', *Political Studies,* 48:4, 802–20.

March, J. and Olsen, J. (1984). 'The New Institutionalism: organizational factors in political life', *American Political Science Review,* 78: 734–49.

Marsh, D., Richards, D. and Smith, M. (2001). *Changing Patterns of Governance: reinventing Whitehall*. Basingstoke: Palgrave Macmillan.

Marshall, J. (2009). *Membership of UK Political Parties*. London: House of Commons Library, Standard Note SN/SG/5125. http://www.parliament.uk/documents/commons/lib/research/briefings/snsg-05125.pdf.

Middlemas, K. (1979). *Politics in Industrial Society: the experience of the British system since 1911*. London: André Deutsch.

Milward, A. (1992). *The European Rescue of the Nation-state*. London: Routledge.

Ministry of Justice (2008). *National Offender Management Service: agency framework document*. London: Ministry of Justice.

Ministry of Reconstruction (1918). *Report of the Machinery of Government Committee*. Cmd 9230.

Moran, M. (1985). *Politics and Society in Britain*. London: Macmillan.

—— (2001). 'Not steering but drowning: policy catastrophes and the regulatory state', *Political Quarterly,* 72:4, 414–27.

—— (2007). *The British Regulatory State: high modernism and hyper-innovation*. Oxford: Oxford University Press.

Moran, M., Rein, M. and Goodin, R. eds, (2008). *The Oxford Handbook of Public Policy*. Oxford: Oxford University Press.

Mughan, A. (2000). *The Media and the Presidentialization of Parliamentary Elections*. Basingstoke: Palgrave Macmillan.

Mullin, C. (2009). *A View from the Foothills: the diaries of Chris Mullin*. Ed. R. Winstone. London: Profile Books.

Nairn, T. (1981). *The Break-Up of Britain: crisis and neo-nationalism*. 2nd edn. London: Verso.

National Equality Panel (2010). An anatomy of economic inequality in the UK: Report of the National Equality Panel. London: Government Equalities Office. http://www.equalities.gov.uk/pdf/NEP%20Report%20bookmarkedfinal.pdf.

Newton, K. and Brymin, M. (2001). 'The National Press and Party Voting in the UK'. *Political Studies,* 49:2, 265–85.

Norris, P. (2001). 'Apathetic landslide: the 2001 General Election', *Parliamentary Affairs,* 54:4, 565–89.

Norris, P. and Lovenduski, J. (1995). *Parliamentary Recruitment: gender, race and class in the British Parliament*. Cambridge: Cambridge University Press.

Norton, P. (1981). *The Commons in Perspective*. Oxford: Martin Robertson.

—— (2005). *Parliament in British Politics*. Basingstoke: Palgrave Macmillan.

North East Lincolnshire Council (2002). *Renaissance: a local cultural strategy for North East Lincolnshire*. Grimsby: North East Lincolnshire Council.

Nugent, N. (2002). *The Government and Politics of the European Union*. 5th edn. Basingstoke: Palgrave Macmillan.

—— ed., (2004). *European Union Enlargement*. Basingstoke: Palgrave Macmillan.

—— (2010). *The Government and Politics of the European Union* 7th edn: Basingstoke: Palgrave Macmillan.

Office of Telecommunications (OFTEL) (2003). *Consumers' Use of Internet*. London: Oftel.

Office for National Statistics (1999). *Social Trends.* London: The Stationery Office.

——— (2008). *Social Trends.* Basingstoke: Palgrave Macmillan.

——— (2009). *Social Trends.* Basingstoke: Palgrave Macmillan.

O'Leary, B. and McGarry, J. (1996). *The Politics of Antagonism: understanding Northern Ireland*, 2nd edn. London: Athlone Press.

——— (2010). *Understanding Northern Ireland: Colonialism, Control and Consociation*, 3rd edn. London: Routledge.

Osborne, D. and Gaebler, T. (1992). *Reinventing Government: how the entrepreneurial spirit is transforming the public sector.* Reading, MA: Addison Wesley.

Parkin, F. (1968). *Middle Class Radicalism.* Manchester: Manchester University Press.

Parry, G., Moyser, G. and Day, N. (1992). *Political Participation and Democracy in Britain.* Cambridge: Cambridge University Press.

Parsons, D.W. (1995). *Public Policy: an introduction.* Aldershot: Edward Elgar.

Pattie, C. and Johnston, R. (2009). 'Voting and Identity' in M. Flinders, A. Gamble, C. Hay and M. Kenny, eds, *The Oxford Handbook of British Politics.* Oxford: Oxford University Press, pp. 461–83.

Pattie, C., Seyd, P., Whiteley, P. (2003). 'Citizenship and civic engagement: attitudes and behaviour in Britain', *Political Studies*, 51:3, 443–68

——— (2004). *Citizenship in Britain: values, participation and democracy.* Cambridge: Cambridge University Press.

Peston, R. (2008).*Who Runs Britain?: and who's to blame for the economic mess we're in.* London: Hodder.

Philips, H. (2007). *Strengthening Democracy: fair and sustainable funding for political parties. the review of the funding of political parties.* Norwich: HMSO.

Pilkington, C. (1998). *Issues in British Politics.* London: Macmillan.

Pimlott, B. and Rao, N. (2002). *Governing London.* Oxford: Oxford University Press.

Public Administration Committee (2008). *Justice Delayed: the ombudsman's report on Equitable Life, volume 1.* HC 41–1.

——— (2009). *Justice Denied: government response to the committee's sixth report of 2008–9.* HC 569.

Pinto-Duschinsky, M. (1981). *British Political Finance 1830–1980.* Washington, DC: American Enterprise Institute.

Prison Reform Trust (2000). *A Hard Act to Follow? Prisons and the Human Rights Act.* London: Prison Reform Trust.

Pulzer, P. (1967). *Political Representation and Elections in Britain.* London: Allen & Unwin.

Putnam, R. (2000). *Bowling Alone: the collapse and revival of American community.* New York: Simon & Schuster.

Pyper, R. (1998) 'Redress of grievances', *Politics Review,* February, 28–33.

——— (2002). 'Making government accountable', *Politics Review,* May, 14–18.

Rawnsley, A. (2010). *The End of the Party: the rise and fall of New Labour.* London: Viking.

Rayner, G. (2009) 'MPs expenses: Questions and Answers', *Daily Telegraph,* 10 May.

Reid, M. (1992). 'Policy networks and issue networks: the politics of smoking', in D. Marsh and R. Rhodes, eds., *Policy Networks in British Government.* Oxford: Clarendon Press.

Reiner, R. (2010). *The Politics of the Police.* 4th edn. Oxford: Oxford University Press.

Rhodes, R. (1988). *Beyond Westminster and Whitehall: the sub-central governments of Britain.* London: Unwin Hyman.

——— (1997). *Understanding Governance: policy networks, governance, reflexivity and accountability.* Buckingham: Open University Press.

——— (1999). *Control and Power in Central-Local Relations.* 2nd edn. Aldershot: Ashgate.

——— ed., (2000). Ed., *Transforming British Government: volume 1, Changing Institutions; volume 2, Changing Roles and Relationships.* Basingstoke: Palgrave Macmillan.

Richards, D. (2007). *New Labour and the Civil Service: reconstituting the Westminster model.* Basingstoke: Palgrave Macmillan.

Robins, L, and Jones, B. eds, (2000). *Debates in British Politics Today.* Manchester: Manchester University Press.

Robson, W.A. (1928/1947). *Justice and Administrative Law.* London: Macmillan.

Royal, T. (2009). 'Regulating the Internet', *Computeractive,* 10 March. http://www.computeractive.co.uk/computeractive/features/2238207/regulating-internet.

Russell, A. and Fieldhouse, E. (2004). *Neither Left Nor Right? The Liberal Democrats and the Electorate: the electoral politics of the Liberal Democrats.* Manchester: Manchester University Press.

Russell, M. (2000). *Reforming the Lords: lessons from abroad.* Oxford: Oxford University Press.

Saga Magazine (2003): 'Tony Blair at fifty: the Saga interview', May 2003, 44–50.

Sanders, D., Clarke, H., Stewart, M., and Whiteley, P. (2001). 'The economy and voting' in P. Norris, ed., *Britain Votes 2001,* Oxford: Oxford University Press, pp. 225–38.

Schon, D. A. and M. Rein. 1994. *Frame Reflection: toward*

the resolution of intractable policy controversies. New York: Basic.

Schumpeter, J. (1943/1976). *Capitalism, Socialism and Democracy.* London: Allen & Unwin.

Scott, R. (1996) *Report of the Inquiry into the Export of Defence Equipment and Dual-use Goods to Iraq and Related Prosecutions.* London: HMSO, HC 115.

Scully, R. and Wyn Jones, R. (2009). 'Elections, Parties and Public Attitudes' in Scully, R. and Wyn Jones, R. eds, *Wales Devolution Monitoring Report January 2009.* London: University College Constitution Unit and Aberystwyth: Institute of Welsh Politics, pp. 70–76.

Select Committee on Public Administration (2001) *Fifth Report, 2000–1, Mapping the Quango State.* www.publications.parliament-UK/pa/cm2001/cmselect/cmpubadmin/HC367.

———— (2003) *Fourth Report, 2003–3 Government by Appointment: opening up the patronage state.* www.publications.parliament-UK/pa/cm2003/cmselect/cmpubadmin/HC165.

———— (2009a) *Justice Denied? The Government's response to the Ombudsman's Report on Equitable Life. Sixth Report, 2008–9.* HC 219.

———— (2009b). *Justice Denied? Government Response to the Committee's Sixth Report of the Session 2008–9. Third Special Report, 2008–9.* HC569.

Senvirante, M. (2002). *Ombudsmen: public services and administrative justice.* London: Butterworths.

Seymour-Ure, C. (1996). *The British Press and Broadcasting since 1945.* 2nd edn. Oxford: Blackwell.

Shaw, E. (2002). 'New Labour in Britain: new democratic centralism?', *West European Politics,* 25:3, 147 – 170

Sikka. P. (2002). 'Show us the money: an international clampdown on tax avoidance is long overdue', *The Guardian,* April 12.

Skelcher, C. (1998). *The Appointed State: quasi-governmental organizations and democracy.* Buckingham: Open University Press.

Smith, M. (1999.) *The Core Executive in Britain.* London: Macmillan.

———— (2000a). 'The core executive', *Politics Review,* September, 2–5.

———— (2000b). 'Prime Ministers, ministers and civil servants in the core executive' in R. Rhodes, ed. *Transforming British Government, volume 1, changing institutions,* London: Palgrave Macmillan, pp. 25–45.

Smith, S. de and Brazier, R. (1998). *Constitutional and Administrative Law,* 8th edn. London: Penguin.

Stationery Office (2001a). *National Intelligence Machinery.* Norwich: The Stationery Office.

———— (2001b). *Regional Trends 2001.* London: The Stationery Office.

———— (2002). *Social Trends 2002.* London: The Stationery Office.

Steinmo, S. (1993). *Taxation and Democracy: Swedish, British and American approaches to financing the modern state.* London: Yale University Press.

Stoker, G. (2004). *Transforming Local Governance: from Thatcherism to New Labour.* Basingstoke: Palgrave Macmillan.

Street, J. (2001). *Mass Media, Politics and Democracy.* Basingstoke: Palgrave Macmillan.

Sunkin, M. (2001). 'Trends in Judicial Review and the Human Rights Act', *Public Policy and Management,* July–September 2001, 9–12.

Sutton Trust (2010) *The Educational Backgrounds of Members of Parliament in 2010.* London: Sutton Trust. http://www.suttontrust.com/reports/MPs_educational_backgrounds_2010.pdf.

Thain, C. and Wright, M. (1995). *Treasury and Whitehall: planning and control of public expenditure.* Oxford: Oxford University Press.

Theakston, K. (1999). *Leadership in Whitehall.* London: Macmillan.

Timmins, N. (1995). *The Five Giants.* London: Harper Collins.

Tonge, J. (2006). *Northern Ireland.* Cambridge: Polity.

———— (2007). 'The return of devolved power-sharing to Northern Ireland', *Politics Review,* November, 8–12.

Turner, A. (2009). *The Turner Review: a regulatory response to the global banking crisis.* London: Financial Services Authority.

Wainwright, M. (2003). 'Cleethorpes bucks trend of decline', *The Guardian,* May 10.

Watts, D. and Pilkington, C. (2005). *Britain in the European Union Today.* Manchester: Manchester University Press.

Webb. P. (2000). *The Modern British Party System.* London: Sage.

Weber. M. (1918/1948), 'Politics as a vocation' in H.Gerth and C.W. Mills, eds, *From Max Weber,* pp. 77–128.

Weir, S. and Beetham, D. (1999). *Political Power and Democratic Control in Britain.* London: Routledge.

White, R.J. (1950), ed., *The Conservative Tradition.* London: Kaye.

Whiteley, P. and Seyd, P. (2002.) *High Intensity Participation: the dynamics of party activism in Britain.* Ann Arbor, MI: University of Michigan Press.

Wilson, D., and Game, C. (2006). *Local Government in the UK: government beyond the centre,* 4th edn. Basingstoke: Palgrave Macmillan.

Wilson, R. (1999). 'The civil service in the new millennium'. www.cabinet-office.gov.uk/1999/senior/rw.

Worcester, R. and Mortimore, R. (2001). *Explaining Labour's Second Landslide.* London: Politico.

Index